PEABODY LANGUAGE DEVELOPMENT KITS

REVISED

Teacher's Manual

LEVEL P

LLOYD M. DUNN, Ph.D.
Affiliate Professor of Special Education,
University of Hawaii at Manoa, Honolulu, Hawaii.
Senior Author of the Series

KATHRYN B. HORTON, M.S.
Associate Professor of Speech and Language Pathology,
Vanderbilt University, Nashville, Tennessee.
Coordinator of Level P

JAMES O. SMITH, Ed.D.
Professor of Special Education, University of New Mexico,
Albuquerque, New Mexico.

AGS®
American Guidance Service, Inc.
Circle Pines, MN 55014-1796

Contents

Preface

The original edition of Level P of the *Peabody Language Development Kits* was published in early 1968 after two years of development, field testing, research, and consequent revision. Level P and the other levels of PLDK were written in response to a recognized need to improve the oral language and cognitive skills of young children, especially those from non-Standard-English-speaking backgrounds.

During the first half of the century, preschool education was designed primarily for children of the middle class; in recent years, however, radical changes have occurred in our perceptions of the value of early education. Many people are now convinced that education before age six significantly influences later school performance in all children, particularly those from the lower economic strata. The development of oral language skills is seen to be a significant need of these children. The importance of early education and language development for handicapped children also became apparent during the late 1960s and the 1970s. Implementing the right of all children to quality preschool education has become a major objective not only in the United States but also in many other societies.

Since its publication in 1968, Level P of the PLDK series has enjoyed widespread use in both general and special preschool programs in the United States and abroad. But over these 13 years, the attitudes and values of our society have changed. We have become more sensitive to both overt and subtle ways in which we teach and reinforce discrimination and prejudice. We have also become even more aware of the need to realize in full the cognitive potential of all children in preparation for the 21st century. The 1981 edition of Level P of the revised PLDK series addresses these issues.

K.B.H./L.M.D./J.O.S.
1/81

PART 1

Introduction

It is not programs but teachers who teach, and this section of the PLDK Level P *Teacher's Manual* has been written with that idea in mind. This section is to enable you to teach effectively Level P of the revised PLDK series (PLDK-R) to help preschoolers develop cognitive and oral language skills. The guide has two parts. Part I describes and explains the program's features and instructional materials, and offers guidelines for teaching the lessons. Part II summarizes the findings of almost two decades of research on the effectiveness of the original PLDK series. We recommend that teachers reread Part I several times during the course of using the 360 lessons.

Program Description

Like its predecessor, the revised edition of Level P of the PLDK series is a self-contained, comprehensive program of lessons and accompanying instructional materials. It is designed to stimulate both language and cognitive development in groups of children whose proficiency in Standard English is at about the four-to-five-year level at the program's outset. It is also useful for above-average children who enter the program at about age three.

Level P contains 360 lessons, each with two activities. The program may be taught in two years by using one lesson per day, or it may be completed in one year by using two lessons per day. Depending on group size, each lesson requires an average of about 30 to 40 minutes.

Each lesson has been written in sufficient detail for use by aides and inexperienced teachers. We encourage the experienced user to adapt the activities to meet the needs of the children in the group. The lessons are designed to be taught in classroom settings to groups of about 20 children, with 10 to 14 being the ideal class size to ensure maximum participation of each child.

We strongly recommend that the lessons be taught in sequence, since they become progressively more difficult. A second reason for teaching the lessons in order is that the activities have been developed in strands — later activities build upon what has been taught in earlier ones. For those who need specific types of activities or who choose not to teach the lessons in sequence, the 720 activities have been indexed by *skill* and *subject* categories.

Major Changes in the Revision

This revision of Level P substantially retains the rationale and organization of the original edition. To improve the original, the following major changes were made:

1. The difficulty of the lessons has been increased to challenge today's more sophisticated children, and to make the activities more appropriate for preschoolers with Standard English backgrounds.
2. Variations have been frequently suggested at the end of activities to make the tasks easier or harder, so that a much wider range of individual differences can be accommodated.
3. Virtually all the activities are new or extensively revised. Only about half are based on original activities.
4. In response to strong demand, lesson content has been spelled out in greater detail so that aides can use the kit more easily than before.
5. Each activity is introduced with a focus statement that briefly summarizes its content.
6. All the activities have been indexed by skill and subject so that users who wish to can select specific types of activities to teach.
7. A concerted effort was made to remove sexual, racial, ethnic, and age biases from the lessons, art, and recordings.

8. Many materials have been added or changed, including manikins, puppets, posters, and stories.
9. Nearly all the picture cards are new, with art that is up-to-date and realistic.
10. Duplication of picture cards with other levels has been dramatically reduced; only a few cards are used in more than one level.
11. Most written language and nationalistic content have been removed from the pictures to make the program more suitable for use in other countries.

Kit Materials and Their Uses

This *Teacher's Manual* is the core of the Level P program. Besides the manual, there are 15 types of materials, which fall into three categories: visual, manipulative, and auditory. These materials are charted in Figure 1 .1 and listed in the appendixes. In the following pages, we discuss the kit components in terms of their physical appearance, reason for inclusion, and use in the program. Level P's variety of instructional materials not only makes it possible for you to take a multi-sensory approach to teaching but also allows you to match materials to the individual needs of your children.

Manipulative Materials

1. COLOR CHIPS. The kit contains 240 color chips in the following eight colors: black, blue, brown, green, orange, red, white, and yellow. Thirty chips of each color are provided so that each child, even in a large group, may have a complete set of eight. Designed the same as those in the original edition, the chips can be linked into chains.

The color chips are used most frequently in activities which involve assembling, matching, counting, and naming, and which focus on the concepts of color, number, and length. The chips are also used in games and in activities involving make-believe. You may wish to use the color chips for additional purposes like these:

- remembering and reproducing sequences of colors
- linking chips in timed activities to increase eye-hand coordination
- distributing chips as tokens for reinforcement of good performance
- using chips as money in "make-believe" activities
- classifying chips by color and/or number

2. MANIKINS. The Level P kit contains two manikins: one that is disassembled and one that is movable. The disassembled manikin has 11 body parts, six facial features, and three hairstyles. The facial features and hairstyles are mylar and will adhere to the surface of the head. The movable manikin is hinged at eight body points and is shown in profile. Both manikins are backed with magnets which allow them to adhere to the surface of the display board.

The manikins can be an aid in teaching about body parts (their locations and functions) and demonstrating the actions of which the human body is capable. The disassembled manikin may also be used in activities which focus on identifying missing or inaccurately placed parts. Since the movable manikin can be posed in many ways, it may be used not only to decide whether certain positions are humanly possible, but also to list all the actions that are suggested by a manikin pose. In fact, we feel that the main usefulness of the movable manikin lies in demonstrating actions: kneeling, running, jumping, sleeping, crawling, reaching, stretching, sitting, lying, and many others.

3. DISPLAY BOARD AND MAGNETIC LEDGES. The Level P kit includes a display board and six magnetic ledges for displaying the cards, the posters, the disassembled and movable manikins, and the magnetic geometric shapes. The board measures 24" x 32" (60cm x 81 cm), and can accommodate at any one time the 60 magnetic geometric shapes, or one or both of the manikins. The metal, table-model board has an easel base and an off-white, washable surface. The six magnetic ledges are each 16" (40 cm) long and will conveniently hold the cards on either the display board or on a metallic chalkboard.

Fifteen cards can be shown at one time on the six ledges, which may also be used to affix the posters to the board for display. The board and ledges are used in most of the program activities to support the use of other materials.

4. MAGNETIC GEOMETRIC SHAPES. The kit's 60 geometric shapes come in four different shapes (circle, square, triangle, and rectangle), three sizes, and five colors (black,

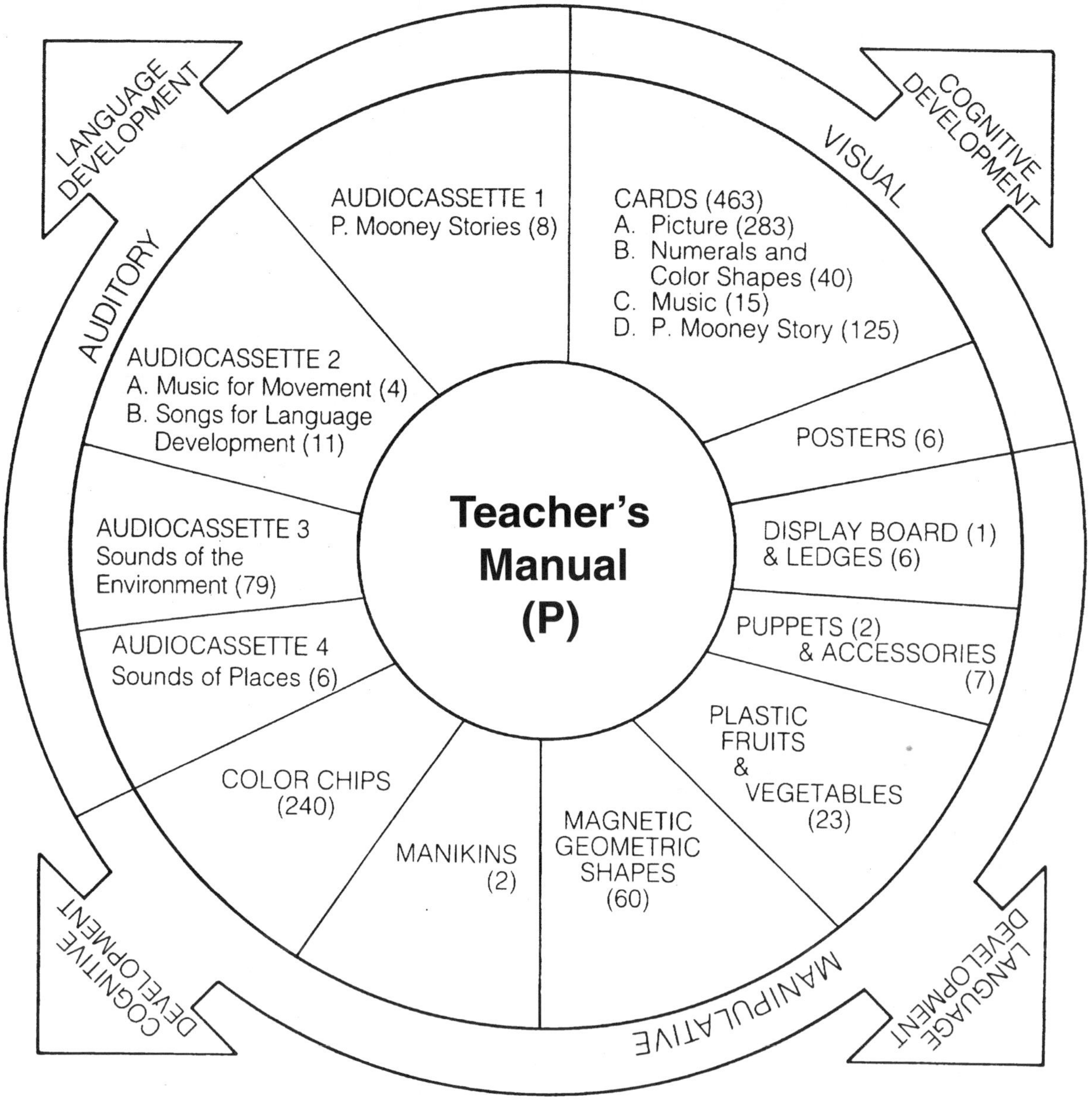

Figure 1.1
Instructional materials for Level 1 of the Peabody Language Development Kits — Revised

blue, green, red, and yellow). The shapes are stored together in a removable container in Case 1. They may be used to teach the concepts of shape, color, number, size, length, width, and height. Their sizes were chosen for maximum flexibility and for safe use with young children.

The magnetic shapes may be used for matching by color, size, and/or shape. They can be classified by color, shape, size, and number and formation of sides. The shapes can also help teach counting and number concepts, sequencing and predicting sequences, comparing, developing eye-hand coordination and visual-perceptual skills, and imaginative design-building.

5. PLASTIC FRUITS AND VEGETABLES.
The 23 plastic fruits and vegetables include eight different kinds of fruit and five vegetables. All 23 pieces are too large to swallow and are therefore safe for young children.

Once the children are able to identify each fruit and vegetable by name, you can use these materials to teach concepts of color, relative size, length, and comparison. By having the children identify a fruit or vegetable by touch alone, you may improve their tactile perception.

The fruits and vegetables are useful in activities that call for sequencing or classifying. They may also be discussed in terms of when or at which meal each would probably be eaten, and are useful as props when the children engage in dramatic play.

6. PUPPETS AND ACCESSORIES. Level P has two puppets with five accompanying accessories. Dressed in his red-and-blue striped shirt and cap, P. Mooney stands ready to help and care for others. As in the original edition, P. Mooney has neither eyes nor ears, yet he can see and hear. His adventures stem from his helping and caring attitude, a characteristic which readily endears him to children.

This edition introduces Zoey, whose name is derived from the Greek word zoe, meaning "life." As her song explains, Zoey's three hats — for discovery, thinking, and action — represent three important aspects of problem solving. Zoey is excited about exploring life.

The two puppets are devices of stimulation and motivation. We recommend that early in the school year you place them in a prominent position in the classroom, so the children may become familiar with the two characters. P. Mooney and Zoey may be used to introduce and close each lesson. The puppets are also highly effective (especially early in the year) with children who are shy, withdrawn, or whose attention spans are short. P. Mooney is used often in lessons which involve describing, naming, talking, and following directions. Zoey appears regularly in thinking, imagining, and problem-solving activities.

The heads of both puppets can be washed in a mild detergent with a soft cloth. To ensure long life, the puppets should be stored away from dust and strong sunlight.

The P. Mooney bag is made of durable, soil-resistant cloth and has an adjustable strap which allows it to be worn by teachers or children. It is large enough to hold 100 cards, the fruits and vegetables, the magnetic shapes, or whatever you wish. The bag is useful for activities involving memory or the recognition of objects by touch. It is especially useful for holding "surprises" or any materials being introduced.

The P. Mooney stick is made of durable, molded plastic and has a replica of P. Mooney's head at one end. Its "magical" ability to "transform" people and things makes it suitable for all activities that involve pantomiming and imagining.

Visual Materials

1. PICTURE CARDS. The kit contains 283 sturdy, full-color, realistic picture cards that are varnished to ensure long life. The cards fall into eight categories: animals, clothing and accessories, face pairs, foods, household items, people, toys, and vehicles.

The card size has been increased to approximately 8" x 9" (20 cm x 23 cm), allowing most items to be recognized by children at some distance from the teacher. Care has been taken to avoid showing extraneous features which may lead children to label incorrectly, or which may distract their attention from the main subject. Each art piece has been carefully researched and realistically drawn. Artwork of people shows them in the ethnic and racial proportions recorded by the United States Census; handicapped people are also depicted.

Early in the program, the cards are used in activities which involve naming, describing, matching, identifying, and talking. In later lessons, they are extensively used in relating, classifying, sequencing, brainstorming, and thinking activities.

2. NUMERALS AND COLOR SHAPES CARDS. The kit contains 40 cards used to teach the concepts of number, shape, and color. They are especially useful for activities involving matching. The cards allow numbers to be matched both as numerals and as counted shapes, and may be used for direct matching of colors and shapes. The cards may also be used for counting and sequencing activities, and to reinforce the meanings of *more* and *less, most* and *least, before* and *after,* and *first* and *last.* Used with the song "Find That Shape (Color, Number)," the cards can reinforce the children's understanding of colors, shapes, and numbers. The last 10 cards of the series may also be adapted for bingolike games when used with the color chips and/or magnetic geometric shapes.

3. MUSIC CARDS. The 15 music cards accompany the program's character songs, songs for language development, and music for movement. As well as giving information on each piece, the cards provide alternate introductions more detailed than what is given in the lessons, and suggest other ways of using the music. We recommend that you use the cards as resources for extended use of the songs and music.

4. STORY CARDS. The 125 story cards accompany the eight P. Mooney stories. P. Mooney is the main character in the stories, which detail the ways he uses his magical P. Mooney bag and P. Mooney stick to help others. The narrative, printed in easy-to-read type, is given on the reverse side of each story picture card.

Besides accompanying the recorded stories, the story cards are primarily used in describing, retelling, and sequencing activities. They may also be used as aids for remembering and acting out the stories.

5. POSTERS. Level P contains six large posters printed on both sides of three heavy-duty, plastic-coated paper sheets. The posters show the four seasons and a variety of places, and include many details of interest to young children. They are used for labeling and describing animals, people, actions, and seasons. Each poster has a recorded sound effects sequence on Audiocassette 4.

In most lessons introducing posters, the P. Mooney stick is used to "transport" everyone to the scene shown. The first lesson about a poster usually involves careful observation and naming. In-depth questioning about what is shown on the poster leads the children to tell about their own experiences in similar places or seasons.

Auditory Materials

Level P auditory materials are recorded on four audiocassettes whose contents are listed in the Appendixes.

1. AUDIOCASSETTE 1: P. MOONEY STORIES. Each of the eight newly recorded stories is recorded on Audiocassette 1, Sides A and B. Early presentation of the stories combines use of the recordings with the story cards. Later, only the recordings are used. The appealing quality of these recordings makes them effective not only in presenting story content, but also in developing listening skills such as comprehension and retention.

2. AUDIOCASSETTE 2: SONGS FOR LANGUAGE DEVELOPMENT AND MUSIC FOR MOVEMENT. Audiocassette 2 contains 10 new pieces of music and several revised songs from the original edition.

3. AUDIOCASSETTE 3: SOUNDS OF THE ENVIRONMENT. Level P's sound effects include sounds of people and things, and sounds of places. The 79 sounds of people and things are in six categories: animals, home, actions, voices, toys, and vehicles. The sounds are realistic and have been recorded with no extraneous background noises. Each is repeated more than once to allow time for thoughtful identification. Each of the sounds has an accompanying picture card. Using sound effects and pictures in combination allows children to match sounds with their origins. Activities using the sound effects might include recalling sound sequences, brainstorming possible sources of each sound, and making up stories about one or more sounds.

4. AUDIOCASSETTE 4: SOUNDS OF PLACES. The sounds of places are auditory companions of the six posters. Each segment has eight to 10 sounds occurring in relatively quick progression against a continuing background sound. The listening task involves distinguishing foreground sounds, assimilating sounds presented in quick succession, and scanning the corresponding poster to locate the visual source of each sound.

The variety of sound materials makes many kinds of listening activities possible. We suggest that you present the individual sounds on Audiocassette 3 before introducing poster sound sequences because of the differences in difficulty.

Purposes of the Program

The PLDK-R program has two main purposes:

1. The primary aim is to stimulate overall oral language skills in Standard English. Especially noticeable should be the improved ability of the children to express ideas in sentences. The program neither drills on rules of grammar, nor stresses speech correction or phonology. Instead, a balanced array of activities is built into the lessons.
2. The second aim of the program is to advance the children's cognitive skills about a year per level. Again, a balanced approach to lesson construction was adopted. Activities do not concentrate on a few skills, such as memory training or brainstorming. Instead, the intent is to stimulate a broad range of divergent and convergent cognitive abilities.

Age of the children and youth	Cognitive and Linguistic Proficiency in Standard English			
	Borderline	Mild disability	Moderate disability	Severe disability
	85*	70*	55*	40*
5-0 to 5-11	P			
6-0 to 6-11	P 1	P		No level recommended for use without considerable modification
7-0 to 7-11	1 2	P 1		
8-0 to 8-11	2 3	P 1 2	P	
9-0 to 9-11	3	1 2 3	P	
10-0 to 10-11		2 3	P 1	*These values are standard score equivalents (IQs or LQs)
11-0 to 11-11		3	P 1	
12-0 to 12-11		3	1 2	
13-0 to 13-11			1 2	
14-0 to 14-11			2 3	
15-0 to 15-11			2 3	
16-0 to 16-11			3	
17 and over			3	

Table 1.1
Appropriate level of the PLDK-R series to use with different groups of children with learning disability, depending upon their cognitive and linguistic proficiency in Standard Enlish, and years needed to complete each level

It is not a primary aim of the PLDK-R series to enhance academic skills. The research, reported in Part II of this manual, does provide some limited evidence that this happens incidentally. On the one hand, it can be argued that children should improve in reading and mathematics skills if they can listen, talk, and think better. On the other hand, the language lessons give no practice in reading, and instruction in arithmetic is incidental to the two main purposes of the program. Obviously, the academic subjects need to be taught well in their own right. We believe the Peabody program will have served its two main purposes if it helps children communicate their ideas more effectively and think more logically.

Target Populations

Pupils

Level P is the first program in the PLDK-R. It is designed to stimulate oral language and cognitive development among groups of children whose cognitive and linguistic proficiency in Standard English is at approximately the four-to-five-year level at the outset of the program. Thus, four-year-old children with average ability and Standard English backgrounds will find the Level P lessons challenging. This program is also designed for five-year-olds who come from backgrounds where a dialect of English, or a language other than English, is spoken in the home. It should also be effective with somewhat older children who have limited proficiency in Standard English, or who have mild to moderate learning disabilities. Bright three-year-olds should also find Level P stimulating.

Instructors

The Level P lessons are intended primarily for regular and special education teachers, Head Start and day-care instructors, and other educators of young children. Community volunteers, teacher aides, and parents can also effectively use the program because the lessons and teacher information are written in considerable detail. All users of Level P will increase the effectiveness of the lessons if they prepare in advance by thoroughly reviewing each lesson and organizing the materials needed, teach the lessons accurately and enthusiastically, and manage the pupils effectively.

Instructors do not need to attend specialized workshops or see training films before using the program. In fact, we do not recommend that such devices be used because they tend to stereotype teaching approaches. Instead, if you want more orientation than a careful study of the kit's guide, lessons, and materials provides, arrange to observe several teachers experienced in the use of the program.

Guidelines for Teaching the Lessons

Over a period of more than a decade, the following effective teaching procedures have evolved, and we recommend you become thoroughly familiar with the lessons before attempting to teach them. Furthermore, instructors with limited experience should restudy these guidelines at least twice more during the course of teaching the program, at evenly spaced intervals.

Lesson Preparation and Modification

Although Level P lessons are written in considerable detail, it would be unfair to your children to present a lesson without adequate preparation. If the children are to learn from a lesson, its intent and focus need to be clear in your mind. You cannot study a lesson while teaching it and expect good results. Each lesson should be taught in a natural, enthusiastic, relaxed, and smooth-flowing manner, and this may best be achieved through advance preparation.

We encourage you to follow the lessons as outlined in the manual, making marginal notes as needed. We also encourage those of you who are experienced teachers and language specialists to create activity variations as soon as you feel comfortable doing so:

We offer these suggestions for lesson preparation:

1. Study the lesson when you are not likely to be interrupted. If you wish, mark the activity parts you plan to emphasize.
2. Review the needs of the children in your group, planning for those who require special attention.
3. Consider each activity and think about whether it should be modified or extended to fit your group's particular needs.
4. Assemble all materials. Recordings should be set up to play, so the flow of the lesson will not be interrupted. Note any key preparation statements detailing the need for extra time and preparation.
5. As you present each activity, evaluate it from the children's perspective as well as from your own. Doing so will make you better able to adapt the lesson to meet the children's needs as well as the lesson's objectives.

In summary, the lessons are written for both inexperienced and experienced users. We do not believe, however, that success can only be achieved by teaching the lessons exactly as written. We encourage you to adapt the activities to your own teaching style without sacrificing the intent or objective of the lesson.

Appropriate Setting and Atmosphere

We feel that each language lesson should be viewed as a special time, an enjoyable break from the day's conventional activities. Try to create a gamelike atmosphere for as many activities as possible. Language time should give the children more opportunities to talk and move about than are usually allowed. Remember that the setting and atmosphere are as important as the materials in making a lesson successful. To create this pleasant environment, keep these principles in mind:

1. Whenever possible, have the children sit close to you in order to increase eye-to-eye contact. The group might sit on mats, cushions, or on the floor. In any event, the lessons should be conducted in a place relatively free of noise and other distractions. In special education settings, a specific area in the room may be reserved for language time.
2. A teacher's manner and attitudes are highly contagious. Be sure to join in the fun with smiles, laughter, and supporting statements. Above all, be enthusiastic and energetic.

3. Teachers are models for children. The way you talk influences the way your children will speak. Your diction and sentence structure should be clear and your tone of voice pleasant. You may wish to tape record yourself during a lesson in order to evaluate your way of speaking.
4. Maintaining group attention is important. The kit materials will help you do so, but equally important is the enthusiasm with which you present the lesson. If your group is easily distracted, you may wish to take a break between the lesson's two activities. But remember that children pay attention to what interests them — so be an interesting teacher.
5. *Remember that PLDK-R is primarily a talking time for the children, not the teacher.* Try to include and involve all the children, even the most retiring. Avoid calling excessively on volunteers, since these are usually the children who least need help. However, when you call on a child who did not volunteer, structure your request and provide assistance to increase the likelihood that the child will respond successfully.

Organizing the Lessons
Please consider these suggestions for the length of the lesson periods, the time during the day when they are best taught, the balance between the activities, and the method of grouping:

1. When the number of children in the group is over 20, the language lesson should normally take 30 to 40 minutes to complete. When the group size is 15 or fewer, the same lesson can usually be presented in about 20 to 30 minutes. When the group size is between 16 and 25, the lesson period may take 25 to 35 minutes. The additional time for the larger group is designed to provide adequate opportunities for all the children to participate in the lesson.
2. We recommend that you teach the lessons at the same time every day, preferably during a period that is relatively free of interruptions. Mid-morning is a desirable time, but the lessons may also be taught successfully later in the day, since they are stimulating and often include physical activity.
3. In general, balance the time between the two activities in a lesson, although less time may be spent on activities less popular with the children. Keep the pace lively, since pre-school children lose interest in lessons that are slow-moving or over-taught.
4. We recommend that you teach the lessons in the order in which they appear in the manuals. For best results, teach them on a regular, daily basis. With less mature children, the two activities may be presented in two sessions separated by an hour or so. However, since the two activities of a lesson are often closely related, it is best to teach them as close as possible to each other. As stated earlier, the program may be taught in two years by using one lesson per day, or it may be completed in one year by using two lessons per day.

Teaching the Activities by Skill and Subject Strands*
We recognize that, in spite of our recommendations, some instructors will pick and choose activities selectively, rather than teach whole lessons consecutively. This approach may have merit for those who wish to modify the Peabody program to fit the *differential diagnosis — prescriptive teaching model,* which is discussed briefly in Part II of this manual. However, we have found no research evidence as yet on the effectiveness of this procedure.

Nevertheless, in response to considerable demand, as a new feature in this revision, the activities have been classified in Appendixes E, F, and G of this manual by *skill* and *subject* categories. Examples of *skill* strands include brainstorming, classifying, describing, identifying, problem solving, sentence building, and sequencing. The complete array of 25 *skills* is indexed in Appendix E, where each is defined and where the activities that stress each of them are listed. Examples of *subject* strands include absurdities, animals, foods, numbers, shapes, sizes, and time. The complete list of 41 will be found in Appendix F, where the activities that focus on each are indexed. There is an additional reference listing in Appendix G.

Here each activity in Level P is listed in order, with the skill and subject strands emphasized in each. Appendix G allows you to search easily through the sequence of activities for those that emphasize particular skills and/or subjects. This activity-by-activity summary may also be helpful to you in the preparation of individual educational plans, particularly in special and

**We would greatly appreciate feedback from users of this system, and suggestions on how to improve it.*

remedial situations. Nevertheless, the classification system we have used is but one of a number that could have been adopted. In fact, there is probably a need for as many organizational systems as there are teaching styles. So you may want to devise your own. The following section may be helpful in this regard.

Using the Focus Statements

Each of the activities in the revised lessons begins with a preview, or more precisely, a focus statement. These statements give a brief summary of the contents of the activity, expressed from the child's point of view. For example, the first one in the kit is: *Guessing the identity of a hidden object, talking about puppets, and then finding P. Mooney.* On three main counts, instructors should find these statements useful. *First,* they provide a "mind set" for studying each activity. *Second,* they will facilitate a search for different types of activities by those teachers who are not comfortable with our *skill* and *subject* categories. *Third,* these focus statements should be helpful if you wish to devise your own classification system.

Encouraging and Reinforcing Pupil Participation

Children in a well-run class learn not only basic concepts but also the skill of participating in a peer group. Most teachers have seen the satisfaction such participation can bring. The following suggestions for encouraging and reinforcing participation may prove helpful:

1. Children should be encouraged to answer when they can; they should never be forced to respond. If you have difficulty holding your children's attention, examine your style of teaching and the classroom atmosphere you have created. Then consider whether what you are teaching is appropriate. You may need to modify lessons so that each child is working successfully at his or her own level. In the Peabody program, a child's failure should be viewed as a failure on the part of the teacher to modify an activity, ask questions the child can answer, or provide hints enabling the child to perform as requested.
2. To encourage the children to participate, use an unpredictable pattern of questioning. For example, call on a child sitting on one side of the group and then on a child in another location. Sometimes call on neighboring children, but do not go around the circle, calling on each one in turn. *As a general rule, the question or request should be posed before calling upon anyone to respond.* This practice helps keep every child alert and attentive. While unison responses are sometimes appropriate, individual responses are usually more desirable. To establish a desired response pattern for an exercise, first call on more able individuals to serve as models. But by the end of each lesson, try to have every child respond satisfactorily at least once.
3. Although some gamelike competition can be effective in teaching the lessons, it can be overdone and may become harmful if it degrades the losers. Greater emphasis should be placed on cooperation. The lessons provide many opportunities for the children to solve problems as a group or in teams. You may wish to emphasize this feature even more.
4. You are urged to stress repetition and overlearning. After a child has performed a newly learned skill successfully, it is extremely important that there be opportunities for repeating it a number of times. You may find many incidental opportunities throughout the day for review, drill, and practice.
5. As the year progresses, play a less dominant role in the activities. Have the children become increasingly active in conducting the lessons.
6. Express appreciation of children's positive efforts. For example, let creative children know that creative thinking is valued. Praise should be given generously, but not overdone. Since most children recognize unearned praise, become sensitive to the amount of encouragement needed to elicit the best performance. Praise group success as well as that of individuals.
7. Tell the children what is expected of them so they will know how to respond correctly. There is no place in the program for harsh criticism or negative comparisons of children's performances. It takes skill to let a child know what is desired without appearing to criticize. We do not believe that unsatisfactory behavior should be ignored. You should explain, however, in a non judgmental way, what the desired behavior is, and/or model it.
8. Praise should often be accompanied by a tangible reward, such as a picture card or a color chip. With mildly retarded and moderately retarded children, you may wish to use tangible rewards more often. Use of the color chips as reinforcers is discussed in the section entitled "Guidelines for Using the Color Chips, Puppets, and Music."

Individualizing Instruction
This program is based on the premise that oral language development takes place through group activities. After all, verbal communication requires at least two participants. The basic form of individualization in this program is the attention the teacher gives each child during the ongoing group lesson. Therefore, please keep in mind that you are teaching *groups of individuals*. Strive to meet each person's needs within the group. At the same time, given the wide range of individual differences within most preschool groups, the need for more intensive individualization through tutoring will become apparent during most lessons. To a considerable degree, the success of the program depends on teachers who take time to identify specific children who need additional help, and then work with them individually between lessons until they perform adequately.

Here are some guidelines for individualizing instruction during the group lessons:

1. As already stated, except to furnish a good model at the outset of an activity, do not call unduly upon volunteers and the more precocious children in your group. Instead, balance participation across the group, going out of your way to draw out shy and slow children. Find ways in which everyone an succeed.
2. As necessary, modify the questions and instructions to challenge each individual in the group. At the end of many activities, we have suggested variations to accomplish this. Since every group is unique, it rests with the teacher to make each lesson a worthwhile, challenging learning experience for every member of the group.
3. During the lesson, ask questions to find out what each child knows and does not know. Each lesson should be viewed as a diagnostic session. This diagnostic approach to teaching will pay off in many ways. It is especially valuable in giving you the necessary information to modify forthcoming lessons as needed, and can suggest where individual tutoring is necessary.
4. Every child in the group deserves equal attention. Do not fail to give any child a successful learning experience, whether that person is a slow, average, or rapid learner. If PLDK-R Level 1 is also being taught in your school, you may have the option of placing children in a different group. The more able children could be transferred to the Level 1 program. In turn, you could take a corresponding number of children who appear especially to need Level P.
5. Every group lesson is a compromise: too easy for some, too hard for others. You may need to modify some activities and break others into smaller units. In still other cases, follow-through activities may need to be developed to establish a skill or concept. During the lessons, be thinking of how to take advantage of the *teachable moments* to help a child learn something new. By carefully considering each situation and using suggested options and variations, you can successfully individualize instruction.

Here are some guidelines for tutoring children in need of individualized teaching after completing a lesson:

1. If possible, the instructor who taught the lesson should provide the needed tutoring. After all, that person observed the deficiency and probably designed away to remediate it. It is imperative that you bring along slower children so they do not fall so far behind that later lessons are beyond their abilities.
2. Teacher aides, including community volunteers, may provide this tutoring under your direction.
3. Peer tutors and cross-age tutors (older children who help younger ones) can also be successful, but you will need to monitor and direct these helpers. Children receiving help from other children often improve because of practice, added attention, and greater opportunities to communicate verbally. At the same time, student tutors often learn by teaching; their self-concept is enhanced through helping others.
4. You might also wish to create personalized follow-through and/or take-home activities for children who are experiencing problems.

Guidelines for Competency Testing*
Some teachers may want to monitor pupil progress with teacher-made tests. Because this is very time consuming, it often works best in team-teaching situations, or where aides can free the teacher for test construction, administration, scoring, record keeping, and

**We would appreciate hearing from those of you who develop your own pool of test items. Either the publisher or the coordinating author can serve as a clearinghouse in sharing them.*

program modification. One can reasonably ask whether this time could be better spent either at tutoring or at extending the lessons, since most teachers informally monitor the progress of their students by questioning while the lesson is being taught and by noting the quality of the responses. The value of this Socratic method of informally testing while teaching cannot be overstressed.

For those who wish to measure pupil progress more formally, the recommended route is by traditional, teacher-made test items. Batteries of these may be given as tests on a weekly or monthly basis. The onus falls on the teacher to decide what is important for the pupils to learn. For example, such items as the following might be developed to test children on the first 30 lessons of Level P:

1. Telling One's Name

Ask: "What is your first and last name?"
(both names to pass)

2. Naming Body Parts

Ask the child to touch his or her

3. Recognizing Animals

Ask the child to answer yes or no to the following ten questions:

A. Is a *cow* an animal?
B. Is a *chair* an animal?
C. Is a *bear* an animal?
D. Is a *dog* an animal?
E. Is a *flower* an animal?
F. Is a *cat* an animal?
G. Is a *duck* an animal?
H. Is a *watch* an animal?
I. Is a *spider* an animal?
J. Is a *goat* an animal?
(eight or more to pass)

4. Following Directions

Ask the child to perform the following actions:

A. "Jump up and down."
B. "Smack your lips."
C. "Walk in place."
D. "Stand on tiptoes."
E. "Clap your hands."
(no errors to pass)

5. Functions of Body Parts

Ask: "What body parts do you use to do these actions?"

A. walking (legs, feet)
B. seeing (eyes)
C. listening (ears)
D. smelling (nose)
E. picking up something (fingers, hands)
(no errors to pass)

6. Naming Animals

Ask the child to name all the animals she or he can think of which make sounds.
(five or more to pass)

7. Clothing

Say: "Show and tell me where on your body you wear these kinds of clothing."

8. Animals and Their Young

Ask the child to answer the following questions:

A. "What is a baby horse called?" (colt)
B. "What is a baby cow called?" (calf)
C. "What is a baby hen called?" (chick)
D. "What is a baby duck called?" (duckling)
E. "What is a baby cat called?" (kitten)
F. "What is a baby dog called?" (puppy)
(five or more correct to pass)

9. Using Past Tense to Name an Action

Say: "Watch closely as I perform an action. Then tell me in a sentence what I did."
(Teacher should perform action and then have child describe action in a complete sentence)

Action	*Child's Response*
A. clap hands	"You *clapped* your hands."
B. snap fingers	"You *snapped* your fingers."
C. whistle"	"You *whistled*."
D. knock on table	"You *knocked* on the table."
E. write on board	"You *wrote* on the board."
F. hum	"You *hummed*." (five or more in a sentence to pass)

10. Remembering Sounds Heard Outside

Say: "Tell me all the things you might hear if you were outside."

(five or more appropriate sounds to pass)

You can keep a class record for each child on pretesting and posttesting to determine what has been learned during the group language lessons, and what still remains to be taught. But the construction of initial sets of items, such as these 10 examples, is just a first step. For repeated use, many will need to be refined, others deleted, and new ones substituted. In this way, a bank of items can be developed for use in subsequent years. Some users may wish to establish such criteria as those suggested above for passing or failing items. If so, these criteria should be adjusted according to the abilities of the children. The standards for average children, for example, should be higher than those for slower children, though some people would contend that the standard for all should be complete mastery. In any event, as the nation's schools move toward a data-based curriculum, teachers, authors, and publishers must become more accountable. One way to accomplish this is through improved pupil evaluation.

Guidelines for Using the Color Chips, Puppets, and Music

Guidelines for Using the Color Chips as Reinforcers (Tokens)

1. In exchange for a desired response, give a child a chip to hold. The object may be to get as many chips as possible during an activity or lesson. The chips may be accumulated on a weekly basis, or linked to see whose chain is longest. Since children may wish to compare their daily scores, you may wish to note their progress in a daily record or a monthly cumulative graph. Strings of chips may be hung on pegs on the wall to compare performances.
2. You do not need to hand out chips for every desired response, except in the initial stages of the program. In fact, intermittent reinforcement is usually more effective than continuous reinforcement.
3. Many children will find the chips reinforcing in their own right. However, from time to time, you may wish to convert the chips into a prize or privilege, especially after the novelty wears off.
4. At first, reinforce small increments of desired behavior; later, set higher standards. But vary the standards to suit the abilities of each child.
5. Never withdraw chips from a child because of unsatisfactory performance. Only use them as positive reinforcers.
6. Adequate reinforcement is essential to learning. You will probably find that a combination of verbal reinforcement (praise) and a token reward (chips) is more effective than either used alone, or than criticism.

(To avoid distractions, you may wish to record points earned during a lesson, and then hand out the chips at the end of a period.)

Guidelines for Using the Puppets

P. Mooney and Zoey are central to Level P and usually become an integral part of the classroom over the course of the program. They are especially useful for getting children to respond and participate. During the first 30 or so lessons, keep the puppets on display in the room. Try to establish their personalities as early as possible. P. Mooney is a thoughtful character, willing to assist anyone in need. Zoey is restless and inquisitive, and will continue to ask probing questions until she solves a problem. She has a great sense of fun and likes to be in the midst of the action. Both characters have magical powers.

In the first lesson, the children find the P. Mooney puppet. The teacher then wears the puppet and acts as puppeteer. Keep in mind that by assuming this role, you are not only establishing the puppet's character but also demonstrating how puppets are used. The first few times that children use the puppets, we suggest you call on persons likely to manipulate them well. This example may ensure greater success for everyone and will help develop favorable attitudes about puppetry.

P. Mooney and Zoey can create a special intimacy in a group of preschoolers. We suggest you become competent in handling the puppets before beginning the program. Here are some ways to make the puppets seem real:

1. Practice in front of a mirror, using a special voice for each puppet.
2. Always keep your eyes on the puppet.
3. Do not let the puppet's head drop. The children should be able to see the puppet's face at all times.

4. Have the children sit as close as possible to you, so everyone can see and hear easily.
5. Always maintain the character of the puppet.
6. Any movements should be made by the puppet who is talking. You might exaggerate them a little to make them meaningful and definite rather than distracting.

Guidelines for Using the Songs for Language Development

The songs in Level P each focus on a linguistic or cognitive principle, as the music cards detail. Music is a potent means of developing and reinforcing verbal skills. Because singing and chanting involve different neurological functions from those required for speaking, these activities help children learn certain kinds of information in a different way — by rote. Music is therefore an excellent tool for teaching oral language skills to all children, but it is especially valuable for children with learning problems. Here are some guidelines for teaching the songs:

1. Introduce the song and have the children listen to it.
2. Talk about what the children have heard, discussing the subject of the song.
3. Play the song again and ask the children to listen for the answer to a question like "What does the song tell us about P. Mooney?" or "Do you hear the words *is* and *are* in the song?"
4. Phrase by phrase, recite the words in the song, having the children repeat them after you.
5. Phrase by phrase, sing or play the song, having the children repeat each phrase after you.
6. Sing the whole song.
7. If there are several verses, do just one or two the first day and the rest another time.
8. You may wish to use one of the puppets to "sing" the song. Children enjoy this, and it often encourages a shy or withdrawn child to participate more fully.

Guidelines for Using the Music for Movement

1. Provide as much space as possible.
2. Introduce the music by having the children listen to the recording.
3. Discuss what the children heard and were reminded of as they listened to the piece. Point out important aspects of the music.
4. Play the recording again, and have the children listen to the rhythm; then lead them in clapping the rhythm while the music is played.
5. Suggest ways to move to the music, such as marching, dancing, and moving arms to draw "sound pictures." Also let the children suggest other movements which fit the music.
6. Beat out the rhythms with rhythm instruments.

Teaching the Program to Children with Special Needs

Education of children with special needs is undergoing sweeping changes in many countries. Over the years, the original PLDK series has been used extensively in both regular and special classrooms, each of which usually functioned as a self-contained operation. The regular teacher and the special education teacher had few shared responsibilities. This pattern began to change in the late 1970s. Today's emphasis is on including all children in the same classes.

We believe this pervasive trend will significantly change how the PLDK-R series is taught. For example, more teachers are made available to serve on instructional teams. Thus, most children with cognitive and linguistic disabilities will have many instructors: regular teachers, resource teachers, and speech/language tutors. These three types of teachers can plan who may best teach a given PLDK-R level to a specific class. This division of labor can direct each teacher's special skills to the needs of particular groups.

We do not advocate any one way of teaching or following through on Level P for students with special needs. Many regular educators find the lessons an effective addition to the regular curriculum. In other cases, the lessons are taught to youngsters with special needs by the resource teacher or the speech/language specialist. We support all of these approaches. The program was not designed to be the exclusive province of any one group of instructors.

The prevalence of language problems is very high for children with special needs. Remedial treatment of language difficulties is most effective in the earlier years. Intensive, concentrated effort is needed to overcome difficulties of this sort. We therefore urge that all children with such problems be given the chance to complete all 360 lessons of the revised Level P.

Evaluation of Program Effectiveness

Evaluation of Level P means determining whether it is helping children reach certain goals. Three types of evaluation are helpful in assessing the impact of Level P on children: 1) descriptive reports based on teacher observations, 2) test items devised and administered by the teacher, and 3) standardized tests. Changes in cognitive and language skills should be measured in any evaluation of program effectiveness. Using several different measurements will increase the accuracy of test results. Possible sources for a test of language skills include the following:

1. Carrow-Woolfolk, E. *Carrow elicited language inventory.* Hingham, Mass.: Teaching Resources Corporation, 1974.
2. Carrow-Woolfolk, E. *Screening test for auditory comprehension of language.* Hingham, Mass.: Teaching Resources Corporation, 1973.
3. Carrow-Woolfolk, E. T*est for auditory comprehension of language.* Hingham, Mass.: Teaching Resources Corporation, 1973.
4. Coughran, L. & Liles, B.Z. *Developmental syntax program.* Hingham, Mass.: Teaching Resources Corporation, 1974 & 1979.
5. Dunn, L.M., & Dunn, L.M. *Peabody picture vocabulary test–revised.* Circle Pines, Minn.: American Guidance Service, 1981.
6. Fluharty, N.B. *Fluharty preschool speech and language screening test.* Hingham, Mass.: Teaching Resources Corporation, 1978.
7. Kirk, S.A., McCarthy, J.J., & Kirk, W.D. *Illinois test of psycholinguistic abilities (rev. ed.).* Champaign, Ill.: University of Illinois Press, 1968.

Some major tests of cognitive skills appropriate for use with preschoolers are as follows:

1. Terman, L.M., & Merrill, MA. *Stanford-Binet test of intelligence.* Norms edition. Boston: Houghton-Mifflin Co., 1973.
2. Wechsler, D. *Wechsler intelligence scale for children.* New York: Psychological Corporation, 1949.
3. Wechsler, D. *Wechsler preschool and primary scale of intelligence.* New York: Psychological Corporation, 1967.

The question of teacher change is also important: discovering whether a teacher makes positive changes in teaching behavior after using the program. We encourage researchers to explore changes in teacher behavior. As Level P was revised, an important goal was to help teachers grow professionally. We are well aware that teachers play a pivotal role in the success of any program. Only future research will show whether an instructor changes teaching behavior or develops new skills in teaching and class management after using a program such as this one.

A Request

This revision was shaped by research studies on the original Level P, by changes in current linguistic and cognitive theory, and by literally hundreds of suggestions sent to us by teachers using the original edition over the last 13 years.

Everyone who has played a part in developing Level P of PLDK-R hopes this program will make a real difference in the everyday lives of children and their teachers. When you see ways in which the program can be improved, please send in your suggestions. These may be mailed to any one of the authors or to the publisher. We will continue to be guided by your recommendations for improving, expanding, or revising this new edition.

PART 2

Rationale and Research

Part II outlines the rationale for the PLDK-R series and summarizes the research on the original edition.

Part II focuses on the use of the PLDK series with children who have potential or evident difficulties in learning Standard English, and in using language as a tool for thought. The reason for this is that, for the past 15 years, the emphasis of the field has been on analyzing and evaluating intervention programs, such as the PLDK series, that teach Standard English to children who first learned a dialect of it or who demonstrate intellectual problems. Only recently has the PLDK series come into general use in teaching oral language facility in English to boys and girls who first learned a *different* language at home. As a result, it will probably take another decade for evidence to accumulate on the effectiveness of the Peabody program as a tool in teaching English as a second language (TESL).

Rationale

What sets people apart from other living things is their skill in verbal communication and their concurrent ability to reason abstractly. It is not surprising, therefore, that the human species has been interested in language and cognition throughout history. Three of the most important functions that language serves are as follows:

1. As a means of communication and social interaction.
2. As a tool for thought involving the higher intellectual processes.
3. As a method for regulating human behavior through influencing a listener's actions and attitudes.

Language is clearly the foundation for much of our social and intellectual behavior.

Professional interest in children's language development and associated disabilities has been especially high in recent years. The 1970s saw more articles, studies, books, and journals published on the topic than any previous decade. Not surprisingly, controversies over the nature and functions of language, and he effectiveness of interventions, have also increased. It is not possible to encapsulate the recent activity here. Instead, the reader is directed to textbooks that survey the field, such as the following: Bloom and Lahey, 1978; Brown, 1973; Dale, 1976; Gluckenberg and Danks, 1975; Ingram, 1976; Karmiloff-Smith, 1979; Lee, 1979; Leonard, 1976; McLean and Snyder-McLean, 1978; Moerk, 1977; Morehead and Morehead, 1976; Schiefelbusch, 1978a & 1978b.

Another major development in the last decade has been the shared and competitive interests of cognitive psychology and psycholinguistics. Even though there is growing recognition that language and thought are intertwined in a complex fashion, different professional groups continue to choose, in an arbitrary way, their own terms to discuss one or the other in an attempt to stake out the domain as their own. A useful procedure to follow to broaden one's knowledge about verbal ability, and to see how closely language and cognition are related, is to study such current books in cognitive psychology as the following: Anderson, 1980; Dodd and White, 1980; Ellis, 1978; Floyd, 1979; Kirby and Biggs, 1980; Klausmeier, Ghatala, and Frayer, 1974; Levin and Allen, 1976; Meeker, 1969; O'Neil and Spielberger, 1979; Posner, 1973; Skemp, 1979; and Whimbey, 1980. We will discuss here only one of the issues: namely, the controversies concerning interventions to stimulate linguistic and cognitive facility.

The Need for Oral Language Intervention

One dimension of this issue relates to the classic *nature/nurture* issue. In the nature/nurture controversy, the naturalists (hereditarians) believe most of our language and intelligence is determined by our biological inheritance. The nurturists (environmentalists) believe that linguistic and thinking skills result largely from environmental stimulation. In the area of psycholinguistics, Chomsky (1957,1968), Lenneberg (1967), and McNeill (1970) are some of the leading hereditarians. They contend that the human brain is genetically programmed to acquire adult syntactic structures. They say that all but severely brain-injured, mentally retarded, and deaf persons develop adult patterns of speech quite naturally, given almost any type of social environment. Similarly, in the area of cognitive development, Piaget is a hereditarian. He has maintained that children develop through identical cognitive stages, in invariant order, at uniform rates across cultures (Piaget, 1951,1952). From the hereditarian position, one can infer that intervention programs to stimulate cognitive and language skills are inappropriate and of no value, except for severely handicapped people.

There are as many environmentalists as there are hereditarians. In the linguistic areas, strict behaviorists argue that oral language is learned through operant conditioning. Speech patterns are built through the process of selectively reinforcing appropriate behaviors (Skinner, 1957, 1968; Staats, 1968). In the area of cognitive development, Bruner (1960) exemplifies the modern environmentalist. He posits that "any subject can be taught effectively in some intellectually honest form to any child at any state of development." From the theoretical position of environmentalists like these, one can infer that programs of instruction are extremely important for the cognitive and linguistic development of children.

Not surprisingly, few educators accept either of these extreme positions in the nature/nurture controversy. Instead, most accept the importance of *interaction*. They contend that both inheritance and environment play important roles and interact with each other, in complex ways, in language and cognitive development. This suggests there are limits to which intervention is likely to be effective, and we authors accept this position.

Children with average and above-average intelligence and reasonably intact central nervous systems and hearing mechanisms, who grow up in an environment where Standard English is spoken, will usually acquire proficiency in that language informally and often incidentally. But many others are not so fortunate in that they do not fit this mold. We join the many persons interested in child development who contend that intervention programs are needed both to teach Standard English to children who learned a dialect of it at home, or a foreign language, and to stimulate the linguistic skills of children who have actual or potential learning difficulties (Fristoe, 1975; Fristoe & Lloyd (in press); Lloyd, 1976; Schiefelbusch, 1978; Schiefelbusch & Lloyd, 1974). The PLDK-R series is such a program.

The Framework for the PLDK-R Series

Having argued that there is a place for interventions to stimulate the language and thought processes of many children, we need to examine the methods of intervention and determine which approach might work best. There are three main strategies. We take the position that each is effective with some children, and each has certain attractive features.

The traditional, early-childhood education method might be described as the "natural unfolding" approach. Here, children as a group are free to interact with one another and their environment in a nonstructured school setting. This approach stresses informality, play, enrichment, child-initiated activities, and teacher response to inquiry. It has been more popular with teachers of younger children than with teachers of older children. It probably has most merit for highly motivated, able youngsters. This "natural unfolding" approach is not central to the PLDK-R program. However, certain of its features are at the heart of the Peabody lessons, such as the use of play to motivate students. Even more fundamentally, the PLDK-R is a group program of instruction.

For less able children, two rather extreme intervention strategies have evolved. One is called the *differential diagnosis — prescriptive teaching* (DD-PT) approach. It is widely advocated by remedial and special educators of learning-disabled children. This is a two-step approach. Step one involves the use of standardized tests of intelligence and language to make a differential diagnosis of critical psycholinguistic and cognitive factors or abilities, based usually on subtest scores. This yields a profile of the child's abilities and disabilities. Step two involves the prescribing and carrying out of remedial procedures to correct the weaknesses.

Arter and Jenkins (1979) contend that advocates of the DD-PT approach usually have in mind underlying weaknesses in the child's higher thought processes, rather than deficiencies in observed behavior. After appraising this intervention strategy, they were led to "challenge the model's validity and suggest that continued advocacy of the model cannot be justified," though the data reviewed hardly appear to warrant this harsh conclusion. In our view, this approach would appear to be most effective for individuals with reasonably good general ability, but who have a specific weakness that lends itself to correction, such as poor word-attack skills in reading.

For four main reasons, this DD-PT approach was not used in the PLDK-R program: 1) serious questions have been raised about the validity, reliability, and mutual independence of subtests on commonly used tests of verbal intelligence and psycholinguistics; 2) there is little evidence that teaching to correct weaknesses is superior to a balanced program of instruction for most children; 3) few teachers have the training to administer individual tests of intelligence and language; and 4) classroom teachers do not have the time to tutor extensively individual children in their areas of weakness. We do recommend, however, that one feature of this approach be used in conjunction with the PLDK-R program. Global pupil progress can best be measured by using standardized instruments as pretests and posttests, administered before and after a level of PLDK-R lessons is taught.

The second intervention strategy popular with teachers of handicapped children is known as the *task-analysis* approach. In this approach, a desired, relatively complex task is identified and then broken down into a hierarchy of simple tasks (or behavioral objectives) to be mastered. The pupil is carefully studied to determine his or her proficiency along this continuum. Typically, teacher-made, criterion-referenced appraisal techniques, rather than standardized tests, are used. Then an intensive tutorial program is designed and implemented to teach the desired behaviors so the child masters the specific objectives. This systematic teaching technique (sometimes called behavior shaping) has been found to be especially effective for severely handicapped pupils.

In contrast with the DD-PT approach, this second model calls for a task to be subdivided into a finer set of specific tasks; no standardized tests are used in the initial diagnosis; and the teacher need only help the child *master* specific behavioral tasks — no attention is given to any underlying process weaknesses. While the two models are quite similar (except for arguments as to whether they deal with surface behavior or underlying processes), they do lead to somewhat different approaches in testing and teaching.

We rejected the task-analysis, behavioral-objectives approach as the basis for the LDK-R series because it is a clinical method requiring intensive individual tutoring. Such an approach is highly structured and can become mechanistic. It is very time consuming, and often is not easily applied to group instruction. However, the feature of continuously monitoring pupil progress by means of nonstandardized tests that measure units of work is a valued procedure, and we recommend that it be used in conjunction with the Peabody program.

The PLDK-R program adopts a third method — an *eclectic* approach. Its five main qualities are these. First, it is *moderately* structured — neither unstructured nor highly structured. Second, it is basically a *group* instructional program, not a tutorial one. Third, standardized tests are recommended only as supplements for placement purposes (to determine which level of the program is appropriate for the child) and for global measures of pupil progress through pretests and posttests. They are not necessary for placement. In fact, a good technique for determining the appropriateness of a given kit level is by a trial placement of the pupil in question. Fourth, PLDK-R is a comprehensive program designed to stimulate an array of cognitive and language skills; it does not teach to specific strengths or weaknesses. Fifth, the program is designed to develop word meaning, phrase meaning, sentence meaning, and, especially, connected discourse meaning (the semantics of language). It does not drill children on articulation/phonology, syntax/grammar rules, or correct pronunciation; but it does encourage good speech modeling.

This last point might lead one to ask: "Why does the program integrate instruction in language and in cognition?" The literature on the commonalities between language and thought at the higher thought process level goes back to Vygotsky (1962). He made the point that children need to be aware of and understand something before they can talk about it. Thus, there is a cyclical relationship between a child using language to map her or his knowledge of the world, and a child needing some knowledge before meaningful expressive language can occur. This construct has led many scholars to conclude that cognitive development is both prerequisite to and interactive with language development (Bloom, 1973; Clark & Clark, 1977; MacNamara, 1972; McLean, 1972; Nelson, 1973,1974; Slobin, 1973).

Language intervention programs, then, need to achieve a balance between already "mapped" or "learned" constructs and new, related constructs for which the child has some demonstrated knowledge. Graham (1976) states that language intervention should use a spontaneous approach with capable youngsters, but be more systematic with less verbal children.

The need for teaching both meaning and expressive language led McLean and Snyder-McLean (1978) to make the following suggestions for a successful intervention strategy:

1. Teach children to talk about things and events, and about relationships involving things and events.
2. Teach children to talk about such topics in terms of their knowledge of them.
3. Teach children to talk about such topics in as many different ways as their knowledge allows.

While these guidelines provided an overall framework for the PLDK-R series, the following two principles were also incorporated into the Peabody program:

1. Language intervention should stress increasingly abstract representational and symbolic thought. Mere repetition and recall will not foster this higher order of intellectual processes. Concern for higher-order thinking has received much emphasis (Bowerman, 1974; Miller & Yoder, 1974; Morehead & Morehead, 1974).
2. Language intervention should stress the social uses of language. A setting should exist for children to receive feedback about their use of language, as well as to experience the effects their language has upon others in a group. Schlesinger (1974) and Yoder and Miller (1972) point out that children must have a reason to talk and a desire to communicate. A natural interactive setting more closely approximates the child's real world than does a structured, clinical environment. A natural setting maximizes the probability that skills will be generalized to other natural settings.

This background of thought furnishes a rationale for the PLDK-R program. It would seem to be equally relevant for teaching English as a second language, for teaching Standard English to girls and boys who first learned a dialect, and for teaching children with learning problems who come from homes where Standard English is spoken.

Research

Almost 20 years of research has accumulated on the efficacy of the Peabody program and its antecedent. This research is summarized below.

The antecedent was a doctoral investigation conducted by James O. Smith (1962a & 1962b), co-author of PLDK, while he was at Peabody College as an advisee of Lloyd M. Dunn, the senior author of the Peabody series. Smith generated 33 lessons as a group, oral-language development program for mildly retarded children in special day classes. Experimental and control groups — 16 pairs — were set up, and lessons were taught to the former at the rate of three per week for only 11 weeks. Significant overall gains were obtained on the original *Illinois Test of Psycholinguistic Abilities* (ITPA) in favor of the experimental group. Approximately one year later, Mueller and Smith (1964) located 13 of the original 16 pairs and readministered the ITPA to them. In this follow-up study, the difference was no longer statistically significant. This finding strongly suggested the need for a longer intervention program to enhance the chances of initial gains becoming long-term advantages.

Work on the original editions of PLDK began with Level 1 in 1964, and was completed with Level P in 1968 (Dunn & Smith, 1965, Dunn & Smith, 1966; Dunn & Smith, 1967; Dunn, Horton, & Smith, 1968). Over this period of time, a number of efficacy studies were conducted, usually with the *experimental* (field-test) version of the original kits, not with the final, refined commercial publications. Three sources of data have accumulated on these experimental editions. First, the efficacy of Level P was researched in studies initiated by Kathryn B. Horton, coordinator of that level of the series. Second, while Dunn was director of the *Institute on Mental Retardation and Intellectual Development* (IMRID) at Peabody College, he and his colleagues conducted several studies on the effectiveness of Levels 1, 2, and 3. The third research base came from independent researchers studying Level 1. These three groups of early studies are summarized below.

Early Studies

Efficacy studies on the experimental edition of Level P. The most extensive field testing was done at two community day-care centers that served inner-city black children in Nashville, Tennessee (Horton, 1968). A group of 25 four- and five-year-old children at one center was taught an early version of the Level P lessons, in addition to their regular preschool program. A group of 28 children at the other center served as the control and received only their regular program. Data was gathered using the following tests: *Peabody Picture Vocabulary Test* (PPVT); *Stan ford-Binet Form L-M* (S-B); the *Illinois Test of Psycholinguistic Abilities* (ITPA); and The Test of Grammar, adapted from Berko (1958). After a seven-month instructional program, the experimental group demonstrated substantially greater gains in intellectual functioning, as seen in Table 2.1. In addition, on the ITPA, the experimental group advanced an average of 7.2 months, while the control group advanced only an average of 3.9 months in language age. The subtests on which the experimental group made the greatest gains were visual-motor association (± 23.4 months), auditory decoding (+16.8 months), and auditory-vocal association (+12.8 months). They regressed in one subtest, auditory-vocal sequential (immediate auditory memory for digits). By contrast, the control group regressed in the following four subtests: vocal encoding (-5.8 months), motor encoding (-3.95 months), auditory-vocal automatic (-5.1 months), and visual-motor sequential (-1.5 months).

Group	Pretest	Posttest	Difference
	Mean S-B IQ Scores		
Experimental group	93.3	102.9	+9.6
Control group	l93.6	91.3	-2.3
	Mean PPVT IQ Scores		
Experimental group	81.0	93.0	+12.0
Control group	71.8	79.6	+7.8

Table 2.1
Mean intelligence test scores on the *Stanford-Binet* and *Peabody Picture Vocabulary Test* before and after seven months of training using the experimental edition of Level P of the original PLDK series with four- and five-year-old inner city African American children

A second study on the effectiveness of the experimental version of the original Level P involved a group of 20 mentally retarded children in residence in a school in Wisconsin. Their IQs clustered around 50, and their mental ages ranged from three to five years. These children were also given seven months of Level P training. Their performances on the ITPA, prior to the program and immediately after it, were compared. The total group was divided into three subgroups, according to their level of functioning in school. As seen in Table 2.2, the mean language age increases were 10.2, 14.2, and 14.0 months, respectively. These were very impressive gains indeed, since the children could only be expected to increase developmentally about 3.5 months in language age during that period of time.

Group	N	Pre-training Mean Language Age (months)	Post-training Mean Language Age (months)	Difference (months)
Adjustment Group	5	26.00	36.2	+10.2
Pre-Kindergarten Group	11	46.8	61.0	+14.2
Kindergarten Group	13	58.0	72.0	+14.0

Table 2.2
Mean language age scores on the *Illinois Test of Psycholinguistic Abilities* before and after seven months of training using the experimental edition of Level P of the PLDK series with mentally retarded children

It was concluded from this field-test research that the experimental Level P lessons could stimulate intellectual and linguistic skills of inner-city black children and moderately mentally retarded children, even over a short period of seven months. The long-term residual effects were not tested.

IMRID efficacy studies on the experimental and commercial editions of the original Levels 1,2, and 3. The most comprehensive IMRID investigation was the *Cooperative Language Development Project.* This project ran from 1964 to 1967, and a follow-up study was conducted in 1968. In this study, 734 inner-city black children in Nashville, Tennessee, over their first three grades, received varying amounts of PLDK instruction taught by: 1) regular teachers alone, 2) a team of two instructors, 3) an itinerant language specialist, and 4) community volunteers with supervision.

Researched as well was the relative effectiveness of teaching the lessons to a whole class, as compared with presenting them twice per day, first to the brighter children and then to the slower children. In the first grade, the children were taught the 180 experimental Level 1 lessons; in the second grade, the 180 experimental Level 2 lessons; and in the third grade, the 180 experimental Level 3 lessons. Also contrasted in the project was the relative effectiveness of the *Initial Teaching Alphabet* (ITA) approach to teaching beginning reading versus a regular textbook program in traditional orthography (TO).

Four reports describe the four stages of this study. Dunn and Mueller (1966) described progress at the end of the first year; Dunn, Pochanart, and Pfost (1967) at the end of the second year; and Dunn, Pochanart, Pfost, and Bruininks (1968) at the end of the third year in school. Dunn and Bruininks (1968a) reported on a fourth-grade follow-up study in which the data were gathered one year after the termination of the three-year intervention program. The results were complex; the following is but a summary:

1. At the end of the three-year experimental phase, PLDK instruction with the experimental versions of Levels 1, 2, and 3 had resulted: in significant gains in language age, as measured by the ITPA; in significant gains in intelligence (10) as measured by the S-B; and in significant school achievement gains, as measured by the *Metropolitan Achievement Tests* (MET). However, only the significant 10 gains were retained in follow-up evaluation at the end of the fourth grade.
2. Generally, children who were taught the PLDK lessons once a day, as a whole class, made as much progress as those in classes where the lessons were taught twice a day, first to the brighter and then to the slower children.
3. The regular teachers alone, the team of two instructors, the itinerant language specialist alone, and the community volunteers were equally effective in teaching the program.
4. Overall, the children who first learned to read by using TA were generally superior to the TO group at posttesting, but essentially all these differences were lost by the time of the follow-up testing.

A second IMRID project, called the *Cooperative Reading Project,* was conducted with a similar group of inner-city black children between 1965 and 1967. Its aim was to measure a greater variety of reading approaches, in combination with the Peabody lessons, using the final *commercial* editions of Levels 1 and 2. The three alternative reading programs were 1) the *Hay-Win go Reading with Phonics*, as a supplement to the *Houghton-Mifflin Reading for Meaning* series; 2) *Initial Teaching Alphabet;* and 3) the *Words in Color* (WIC) program. Each method was either combined or not combined with PLDK instruction. Successive reports of this project can be found in Dunn, Neville, Bailey, Pochanart, and Pfost (1967), and in Dunn, Neville, Pfost, Pochanart, and Bruininks (1968), with a follow-up by Dunn and Bruininks (1968b) after the third grade. The results were mixed, but the major findings were:

1. PLDK instruction facilitated the development of linguistic skills more than intellectual and academic skills.
2. Generally, the first reading approach (basic reader supplemented with phonic drills) was somewhat superior, with few significant differences among the three reading approaches.

The results of the *Cooperative Language Development Project* and the *Cooperative Reading Project* are outlined in Table 2.3.

Researcher	Year	CA**	IQ***	Duration of Treatment	Results****
Cooperative Language Development Project					
1. Dunn & Mueller	1966	$\bar{X} = 6.4$	$\bar{X} = 84.55$ SD = 11.32	First-grade school year	PLDK groups made significant LA gains over non-PLDK groups. PLDK with ITA groups made significant IQ gains — gains greater for boys than girls in these groups. ITA combined with PLDK suggested to enhance school achievement.
2. Dunn, Pochanart, & Pfost	1967	$\bar{X} = 7.4$	$\bar{X} = 84.86$ SD = 10.82	Second-grade school year	Second-year PLDK group made significant reading gains over non-PLDK and PLDK-for-only-a-year groups. PLDK group made significant LA gains over non-PLDK. IQ gains were made but not significant.
3. Dunn, Pochanart, Pfost, & Bruininks	1968	$\bar{X} = 8.4$	$\bar{X} = 84.93$ SD = 14.73	Third-year school year	PLDK group with ITA made significant IQ gains. Second- and third-year PLDK groups with ITA made signifant LA gains (length of program related to amount of gains made — the longer in related to amount of gains made-the longer in PLDK, the greater the gains). Gains in reading achievement occurred but were not significant.
4. Dunn & Bruininks	1968a	$\bar{X} = 9.4$	$\bar{X} = 90.38$	No PLDK treatment during fourth-grade school year	Significant IQ gains remained. Significant achievement gains were lost except when ITA was paired with two or three years of PLDK instruction.
Cooperative Reading Project					
1. Dunn, Neville, Bailey, Pochanart, & Pfost	1967	$\bar{X} = 6.2$	$\bar{X} = 86.87$	First-grade school year	Significant IQ gains by PLDK group over controls. No significant LA gains by PLDK group over controls. Boys made greater LA gains than girls. PLDK group significantly better in connected speech production. No significant differences in reading.
2. Dunn, Neville, Pfost, Pochanart, & Bruininks	1968	$\bar{X} = 7.2$	$\bar{X} = 86.73$ SD = 10.77	Second-grade school year	No significant differences between PLDK and non-PLDK groups for IQ, LA, Mat. Girls in PLDK made significant MA gains in both the 1-year and 2-year groups. Boys made significantly greater LA gains than girls. Two-year WIC groups with PLDK made significantly more LA gains than 1-year PLDK or non-PLDK groups. Two-year PLDK and non-PLDK groups did significantly better on MAT written language than the 1-year PLDK group.
3. Dunn & Bruininks	1968b	$\bar{X} = 8.2$	$\bar{X} = 88.65$	No PLDK treatment during third-grade school year	IQ scores fell to original levels for most groups even though differential gains for some had been significant. Gains remained on LA for PLDK groups in one of two analyses of data. Creative thinking was significantly better for 1- and 2-year PLDK groups. Significant differences were in favor of PLDK groups in one of two analyses of data on MAT.

Table 2.3
Summary of major IMRID efficacy studies on the experimental versions of Levels 1,2, and 3 of the original edition of the PLDK series*

*The language development project used the experimental editions of Levels 1, 2, and 3. The reading project used published editions of Levels 1 and 2. In both projects, teachers were requested to use the materials as recommended.
**CA reported is approximation of ages at beginning of each treatment period.
***IQ reported was taken from the Stanford-Binet results (1960 edition).
****Results reported are limited to those directly related to use of PLDK.

In a third project, the commercial versions of the original Level 1 and 2 lessons were taught to an initial pool of 283 mildly retarded, special-class children over a two and one-half year period (Dunn, Nitzman, Pochanart, & Bransky, 1968). In contrast to a control group, the experimental group of children gained significantly in language and cognitive skills but not in school achievement. There was an "initial spurt" phenomenon, with most of the gains occurring in the first school year. There was no follow-up to determine how long lasting the effects were.

One other IMRID study bears reporting. Hausman and Apffel (1968) analyzed the ITPA profiles of subjects in the *Cooperative Reading Project* who were taught Levels 1 and 2of the commercial versions of the kits. In contrast to the control curricula, they found that the Peabody lessons were especially effective in enhancing the ability of inner-city black children to express their ideas in words (vocal encoding) and to remember sequences of symbols (auditory-vocal sequencing). They suggested that the Peabody lessons be supplemented with grammar exercises to correct further the major oral language deficits. However, in scanning the ITPA profile, one can see that the growth in all nine subtests was remarkably equal, with unusual improvements in the two areas cited.

Independent research on the experimental version of Level 1. Several studies, independent of IMRID, were conducted using the experimental version of the original Level 1. Table 2.4 summarizes these results.

Milligan (1965, 1966) taught some of the Level 1 lessons (experimental edition) to normal kindergarten children over a period of six months. As measured with the ITPA, the experimental group made greater gains than the control group on total language age, auditory association, and verbal expression. There was no support for significant achievement gains based on the *Metropolitan Readiness Test.*

Another study using the experimental edition of Level 1 was conducted by Carter (1966), with only a 10-week treatment period for

Researcher	Year	Population	CA	IQ	Use of Materials	Duration of Treatment	Results
Milligan	1965 (1966)	Normal kindergarten	Kindergarten age range	(not given)	Standard as recommend-ed	6 months; 40-to-45-minute daily sessions	PLDK group made greater gains on LA, AA, and VE. Significant support on AA & VE. No support for achievement gains.
Carter	1966	Culturally diverse; low SES	$\bar{X}$ = 6.75 Ranged from 6.1 to 8.2	$\bar{X}$ = 75 Ranged from 62 to 91	Standard as recommend-ed, first 40 lessons	10 weeks; 1 hour, 4 days per week	Significant support for LA, IQ, & MA gains. No support for achievement gains (at that time).
Ensminger	1966	Slow learners	Ranged from 6.1 to 7.9; ranged from 7.1 to 9.9	Ranged from 70 to 95	Standard as recommend-ed, 132 lessons	6 1/2 months; 30-45-minute sessions	Significant support for VE & AA. None for MA. Younger group made greater gains.
Forgnone	1966 (1976)	EMR	Ranged from 7.0 to 11.0	Ranged from 50 to 80	Standard with Frostig, 58 lessons	3 months; daily sessions	No significant support for LA, IQ, or achievement gains.
Gibson	1966 (1967)	EMR	Ranged from 6.5 to 9.0	$\bar{X}$ = 76.34	Standard as recommend-ed, first 45 lessons	6 months	No significant support for LA. Slight gains on selected direct measures of VE. No support for MA.

Table 2.4
Summary of early efficacy studies done independently of the authors with the experimental version of Level 1 of the original edition of the PLDK series

socioeconomically disadvantaged rural black students. Rather surprisingly, considering the short period of intervention, Carter found that the PLDK groups, when compared with control groups, made significant gains in language age, IQ, and mental age. He found no support for significant achievement gains as measured by the *Lee-Clark California Reading Test.* However, several follow-up studies, to be reported later in this guide, indicate that the reading achievement gains appeared at a later age.

Ensminger (1966) conducted a study on mildly retarded subjects enrolled in special day classes. He concluded that the PLDK group, as measured with the ITPA, exhibited significant improvement in verbal expression and auditory association. However, no significant changes occurred in overall language age or mental age. Ensminger then divided his subjects into younger and older age groups. From this analysis, it appeared that younger subjects made greater gains in language age, as compared with the younger control subjects, but the gain did not reach the .05 level of significance.

Forgnone (1966, 1976) taught the first 58 experimental lessons of Level 1 to some mildly retarded, special-class subjects who were involved in a study primarily to measure the efficacy of the *Frostig Visual Perception Program.* He found no significant effects from the lessons on verbal, intellectual, or academic progress from this short treatment program.

Gibson (1966,1967) taught the same set of lessons for a period of six months to some mildly retarded subjects. No significant increases in language or mental age were obtained in this same short period of time.

One major conclusion can be drawn from this cluster of studies. Short-term programs of instruction, lasting a few weeks or months, generally are not very effective. These results would very likely have been largely the same had the final, commercial edition been used. There is cumulative evidence that longer treatment periods are necessary to produce significant pupil progress, though an "initial spurt" effect sometimes occurs.

Later Research

A considerable number of efficacy studies were conducted using lessons from the published, original editions of Levels P, 1, 2, and 3. This research is presented below. Several studies used Levels P and 1. It appears that very few studies used Levels 2 and 3; however, in some cases the level used was not reported. No attempt is made to present a comprehensive analysis of each study. Instead the reader is referred to the original sources for more extensive information.

Later research on Level P. Several studies reporting on the effectiveness of Level P are summarized in Table 2.5.

The effectiveness of Level P with disadvantaged children has been rather well researched, and the findings are quite consistent. Howe (1972), Jones (1970), McConnell, Horton, and Smith (1969), Miller (1977), Parker (1969, 1970), and Woodhead (1976) all found significant support for Level P. However, after only three months of intervention, the various findings, based on ITPA total language age scores and 10 scores, were mixed. After nine months, gains were generally significant. In summary, Level P appears to be effective in stimulating gains among disadvantaged children in the cognitive and language areas, and even in social competency. Its effects on reading readiness are questionable, although gains were made in some instances.

The research on the effectiveness of Level P with moderately retarded children is less supportive. Happ and Lyon (1972) reported progress in functional language, and Shiach (1973) found significant gains on language measures. However, Leiss and Proger (1974) and Proger and Leiss (1976) conducted a three-year study (Leiss & Proger, 1977) in which Level P was used during the second and third years. Their purpose was to compare the effects of Level P and *Distar* (Engelmann & Osburn, 1970) on trainable children. *Distar* groups gained more on all measures, except that, in the third year, the PLDK-P group made significantly greater gains on auditory association. Leiss and Proger acknowledge the weakness of their research design since, for practical reasons, nonverbal children were assigned to the PLDK-P group, and children with some words and phrases were assigned to a combined Distar — PLDK-P group. Thus the Distar groups had a clear advantage in functional language skills. Nevertheless, the results do seem to support other studies to be noted later in this guide (Guess, Rutherford, Smith, & Ensminger, 1970; Guess, Smith, & Ensminger, 1971) in which the contents of the PLDK lessons were found to be too advanced for trainable children. Apparently, concepts presented to these youngsters need to

Researcher	Year	Population	CA	IQ	Use of Materials	Duration of Treatment	Results
McConnell, Horton, & Smith	1969	Urban; low SES	Ranged from 2.67 to 5.91	$\bar{X}$ = 92	Standard as part of total program	9 months; first 85 to 90 lessons	Significant support for S-B IQ gains. No significant support for PPVT gains. Significant gains made on LA. Significant gains made on MRT.
Parker	1969a 1969b 1970	Comparison-middle SES caucasian; experimental-low SES black. Each group had matched controls	4-year-olds	$\bar{X}$ = 95	Standard	One group = 9 months; one group = 3 months	Significant support for 9-month group on IQ, VA, VE, VC, ASM, VSM. Three-month group made no significant gains. Nine-month group resulted in no significant differences., although there were initial gains. No significant support for MRT gains.
Jones	1970	Urban; low SES	Ranged from 4 to 6	(not given)	Standard; approxi-metely 56 lessons	2 1/2 months (estimate); daily	Significant support on ITPA total and IQ for pre-post gains. Significant gains occurred for regular preschool and regular preschool with PLDK.
Happ & Lyon	1972	TMR	5 to 9	MA ($\bar{X}$) = 2.5	Modified to lowered needs of TMR	(not specified)	More functional language observed. No data.
Howe	1972	Low SES	Pre-school, 3- & 4-year-olds	Approximately 100	Standard, with story reading & discussion added	Full year school	Significant support on VA. Greater gains on PPVT. Distar group made greater gains on AM. PLDK enhanced conceptual processes. Distar enhanced memory.
Shiach	1973	Severely subnormal	$\bar{X}$ = 11.67	$\bar{X}$ = 44.5	Standard	Full year school	Significant support on VE, ME, and total LA.
Leiss & Proger	1974	TMR	Ranged from 7 to 14	First group ranged from 21 to 43; second group ranged from 44 to 53	Standard	7 1/2 months	For high-IQ group, PLDK was significantly better than for low-IQ group. Distar groups were significantly better than PLDK groups. Low IQ-PLDK did significantly worse than either Distar group.
Proger & Leiss	1976	TMR	Ranged from 7 to 14	First group ranged from 21 to 43; second group ranged from 44 to 53	Standard	7 1/2 months	Significant suport for improved MA. Distar groups were significantly better on VA, VE, GC, PPVT, Spencer Memory for Sentences, & Distar placement.
Woodhead	1976	Low SES	$\bar{X}$ = 4.2 Ranged from 3.4 to 5.0	$\bar{X}$ = 100.9	Standard, with minimal modifications to British Educational System	Full year school (estimate)	Significant support on VA, VE.Greater gains on GC, AA, ASM.
Miller	1977	Low SES	$\bar{X}$ = 4.2	(not given)	Standard	7 months (approximate-ly); first 85 to 90 lessons	Significant support on Cain Levine Social Competency Scale. No significant support on Preschool Inventory, although greater gains were made.

Table 2.5
Summary of later research on Level P of the original edition of the PLDK series

Researcher	Year	Population	CA	IQ	Use of Materials	Duration of Treatment	Results
Mitchell	1967	Culturally diverse; Head Start pre-first graders	Summer before first grade	(not given)	Standard; 25 lessons	Summer of 1966	No significant support on total language score. PLDK gains made. Mean raw score greater on post-test than pre-test. Differential effect on ITPA, AV.
Gazdic	1971	"High risk" first graders	(not given)	$\bar{X}$ = 93.78 Ranged from 75 to 111	Standard, development al first-grade program	Full school year	No significant support.
Schifani	1971	EMR	Ranged from 9 to 13	Ranged from 50 to 80	Standard	9 months	Significant support for LA gains.
Marchand, Buelde, & Woodward	1974	L.D. language problems; French-speak-ing Canadian	Ranged from 5.75 to 7.75	Ranged from 85 to 134	Modified in vocabulary, creativity, & sequencing	4 months	Significant results. Pre-post gain design. Significant for listening, Wepman, ITPA.
Campbell, Moffat, & Bracket	1978	EMR	Ranged from 6 to 9	Ranged from 50 to 75	Standard; Lessons 1-5 & 13-53	2 1/2 months; 45 sessions; 30 min. daily	Significant support for mathematics achievement gains.

Table 2.6
Summary of later research on Level 1 of the original edition of the PLDK series

be simpler and more functional. Also, the learning environment needs to be more highly structured than PLDK provides on its own.

Later research on Level 1. A summary of Level 1 research is found in Table 2.6. The findings in it need to be considered along with the early studies reported in Tables 2.3 and 2.4. Clearly, the results were mixed. In the later research, significant gains were consistently made with mildly retarded subjects. Schifani (1971) found significant gains for ITPA language age after nine months of PLDK instruction. Campbell, Moffat, and Bracket (1978) report a study unique in PLDK research. Their primary area of investigation was mathematics achievement (specifically, computation and application) as measured by the *Stanford Achievement Test.* They found that the PLDK group, after only two and one-half months, made significant mathematics achievement gains between pretesting and posttesting, when compared with the controls.

Mitchell (1967) and Gazdic (1971) found no significant support for ITPA language gains with high-risk pre-first graders and first graders. Mitchell conducted research using Level 1 with summer Head Start children before their first-grade year. Level 1 was the lowest level available at the time, and so the possibility exists that it was too advanced.

With French-speaking Canadian children with language problems, Marchand, Buelde, and Woodward (1974) obtained significant ITPA results after only four months of intervention.

More research has been done with Level 1 than with any of the other levels. Additional evidence on its effectiveness is presented later in this guide when an overall research analysis is reported.

Later research with a combination of levels and with Levels 2 and 3. Some studies have used combinations of Levels P, 1,2, and 3 to match a wide range of pupil abilities. One study used the experimental version of the original Level 3. These are summarized in Table 2.7.

Except for the IMRID studies reported earlier, no independent study was found that tested the efficacy of Level 2 in isolation, and there was only one that tested Level 3.

Researcher	Year	PLDK Levels	Population	CA	IQ	Use of Materials	Duration of Treatment	Results
Cross	1968	3 (exp.)	Third-grade regular class divided into low and high groups	$\bar{X}$ = 8.26 Ranged from 7.6 to 8.8	$\bar{X}$ = 100 Ranged from 74 to 138	Standard	6 months	Significant support for IQ gains for low-achieving students. No significant support for PPVT gains. Significant support for increase in number of responses for low-achieving. PLDK enhances reading on ITBS for regular class students.
Guess, Rutherford, Smith, & Ensminger	1970	P, 1, 2	Severely retarded in residential facility	$\bar{X}$ = 13 Ranged from 4 to 18	$\bar{X}$ = 33 Ranged from 14 to 61	Standard for Levels 1 and 2. Level P was extensively modified for lowest IQ students.	9 months	Significant support for IQ gains for combined PLDK and special class group over those receiving none. Significant support for PLDK group with LA over group with no treatment and group with only special class.
Saudergras, Madsen, & Thompson	1971	P & 3	Regular combined second- and third-grade students; culturally diverse	$\bar{X}$ = 8.5	$\bar{X}$ = 77	Adapted as part of eclectic, prescriptive, learning center program	3 months; 15-minute sessions, 3 days a week	Support based on Sheldon Reading Inventories. Significant support for total prescriptive program.
Guess, Smith, & Ensminger	1971	P, 1, 2	Severely retarded in residential facility	Same as above	Same as above	Same as above	18 months total (follow-up of above)	Significant support for IQ gains for 1-to-9-month group. No significant support for IQ for 1-to-18 and 9- to-18. Significant support for ITPA total LA gains for 9-to18 and 1-to-18.
Lovitt & Smith	1972	P, 1, 2, & 3	Learning disability (single subject study)	9	(not given)	Picture cards only, pulled from each level	28 days (sessions)	Verbal responses significantly changed according to instructions given for beginning a sentence and length of response.
Carter	1975	1 & 2	Random sample from 84 EMR & 6 TMR	$\bar{X}$ = 12.2	$\bar{X}$ = 63	Selected lessons 1 & 2 for specific auditory discrimina-tion training	6 weeks; daily 30-minute sessions	Significant support for Wepman Auditory Discrimination gains.

Table 2.7
Summary of later research on levels 2 and 3, and combined levels of the original edition of the PLDK series

The Level 3 study was conducted by Cross (1968), who conducted a six-month study using the experimental lessons of that level. The children were regular-class third graders, one group of whom was at or below the 33rd percentile in total language skills as measured by the *Iowa Tests of Basic Skills* (ITBS). The other group consisted of students who were above the 33rd percentile. The low-achieving PLDK group made significant *Stan ford-Binet* 10 gains. There were also significant gains for number of responses made to a silent movie stimulus for low-achieving students, and a significant increase in ITBS reading scores for the high-achieving group. This latter finding is especially important, since few studies have reported reading achievement gains. Carter (1967), as previously discussed, also found reading gains one year after first-grade PLDK lessons. The research of both Carter and Cross suggests the possibility that reading gains may occur at second and third grade. Neither study says which basal reader was used. However, since many basal readers do not focus on comprehension skills until the second and third grade, there may have been little interaction between the Peabody lessons and the reading test scores until that time.

Two studies (Guess, Rutherford, Smith, & Ensminger, 1970; Guess, Smith, & Ensminger, 1971) found significant support for Levels P, 1, and 2 when used with severely retarded children in residential facilities. However, Level P had to be extensively modified to stimulate appropriate behaviors. Significant 10 gains and ITPA total LA gains were made after the first nine months by the group receiving PLDK lessons. However, no extra growth was noted when treatment extended for another nine months, suggesting again that an "initial spurt" phenomenon may have occurred. Another finding was that psychiatric aides, without prior teacher training, could teach the PLDK lessons effectively. This finding is supported by Howe (1971, 1972). He found that paraprofessionals, in this case community aides who enrolled in a training program, were effective in teaching the PLDK lessons in a community preschool. Both sets of studies, as well as the IMRID study reported earlier, agree that aides can be effective instructors of PLDK lessons.

Three other studies represent unusual uses for the PLDK lessons. Lovitt and Smith (1972) used only the picture cards to serve as stimuli for verbal responses. They found that such responses were significantly improved after instruction was given in how to begin a sentence. Saudergras, Madsen, and Thompson (1971) used Fessons from Levels P and 3 as part of a total prescriptive program in a learning center. Children needing specific skills were given selected instruction to remediate their language difficulties. The authors concluded that this approach was effective. Carter (1975) used selected lessons in Levels 1 and 2 to stimulate auditory discrimination, and subjects made significant gains on the *Wepman Auditory Discrimination Test*. Carter's findings suggest that this procedure stimulates auditory discrimination.

Later research on unspecified levels. Several studies used the original PLDK lessons, but the levels used were not reported. Therefore, these studies are analyzed according to population and duration of instruc tion. They are summarized in Table 2.8.

Discussed first are three studies involving socioeconomically disadvantaged subjects. Beidler (1968) used a language arts program, along with PLDK lessons, for seven months with such children in the primary grades. No significant gains were found except in word recognition, a result hard to understand since PLDK involves no written language. With four-year-old youngsters, Richmond (1970) found no significant gains over controls from using PLDK lessons for a year. This finding seems incompatible with much of the other evidence. With rural kindergarten children, Clasen, Spear, and Tomaro (1969), after PLDK lessons were taught for only eight weeks, reported significant overall gains for ITPA language age. And, rather remarkably, this gain persisted after one year in two of the ITPA subtests, visual perception and visual association.

Next reported are two studies whose subjects were mildly retarded children. After a 15-week instruction period, Rabush (1973) found that the *Syntax Teaching Program* was more effective than PLDK for low-verbally-performing retarded children. This finding is consistent with the authors' initial recognition that syntactical patterns are not emphasized in PLDK lessons. A unique study was conducted by Riegel, Taylor, and Danner (1973). They used two treatments, PLDK lessons and strategy training, to investigate the improvement of recall and sorting skills. Because PLDK does not directly teach sorting, more significant results for sorting skills were obtained by the strategy-training group. However, no significant differences were found between the groups on total recall.

Later research on long-term PLDK effects. The ultimate goal of any treatment is to have long-term positive effects. In the IMRID studies, some evidence showed that the effects of teaching the PLDK lessons faded out by the fourth grade follow-up. However, Carter has found more positive effects.

As reported earlier, Carter (1966a, 1966b) conducted a study with low socioeconomic students in the first grade. The experimental group received PLDK language training with the regular class curriculum, and the control group received the regular class curriculum only. PLDK instruction extended only over a 10-week period, and Carter used the experimental edition of Level 1. He found significant S-B 10 and mental age gains, as well as overall ITPA

Researcher	Year	Population	CA	IQ	Use of Materials	Duration of Treatment	Results
Beidler	1968	Low SES in regular classes	Grades K, 1, & 2	(not given)	Standard, used with regular language arts program	7 months	No significant support for K, 1, or 2 on Otis Lennon MA, Reading, and Listening. Significant support for second graders on Word Recognition.
Clasen, Spear, & Tomaro	1969	Low SES; rural	(not given)	(not given)	Standard, with games and other language-building activities	8 weeks; daily	Significant support for ITPA. Significant support one year later for kindergartners on VR, VA. No significant support for IQ gains.
Richmond	1970	Low SES	4-year-olds	(not given)	Standard	Full school year	No significant support for PLDK over regular program. Both groups made significant pre-post gains.
Rabush	1973	Low-verbally-performing students	Ranged from 4 to 14	(not given)	Standard	15 weeks; 60 sessions; 30 minutes each	No significant support for PLDK. Syntax Teaching Program was more effective on direct measure of verbal expression.
Riegel, Taylor, & Danner	1973	EMR	SIS group $\bar{X}$ = 8.3 PLDK group $\bar{X}$ = 7.7	SIS group $\bar{X}$ = 72.5 PLDK group $\bar{X}$ = 72.3	Standard	4 weeks	PLDK and SIS (strategy training) no significant differences on total recall. SIS positively significant on sorting and recall clustering.

Table 2.8
Summary of later research on unspecified levels of the original edition of the PLDK series

language age gains. Results were significant upon pretest and posttest analysis, as well as significantly different from the control group scores. There was, however, no significant difference between pre- and post-scores or control group comparisons on reading achievement, as measured by the *Lee-Clark Reading Test.*

Twenty months (1 .8 years) after the initial testing, Carter (1967) found that significant gains had been maintained. By that time, the children were in the middle of the second grade. One extraordinary finding was that significant reading achievement differences emerged in favor of the experimental PLDK group when the *California Reading Test* and the *Durrell Analysis of Reading Difficulty* were used. In summary, 10, MA, and LA gains remained significantly superior to the controls, and a significant reading differential emerged after 20 months.

Approximately one year later, when the children were in the third grade, the same significant differences continued to be evident (Carter, 1969, 1971). The experimental group (24 of the original 32) had not reached "grade level," but were achieving significantly better than their controls, who had not received PLDK lessons. Experimental group IQ, MA, and LA scores continued to be significantly higher than those for the control group.

Carter and Capobianco (1976) published another follow-up report when most of the subjects had completed the seventh grade. They also located records on 17 of the original 32 pairs. Once again, significant gains were maintained.

Needless to say, Carter and his associates have presented interesting long-term results, after PLDK lessons were taught for only 10 weeks in the first grade. However, since the long-term effects are so positive, and so divergent from the follow-up IMRID study, there is a clearly indicated need for additional research on the long-term effects of the PLDK lessons.

Overall Research Analyses

The foregoing review of individual research shows a pattern of mixed results. Some studies report positive gains, and others no significant progress. This raises the basic question: Under what circumstances, for what groups of children, and in which areas, does the PLDK program work? Several review articles throw considerable light on this query.

Hammill and Larsen (1974) reviewed the results of 39 studies reporting on the effectiveness of a variety of language intervention programs. In 31 of the 39 studies, PLDK was used as the program of instruction. In all cases, the ITPA was used as a measure of pupil improvement in language functioning. These reviewers were especially interested in determining which subtests (psycholinguistic processes), if any, were stimulated by the training programs. From an analysis of the data, they concluded: "The effectiveness of psycholinguistic training has not been conclusively demonstrated. Therefore, the rapid expansion of psycholinguistic training programs seems unwarranted."

This negative finding precipitated two replies. In the first, Minskoff (1975) argued that such a conclusion was not warranted because so many studies had design weaknesses, the treatments extended over too short a time, and too few subjects were used. After reinterpretation of the data, she concluded that psycholinguistic training can be effective.

The second reply was by Lund, Foster, and McCall-Perez (1978), who reanalyzed 24 of the 39 studies reviewed by Hammill and Larsen. They reported finding a number of cases of inaccurate reporting, inappropriate categorization, and misinterpretation which invalidated the conclusions. Their conclusion was that some studies showed significant gains and others did not. Thus no black-and-white indictment was justified.

In a reply, Hammill and Larsen (1978) conceded they had made some errors in reporting the data. However, they continued to argue that the inconclusive and mixed results, in and of themselves, demonstrated that the effectiveness of psycholinguistic process training had yet to be *conclusively* demonstrated. Clearly, the word *conclusively* made their observation technically accurate, but hardly justified the extreme course of action they proposed, namely to condemn all psycholinguistic training programs.

The controversy remained unresolved until Kavale (1980, in press) reported the results of his reanalyses of these efficacy studies. Hammill and Larsen simply used *inferential tests of significance* to report each study as producing "passing" or "failing" results. Kavale spotted this all-or-none weakness that was used to analyze the data. So he proceeded to conduct a meta-analysis on the same data, using procedures developed by Glass (1976, 1977). The results were based on the original 39 studies. These data represented approximately 1,850 experimental and control subjects, who averaged 7.5 years of age with a mean 10 of 82, and who received an average of only 50 hours of psycholinguistic training. This meta-analysis was based on the large samples and thus was able to shed light on the magnitude of the treatment effects. The major results were as follows:

1. Overall, the subjects receiving psycholinguistic training stood at the 65th percentile of the average for the control group, who stood at the 50th percentile. This 15-percentage differential was considered substantial enough to justify psycholinguistic training.
2. The PLDK program was found to be more effective than the others cited in the report. Included were highly structured programs, perceptual-motor training, and ITPA-based instruction. It was suggested that the moderately structured and sequential nature of PLDK lessons was the major factor contributing to its greater effectiveness.
3. The PLDK lessons stimulate all nine ITPA subtests. The average effects are rank-ordered below:

Vocal expression	0.77
Manual expression	0.53
Auditory association	0.49
Visual association	0.45
Visual sequential memory	0.42
Auditory sequential memory	0.34
Auditory reception	0.32
Grammatic closure	0.11
Visual reception	0.10

As designed, the Peabody lessons are especially effective in teaching children to express themselves well. They do not teach well the rules of grammar, or how to classify pictures from memory.

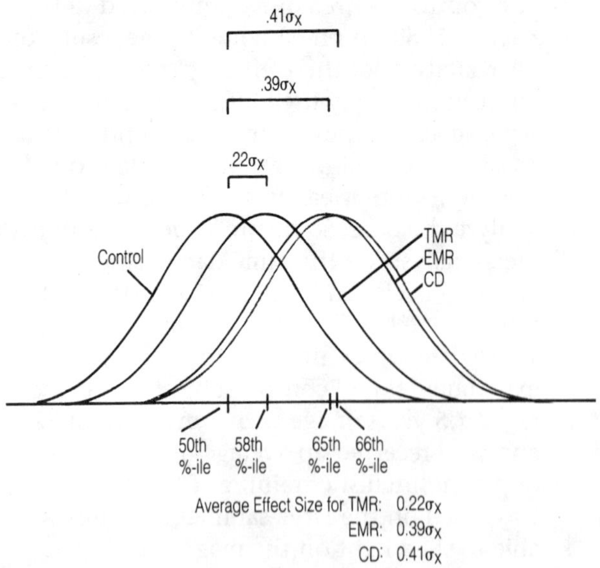

Figure 2.1
Differential effects of language intervention in IPTA scores for culturally disadvantaged, educable mentally retarded, and trainable mentally retarded subjects (Kavale, 1980; Kavale, in press)

4. PLDK lessons were found to be slightly more effective for low socioeconomic children, often black, than for mildly retarded and learning disabled children. The differences, however, were minimal. The program did not work well, as written, for trainable mentally retarded children. The average effect size for the three groups is shown below in Figure 2.1.

5. The program worked equally well with preschool and elementary level children.

The more sensitive meta-analysis brought the findings of existing research reports into focus. An overall pattern now has been discerned. Another decade or more of efficacy studies is needed to sharpen the conclusions. It is to be hoped that a body of knowledge will emerge on the effectiveness of the PLDK-R lessons in teaching English as a second language. PLDK-R is not designed to work with all children. The task is to determine more precisely under which circumstances and for which children it works best.

Notice

We urge researchers investigating the effectiveness of the PLDK-R series to mail copies of both their unpublished and published reports to the publisher or the authors.

References

Anderson, J .R. *Cognitive psychology and its implications.* New York: W. H. Freeman, 1980.

Arter, J.A., & Jenkins, J.R. Differential diagnosis — prescriptive teaching: A critical appraisal. *Review of Educational Research,* 1979,49, 517-555.

Beidler, A.E. The effects of the Peabody Language Development Kits on the intelligence, reading, listening and writing of disadvantaged children in the primary grades (Doctoral dissertation, Lehigh University, 1968). *Dissertation Abstracts International,* 1969,29, 3760A-3761 A.
(University Microfilms No. 69-7322).

Berko, J. The child's learning of English morphology. *Word,* 1958, 44, 150-177.

Bloom, L. *One word at a time: The use of single word utterances before syntax.* The Hague: Mouton, 1973.

Bloom, L., & Lahey, M. *Language development and language disorders.* New York: John Wiley & Sons, 1978.

Bowerman, M.F. Discussion summary: Development of concepts underlying language. In R. L. Schiefelbusch & L. L. Lloyd (Eds.), *Language perspectives: Acquisition, retardation and intervention.* Baltimore: University Park Press, 1974.

Brown, R. *A first language: The early stages.* Cambridge: Harvard University Press, 1973.

Bruner, J.S. *The process of education.* Cambridge: Harvard University Press, 1960.

Campbell, J., Moffat, K., & Brackett, L. The effect of language instruction on the math skills of retarded children. *Mental Retardation, 1978, 16,167-169.*

Carter, J.L. The effect of a group language stimulation program upon Negro culturally disadvantaged first grade children. (Doctoral dissertation, University of Texas, 1966). *Dissertation Abstracts International,* 1967, 27(A), 2870A. (University Microfilms No. 67-3261). (a)

Carter, J.L. The effect of a language stimulation program upon first grade educationally disadvantaged children. *Education and Training for the Mentally Retarded,* 1966, 1, 169-174. (b)

Carter, J.L. *The long range effects of a language stimulation program upon Negro educationally disadvantaged first grade children.* Houston, Texas: Houston University, 1967. (ERIC Document Reproduction Service No. ED 013276).

Carter, J.L. *Follow-up study of the effects of a language stimulation program upon Negro educationally disadvantaged first grade children.* Final report, 1969. (ERIC Document Reproduction Service No. ED 035714).

Carter, J.L. An analysis of the effects of a language development program with first grade children of the New Orleans education improvement project. *Journal of Negro Education,* 1971, 40, 352-355.

Carter, J.L. Auditory discrimination and training for educable retarded children. *Education and Training of the Mentally Retarded,* 1975,10, 94-95.

Carter, J.L., & Capobianco, R.J. A systematic language stimulation program —revisited. *Education and Training of the Mentally Retarded,* 1976, 11, 112-116.

Chomsky, N. *Syntactic structures.* The Hague: Mouton, 1950.

Chomsky, N. Language and the mind. *Psychology Today,* 1968, 1, 48-51, 66-68.

Clark, H.H., & Clark, E.V. *Psychology and language.* New York: Harcourt Brace Jovanovich, 1977.

Clasen, R.E., Spear, J.E., &Tomaro, M.P. A comparison of the relative effectiveness of two types of preschool compensatory programming. *Journal of Educational Research,* 1969, 62, 401-405.

Cross, D.P. The effects of a group language development program with normal third grade subjects: A summary (Doctoral dissertation, University of Kentucky, 1968). *Dissertation Abstracts International,* 1968,29, 181 9A. (University Microfilms No. 68-17, 372).

Dale, P.S. *Language development:* Structure and function (2nd ed.). New York: Holt, Rinehart & Winston, 1976.

Dodd, D., & White, R. *Cognition: Mental structures and processes.* Boston: Allyn & Bacon, 1980.

Dunn, L.M., & Bruininks, RH. Efficacy of the Peabody Language Development Kits and the Initial Teaching Alphabet with southern disadvantaged children in the primary grades: A follow-up report after the fourth grade. *IMRID papers and reports.* Nashville, Tenn.: George PeabodyCollege, 1968, V(14). (ERIC Document Reproduction Service No. ED 043 724). (a)

Dunn, L.M., & Bruininks, R. H. The effectiveness of three reading approaches and an oral language stimulation program with disadvantaged children in the primary grades: A follow-up report after the third grade. *IMRID papers and reports.* Nashville, Tenn.: George Peabody College, 1968, V(1 3). (b)

Dunn, L.M., Horton, KB., & Smith, J.O. *Peabody Language Development Kits: Level P* (1st ed.). Circle Pines, Minn.: American Guidance Service, 1968.

Dunn, L.M., & Mueller, M.W. The effectiveness of the Peabody Language Development Kits and the Initial Teaching Alphabet with disadvantaged children in the primary grades: After one year. *IMRID Monograph #2.* Nashville, Tenn.: George Peabody College, 1966.

Dunn, L.M., Neville, D., Bailey, C.F., Pochanart, P., & Pfost, P. The effectiveness of three reading approaches and an oral language stimulation program with disadvantaged children in the primary grades: After one year. *IMRID Monograph #7.* Nashville, Tenn.: George Peabody College, 1967.

Dunn, L.M., Neville, D., Pfost, P., Pochanart, P., & Bruininks, R.H. The effectiveness of three reading approaches and an oral language stimulation program with disadvantaged children in the primary grades: A final report after two years of the Cooperative Reading Project. *IMRID Monograph #10.* Nashville, Tenn.: George Peabody College, 1968.

Dunn, L.M., Nitzman, M., Pochanart, P., & Bransky, M. Effectiveness of the Peabody Language Development Kits with educable mentally retarded children: A report after two and one-half years. *IMRID papers and reports.* Nashville, Tenn.: George Peabody College, 1968, V(15). (ERIC Document Reproduction Service No. ED 043 185).

Dunn, L.M., Pochanart, P., & Pfost, P. The effectiveness of the Peabody Language Development Kits and the Initial Teaching Alphabet with disadvantaged children in the primary grades: After two years. *IMRID Monograph #6.* Nashville, Tenn.: George Peabody College, 1967. (ERIC Document Reproduction Service No. ED 026 125).

Dunn, L.M., Pochanart, P., Pfost, P., & Bruininks, R.H. The effectiveness of the Peabody Language Development Kits and the Initial Teaching Alphabet with disadvantaged children in the primary grades: A report after the third grade of the Cooperative Language Development Project. *IMRID Monograph #9.* Nashville, Tenn.: George Peabody College, 1968. (ERIC Document Reproduction Service No. ED 043 723).

Dunn, L.M., & Smith, J.O. *Peabody Language Development Kits: Levels #1, #2, & #3* (1st ed.). Circle Pines, Minn.: American Guidance Service, 1965, 1966,1967.

Ellis, H.C. *Fundamentals of human learning, memory, and cognition* (2nd ed.). Dubuque, Iowa: W. C. Brown, 1978.

Engelmann, S., & Osborn, J. *Distar: An instructional system for language instruction.* Chicago: Science Research Associates, 1970.

Ensminger, E.E. The effects of a classroom language development program on psycholinguistic abilities and intellectual functioning of slow learning and borderline retarded children (Doctoral dissertation, University of Kansas, 1966). *Dissertation Abstracts International,* 1966, 27(B), 2158B-2159B. (University Microfilms No. 66-13,029).

Floyd, A. *Cognitive development in the school years.* New York: Halsted Press, 1979.

Forgnone, C. Effects of group training in visual perception and language development upon the visual perception and psycholinguistic abilities of retarded children (Doctoral dissertation, George Peabody College, 1966). *Dissertation Abstracts International,* 1967, 27(A), 1197A-1198A. (University Microfilms No. 66-11, 225).

Forgnone, C. Effects of visual perception and language training upon certain abilities of retarded children. *Education and Training of the Mentally Retarded,* 1976, 11, 212-217.

Fristoe, M. *Language intervention systems for the retarded.* Montgomery, Ala.: Alabama State Department of Education, 1975.

Fristoe, M., & Lloyd, L.L. *Language intervention systems.' A clinical and educational guide.* Baltimore: University Park Press, in press.

Gazdic, J.M. *An evaluation of a program for those children ascertained to be not ready for regular first grade placement.* Unpublished Master's thesis, Northeastern Illinois State College, 1971.

Gibson, R. *Effectiveness of a supplemental language development program with educable mentally retarded children* (Doctoral Dissertation, University of Iowa, 1966). Dissertation Abstracts International, 1967,27(A), 2726A-2727A. (University Microfilms No. 67-2620).

Gibson, R. *Effectiveness of the Peabody Language Development Program with a class of educable mentally retarded children.* Presented at the 1967 National Meeting of the American Association on Mental Deficiency, Denver, Colorado, May 20, 1967.

Glass, G.V. Primary, secondary, and meta-analysis of research. *Educational Researcher,* 1976,5,3-8.

Glass, G.V. Integrating findings: The meta-analysis of research. In L. S. Shulman (Ed.), *Review of research in education,* 1977, 5, 351-379.

Gluckenberg, S., & Danks, J.H. *Experimental psycholinguistics: An introduction.* New York: John Wiley & Sons, 1975.

Graham, L.W. Language programming and intervention. In L. L. Lloyd (Ed.), *Communication assessment and intervention strategies.* Baltimore, Maryland: University Park Press, 1976.

Guess, D., Rutherford, G., Smith, J.O., & Ensminger, E.E. Utilization of sub-professional personnel in teaching language skills to mentally retarded children: An interim report. *Mental Retardation,* 1970, 8, 17-23.

Guess, D., Smith, J.O., & Ensminger, E.E. The role of nonprofessional persons in teaching language skills to mentally retarded children. *Exceptional Children,* 1971, 37, 447-453.

Hammill, D.D., & Larsen, S.C. The effectiveness of psycholinguistic training. *Exceptional Children,* 1974, 41, 5-14.

Hammill, D.D., & Larsen, S.C. The effectiveness of psycholinguistic training: A reaffirmation of position. *Exceptional Children,* 1978,44, 402-414.

Happ, F.W., & Lyon, S. Communicative skills for trainables. *Mental Retardation,* 1972, 10, 38-39.

Hausman, R.M., & Apffel, J.A. Differential effects on the ITPA (Illinois Test of Psycholinguistic Abilities) profile of the final version of the Peabody Language Development Kits (Levels #1 and #2) with young disadvantaged Negro children. *IMRID papers and reports.* Nashville, Tenn.: George Peabody College, 1968, V(24). (ERIC Document Reproduction Service No. ED 105476).

Horton, K.B. *Summary of field testing of PLDK-P on which pre-program and post-program test data was accumulated and analyzed.* Unpublished memorandum, Circle Pines, Minn.: American Guidance Service, 1968.

Howe, A.C. *The Heman Street preschool. Preliminary report,* 1971. (ERIC Document Reproduction Service No. ED 057917).

Howe, A.C. *The Heman Street preschool 1971-72 report,* 1972. (ERIC Document Reproduction Service No. ED 070512).

Ingram, D. *Phonological disability in children.* New York: Elsevier, 1976.

Jones, E.L.H. The effects of a language development program on the psycholinguistic abilities and 10 of a group of preschool disadvantaged children (Doctoral dissertation, University of Arkansas, 1970). *Dissertation Abstracts International,* 1970, 31, 2761A-2762A. (University Microfilms No. 70-26, 204).

Karmlloff-Smith, A. *A functional approach to child language.* Cambridge: Cambridge University Press, 1979.

Kavale, K. Psycholinguistic training programs: Are there differential treatment effects? Unpublished research report, University of California at Riverside, 1980.

Kavale, K. Functions of the Illinois Test of Psycholinguistic Abilities: Are they trainable? *Exceptional Children,* in press.

Kirby, JR., & Biggs, J.B. (Eds.). *Cognitive development and instruction.* New York: Academic Press, 1980.

Klausmeier, H.J., Ghatala, E. S., & Frayer, D.A. *Conceptual learning and development: A cognitive view.* New York: Academic Press, 1974.

Lee, V. (Ed.). *Language development.* New York: Wiley, 1979.

Leiss, R.H., & Proger, B.B. *Language training for trainable mentally retarded. Annual project report: Second Year: ESEA Title Ill.* Norristown, Penn.: Montgomery County Intermediate Unit No. 23, 1974. (ERIC Document Reproduction Service No. ED 097 789).

Leiss, R.H., & Proger, B.B. *Language training for trainable mentally retarded children: ITPA, Peabody, and Distar techniques.* Paper presented at the annual meeting of the American Educational Research Association (New York), 1977. (ERIC Document Reproduction Service No. ED 140 527).

Lenneberg, E. H. *Biological foundations of language.* New York: Wiley, 1967.

Leonard, L.B. *Meaning in child language: Issues in the study of early semantic development.* New York: Grune & Stratton, 1976.

Levin, J.R., and Allen, V.L. (Eds.). *Cognitive learning in theories and strategies.* New York: Academic Press, 1976.

Lloyd, L.L. (Ed.). *Communication assessment and intervention strategies.* Baltimore: University Park Press, 1976.

Lovitt, T.C., & Smith, J.O. Effects of instructions on an individual's verbal behavior. *Exceptional Children,* 1972, 38, 685-693.

Lund, K.A., Foster, G.E., & McCall-Perez, F.C. The effectiveness of psycholinguistic training: A reevaluation. *Exceptional Children,* 1978, 44, 310-318.

MacNamara, J. Cognitive basis of language learning in infants. *Psychological Review, 1972,* 79,1-13.

Marchand, S.J., Buelde, M., & Woodward, R. Improving English in division I. *Saskatchewan Journal of Educational Research and Development,* 1974, 4, 16-22.

McConnell, F., Horton, KB., & Smith, B.R. Effects of early language training for culturally disadvantaged preschool children. *Journal of School Health,* 1969, 39, 661-665.

McLean, J.E. Introduction: Developing clinical strategies for language intervention with mentally retarded children. In J. E. McLean, D. Yoder, & R. L. Schiefelbusch (Eds.), *Language intervention with the retarded. Developing strategies.* Baltimore: University Park Press, 1972.

McLean, J.E., & Snyder-McLean, L.K. *A transactional approach to early language training.* Columbus, Ohio: Charles E. Merrill, 1978.

McNeill, D. *The acquisition of language: The study of developmental psycholinguistics.* New York: Harper & Row, 1970.

Meeker, M.N. *The structure of intellect: Its interpretation and uses.* Columbus, Ohio: Charles E. Merrill, 1969.

Miller, J., & Yoder, D. Ontogenetic language teaching strategy for retarded children. In R. L. Schiefelbusch & L. L. Lloyd (Eds.), *Language perspectives: Acquisition, retardation and intervention.* Baltimore: University Park Press, 1974.

Miller, L.B. *Four preschool programs: Their dimensions and effects — II. Final report.* Unpublished manuscript, Louisville, Kentucky: University of Louisville, 1977.

Milligan, J.L. *A study of the effects of a group language development program upon the psycholinguistic abilities and later beginning reading success of kindergarten children.* Pullman, Wash.: Washington State University, 1965. (ERIC Document Reproduction Service No. ED 031 315).

Milligan, J.L. A study of the effects of a group language development program upon the psycholinguistic abilities of normal kindergarten children (Doctoral dissertation, University of Kansas, 1966). *Dissertation Abstracts International,* 1967,28(A), 1007A. (University Microfilms No. 67-10, 825).

Minskoff, E.H. Research on psycholinguistic training: Critique and guidelines. *Exceptional Children,* 1975,42, 136-144.

Mitchell, R.S. A study of the effects of a specific language training on psycholinguistic scores of Head Start pupils (Doctoral dissertation, The Florida State University, 1967). *Dissertation Abstracts International,* 1968,28, 1 709A-1 71 Q.A. (University Microfilms No. 67-14, 455).

Moerck, E.L. *Pragmatic and semantic aspects of early language development.* Baltimore: University Park Press, 1977.

Morehead, D.M., & Morehead, A. A Piagetian view of thought and language during the first two years. In R. L. Schiefelbusch and L.L. Lloyd (Eds.), *Language perspectives: Acquisition, retardation and intervention.* Baltimore: University Park Press, 1974.

Morehead, D.M., & Morehead, A. (Eds.). *Normal and deficient child language.* Baltimore: University Park Press, 1976.

Mueller, M., & Smith, J.O. The stability of language age modifications over time. *American Journal of Mental Deficiency.* 1964, 68, 537-539.

Nelson, K. Structure and strategy in learning to talk. *Monographs of the Society for Research in Child Development,* 1973, 38, (1 & 2, Serial No. 149).

Nelson, K. Concept, word and sentence: Interrelations in acquisition and development. *Psychological Review,* 1974, 81, 267-285.

O'Neil, H.F., & Spielberger, C. (Eds.). *Cognitive and affective learning strategies.* New York: Academic Press, 1979.

Parker, R. K. *Wakulla County preschool. Final report.* Tallahassee, Florida: Florida State University, 1969. (ERIC Document Reproduction Service No. ED 039 022).

Parker, R. K. *The effectiveness of special programs for rural isolated four-year-old children:* Wakulla County preschool. Tallahassee, Florida: Florida State University, 1970. (ERIC Document Reproduction Service No. ED 056 743).

Piaget, J. *The child's conception of the world.* New York: Harcourt, Brace & World, 1951.

Piaget, J. *The origins of intelligence in children.* (2nd ed.) New York: International University Press, 1952.

Posner, M.l. *Cognition: An introduction.* Glenview, Ill.: Scott, Foresman, 1973.

Proger, B.B., & Leiss, R.H. *Language training for TMR children; Third year results and comparison with first two years; The Peabody, Distar, and ITPA programs: ESEA Title Ill.* Norristown, Penn.: Montgomery County Intermediate Unit No. 23, 1976. (ERIC Document Reproduction Service No. ED 126647).

Rabush, D.R. A comparative study of the syntax teaching program and the Peabody Language Development Kit as they affect oral expressive language in children who demonstrate retarded verbal behavior (Doctoral dissertation, University of Denver, 1973). *Dissertation Abstracts International,* 1973, 34 (6-A), 3192A-3193A. (University Microfilms No. 73-29, 654).

Richmond, E.J. The effect of the use of the Peabody Language Development Kit upon intellectual functioning and achievement of disadvantaged preschool children. (Doctoral dissertation, University of Alabama, 1970). *Dissertation' Abstracts International,* 1971, 31(12), 7643B-7644B. (University Microfilms No. 71-9134).

Riegel, R.H., Taylor, A.M., & Danner, F.W. *The effects of training in the use of a grouping strategy on the learning and memory capabilities of young EMR children,* 1973. (ERIC Document Reproduction Service No. ED 104050).

Saudergras, R.A., Madsen, C.H., & Thompson, F. Prescriptive teaching in language arts remediation for Black rural elementary school children. *Journal of Learning Disabilities,* 1971, 3, 364-370.

Schiefelbusch, R.L. (Ed.). *Bases of language intervention.* Baltimore: University Park Press, 1978. (a)

Schiefelbusch, R. L. (Ed.). *Language intervention strategies.* Baltimore: University Park Press, 1978. (b)

Schiefelbusch, R.L., & Lloyd, L.L. (Eds.). *Language perspectives — Acquisition, retardation and intervention.* Baltimore: University Park Press, 1974.

Schifani, J.W. The relationship between the Illinois Test of Psycholinguistic Abilities and the Peabody Language Development Kit with a select group of intermediate educable mentally retarded children (Doctoral dissertation, University of Alabama, 1971). *Dissertation Abstracts International,* 1972,32, 5076A. (University Microfilms No. 72-8466).

Schlesinger, I.M. Relational concepts underlying language. In R. L. Schiefelbusch and L. L. Lloyd (Eds.), *Language perspectives: Acquisition, retardation and intervention.* Baltimore: University Park Press, 1974.

Shiach, G.M. The effectiveness of a Peabody Language Development Kit with severely subnormal children. *British Journal of Educational Psychology,* 1973,43, 294-297.

Skemp, R.R. *Intelligence, learning and action.* New York: Wiley, 1979.

Skinner, B.F. *Verbal behavior.* New York: Appleton-Century-Crofts, 1957.

Skinner, B.F. *The technology of teaching.* New York: Appleton-Century-Crofts, 1968.

Slobin, D.l. Cognitive prerequisites for the development of grammar. In D. I. Slobin & C. Ferguson (Eds.), *Studies of child language development.* New York: Holt, Rinehart & Winston, 1973.

Smith, J.O. Effects of a group language development program upon the psycholinguistic abilities of educable mental retardates. *Peabody College Research Monograph Series in Special Education ,* No. 1. Nashville, Tenn.: George Peabody College, 1962. (a)

Smith, J.O. Group language development for educable mental retardates. *Exceptional Children,* 1962,29, 95-101. (b)

Staats, A.W. *Learning, language and cognition.* New York: Holt, Rinehart & Winston, 1968.

Vygotsky, L.S. *Thought and language.* New York: Wiley, 1962. Whimbey, A. Intelligence can be taught. New York: E. P. Dutton, 1980.

Woodhead, M. (Ed.). *An experiment in nursery education: Report of the National Foundation for Educational Research pre-school project.* Windsor, England: NFER Publishing, 1976.

Yoder, D.E., & Miller, J.F. What we may know and what we can do: Input toward a system. In J. E. McLean, D. E. Yoder & R. L. Schiefelbusch (Eds.), *Language intervention with the retarded: Developing strategies.* Baltimore: University Park Press, 1972.

Lessons

1

MATERIALS*

ACTIVITY 1

Puppets

P. Mooney

ACTIVITY 2

Puppets

P. Mooney

**NOTE: All materials are listed in the appendix to the Teacher's Guide.*

1 Focus: guessing the identity of a hidden object, talking about *puppets,* and then finding P. Mooney

Before the lesson, hide the puppet where the children can easily find it.

Introduce the program by saying:

Something interesting is hidden in the room. What do you think it might be?

After each guess, give clues. If no one guesses correctly, say:

I have hidden a special puppet. What is a puppet?

Encourage the children to talk about puppets. Summarize their remarks:

Yes, a puppet may look like a doll. You can put your hand Into a puppet and use your fingers to move its head and arms or its mouth, if it has one. Now let's look for the puppet.

During the search, give clues as necessary. When someone finds the puppet, have that child bring it to you, and ask the other children to clap for him or her.

2 Focus: talkng with P. Mooney, and telling first and last names

Put P. Mooney on your hand and have him say:

Hello, everyone! I am glad you found me! I am a puppet. See how I move my head and arms. (Demonstrate) **Have you ever known anyone named P. Mooney?** (Pause) **That is my name. Let's all say it together.**

After the children have said his name in unison several times, the puppet continues:

Now that you know my name, I want to know yours. When I call on you, please come up, shake my hand, and tell me your first and last names in a sentence.

Each time a child does so, have the puppet respond with such phrases as these:

1. **I am happy to meet you, (Rosa Ortega).**
2. **Hello, (Clarence Melnick).**
3. **How are you, (Katie O'Neill)?**
4. **I like your name, (Ray Baxter).**

When every child has met P. Mooney, the puppet concludes:

I enjoyed meeting all of you. I must go now, but I will come back soon to see you again. Good-bye!

After each lesson in the program, individuals who have difficulty demonstrating proficiency in the skills you consider appropriate and important for them to learn should be tutored. Aides could help you with this task.

2

MATERIALS*

ACTIVITY 1

Puppets

P. Mooney

ACTIVITY 2

Puppets

P. Mooney

1 Focus: describing P. Mooney while pointing out or touching his body parts and accessories

Hold the puppet and point to it as you say:

Here is our new friend. What is his name? (Encourage unison response) **Yes, this is P. Mooney. Let's describe what he looks like.**

Have the children point to or touch the features described. Encourage discussion with questions like these:

1. **What does P. Mooney wear on his head?**
2. **What is under P. Mooney's nose?** (Pause) **Do you know anyone else who has a moustache?**
3. **P. Mooney has a funny nose. Does it remind you of anything?**
4. **What colors are the stripes in P. Mooney's shirt?**
5. **Why does P. Mooney wear a bag? What might he carry in the bag?**

If the children mention the puppet's lack of eyes and ears, say:

Yes, he does not have eyes or ears. But P. Mooney does not need them, because he is magical. His magic helps him see without eyes and hear without ears.

Continue discussion as time and interest suggest.

2 Focus: following directions in the game P. Mooney Says

Ask the children to stand before you. Have P. Mooney say:

Let's play a game called P. Mooney Says. First I will say, "P. Mooney says," and then I will tell you to do something. Please do it until you hear "P. Mooney says, 'Stop'. " Here we go!

Have P. Mooney give commands like these:

P. Mooney says . . .

1. **Jump up and down. Stop.**
2. **Clap your hands. Stop.**
3. **Walk on your tiptoes. Stop.**
4. **Smack your lips. Stop.**
5. **Blink your eyes. Stop.**
6. **Swing your arms. Stop.**
7. **Wave good-bye to me.**

As the children wave, the puppet waves back and says:

This ends our game. We will have more fun together soon. Good-bye!

3

MATERIALS*

ACTIVITY 1

Cards
Music
324

Puppets
P. Mooney

Audiocassette 2
Side A, Song 1,
"I'm P. Mooney"

ACTIVITY 2

Cards
Music
(same as for Activity 1)

Puppets
P. Mooney

Color Chips
Container
10 per child, assorted colors

P. Mooney Bag

Audiocassette 2
Side A, Song 1,
"I'm P. Mooney"

Teacher provides
Audiocassette player*

**NOTE: In the lessons after this one, the audiocassette player will not appear on the materials list. Continue to provide one whenever a lesson calls for the audiocassette player to be used.*

1 Focus: listening to and retelling the song "I'm P. Mooney"

Before the lesson, hide the puppet nearby.

Hold the music card and say:

Let's listen to a new song about a friend of ours. Please listen carefully. I will ask questions after the song.

Play the song once or twice. When it ends, ask questions like those listed below to check comprehension. If the children need help, slowly say or sing the words again.

1. **Whom is the song about?**
2. **What does the song tell us about P. Mooney?**
3. **What does he wear on his head?**
4. **What does he have under his nose?**
5. **What kind of nose does P. Mooney have?**
6. **What kind of shirt does he wear?**
7. **What does P. Mooney have that is colored bright orange?**
8. **What does P. Mooney have that is magic?**

Take out the puppet and have a child hold it. Play the song again and ask a second child to point to each feature as it is mentioned. Repeat this procedure several times with other pairs of children. Invite the children to join you in singing along with the recording.

2 Focus: talking about the P. Mooney bag and the color chips, and then marching while singing the song "I'm P. Mooney"

Make a color chip necklace of assorted colors for each child. Put the necklaces into the bag.

Place the bag on your lap, and put P. Mooney on your hand. Have him point to the bag as he says:

This is my P. Mooney bag. It is often full of surprises. Do you think there is something in it now? (Pause) **Yes, it does look lumpy and bumpy and interesting today. Let's talk about what might be inside.**

After the children have speculated about the bag's contents, have P. Mooney invite each child in turn to pull a necklace from the bag. The puppet then continues:

My bag did hold a surprise for everyone. Now you each have something to wear around your neck: a color chip necklace. Please put on your necklace. We are going to march around the room and sing my song.

Give the puppet to a child and have the other children line up behind him or her. Play the song and invite the children to sing as they march. Change the leader each time you repeat the song. To conclude, ask the children to take their necklaces apart and put the chips into the container.

4

MATERIALS*

ACTIVITY 1

Color Chips

Half (about 120), assorted colors

ACTIVITY 2

Color Chips

Container

Half (about 120), assorted colors

1 Focus: linking color chips to make a circle, and then marching and dancing around it while singing

Sit in a circle with the children and give each child an equal number of chips. Hold two chips and say:

Each of you has a pile of color chips. These chips can be linked together, like this. (Demonstrate) **Now link your chips to make a chain.**

Help as needed. Continue:

Now let's link the chains into one large circle.

When the children have done so, help them place the circle on the floor. Then say:

Please watch me and listen as I sing about our circle. Then we will sing and act out the words together.

Sing or chant these verses, using gestures, to the tune or rhythm of "Here We Go 'Round the Mulberry Bush":

We march around the color chips,
(March around circle)

The color chips, the color chips.

We march around the color chips,

And then we all sit down.
(Stop and sit down)

We dance around the color chips,
(Dance around circle)

The color chips, the color chips.

We dance around the color chips,

And then we turn around.
(Stop and turn around)

Repeat, inviting the children to join you. Continue as time and interest suggest.

2 Focus: following directions that stress the positional words *into, out, inside,* and *outside*

Leave the color chip circle from Activity 1 on the floor.

Ask the children to stand outside the color chip circle. Demonstrating as necessary, stress the positional words as you give instructions like these:

1. **Walk around the *outside* of the circle, in this direction.** (Point) **. . . Stop.**
2. **Jump *into* the circle.**
3. **Step *out of* the circle.**
4. **Hop *into* the circle.**
5. **Walk around the *inside* of the circle, in this direction.** (Point) **. . . Stop.**
6. **Jump *out of* the circle.**
7. **Tiptoe around the *outside* of the circle, in this direction.** (Point) **. . . Stop.**
8. **Step *into* the circle.**
9. **Hop *out of* the circle.**

To conclude, ask the children to take the circle apart and put the color chips into the container.

5

MATERIALS*

ACTIVITY 1

P. Mooney Bag

ACTIVITY 2

P. Mooney Bag

1 Focus: describing imaginary contents of the P. Mooney bag

Wear the bag and say:

P. Mooney's bag is magical, so it contains all kinds of surprises. (Peek into bag) **We might find a dragon inside, or a mouse, or a train! If you could pick anything you wanted from the P. Mooney bag, think about what it would be. Let's take turns wearing the P. Mooney bag. When it is your turn, peek into the bag and tell us in a sentence what you are pretending to find. I will go first.** (Peek into bag) **I found a (tiny black kitten).**

Help children as necessary by asking questions like these:

1. **What did you find?**
2. **What color is your surprise?**
3. **How big is it?**
4. **What can you do with it?**

2 Focus: identifying imaginary objects pulled from the P. Mooney bag and whose uses are pantomimed

Wear the bag and say:

I wonder if we have found *all* the surprises in P. Mooney's bag. I am going to reach down to the very bottom. (Reach into bag) **I found something. Guess what it is from my actions.**

As necessary, give clues as you pantomime actions for items like these:

1. ***balloon:* blow it up, and tie a knot in its neck**
2. ***ice-cream cone:* eat it**
3. ***ball:* bounce it**
4. ***roller skates:* put them on, stand up, and skate**
5. ***piece of wrapped candy:* unwrap it, put it into your mouth, chew it, and swallow**
6. ***hairbrush:* brush your hair**

Continue with other actions you feel may interest the children.

6

MATERIALS*

ACTIVITY 1

Cards

Stories

339-352

Audiocassette 1

Side A, Story 1,

"How P. Mooney Got the P. Mooney Stick"

ACTIVITY 2

Cards

Music

324

Audiocassette 2

Side A, Song 1,

"I'm P. Mooney"

1 Focus: listening to the story "How P. Mooney Got the P. Mooney Stick," and then answering questions

Hold the 14 story cards and say:

Today we are going to hear a new story about how P. Mooney got his magic stick. Please listen carefully, so you will remember what happens.

Play the recording. During the narration, show the cards in turn as you scan the printed copy on the back of each picture. After showing each card, lay it facedown in a pile on your lap. When the story ends, lead the discussion with questions like these:

1. **What was P. Mooney doing the day he found the little sick tree?**
2. **How did he help the tree?**
3. **Why did P. Mooney have trouble finding the tree when he came back to the forest?**
4. **How did the tree thank P. Mooney?**

2 Focus: singing and acting out the song "I'm P. Mooney"

Have the children stand facing you. Hold the music card and say:

P. Mooney's song tells us about him. Let's sing his song again. Today we will also act out the words.

Act as if you are P. Mooney as the song is played. Repeat as desired.

1. **What do you see when you look at me?**

   A fellow with a cap on his head, (Hold bill of imaginary cap)

   A small moustache, (Lay forefinger across upper lip)

   A very large nose, (Point to nose)

   And a shirt of blue and red. (Place hands on chest)

Chorus:

I'm P. Mooney, P. Mooney;

Oh, come and spend some time with me.

I'm P. Mooney, P. Mooney;

I hope you'll remember me.

2. **What do you see when you look at me?**

   A fellow who likes to have fun!

   With my bright orange bag (Pull open imaginary bag)

   And my magic stick, (Wave imaginary stick in the air)

   I have something for everyone!

(Repeat chorus)

7 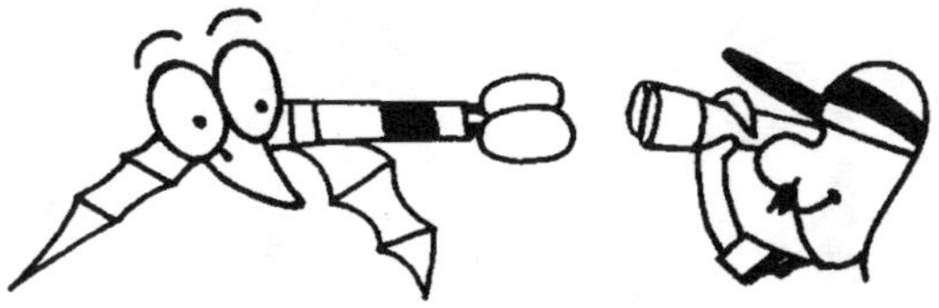

MATERIALS*

ACTIVITY 1

Cards
Stories
352

P. Mooney Stick

Puppets
P. Mooney

ACTIVITY 2

P. Mooney Stick

1 Focus: finding and talking about the P. Mooney stick

Before the lesson, hide the stick where the children can easily find it.

Ask the children to stand before you. Put P. Mooney on your hand. He says:

Hello, everyone! Today I want to show you my special stick — the P. Mooney stick. It is inside my bag.

Have P. Mooney look into the small bag around his neck. He shouts:

Oh, no! It's gone! My stick is gone! Maybe it fell into the ocean! Maybe a whale ate it! (Show card 352) **Here is a picture of the P. Mooney stick. Please help me find it.**

During the search, give hints as necessary. When the stick is found, have the finder give it to P. Mooney, who holds it and exclaims:

Thank you very much for finding my magic stick! I was afraid it was lost forever. You have made me feel much better. Now you may look at the P. Mooney stick.

Let the children take turns holding the stick and discussing it with P. Mooney.

2 Focus: talking about the imaginary powers of the P. Mooney stick, and then pretending to be transformed into animals and pantomiming them

Hold up the stick and say:

P. Mooney's stick is magical. What magical things do you think it can do?

Encourage discussion before continuing:

P. Mooney's stick might change us into whatever we like. Today let's use it to turn ourselves into animals.

Wave the stick as you say:

Mooney Magic,

Do a trick!

Make *rabbits*,

P. Mooney Stick!

Encourage the children to hop around the room like rabbits. After a short while, let the children decide what animal they wish to be next. Suggestions: duck, chicken, dog, cat, kangaroo. For each pretended change, wave the stick and repeat the rhyme. Continue as time and interest permit. Conclude by waving the stick and saying:

Eenie, Mooney,

Macaroony!

Now let's be

You and me.

8

MATERIALS*

ACTIVITY 1

Magnetic Shapes
1 per child (excluding large black shapes)

P. Mooney Bag

ACTIVITY 2

Display Board
3 ledges

Magnetic Shapes
1 per child
4 large black shapes

P. Mooney Bag

1 Focus: talking about *magnetism*, and testing the magnetic shapes on classroom objects

Put the shapes into the bag.

Shake the bag and ask:

Is the P. Mooney bag empty today? (Pause) **How do you know it has something inside?** (Encourage individual responses) **Yes, you can see and hear that something is in the bag. Let's feel it and guess what it contains.**

Hold the top closed as children take turns guessing the contents. Then say:

Now let's see what surprises are in P. Mooney's bag.

Have each child select a shape before you continue:

Each of you is holding a shape. We say these shapes are *magnetic* because they stick to metals which contain iron. Each shape has a small magnet on the back. Let's test our magnetic shapes on things in the classroom.

When a child finds something the shape sticks to, have the child name the object before you add, "Yes, a (tricycle) is made of a metal that contains iron, so your magnetic shape sticks to it." Make sure every child finds an iron or steel item to test. Conclude by having the children return the shapes to the bag.

2 Focus: talking about the display board, and sorting the magnetic shapes

Have the bag of shapes within reach.

Point to the board as you say:

This is our display board. Watch as I put these shapes and ledges upon it.

Arrange the four large black shapes at the top of the board, and use the ledges as vertical dividers, like this:

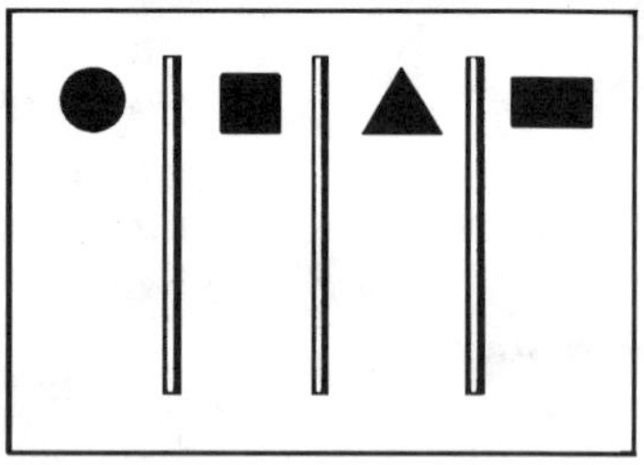

Ask:

Why do the shapes and the ledges stick to the board? (Encourage discussion before continuing) **Yes, these ledges and shapes are magnetic. Because they are sticking to the board, we know the board must contain iron.**

Point to the board as you say:

These shapes are all the same color, but each looks different from the others. Let's each choose a shape from the bag and put it under the shape it looks like.

Help as necessary, commenting on correct matches. Name the shapes only if the children ask. Repeat as time and interest suggest.

9

MATERIALS*

ACTIVITY 1

Cards
Stories
339-352

Display Board
6 ledges

P. Mooney Stick

ACTIVITY 2

P. Mooney Stick

1 Focus: retelling the story "How P. Mooney Got the P. Mooney Stick"

Set the ledges horizontally on the board to hold the 14 story cards.

Place the cards facedown on your lap. Hold up the P. Mooney stick and say:

This stick belongs to someone we know. Whose stick is it? (Pause) **Yes, it is P. Mooney's stick. We have heard a story about it. Let's look at the story cards again and tell what is happening in each picture.** (Show card 339) **What is happening in this picture, (Nicola)?** (Pause) **What else does this picture show, (Kevin)?**

Refer to the printed part of the story on the back of each card as you show the rest of the cards in order, encouraging individuals to continue the story. If necessary, ask questions to help them remember important details. As the cards are described, have them placed in three rows on the board in left-to-right sequence as seen by the group.

2 Focus: naming children in a P. Mooney-stick game

Stand with the children. Hold the stick and say:

We are going to use the P. Mooney stick to play a new game. But first, let's learn a rhyme to say during the game. It goes like this:

> **(Christina), be nimble; (Christina), be quick;**
>
> **(Christina), step over P. Mooney's stick!**

Repeat the rhyme with the children until most of them know the words. Then explain:

Now we are ready to play the game. I will put the P. Mooney stick on the floor. While everyone says the rhyme together, you will take turns stepping over the stick. You may go first, (Christina).

Use each child's name in the rhyme as he or she steps over the stick. Then repeat the procedure, having the children jump over the stick as they say:

> **(Jason), be nimble; (Jason), be quick;**
>
> **(Jason), jump over P. Mooney's stick!**

Continue until everyone has had a turn, or as long as time and interest suggest.

10

MATERIALS*

ACTIVITY 1

Display Board

Magnetic Shapes
All
Container

ACTIVITY 2

Cards
Music
335

Display Board

Magnetic Shapes
1 large circle
2 medium circles
2 small circles

Audiocassette 2
Side B, Song 12, "Rhythm Walk"

1 Focus: identifying and building magnetic shape constructions, and then describing them

Say:

I am going to build something with our magnetic shapes. Please watch and try to figure out what I am making.

Place a large triangle above a large square, like this:

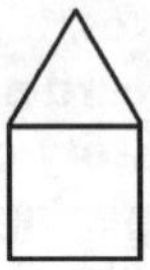

Let volunteers identify your work in sentences such as "You made a house" or "That is a house." Then invite several children in turn to make additional houses on the board. Remove the shapes and repeat the procedure, using the ideas below. As you position each shape, encourage the children to guess what you are making. Conclude by letting five volunteers each assemble one of the groupings below. Each child who makes one should describe it in a sentence for the group.

snowman

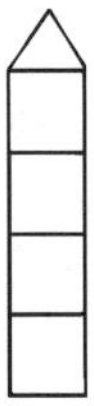

rocket

tree

butterfly

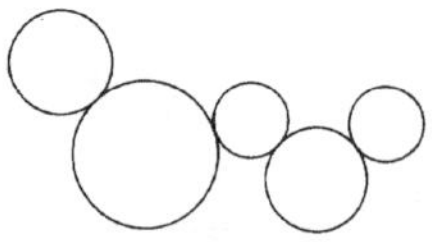

caterpillar

2 Focus: listening to the music "Rhythm Walk," and then moving like a caterpillar

Have the caterpillar construction from Activity 1 left on the board.

Hold the music card and say:

As you listen to this new piece of music, look at the board. The music may remind you of something you see there.

Play the music and encourage the children to tell what it sounds like to them. Accept all responses. Then continue:

Does the music remind you of the way a caterpillar crawls along? (Pause)
We are going to pretend that all of you together are one long caterpillar. First let's practice moving our bodies up and down.

Play the song and demonstrate the action: move from a standing position to a half-squat in time to the music. When the children can move correctly, line them up in single file. Each should hold the preceding child's waist. Repeat the music and have the children move up and down, not in unison, to the music, creating a wave-like effect as they imitate a caterpillar crawling around the room. Change leaders and continue as long as time and interest suggest.

Keep in Mind . . .
After each lesson in the program, individuals who have difficulty demonstrating proficiency in the skills you consider appropriate and important for them to learn should be tutored. Aides could help you with this task.

11

MATERIALS*

ACTIVITY 1

P. Mooney Bag

Teacher provides

2 fresh red apples

ACTIVITY 2

Teacher provides

1 fresh red apple

1 Focus: describing and talking about *apples*

Put the apples into the bag.

Wearing the bag, say:

Today the P. Mooney bag contains two surprises. You can eat them. What do you think they could be? (Encourage individual responses) **Please come and take the surprises out of the bag, (Betty Jean), so we can see what they are.**

Place the apples where everyone can see them. Then lead a discussion about apples, asking questions like these:

1. **What are these called?**
2. **What color are these apples?**
3. **What other colors can apples be?**
4. **What is the outside cover of an apple called?**
5. **What part holds an apple to the tree?**
6. **What are some things we can make out of apples?** (jelly, juice, pie, sauce, dried-apple doll heads)
7. **Do you like apples? Why? Why not?**
8. **If you had some apples, what would you do with them?**

Summarize the discussion:

We have learned a lot about apples — what they look like, what parts they have, and what we can make from them.

2 Focus: identifying red objects while chanting an action rhyme

Hold up the red apple and ask:

What color is this apple? (Pause) **Yes, it is red. There are some other things in this room that are red, too. Let's look for them together. I know a rhyme we can say while we are looking:**

Look up and down and all around!
Something *red* will soon be found.

Repeat the rhyme several times with the children before you lead them in walking around the room and chanting. Each time the rhyme is finished, stop and let the children take turns pointing out and naming red objects in a sentence such as "Here is a red (crayon)." Continue until everyone has had a turn, even if some items are repeated.

12

MATERIALS*

ACTIVITY 1

Fruits & Vegetables

3 apples

Teacher provides

1 fresh apple

ACTIVITY 2

Teacher provides

1 fresh apple

1 table knife

1 Focus: comparing real and plastic apples by sight, smell, and touch

Place the four apples where everyone can see them. Sit with the apples within reach as the children sit facing you. Ask them to tell you which apple is different from the rest. If no one can explain, pass the apples around, encouraging the children to handle and smell them. If necessary, point out such differences as color, weight, smell, size, and texture. Then ask the question again. When the real apple has been identified, say:

Yes! One of the apples is real, but the rest are not real. They are artificial. They are made of plastic. Let's play a game to see if you can tell which apple is real and which is not real.

Invite one child to stand beside you. Continue:

Close your eyes, (Jackson). (Pause) **Now I will put the real apple into one of your hands, and a plastic apple into the other.** (Do this) **Which is the real apple, (Jackson)?**

When the child chooses, ask, "Why did you choose this apple?" The child should respond in a sentence such as "I know this is the real apple, because it is heavier" or "This is the real apple. I know because of the smell." Continue with other children.

2 Focus: talking about apples, and then saying and pantomiming a rhyme about planting an apple seed

Hold the fresh apple and say:

Let's talk some more about how apples grow. Apples grow on what kind of plant? (Pause) **Yes, apples grow on apple trees. How would you take care of an apple tree if you wanted it to grow big, juicy apples?**

Discussion should include mention of water, sunlight, and fertilizer. Then take the knife and say:

Now watch while I cut the apple in half.

Pass the halves around and let the children take turns describing what they see. Elaborate on the previous lesson. Descriptions should include naming these apple parts: seeds, core, flesh, skin, and stem. Then ask:

What might happen if we planted one of these seeds? (Encourage individual responses) **I know a rhyme we can say while we pretend to grow our own apples. Please listen carefully and watch me as I act out the words for you the first time. Then we will do it together.**

Present this rhyme* with gestures:

Here's a little apple seed.

(Hold imaginary seed in one hand; point with other)

Plant it in the ground.
(Pretend to plant seed)

Give it water every day.
(Pretend to water plant)

Weed it all around.
(Pretend to pull weeds)

Now the tree is growing,

(Hang head and arms down; gradually lift them up)

Reaching to the sky.

We can pick the apples now
(Pretend to pick apples)

And make an apple pie!

(Pretend to put pie into oven, close oven door, and rub stomach happily)

Invite the children to join you in performing the rhyme several times.

OPTIONAL: Conclude by giving each child a piece of the apple.

**NOTE:
This rhyme is by Sharon Holland.*

13

MATERIALS*

ACTIVITY 1

Cards

Stories

353-368

Puppets

P. Mooney

Audiocassette 1

Side A, Story 2,

"P. Mooney and Mr. Nobody"

ACTIVITY 2

Display Board

6 ledges

Cards

Stories

(same as for Activity 1)

1 Focus: listening to the story "P. Mooney and Mr. Nobody"

Place the 16 story cards on your lap, and put P. Mooney on your hand. He says:

Hello, everyone! Today we are going to hear a new story. The story tells how I met one of my best friends, whose name is Mr. Nobody. Let's listen to find out why Mr. Nobody' has such a funny name.

Set the puppet aside and play the song. During the narration, show the story cards in turn as you scan the printed copy on the back of each picture. After showing each card, lay it facedown in a pile on your lap.

2 Focus: talking about Mr. Nobody, and then retelling the story "P. Mooney and Mr. Nobody"

Still holding the cards, say:

Let's remember the story together. What is the name of P. Mooney's friend? (Encourage unison response) **Why is he called Mr. Nobody?**

If no one can explain, say:

Mr. Nobody's last name is two words put together: *no* and *body*. His name is Mr. (say name in two parts) **No-body because he seemed to have *no body*. When we say his name fast, it comes out Mr.** (say name normally) **Nobody.**

Continue with these or similar questions in story sequence:

1. **How did P. Mooney help Mr. Nobody?**
2. **How did Mr. Nobody feel after P. Mooney helped him? Why?**
3. **What did you like — or not like — about the story?**

Then say:

Let's look at the story cards again while we take turns telling what is happening in each picture. (Show card 353) **What is happening in this picture, (Helen)?** (Pause) **What else does this picture show, (Tommy)?**

Show the rest of the cards in order, encouraging individuals to continue the story. If necessary, ask questions to help the children remember important details. As the cards are described, have them placed in three rows on the board in left-to-right sequence as seen by the group. As necessary, remove cards to make room for others as you proceed.

14

MATERIALS*

ACTIVITY 1

None

ACTIVITY 2

None

1 Focus: imitating pantomimed actions, and then identifying the actions and body parts used

Ask the children to stand before you. Say:

We can use our body parts to do many different things. Watch carefully, and then do what I am doing.

Pretend to smell something. Encourage the children to join you. Then ask:

What were we pretending to do? (Pause) **Yes, we were pretending to smell something. Which body part do we use to smell?** (Pause) **Yes, we use our noses to smell.**

Continue with these actions and body parts:

1. **walking** (legs, knees, feet, toes)
2. **bending** (elbows, knees, fingers, wrists, neck, waist)
3. **eating** (mouth, lips, tongue, teeth, jaws)
4. **listening** (ears)
5. **picking up** (fingers, hands, arms, mouth, toes if we must)
6. **blinking** (eyes, eyelids)
7. **kicking** (feet, legs, toes)
8. **stretching** (all body parts)

End by inviting the children to stand on tiptoe and stretch.

2 Focus: singing an action song about uses of the *mouth, feet,* and *hands*

With the children still standing, say:

I know a song that is fun to sing and act out. Please listen as I go through it for you the first time. Then we will do it together.

Sing or chant the following words to the tune or rhythm of "The Farmer in the Dell":

We use our mouths to sing,
(Point to mouth)
We use our mouths to sing,
Hi-ho the derry-o,
We use our mouths to sing.

Continue with verses that begin as follows:

We use our feet to march, etc.
(March in place)
We use our hands to clap, etc.
(Clap hands)

Invite the children to join you in repeating the verses and movements. Ask volunteers to lead the group as everyone sings the song again.

VARIATION: To make the activity *harder,* invite the children to make up more verses.

15

MATERIALS*

ACTIVITY 1

Display Board

Manikin, Disassembled

Body parts

Facial features

Short hair

ACTIVITY 2

None

1 Focus: talking about and assembling the manikin

Hold the pieces of the manikin on your lap. Say:

I am going to put something like a puzzle onto the board.

Place the manikin pieces onto it in random order. Ask:

What do you think this is?

Encourage the children to guess. Then have them watch you assemble the complete figure before you explain:

This doll is called a *manikin*. Let's say the word together: *manikin*. Do you hear another word in *man-ikin*. (Pause) **Yes, the word *manikin* contains the word *man*. All these pieces together form a *man*ikin that looks like a person.**

Remove the pieces and invite several children to reassemble the figure. Hand out the pieces one at a time. As needed, guide the children with cues such as "Place the head at the top" or "Connect the foot to the leg." Let the children take turns assembling the manikin as long as time and interest permit.

2 Focus: talking about and singing an action song about *mouths, feet,* and *hands*

Ask the children to stand before you. Say:

Let's talk about what we can do with our mouths. (Encourage individual responses) **Yes, we use our mouths when we sing. We use our mouths to eat and whistle. We use our mouths to talk and kiss. Let's sing about some of the ways we use our mouths. I will go through the song for you the first time. Then we will sing and act it out together.**

Sing or chant these words to the tune or rhythm of "The Farmer in the Dell":

We use our mouths to sing (chant),
(Point to mouth)

We use our mouths to sing (chant);

Hi-ho the derry-o,

We use our mouths to sing (chant).

Continue with verses that begin as follows:

We use our mouths to eat, etc.
(Pretend to eat)

We use our mouths to kiss, etc.
(Pretend to kiss)

Repeat the activity for feet (march, kick, walk) and hands (clap, draw, eat).

Keep in Mind . . .
After each lesson in the program, individuals who have difficulty demonstrating proficiency in the skills you consider appropriate and important for them to learn should be tutored. Aides could help you with this task.

16

MATERIALS*

ACTIVITY 1

Cards

Animals

1-20

Display Board

6 ledges

ACTIVITY 2

Cards

Animals

1* 5* 6* 9* 11* 12* 15* 19*

Display Board

6 ledges

**NOTE: Cards followed by an asterisk were also used in Activity 1.*

1 Focus: finding and naming animal cards

While the other children cover their eyes, have several children help you hide the 20 animal cards, picture sides hidden, around the room.

Ask the children to stand before you. Say:

When we go on a hunt, we look for things. Today we will go on an animal hunt. Many animal pictures are hidden in the room. Let's find them all. Please bring the cards you find, and sit in front of the board.

Give clues as necessary. When all the children are seated, they are then to take turns placing their cards on the board and naming the animals in a sentence like "This animal is a (bear)." Remove the cards from the board to make room as you proceed. Continue until all cards have been identified.

VARIATION: To make the activity *harder,* say, "Tell us something about a (bear)."

2 Focus: identifying animals from their descriptions

Display the eight animal cards on the board.

Say:

Now let's play a guessing game. I will tell you something about one of these animals. (Point to cards on display) **You are to guess which animal I mean.**

Present the following sets of clues. Pause after each clue, to give the children time to think and respond.

1. **This animal is small. . . . It has feathers. . . . It has wings. . . . It lives in a tree. . . . What animal is it?** (bird)
2. **This animal is large. . . . It growls. . . . It likes to eat honey. . . . What animal is it?** (bear)
3. **This animal is small. . . . It is yellow. . . . Its mother is a hen. . . . Its father is a rooster. . . . It pecks on the ground to find its food. . . . What animal is it?** (chick)
4. **This animal is very large. . . . It is gray. . . . Sometimes it lives in a circus. . . . It has a long nose called a trunk. . . . It has big floppy ears. . . . What animal is it?** (elephant)
5. **This animal is very small. . . . It has two beautiful wings. . . . It flies from flower to flower. . . . What animal is it?** (butterfly)
6. **This animal is large. . . . It is black with white spots. . . . It gives us milk. . . . What animal is it?** (cow)
7. **This animal is small. . . . It swims in the water. . . . It is gold. . . . What animal is it?** (goldfish)
8. **This animal is usually a pet. . . . It barks. . . . It has shaggy brown hair. . . . What animal is it?** (dog)

17

MATERIALS*

ACTIVITY 1

Display Board
4 ledges

P. Mooney Stick

Poster 1

ACTIVITY 2

Cards
Animals
8 11 13 31
Music
325

Display Board
4 ledges

Audiocassette 2
Side A, Song 2,
"The Is-Are Song"

1 Focus: naming items on the poster "Farm in Spring," and then talking about farm life

Do not display the poster until asked to do so.

Hold up the stick and say:

P. Mooney's magic stick is going to send us on a magical trip. Where do you think it might take us?

Encourage the children to guess. Then wave the stick and say this rhyme:

Mooney Magic, zing and zip!

Take us on a P. Mooney trip.

Use the ledges to place the poster on the board. Ask:

Where are we? (Encourage unison response) **Yes, we are on a farm.**

Let the children take turns pointing out and naming something they see on the poster that has not been mentioned. If no one notices P. Mooney on the farm, ask the children to look for him there. Then continue the discussion with questions like these:

1. **Have you ever visited a farm?** (Pause) **What was it like?** (Encourage children to discuss their experiences)
2. **What is a farmer?**
3. **Could both women and men be farmers?**
4. **What animals live on a farm?**
5. **What plants do farmers grow?**

Accept all appropriate answers and add instructive comments. End by waving the stick again as you say:

Mooney Magic, do a trick;

Take us back, P. Mooney Stick!

2 Focus: listening to and singing "The Is-Are Song"

Place the four animal cards on the board in this order: 11, 13, 8, and 31.

Review the animal card labels with the children. Then hold the music card and say:

Let's learn a new song about the sounds animals make. Please listen to the words and sing with me as soon as you can.

Play the song and refer to the music card as you sing along with the recording, pointing to each animal card as the animal is mentioned. Emphasize the verb forms and plurals. Repeat the song with the children until they are familiar with the words.

18

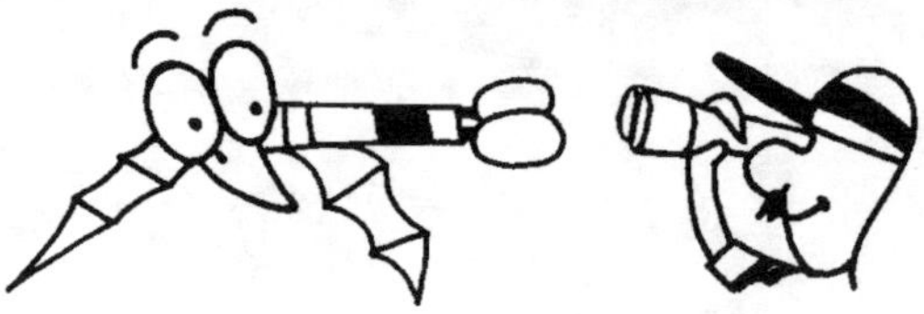

MATERIALS*

ACTIVITY 1

Cards

Animals

3 5 8 11 12 13 21
25 26 27 31 36

Music

325

Audiocassette 2

Side A, Song 2,
"The Is-Are Song"

ACTIVITY 2

Cards

Animals

12*

Display Board

I ledge

**NOTE: Cards followed by an asterisk were also used in Activity 1.*

1 Focus: singing "The Is-Are Song" while naming animals and imitating their sounds

Review the animal card labels with the children. Select four children and ask them to stand facing the group. Going from left-to-right as seen by the class, hand each of the four an animal card, in this order: 11, 13, 8, 31. Ask:

Do you remember the song we learned about the sounds animals make? (Pause) **Let's sing it again. Then we will choose other animal sounds to sing about.**

Play the song and have each standing child hold out the card when the animal is mentioned. Each time, stress the plurals and encourage the children to sing and make the animal sound with you. Repeat two or three times before suggesting:

Let's sing about four more animals.

Let four other children each hold one of these cards, in this order: 3, 21, 27, 5. Then play the song (instrumental version) and lead the children in singing the new verses. Repeat the procedure with the four remaining cards, in this order: 12, 26, 25, 36.

2 Focus: saying an action poem about a *dog* while stressing the use of *is, are,* and plurals

Display animal card 12.

Have the children stand facing you and the board. Point to the card and ask:

What animal is this? (Pause) **Yes, it is a dog. I know a rhyme about a happy dog. Please listen and watch as I say and act out the words. Then we will practice the rhyme together.**

Recite the following poem* with gestures:

This is my nose; (Point to nose)
This is my mouth; (Point to mouth)
This is my coat so shaggy.
(Rub chest and arms)
This is my head;
(Place both hands on head)
This is my tail
(Hold hands together behind back)
That is so long and waggy.
(With hands behind back,
wiggle hips)

These are my legs; (Point to legs)
These are my paws;
(Hold hands up like paws)
These are my teeth so snappy.
(Point to teeth and snap them)
These are my eyes; (Point to eyes)
These are my ears
(Place hands with fingers bent on either side of head)
That stand up when I'm happy.
(Straighten fingers)

As you repeat the poem line by line, perform the actions with the children. Then lead the group again in the words and actions. Continue as long as time and interest suggest, fading out your participation as much as possible.

**NOTE: This rhyme is by Margie Donnelly.*

19

MATERIALS*

ACTIVITY 1

Cards
Stories
369-385

Audiocassette 1
Side A, Story 3,
"P. Mooney and Zoey"

ACTIVITY 2

Puppets
Zoey
Discovery hat

1 Focus: listening to the story "P. Mooney and Zoey," and then answering questions about it

Say:

Today you are going to hear a new story. It is about Zoey, who is a special friend of P. Mooney's. Let's listen together.

Play the story. During the narration, show the story cards in turn as you scan the printed copy on the back of each picture. After showing each card, lay it facedown in a pile on your lap. Afterwards, review the major points with questions like these:

1. **How did P. Mooney get caught inside his bag?**
2. **How did Zoey rescue P. Mooney?**
3. **What might have happened to P. Mooney if Zoey had not found him?**
4. **What kind of person do you think Zoey is?**

2 Focus: describing one's appearance or clothes to Zoey

Place Zoey (wearing her discovery hat) on your hand. She asks:

Do you know who I am? (Encourage unison response) **Yes, my name is Zoey. Today I am wearing my discovery hat as I find out who you are. Let's play a game using your names. I will cover my eyes. When I call on you, say, "Hello, Zoey." Then tell me what you look like or what you are wearing. I will try to discover who you are. Let's begin.** (Cover puppet's eyes) **Say hello to me and then tell me what you look like, (Pamela).**

Zoey should encourage as full a description as possible, and stress the use of sentences. After each response, Zoey should look over all the children before inviting the right child to come and shake her hand. Have the puppet occasionally choose the wrong child and invite the class to correct her.

20

MATERIALS*

ACTIVITY 1

Cards

Music

326

Puppets

Zoey

All 3 hats

Audiocassette 2

Side A, Song 3, "Zoey"

ACTIVITY 2

Puppets

Zoey

All 3 hats

1 Focus: listening to and singing the song "Zoey," and naming her three hats

Place Zoey (wearing her discovery hat) on your hand. She says:

Hello, girls and boys! You are going to hear a new song about my hats. For each verse, I will change the hat I am wearing. Please listen carefully, so you will be able to sing along later.

Play the song and change Zoey's hats as indicated. Then the puppet continues:

Let's listen again to the first verse, which tells when I wear my discovery hat.

After hearing the verse, the group should tell Zoey when she wears her discovery hat. Repeat this procedure with the next two verses. Then have Zoey lead the group in singing the song as several children take turns switching her hats verse by verse. Repeat several times, to give other children a turn.

2 Focus: talking about *thinking, discovery,* and *action,* and then playing an action game to identify Zoey's hats

Hold Zoey (wearing her thinking hat), point to her, and say:

Zoey is wearing her thinking hat because she is ready to think. Are you ready to think? (Pause) **Think about an animal.** (Pause) **What animal are you thinking about right now?** (Encourage individual responses) **What do we mean when we say we are thinking?**

After the discussion, switch Zoey's thinking hat to her discovery hat and say:

Now Zoey is wearing her discovery hat. Are you ready to discover something? (Pause) **What food would you like to discover right now?** (Encourage individual responses) **What do we mean when we say we made a discovery?**

After the discussion, switch Zoey's discovery hat to her action hat and say:

Now Zoey is wearing her action hat. Are you ready for action? (Pause) **What actions can we do right now?** (Encourage individual responses) **What does the word *action* mean?**

After the discussion, say:

Let's play a Zoey hat game. I will change Zoey's hats. Please make the same movements I do for each hat you see her wearing. Let's practice them before we play.

Suggested movements:

thinking hat — put chin in palm of hand and pretend to think

discovery hat — shade eyes with one hand as you look around

action hat — run in place

Repeat the game one or more times, fading out your participation as much as possible. Vary the order in which you put the hats on the puppet.

Keep in Mind . .
After each lesson in the program, individuals who have difficulty demonstrating proficiency in the skills you consider appropriate and important for them to learn should be tutored. Aides could help you with this task.

21

MATERIALS*

ACTIVITY 1

Cards
Music
326

Puppets
Zoey
All 3 hats

Audiocassette 2
Side A, Song 3, "Zoey"

ACTIVITY 2

Cards
Stories
369-385

Display Board
6 ledges

1 Focus: listening to, singing, and acting out the song "Zoey"

Stand beside the audiocassette player and have the children stand before you. Place Zoey (wearing her discovery hat) on your hand. She says:

Let's listen again to the song about my three hats. Sing the song and do the actions for the hat you see me wearing. When the song tells about my discovery hat, shade your eyes and look all around, like this. (Demonstrate with puppet) **When the song mentions my thinking hat, put your chin in your hand and pretend to think, like this.** (Demonstrate with puppet) **During the verse about my action hat, run in place, like this.** (Demonstrate)

Play the song, calling on different children to change the puppet's hats verse by verse. The rest of the children should sing along. Repeat as time and interest suggest.

2 Focus: retelling the story "P. Mooney and Zoey"

Place the cards facedown on your lap and say:

Let's retell the story of how P. Mooney met Zoey. I will show the story cards while you take turns telling what is happening in each picture. (Show card 369) **What is happening in this picture, (Erik)?**

Show the rest of the cards in order, encouraging individuals to continue the story. If necessary, ask questions to help them remember important details. As the cards are discussed, have them placed on the board in left-to-right order as seen by the group.

22

MATERIALS*

ACTIVITY 1

Cards

Animals

21-38

Display Board

6 ledges

ACTIVITY 2

Cards

Animals

1-20

21-38*

Display Board

6 ledges

**NOTE: Cards followed by an asterisk were also used in Activity 1.*

1 Focus: finding and naming animal cards

While the other children cover their eyes, have several children hide the 18 animal cards, picture sides hidden, around the room.

Ask the children to stand before you. Say:

Today we will go on another animal hunt. Let's find all the animal pictures hidden in the room. Please bring the cards you find, and sit in front of the board.

Give clues as necessary. When all the children are seated, they are then to take turns placing their cards on the board and naming the animals in a sentence like "This animal is a (horse)." Remove cards from the board to make room as you proceed. Continue until all cards have been identified.

VARIATION: To make the activity *harder,* call on children to tell something about each animal named.

2 Focus: identifying animals that make sounds, and imitating these sounds

Display as many animal cards as you can on the board.

Hold the remaining animal cards, point to the board, and say:

Let's look at all these pictured animals and decide which of them make sounds. I will point to each card in turn. When I call on you, tell me whether the animal makes a sound. If it does, please imitate the sound for us.

As you proceed, remove the cards of soundless animals. Continue until all 38 animals have been considered.

23

MATERIALS*

ACTIVITY 1

Puppets

Zoey

Thinking hat

ACTIVITY 2

None

1 Focus: identifying body parts from questions about actions

Place Zoey (wearing her thinking hat) on your hand and have her say:

I am wearing my thinking hat. Pretend you are wearing yours, too. (Pause) **We are going to think hard today. I will ask you some questions about body parts. Try to figure out which parts I mean.**

Zoey should call on individuals to answer each question and then have all the children perform the action named. Another child should then describe the action in a sentence like "We (hug) with our (arms)."

What body parts can . . .

1. **hug someone?** (arms, hands)
2. **open and close?** (mouths, eyes)
3. **wave good-bye?** (arms)
4. **wiggle?** (toes, fingers)
5. **nod?** (head)
6. **wink and blink?** (eyes)
7. **scratch?** (fingers, fingernails, toes, toenails)
8. **help us eat?** (teeth, mouth, jaws)

OPTIONAL: Continue by having children hold Zoey and make up more questions about body parts.

2 Focus: naming body parts, and then following directions while singing

Ask the children to stand in a circle around you. Say:

We are going to sing about body parts. First, let's make sure that you know the body parts mentioned in the song. Please name the parts as I point to them.

Point to the head, nose, legs, toes, ears, and mouth of several children as the group responds in unison. Continue:

Watch me and listen as I go through the song for you the first time. Then we will sing and act out the words together.

Demonstrate the actions as you sing or chant these words to the tune or rhythm of "Here We Go Looby Lou":

1. **Everyone, touch your head.**
   (Touch head)
   Everyone, touch your nose.
   (Touch nose)
   Everyone, touch your legs.
   (Touch legs)
   Now, everyone, touch your toes!
   (Touch toes)

Chorus:

Now we turn 'round and 'round.
(Turn around in place, stepping in rhythm with song)
Now we turn 'round and 'round.
Now we turn 'round and 'round.
Now, everyone, touch your toes!
(Touch toes)

2. **Everyone, touch your mouth.**
   (Touch mouth)
   Everyone, touch your nose.
   (Touch nose)
   Everyone, touch your ears.
   (Touch ears)
   Now, everyone, touch your toes!
   (Touch toes)

(Repeat chorus)

Invite the children to join in as you repeat the words and actions together. Continue as time permits.

24

MATERIALS*

ACTIVITY 1

Cards
Clothing
39-54

P. Mooney Bag

ACTIVITY 2

Cards
Clothing
(same as for Activity 1)
Music
325

Audiocassette 2
Side A, Song 2,
"The Is-Are Song"

1 Focus: naming dothing in sentences

Put the 16 clothing cards into the bag.

Wear the bag and say:

P. Mooney's bag is full today. What might be inside it?

Call on several children in turn. After each guess, give clues. If no one guesses correctly, tell the class that the bag contains clothing cards. Continue:

Each of you is to come up and take a card from the bag. You choose first and show everyone your card, (Denise). Tell us what you chose in a sentence.

The child should respond with a sentence such as "This is a (jacket)." Continue with other children. If necessary, help by asking, "Are you holding (mittens), or a (cap)?" Accept suitable synonyms. Continue until all cards have been named. If your class is large, return cards to the bag, so that everyone has at least one turn.

OPTIONAL: Have the children discuss each item in detail.

2 Focus: singing "The Is-Are Song" while naming clothing and showing where it is worn

Give four children each a clothing card and ask them to stand facing the group. Line them up, left-to-right as seen by the class, with the cards in this order: 39, 40, 41, and 42. Point to the four cards and say:

Let's sing about these pictured clothes and where they are worn.

Refer to the music card as you play the song (instrumental version) and lead the children in singing the verses given below. Have each standing child hold up the card when the garment is mentioned. At the end of each verse, have the children show where the item of clothing is worn.

1. **Blouse is one; blouses are two. Where would I put a blouse on you?**
2. **Bonnet is one; bonnets are two. Where would I put a bonnet on you?**
3. **Bootie is one; booties are two. Where would I put booties on you?**
4. **Boot is one; boots are two. Where would I put boots on you?**

Repeat the song with other groups of four, using different cards each time. Continue as long as time and interest permit.

25

MATERIALS*

ACTIVITY 1

Cards

Foods

137 138 141 144
145 146 147 150

Fruits & Vegetables

3 apples

3 bananas

Lemon

3 oranges

Peach

3 pears

Pineapple

3 strawberries

ACTIVITY 2

Fruits & Vegetables

1 of each kind of fruit

P. Mooney Bag

1 Focus: matching fruits with their pictures, and then naming and talking about the fruits

Give each child either one fruit or one card. Be sure the sets match. Take a card or fruit yourself, if necessary. Set aside whatever spares are left. Say:

Some of you are holding fruit cards, and some of you are holding fruits. Try to find someone else holding the kind of fruit you have. There may be more than one other person, so look carefully. Then come and sit in front of me with your partners.

When the groups are assembled, point to one of them and say:

Tell me in a sentence what fruit you are holding.

The group should respond with a sentence such as "We are holding (oranges)" or "We have (oranges)." Continue with the other groups. Then ask questions like these to promote discussion:

1. **Which fruits have stems?**
2. **Which fruits must we peel before we eat them?**
3. **Which fruits have seeds?**
4. **Which fruits give us juice?**

2 Focus: naming fruits from memory

Put the eight plastic fruits into the bag.

Wear the bag and say:

Let's play a remembering game. First, I will take out two fruits and show them to you. Look at them carefully and whisper their names to help you remember them. Then I will put them back into the bag and ask one of you to tell me in a sentence which fruits you saw.

The child you call on should answer with a sentence such as "I saw an (apple) and a (strawberry)" or "You had a (banana) and a (pineapple)." Continue until everyone has had at least one turn.

VARIATION: To make the activity *harder,* hold up three fruits at a time.

26

MATERIALS*

ACTIVITY 1

Cards

Animals

1 2 7 8 9 10 11
12 13 14 18 20 21
22 23 24 27 28 29
32

Display Board

6 ledges

P. Mooney Bag

ACTIVITY 2

Cards

Animals

(same as for Activity 1)

Music

325

Display Board

6 ledges

Audiocassette 2

Side A, Song 2,
"The Is-Are Song"

1 Focus: naming, describing, and relating adult animals and their young

Put the 20 animal cards into the bag.

Wear the bag and say:

P. Mooney's bag holds surprises for everyone. What do you think they might be today?

Encourage the children to guess before you continue:

Let's find out. Pull a surprise from the bag and show us what it is, (George). (Pause) **What kind of animal do you have?** (Pause) **Tell us something about it.** (Pause) **Now put your card on the board.**

Continue with other children. Each child should describe the pictured animal in sentences like "I have a (calf). It has (four legs, two ears, and a tail)." Encourage the children to give complete descriptions. If necessary, ask questions or give clues. Remove the cards from the board to make room as you proceed. When every child has had a turn, collect the cards and say:

Now let's put the animals together in families. (Show card 21)

What baby animal belongs to this horse, (Carmen)? (Pause)

Yes, the colt and the horse belong together.

Have the child display the two cards together on the board. When the board is full, remove a few pairs to make room for the remaining cards. Continue until all cards have been paired.

2 Focus: singing "The Is-Are Song" while naming animals and imitating their sounds

Keep the animal pairs from Activity 1 on display. Point to the cards on display and say:

Let's sing about these animals and imitate their sounds. I will play just the music for you before we begin. Play the song (instrumental version) without singing. Repeat the recording as you lead the children in singing verses like these:

1. **Hen is one; hens are two. What do they say when they talk to you?** (cluck, cluck)
2. **Chick is one; chicks are two. What do they say when they talk to you?** (peep, peep)

Continue in this manner with the remaining animal cards, adding those not on the board as they are needed.

27

MATERIALS*

ACTIVITY 1

Cards

Animals

1 3 5 8 11 12 13
15 16 17 18 20 21

Display Board

6 ledges

Audiocassette 3

Side A, Selection 1,
"Sounds of Animals"

ACTIVITY 2

Puppets

P. Mooney

1 Focus: listening to "Sounds of Animals," and then identifying and imitating each of them

In random order, display the 13 animal cards on the board.

Review the animal card labels with the children. Then say:

Sometimes we can name an animal by hearing its sound. Let's listen to some new animal sounds. When you decide which animal is making a sound, please point to its picture on the board. Then we will name it together and imitate its sound.

Play only the first sound (bear) before having the class say in unison, "This is a bear." Have a child find and hold up the picture of a bear as you say:

A bear makes this sound: grrr. A bear growls. Let's all growl like bears.

Repeat this procedure with the remaining sounds and cards.

2 Focus: following directions to imitate animal sounds in the game P. Mooney Says

Ask the children to stand before you. Place P. Mooney on your hand and have him say:

Let's play P. Mooney Says. First I will say, "P. Mooney says," and then I will tell you to make an animal sound. Make the sound over and over until you hear "P. Mooney says, 'Stop.' "If I do not begin by saying, "P. Mooney says," don't make the sound at all. Let's practice before we play.

Practice by having the puppet say:

1. **P. Mooney says, "Growl like a bear-"** (Make sure everyone growls)
2. **P. Mooney says, "Stop."** (Make sure everyone stops)
3. **Growl like a bear.** (Make sure everyone remains silent and understands why)

When the children are ready, have P. Mooney give commands like these:

1. **P. Mooney says, "Buzz like a bee."**
2. **P. Mooney says, "Stop."**
3. **P. Mooney says, "Cluck like a hen."**
4. **Stop.**
5. **P. Mooney says, "Stop."**
6. **P. Mooney says, "Bark like a dog."**
7. **P. Mooney says, "Stop."**
8. **P. Mooney says, "Moo like a cow."**
9. **P. Mooney says, "Stop."**
10. **Meow like a cat.**
11. **P. Mooney says, "Meow like a cat."**
12. **P. Mooney says, "Stop."**

Continue as long as the game is fun and time permits.

28 

MATERIALS*

ACTIVITY 1

Cards

Stories

386-398

Audiocassette 1

Side A, Story 4,

"The Elephant That Did Not Know How to Listen"

ACTIVITY 2

Cards

Music

335

Audiocassette 2

Side B, Song 12,

"Rhythm Walk"

1 Focus: listening to and retelling the story "The Elephant That Did Not Know How to Listen"

Place the 13 story cards on your lap and say:

Someone we all know has an elephant for a friend. What friend of ours might also be friends with an elephant?

If no one mentions P. Mooney, give hints until his name is guessed. Then continue:

Today's story tells how P. Mooney helped Elbert the Elephant learn how to listen. Please listen carefully, because I will ask you to retell the story afterwards.

Play the story. During the narration, show the story cards in turn as you scan the printed copy on the back of each picture. After showing each card, lay it facedown in a pile on your lap. Then hold up each card again in turn as volunteers retell the story. Prompt as necessary.

2 Focus: pantomiming elephants to the music "Rhythm Walk" in a stop-go listening game

Stand with the children. Say:

Let's pretend we are elephants, like this: Bend over and hold your hands together. Take big steps and swing your hands from side to side. (Demonstrate) **Try it.**

Let the children practice before you continue:

Now let's play a listening game. While the music is playing, walk like an elephant. But when the music stops, stop where you are! (Demonstrate)

Play the music. From time to time, stop the music so the children may stop. Continue as long as the game is fun and time permits.

29

MATERIALS*

ACTIVITY 1

Display Board

Teacher provides

Bell

Glass

Pen

Sheet of paper

ACTIVITY 2

Cards

Music

327

Audiocassette 2

Side A, Song 4, "Elbert's Song"

1 Focus: identifying classroom objects by their sounds

Before the lesson, set up the board and hide the items listed under Materials behind it.

Say:

Elbert learned how to be a good listener. Let's find out if you know how to listen, too. I will go behind the board and make some sounds. Try to figure out how I make each one. When I call on you, tell me in a sentence what I did.

Call on volunteers to identify these sounds:

1. **clap hands**
2. **ring bell**
3. **snap fingers**
4. **tap glass with pen**
5. **cluck with tongue**
6. **crumple sheet of paper**
7. **whistle**
8. **knock on board**
9. **scratch board**
10. **hum**

The children you call on should respond in complete sentences such as "You clapped your hands." As necessary, repeat or add sounds to give each child a turn.

VARIATION: To make the activity *harder,* let the children take turns making sounds behind the board for the class to identify.

2 Focus: listening to, talking about, and singing "Elbert's Song"

Say:

Before he met P. Mooney, Elbert could not understand the sounds he heard. Let's listen to his song to find out how his problem was solved.

Play the song, and then ask questions like these:

1. **Who is singing this song?**
2. **What does the song tell you about Elbert?**
3. **What does the song ask us to do?**
4. **Do you sometimes not pay attention to what you hear?**

If necessary, play the song again to promote discussion. Once the children understand that they should "listen to the sounds of the world," play the song again and encourage everyone to sing the chorus. Repeat as desired.

30

MATERIALS*

ACTIVITY 1

None

ACTIVITY 2

Cards

Music

327

Audiocassette 2

Side A, Song 4,

"Elbert's Song"

1 Focus: listening to and remembering environmental sounds, and then talking about them

If feasible, open all classroom doors and windows, or take the group outdoors.

Say:

Let's listen to the sounds of the world the way Elbert does. Ue down on the (floor, ground). (Pause) **Close your eyes and listen carefully. Try to remember all the sounds you hear. In a little while, we will talk about them.**

The children you call on should name the sounds in sentences such as "I heard someone giggling" or "I heard a bird singing." Repeat as often as time and interest suggest.

2 Focus: singing "Elbert's Song," and moving to the music

Play the song and encourage the children to sing the chorus. Then say:

Let's move around the room to the music of Elbert's song. When the music is slow, walk like a big, slow elephant. When the music is fast, sing along and move quickly in any way you like.

Play the song as the children move around the room in rhythm with the music. Repeat as often as time and interest suggest.

31

MATERIALS*

ACTIVITY 1

None

ACTIVITY 2

Cards

Stories

388

Display Board

1 ledge

1 Focus: identifying classmates' voices in a listening game

Say:

Let's play a listening game. One of you will pretend to be Elbert the Elephant. That person will face the group and stand with eyes closed. Everyone else will change places. Then I will have someone call out, "Elbert the Elephant!" The person pretending to be Elbert must guess who spoke.

If the guess is correct, the child continues to play Elbert. If the guess is incorrect, the group should name the caller in unison. The child who called out then becomes Elbert for the next turn. If feasible, continue until each child has played Elbert.

2 Focus: changing first consonants of names in a rhyming activity

Display the story card on the ledge of the board.

Have the children sit before you. Point to the card on display and say:

Elbert's ear elevators helped him listen. He loved discovering new sounds. Let's have fun playing with names in a rhyming game. First, we will make up names that sound like *Elbert*. *Melbert* and *Telbert* sound like *Elbert*. Can you think of any others?

Help the children use various consonants to begin more names. Then continue:

Now let's make up real or silly words that sound like my name.

Use your first or last name and help as necessary. Once the children understand the game, have them volunteer their own names for use.

32 

MATERIALS*

ACTIVITY 1

Cards
Toys
226-246

Teacher provides
Cardboard box big enough to hold cards

ACTIVITY 2

Cards
Toys
(same as for Activity 1)
Music
337

Display Board
6 ledges

Audiocassette 2
Side B, Song 14,
"Rag March"

1 Focus: naming and describing toy cards

Put all 21 toy cards into the box.

Ask the children to sit before you. Place the box on your lap and say:

Let's pretend this is a toy box with many toys in it. Each of you may shake the box and take out a toy card. Then you are to name the toy and tell us at least two things about it.

Help as necessary. Continue until all the cards have been used.

2 Focus: following directions using *positional words,* and parading to the music "Rag March"

Display 12 toy cards on the board and have the remaining cards handy.

Have each child come up and choose a toy card from those on display. Add the remaining cards to the board as needed. Then say:

Now let's line up and have a toy parade. (Drum), please stand here. (Point) **(Ball), stand *in front of* the (drum). (Puzzle), stand *behind* the (ball). (Doll buggy), stand *beside* the (ball).**

Continue to stress the words *behind, beside,* and *in front of* as the children line up in pairs. When the line is complete, play the music and let the children march around the room. Change leaders frequently and continue as long as time and interest suggest.

VARIATION: To make the activity *harder,* have the children choose their positions in sentences such as "I would like to stand beside the (puzzle)."

33

MATERIALS*

ACTIVITY 1

Cards

Clothing

55-73

P. Mooney Bag

ACTIVITY 2

Cards

Clothing

39 44 46 48 49 52
53 54 56*
58* 59* 62* 63*
64* 66* 67*

Display Board

6 ledges

**NOTE: Cards followed by an asterisk were also used in Activity 1.*

1 Focus: naming dothing in sentences

Put the 19 clothing cards into the bag.

Wear the bag and say:

P. Mooney's bag is full today. It has more pictures of clothes in it. Each of you is to come up and take a card from the bag. You choose first and show everyone your card, (Jonathan). Tell us what it is in a sentence.

The child should use a sentence such as "This is a (shirt)." Continue with other children. If necessary, help by asking, "Are you holding a (sweater), or a (wristwatch)?" Accept suitable synonyms. Continue until all cards have been named.

2 Focus: classifying and naming clothing in the game I Spy

Display the 16 clothing cards on the board.

Say:

Let's use these cards to play a game called I Spy. The words *I spy* mean "I see." I will ask you to find all the clothes that are the same in some way. Please look carefully, because there may be more than one right answer. Use sentences. Who spies all the clothing with buttons?

The child you call on should point to the correct cards and identify them in a sentence such as "I spy a coat, a suit, and a shirt that have buttons." Help as necessary. Continue with questions like these:

1. **Who spies clothing that covers the head?** (snowsuit, jacket, raincoat)
2. **Who spies clothing with sleeves?** (jacket, girl's pajamas, boy's shirt, sweater, coat, dress, suit, snowsuit, raincoat, knit shirt)
3. **Who spies clothing with buckles?** (snowsuit, jeans, overalls)
4. **Who spies clothing with pockets?** (coat, suit, snowsuit, jacket, jeans, overalls, raincoat, boy's shirt)
5. **Who spies clothing with zippers?** (snowsuit, jeans, overalls)
6. **Who spies clothing that is blue?** (suit, snowsuit, jeans, overalls, boy's shirt, knit shirt)
7. **Who spies clothing with lace?** (slip, blouse)
8. **Who spies clothing with something that ties on it?** (dress, snowsuit, raincoat)

34

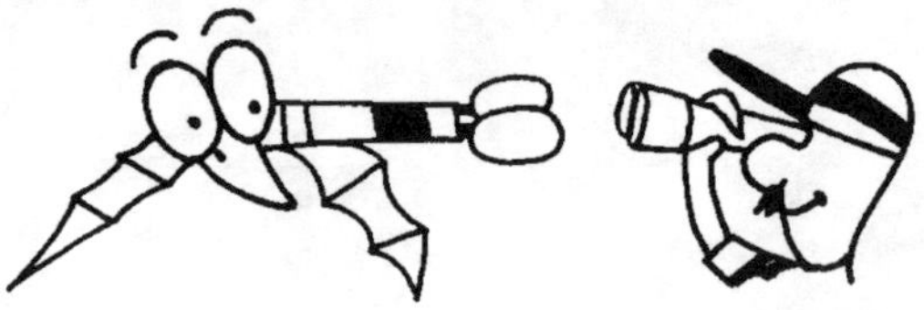

MATERIALS*

ACTIVITY 1

Color Chips
I red per child
I green per child

Display Board
4 ledges

Poster 1

ACTIVITY 2

Cards
Music
328

Audiocassette 2
Side A, Song 5, "If and Then Go Together"

1 Focus: matching red and green chips to similarly colored objects on the poster "Farm in Spring," and then naming the items

Use the ledges to display the poster on the board.

Give each child a red and a green color chip. Say:

Let's have a color hunt. If you have a red color chip, show it to me. (Pause) **Yes! Everyone has a red chip. Look for red things on the poster.** (Pause) **Please come up here and point to something red on the poster, (LaTanya).** (Pause) **What did you find?**

The child should answer in a sentence such as "Here is a red (bam)." Continue until everyone has had a turn, even if some objects are named more than once. Then ask:

What color is the grass on the farm? (Pause) **Yes, it is green. If you have a green chip, hold it up.** (Pause) **Yes! Now let's look for green things on the poster.**

Continue as before.

VARIATION: To make the activity *harder,* ask the child to tell something about the item. For example: "Farm animals sleep in a barn."

2 Focus: brainstorming *tall* and *small* animals, and then singing the song "If and Then Go Together"

Say:

Let's talk about very small animals and very tall animals. Please name animals that are small enough to hold in your hands. (Encourage individual responses) **Now name some animals that are taller than you are.**

When several tall animals have been named, ask the children to stand as you continue:

Let's sing a new song about a very small animal — an ant — and a very tall animal — a giraffe. Use your fingers to show me how small an ant is. (Demonstrate by holding your thumb and forefinger close together) **Now show me how high a giraffe might be.** (Demonstrate by standing on tiptoe and reaching up) **When the song mentions the ant, use your fingers to show how small it is. When the song mentions the giraffe, reach up high, as though you were petting it. Sing along when you know the words.**

Play the song and lead the children in singing and acting out each verse. Repeat as time permits.

35

MATERIALS*

ACTIVITY 1

Display Board
4 ledges

P. Mooney Stick

Poster 1

ACTIVITY 2

Display Board
4 ledges

P. Mooney Stick

Poster 1

1 Focus: classifying and naming animals on the poster "Farm in Spring" in the game I Spy

Use the ledges to display the poster on the board.

Point to the poster with the stick as you say:

Let's play I Spy with the farm animals on this poster. Remember, the words I spy mean "I see." I will ask you a question about animals. When I call on you, point with the stick to the right animal and name it in a sentence. Please look carefully, because there may be more than one correct answer. Let's begin. (Pause) **Raise your hand if you spy an animal with horns.**

The child you call on should respond in sentences such as "I spy an animal with horns. It is a (cow, goat)." Help as necessary. Continue with questions like these:

1. **Who spies an animal with a tail?** (fox, raccoon, dog, goat)
2. **Who spies an animal with spots?** (pig, frog, fawn, fish)
3. **Who spies an animal that flies?** (dragonfly, bird, bee, owl)
4. **Who spies an animal that swims?** (frog, duck, fish, turtle)
5. **Who spies an animal that may sleep in a barn?** (pig, horse, cow, goat)

VARIATION: To make the activity *harder,* allow the children to take tums asking the group similar questions.

2 Focus: brainstorming animals with certain characteristics, and then pantomiming the animals

Stand with the children and hold the stick as you say:

P. Mooney's magic stick is going to change you into animals. As I wave it and say a magic verse, decide which animal you want to be that fits the description.

Wave the stick and say:

Mooney Magic, do a trick!

Make animals with horns, P. Mooney Stick!

Have every child in turn name an animal with horns before you allow the children to pantomime their animals. Help as necessary. Continue, repeating the rhyme about animals like these:

1. **animals with tails**
2. **animals with spots**
3. **animals that fly**
4. **animals that swim**

Conclude by waving the stick as you say:

Eenie, Mooney,
Macaroony!
Now let's be
You and me!

36

MATERIALS*

ACTIVITY 1

Puppets

Zoey

Discovery hat

ACTIVITY 2

None

1 Focus: identifying single and multiple body parts

Put Zoey (wearing her discovery hat) on your hand. The puppet says:

I am wearing my discovery hat because I have made a discovery about our bodies. I have *one* nose. (Point to Zoey's nose) **But look at my eyes.** (Point to Zoey's eyes) **I have *more than one* eye. How many do I have?** (Encourage unison response) **That is right; I have *two* eyes. I discovered that we have *one* of some body parts and *more than one* of others. Let's name the body parts of which we have only *one*. You go first, (Sam).**

If the class agrees that a person has only one of the body part named, have them point to it as they say with Zoey, "We have *one* (mouth)." When all single body parts have been named, continue with body parts of which there are two and more than two.
Suggested body parts:

one	*two*	*more than two*
1. mouth	**1. arms**	**1. teeth**
2. nose	**2. hands**	**2. hair**
3. stomach	**3. elbows**	**3. fingers**
4. head	**4. feet**	**4. toes**
5. neck	**5. knees**	**5. fingernails**
6. back	**6. legs**	
7. body	**7. eyes**	
8. tongue	**8. ears**	
9. chin	**9. eyebrows**	
	10. lips	

2 Focus: chanting an action rhyme stressing "one" and "two" body parts

Stand with the children and say:

I know a rhyme about parts of our bodies. Please listen to the words and act them out with me.

Act out the words with the children as you say:

Use one hand to tap, tap, tap.
(Tap head)

Use two hands to clap, clap, clap.
(Clap hands)

Use one eye to wink, wink, wink.
(Wink one eye)

Use two eyes to blink, blink, blink.
(Blink both eyes)

Use one foot to hop, hop, hop.
(Hop on one foot)

Use two feet to jump, jump, jump.
(Jump)

Repeat the rhyme, encouraging the children to join you in both saying the words and doing the actions. Continue as time and interest suggest.

37

MATERIALS*

ACTIVITY 1

Display Board
Manikin, Disassembled
Body parts

ACTIVITY 2

None

1 Focus: relating one's own and the manikin's body parts, then describing their actions

Ask several children to help you place the manikin pieces on the board in random order. Then ask:

What do you see on the board?

(Encourage individual responses)

Yes, these are manikin body parts. Please point to the body part I name. Everyone, point to your own head. (Pause) **Now please come up and find the manikin head, (Clare).** (Pause) **Tell us something that you can do with your head, (Clare).**

The child should answer in a sentence such as "I can nod (shake, turn, think with) my head." Continue with the other body parts displayed. Give everyone a turn, even if some parts are named more than once.

VARIATION: To make the activity harder, have the children name more than one function of each body part.

2 Focus: evaluating statements on actions of body parts, and correcting the statements while stressing not

Say:

Let's pretend that you are teachers and that I am a child in your class. You must find out if I know what our body parts can do. If what I say is true, tell me so in a sentence. If I say something that is not true, please tell me.

Say sentences such as those given below. Each time, the children should respond in unison by saying, "Yes, we (clap) with our (hands)" or "No, we do not (nod) with our (toes)." Then let a child give the correct response, such as "We nod with our heads."

1. **We clap with our hands.**
2. **We nod with our toes.**
3. **We smell with our ears.**
4. **We walk with our legs.**
5. **We wiggle our teeth.**
6. **We listen with our knees.**
7. **We talk with our mouths.**
8. **We blink our elbows.**
9. **We wave with our hands.**
10. **We scratch with our fingers.**

VARIATION: To make the activity harder, have the children make up their own statements to be corrected by the class.

38

MATERIALS*

ACTIVITY 1

Cards

Foods

103 139 143 148 151

Fruits & Vegetables

Carrot

Corn

Potato

Tomato

ACTIVITY 2

P. Mooney Bag

Fruits & Vegetables

Carrot

Corn

Onion

Potato

Tomato

1 Focus: matching *vegetables* with their pictures, and then naming the vegetables

Give each child either one vegetable or one card. Be sure the sets match. Take a card or vegetable yourself, if necessary. Set aside whatever spares are left. Say:

Some of you are holding vegetable cards, and some of you are holding vegetables. Try to find someone else who is holding the kind of vegetable you have. Then come and sit in front of me with your partners.

When the groups are assembled, point to one of them and say:

Tell me in a sentence what vegetable you are holding.

The group should name the vegetable in a sentence such as "We are holding (onions)" or "We have (onions)." Continue with the other groups. If there are children who did not have a chance to participate, redistribute the cards and vegetables, and repeat the procedure.

VARIATION: To make the activity *harder,* ask questions like these:

1. **Which vegetables grow under the ground?**
2. **Which vegetables must we peel before we eat them?**
3. **Which vegetables give us juice?**
4. **How do you like to eat each of these vegetables?**

2 Focus: naming *vegetables* from memory

Put the five plastic vegetables into the bag.

Wear the bag and say:

Let's play a remembering game. First, I will hold up two vegetables and you will look at them carefully. Whisper the names of the vegetables to yourself to help you remember them. Then I will put them back into the bag and ask one of you which vegetables you saw. Answer in sentences.

Each child you call on should respond in a sentence such as "I saw a (potato) and a (carrot)" or "You had (corn) and an (onion)." Continue until everyone has had at least one turn.

VARIATION: To make the activity *harder,* hold up three vegetables at a time.

39

MATERIALS*

ACTIVITY 1

Display Board
4 ledges

Poster 1

ACTIVITY 2

Cards
Music
328

Display Board
4 ledges

Poster 1

Audiocassette 2
Side A, Song 5,
"If and Then Go Together"

1 Focus: comparing animal sizes on the poster "Farm in Spring"

Use the ledges to display the poster on the board.

Point to the poster and say:

Let's look for large and small animals on this farm. I will ask one of you to find a certain kind of animal. Then that person will come up, point to the animal on the poster, and tell us about it. Let's begin. Find an animal that is larger than the spider, (Larry). (Pause) **Yes! Repeat after me: The (goat) is larger than the spider.** (Pause) **Find another animal larger than the spider, (Debbie).**

Continue with the commands given below. Since there are many correct responses, several children may participate each time. Let children who are able say the sentence without prompting.

Find an animal that is . . .

1. ***larger*** **than a dog.**
2. ***smaller*** **than a duck.**
3. ***smaller*** **than a cow.**
4. ***larger*** **than a bird.**
5. ***smaller*** **than a horse.**

Conclude with these directions:

6. **Find the *largest* animal on the poster.**
7. **Find the *smallest* animal on the poster.**

2 Focus: singing the song "If and Then Go Together" about tall and small animals

Stand beside the audiocassette player and the poster, with the children standing before you. Say:

We have been talking about large and small animals. Let's sing again the song about an ant and a giraffe. When the song tells you about an ant, use your fingers to show how small an ant is. When the song tells you about the giraffe, show me how tall a giraffe might be.

Play the song. If necessary, demonstrate the size of an ant by holding your thumb and forefinger close together. Demonstrate the size of a giraffe by standing on tiptoes and reaching up with both arms. Repeat the recording, encouraging the children to sing along. Then continue:

Now that you know the song, let's make up a verse about one of the small animals shown on the poster. Which small animal do you choose?

When the choice is made, play the song (instrumental version) and lead the children in singing the new verse. Repeat the procedure with a tall animal. Continue with other animals as time and interest suggest.

40

MATERIALS*

ACTIVITY 1

Cards

Stories

369-385 (optional)

Audiocassette 1

Side A, Story 1,

"P. Mooney and Zoey"

ACTIVITY 2

Cards

Music

326

Puppets

Zoey

All 3 hats

Audiocassette 2

Side A, Song 3,

"Zoey"

1 Focus: listening to the story "P. Mooney and Zoey," and then answering questions about it

Say:

Let's listen again to the story of how P. Mooney and Zoey became friends. This time we will not look at the pictures. Please listen very carefully, because later we will talk about what happens in the story.

Play the story. Lead the discussion with questions like these:

1. **What was P. Mooney doing the day he met Zoey?**
2. **What happened to P. Mooney in the story?**
3. **How did Zoey help P. Mooney?**
4. **What might have happened if Zoey had not come along to help P. Mooney?**
5. **What kind of person do you think Zoey is?**
6. **Do you like the story about Zoey? Why? Why not?**

OPTIONAL: If necessary, use the story cards as cues.

2 Focus: singing and acting out the song "Zoey"

Stand beside the audiocassette player, with the children standing before you. Place Zoey (wearing her discovery hat) on your hand. She says:

Let's sing the song about my hats. Please do the actions for each hat you see me wearing. Let's begin with my discovery hat.

Play the song and switch Zoey's hats as indicated in each verse. If necessary, rehearse the actions:

discovery hat — shade eyes with one hand and look around

thinking hat — put chin in palm of hand and pretend to think

action hat — run in place

Let the children take turns switching Zoey's hats as the song is repeated.

Keep in Mind . .
After each lesson in the program, individuals who have difficulty demonstrating proficiency in the skills you consider appropriate and important for them to learn should be tutored. Aides could help you with this task.

41

MATERIALS*

ACTIVITY 1

Display Board

Manikin, Disassembled
Body parts
Curly hair
Facial features

ACTIVITY 2

Cards
Music
329

Audiocassette 2
Side A, Song 6,
"The Not Song"

Teacher provides
Record player

1 Focus: evaluating what is wrong with the manikin, and reassembling it correctly

Ask two children to assemble the manikin on the board. Then say:

(Mark) and (Francesca) did a good job of putting the manikin together. Now let's play a game with it. While you cover your eyes, I will change some of the manikin's parts around. Then all of you are to tell me in a sentence what I changed.

When the children's eyes are covered, switch the manikin's hands and feet. After the class identifies the changed parts, ask a child to return them to the right positions. Repeat the procedure with these body part changes:

1. **take off head**
2. **turn trunk upside down**
3. **remove one arm**
4. **switch arms and legs**
5. **exchange mouth and nose**
6. **exchange feet and hands**
7. **attach arms to the head**
8. **take off one arm**
9. **put ears on knees**
10. **turn over ears**
11. **place neck between one shoulder and arm**

2 Focus: singing and acting out "The Not Song"

Stand beside the audiocassette player, with the children standing before you. Say:

Let's sing a new song about body parts. Please watch as I go through the song for you the first time. I will point to the body parts as they are mentioned. Then we will do the song together.

Play the song and sing these verses with gestures:

1. **This is my head. This is my head.**
   (Point to head)

   This is not my head. This is not my head. (Point to foot)

   This is my head. This is my head,
   (Point to head)

   And this is a part of me.
   (Point to head)

2. **This is my foot. This is my foot.**
   (Point to foot)

   This is not my foot. This is not my foot. (Point to head)

   This is my foot. This is my foot,
   (Point to foot)

   And this is a part of me.
   Point to foot)

Invite the children to join you in repeating the song. Continue as time permits.

42

MATERIALS*

ACTIVITY 1

Cards

Toys

247-266

Teacher provides

Cardboard box large enough to hold the toy cards

ACTIVITY 2

Cards

Toys
(same as for Activity 1)

Music

329

Audiocassette 2

Side A, Song 6,
"The Not Song

1 Focus: naming and describing toys

Put the 20 toy cards into the box.

Place the box on your lap and say:

There are different toys in our toy box today. Think about what toy you would like to find in it. When I call on you, shake the box and pick a toy card. Then you are to tell us at least two things about the toy you picked.

Help as necessary. Continue until all the cards have been used.

2 Focus: singing "The Not Song" while naming toys

Stand beside the audiocassette player, with the children standing before you. Give card 258 to one child and 254 to another. Have these two children stand facing the group and holding up the cards. Play the song (instrumental version) and sing the verses given below, pointing to the card when a toy is mentioned.

1. **This is my top. This is my top**
   (Point to top)

   This is not my top. This is not my top
   (Point to swing)

   This is my top. This is my top.
   (Point to top)

   And this is a toy for me.
   (Point to top)

2. **This is my swing. This is my swing.**
   (Point to swing)

   This is not my swing. This is not my swing (Point to top)

   This is my swing. This is my swing.
   (Point to swing)

   And this is a toy for me.
   (Point to swing)

Invite the group to join you in repeating the song. Continue as time permits with other pairs of children and toy cards.

43

MATERIALS*

ACTIVITY 1

Cards

Toys

228 229 236 237
238 240 243 248
251 258 260 266

Display Board

6 ledges

Audiocassette 3

Side B, Selection 2,
"Sounds of Toys"

ACTIVITY 2

P. Mooney Stick

1 Focus: listening to "Sounds of Toys," and then identifying each one

Display the 12 toy cards on the board.

Begin by reviewing the names of the toys. Then point to the cards on display and say:

Please listen to some new sound effects and try to tell which of these toys might make each sound we hear.

Play the sound effects, one sound at a time. After the children have identified the sound in unison, one child may then point to the corresponding picture and name it in a sentence such as "We heard the (train set)" or "That was the (guitar)." Continue with all twelve sounds. Then turn over the cards so that the pictures are hidden. Play the sound effects in random order and have the children identify them without seeing the pictures. When a sound is correctly identified, turn over the corresponding card for verification. If necessary, use the pictures as cues.

2 Focus: describing actions of children while stressing the past tense in a P. Mooney-stick game

Ask the children to stand before you. Hold the stick and say:

We are going to use P. Mooney's stick to play a game we have played before. First, let's practice the rhyme we will say. It goes like this:

(William), be nimble; (William), be quick;

(William), step over P. Mooney's stick!

Repeat the rhyme with the children until most of them know the words. Then explain:

Now we are ready to play the game. I will put the P. Mooney stick on the floor. (Do this) **While everyone says the rhyme, you will take turns stepping over the stick. You may go first, (William).**

Use each child's name in the rhyme as she or he steps over the stick. Then stress the past tense as you lead the class in saying, "(Sheila) stepped over the P. Mooney stick." After everyone has had a turn, repeat the procedure, having the children jump over the stick as the group says:

(Rodney), be nimble; (Rodney), be quick;

(Rodney), jump over P. Mooney's stick!

Continue until everyone has had a turn.

44

MATERIALS*

ACTIVITY 1

Cards

People

202 204 205 211
214 215 219 220
221

Display Board

ACTIVITY 2

Cards

Music

330

Puppets

P. Mooney

Audiocassette 2

Side A, Song 7,
"Hi Ho, Pal"

1 Focus: sequencing people from youngest to oldest, and then talking about them

Display the nine people cards in random order on the board.

Ask the children to sit before you. Point to the cards, and ask:

Which of these people do you think is the youngest?

As necessary, give clues until the baby is identified. Have a child place this card at the far left on the top ledge. Then ask:

Which person is the oldest?

Give clues until either the older man or the older woman is named. Have that card placed at the far right on the bottom ledge. Continue in this way until all the cards have been sequenced by age in left-to-right order as seen by the group. Encourage the children to talk about their choices. Continue discussion of the cards with questions like these:

1. **What is the (older man) doing?**
2. **What might be the (girl's) first name?**
3. **Who do you think is having the most fun? Why do you think so?**
4. **Whom would you choose for a friend? Why?**
5. **Do any of these people remind you of someone you know? Who?**
6. **Some of these people look as though they are about to say something; what do you think they might say?**

2 Focus: singing the song "Hi Ho, Pal" while telling first and last names

Stand beside the audiocassette player, with the children standing before you. Put P. Mooney on your hand and have him say:

When we meet people, we need to learn their names. My name is P. Mooney. Please listen to a new song about learning names. Then we will sing it together.

Play the song once. Then P. Mooney continues:

Now let's sing together. When I point to you, tell me your first and last names.

Play the song. After the words "learning names," the puppet says, "My name's P. Mooney. What's yours?" and then points to four children in turn. Each should reply, "My name's (Joanie Robb). What's yours?" Repeat the song until everyone has had a turn.

45

MATERIALS*

ACTIVITY 1

Cards

People

200 201 203 206
207 208 209 210
212 213 216 217
218

Display Board

6 ledges

ACTIVITY 2

Cards

People
(same as for Activity I)

Display Board

6 ledges

1 Focus: naming and talking about workers

Display the 13 people cards on the board.

Point to the pictures on display, and have the workers named and discussed in turn. Then say:

These people all work. If you could be any one of them or some other kind of worker, who would you be, (Vernon)? (Pause) **Why?**

Continue with other children. Expand their understanding of work by suggesting and discussing occupations such as homemaker, reporter, judge, cook, and truck driver. Accept all responses.

2 Focus: identifying workers from pantomimed actions

Keep the 13 people cards from Activity 1 on display.

Point to the board and say:

Let's take turns pretending to do what these people are doing. During your turn, the rest of us will guess what you are doing and who you are pretending to be.

Call on individuals to stand before the group and perform. Provide help as necessary. Encourage the others to use sentences when they describe the actions and name the workers. Continue until everyone has had a turn at acting.

46

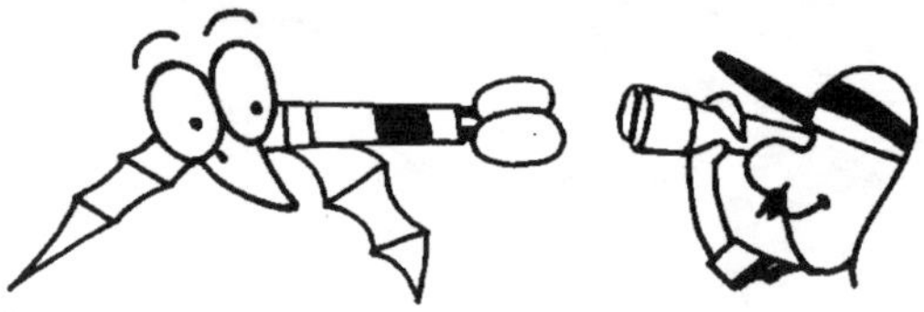

MATERIALS*

ACTIVITY I

Display Board

Magnetic Shapes

Large black circle

Large black triangle

1 medium circle per child

1 medium triangle per child

ACTIVITY 2

Cards

Music

330

Magnetic Shapes

Circles for half the class & self

Triangles for half the class

Audiocassette 2

Side A, Song 7,

"Hi Ho, Pal"

1 Focus: listening to a story about shapes, and then building magnetic shape constructions

Set up the board. Place the large black triangle near one edge and the large black circle in the center. Have the other circles and triangles handy.

Say:

Today I will tell you a story about two shapes. Please listen and watch.

Moving the shapes as indicated, read this story aloud:

Once there was a circle. It was round and fat and had no corners. (Trace circle with finger) **This circle was happy. It loved to play and could roll around and around like a bicycle wheel.** (Make circle go around and around) **It could also bounce like a ball.** (Make circle hop across board) **One day the circle was having such a good time rolling and bouncing that it forgot to look where it was going. All at once, it bumped into something.** (Have circle bump into triangle)

"Oh, excuse me," said the circle. "I didn't see you. My name is Circle. Who are you?"

"I am called Triangle," said the other shape, who had three straight sides (trace sides with finger) **and three corners.** (Point to corners in turn)

"Would you like to play?" asked the circle. "I am tired of rolling and bouncing by myself. I would like to roll and bounce with you."

"I wish I could," said the triangle, "but I can't roll and I can't bounce. All I can do is slide on my sides, like this."

(Make triangle slide on one side)

"Oh, dear," said the circle. "You can't roll or bounce, and I can't slide. But can we work together?"

The triangle thought for a moment. "You know," he said, "if we did things together, we could have fun."

"That's it!" exclaimed the circle. "If you hop on top of me, we can pretend that we are a clown's head." (Demonstrate, like this: △○)

The triangle said, "If I stand on one of my corners and you jump on top of me, we can pretend that we are an ice-cream cone!" (Demonstrate, like this: ○▽)

The circle and the triangle had never had so much fun or laughed so hard. So the two shapes played together and pretended to be many things. What do you think they might have pretended to be?

Give each child a circle and a triangle. If there are more than 14 children, have them work in pairs. The children may then arrange the shapes as they like before telling the group in sentences what they have built. As necessary, give help. Items might include: ○△ moon coming over mountain, ○▽ baby wearing bib, ◁○ tadpole.

2 Focus: singing the song "Hi Ho, Pal" while naming shapes

Stand beside the audiocassette player, with the children standing before you. Give each child a shape and keep one circle for yourself. Say:

Let's sing "Hi Ho, Pal" about the shapes we are holding. When it is your turn, tell us the name of your shape. I will go first.

Play the song. After the words "learning names," say, "My name's Circle. What's yours?" and point to a child. Continue with others and repeat the recording until everyone has had a turn.

47

MATERIALS*

ACTIVITY 1

Cards

Foods

94-114

Teacher provides

Large brown paper bag

ACTIVITY 2

Cards

Foods

(same as for Activity 1)

Display Board

2 ledges

1 Focus: naming and describing foods

Put all 21 food cards into the paper bag and put it on the floor in front of you.

Ask the children to sit before you. Point to the bag and say:

This paper bag is full of food cards. Let's pretend it contains real foods. Now let's each choose a card to name and describe.

Call on everyone in turn. If a child experiences difficulty, ask:

What food do you have, (Sarah)? (Pause) **Yes, your food is a (doughnut). Tell us something about it.**

The child should respond in a sentence such as "A doughnut has a hole in it." Continue until everyone has had a turn and all the cards are described. Help when necessary by asking questions about the color, taste, smell, texture, or temperature of the foods.

2 Focus: naming *foods* from memory

Hold the 21 food cards on your lap and say:

We are going to use our food cards to play a shopping game. Let's pretend that we went shopping and bought these three foods.

Place food cards 94, 95, and 96 on the board. Point to each card for the children to name as you all say, "We went shopping and we bought bacon, green beans, and red beans." Continue:

Now I will turn over the cards so that you cannot see the pictures. (Do so) **What did we buy when we went shopping?**

Have individuals answer with the above sentence model. Using new cards each time, repeat the procedure as time and interest suggest.

VARIATIONS: To make the activity *harder,* use more than three food cards. To make it *easier,* use only one or two cards.

48

MATERIALS*

ACTIVITY 1

Color Chips
30 green
30 red
30 yellow

Fruits & Vegetables
3 apples
3 bananas
Corn
Lemon
3 pears
Pineapple
3 strawberries
Tomato

P. Mooney Bag

ACTIVITY 2

Cards
Music
336

Fruits & Vegetables
I per child

Audiocassette 2
Side B, Song 13,
"Round Dance"

1 Focus: matching color chips with fruits and vegetables, and then describing the fruits and vegetables

Put the chips into the bag.

Ask the children to sit in a circle. Place the 16 fruits and vegetables in the center. Wearing the bag, stand inside the circle and say:

Let's play a game with these fruits and vegetables. Come and take a chip from the bag, (Jimmy John). What color did you choose? (Pause) **Yes, your chip is (yellow). Please find a (yellow) fruit or vegetable.**

When a match is made, help the child use the color to describe the fruit or vegetable in a sentence such as "This banana is yellow" or "The corn has yellow kernels." Continue with other children. Leave all the fruits and vegetables in the center, but encourage the children to vary their choices. Check to be sure the children can distinguish between red, green, and yellow. If time and interest permit, each child may draw a second chip and have another turn.

VARIATION: To make the activity *harder,* have each child match two different chips to a fruit or vegetable that has both colors.

2 Focus: naming fruits and vegetables in a stop-go listening game using the music "Round Dance"

Let each child choose a fruit or vegetable. Have the children stand in a circle as you say:

Let's play a game. Put your fruit or vegetable on the floor in front of you. While the music plays, join hands and move in a circle around the fruits and vegetables. When the music ends, stop and pick up the item in front of you. Then each of you will name what you are holding.

Play the music as the children move. Then stop the audiocassette player and say, "Stop!" The children are to lift up and name their fruits and vegetables in rapid succession before putting them back on the floor. Continue as time and interest suggest.

49

MATERIALS*

ACTIVITY 1

Cards

Toys

228 229 230 232
237 240 241 242
247 250 251 252
257 258 259 262
263 264 265 266

Display Board

6 ledges

ACTIVITY 2

None

1 Focus: talking about toys

Display 15 of the toy cards and keep the other five handy.

Say:

Let's pretend the board is a toy shop with many different toys for sale. Look at them carefully, because we are going to talk about each one.

Lead discussion of each toy with questions like these:

1. **What is this toy called?**
2. **Where could you play with a (ball)?**
3. **What body parts do you use when you play with a (ball)?**
4. **How does a (ball) move?**
5. **Name some of the ways you might play with this (ball).**

Continue with the remaining cards, replacing those already discussed. Encourage imaginative responses.

2 Focus: following directions in pantomiming uses of toys

Ask the children to stand before you. Say:

Let's play a game. I will give a direction to all or some of you. Listen very carefully. Pretend to blow up a balloon, (Mei-Ling, Rocco, and Joyce). (Pause) **Yes, you followed my directions.**

Repeat this procedure with the actions listed below. Call on one to four children at a time, or everyone. Be sure to give the direction before saying the name(s).

1. **Pretend to bounce a ball, (Emilio, Yvette, and Adam).**
2. **Pretend to crawl through a tunnel, (Malita, Stewart, and Ruth).**
3. **Pretend to roller skate, (everyone).**
4. **Pretend to play a guitar, (Cameron and Rebecca).**
5. **Pretend to blow a whistle, (everyone).**
6. **Pretend to be a doctor or nurse, (Brady, Lydia, and Steve).**
7. **Pretend to use a rake, hoe, or shovel, (everyone).**
8. **Pretend to jump rope, (Carlotta, Alvin, Bethany, and Charles).**
9. **Pretend to use a shovel and pail, (Margaret and Philip).**
10. **Pretend to sit on the teeter-totter, (Coretta and Donald).**
11. **Pretend to use a wagon, (everyone).**
12. **Pretend to play with a top, (Linda).**
13. **Pretend to climb a jungle gym, (Scott, Judy, Patrick, and Megan).**
14. **Pretend to ride a tricycle, (Juan and Louise).**
15. **Pretend to use a dump truck, (Darcey).**
16. **Pretend to play in the sandbox, (Miranda, Bud, and Jane).**

50

MATERIALS*

ACTIVITY 1

Cards

Household Items

153-176

Display Board

6 ledges

P. Mooney Bag

ACTIVITY 2

Cards

Household Items

155* 156* 163*
168* 170* 172*

Music

330

Display Board

I ledge

Audiocassette 2

Side A, Song 7,
"Hi Ho, Pal"

**NOTE: These cards were also used in Activity 1; this explanation will no longer be provided.*

1 Focus: naming and describing household items

Set up the board and use five ledges to outline a simple house. Place one ledge in the center, like this: Put the 24 cards into the bag.

Wear the bag and say:

Let's look at some pictures of things often found in a house. When I call on you, take a card from the bag and put it on this ledge. (Point to ledge inside "house") **Then you may tell us all about the card you picked.**

The child should name and describe the item. Help as necessary and conclude the discussion by saying, "Now we have a Clamp) for the house." Lay the card aside and continue with other children until all cards have been used.

2 Focus: singing the song "Hi Ho, Pal" while pantomiming the use of *household items*

Stand beside the audiocassette player and board, with the children standing before you. Hold the six household cards and say:

Let's pretend to use some of the things we could find in a house. (Display card 168 on board) **How do we use an iron, (Matthew)?** (Pause) **Yes! We use it to iron clothes, like this.**

Demonstrate by moving a fist back and forth at waist level. Have the class join you. Remove the card and repeat the procedure with the other cards. Then play the song (instrumental version). Lead the children in pantomiming ironing clothes as you sing.

Hi ho, pal;

Hi ho, chum.

I'm your friend;

Let's have some fun

ironing clothes

Continue by replaying the song and singing more verses with actions: brushing hair, cuffing meat, mopping floors, sweeping floors, and drinking tea.

51

MATERIALS*

ACTIVITY 1

Display Board
4 ledges

Poster 3

ACTIVITY 2

Display Board
4 ledges

Cards
Toys
228 229 230 231
232 233 234 236
237 240 241 242
243 246 249 250
251 253 254 256
258 259 260 262
263 265

P. Mooney Bag

Poster 3

1 Focus: talking about the poster "Department Store"

Use the ledges to display the poster on the board.

Point to the poster as you ask:

What is this place called? (Pause) **Yes, it is a department store. P. Mooney is somewhere inside. See if you can find him.** (Pause) **Where did you find P. Mooney?**

Discuss the contents of the poster with the children. Make sure every child has a chance to participate. Then continue with questions like these:

1. **Have you ever been to a store like this one?**
2. **How was the store you visited different?**
3. **How was the store the same?**
4. **How many floors does this store have?**
5. **Would you like to work in a store like this? Why? Why not?**
6. **Where would you like to work in this store?**

Continue until all children have participated.

2 Focus: matching and comparing toy cards with toys in the poster "Department Store," and naming the toys

Put the 30 toy cards into the bag.

Wear the bag and say:

Today P. Mooney's bag contains pictures of toys. Let's see if this department store sells the same kinds of toys. Look carefully, because some toys may not be exactly the same. Pick a card from the bag, (Tamika), and tell us what it is in a sentence. Then find the same toy on the poster.

After naming the toy card in a sentence, each child should find a similar toy on the poster and identify it in another sentence such as "Here is another balloon."

VARIATION: To make the activity *harder*, have the children talk about how the toys on the card and the poster are alike and how they are different.

52

MATERIALS*

ACTIVITY I

None

ACTIVITY 2

Cards

Music

329

Audiocassette 2

Side A, Song 6,

"The Not Song"

1 Focus: evaluating and correcting statements about movements of body parts

Say:

I am going to say something silly. Listen carefully and tell me what is wrong with this sentence: We see with our nose. (Pause) **You are right. We don't see with our nose — we see with our eyes. What do we do with our nose?** (Encourage individual responses) **Yes! We (smell, blow) with our nose.**

Help the children respond as above to statements like these:

1. **We wave with our feet.**
2. **We scratch with our head.**
3. **We smile with our ears.**
4. **We tiptoe with our hands.**
5. **We think with our teeth.**
6. **We wave with our nose.**
7. **We chew with our eyes.**
8. **We whistle with our arms.**

2 Focus: singing and acting out "The Not Song" to name body parts

Stand beside the audiocassette player, with the children standing before you. Hold the music card and ask:

Do you remember the song about parts of our bodies? (Pause) **Let's sing it again and act out the words together.**

Play the song several times and lead the children in singing and doing the actions indicated on the card. Continue by playing the song (instrumental version) and singing more verses like these:

This is my hand, etc. (Point to hand)
This is not my hand, etc. (Point to leg)
This is my arm, etc. (Point to arm)
This is not my arm, etc. (Point to head)
This is my leg, etc. (Point to leg)
This is not my leg, etc. (Point to eye)
This is my elbow, etc. (Point to elbow)
This is not my elbow, etc. (Point to knee)
This is my thumb, etc. (Point to thumb)
This is not my thumb, etc. (Point to elbow)
This is my ankle, etc. (Point to ankle)
This is not my ankle, etc. (Point to neck)

53

MATERIALS*

ACTIVITY 1

Cards
Foods
115-136

Teacher provides
Large brown paper bag

ACTIVITY 2

Cards
Foods
(same as for Activity 1)

Display Board
2 ledges

1 Focus: naming and describing foods

Put the 22 food cards into the paper bag and put it on the floor in front of you.

Point to the bag and say:

Our shopping bag is full of food cards. Let's pretend that it contains real foods again. I wonder what kinds of foods we will find today. Let's each choose a card to name and describe.

Pass the bag to each of the children. If a child has difficulty, ask:

What food do you have, (Howard)? (Pause) **Yes, your food is (milk). Tell us something about it.**

The child should respond in a sentence such as "Cows give us milk." Continue until everyone has had a turn. Help when necessary by asking questions about the color, taste, smell, texture, or temperature of the foods.

2 Focus: naming *foods* from memory

Place the 22 food cards on your lap and say:

We are going to use our food cards to play a shopping game. Let's pretend that we went shopping and bought these foods.

Place food cards 115,116, and 117 on the board. Point to each card for the children to name as you all say, "We went shopping and we bought jam, jello, and orange juice." Continue:

Now I will turn over the cards so that you cannot see the pictures. (Do so) **What did we buy when we went shopping?**

Have individuals answer with the above sentence model. Using new cards each time, repeat the procedure as time and interest suggest.

VARIATIONS: To make the activity *easier*, use only one or two cards at a time. To make it *harder*, use more than three cards.

54

MATERIALS*

ACTIVITY 1

Cards

Foods

103 109 110 113
118 129 130 131
132 133 134 137

Display Board

6 ledges

Teacher provides

3 chairs

1 table

ACTIVITY 2

Fruits & Vegetables

Potato

1 Focus: pretending to be in a restaurant, and naming *foods*

Display the 12 food cards on the board. Group three chairs around a table near the board.

Say:

Let's pretend that we are choosing foods in a restaurant. These cards are the menu. (Point) **A menu tells us what foods the restaurant serves. A restaurant has cooks to prepare the food, waiters to serve it, and customers to eat it. You may be the cook, (Kimberly). Come and stand by the food.** (Pause) **You may be the waiter, (Martin). Stand over here by the table.** (Pause) **You may be the customers, (Shirley, Brendan, and Elena). Customers are people who come to eat at the restaurant. Customers, please sit here at the table.** (Pause) **Now, each customer may look at the menu and name three foods.**

Encourage the children to act their parts imaginatively as the "cook" hands the selected cards to the "waiter," who then gives them to the "customers." Have the cards put back on the board, and repeat the game with a new cast. Continue until every child has participated.

2 Focus: counting in a chanting game

Stand in a circle with the children. Hold up the plastic potato and ask:

What am I holding? (Encourage unison response) **You are right. This is a potato. Today we are going to learn a chant about potatoes. Please listen while I say it.**

Present this rhyme:

One potato, two potatoes,
Three potatoes, four;
Five potatoes, six potatoes,
Seven potatoes, more.

Repeat the rhyme several times, encouraging the children to join you as they learn the words. Then say:

Now let's play a game. We will pass the potato from person to person while we say the chant. Whoever is holding the potato when we say "more" should sit down. Let's begin.

Continue until all of the children but one are seated. Then have the group clap for the last child standing. Repeat as time permits.

55

MATERIALS*

ACTIVITY I

Cards

Stories

399-418

Audiocassette 1

Side B, Story 5,

"P. Mooney, Ophelia,

and the Where-Bear"

ACTIVITY 2

Cards

Stories

404-415*

P. Mooney Bag

Puppets

P. Mooney

Zoey

Action hat

Teacher provides

1 chair

1 Focus: listening to the story "P. Mooney, Ophelia, and the Where-Bear," and answering questions about it

Hold the 20 story cards on your lap and say:

Today we are going to hear a new story about a little girl named Ophelia. Ophelia has a problem that P. Mooney and the Where-Bear help her solve. Please listen carefully, so you will remember what happens.

Play the story. During the narration, show the story cards in turn as you scan the printed copy on the back of each picture. After showing each card, lay it facedown in a pile on your lap. When the story ends, lead the discussion with these questions:

1. **What was Ophelia's problem?**
2. **How did P. Mooney help Ophelia?**
3. **What is unusual about the Where-Bear?**
4. **Have you ever needed a Where-Bear to help you find your way home? When?**

2 Focus: following directions that stress *positional words*

Put the bag on a chair at the front of the room. Have P. Mooney and Zoey (wearing her action hat) available.

Two children should each hold a puppet and stand beside the chair. Ask the rest of the children to sit facing it. Hold the 12 story cards and say:

P. Mooney and Zoey are going to play a game with us today. We will use the words that the Where-Bear knows. First, I will show either P. Mooney or Zoey a story card. Then I will ask that puppet to move in the direction shown on the card.

Use the instructions given below. As each puppet is made to perform successfully, have the class applaud. Continue with other children until everyone has had a turn operating a puppet.

1. **Fly *up*, Zoey.** (Show 404)
2. **Fly *down*, P. Mooney.** (Show 405)
3. **Go *over* the chair, Zoey.** (Show 406)
4. **Go *under* the chair, P. Mooney.** (Show 407)
5. **Stand *beside* the chair, Zoey.** (Show 408)
6. **Go *between* the chair legs, P. Mooney.** (Show 409)
7. **Go *behind* the chair, Zoey.** (Show 410)
8. **Walk *in front of* the chair, P. Mooney.** (Show 411)
9. **Go *around* the chair, Zoey.** (Show 412)
10. **Go *through* the chair legs, P. Mooney.** (Show 413)
11. **Go *into* the bag, Zoey.** (Show 414)
12. **Sit *on* the chair, P. Mooney.** (Show 415)
13. **Hold *up* (Andre's) hand, Zoey.** (Show 404)
14. **Put your head *down,* P. Mooney.** (Show 405)
15. **Peek *over* the picture card, Zoey.** (Show 406)
16. **Put Zoey's action hat *under* the chair, P. Mooney.** (Show 407)
17. **Stand *beside* P. Mooney, Zoey.** (Show 408)
18. **Stand *between* (Stephanie) and (Clint), P. Mooney.** (Show 409)
19. **Hide *behind* someone, Zoey.** (Show 410)
20. **Dance *in front of* the children, P. Mooney.** (Show 411)
21. **Put your arms *around* P. Mooney, Zoey.** (Show 412)
22. **Go *through* the P. Mooney bag strap, Zoey.** (Show 413)
23. **Peek *into* a pocket, P. Mooney.** (Show 414)
24. **Hop *on* the floor, Zoey.** (Show 415)

56

MATERIALS*

ACTIVITY 1

Cards
Stories
399-418

ACTIVITY 2

Puppets
P. Mooney

1 Focus: retelling the story "P. Mooney, Ophelia, and the Where-Bear"

Say:

P. Mooney has a friend who knows exactly *where* to go. Which friend am I talking about? (Pause) **Yes, when Ophelia was lost, the Where-Bear helped her get where she wanted to be. Now let's look at the story cards again while we take turns telling what happened. Use sentences.**

Show the pictures in order and call on children to retell the story. If necessary, ask questions to help them remember important details. Stress the positional words. Then show story cards 404 through 415 again, this time in random order. As you show each card, ask questions like "Where is the Where-Bear in this picture? Is he (*in* the box or *under* the box)?" Encourage the children to use sentences as they describe the Where-Bear's positions.

2 Focus: following directions using *positional* words in the game P. Mooney Says

Stand with the children and put P. Mooney on your hand. He says:

Let's play P. Mooney Says. If you do not hear the words "P. Mooney says" before a command, then don't do anything!

The puppet should omit the phrase about half the time. Suggested instructions:

P. Mooney says . . . .

1. **Sit *down* on the floor.**
2. **Hold your hands *over* your head.**
3. **Stand *up*.**
4. **Hold your fingers *under* your chin.**
5. **Put your finger *in* your hair.**
6. **Put your hand *on* your head.**
7. **Stand *beside* another person.**
8. **Stand *between* me and the door.**
9. **Turn *around*.**
10. **Put your hands *behind* your back.**
11. **Run your fingers *through* your hair.**
12. **Put your little finger *in front* of your nose.**
13. **Bend *down* and touch the floor.**
14. **Reach *up* toward the sky.**
15. **Cross one leg *over* the other one.**
16. **Put one hand *under* the other one.**
17. **Walk *around* me in a circle.**
18. **Put your head *on* your folded arms.**
19. **Link your arms *through* each other.**
20. **Sit *in front* of me.**

VARIATION: To make the activity *easier,* demonstrate commands which were not understood, and then have the children repeat the action.

57

MATERIALS*

ACTIVITY 1

Cards

Household Items

177-199

Display Board

6 ledges

P. Mooney Bag

ACTIVITY 2

Cards

Household Items

179* 180* 184*
190* 192* 194*
197*

Music

330

Display Board

1 ledge

Audiocassette 2

Side A, Song 7,
"Hi Ho, Pal"

1 Focus: naming and describing household items

Set up the board and use five ledges to outline a simple house. Place one ledge in the center, like this:

Put the cards into the bag. Wear the bag and say:

Let's look at some new pictures of things often found in a house. When I call on you, take a card from the bag and put it on this ledge. (Point) **Then you are to name and describe the picture you picked.**

Help the child you call on as necessary and conclude the discussion by saying, "Now we have an (audiocassette player) for the house." Lay the card aside and continue with other children until all cards have been used.

2 Focus: singing the song "Hi Ho, Pal" while pantomiming the use of *household items*

Stand beside the audiocassette player and board, with the children standing before you. Hold the seven household cards and ask:

Let's pretend to use some of the things we could find in a house. (Display card 184 on the board) **How do we use soap, (Rhonda)?** (Pause) **Yes! We use it to wash our hands, like this.**

Demonstrate by pretending to rub soap lather on both hands. Have the class join you. Remove the card and repeat the procedure with the other cards. Then play the song (instrumental version). Refer to the music card as you sing with the children about "washing hands," and lead them in pantomiming the action. Continue with one of these actions per verse:

1. **stirring sauce — pretend to hold saucepan in one hand and stir with the other**
2. **cutting cloth — open and clench fist as you move hand forward**
3. **phoning friends — pretend to punch buttons and talk into the mouthpiece**
4. **blowing nose — pretend to pull tissue from box and blow your nose**
5. **fixing things — pretend to hammer a nail, use a screwdriver, measure with a tape, or pinch and twist with pliers**
6. **cleaning rugs — pretend to move vacuum cleaner back and forth over rugs**

58

MATERIALS*

ACTIVITY I

Color Chips
30 black
30 blue
30 yellow
Container

P. Mooney Bag

ACTIVITY 2

Color Chips
30 black
30 blue
30 yellow

1 Focus: naming the color of and counting color chips in bracelets, and then finding and naming objects of the same color

Make each child a bracelet with four color chips of the same color. Put the bracelets into the bag.

Wearing the bag, sit with the children in a circle and say:

Please come and choose a bracelet from the P. Mooney bag (Simon). What color is your bracelet? (Pause) **Yes, it is (blue). Now tell us how many chips your bracelet has.** (Pause) **Yes, it is made out of four chips.**

Have the child name four (blue) classroom objects. The child may then put on the bracelet. Continue with other children until everyone is wearing a bracelet.

2 Focus: singing in a game that stresses blue, black, and yellow

Have the children continue to wear their bracelets from Activity 1.

Ask the children to stand in a circle. Say:

Now let's play a game called Go In and Out the Windows. Everyone with blue bracelets, please line up inside the circle. Everyone else, join hands and raise them high to make windows. Blues, please move in and out the windows as I sing.

If necessary, demonstrate. Then sing or chant the verse given below to the tune or rhythm of "Go In and Out the Windows." Encourage the children to join you as soon as they are familiar with the words.

***Blues*, go in and out the windows;**
***Blues*, go in and out the windows;**
***Blues*, go in and out the windows**
As you have done before.

Repeat the verse until the children wearing blue bracelets have gone through all the windows once or more. Continue with the remaining colors.

59

MATERIALS*

ACTIVITY 1

Display Board

Magnetic Shapes
All
Container

ACTIVITY 2

Display Board

Magnetic Shapes
All
Container

1 Focus: listening to a story about shapes, and then building magnetic shape constructions

Set up the board and place the large black triangle and the large black circle near its center. Near the board's left edge, place the large black square and the large black rectangle. Have at hand the container with all the remaining shapes.

Ask:

Do you remember the story about the circle and the triangle? What did they like to do when they played together? (Encourage individual responses) **Yes, they pretended to be many things. I have a new story about shapes for you. Please watch and listen.**

Read this story as you move the shapes on the board:

One bright day, the circle and the triangle were out playing together. All of a sudden, they heard someone coming. "I have an idea," said the circle. "I will jump on top of you. Then whoever is coming will have to guess what we are pretending to be." So the circle jumped on top of the triangle, and they both were very still. (Demonstrate, like this:)

Along came two shapes who looked very much alike. (Move square and rectangle toward center of board) **They each had four straight sides and four corners. One of the shapes was a square; all of the square's sides were the same length.** (Point to square's sides) **The other shape was a rectangle. Two of the rectangle's sides were longer than its other two sides.** (Point to longer sides of rectangle, then to shorter sides) **Suddenly they saw a strange sight: the circle on top of the triangle.**

"Look!" said the square. "There is the sun sitting right on top of that mountain."

"Don't be silly," said the rectangle. "That is a baby wearing a bib."

The circle and triangle started to laugh so hard that the circle rolled right off the triangle. (Demonstrate) **The square and the rectangle were very surprised. What they had thought was the sun on a mountain or a baby wearing a bib was really just two other shapes.**

"What other things can you make yourselves look like?" asked the square and rectangle.

"Lots of things," said the triangle. The circle and triangle then made many things for the other two shapes to guess. (Let children suggest what these patterns represent:)

After that, the circle said, "I have an idea. Since we are all different, let's play together and pretend to be even more things." Everyone agreed. So the square and triangle made a house. (Have a child place the square and triangle like this:) **The rectangle and triangle pretended to be a rocket. ( ) The circle and square pretended to be a lamp. ( ) And, all together, the four shapes pretended to be a person.) Now let's think of more things our shapes could pretend to be.**

Depending on class size, give each child two, three, or four shapes. Help the children use the shapes to make things on the floor before they tell the group what the shapes represent. Praise all efforts.

2 Focus: identifying shapes by color or shape

Have two children place the shapes on the board.

Say:

Now let's play a look-and-find game. I will tell you what to look for. The person who finds the shape I am talking about will take it off the board and hold it up. Let's try. Find a (circle), (Mary Beth). (Pause) **Now tell us in a sentence what you found.** (Pause) **Yes, you found a (circle). Find a (green) shape, (Roy).** (Pause) **What did you find?** (Pause) **Yes, you found a (green) shape.**

Continue with other children. Each direction should mention only shape or color, not both. Help as necessary. Continue until all shapes have been used. Conclude by having the children return them to the container.

VARIATION: To make the activity *harder,* give directions that mention both color and shape, such as "Find a red triangle."

60

MATERIALS*

ACTIVITY 1

Cards

Household Items

156 157 160 161
165 173 176 179
184 185 188 190
195

Color Chips

1 blue

1 green

1 red

1 yellow

Display Board

6 ledges

ACTIVITY 2

Color Chips

4 blue, 4 green,
4 red, or 4 yellow
per child

1 Focus: naming and matching colors and household items

Display the 13 household cards on the board.

Hold the chips and say:

Let's play a look-and-find game. (Hold up blue chip) **What color is this?** (Pause) **Yes, it is blue. I see something blue on the board. We use it to make our hair look nice. What is it, (Abe)?** (Pause) **Yes, it is a brush.**

Continue with the statements given below. For each, pause to let the group name the color of the chip you hold up. Then have a child name the household item in a sentence.

1. **1 see something *red*. We use it to brush our teeth. What is it?** (toothbrush)
2. **I see something *blue*. We use it to wash clothes. What is it?** (laundry soap)
3. **I see something *yellow*. We wash our hands with it. What is it?** (hand soap)
4. **I see something *red*. I can talk on it to a friend. What is it?** (telephone)
5. **I see something *yellow*. We use it to scrub floors. What is it?** (scrub brush)
6. **I see something *green*. We use it with a mop. What is it?** (pail)
7. **I see something *blue*. We fix our hair with it. What is it?** (comb)
8. **I see something *yellow*. We cook our food on it. What is it?** (stove)
9. **I see something *red*. We use it when we cook. What is it?** (saucepan)
10. **I see something *green*. We use it when we sweep. What is it?** (dustpan)
11. **I see something *red*. We can hear a weather report or music on it. What is it?** (radio)

2 Focus: linking color chips to make bracelets, and then following directions involving colors

Have each child make a bracelet out of either four green, four red, or four yellow color chips. Then say:

Let's use your bracelets to play a game. First, let's be sure you each know what color your bracelet is. If it is blue, hold it up. (Pause) **If it is *green*, hold it up.** (Pause) **If your bracelet is *red*, show it to me.** (Pause) **If it is *yellow*, hold it up.** (Pause) **Very good. Put on your bracelet. When I name your color, please do what I say.**

Occasionally include everyone and vary the colors as you give commands like those below. Help as necessary and check to see that the right children respond each time.

1. **Blink your eyes, *reds*.**
2. **Scratch your heads, *greens*.**
3. **Clap your hands, *yellows*.**
4. **Stand up, *everyone*.**
5. **Rub your stomachs, *blues*.**
6. **Wiggle your fingers, *reds*.**
7. **Pat your knees, *blues*.**
8. **Shake your heads, *everyone*.**
9. **Blow kisses, *greens*.**
10. **Make funny faces, *yellows*.**
11. **Sit down, *blues*.**
12. **Turn around two times, *reds*.**
13. **Wave your arms, *everyone*.**
14. **Run in place, *yellows*.**
15. **Smack your lips, *greens*.**
16. **Make happy faces, *everyone*.**

Keep in Mind.
After each lesson in the program, individuals who have difficulty demonstrating proficiency in the skills you consider appropriate and important for them to learn should be tutored. Aides could help you with this task.

61

MATERIALS*

ACTIVITY 1

Display Board

Magnetic Shapes
Large green circle
Large red circle
Large yellow circle

ACTIVITY 2

Magnetic Shapes
Large green circle
Large red circle

1 Focus: talking about traffic lights

Place the three large circles on the board, like this:

(L) **Red**
(L) **Yellow**
(L) **Green**

Point to the shapes on display as you say:

Let's pretend that the shapes are a traffic light. Where do we see traffic lights, (Eleanor)? (Pause) **Yes, traffic lights are placed where busy streets cross each other.**

Continue the discussion with questions like these:

1. **What do traffic lights tell people?**
2. **How many colors do traffic lights have? Name the colors.**
3. **What does a red light mean? A yellow light? A green light?**
4. **What color should the light be when we walk across a street?**
5. **What could be used in place of traffic lights?** (traffic officer, stop signs)
6. **Why should everyone obey traffic lights?**

Accept all appropriate responses.

VARIATION: To make the activity *harder,* have the children also talk about what would happen if there were no traffic lights.

2 Focus: following directions during the color game Red Light, Green Light

Ask the children to stand shoulder-to-shoulder in a line at the end of the room or playground. Choose a child to be the first leader. That child is to stand facing the group, holding the red circle in one hand and the green circle in the other. Say:

We are going to play a game called Red Light, Green Light. (Felipe) will be our first leader. When (Felipe) holds up the "green light," take very small steps towards (him). Keep moving until (he) holds up the "red light." Then stop until you see the "green light" again.

When the players reach the leader, select a new one and have the rest of the group return to the starting point. Repeat the game, changing the kind of movements the children are to make. Continue as long as they enjoy the game. Suggested movements:

1. **sliding steps**
2. **walking on tiptoe**
3. **walking with knees together**
4. **walking heel-to-toe**
5. **hopping**

VARIATION: To make the activity *easier,* serve as leader yourself.

62

MATERIALS*

ACTIVITY I

Cards

Stories (optional)

386-398

Display Board (optional)

6 ledges (optional)

Audiocassette 1

Side A, Story 4, "The Elephant That Did Not Know How to Listen"

ACTIVITY 2

Cards

Animals

23 25 26 27 29
31 32 34 35 36

Display Board

6 ledges

Audiocassette 3

Side A, Selection 1, "Sounds of Animals"

1 Focus: listening to and talking about the story "The Elephant That Did Not Know How to Listen"

Hold the 13 story cards on your lap and ask:

Do you remember the story about the elephant that did not know how to listen? (Pause) **What is the elephant's name?** (Pause) **Yes, his name is Elbert. Let's listen to the story again. Then we will talk about what happens in it.**

Play the story without showing the cards. Then lead the discussion with questions like these:

1. **What happened as P. Mooney was driving his Rock Roller on the country road?**
2. **What was Elbert's problem?**
3. **Tell us what happened when P. Mooney and Elbert played their game.**
4. **How did P. Mooney help Elbert?**
5. **Why is it important to be a good listener?**
6. **How could you help yourself become a better listener?**

OPTIONAL: If necessary, place the cards on the board as memory cues.

2 Focus: listening to "Sounds of Animals," and then identifying and imitating each of them

In random order, display the 10 animal cards on the board.

Say:

Elbert learned to recognize animals by their sounds. Look at the pictures on the board as we listen to some animal sounds. Try to figure out which animal is making the sound you hear.

Play the sound effects, one sound at a time. After each sound, ask a child to come and point to the correct picture as the group names the animal in a sentence like "We heard a (lion)." The children may then imitate the sound. When all ten sounds have been identified, remove the cards. Play the sounds again in random order and ask the group to name each animal in a sentence.

VARIATION: To make the activity *harder,* play two sounds each time and have the group identify the sounds in the right order.

63

MATERIALS*

ACTIVITY I

Display Board

Manikin, Disassembled

Body parts

Facial features

Long hair

Manikin, Movable

ACTIVITY 2

Display Board

Manikin, Movable

1 Focus: comparing the disassembled and movable manikins

Ask two children who need the experience to assemble the disassembled manikin on the left side of the board. Hold the movable manikin on your lap and say:

(Charlotte) and (Quincy) did a good job of putting the manikin together. The manikin on the board is like a cardboard doll cut into pieces to make a puzzle. Today I have a new kind of manikin to show you.

Let the children take turns manipulating the movable manikin as they pass it around. Then have a child put it on the right side of the board. Point to the two figures and say:

Look! The two manikins are different from each other. Let's think of ways in which they are not the same. Name one difference, (Samantha).

Help as necessary, encouraging the children to name differences like these:

1. **one comes apart, the other does not**
2. **one can be moved into different positions, the other cannot**
3. **one faces forward, the other faces sideways**

Then ask the children how the manikins are the same. Encourage them to name similarities like these:

1. **both look like people**
2. **both have body parts**
3. **they are about the same size**

2 Focus: imitating and describing manikin positions

Display the movable manikin on the board.

Stand beside the board, with the children standing before you. Say:

Please watch as I change the position of this manikin. Then we will do what it is doing and describe what we did.

Place the manikin in positions like those listed below. Each time, lead the children in imitating the manikin's pose and have them describe it in a sentence like "We are (bending) our (knees)." Suggested actions:

1. **bending knees**
2. **nodding head**
3. **lifting arms over head**
4. **touching chin to chest**
5. **standing on tiptoes**
6. **holding arms straight out**
7. **touching toes**
8. **looking at ceiling**
9. **waving hands**
10. **curling up in a ball**

64

MATERIALS*

ACTIVITY 1

Cards
People
200-221

ACTIVITY 2

Cards
Music
331

Audiocassette 2
Side B, Song 8,
"Today, Yesterday, and Tomorrow"

1 Focus: brainstorming what legs and arms can do, and then describing actions shown on people cards

Hold the 22 people cards on your lap and say:

Let's think about how we can use our arms and legs. Name something you can do with your arms, (Cliff). (Pause) Yes, you can (hug someone) with your arms. What else can you do with your arms, (Josie)?

Continue with other children. As necessary, give clues. Accept such answers as reaching, holding, swinging, hugging, pushing, bending, and balancing. Then say:

Name something you can do with your legs.

Continue as before. Accept answers like bending, walking, jumping, and kicking. Point out that many actions require feet and legs or hands and arms. Brainstorm these actions with the children before saying:

Now let's look at some pictures of people who are using their arms and legs. Here is the first one. (Show card 200) **What is this person called?** (Encourage unison response) **Yes, this person is called an acrobat. Now let's talk about what he is doing.**

Call on children to describe the actions in sentences such as "The acrobat is swinging by his legs." Continue in this way with the remaining people cards, stressing action words such as *holding, pumping, driving, reaching, writing, bouncing,* and *pushing.*

2 Focus: listening to, singing, chanting, and acting out the song "Today, Yesterday, and Tomorrow"

Hold the music card and say:

Let's learn a new song. The song tells what we *do* today, what we *did* yesterday, and what we *will* do tomorrow.

Play the first verse. Then ask:

What did the song say that we do today? (Pause) **Yes! Today we *walk*. What did the song say we did yesterday?** (Pause) **You are right; yesterday we *walked.* What does the song say we will do tomorrow?** (Pause) **Very good! Tomorrow we *will walk*. Let's listen again and sing the words. When the voice part ends, we will walk in place.**

Ask the children to stand. Play the first verse again and encourage the children to walk in place during the instrumental section. Refer to the music card as you continue in this way with the second and third verses.

65

MATERIALS*

ACTIVITY 1

Display Board

4 ledges

Magnetic Shapes

All

ACTIVITY 2

Magnetic Shapes

Large black circle

Large black rectangle

Large black square

Large black triangle

Teacher provides

1 chair

Identical socks

1 Focus: comparing shapes in a group, and then identifying the one that does not belong

Set up the board and use the ledges to make a large square in the center like this:

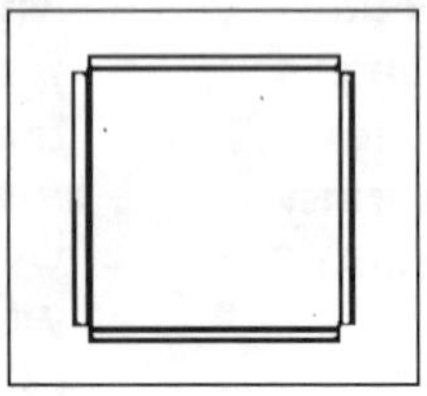

Ask several children to put the shapes around the square. Say:

Please put three small circles and one small triangle inside the square, (David).

Point to the four shapes and ask another child:

Which of these four shapes does not belong with the others? (Pause) **Yes, the triangle is different in shape from the three circles.**

Remove the shapes and continue with other combinations such as those listed below. The children should explain their choices in sentences like "This shape does not belong because it is a square and the other shapes are circles" or "This is a triangle and the other shapes are squares."

1. **three circles, one square**
2. **three squares, one triangle**
3. **three rectangles, one circle**
4. **three triangles, one rectangle**
5. **three squares, one circle**
6. **three rectangles, one triangle**

2 Focus: identifying by touch shapes hidden in socks

Place a chair next to yours.

Hold the shapes and socks as you say:

Let's find out if you can name shapes by feeling them. First, let's look at these shapes and name them together.

Afterwards, let four children each put a shape into one of the socks. Place the socks on the chair and invite still another child to select one and feel the shape inside. Then the child is to name the shape in a sentence such as "There is a (square) in the sock" before pulling it out for everyone to see. If the shape is identified correctly, have the group name it together. The child then puts the shape back into its sock and scrambles the four socks. Continue with other children until everyone has had a turn.

66

MATERIALS*

ACTIVITY 1

None

ACTIVITY 2

Cards

Music

331

Audiocassette 2

Side B, Song 8,

"Today, Yesterday, and Tomorrow"

1 Focus: identifying actions of people by their sounds

Say:

We can make sounds with our body parts. Let's play a listening game. After you close your eyes, I will make a sound. Then I will ask you to tell me what sound I made and what body parts I used.

After each action, have a child name it in a sentence such as "You (clapped) with your (hands)." Then lead the group in doing it together. Suggested actions:

1. jumping
2. scratching
3. coughing
4. running
5. humming
6. laughing
7. stamping
8. sniffing
9. marching
10. whistling
11. sneezing
12. snapping fingers
13. clicking tongue
14. teeth chattering
15. panting

2 Focus: singing, chanting, and acting out the song "Today, Yesterday, and Tomorrow"

Holding the music card, stand in a circle with the children and say:

Let's move as we sing "Today, Yesterday, and Tomorrow." When the song mentions walking, we will walk around the circle in this direction. (Point) **When the song mentions clapping, stand still and clap in rhythm with the music. When the song mentions sneezing, pretend to sneeze loudly!**

Play the song and encourage the children to sing and act out the words. Repeat the three verses until the children are able to sing along. Then play the song (instrumental version) and lead the children in singing and acting out verses about these verbs: *march, cough, sniff,* and *jump.*

67

MATERIALS*

ACTIVITY 1

Cards

Stories

399-418

ACTIVITY 2

Teacher provides

1 book

2 chairs

1 table

1 Focus: retelling the story "P. Mooney, Ophelia, and the Where-Bear," and answering questions about the Where-Bear's positions

Hold the 20 story cards and say:

Let's see how much you remember about the story of Ophelia and the Where-Bear. I will show you the pictures from the story. Please tell me what is happening in each picture.

Show the pictures in order as the children use sentences to retell the story. If necessary, ask questions to help the children remember important details. During the discussion, stress the positional words. Then show cards 404 through 408 in any order. As you show each card, ask questions such as "Where is the Where-Bear in this picture? Is he (*in* the box) or (*under* the box)?" The children should describe the Where-Bear's position in sentences.

2 Focus: singing an action song about *positional* words

Place two chairs three feet apart in an activity area. Place a book on the floor in another area. In a third area, place a table large enough for a child to crawl under it.

Stand with the children and say:

Let's learn a song using words from the Where-Bear's story. As we sing, we will go where the song tells us. Let's pretend to go through a cave first.

Have half the class line up in two rows facing each other. These rows then form a "cave" by raising their arms and touching the fingers of the children facing them. Ask the other half of the class to line up and march through the "cave" as everyone sings or chants this verse to the tune or rhythm of "The Farmer in the Dell":

Oh, *through* the cave we march.
Oh, *through* the cave we march.
Hi-ho, the derry-o,
Oh, *through* the cave we march.

Reverse the groups and repeat the activity. Then have all the children line up. Lead them in singing and acting out the words of each of these verses:

***Around* the table we hop, etc.**
***Between* two chairs we march, etc.**
***Under* the table we crawl, etc.**
***Over* the book we jump, etc.**

68

MATERIALS*

ACTIVITY 1

Cards

Household Items

153 154 162 188

155-199,1 per child

ACTIVITY 2

Cards

Household Items

155-199, 1 per child

1 Focus: classifying household objects by location

Give each child a household card. With the children standing before you, hold cards 153, 154, 162, and 188 as you say:

Let's pretend that our classroom is a house with four rooms. Our house has a kitchen (show 188)**, a bathroom** (show 153)**, a bedroom** (show 154)**, and a living room** (show 162)**. Look at your cards.** (Pause) **If the item on your card belongs in a kitchen, come and stand here.** (Point)

When the group has assembled, discuss with the class whether each of those items belongs in a kitchen. If a wrong choice has been made, have the class suggest another room for that item. Then have the class complete this sentence as the cards are raised in turn: "In the kitchen, we have a(n) (iron), a (refrigerator), a (saucepan), and a (knife)." Repeat this procedure for the other three rooms.

2 Focus: following directions using positional words

Have the children keep their cards from Activity 1 and remain standing in their four groups.

Say:

Now that you are each in one of the four rooms of our house, let's play a game. I will give some directions. Please listen carefully to see if I am talking about the room in which your object belongs. If I am, do what I say.

After each command, be sure that the right children respond. Each time, ask one child who moved to name the action in a sentence such as "I jumped up and down." Suggested instructions:

1. **If you belong in the (kitchen), jump *up* and *down*.**
2. **If you belong in the (bathroom), turn *around*.**
3. **If you belong in the (living room), put your hand *between* your knees.**
4. **If you belong in the (bedroom), run your fingers *through* your hair.**
5. **If you belong in the (kitchen), put your hand *under* your chin.**
6. **If you belong in the (bathroom), put your hand *over* your eyes.**
7. **If you belong in the (living room), put your elbows *on* your knees.**
8. **If you belong in the (bedroom), put your arms *beside* your body.**

VARIATION: To make the activity *harder,* combine two commands, like this: "If you belong in the bedroom, put your hand *under* your chin, and jump *up* and *down*."

69

MATERIALS*

ACTIVITY 1

Cards

Toys

226 233 234 243
246 249 251 253
260 262 263 265

Display Board

6 ledges

ACTIVITY 2

Cards

Music

328

Audiocassette 2

Side A, Song 5,
"If and Then Go
Together"

1 Focus: classifying and talking about toys with wheels

Display the 12 toy cards on the board.

Point to the board and ask:

Do all the toys on these cards have wheels? (Pause) **No, not all of them have wheels. Please name in a sentence one toy with wheels, (Sally).** (Pause) **Yes! The (tricycle) has wheels. Name another toy with wheels, (Nhieu).**

Continue until all toys with wheels have been named. The children should respond in sentences. Then remove all cards of toys without wheels. Lead a discussion of wheels — their shape, function, and number on each toy — with questions like these:

1. **What makes these toys able to move?**
2. **How do wheels move?**
3. **What shape are wheels?**
4. **How many wheels does (each toy) have? Let's count them.**
5. **What other things have wheels?**

2 Focus: singing and acting out the song "If and Then Go Together" about wheels

Ask the children to stand in a circle. Hold the music card and say:

Let's learn a song about wheels. I will sing it for you while we do the actions. Please sing along when you can.

Play the song (instrumental version) and lead the children in performing the actions as you sing these verses:

1. **If you are a wheel, then you are round.** (Draw circle in air) **If you are a wheel, then you are round.** (Draw circle in air)

   If you are a wheel, then you are round. (Draw circle in air) **If and then go together.**

2. **If you are a wheel, then you can roll.** (Move hands in circular motion before chest)

   If you are a wheel, then you can roll. (Move hands in circular motion before chest)

   If you are a wheel, then you can roll. (Move hands in circular motion before chest)

   If and then go together.

Repeat several times or until the children know the words.

VARIATION: To make the activity *easier,* do not ask the children to do the actions as they sing.

70

MATERIALS*

ACTIVITY 1

Display Board

Magnetic Shapes

All

Container

ACTIVITY 2

Cards

Music

338

Audiocassette 2

Side B, Song 15,

"Contrasts"

1 Focus: identifying magnetic shapes by shape and color

Ask two children to place all 60 shapes onto the board.

Point to the shapes and say:

We are going to play a looking game with these shapes. I will tell you what to find. The person who finds the shape I am talking about will take it off the board and hold it up. Find a (yellow circle), (Janella).

Have the child tell the group, "I found a (yellow circle)." Continue with other children. Each direction should mention color and shape only. Continue until everyone has had at least one turn. Conclude by having the children return all the shapes to the container.

VARIATION: To make the activity *harder,* have the children ask each other for specific shapes.

2 Focus: talking about, listening to, and moving to the music "Contrasts"

Say:

When two things are very different, we say they contrast with each other. Please isten and try to figure out why this new piece of music is named "Contrasts."

Play the song. Then ask:

Did you hear how the music changed? (Pause) **How did it change?** (Encourage individual responses) **Yes, this music is fast at first and then slow. Let's listen again and move as the circle and the triangle did in the story. When the music begins, jump and bounce the way a circle or a ball would. But when the music changes, slide the way a triangle would, as if you were skating.**

Ask the children to stand. Play the music and encourage the group to jump or slide at the correct times. Demonstrate if necessary. If time and interest permit, repeat the song a third time.

71

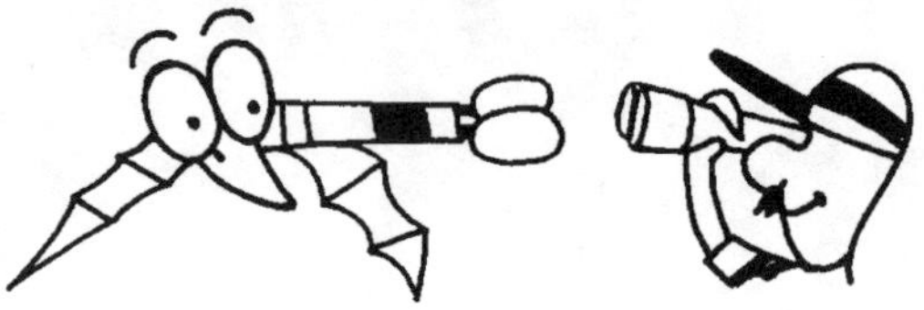

MATERIALS*

ACTIVITY 1

Cards

Toys

228 229 231 239
245 248 250 252
256 258 261 264

Display Board

6 ledges

Puppets

Zoey

Thinking hat

ACTIVITY 2

Puppets

P. Mooney

1 Focus: identifying toys from descriptions

Display the 12 toy cards on the board.

Put Zoey (wearing her thinking hat) on your hand. Have her point to the board as she says:

Today I will ask you some riddles about these toys. Please listen and guess which toy I am describing.

Have the children respond in unison to riddles like those given below. The puppet should expand brief answers by saying, "Good thinking! It is a (ball)."

1. **This toy is round, and you can bounce it.** (ball)
2. **This toy has pages with pictures on them.** (book)
3. **This toy is an animal on which you can ride.** (rocking horse)
4. **This toy has pieces that go together to make a picture.** (puzzle)
5. **This toy spins and hums.** (top)
6. **You can ride down a snowy hill on this toy.** (sled)
7. **You have to climb a tree to get into this toy.** (tree house)
8. **This toy is made out of metal, and it looks somewhat like a person.** (robot)
9. **This toy is fun to hug and take to bed with you.** (teddy bear)
10. **This toy is filled with something found at the beach.** (sandbox)
11. **You have to blow up this toy.** (balloon)
12. **You can move through this toy on your hands and knees.** (tunnel)

VARIATION: To make the activity *harder,* do not show the correct toy card until the riddle is solved.

2 Focus: following directions that stress *counting* while playing the game P. Mooney, May We?

Ask the children to stand shoulder-to-shoulder in a single line. Put P. Mooney on your hand and have him say:

Let's play a game called P. Mooney, May We? When I tell all of you to do something, ask, "P. Mooney, may we?" together. You may move after I say, "Yes, you may." Let's begin. (Pause) **Hop forward two times!**

Have them count each hop aloud together. Continue with instructions like those given below, making sure the children move and count correctly. As necessary, demonstrate.

1. **Take two giant steps.**
2. **Clap your hands four times.**
3. **Take four small steps.**
4. **Turn around two times.**
5. **Pat your stomach three times.**
6. **Take one giant step backwards.**
7. **Stamp your feet two times.**
8. **Nod your head one time.**
9. **Jump forward three times.**
10. **Touch your toes four times.**
11. **Step sideways one time.**
12. **Take three small steps backwards.**
13. **Take five small steps forward.**
14. **Clap your hands behind your back two times.**
15. **Slide your feet four times.**
16. **Sit down two times.**

VARIATIONS: To make the activity *harder,* have a child ask after each instruction, "P. Mooney, may we (take two giant steps)?" Or increase difficulty by combining two instructions, like this: "Take two giant steps, and clap your hands four times." Have the children count each action aloud.

72

MATERIALS*

ACTIVITY 1

Color Chips
Half (120)

ACTIVITY 2

Cards
Music
337

Color Chips
Half (120)

Audiocassette 2
Side B, Song 14,
"Rag March"

1 Focus: linking color chips in chains while stressing *long* and *longer*

Pile the chips on the floor, and have the children sit around them in a circle. Say:

I will give each of you a handful of color chips to link together in a chain. Then we will connect the chains to make a circle.

Give out unequal numbers of chips, so that the chains will vary in length. While the children are linking their chips, comment on the fact that a *long* chain grows *longer* as chips are added. When all the chips have been used, help the children link the individual chains to make one large circle on the floor.

2 Focus: walking to the music "Rag March" in a stop-go listening game

Leave the color chip circle from Activity 1 on the floor.

Have the children stand around the color chip circle. Stand beside the audiocassette player as you say:

Now let's play a listening game. While the music plays, walk around the circle in this direction. (Point) **When the music stops, pretend to freeze by standing very still. When the music begins again, walk around the circle in the opposite direction.** (Point)

Play "Rag March" as the children walk, occasionally stopping the music to give them a chance to "freeze." Continue as time and interest suggest.

73

MATERIALS*

ACTIVITY 1

Cards

Animals

1-38, 1 per child

ACTIVITY 2

Cards

Animals

(same as for Activity 1)

1 Focus: classifying and naming animals and their characteristics

Ask the children to sit before you. Give each child an animal card. Have the children name their animals before you say:

Let's play an animal game together. I will ask a question about animals. If your animal is an answer to my question, please stand up and show us your card. Then I will ask each. of you to point to the body part I mentioned and to say a sentence about your animal.

Ask questions like those given below, checking to see that the right children respond. Each child should point to the feature you mentioned and name the animal by saying, "Here are the (ears) on the (bear)."

Which animals . . .

1. **have claws?**
2. **have wings?**
3. **have feathers?**
4. **have fur?**
5. **have ears?**
6. **have whiskers?**
7. **have beaks?**
8. **have two legs?**
9. **have four legs?**
10. **have more than four legs?**
11. **look soft to touch?**
12. **can hop?**
13. **can swim?**
14. **make sounds?**

2 Focus: naming *animals* from memory

Have the children continue to hold their animal cards from Activity 1.

Ask three children to stand facing the group. Have the three hold up their cards as you say:

Let's name these animals as I point to each one. (Do this) **Now as I point to the cards, whisper the names of the animals to yourself. It will help you remember them if an animal runs away.** (Pause) **Now please cover your eyes with your hands.**

When the children's eyes are covered, turn over the card of one standing child. Then have the class uncover their eyes and tell you which animal is missing. Continue with other groups of three.

VARIATIONS: To make the activity *harder,* change the order of the three children each time. To make it even more difficult, use four or five children and turn over two cards. To make the activity *easier,* have only two children face the group.

74

MATERIALS*

ACTIVITY I

Audiocassette 3
Side A, Selection 1,
"Sounds of Animals"

ACTIVITY 1

P. Mooney Stick

1 Focus: listening to "Sounds of Animals," and then identifying and talking about each of them

Say:

Let's pretend that we have gone camping. It is late at night, and we are lying in our sleeping bags. Lie down, everyone. (Pause) **Soon we will go to sleep. Before we do, let's be very quiet and listen for sounds of animals.**

Play the first sound effect. Then whisper:

What was that? (Encourage unison response) **Yes, it was a bear. Did you hear the growl?** (Pause) **Now lie back. Let's listen for another sound.**

Continue with the remaining sound effects. Then discuss with the children whether those animals might be heard on a real camping trip.

2 Focus: pantomiming the actions of animals

Hold the P. Mooney stick and say:

Now let's use Mooney magic to change us into animals. Here we go!

Wave the stick over the group as you chant each rhyme. Allow the children to pantomime each animal in turn.

1. **Eenie-meenie-Mooney-mat, Turn each one into a *cat*.**
2. **Eenie-meenie-Mooney-mare, Turn each one into a *bear*.**
3. **Eenie-meenie-Money-mird, Turn each one into a *bird*.**
4. **Eenie-meenie-Mooney-mog, Turn each one into a *dog*.**
5. **Eenie-meenie-Mooney-muck, Turn each one into a *duck*.**
6. **Eenie-meenie-Mooney-my, Turn each one into a *butterfly*.**
7. **Eenie-meenie-Mooney-mick, Turn each one into a *chick*.**
8. **Eenie-meenie-Mooney-morse, Turn each one into a *horse*.**

End by waving the P. Mooney stick as you say:

Eenie-meenie-Mooney-me,

Now let's be you and me.

75

MATERIALS*

ACTIVITY 1

Cards

Household Items

155 157 158 161
166 167 168 169
170 171 175 179
180 181 183 185
191 196 197 199

Display Board

Puppets

6 ledges

ACTIVITY 2

Puppets

P. Mooney

1 Focus: identifying household items from questions about their use

Place on the board these 10 household cards: 155, 157, 158, 161, 166, 167, 168, 169, 170, and 171. Stack the remaining cards.

Begin by having the class name the items on display as you point to each card in turn. Then ask:

Where could all these things be found? (Pause) **Yes, they might be found in a house. Now let's play a thinking game. I will say part of a sentence. Then I will ask one of you to tell us which item on the board finishes the sentence.**

After each sentence is finished, have the group repeat the entire sentence with you. Continue until everyone has had a turn, even if some items must be repeated.

1. **We sit in a _______ .** (chair)
2. **When it gets dark, we turn on a _______ .** (lamp)
3. **We eat peas and carrots with a _______ .** (fork)
4. **We iron clothes with an _______ .** (iron)
5. **We drink milk from a _______ .** (glass)
6. **We iron clothes on an _______ .** (ironing board)
7. **We cut meat with a _______ .** (knife)
8. **We sweep the kitchen floor with a _______ .** (broom)
9. **When our hair is tangled, we fix it with a _______** (comb)
10. **We scrub the bathroom floor with a _______ .** (scrub brush)

Replace the cards on the board with the stacked cards and continue:

11. **We wash dishes in a _______ .** (sink)
12. **We watch programs on the _______ .** (television)
13. **We clean the rugs with a _______ .** (vacuum cleaner)
14. **We sew with a _______ .** (sewing machine)
15. **We cook spaghetti sauce in a _______ .** (saucepan)
16. **We throw papers into the _______ .** (wastebasket)
17. **We brush our teeth with _______ .** (toothpaste)
18. **We eat dinner from a _______ .** (plate)
19. **We cut paper with _______ .** (scissors)
20. **We wash the laundry with _______ .** (laundry soap)

VARIATION: To make the activity *harder,* do not use cards as cues, and accept all logical answers.

2 Focus: following directions to pantomime the use of household objects in the game *P. Mooney Says*

Ask the children to stand before you. Put P. Mooney on your hand and have him say:

Let's play P. Mooney Says and pretend to use some of the things found in a house. When I say "P. Mooney says," pretend to use the object I name. But listen carefully. If you do not hear "P. Mooney says, "then don't do anything!

Have the puppet give the directions below, omitting "P. Mooney says" about half the time. Demonstrate the actions as necessary.

P. Mooney says .

1. **Pretend to iron clothes.**
2. **Pretend to mop the floor.**
3. **Pretend to eat soup with a spoon.**
4. **Pretend to comb your hair.**
5. **Pretend to cut paper with scissors.**
6. **Pretend to sit on a chair.**
7. **Pretend to drink milk from a glass.**
8. **Pretend to wash dishes in a sink.**
9. **Pretend to sweep the floor.**
10. **Pretend to brush your teeth.**
11. **Pretend to scrub the floor with a brush.**
12. **Pretend to comb your hair.**
13. **Pretend to eat with a fork.**
14. **Pretend to turn on a lamp.**
15. **Pretend to wash a plate.**
16. **Pretend to stir the soup in the saucepan.**
17. **Pretend to thread the needle on the sewing machine.**
18. **Pretend to use the laundry soap on your socks.**
19. **Pretend to be watching television.**
20. **Pretend to vacuum your room.**

76

MATERIALS*

ACTIVITY 1

Cards

Clothing

39 42 46 48 49 50
52 56 58 59 60 67
62 63 64 65 71 72

Display Board

2 ledges

ACTIVITY 2

Cards

Pictures from Several Categories

43 49* 59* 60* 97
103 106 118 228
230 236 251

Music

332

Display Board

6 ledges

Audiocassette 2

Side B, Song 9, "Things That Go Together"

1 Focus: sequencing and talking about putting on clothing while stressing *first, next,* and *last*

Stack the 18 clothing cards in this order: 48, 49, 67, 59, 50, 64, 63, 46, 56, 39, 62, 71, 52, 58, 72, 65, 60, and 42.

Hold the stacked cards and say:

Let's think about how we dressed this morning. What piece of clothing did you put on *first*, (Shanda)? (Pause) **What did you put on *next*?** (Pause) **What did you put on *last*?**

Ask several other children the same questions. Then say:

Now let's talk about other clothes. I will show you some pictures.

Display cards 48, 49, and 67. Then ask:

Which of these would you put on first? (Pause) **Which would you put on next?** (Pause) **Which would you put on last?** (Pause) **What would happen if you put on the jacket first, the jeans next, and the sweater last?**

After the discussion, have a child place the three cards on the board in left-to-right order as seen by the class. Continue with these groups of clothes:

1. 59, 50, and 64

2. 63, 46, and 56

3. 39, 62, and 71

4. 52, 58, and 72

5. 65, 60, and 42

2 Focus: classifying and naming *clothing, toys,* and *foods,* and then singing the song "Things That Go Together"

On the top ledge, in this order, place clothing cards 59, 49, 60, and 43. On the middle ledge, place toy cards 228, 236, 230, and 251. On the bottom ledge, place food cards 97, 118, 103, and 106.

Stand beside the audiocassette player, with the children standing before you. Say:

Today we are going to learn a new song called "Things That Go Together." Look at the cards on the top ledge. (Pause) **What is one word that we use to talk about all these things?** (Encourage unison response) **Yes! These are clothes. Let's name them together.**

Point to each card in turn as the group names the clothes. Repeat this procedure with the cards on the middle and bottom ledges. Then continue:

Now let's sing "Things That Go Together." When I point to the clothes, name them with the song.

Play the song and refer to the music card, pointing to each clothing card. Continue with the toy and food cards. Repeat the song until the children are familiar with the words.

77

MATERIALS*

ACTIVITY 1

Cards
Stories
419-432

Audiocassette 1
Side B, Story 6,
"P. Mooney and the Kiwi"

ACTIVITY 2

None

1 Focus: listening to the story "P. Mooney and the Kiwi"

Hold the 14 story cards and say:

Today we are going to listen to a new story called "P. Mooney and the *Kiwi*." Let's say the word kiwi together. (Encourage unison response) **Kiwis are birds that live in a country called New Zealand. They are different from most birds because they cannot fly, even though they have wings. Let's listen to the story about this special bird, the Kiwi.**

Play the story. During the narration, show the story cards in turn as you scan the printed copy on the back of each picture. After showing each card, place it facedown in a pile on your lap.

2 Focus: talking about the story "P. Mooney and the Kiwi" while stressing that everyone is special

Say:

The Kiwi learned something very important from P. Mooney. Let's talk about what the Kiwi learned.

Lead the discussion with questions like these:

1. **What was the Kiwi's problem?**
2. **How did P. Mooney help the Kiwi?**
3. **How did the "Me" button make the Kiwi feel?**
4. **What did the Kiwi learn?** (everyone is important)
5. **Do you ever wish that you were someone else? Why?**

End the discussion by saying:

The Kiwi is special because there is no one else like him. Each of you is special, too, because there is no one else in the whole world just like you. You look and act different from everyone else. You cannot do everything, but each of you can do many things well.

Have the children take turns telling what they think they can do well. Help as necessary and pay extra attention to those children whose self-confidence needs building.

78

MATERIALS*

ACTIVITY 1

Cards

Stories

423-428

Display Board

4 ledges

ACTIVITY 2

Cards

Music

328

Stories

(same as for Activity 1)

Audiocassette 2

Side A, Song 5,

"If and Then Go Together"

1 Focus: remembering the story "P. Mooney and the Kiwi," and then thinking about the Kiwi's comparisons

Display the six story cards on the board, picture sides hidden.

Say:

Before P. Mooney pinned the shiny "Me" button onto the Kiwi's chest, the Kiwi said some things about himself that were not true. What were some of the things he said?

Call on volunteers to respond in sentences such as "The Kiwi said he was (bigger than an elephant)." If necessary, give clues until the children recall all the Kiwi's remarks about these animals: elephant, mouse, kangaroo, leopard, giraffe, and bird. Then continue:

Now let's pretend that I am the Kiwi and each one of you is P. Mooney. I will say what the Kiwi said in the story. Then you may correct me.

Turn over the corresponding story card as you say each statement listed below. The children should respond together in sentences such as "No! You are *not* (bigger than an elephant)" or "No! You *cannot* (jump higher than a kangaroo)."

1. 423•**I am bigger than an elephant.**
2. 424•**I am smaller than a mouse.**
3. 425•**I can jump higher than a kangaroo.**
4. 426•**I can run faster than a leopard.**
5. 427•**I am taller than a giraffe.**
6. 428•**I can sing better than a bird.**

Repeat the six statements, allowing volunteers to respond as before.

VARIATION: To make the activity *harder,* have the children correct your statements, like this: "You are (smaller than an elephant)."

2 Focus: singing and acting out the song "If and Then Go Together" to describe the animals in the story "P. Mooney and the Kiwi"

Stand beside the audiocassette player, with the children standing before you. Say:

Let's sing about the animals that were in the Kiwi's story. (Show card 423) **We will sing about the elephant first.**

Play the song (instrumental version) and refer to the music card as you lead the children in singing and acting out this verse.

If you are an elephant, then
you are large.
(Hold arms outstretched)
If you are an elephant, then
you are large.
(Hold arms outstretched)
If you are an elephant, then
you are large.
(Hold arms outstretched)
If and then go together.

Continue with these story cards and verses:

1. 424•**If you are a mouse, then you are small, etc.** (Hold index fingers close together)
2. 425•**If you are a kangaroo, then you can jump, etc.** (Jump up and down)
3. 426•**If you are a leopard, then you can run, etc.** (Run in place)
4. 427•**If you are a giraffe, then you are tall, etc.** (Stand on tiptoes and reach up with arms)
5. 428•**If you are a bird, then you can sing, etc.** (Smile and wave arms as if leading a choir)

VARIATIONS: To make the activity *easier,* sing the song without actions. To make it *harder,* have the children make up more verses about the story animals.

79

MATERIALS*

ACTIVITY 1

None

ACTIVITY 2

None

1 Focus: talking about faces, and then saying an action poem about parts of the face

Say:

Faces do not look alike, but all faces have the same parts. What parts of the face are the same on everybody? (Encourage individual responses) **Yes, everyone has two eyes, a nose, a mouth, and two ears; but every face is different in some way. Today we are going to learn a poem about faces.**

Point to each face part as it is mentioned in this poem:*

When I get up, I check my face,
(Use finger to outline face)
Just to make sure it's all in place.
My eyes both open (I've got two),
(Point to eyes)
Looking for wonderful things to do.
My nose gets ready, I can tell,
(Point to nose)
Ready to sneeze and sniff and smell.
My mouth is helpful when I say,
Point to mouth)
"I've got a lot to do today."
My ears both listen, so I know
(Point to ears)
That then it's time for me to go.

**NOTE:*
This rhyme is by Sharon Holland.

Invite the children to join you in repeating and acting out the poem several times.

2 Focus: imitating and naming facial movements

With the children still seated, say:

We can do many things with our faces. Please watch what I do.

Wink several times before asking, "What did I do with my face?" Call on someone to respond in a sentence such as "You winked one eye." Continue by calling on volunteers to demonstrate facial actions. After each action, have a second child describe it in a sentence. Help as necessary. Suggested actions:

1. **blink eyes rapidly**
2. **open and close mouth several times**
3. **wrinkle nose**
4. **smile with mouth closed**
5. **move eyebrows up and down**
6. **pucker lips**
7. **grin, showing teeth**
8. **yawn, opening mouth very wide**
9. **close eyes**
10. **puff cheeks out Continue until everyone has had a turn.**

Continue until everyone has had a turn.

80

MATERIALS*

ACTIVITY 1

Cards

Face Pairs

74 76 78 80 82 84
86 88 90 92

Display Board"

5 ledges

ACTIVITY 2

Cards

Music

325

Audiocassette 2

Side A, Song 2
"The Is-Are Song"

1 Focus: classifying and describing head and facial features

Display the 10 face pair cards on the board.

Point to the cards on display and ask:

What do you see on the board? (Encourage unison response) **Yes, you see some new cards that show many different faces. But let's see if we can find the faces that are the same in certain ways. Please show me a face that is smiling, (Louis).** (Pause) **Yes, that face is smiling. You may take the card off the board.**

Continue until all six smiling faces have been identified. Then put these cards back on the board and continue with the facial features listed below. Always replace all cards before you call for the next feature.

1. **faces that are frowning**
2. **faces with both eyes open**
3. **faces with one eye open and one eye closed**
4. **faces with both eyes closed**
5. **faces of heads with long hair**
6. **faces of heads with short hair**

VARIATION: To make the activity *harder,* conclude by showing the cards in turn and asking children to describe each face.

2 Focus: singing and acting out "The Is-Me Song" while naming facial parts

Say:

Let's sing about our face parts. Listen and watch carefully as I go through the song for you the first time. Then we will do it together.

Play the song (instrumental version) and sing:

1. **Face is one; faces are two.**

   How do I look when I frown at you? (Frown)

Invite the children to join you in singing the verse. Continue with these verses:

2 **Eye is one; eyes are two.**

   What do you do when they blink at you? (Blink eyes)

3. **Nose is one; noses are two.**

   What do you do when they sniff at you? (Sniff)

4. **Lip is one; lips are two.**

   What do I do when I'm kissing you? (Kiss)

5 **Ear is one; ears are two.**

   What do you do when they listen to you? (Cup ears with hands)

6. **Mouth is one; mouths are two.**

   What do you do when they smile at you? (Smile)

7. **Voice is one; voices are two.**

   What do you do when they giggle at you? (Giggle)

Have the children make up more verses about face parts as long as time and interest permit.

Keep in Mind.
After each lesson in the program, individuals who have difficulty demonstrating proficiency in the skills you consider appropriate and important for them to learn should be tutored. Aides could help you with this task.

81

MATERIALS*

ACTIVITY 1

Display Board
4 ledges

P. Mooney Stick

Poster 2

ACTIVITY 2

Display Board
4 ledges

Poster 2

Teacher provides
Chalk or masking tape
Balance beam or plank (optional)

1 Focus: naming items on the poster "Circus," and then talking about circus experiences

Do not display the poster until asked to do so.

Hold the stick and say:

P. Mooney's stick is going to send us on a magical Mooney trip. Where do you think it might take us?

After the children have guessed, ask them to close their eyes as you wave the stick and say:

Mooney Magic, zing and zip!

Take us on a P. Mooney trip.

Quickly use the ledges to place the poster on the board. Then say:

Open your eyes! Where are we? (Encourage unison response) **Yes, we are at the circus.**

Encourage the children to point out and describe the circus items of special interest to them. If no one notices P. Mooney on the poster, ask the children to look for him there. Then continue the discussion with questions like these:

1. **Have you ever been to the circus? What was it like?** (Encourage children to discuss their experiences)
2. **What is a circus performer?**
3. **Where do the circus performers do their acts?**
4. **Why are some animals kept in cages?**
5. **Would you like to work in a circus? What would you like to do? Why?**

Accept all appropriate answers and add instructive comments. End by waving the stick as you say:

Mooney Magic, do a trick!

Take us back, P. Mooney Stick!

2 Focus: pantomiming the actions of tightrope walkers

Using masking tape or chalk, make one straight line at least 12 feet (four meters) long on the floor, where the children will be able to walk on it. Leave the poster from Activity 1 on display.

Stand with the children and ask:

What is P. Mooney doing in the poster, (Suzanne)? (Pause) **Yes, he is riding his Chaincycle along the tightrope. Even if we don't have a Chaincycle, we can pretend that we are tightrope walkers. Imagine that this line on the floor is a tightrope high in the air. Let's pretend to walk on the rope without falling off. First I will show you how.**

Demonstrate by holding your arms out to the sides and swaying as you carefully walk the length of the line. Let the children take turns walking on the imaginary tightrope. Continue as long as time and interest permit.

VARIATiON: To make the activity *harder,* have the children walk on a balance beam or plank, if available.

82

MATERIALS*

ACTIVITY 1

Display Board
4 ledges

Poster 2

ACTIVITY 2

Display Board
4 ledges

Poster 2

Audiocassette 4
Side A, Selection 2,
"Sounds of the Circus"

1 Focus: thinking about "who might say that" on the poster "Circus"

Use the ledges to display the poster on the board.

Point to the poster and say:

Look at all these people and animals! I will say a sentence that one of them might say. Please try to figure out who is speaking. Are you ready? (Pause) **Who might say, "The next act will be Susie and her pony Blaze, doing tricks"?** (Pause) **Yes, you are right. The ringmaster might say that.**

Have a volunteer come and point to the ringmaster. Then continue with these statements:

1. **"Balancing such a long stick in the air is not easy!"**
2. **"Did you ever ride on only one wheel?"**
3. **"I hope that loud noise won't hurt my ears!"**
4. **"Standing on my two front paws is a real trick!"**
5. **"Look, no hands!"**
6. **"I hope those two balls don't roll out from under our feet!"**
7. **"Let's play a marching song next."**
8. **"I have the longest legs in the circus!"**
9. **"Such a little dog doesn't need such a strong leash!"**
10. **"Why did you chain me to this wagon?"**
11. **"I hope that man's whip doesn't hit us!"**
12. **"I am talking through this so that everyone can hear me."**
13. **"Don't you wish you were as strong as I am?"**
14. **"I have never pulled a wagon with such a heavy load!"**
15. **"Oh, Daddy, we are having so much fun!"**
16. **"I had better blow this out right now before the big explosion!"**
17. **"We are the three biggest things in this whole circus!"**
18. **"Don't let go of my arms!"**
19. **"Did you ever stand on someone's shoulder so high up in the air?"**
20. **"We are swinging around and around."**

2 Focus: listening to "Sounds of the Circus" and then identifying each of them

Leave the poster from Activity 1 on display.

Say:

Many interesting sounds can be heard at a circus. Look at the poster as we listen for the first time to these circus sounds.

Play the sounds and then say:

Let's listen again and try to figure out what is making each sound.

Play the circus sounds again. Then have a volunteer come up and point to the correct items as you play the circus sounds a third time. Continue with other children until they all seem familiar with the sound effects.

83

MATERIALS*

ACTIVITY I

Display Board

Magnetic Shapes
All

ACTIVITY 2

Cards
Music
336

Display Board

Magnetic Shapes
All circles
All squares
Container

Audiocassette 2
Side B, Song 13,
"Round Dance"

1 Focus: classifying *shapes,* and then sequencing them by size

Let several children sort the shapes into piles of circles, squares, triangles, and rectangles on the floor in front of the board.

Say:

Let's use the shapes to play a game called Copycat. What is a copycat? (Encourage individual responses) **Yes, a copycat is someone who does the same thing another person does. I will put three shapes on the board in a certain order, and ask one of you what I did. Then that person will become a copycat by doing the same thing with the same kind of shapes, but a different color.**

Choose three circles of one color and arrange them on the board like this:

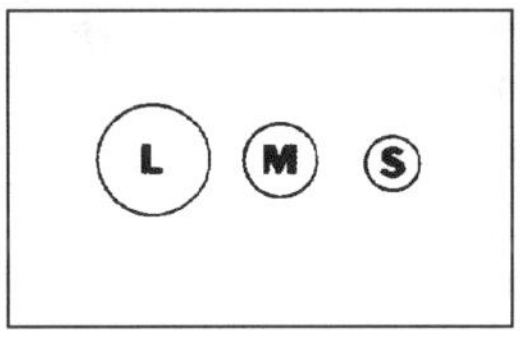

The child you call on should describe your actions in sentences like these:

***First,* you put up a *large* (black) circle.**

***Next,* you put up a *medium* (black) circle.**

***Last,* you put up a *small* (black) circle.**

If necessary, help the child reproduce the order of circles with another color. Continue with other children. When all circles have been used, remove them from the board and set new patterns with the squares, triangles, and rectangles in turn. Continue until everyone has had at least one turn.

2 Focus: describing shapes in a stop-go listening game using the music "Round Dance"

Leave a pattern of squares and one of circles from Activity 1 on display. Place the remaining circles and squares into the container.

Ask the children to stand in a circle. Have each child pick a shape from the container. Stand next to the audiocassette player and say:

Let's play a game. When the music starts, pass your shapes in this direction. (Point) **Continue as long as you hear the music. When it stops and I call on you, describe your shape in a sentence like "I have a small yellow circle" or "I am holding a large red square." Let's begin.**

Play the music for a short while before stopping the audiocassette player and calling on several children. Continue until every child has had a turn.

VARIATION: To make the activity *easier,* have everyone compare the size of his or her shape with that of shapes on the board.

84

MATERIALS*

ACTIVITY 1

Cards

Foods

97 98 101 102
103 104 105 109
111 112 115 117
118 119 120 122
123 125 127 136
138 139 140 141
142 143 147 148
150 152

Color Chips

All

Container

Display Board

6 ledges

Puppets

P. Mooney

ACTIVITY 2

Cards

Foods

(same as for Activity 1)

Display Board

6 ledges

1 Focus: pretending to select and pay for groceries while stressing counting

Display any 12 food cards on the board.

Have the stacked cards within reach. Put P. Mooney on your hand. He says:

Let's use color chips for money as we shop for foods.

Have each child take four chips from the container. P. Mooney continues:

I am the storekeeper and the board is my store. Look at all the foods I have for sale. Please stand up and tell me in a sentence which food you would like to buy, (Shirley). (Pause) **You would like to buy some (cheese). It costs three color chips, please.** (Pause) **Thank you.**

Continue with other children, varying prices. Have the children take their purchases back to their seats. Once the children understand the game, allow them to take turns holding P. Mooney and being the storekeeper. Help any child who has difficulty in counting out the proper number of chips. Restock the store with the remaining cards from time to time. Continue until everyone has purchased at least one food and all the cards have been used.

VARIATION: To make the activity *harder,* give each child more than four chips and charge higher prices for the foods.

2 Focus: classifying foods according to whether or not they need refrigeration

Have the children continue to hold their cards from Activity 1. Arrange the ledges on the board like this:

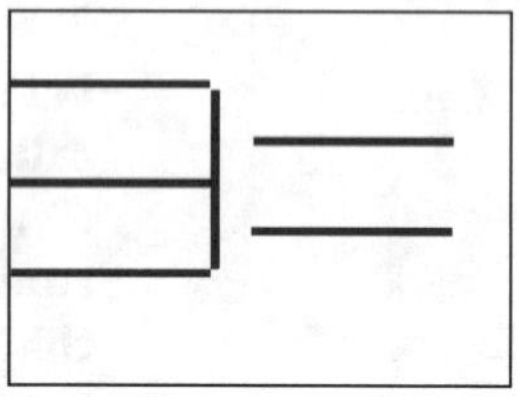

Say:

Each of you is holding foods from P. Mooney's store. Some foods must be kept in the refrigerator. Why? (Encourage individual responses) **You are right; some foods must be kept cool, so that they will not spoil. Where do we keep food that does not need to be in the refrigerator?**

Accept all plausible answers. If no one mentions a shelf, suggest it. Continue:

Now look at your food and decide if it belongs in the refrigerator or on a shelf. Let's take turns putting the foods away. Put food that will spoil into this "refrigerator." (Point) **Food that will *not* spoil should be put on these "shelves."** (Point)

Each child should explain a choice by saying, "(Cheese) is kept in the refrigerator because it will spoil" or "(Nuts) are kept on a shelf because (they) do not spoil quickly." Help as necessary, and remove cards as the ledges become full. Continue until every child has had a turn.

85

MATERIALS*

ACTIVITY 1

Cards
Stories
419-432

Display Board
6 ledges

Audiocassette 1
Side B, Story 6,
"P. Mooney and the Kiwi"

ACTIVITY 2

None

1 Focus: listening to and retelling the story "P. Mooney and the Kiwi"

Hold the 14 story cards and say:

Let's listen again to the story "P. Mooney and the Kiwi." Then we will talk about what happens in it. Remember, the Kiwi is a special friend of P. Mooney's.

Play the story. During the narration, show the story cards in turn, scanning the printed copy on the back of each picture. When the story ends, say:

Now let's see if you can tell the story. Please tell me what is happening in each picture.

Show the pictures in order as the children retell the story. Ask questions to help them remember important details. After each card is discussed, let several children act out what happens in it. Then have the cards placed on the board in a left-to-right sequence as seen by the group.

2 Focus: brainstorming *actions,* and then saying an action rhyme

Stand with the children and say:

Now let's think about things that we can do.

Encourage the children to mention actions like walking, jumping, bending, coughing, tapping, and giggling. If necessary, ask questions to stimulate discussion. Then continue:

Let's learn a rhyme about some of the things we can do. Please listen and watch me. Then we will say and act out the rhyme together.

Say the following rhyme with gestures:

I can smile; (Smile)

I can frown. (Frown)

I can turn upside down. (Bend over and look between legs)

I can run; (Run in place)

I can clap. (Clap hands)

I can take a little nap.

(Place palms together, lay cheek against hands, close eyes)

I can stretch; (Stretch)

I can bend. (Bend over)

I can whisper to a friend. (Whisper the word *whisper*)

I can jump; (Jump up and down once)

I can sing. (Sing the word *sing*)

I can do many things.

Invite the children to join you in repeating the rhyme and actions. Continue as time permits.

86 

MATERIALS*

ACTIVITY 1

Cards

Face Pairs

74 through 93, 1 per child

ACTIVITY 2

Cards

Music

329

Audiocassette 2

Side A, Song 6,

"The Not Song"

1 Focus: talking about being *happy* and *sad*

Give each child a card. Say:

Please look at the face on the card I gave you. If it is a happy face, come and sit facing me on this side. (Indicate your right side) **If your card has a sad face, come and sit facing me on this side.** (Indicate your left side)

Help as necessary until the groups are seated. Then ask:

How can you tell whether a face is happy or sad? (Encourage individual responses) **Yes, sometimes we can learn whether someone is happy or sad by looking at that person's mouth. What are other ways to tell whether someone is happy?**

Accept all reasonable responses and then ask how sadness is shown. Continue the discussion by asking each child these questions:

1. **What makes you happy?**
2. **What makes you sad?**

Encourage the children to respond in complete sentences.

2 Focus: singing and acting out "The Not Song" about *smiling* and *frowning*

Stand beside the audiocassette player, with the children standing before you. Say:

Show me how your face looks when you are happy.

Encourage the children to look at each other as they smile. Continue:

What does your face do when you are happy? (Encourage unison response) **Yes! When you are happy, you *smile*. Now show me how your face looks when you are sad or angry.**

Have the children look at each other as they frown. Then say:

What does your face do when you are sad? (Encourage unison response) **Very good; you *frown* when you are sad or angry. Let's learn a song about a smile and a frown. Please listen and watch what I do.**

Play the song (instrumental version) and refer to the music card as you sing and act out these verses:

1. **This is a smile; this is a smile.** (Smile)

   This is not a smile; this is not a smile. (Frown)

   This is a smile; this is a smile, (Smile)

   And this is a part of me. (Smile)

2. **This is a frown; this is a frown.** (Frown)

   This is not a frown; this is not a frown. (Smile)

   This is a frown; this is a frown, (Frown)

   And this is a part of me. (Frown)

Invite the children to join you in repeating the song and actions. Continue as time and interest suggest.

87 

MATERIALS*

ACTIVITY 1

Cards

Animals

1 5 8 14 17
19 25 28 30 31
33 34 35 36 37
38

Display Board

6 ledges

ACTIVITY 2

Cards

Animals

(Same as for Activity 1)

Music

332

Display Board

6 ledges

Audiocassette 2

Side B, Song 9, "Things That Go Together"

1 Focus: identifying *animals* from incomplete names

Place on the board all the 16 listed animal cards except 38.

Hold card 38. Point to the cards on display and say:

Let's use these animals to play a listening game. I will say the last part of an animal's name. Listen carefully and tell me which animal I am trying to name. oldfish. (Pause) **Yes, that is right. It is a goldfish.**

Have a child point to the corresponding card. Remove it and display card 38 in its place. Continue with the word endings given below. The children should respond in sentences. Stress the first consonant as you repeat the animal's name.

1. _ion
2. _ird
3. _urtle
4. _abbit
5. _erbil
6. _pider
7. _orm
8. _urkey
9. _ooster
10. _oad
11. _quirrel
12. _ear
13. _at
14. _uckling
15. _iglet

2 Focus: singing the song "Things That Go Together" to name animals

Leave the 15 animal cards from Activity 1 on display.

Hold up card 38, point to the 15 animal cards on display, and say:

Let's sing "Things That Go Together" about some of these animals. I will ask four of you each to hold up a card. Then we will sing a verse about those four animals.

Have each child with a card hold it up for the group to name. Then play the song (instrumental version) and sing with the children, inserting the names of the four animals. Continue with other groups of four until everyone has had a turn.

88

MATERIALS*

ACTIVITY 1

Fruits & Vegetables
All

ACTIVITY 2

Fruits & Vegetables
1 of each kind

P. Mooney Bag

1 Focus: classifying and naming *fruits* and *vegetables*

Sit in a circle with the children and place the fruits and vegetables in the center. Say:

Let's play a game to see how fast you can find all the foods I name.

Give at least one of the following commands to each child in the group. After a child has selected the correct foods, ask:

What did you find, (Inez)?

The child should respond in a sentence such as "I found all the (bananas)." Have the selected foods returned to the center of the circle before giving the next command.

Find all the . . .

1. **bananas.**
2. **apples.**
3. **pears.**
4. **strawberries.**
5. **oranges.**
6. **foods that have green leaves.**
7. **red foods.**
8. **yellow foods.**
9. **foods that could be eaten in one bite.**
10. **foods that cannot be eaten in one bite.**

VARIATION: To make the activity *harder,* ask individuals to find all the fruits or all the vegetables.

2 Focus: identifying by touch fruits and vegetables hidden in the P. Mooney bag

Put the 13 fruits and vegetables into the bag.

Wear the P. Mooney bag and say:

Now let's find out if you can name the fruits and vegetables by feeling them. I will ask two or three of you to stand beside me, face the class, and put your hands behind your back. Then I will give you each a food from the P. Mooney bag. You must feel the food and tell us what it is without looking at it.

If necessary, give clues until the food is identified correctly. Then the child should show the food to the group and say, "This is a (pineapple)." Continue with other threesomes until every child has had at least one turn.

VARIATION: To make the activity *easier,* let the children handle the fruits and vegetables before the items are put into the bag.

89

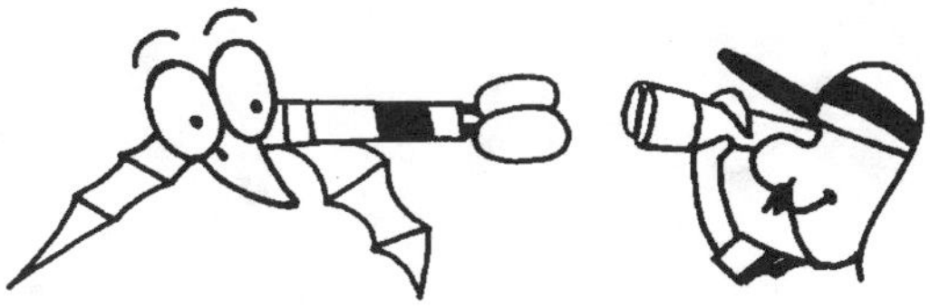

MATERIALS*

ACTIVITY 1

Display Board

4 ledges

Poster 2

ACTIVITY 2

Cards

Animals

25

1 Focus: identifying and naming items on the poster "Circus" while stressing numbers and actions in the game I Spy

Use the ledges to fasten the poster to the board.

Say:

Let's play I Spy with the circus poster. I will spy something on the poster and tell you about it. Try to figure out what I see. Answer together.

Emphasize the number clues in each description given below. When the group responds, count the objects aloud with them. One child may then give the answer in a sentence such as "You see two lions."

1. **I spy *two* animals in a cage. What do I see?** (lions)
2. **I spy *one* animal riding on a wagon. What do I see?** (gorilla)
3. **I spy *three* people making music. Whom do I see?** (band)
4. **I spy someone riding on *one* wheel. Whom do I see?** (unicycle rider)
5. **I spy an animal standing on only *two* legs. What do I see?** (pony, dog)
6. **I spy *three* animals doing a trick together. What do I see?** (elephants)
7. **I spy *one* person riding alone on the high wire. Whom do I see?** (P. Mooney)
8. **I spy *four* people doing the same trick. Whom do I see?** (swinging acrobats)
9. **I spy *three* people on the trapeze. Whom do I see?** (trapeze artists)
10. **I spy *three* people standing on two balls. Whom do I see?** (acrobats)
11. **I spy *four* people in funny costumes. Whom do I see?** (clowns)
12. **I spy *two* dogs. Can you find them?**
13. **I spy *one* person standing on top of another. Whom do I see?** (high wire artists)
14. **I spy *two* people riding animals. Where are they?** (on horse and elephant)

2 Focus: talking about *lions,* and then chanting an action rhyme about the zoo

Ask the children to stand before you. Hold up card 25 and say:

If we went to a circus, we might see this animal. What is it? (Encourage unison response) **Yes, it is a lion. Who has seen a real lion?** (Pause) **Please tell us about it, (Tom). Where did you see it?**

Encourage the children to tell their experiences. If no one mentions the zoo, suggest it. Then say:

Let's learn a rhyme about visiting lions at the zoo. Please listen and watch as I go through the rhyme the first time. Then we will do it together.

Set the card aside and recite the following rhyme* with gestures:

One, two;
Off to the zoo! (March in place)

Three, four;
Lions roar! (Stop and roar)

Five, six;
We're in a fix! (Shake with fear)

Seven, eight;
Run for the gate! (Run in place)

Nine, ten;
Let's go again! (March in place)

Invite the children to join you in repeating the rhyme and actions. Continue as time and interest permit.

**NOTE:*
This rhyme is by Sharon Holland.

90

MATERIALS*

ACTIVITY 1

Cards
Pictures from Several Categories
19 117 132 139 144 149 162 189 200

Color Chips
20 orange

Display Board
5 ledges

Fruits & Vegetables
Carrot
2 oranges

P. Mooney Bag

Puppets
Zoey
Discovery hat

ACTIVITY 2

Cards
Pictures from Several Categories
(same as for Activity 1)

Display Board
5 ledges

P. Mooney Bag

Puppets
Zoey
Thinking hat

1 Focus: naming and comparing *orange items* pulled from the P. Mooney bag, and then brainstorming other orange items

Put the oranges, the carrot, the nine picture cards, and two necklaces made of 10 orange color chips each into the bag.

Hold the bag on your lap. Put Zoey (wearing her discovery hat) on your hand and have her say:

The P. Mooney bag is full of surprises today. Let's discover what it holds.

Let volunteers each choose and name an item before displaying it on the board (if it is a card) or placing it on the floor in front of the board (if it is an item other than a card). When all items have been chosen, Zoey continues:

These things are all the same in one way. What is it?

If no one notices that everything is orange, the puppet should ask:

Are they all food? (Pause) **Are they all round?** (Pause) **Are they all the same color?** (Pause) **Yes, they are the same color. What color are they?** (Encourage unison response) **Yes, they are all orange. That is how they are the same!**

End by having the children name other orange items. If no one notices that the decal on the kit case is orange, mention this.

2 Focus: identifying *orange items* from their descriptions in riddles

Hang the bag on a corner of the board, on which are displayed the cards from Activity 1. Replace Zoey's discovery hat with her thinking hat.

Say:

Let's play a thinking game. I will say a riddle about something on the board. Raise your hand if you have an answer for the riddle. Then you may put Zoey on your hand and have her answer.

Pause after each clue to give the children time to think. Have volunteers hold Zoey and answer through her. Present riddles like these:

1. **I am orange. . . I grow in a garden. . . Rabbits like to eat me. . . What am I?** (carrots)
2. **I am orange. . . I am a kind of food. . . You can eat me with a spoon. . . .What am I?** (soup)
3. **I am orange. . . I often have surprises inside me. . . I belong to P. Mooney. . . What am I?** (P. Mooney bag)
4. **I am orange. . . I have fins and a tail. . . I swim very well. . . What am I?** (goldfish)
5. **I am orange. . . I am something to wear. . . The man who wears me works in a circus. . . What am I?** (acrobat's costume)
6. **I am orange. . . You can find me in a house. . . People like to sit on me. . . What am I?** (couch)

7. **I am orange. . . I am a kind of food. . . You can drink me. . . What am I?** (orange juice)
8. **I am orange. . . I am found in a house. . . You can eat lunch on me. . . What am I?** (table)
9. **I am orange. . . I am round. . . I have a name the same as my color. . . What am I?** (orange)
10. **I am orange. . . I am round. . . You can carve a face in me. . . What am I?** (pumpkin)
11. **I am orange. . . I grow on a vine in the field or garden. . . You can use me to make good pies. . . What am I?** (pumpkin)
12. **I am orange. . . I have four legs. . . You put things on me. . . What am I?** (table)
13. **I am orange. . . I am something to eat. . . You buy me in bunches at the store. . . What am I?** (carrots)
14. **I am orange. . . I am a food. . . Sometimes I am smooth and sometimes I have pieces of vegetables and meat in me. . . What am I?** (soup)
15. **I am orange. . . I live in water. . . I get air through my gills. . . What am I?** (goldfish)
16. **I am orange. . . I am a piece of furniture. . . You can take a nap on me. . . What am I?** (couch)
17. **I am orange. . . You can squeeze me out of a fruit. . . I can be poured into a glass. . . What am I?** (orange juice)
18. **I am orange. . . I love to hang upside down. . . swing through the air. . . what am I?** (acrobat)
19. **I am orange. . . You can carry many things in me. . . I belong to P. Mooney. . . What am I?** (P. Mooney bag)
20. **I am orange. . . You can peel the skin off me. . . I am good to eat. . . What am I?** (orange)

We recommend that you read again Part I of the Teacher's Guide at about this point. This should remind you of ways to teach the lessons for maximum efficiency.

91

MATERIALS*

ACTIVITY 1

Audiocassette 3
Side A, Selection 3,
"Sounds of People - Actions"

ACTIVITY 2

Cards
Music
333

Audiocassette 2
Side B, Selection 10,
"Make a Sound"

1 Focus: listening to "Sounds of People — Actions," and then identifying and imitating these actions

Say:

People can make many different kinds of sounds. Let's listen to some new sound effects and find out if we can tell what a person is doing just from the sound we hear.

Play the first sound. Ask:

What did you hear? (Encourage unison response) **You are right. That was the sound of a person clapping. Let's listen to more sounds.**

Continue with the remaining sounds. Then play the sound effects again. Volunteers should identify each in a sentence such as "I heard a person (walking)." Invite the children to imitate each action as you play the sound effects a third time.

2 Focus: listening to, singing, and acting out the song "Make a Sound" while stressing *loud, louder, loudest*, and *soft, softer, softest*

Say:

I will clap three times. Listen for how loudly I clap.

Clap your hands three times, making each sound louder than the last. Then ask:

What happened when I clapped my hands? (Encourage responses from several children) **You are right; each time I clapped, I made a louder sound. First I clapped *loud.*** (Clap hands) **Then I clapped louder. (Clap hands hard) Then I clapped the *loudest* of all.** (Clap hands very hard) **Now listen as I clap my hands again.**

Clap your hands three times again, making each clapping sound softer than the last. Repeat the above questioning, emphasizing the words *soft, softer,* and *softest.* Continue:

Now let's learn a new song about making loud and soft sounds with our hands and voices.

Play the sounds and encourage the children to listen carefully. Play the four verses of the recording a second time and lead the children in doing the appropriate actions and singing. Repeat the recording as time and interest permit.

92

MATERIALS*

ACTIVITY 1

None

ACTIVITY 2

Cards

Toys

235

Music

336

Audiocassette 2

Side B, Song 13,

"Round Dance"

1 Focus: brainstorming and talking about *toys*

Say:

Let's see how many different toys you can name.

The children should name all they can without repeating. Then continue:

If you could have any toy in the whole world, (Carolyn), what would it be? (Pause) **Why would you like to have a (bicycle), (Carolyn)?**

Continue with other children. Encourage them to respond in sentences.

2 Focus: pantomiming the movements of rag dolls to the music Round Dance

Stand beside the audiocassette player, with the children standing before you. Show the toy card and say:

If we were rag dolls like Raggedy Ann and Raggedy Andy, how would we move? (Encourage individual responses) **Yes, we would be floppy. Let's find out what being floppy feels like.**

Set the card aside and demonstrate by letting your head loll as you bend at the waist, hang your arms loosely, and take shuffling, sliding steps. Invite the children to imitate you and to invent their own floppy movements. Then play "Round Dance" and encourage the children to dance like rag dolls. Allow them to dance alone or with partners, if they wish. End by suggesting that the children collapse like rag dolls.

93 

MATERIALS*

ACTIVITY 1

None

ACTIVITY 2

None

1 Focus: naming parts of the head, and then describing their functions

Say:

Our heads have many parts. Let's name as many parts of the head as we can. Then we will talk about what each part can do for us. (Point to eyes) **What do we call these?** (Encourage unison response) **Yes, these are my eyes. I can blink my eyes.** (Demonstrate) **What are some other things you can do with your eyes?**

Each child should respond in a sentence such as "I can see with my eyes" or "I can close my eyes." Continue with the parts listed below. Adjust the number under discussion to suit your class. As necessary, give clues. Encourage the children to look at one another before they answer.

1. eyes	**10. teeth**
2. nose	**11. tongue**
3. mouth	**12. nostrils**
4. ears	**13. skin**
5. hair	**14. jaws**
6. lips	**15. gums**
7. eyelids	**16. forehead**
8. eyelashes	**17. chin**
9. cheeks	**18. scalp**

2 Focus: saying an action rhyme about the body

Stand in a circle with the children and say:

Let's move our bodies as I say a rhyme. When I stop at the end of a line, we will all do what the rhyme says.

Lead the children in acting out the words as you say this rhyme:

With your hand,
Touch your nose. (Touch nose)
Now bend down and touch your toes. (Touch toes)

Just for fun,
Run, run, run. (Run in place)
Now reach up and touch the sun. (Reach arms up)

Buzz, buzz, buzz,
Like a bee. (Make buzzing sound)
Now bend down and touch your knee. (Touch knee)

Wink one eye; (Wink)
Blink two eyes. (Blink)
Now reach up and touch the skies. (Reach arms up)

Clap your hands. (Clap hands)
Stamp the ground. (Stamp ground)
Isn't that a happy sound?

Say the rhyme again and have the children repeat each line after you as they do the actions. Continue as time and interest permit.

94

MATERIALS*

ACTIVITY I

Cards

Toys

226-266, 1 per child

Color Chips

30 blue

30 green

30 orange

30 red

30 yellow

Container

ACTIVITY 2

Color Chips

60, assorted colors

1 Focus: matching color chips with toy cards, and then describing the toys

Put the 150 chips into the container.

Ask the children to sit in a semicircle. Spread the toy cards, face up, on the floor in front of them. Let each child take two chips of different colors from the container. Say:

Let's find pictures of toys with the same colors as your chips. What colors do you have, (Arthur)? (Pause) **Yes, your chips are (yellow) and (red). Do you see one toy that has both those colors?**

The child should place the two chips on the chosen picture and then name the toy and the colors by saying, "The (ball) is (yellow) and (red)." Continue until everyone has had a turn. If time and interest suggest, let the children again choose two chips of different colors and repeat the activity.

2 Focus: linking color chips to make a chain, and then following directions that stress *positional words*

Give each child an equal number of chips to link into chains. Then help them link their individual chains into one long chain. Say:

Let's use this chain to play a following-directions game. Please listen carefully, so you will know what to do.

Have two children each hold one end of the chain as they stand several feet (a meter or two) apart. Ask the other children to line up in single file. The two children holding the chain should raise or lower it as needed for each of the commands listed below. After each action, have a child describe it in a sentence such as "We (walked) *under* the chain" or "We (hopped) *over* the chain."

1. **Run *under* the chain.**
2. **Jump *around* the chain.**
3. **Jump *over* the chain.**
4. **Run *around* the chain.**
5. **Crawl *under* the chain.**
6. **Walk *under* the chain.**
7. **Step *over* the chain.**
8. **Walk *around* the chain.**

95

MATERIALS*

ACTIVITY 1

Cards

Stories

433-450

Audiocassette 1

Side B, Story 7,

"Terrapin Turtle's Travel Troubles"

ACTIVITY 2

Cards

Music

338

P. Mooney Stick

Audiocassette 2

Side B, Song 15,

"Contrasts"

1 Focus: listening to the story "Terrapin Turtle's Travel Troubles," and answering questions about it

Hold the 18 story cards and say:

Let's listen to a new story called "Terrapin Turtle's Travel Troubles." The name of the story is fun to say. Let's say it together. (Do this) **Now let's find out why the turtle had trouble going places. We will talk about the story after we listen to it.**

Play the story as you follow the printed narrative on the backs of the cards. Then lead the discussion with questions like these:

1. **What is the name of P. Mooney's friend?**
2. **Why was this story called "Terrapin Turtle's Travel Troubles"?**
3. **What were some of the ways to travel that P. Mooney suggested to Terrapin Turtle?**
4. **How were Terrapin Turtle's travel troubles solved?**
5. **What is your favorite way to travel?**

VARIATION: To make the activity *harder,* play the story without showing the cards.

2 Focus: pantomiming the movements of turtles to the music "Contrasts" while stressing *fast* and *slow*

Hold the stick and say:

Terrapin Turtle needed a fast way to travel. Now let's use Mooney magic to pretend we are turtles like Terrapin. When the music is slow, we will move very slowly, as turtles usually do — but when the music is fast, we will slide and glide quickly on Mooney skates. Here we go!

Wave the stick as you chant:

Mooney Magic, do a trick.

Make turtles, P. Mooney Stick!

Play the music as the children crawl to pantomime turtles. When the music changes to the faster tempo, they should pretend to strap on Mooney skates and go fast. Play the music several times and praise all good efforts. End by waving the stick as you say:

Eenie-meenie-Mooney-me;

Now let's be you and me.

96

MATERIALS*

ACTIVITY 1

Cards

Vehicles (optional)

267-283

ACTIVITY 2

Cards

Music

333

Audiocassette 2

Side B, Song 10,

"Make a Sound"

1 Focus: brainstorming and comparing *vehicles*

Say:

A vehicle is something that takes people or things from one place to another. Let's say that word together.

After saying the word *vehicle* several times with the children, continue:

In the story, Terrapin Turtle imagined that he was riding in different vehicles. Let's think about all the ones we could use.

Help the children name all the vehicles they can. Then continue:

Now let's decide which vehicles are faster or slower than others. Which is faster, an (airplane) or a (balloon)? (Encourage unison response) **Yes, you are right. An airplane is faster than a balloon.**

Continue with the questions listed below. The children should respond in sentences.

1. **Which is *faster*, a motorcycle or a bicycle?**
2. **Which is *slower*, a rowboat or a ship?**
3. **Which is *slower*, a helicopter or a jet?**
4. **Which is *faster*, a car or an ambulance?**
5. **Which is *faster*, a hot air balloon or a space capsule?**
6. **Which is *faster*, a horse and wagon or a camping trailer?**
7. **Which is *slower*, a fire truck or a school bus?**
8. **Which is *slower*, a sailboat or jet boat?**
9. **Which is *faster*, a tractor or a horse?**
10. **Which is *faster*, a police car or a tow truck?**
11. **Which is *slower*, a submarine or a canoe?**
12. **Which is *faster*, a train or an airplane?**

OPTIONAL: If the children have difficulty with the question, use the 17 vehicle cards as cues.

2 Focus: singing and acting out the song "Make a Sound" while stressing *slow* and *fast*

Ask the children to sit before you on the floor. Say:

Some ways to travel are fast, and other ways are slow. Let's learn a song about rowing a boat and doing a dance. Sometimes we will pretend to row a boat quickly, and sometimes we will pretend to row slowly. Then we will do a slow dance before we do a fast dance. Please listen and watch what I do.

Play the song and refer to the music card as you sing the verses with gestures. Invite the children to join you in repeating the song as long as time and interest permit.

97

MATERIALS*

ACTIVITY 1

Cards

People

200 201 203 206 207
208 209 210 212 213
216 217 218

Display Board

6 ledges

Puppets

Zoey

Thinking hat

ACTIVITY 2

Cards

Music

333

Audiocassette 2

Side B, Song 10,
"Make a Sound"

1 Focus: identifying *people* from descriptions in riddles

In random order, display the 13 people cards on the board.

Review the card labels with the children. Place Zoey (wearing her thinking hat) on your hand. Have her point to the cards as she says:

I know some riddles about these people. Please listen carefully and try to figure out which person I am describing. Then tell me in a sentence who it is.

Each time, the group or a volunteer should answer Zoey in a sentence such as "You are a (dentist)." Zoey may then invite a child to point to the right card.

1. **I work in a school. You come to see me almost every day if you are in my class. Who am I?** (teacher)
2. **I wear a white coat. I use a small mirror to look at people's teeth. Who am I?** (dentist)
3. **I have black curly hair. I am looking at my watch. Who am I?** (doctor)
4. **I have a green glove. I am waving to you. Who am I?** (clown)
5. **I am wearing waterproof boots, coat, and hat. I am moving a hose. Who am I?** (fire fighter)
6. **I am wearing a yellow shirt. I am using a pair of scissors. Who am I?** (barber)
7. **I wear a red suit. I write with a stick of chalk. Who am I?** (teacher)
8. **I wear a blue uniform. I bring people news. Who am I?** (mail carrier)
9. **I comb and cut people's hair while they sit in my chair. Who am I?** (barber)
10. **I work in an office. I check people's teeth and fill their cavities. Who am I?** (dentist)
11. **I might work in an office or a hospital. I try to help sick people get well again. Who am I?** (doctor)
12. **I grow corn and wheat. I plow the field and milk the cows. Who am I?** (farmer)
13. **I work in a circus. I swing through the air on my trapeze. Who am I?** (acrobat)
14. **I can fly to the moon in my space capsule. Who am I?** (astronaut)
15. **I work in a circus. I wear a big baggy costume. I hope you think I am funny. Who am I?** (clown)
16. **I drive my truck to a fire and try to put out the fire. Who am I?** (fire fighter)
17. **I work in a store. I sell fruits, vegetables, and meat. Who am I?** (grocer)
18. **I drive my truck to your house and bring letters and packages. Who am I?** (mail carrier)
19. **I work with the doctor in an office or a hospital. I help to make sick people feel better. Who am I?** (nurse)
20. **I protect you from people who break the law. Call me if someone robs your house, and I will try to catch the robber. Who am I?** (police officer)

VARIATION: To make the activity *harder,* do not use the cards.

2 Focus: singing and acting out the song "Make a Sound" while stressing *loud* and *soft*

Sit beside the audiocassette player, with the children standing before you. Say:

People can clap and sing. Let's make those sounds as we sing the song again.

Play the song and refer to the music card as you lead the children in singing and doing the actions. Repeat as time and interest permit.

98 

MATERIALS*

ACTIVITY 1

Display Board

Manikin, Disassembled

Body parts

Facial features

Short hair

ACTIVITY 2

Puppets

P. Mooney

1 Focus: evaluating what is wrong with the manikin, and then reassembling it correctly

Set up the board and ask two children to assemble the manikin upon it.

Say:

We are going to use the manikin to play a game. While you keep your eyes covered, I will move one of the manikins s parts. Let's see if you can figure out what I did.

When the children have covered their eyes, place the manikin's mouth on its stomach. A volunteer may then describe the change in a sentence such as "The mouth is on the stomach." Then have another child return the mouth to its proper place. Continue with changes like these:

1. **turn the head upside-down**
2. **switch arms and legs**
3. **switch feet and hands**
4. **switch eyes and ears**
5. **reverse feet**
6. **reverse hands**
7. **turn nose upside-down**
8. **switch nose and mouth**

2 Focus: following directions in the game P. Mooney Says while stressing *positional words*

Ask the children to stand before you. Place P. Mooney on your hand and have him say:

Let's have some fun playing my favorite game, P. Mooney Says. Today I will tell you where to put a part of your body. But listen carefully. If you do not hear "P. Mooney says," then don't move!

Have the puppet give commands like those below, omitting the phrase "P. Mooney says" about half the time. Check to make sure that the children move correctly. Have the puppet repeat any command a child misunderstands.

P. Mooney says . . .

1. **Put your hands *on* your stomach.**
2. **Put your ear *on* your shoulder.**
3. **Put your face *in* your hands.**
4. **Put your fingers *over* your eyes.**
5. **Put one hand *behind* your back.**
6. **Put your nose *on* your knee.**
7. **Put your head *between* your legs.**
8. **Sit *on* your hands.**
9. **Put your thumb *in* your mouth.**
10. **Put your hands *between* your feet.**

Continue as time and interest suggest.

99

MATERIALS*

ACTIVITY 1

Display Board
4 ledges

Poster 1

Audiocassette 4
Side A, Selection 1, "Farm in Spring"

ACTIVITY 2

None

1 Focus: listening to "Sounds of the Farm in Spring," and then identifying each of them

Do not display the poster until asked to do so.

Say:

Close your eyes and listen carefully as I play some new sounds we might hear at a special place. Try to guess where we might be.

Play the sound effects of "Farm in Spring." Afterwards, ask:

Where might we hear those sounds?

When the children answer, "A farm," use the ledges to fasten the poster to the board. If the children cannot answer, display the poster and ask them again. Then say:

Let's listen to the farm sounds again. Look at the poster this time and try to figure out what is making each sound.

Repeat the sounds and then call on children to name the sounds and point out their sources on the poster. Continue until all sounds and sources have been identified.

2 Focus: talking about farm work, and then saying and pantomiming a rhyme about planting an apple seed

Ask:

What kind of work do farmers do?

If no one mentions that farmers grow fruits and vegetables, suggest this. Then continue:

Let's pretend to be farmers as we say a rhyme about planting an apple seed. Please listen and watch as I go through it for you the first time. Then we will do it together.

Recite this rhyme with gestures:

Here's a little apple seed.
(Hold imaginary seed in one hand, point with other)

Plant it in the ground.
(Pretend to plant seed)

Give it water every day.
(Pretend to water plant)

Weed it all around.
(Pretend to pull weeds)

Now the tree is growing,
(Hang head and arms down)

Reaching to the sky.
(Gradually lift head and arms up)

We can pick the apples now
(Pretend to pick apples)

And make an apple pie!
(Pretend to put pie into oven, close oven door, and rub stomach happily)

Invite the children to join you in repeating the rhyme and actions several times.

100 

MATERIALS*

ACTIVITY 1

Cards

Animals

3	5	6	7	8	9
10	11	12	13	14	18
20	21	22	26	27	30
31	32	33	36	37	38

Display Board

4 ledges

P. Mooney Bag

Poster 1

ACTIVITY 2

Display Board

4 ledges

Cards

Music

325

Poster 1

Audiocassette 2

Side A, Song 2,

"The Is-Are Song"

1 Focus: matching animal cards with animals in the poster "Farm in Spring," and then naming the animals

Use the ledges to fasten the poster to the board. Put the 24 animal cards into the bag.

Wear the bag and say:

Today the P. Mooney bag contains pictures of animals found on the farm. Let's see if you can match the animals on the cards with those on the poster.

Each child is to take an animal card and identify it in a sentence such as "This is a (horse)" before finding the same kind of animal on the poster. If there is more than one poster animal, the child should count and identify them by saying, "Here are (five horses)." Continue until every child has had a turn or until all the animal cards have been used.

VARIATION: To make the activity *harder,* have each child also tell how animals in the same family are the same and how they are different.

2 Focus: singing "The Is-Are Song," and then imitating animal sounds

Hold the music card and say:

Let's sing about the sounds farm animals make. Come up and choose an animal on the poster, (Delores).

Have the child point to the animal as you play the song (instrumental version) and lead the group in singing. Refer to the music card and stress the plurals as you sing. The children should end the verse by making the animal sound. Continue with other animals chosen by the children.

Keep in Mind...
After each lesson in the program, individuals who have difficulty demonstrating proficiency in the skills you consider appropriate and important for them to learn should be tutored. Aides could help you with this task.

101

MATERIALS*

ACTIVITY 1

Cards

Stories

353-368

Audiocassette 1

Side A, Story 2,

"P. Mooney and Mr. Nobody"

ACTIVITY 2

None

1 Focus: listening to the story " P. Mooney and Mr. Nobody," and talking about missing body parts

Say:

Let's listen again to the story " P. Mooney and Mr. Nobody." Mr. Nobody's last name is made of two words: *no* and *body.* Let's say it together. (Do this) **He was called "Mr. Nobody" because no one could see him. After we hear Mr. Nobody's story, we will talk about his body parts.**

Play the story. During the narration, show the story cards in order as you scan the printed copy on the back of each picture. After showing each card, lay it facedown on your lap. When the story ends, say:

Now let's pretend that the P. Mooney magic is wearing off and Mr. Nobody's body parts are disappearing. (Show card 365) **What body parts are missing in this picture?**

Show story cards 361 through 365 in reverse order as the children take turns naming the body parts missing from each picture.

2 Focus: imitating body movements, and moving imaginatively

Have the children stand before you. Say:

Our body parts are like Mr. Nobody's, but we do not need magic to let other people see us. We can watch one another do exercises right now. Please listen and then do what you see me doing.

Say sentences like those given below. Each time, invite the children to join you in doing the action.

1. **I clap my hands.**
2. **I jump up and down.**
3. **I blink my eyes.**
4. **I reach up high.**
5. **I run in place.**
6. **I touch my toes.**
7. **I touch my nose.**
8. **I open and close my mouth.**

Repeat as time and interest suggest. If children are able, have them join in saying the descriptions.

102

MATERIALS*

ACTIVITY 1

Display Board

Manikin, Movable

ACTIVITY 2

Cards

Music

338

Audiocassette 2

Side B, Song 15, "Contrasts"

1 Focus: thinking about and imitating the manikin's positions

Set up the board and put the manikin on it.

Stand beside the board, with the children standing facing you. Say:

Watch carefully as I move the manikin into different positions. Then try to do the same thing with your own body. Our bodies won't be able to do everything the manikin can. But let's try!

Position the manikin as indicated below. Help the children decide whether their bodies can move that way as they attempt to imitate each of the poses.

1. **bend legs backwards**
2. **turn head upside down**
3. **lift arms over head**
4. **turn hands back on arms**
5. **touch chin to chest**
6. **nod head**
7. **look at the ceiling**
8. **touch nose with foot**
9. **bend legs forward from knee**
10. **turn feet upside down**
11. **stand on tiptoe**
12. **touch head with your toes**
13. **touch stomach with your toes**
14. **touch bottom with elbow**
15. **bend backwards at waist**
16. **curl up in a ball**

2 Focus: listening to and talking about the music "Contrasts," and then moving to it imaginatively

Hold the music card and say:

Let's listen to some music and think about how we would move to it. Imagine what animals or other things might move that way, too.

Play the music. Afterwards, have the children describe how the changes in tempo would affect their movements. Then discuss what they imagined while listening. Continue:

Now let's play the music again. Move the way it makes you feel as you hear it.

Play the music and move in response to it with the children. Assist any child who has difficulty with changes in tempo. Praise all efforts.

103

MATERIALS*

ACTIVITY 1

None

ACTIVITY 2

Puppets

Zoey

Action hat

1 Focus: describing clothing while stressing numbers and colors

Say:

Your clothes are many different colors, and you are wearing only one of some items and two of others. Let's take turns describing our clothes by color and number. You may go first, (Oliver). Tell us in a sentence about something you are wearing.

The child should specify the color and number of items as they are named in a sentence such as "I am wearing (a green shirt, blue overalls, two white socks, and two blue tennis shoes)." Continue with other children.

VARIATION: To make the activity *easier,* have the children name their clothes without descriptive words.

2 Focus: following directions involving clothing

Stand with the children. Place Zoey (wearing her action hat) on your hand. She says:

I am wearing my red action hat, so let's play an action game. I will tell you to do something if you are wearing a certain item. Please listen carefully and look at your clothes to see if you should move.

After Zoey gives each command listed below, check to see that the right children are moving.

1. **If you are wearing a *shirt,* then clap your hands.**
2. **If you are wearing *underwear,* then turn around two times.**
3. **If you are wearing *socks,* then jump up and down.**
4. **If you are wearing a *sweater,* then make a funny face.**
5. **If you are wearing a *dress,* then run in place.**
6. **If you are wearing *shoes,* then touch your toes.**
7. **If you are wearing *jeans,* then reach up high.**
8. **If you are wearing a *skirt,* then sit down on the floor.**
9. **If you are wearing a *hat,* then stand on your head.**
10. **If you are wearing a *belt,* then wave your hand.**
11. **If you are wearing a *jacket,* then twist your body.**
12. **If you are wearing *shorts,* then kneel on both knees.**
13. **If you are wearing a *scarf,* then slide across the floor.**
14. **If you are wearing *trousers,* then turn around quickly.**
15. **If you are wearing a *blouse,* then bend down two times.**
16. **If you are wearing *shoes,* then shake all over.**

Continue as time and interest suggest.

VARIATION: To make the activity *harder,* add color to each direction, like this: "If you are wearing a red shirt, then clap your hands."

104

MATERIALS*

ACTIVITY 1

Cards

Clothing

39 40 41 42 43 47
49 58 60 61 62 65
67 69 71 72

Display Board

2 ledges

Manikin, Movable

P. Mooney Bag

ACTIVITY 2

Display Board

1 ledge

Cards

Clothing

42* 43* 58* 65*

Music

325

Audiocassette 2

Side A, Song 2,
"The Is-Are Song"
(instrumental)

1 Focus: naming and classifying clothing which is worn on the top half and on the bottom half of the body

Set up the board and put the manikin near the left edge of it. Place the ledges so they touch the manikin's waist and feet, like this:

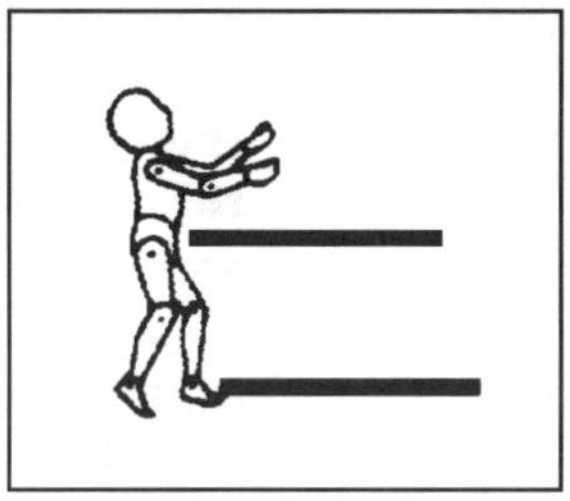

Put these clothing cards into the bag: 40, 41, 42, 43, 47, 60, 61, and 65. Stack clothing cards 39, 49, 58, 62, 67, 69, 71, and 72.

Holding the bag on your lap, say:

The P. Mooney bag contains pictures of clothes that the manikin might wear. Let's decide whether they would be worn on the manikin's top half (point to top ledge) **or on the manikin's bottom half.** (Point to bottom ledge) **Come and pick a card from the bag, (Corinne).** (Pause) **What did you choose?** (Pause) **Would the (cap) go on the top or on the bottom half?**

The child should respond in a sentence such as "The (cap) would go on the (top half) of the manikin" and then place the card on the proper ledge. Continue with other children. As the ledges are filled, remove and set aside the cards. Proceed until the bag is empty. Then put the remaining cards into the bag and continue in the same manner.

2 Focus: singing "The Is-Are Song" while naming clothing and showing where it is worn

Stand beside the audiocassette player and the board, with the children standing and facing you. Place card 42 on the ledge and say:

Let's sing about were we would wear these boots. When the song asks "Where would I put some boots on you?", show me where boots are worn.

Play the song (instrumental version) and refer to the music card as you sing:

1. **Boot is one; boots are two. Where would I put some boots on you?**

Encourage the children to show you by pointing where boots are worn as they join you in repeating the verse. A child may then answer the song's question with a sentence such as "You would put boots on my feet." Continue with these verses:

2. **Cap is one; caps are two. Where would I put a cap on you?**
3. **Shirt is one; shirts are two. Where would I put a shirt on you?**
4. **Sock is one; socks are two. Where would I put some socks on you?**

105

MATERIALS*

ACTIVITY 1

Display Board
4 ledges

Poster 3

Audiocassette 4
Side A, Selection 3, "Sounds of the Department Store"

ACTIVITY 2

Color Chips
5 per child

Display Board
4 ledges

Poster 3

Puppets
P. Mooney

1 Focus: listening to "Sounds of the Department Store," and then identifying each while looking at the poster "Department Store"

Do not display the poster until asked to do so.

Say:

Close your eyes and listen as I play some sounds we might hear at a special place. Try to guess where we might be.

Play the audiocassette sound effects. Then ask:

Where might you hear those sounds?

If no one guesses correctly, give hints and ask the question again. Then use the ledges to fasten the poster to the board. Say:

Yes, this is a department store. Let's listen again to the sounds you might hear there. As you listen, look at the poster and decide what might be making each sound.

Play the sound effects several times, and let the children take turns naming and pointing out the source of each sound.

VARIATION: To make the activity *harder,* have the children think of other sounds which might be heard in a department store.

2 Focus: pretending to shop at the department store while stressing counting

Leave the poster from Activity 1 on display.

Give each child five color chips. Put P. Mooney on your hand. Have him point to the poster as he says:

Let's use our color chips for money to shop at this department store. I will be the salesperson. You will be the shoppers and may choose something to buy. Please come to the store, (Karl), and tell us what you want to buy. (Pause) **You would like some (red blocks) from the toy department. That will be five color chips, please.** (Pause) **Thank you.**

The child should pretend to carry the purchase away. Continue with other children. Once they understand the game, allow them to take turns holding P. Mooney and being the salesperson. Assist any child who has difficulty counting out five chips.

VARIATION: To make the activity *harder,* give children more than five chips apiece and have them vary the prices.

106

MATERIALS*

ACTIVITY 1

Color Chips

All

Container

ACTIVITY 2

Color Chips

Container

1 set of 8 colors

Puppets

P. Mooney

1 Focus: identifying brown color chips, and finding and naming objects of the same color

Sit with the children in a circle, and place all the chips in the center. Ask:

Who can find a brown color chip? (Pause) **Yes, your chip is brown, (Yolanda). Let's find the rest of the brown chips and pile them together here.** (Indicate activity area)

When all brown chips have been identified, the children may each take one and look for something brown in the room. Ask them to stand beside what they find. Let the children take turns naming their brown objects in a sentence such as "I found a brown (crayon)." Help as necessary, and continue until everyone has had a turn. Have the children return all the chips to the container.

2 Focus: identifying colors from rhyming words

Link the set of eight chips into a chain.

Ask the children to sit in a circle with you. Place P. Mooney on your hand. Have him hold up the chain and say:

Here is a chain of many colors. Let's name the colors as I point to each chip. (Point) ***Red.*** (Pause) **Yes, this chip is red.**

Continue with the remaining seven colors. Each time, make sure the children know the color before you go on to the next. Afterwards, the puppet says:

Now let's play a listening game. I will say a word that rhymes with a color. Name the color for me. Let's try. What color sounds like *bed*? (Pause) **Yes, *red* sounds like *bed*.**

Continue with questions like those listed below. If the children have difficulty, lead them in naming the colors on your chain until they find the right one.

1. **What color rhymes with *mellow?***
2. **What color rhymes with *glue?***
3. **What color rhymes with *preen?***
4. **What color rhymes with *porange?***
5. **What color rhymes with *crown?***
6. **What color rhymes with *flack?***
7. **What color rhymes with *sight?***

VARIATION: To make the activity *harder,* have P. Mooney call on individuals to name other rhyming words for the class to match with the color chip chain.

107

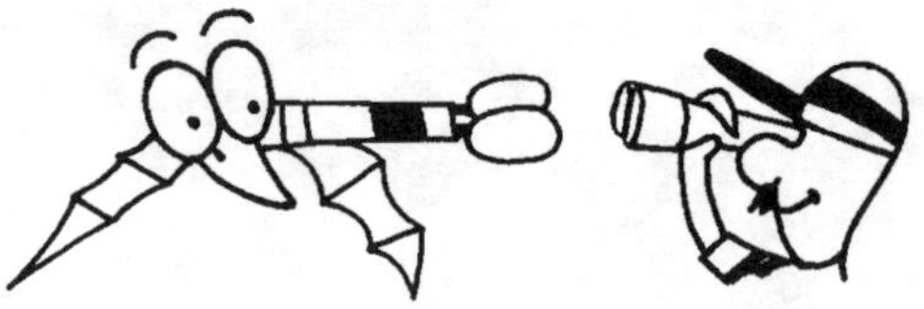

MATERIALS*

ACTIVITY 1

Cards

Animals

1-38

ACTIVITY 2

P. Mooney Stick

1 Focus: brainstorming animals that move in certain ways

Hold the 38 animal cards and say:

Animals move in many different ways. Some animals can fly. Use a sentence to name an animal that can *fly*, (Nathan).

The child should respond in a sentence like "A (butterfly) can fly" or "A (bird) flies." Continue with other children, encouraging them to think of as many flying animals as they can. As necessary, give clues and use the cards as cues. Then ask the class to name animals that move in each of these ways:

1. **hop**
2. **walk**
3. **crawl**
4. **swim**
5. **gallop**
6. **climb**

2 Focus: describing and pantomiming animal movements

Stand with the children. Hold the stick and say:

Let's move like animals. The P. Mooney stick will turn us into rabbits first. How do rabbits move?

Encourage the children to describe thoroughly how rabbits move. Then wave the stick as you say:

Eenie, Mooney,

Macaroony!

What are we today?

We are all hopping rabbits;

Now it's time to play!

Encourage the children to hop around the room. After a short while, "change" the children into an animal listed below, and have them imitate its movements. Repeat this procedure with each remaining animal.

1. **climbing squirrels**
2. **galloping horses**
3. **swimming goldfish**
4. **crawling bugs**
5. **flying butterflies**

End by waving the stick as you say:

Eenie, Mooney,

Macaroony!

Now let's be

You and me!

108

MATERIALS*

ACTIVITY 1

Cards
Stories
339-352

Display Board
6 ledges

ACTIVITY 2

P. Mooney Stick

1 Focus: identifying story cards of "How P. Mooney Got the P. Mooney Stick," and then retelling the story

Set up the board and ledges. Display the 14 story cards in random order.

Point to the cards on display as you say:

P. Mooney has a special stick. Today let's remember how he found it. But the story cards are out of order! (Point) **The story is all mixed up. I will read a sentence from the story. Then we will find the card that shows what is happening.**

After reading one of the sentences listed below, ask a child to find the corresponding card, to be placed in the upper left-hand corner of the board. The child should then tell the part of the story shown on the card. Continue, having the cards placed in left-to-right order.

1. **One day P. Mooney was flying around in his High Flyer and looking for forest fires.**
2. **He looked down and saw a poor little tree drooping all its branches.**
3. **He landed the High Flyer, got out, and looked carefully at the little tree.**
4. **He reached down into his P. Mooney bag and took out some wooden stakes to prop up the tree limbs.**
5. **He took his watering can and poured plenty of water around the roots of the tree.**
6. **Then he snipped a few branches from the older trees that were shading the young tree from the sun, so that the little tree could get plenty of sunlight.**
7. **Then he looked at the little tree. Already it seemed healthier.**
8. **When P. Mooney flew back to the forest, he looked down at the little tree, which now looked much better.**
9. **He visited the little tree and was delighted to see how much it had grown.**
10. **P. Mooney saw a very strange branch growing from the little tree's trunk.**
11. **Two weeks later, he visited the tree again and saw that the strange branch had grown much longer.**
12. **He was so excited when he saw that the little branch had a head just like his.**
13. **He reached down into his P. Mooney bag and pulled out a little saw. Very carefully, he sawed off the P. Mooney stick close to the trunk of the little tree.**
14. **P. Mooney thanked the little tree and said good-bye. He put his new P. Mooney stick over his shoulder and walked off through the forest, feeling very happy.**

2 Focus: identifying one's name from rhyming words in a P. Mooney-stick game

Stand with the children in a circle. Hold the stick and say:

We are going to use the P. Mooney stick to play a game. First let's practice the rhyme we will say:

> **(Betty), be nimble; (Betty), be quick.**
> **(Betty), jump over the P. Mooney stick.**

Practice the rhyme several times with the children before continuing:

Our game will be a little different this time we play it. Instead of saying your name in the rhyme, I will say a word that sounds like your name. Listen carefully, so you will know when to move. I will let (Betty) go first.

Lay the stick on the floor and lead the group in saying:

> **(Metty), be nimble; (Metty), be quick.**
>
> **(Metty), jump over the P. Mooney stick.**

Continue with rhymes for other children's names as the game is repeated. Use the names in random order, and continue until everyone has had a turn.

109

MATERIALS*

ACTIVITY 1

None

ACTIVITY 2

Cards

Music

324

Puppets

P. Mooney

Audiocassette 2

Side A, Song 1,

"I'm P. Mooney"

1 Focus: identifying things from riddles, and then describing the items

Say:

Let's play a guessing game. Listen to each clue and guess the answer. We will talk about the answer to each riddle.

Pause after each clue in the sets given below. When the answer is guessed, call on several children to describe the item in sentences.

1. **I am thinking about an animal that has two feet. . . . It has feathers. . . . It lives in nests and can fly.** (bird)
2. **I am thinking about an animal that has four feet and a long tail. . . . It has soft fur. . . . It purrs and says meow.** (cat)
3. **I am thinking about an animal that lives on land and in the water. . . . It is round and has a hard shell. . . . It has four short legs and moves very slowly.** (turtle)
4. **I am thinking about two pieces of clothing that look the same. . . . They are used when it rains or snows. . . . They keep your shoes and feet from getting wet.** (boots)
5. **I am thinking about a fruit that is round and usually red. . . . It is juicy and good to eat. . . . . It grows on a tree.** (apple)
6. **I am thinking about an animal that has feathers. . . . It has two feet and wings. . . . It lays eggs for us to eat.** (hen)
7. **I am thinking about two pieces of clothing that look the same. . . . You put them on when it's cold outside. . . . They keep your hands warm.** (mittens or gloves)
8. **I am thinking about something that is large and round. . . . It is orange. . . . You can make it into a jack-o'-lantern at Halloween.** (pumpkin)
9. **I am thinking about a person who colors his face. . . . He wears funny clothes and does tricks at the circus. . . . He makes people laugh.** (clown)
10. **I am thinking about something you can buy at the store. . . . It is small and wrapped in paper. . . . It should not be eaten but only chewed.** (chewing gum)
11. **I am thinking about something that is long and narrow. . . . It is sharp on one side. . . . You use it to cut your food into pieces.** (knife)
12. **I am thinking about a toy that is round. . . . It stretches and gets bigger. . . . It may break if you blow too much air into it.** (balloon)
13. **I am thinking about someone who is our friend. . . . He has a round nose. . . . He has a blue-and-red striped shirt.** (P. Mooney)

2 Focus: singing, acting out, and retelling the song "I'm P. Mooney"

Stand beside the audiocassette player, with the children standing before you. Place P. Mooney on your hand. He says:

Let's listen to my song again. As you listen, try to remember what my song tells you about me.

Refer to the music card as you play the song. Afterwards, have P. Mooney discuss the song's major points with the children. Repeat the recording several times, letting the puppet lead the children in singing and acting out the words.

110

MATERIALS*

ACTIVITY 1

Cards

Foods

99 100 103 108
109 110 114 116
121 125 127 128
132 133 134 136
137

ACTIVITY 2

Cards

Foods (optional)

(same as for Activity 1)

Music

332

Display Board (optional)

6 ledges (optional)

Audiocassette 2

Side B, Song 9, "Things That Go Together"

1 Focus: thinking and talking about how foods are eaten

Hold the 17 stacked food cards and say:

Sometimes we use our hands to hold the food we are eating, and sometimes we use knives, forks, and spoons. (Show card 100) **What would we use to eat cereal with milk on it?** (Encourage unison response) **Could we eat it with something other than a spoon?** (Pause) **What would happen if you used a fork (a knife or your hands) to eat cereal and milk?**

Call on volunteers to answer. Continue with the remaining cards.

2 Focus: singing the song "Things That Go Together" to name foods one likes

Say:

Let's sing "Things That Go Together." Think about what you like to eat. (Pause) **When I point to you during the song, name a food you like.**

Play the song (instrumental version) and point to four children in turn during the verse. Repeat with other children and a new selection of foods each time. Continue until everyone has had a turn.

VARIATION: To make the activity *easier,* place the food cards from Activity 1 on the board in groups of four for each verse.

111

MATERIALS*

ACTIVITY 1

Fruits & Vegetables
All fruits

P. Mooney Bag

ACTIVITY 2

Cards
Music
325

Fruits & Vegetables
2 apples
2 bananas
2 oranges
2 strawberries

Audiocassette 2
Side A, Song 2,
"The Is-Are Song"

1 Focus: naming fruits and remembering the sequence in which they were arranged

Put the fruits into the bag.

Wear the bag and say:

Please watch carefully as I take some fruits from the P. Mooney bag. We will name them together. Then you may whisper their names to yourself to help you remember them.

Place an apple, an orange, and a banana in a row on the floor in front of you. Have the fruits named in left-to-right order as seen by the group. Continue:

Now let's see if you are good detectives. While you are not looking, I will change around two of the fruits. See if you can tell which fruits were changed.

After the children cover their eyes with their hands, exchange the banana and the orange. Then ask the children to look again as you call on volunteers to tell what fruits were changed. Expand brief responses by saying, "Yes, the orange and the banana were changed around." Continue by having a child choose and arrange the fruits before another child changes their order.

VARIATION: To make the activity *harder,* use more than three fruits.

2 Focus: singing and acting out "The Is-Are Song" while naming fruits

Put the eight fruits on a table in front of you.

Stand beside the audiocassette player, with the children standing before you. Point to the fruits and say:

Let's sing about these fruits.

Play the song (instrumental version) and refer to the music card as you lead the children in singing the verses given below. Each time, hold up the right number of fruits and stress the verb forms and plurals.

1. **Apple is one;** (Hold up one apple)
   Apples are two. (Hold up two apples)
   I can bite an apple; can you?
   (All pretend to bite an apple)
2. **Banana is one;** (Hold up one banana)
   Bananas are two.
   (Hold up two bananas)
   I can peel a banana; can you?
   (All pretend to peel bananas)
3. **Orange is one;** (Hold up one orange)
   Oranges are two.
   (Hold up two oranges)
   I can squeeze an orange; can you?
   (All pretend to squeeze oranges)
4. **Strawberry is one;** (Hold up one strawberry)
   Strawberries are two.
   (Hold up two strawberries)
   I can pick strawberries; can you?
   (All pretend to pick strawberries)

Repeat, asking children to hold up the fruits for each verse. Continue as time and interest suggest.

112

MATERIALS*

ACTIVITY 1

Cards

Clothing (optional)

39 42 43 44 46 49
50 55 57 63 65 67

Display Board (optional)

6 ledges (optional)

ACTIVITY 2

None

1 Focus: identifying clothing from their descriptions in riddles using rhyming words, and then talking about the words

Say:

Let's play a listening-and-thinking game. After I say each riddle, I will give you the answer and a word that rhymes with it. You must tell me which word is the answer. Let's try. I am something in which you can carry money. Am I a *purse* or a *nurse?* (Pause) **Yes, I am a *purse.***

Each time, the children are to say the correct word in unison. Make sure the children understand both words by saying, "Yes, you know what a (purse) is, but what is a (nurse)? (Pause) That's right; a (nurse) is (someone who takes care of sick people)."

Suggested riddles:

1. **A girl would wear me under a dress. Am I a *lip* or a *slip?***
2. **I keep you warm when it's cold outside. Am I a *goat* or a *coat?***
3. **You wear me on your feet. Am I *socks* or a *box?***
4. **A girl would wear me with a skirt. Am I a *blouse* or a *mouse?***
5. **You wear me on your head. Am I a *map* or a *cap?***
6. **I keep you from getting too cool. Am I a *sweater* or a *letter?***
7. **I keep your feet dry in rain and snow. Am I your *suits* or your *boots?***
8. **A girl would wear me. Am I a *dress* or a *mess?***
9. **I keep your hands warm in winter. Am I your *mittens* or your *kittens?***
10. **You wear me on your finger. Am I a *wing* or a *ring?***
11. **You like to wear me when you play. Am I *beans* or *jeans?***

VARIATION: To make the activity *easier,* display the 12 clothing cards as you present the riddles.

2 Focus: imagining, talking about, and acting out wearing clothes

Stand with the children and say:

Let's imagine what it would be like if we put on our clothes the wrong way. What would happen if we put both legs into just one leg of our pants? (Encourage individual responses) **Show me how you would walk if you had both legs in one pants leg.**

When the children have done so, continue with the situations listed below. In each case, the children should discuss how they would look and feel before showing you how they would move.

1. **shoes worn backwards**
2. **cap worn over eyes**
3. **shoes tied together**
4. **arms inside shirt**
5. **jacket on backwards with hood pulled up**
6. **high-heeled shoes on the wrong feet**

113

MATERIALS*

ACTIVITY 1

Display Board
4 ledges

Magnetic Shapes
20 large
20 small

ACTIVITY 2

Cards
Music
334

Magnetic Shapes
20 large

Audiocassette 2
Side B, Song 11,
"Find That Shape"

1 Focus: classifying magnetic shapes by shape or color

Set up the board and use the ledges to make a large square in the center, like this:

Ask two children who need the experience to go to the board and arrange the 40 shapes outside the square.

Say:

Let's see how fast you can find the shapes I ask you to get. Put them inside this square. (Point) **Find all the (circles), (Doris and Randy).**

When all the correct shapes are inside the square, say, "Tell us what you found, (Doris and Randy)." The children should each respond in a sentence such as "I found all the (circles)." Then let them choose two other children, and repeat the procedure, using these commands:

1. **Find all the *squares*.**
2. **Find all the *triangles*.**
3. **Find all the *rectangles*.**
4. **Find all the *red shapes*.**
5. **Find all the *blue shapes*.**
6. **Find all the *yellow shapes*.**
7. **Find all the *green shapes*.**
8. **Find all the *black shapes*.**

Continue until everyone has had a turn.

2 Focus: singing and acting out the song "Find That Shape"

Have the children stand in a large circle. Ask two children to spread out the shapes on the floor inside the circle. Say:

Let's take turns finding shapes as we sing a new song. When it is your turn, find the shapes that are asked for in the song and hold them up.

Invite five children to stand inside the circle. Play the song and refer to the music card as you lead the children in singing the four verses. As the song progresses, check to be sure that the five children in the center each find and hold up the correct shape for each verse. Repeat the song with other groups of five. Continue until everyone has had a turn.

114

MATERIALS*

ACTIVITY 1

Cards

Household Items

154 161 162 164
165 169 173 176
179 183 188 189
192 196

Display Board

6 ledges

Puppets

Zoey

Thinking hat

ACTIVITY 2

None

1 Focus: identifying household items from descriptions of color and function

Display the 14 household cards on the ledges of the board.

Place Zoey (wearing her thinking hat) on your hand. She says:

Let's solve some riddles about things found in a house. I will give you two clues about a household item. The first clue will be its color; the second clue will be how it is used. When I call on you, please name the household item in a sentence and point to its card.

Zoey should use these statements:

1. **I am thinking of something red.** (Pause) **It is used when we cook soup.** (saucepan)
2. **I am thinking of something in a blue container.** (Pause) **We use it to blow our nose.** (facial tissues)
3. **I am thinking of something red.** (Pause) **It plays music.** (radio)
4. **I am thinking of something orange.** (Pause) **Two or three people could sit on it.** (couch)
5. **I am thinking of something green.** (Pause) **We use it to carry water.** (pail)
6. **I am thinking of something blue.** (Pause) **We sleep on it.** (bed)
7. **I am thinking of something orange.** (Pause) **We sit at it to eat breakfast.** (kitchen table)
8. **I am thinking of something green.** (Pause) **We use it when we iron clothes.** (ironing board)
9. **I am thinking of something yellow.** (Pause) **It holds beans while they are baking.** (baking dish)
10. **I am thinking of something in a red-and-white tube.** (Pause) **We use it when we brush our teeth.** (toothpaste)
11. **I am thinking of something green.** (Pause) **We use it when we wash the dishes.** (kitchen sink)
12. **I am thinking of something blue.** (Pause) **We use it to comb our hair.** (comb)
13. **I am thinking of something yellow.** (Pause) **We use it when we bake cookies, boil water, roast turkeys, and cook many other foods.** (stove)
14. **I am thinking of something green.** (Pause) **We use it to pick up dust after we sweep.** (dustpan)

2 Focus: identifying pantomimed household items

Say:

Please watch as I pretend to use something you might have at home.

As you pantomime sweeping with a broom, ask:

What am I doing? (Encourage children to respond in sentences)

Yes, I am (sweeping with a broom). Let's do it together.

Continue with these actions:

1. **combing hair**
2. **drinking from a cup and saucer**
3. **ironing on an ironing board**
4. **mopping the floor**
5. **talking on the telephone**
6. **taking a bubble bath**
7. **watching television**
8. **brushing teeth**
9. **washing dishes in the kitchen sink**
10. **cutting cloth with scissors**
11. **dancing to a record on the record player**
12. **scrubbing the floor with the scrub brush and pail**

Continue by having the children take turns doing their own pantomimes for the group to identify. Help as necessary.

115

MATERIALS*

ACTIVITY 1

Cards

Numerals & Color Shapes

314-323

Color Chips

Container

I set of 8 colors per child

I set of 8 colors for self

P. Mooney Bag

ACTIVITY 2

Cards

Music

334

Color Chips

Container

1 set of 8 colors per child

Audiocassette 2

Side B, Song 11, "Find That Shape"

1 Focus: naming and matching colors in the game Color Bingo

Put your eight chips into the bag.

Have the children sit in pairs on the floor before you, and hand out one set of eight chips, all colors, to each child. Give each pair one of the number cards and have them name the colors on their cards. Then hold the bag and say:

Let's play a game called Color Bingo. I will show you a chip from the P. Mooney bag. Name the color of the chip, and then look on your card to see if it has the same color. If so, take your matching chips and place them upon that color on the card. We will see whose card first has two chips on every color. When you have matched all four colors, say, "Bingo!"

Hold up a color chip from the bag and check to see that the children respond correctly. Continue until one pair has two chips on each of a card's four colors. Ask each child of the pair to name the colors. Then have all the children exchange cards, and repeat the game. When the children understand the game, have the winners take turns holding up chips for the group. Continue as time and interest suggest.

2 Focus: singing and acting out the song "Find That Color"

Give each child a set of eight chips, all colors.

Ask the children to sit in a circle. Have them place their chips on the floor in front of them. Say:

Let's sing a song about finding colors. Please listen carefully and hold up the color chip you are asked to find. I will go through the song the first time. Then we will do it together.

Play the song (instrumental version) and refer to the music card as you sing this verse:

Find yellow, find yellow.
(Hold up yellow chip)

Can you find the color yellow?

Find yellow; find yellow.

Can you find that color?

Invite the children to join you as you repeat the verse. Continue with other verses, using the remaining colors: black, blue, brown, green, orange, red, and white. Once the children know the song, let them take turns choosing the color for each verse. Repeat as time and interest suggest.

116

MATERIALS*

ACTIVITY 1

Cards

Stories

353-368

ACTIVITY 2

Cards

Stories

(same as for Activity 1)

Display Board

6 ledges

1 Focus: retelling the story "P. Mooney and Mr. Nobody"

Hold the 16 story cards and say:

One of our stories is about someone who could not be seen when P. Mooney first met him. What is his name? (Encourage unison response) **Yes, his name is Mr. Nobody. Let's look at the story cards and tell his story. Then we will talk about it together.**

Show the cards in sequence one by one as the children take turns describing the action shown. Then lead the discussion with questions like these:

1. **What was P. Mooney doing when he met Mr. Nobody?**
2. **What were some things that happened to Mr. Nobody when people could not see him?**
3. **How did P. Mooney help Mr. Nobody?**
4. **What happened when Mr. Nobody said nice things about himself?**
5. **How do you think Mr. Nobody felt after P. Mooney helped him?**

2 Focus: talking about the story "P. Mooney and Mr. Nobody," and sequencing the story cards

Display the 16 story cards in random order on the board ledges.

Ask:

What do you think Mr. Nobody would be doing now if P. Mooney had not come along to help him?

Accept all suggestions, making comments such as "Yes, that could have happened!" Then ask:

What did P. Mooney have in his bag that could help Mr. Nobody? (Encourage unison response) **Yes, he had the special book of P. Mooney magic.**

Place card 360 on the upper left ledge of the board, moving the other cards if necessary. Then say:

When P. Mooney shared his P. Mooney magic, Mr. Nobody began to appear. Let's look at the other cards and put them in the right order.

Help as necessary with questions such as "What body part began to show first?" and "After Mr. Nobody's hands appeared, what body part began to show next?" Call on volunteers to answer in sentences such as "Then Mr. Nobody's (body) appeared." As the cards are chosen, have them placed on the board in left-to-right order as seen by the group. Continue until the sequence is complete.

117 

MATERIALS*

ACTIVITY 1

None

ACTIVITY 2

Cards

Music

332

Audiocassette 2

Side B, Song 9, "Things That Go Together"

1 Focus: imagining and talking about being invisible

Ask the children to sit before you. Say:

Before Mr. Nobody met P. Mooney, he was invisible. Let's close our eyes and think what it would be like if no one could see us. (Pause) **What are some things that you might do if you could not be seen?**

Encourage discussion, and comment on imaginative responses. Then say:

Now let's pretend that Mr. Nobody is still invisible.

Stimulate discussion with questions like these:

1. **What would happen if Mr. Nobody came to dinner at your house?**
2. **How would we be able to play games with Mr. Nobody?**
3. **If Mr. Nobody needed help, how would we find out?**
4. **How could we make Mr. Nobody feel that he was part of our group?**
5. **How would we know when Mr. Nobody was sad (or happy)?**

Conclude with discussion of these questions:

Mr. Nobody did not like it when no one could see him. Would you like being invisible? Why or why not?

2 Focus: singing the song "Things That Go Together" while naming and doing actions

With the children gathered around you, say:

Let's do some actions with our bodies. Watch me and do what I do. (Turn around) **What did we do?** (Pause) **Yes, we turned around.**

Have the children imitate and then name together the following actions: turn, clap, twist, wave. Then play the song (instrumental version) and refer to the music card as you lead the children in doing the actions and singing this verse:

1. **There are things that go together,**
   Belong together.
   There are things that go together
   In a group like this:
   Turn, clap, twist, wave.
   There are things that go together,
   And they are ACTIONS!

Continue as above with verses about these groups of actions:

2. **kneel, stretch, bend, jump**
3. **hop, slide, reach, shake**

118

MATERIALS*

ACTIVITY 1

Cards

Vehicles

267 268 270 272
273 274 275 276
279 280 282

Display Board

6 ledges

Audiocassette 3

Side B, Selection 3, "Sounds of Vehicles"

ACTIVITY 2

Cards

Vehicles

267* 268* 269 270*
271 272* 273* 274*
275* 276* 277 278
279* 280* 281 282*
283

Display Board

6 ledges

Puppets

Zoey

Thinking hat

1 Focus: listening to the "Sounds of Vehicles," and then identifying each one

Display the 11 transportation cards on the board.

Review the card labels with the children. Then say:

Sometimes we can recognize a way to travel by hearing its sound. Let's listen to some new sound effects made by vehicles. Try to figure out which one makes the sound you hear.

Play the sound effects, one sound at a time. Stop after each sound and have the children talk about what could make it. When the group identifies the sound correctly, invite a child to point to the corresponding card. Remove the cards and play the sound effects again, in random order. This time, volunteers should identify the vehicle by saying, "I heard an (airplane)." If a child has difficulty, repeat the sound. Continue until everyone has had a turn.

2 Focus: thinking and talking about vehicles appropriate for different trips

Display transportation cards 267 through 278. Stack cards 279 through 283.

Have Zoey (wearing her thinking hat) within reach. Hold the stacked cards on your lap. Say:

Zoey is going to do some traveling. You are to take turns pretending to be Zoey and deciding what vehicle to use.

Let volunteers respond through Zoey. Accept all feasible answers for each of the situations listed below. When a vehicle is chosen, ask the children to give their reasons for choosing it.

1. **The first place Zoey plans to visit is the moon. What vehicle should she use?** (space capsule)
2. **Zoey wants to go fishing in the middle of the lake. How could she get there?** (rowboat)
3. **P. Mooney and Zoey are going camping. What should they use to go on their trip?** (camping trailer)
4. **Zoey wants to ride to school with all of you. How will you go?** (school bus)
5. **Zoey has a very sick friend who needs to get to the hospital right away. Which vehicle is right for this job?** (ambulance)

Remove the cards chosen for the first five trips, and display the stacked cards. Continue as before.

6. **Zoey is planning to go to the library. Tell me all the ways she could get there.** (bicycle, bus, car, etc.)
7. **Zoey is planning to go across the ocean to Africa to do some exploring. Can you help her decide how to get there?** (jet, ship)
8. **Zoey must get to a fire as fast as she can. How can she get there fast?** (police car, fire truck)
9. **Zoey wants to go to a faraway country very fast. How could she get there?** (jet)
10. **Zoey wants to help deliver the mail. What vehicle would be right for this job?** (mail truck)
11. **Zoey wants to be able to look down on the tops of trees. What vehicle should Zoey use?** (jet, helicopter)
12. **Zoey has just bought a new refrigerator, and needs to go to the store and get it. What vehicle should she use?** (pick-up truck)
13. **P. Mooney's Rock Roller has broken down, and Zoey wants to help him move it to a service station. What vehicle could do this job?** (tow truck)
14. **Zoey would like to take a trip across the country. Tell me all the ways Zoey could do this.** (train, jet, car, bus, etc.)

End by placing Zoey on your hand and having her thank the children for their help.

119

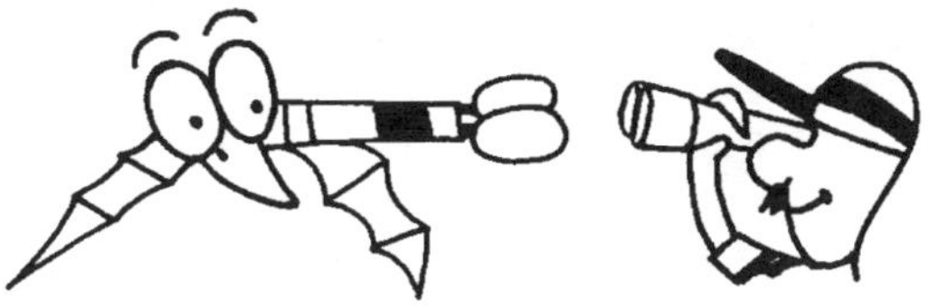

MATERIALS*

ACTIVITY 1

None

ACTIVITY 2

None

1 Focus: imagining and talking about trips and vehicles in which to travel

Say:

Let's pretend that we can go wherever we want and that we can choose any vehicle to take us there. I would like to travel (to a faraway island by ship). Where would you go and what vehicle would you use, (Eileen)?

Call on other children in turn to answer in sentences. Encourage them to discuss their wishes in detail. Help as necessary, and continue until everyone has had a turn.

VARIATION: To make the activity *easier,* have each child name only a destination or a means of transportation.

2 Focus: pantomiming movements of vehicles

Stand with the children and say:

Let's pretend that we are riding in some vehicles. First we will travel in a police car.

Invite the children to pretend they are driving police cars. They may imitate police sirens or pretend to talk over a two-way radio. Continue with such vehicles as these:

1. **helicopter — rotate one arm above head while moving; make chop-chop noises**
2. **airplane — hold arms out on sides while moving; make zooming noises**
3. **bicycle — pretend to hold handlebars while moving; imitate bicycle bell**
4. **rowboat — sit on floor, extend arms, and pretend to row**
5. **train — stand with clenched fists and move arms in circles at sides; make chugging noises**

120

MATERIALS*

ACTIVITY 1

Display Board
4 ledges

P. Mooney Stick

Poster 6

ACTIVITY 2

Cards
Pictures from Several Categories
8 12 40 47 114
149 161 180 202
203 207 229 251
262 267 269 282

Display Board
4 ledges

P. Mooney Bag

Poster 6

1 Focus: naming items on the poster "Town in Fall," and talking about the season

Use the ledges to fasten the poster to the board.

Hold the stick and point to the poster as you say:

P. Mooney's magic stick is going to send us on a visit to this town. Let's go!

Wave the stick and say:

Mooney Magic, zing and zip!

Take us on a Mooney trip!

Set the stick aside and continue:

Now that we are in the town, let's talk about what is here. Please tell us in a sentence about something you see, (Salvatore). (Pause) **Yes, (that little girl lost her balloon).**

Have each child use a sentence to name something on the poster. Encourage a variety of choices. If no one notices P. Mooney on the poster, ask the children to look for him there. Conclude with discussion of these questions:

1. **What do you think is the most interesting thing in this town?**
2. **What season of the year is it in this town? How can you tell?**

2 Focus: naming, matching, and comparing picture cards with items in the poster "Town in Fall"

Leave the poster from Activity 1 on display. Put the 17 picture cards into the bag.

With the children still seated before the poster, wear the bag and say:

P. Mooney's bag is full of pictures. Let's see if we can match them with some things on the poster.

The child you call on should select a card and identify it in a sentence such as "This is a (cat)" before finding a matching poster item and saying, "Here is another (cat)." Lead group discussion of how the two items are the same and how they are different. Repeat this procedure with each of the remaining cards.

Keep in Mind...
After each lesson in the program, individuals who have difficulty demonstrating proficiency in the skills you consider appropriate and important for them to learn should be tutored. Aides could help you with this task.

121

MATERIALS*

ACTIVITY 1

Display Board
4 ledges

Poster 6

ACTIVITY 2

Cards
Music
331

Display Board
4 ledges

Poster 6

Audiocassette 2
Side B, Song 8,
"Today, Yesterday, and Tomorrow"

1 Focus: classifying and describing people doing activities on the poster "Town in Fall"

Use the ledges to fasten the poster to the board.

Point to the poster and say:

Look at the people in this town. The ones who are working are called workers. Let's take turns finding *workers* and talking about what kind of work they are doing.

Volunteers may then point out and describe working people by saying, "Here is a worker. This worker is (washing the window)." When all workers have been identified, have the children look for and describe these people:

1. ***riders*— people who are riding**
2. ***climbers*— people who are climbing**
3. ***buyers*— people who are buying**
4. ***walkers*— people who are walking**
5. ***flyers*— people who are flying**
6. ***players*— people who are playing**
7. ***drivers*— people who are driving**
8. ***sellers*— people who are selling**

2 Focus: singing, chanting, and acting out the song "Today, Yesterday, and Tomorrow"

Leave the poster from Activity 1 on display

Stand beside the audiocassette player, with the children standing before you. Say:

Let's sing as we do some of the actions you see on the poster.

Play the song (instrumental version) and refer to the music card as you lead the children in singing these verses with regular verbs:

1. **Today I walk. Yesterday I walked.**
   Tomorrow I will walk.
   Today I walk. Yesterday I walked.
   Tomorrow I will walk.
   Walk! Walked! Will walk!
   (After these verbs are chanted, walk in place)
2. **Climb! Climbed! Will climb!**
   (After these verbs are chanted, move arms and legs as if climbing)
3. **Play! Played! Will play!**
   (After these verbs are chanted, pretend to bounce a ball)

Stop the music and review the irregular verb forms with the children, like this:

If we went for a *ride* yesterday, we would say that yesterday we . . . what? (Pause) **Yes, yesterday we *rode*. If we decide to go for a ride tomorrow, we say that tomorrow we . . . what?** (Pause) **Yes, tomorrow we *will ride*.**

Play the song and continue with these verbs:

4. **Ride! Rode! Will ride!**
   (Pretend to ride a bike)
5. **Buy! Bought! Will buy!**
   (Pretend to give money and ake goods)
6. **Fly! Flew! Will fly!** (Pretend to fly)
7. **Drive! Drove! Will drive!**
   (Pretend to drive a car)
8. **Sell! Sold! Will sell!**
   (Pretend to take money and give goods)

Stress the verb forms as you repeat the song and actions with the children. Continue as time and interest suggest.

122

MATERIALS*

ACTIVITY 1

Audiocassette 3

Side B, Selection 1,

"Sounds of People - Voices"

ACTIVITY 2

Cards

Music

333

Audiocassette 2

Side B, Song 10,

"Make a Sound"

1 Focus: listening to "Sounds of People — Voices," and imagining and talking about the people

Say:

When we hear people's voices, we can sometimes guess what they might look like and what they might be doing. Let's listen to some voices now. After each one, I will ask you some questions.

Play the sound effects. For each voice, call on volunteers to answer these questions:

1. **What did that person say?**
2. **Who might that person be?**
3. **Was that a (man or woman /boy or girl) speaking?**
4. **How old do you think that person is?**
5. **What do you think that person might look like?**
6. **What do you think that person might be doing?**

Continue until all voices have been discussed.

2 Focus: brainstorming ways one uses one's voice, and then singing and acting out the song "Make a Sound"

Hold the music card and say:

People use their voices to speak. What else can we do with our voices?

Lead the children in thinking of ways they use their voices. If no one mentions singing, suggest it. Then continue:

Let's use our voices to sing. Please listen to this song again and sing it with me.

Play the song and refer to the music card as you lead the children in singing the four verses. Repeat the song as time and interest suggest. Each time the song is repeated, ask a child or a pair of children to lead the group.

123

MATERIALS*

ACTIVITY 1

Cards

People

200 201 203 206
207 208 210 212
213 216 217

Display Board

6 ledges

Puppets

Zoey

Thinking hat

ACTIVITY 2

Cards

Toys

248

Music

335

Audiocassette 2

Side B, Song 12,
"Rhythm Walk"

1 Focus: identifying workers from their descriptions in riddles, and then talking about workers

Display the 11 people cards on the board.

Place Zoey (wearing her thinking hat) on your hand and have her say:

Hello! What hat am I wearing today? (Encourage unison response) **Yes, I am wearing my thinking hat, because my job today is thinking.** (Point to board) **These people wear special clothes when they are working, too. Let's play a thinking game. Here are some riddles about the people whose pictures you see. Try to figure out whom I am describing.**

Have Zoey give the following sets of clues, pausing after each clue to give the children time to think. After each riddle has been solved, ask several children to talk about people they know who do that kind of work.

1. **I have a white uniform. . . . I help people when they don't feel well. . . . I work with a doctor. . . . Who am I?** (nurse)
2. **I am wearing a hat. . . . I wear a big badge. . . . have a car with a light on top and a two-way radio. . . Who am I?** (police officer)
3. **I wear a blue uniform. . . . I carry a big bag full of things. . . . Who am I?** (mail carrier)
4. **I am wearing gloves. . . . People think that I look funny. . . . Who am I?** (clown)
5. **I am wearing a yellow shirt. . . . When people come to see me, they sit in a chair that goes up and down and around- . . . I use scissors when I work. . . . Who am I?** (barber)
6. **I wear a helmet when I work. . . . My suit covers every part of me. . . . Who am I?** (astronaut)
7. **I am wearing a white shirt. . . . I use a special light to help me see what I am doing when I work. . . . Who am I?** (dentist)
8. **I wear an apron. . . . I sell things to people. . . . Who am I?** (grocer)
9. **I wear boots when I am working. . . . A special coat helps keep me dry because I use a lot of water. . Who am I?** (fire fighter)
10. **I like to wear bright colors so you can see me when I am far away. . . . I use a swing when I am working. . . . Who am I?** (acrobat)
11. **I often wear a white coat when I work. . . . When you don't feel well, you might come to see me. . . . I work in an office and a hospital. . . . Who am I?** (doctor)

2 Focus: talking about robots, and then pantomiming robots to the music "Rhythm Walk"

Hold the toy card and ask:

What is a robot? (Pause) **Yes, a robot is a machine that can do many of the things that people can do. Robots can walk and talk. Sometimes we play with robots and sometimes they work for us. Let's think about different ways robots can work.**

Encourage the children to think of and discuss many kinds of work that robots might do, such as these:

1. **guiding and controlling traffic, airplanes, ships, cars**
2. **collecting and sending information by telephone**
3. **building cars on an assembly line**
4. **cleaning houses and factories**
5. **handling and lifting dangerous materials**
6. **testing soil on faraway planets like Mars**

7. **entertaining people on television and in movies**
8. **washing clothes and dishes**

Ask the children to stand. Continue:

Let's pretend that we are robots and move as they do. I will show you how I think a robot moves.

Demonstrate like this: bend your arms up at the elbows, keep your knees stiff as you move forward by shuffling your feet rapidly, and move your arms back and forth slowly. Then play the music as the children imitate robots. Encourage them to move their feet in time with the music.

124

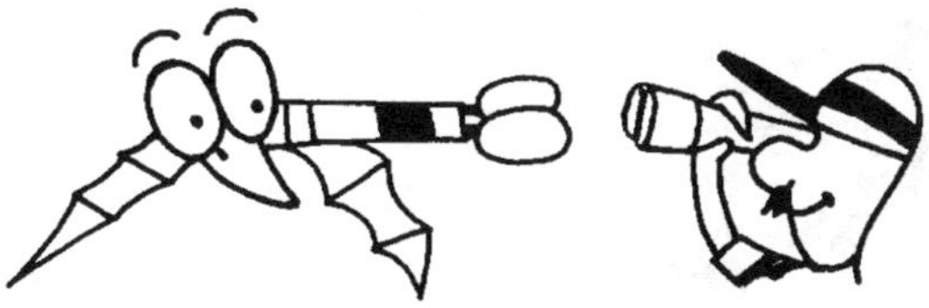

MATERIALS*

ACTIVITY 1

Cards
Stories
451-463

Audiocassette 1
Side B, Story 8,
"P. Mooney and the Gasless Goose"

ACTIVITY 2

None

1 Focus: listening to the story "P. Mooney and the Gasless Goose"

Hold the 13 story cards on your lap and say:

Today you are going to hear a new story. It is about a friend of P. Mooney's called Gasless Goose.

Play the story. During the narration, show the story cards in turn as you scan the printed copy on the back of each picture. After showing each card, lay it facedown in a pile on your lap.

2 Focus: talking about interesting words in the story "P. Mooney and the Gasless Goose"

Say:

The Gasless Goose story has a lot of interesting words in it. Let's talk about some you may not know.

Stress the italicized words as you read aloud the following parts of the story. Comment on the children's definitions, helping as necessary. When possible, allow the children to act out the words or phrases.

1. **"P. Mooney went *strolling* along Gander Bay."** (question) **What do you do when you go strolling?**
2. **"A bit of *sightseeing* seemed proper to do."** (question) **What are you doing when you are sightseeing?**
3. **". . . he'd been careful to pack a P. Mooney gadget deep down in his *sack*."** (question) **How would you pack a sack?**
4. **"*Binocular goggles* of yellow and green."** (question) **What are binocular goggles?**
5. **"And why does he stand on that tree *limb* and sigh?"** (question) **What is a tree limb?**
6. **"He *flipped* a few times and then crashed on a rock."** (question) **How would you flip?**
7. **"And 'Gangway!' he yelled as he *pedaled* away."** (question) **When you are pedaling, what are you doing?**
8. **"'Fill 'er up!' said the goose with a honk loud and *shrill*."** (question) **What is a shrill sound like?**

125

MATERIALS*

ACTIVITY 1

Color chips

5 per half the class

15 per half the class

20 for self

Teacher provides

1 envelope per child

ACTIVITY 2

Color Chips

5 per half the class

15 per half the class

20 for self

1 Focus: linking chips to make long and short "snakes," and then sorting them by length

Put five chips into each envelope for the children in half your class. Put 15 chips into each envelope for the other children. Make yourself two chains of five and 15 chips, respectively.

Sit in a circle with the children. On the floor near the center, place your chains about three feet (one meter) apart. Arrange the chains to resemble "wiggly snakes," like this:

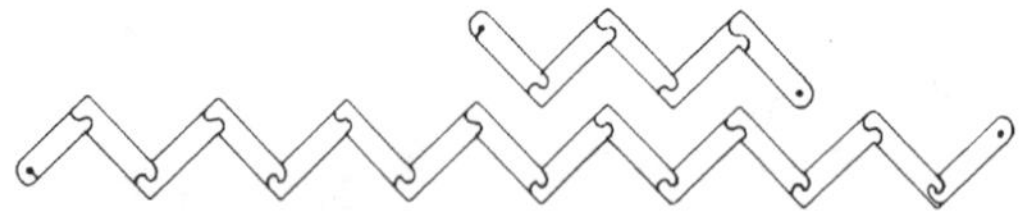

Point to them and say:

Let's pretend that these chains are wiggly snakes. How are they different from each other, (Norma)? (Pause) **Yes! They are different colors and different sizes. One is long, and the other is short. Show me the long "snake," (Victor).** (Pause) **Yes! Which is the short "snake," (Queenie)?** (Pause) **Very good. Now you may each make your own "snake."**

Give an envelope to each child and have them link their chips together. When the chains are complete, the children are to take turns guessing whether their "snakes" are long or short before placing them next to the "snake" that is the same length on the floor. Each child should describe her or his chain by saying, "My snake is long" or "This snake is short." Continue until everyone has had a turn. Conclude by having the children make two chains, one longer than the other, by linking the short chains together and the long chains together.

2 Focus: following directions about color chip chains while stressing positional words and *long* and *short*

Place the two chains from Activity 1 about 10 feet (three meters) apart on the floor.

Have the children line up in single file, with the leader facing the chains. Say:

Let's use these two "snakes" to play a following-directions game. Please listen carefully to each direction, so you will know what to do.

Give commands such as those listed below, and check to make sure that the children respond correctly. After each response, lead the children in chanting together, "We walked *between* the snakes,"' "We jumped *around* the short 'snake,"' and so on. Change the leader occasionally.

1. **Walk *between* the "snakes."**
2. **Jump *around* the short "snake."**
3. **Jump *over* the long "snake."**
4. **Walk *beside* the long "snake."**
5. **Tiptoe *around* the short "snake."**
6. **Hop *between* the "snakes."**
7. **Step *over* the long "snake."**
8. **Walk *beside* the short "snake."**

Continue as time and interest permit.

126 

MATERIALS*

ACTIVITY 1

Cards

Animal

1 8 11 19
25 26 27 30
33 34 37 38

Display Board

6 ledges

ACTIVITY 2

Cards

Animals

25*

1 Focus: naming animals, and then classifying them by where they might live

Display the 12 animal cards on the board.

Point to the cards on display and say:

Let's name all these animals and talk about where they might live.

When the animals have been named, ask:

Would these animals all live together? (Pause) **You are right. These animals would live in many different places. I will ask you some questions about where each of them might live.**

Continue by asking the questions listed below. The children should answer in sentences such as "A (squirrel) lives in a (tree)" or "A (spider) might live in a (barn)." Accept all feasible answers.

Which animal(s) might live . . .

1. in a tree?

2. in a barn?

3. in a cave?

4. in a house?

5. in a pond?

6. in a zoo?

7. in the ground?

Conclude by asking the children to think of other places where animals might live.

2 Focus: saying and acting out a counting rhyme about lions

Stand with the children. Hold up card 25 and ask:

Where do we usually go to see lions like this one? (Encourage unison response) **Let's say a rhyme about going to the zoo to visit the lions. I will go through it for you the first time. Then we will do it together.**

Set the card aside. Say the following rhyme* with gestures. Then invite the children to join you in repeating it.

One, two;
Off to the zoo!
(March in place)
Three, four;
Lions roar!
(Stop and roar)
Five, six;
We're in a fix!
(Huddle and shake with fear)
Seven, eight;
Run for the gate!
(Run in place)
Nine, ten;
Let's go again!
(March in place)

Repeat as long as time and interest suggest.

**NOTE:*
This rhyme is by Sharon Holland.

127

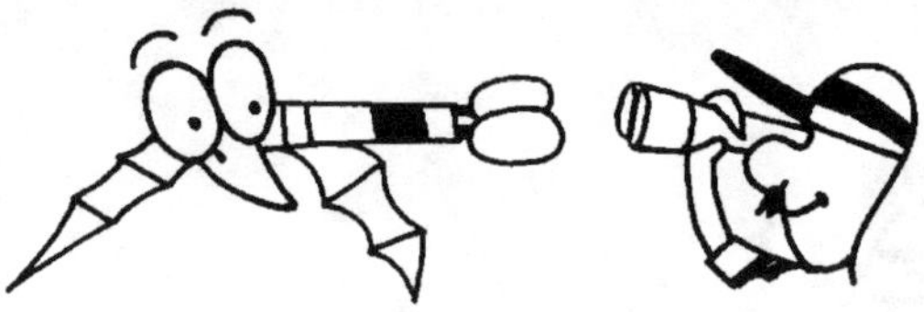

MATERIALS*

ACTIVITY 1

Cards

Stories

451-463

Audiocassette 1

Side B, Story 8,

"P. Mooney and the Gasless Goose"

ACTIVITY 2

None

1 Focus: listening to the story "P. Mooney and the Gasless Goose," and then talking about rhyming and defining rhyming words from the story

Hold the 13 story cards and say:

Let's listen again to the story of how P. Mooney helped the Gasless Goose.

Play the story. During the narration, show the story cards in turn as you scan the printed copy on the back of each picture. After showing each card, lay it facedown in a pile on your lap. Say:

The Gasless Goose story sounds different from the other stories we have heard. How is it different?

If no one mentions that the story is rhymed, point this out by saying:

The story about Gasless Goose is a poem, because many words in the story sound the same. When words sound alike, we say that they *rhyme.* All words that sound alike are called *rhyming words.* Let's take some words from the story and tell what they mean. Then we will think of other words that sound the same.

Call on children to define each of the words listed below. If necessary, give a definition before the children take turns thinking of rhymes for the word. Accept all rhyming words, real and nonsensical.

1. sack
2. tree
3. wings
4. game
5. stump
6. rock
7. gas
8. thunder
9. pipes
10. bill

2 Focus: pantomiming parts of the story "P. Mooney and the Gasless Goose"

Have the children stand several feet apart from each other. Say:

Let's pretend to be P. Mooney and Gasless Goose as we act out what they did in the story.

Give the children time to act out each of these situations:

1. **Pretend that you are P. Mooney gazing around through goggles.**
2. **Pretend that you are a strange goose standing on the end of a tree limb and trying to fly.**
3. **Pretend that you are P. Mooney pedaling your Chaincycle on the way to help Gasless Goose.**
4. **Pretend that you are P. Mooney reaching deep down inside the P. Mooney bag and searching for goose gas.**
5. **Pretend that you are Gasless Goose with the Flying Machine, and fly away into the distance.**

128

MATERIALS*

ACTIVITY 1

Display Board
4 ledges

Poster 3

ACTIVITY 2

None

1 Focus: thinking about "who might say that" on the poster "Department Store"

Use the ledges to display the poster on the board.

Point to the poster and say:

If we were to visit this department store, we would hear people talking. Let's play a game called Who Might Say That? As I say a sentence, please look at the poster and decide what person or animal might be speaking. Here's the first sentence: "If we fly around once more, I will be dizzy." Who might say that, (Daniel)? (Pause) **Yes, a girl riding in one of the toy airplanes might say that. Tell us why you think so.**

(Daniel) should point out and describe (his) choice while explaining it. Continue in this way with the sentences below. Give clues, if necessary.

1. **"When you go up, I come down."**
2. **"Look at yourself in the mirror; do you like the way you look wearing your new coat?"**
3. **"Daddy, I need a new pair of shoes."**
4. **"Mommy, may I have this book?"**
5. **"Look how fast that red car goes!"**
6. **"Look, I am hanging upside down!"**
7. **"I don't think this pail will hold any more sand."**
8. **"Mama, I want to look at those drums."**
9. **"Around and around I go."**
10. **"Jumping is fun."**
11. **"Mother, may I get in the red car and try to drive it?"**
12. **"Look how fast I slide down."**
13. **"I like this orange coat. It fits just right."**
14. **"I will have a chocolate soda, please."**
15. **"Open the door and let me come in, too."**

2 Focus: evaluating the classification of items in a following-directions game that stresses *if* and *then*

Ask the children to stand before you. Say:

Now let's play a following-directions game. I will give you a direction in a sentence containing the words *if* and *then*. If the first part of my sentence is *true*, follow the direction. If the first part of the sentence is *not true*, don't move. Let's begin.

Give directions like those listed below. Each time, check to see that the children have responded correctly before you proceed. After each command, the children should describe their response in a sentence such as "We clapped our hands" or "We did not stamp our feet."

1. ***If* a doll and a drum are both toys, *then* clap your hands.**
2. ***If* a boy and a woman are both people, *then* turn around.**
3. ***If* a coat and a car are both clothes, *then* stamp your feet.**
4. ***If* a robot and a raincoat are both clothes, *then* jump up.**
5. ***If* a seesaw and a slide are both toys, *then* blink your eyes.**
6. ***If* a jump rope and ice cream are both food, *then* clap your hands.**
7. ***If* a bicycle and a balloon are both toys, *then* jump up.**
8. ***If* an airplane and a toy are both ways to travel, *then* turn around.**
9. ***If* a chair and a stool are both furniture, *then* stamp your feet.**
10. ***If* a baby and a dog are both people, *then* blink your eyes.**

VARIATION: To make the activity *harder,* give the children two commands at once.

129

MATERIALS*

ACTIVITY 1

Cards

Toys

226 228 230 229
233 236 237 240
242 243 244 245

Display Board

6 ledges

ACTIVITY 2

Cards

Music

337

Audiocassette 2

Side B, Song 14, "Rag March"

1 Focus: identifying toys from their descriptions in riddles, and then describing the toys

Set up the board with ledges and display the 12 toy cards.

Say:

Today let's play a detective game and take turns being detectives. I will ask a riddle about one of these toys. (Point to board) If you think you know the answer, you may tell us in a sentence which toy I mean.

Pause between clues as you ask the following riddles, one at a time. After each, a child is to answer with a sentence such as "That toy is a *drum.* " Continue in this way with the remaining riddles.

1. **This toy can make music. . . . It has strings for you to strum. . . . What is it?** (guitar)
2. **This toy turns around and around. . . . You jump while playing with it. . . . What is it?** (jump rope)
3. **You can bounce and roll this toy. . . . It is round. . . . What is it?** (ball)
4. **This toy has two wings. . . . It can fly through the air. . . . What is it?** (airplane)
5. **You can push this toy. . . . A doll can ride inside it. . . . What is it?** (doll buggy)
6. **This toy is fun at the beach or in the sandbox. . . . It can help you make castles, houses, or tunnels out of sand. . . . What is it?** (pail and shovel)
7. **You can beat on this toy to make a thumping sound. . . . It is fun to hold when you march in a parade. . . . What is it?** (drum)
8. **This toy has many pieces. . . . You can put the pieces together to make a picture. . . . What is it?** (puzzle)
9. **This toy can be small or large. . . . It must be filled with air. . . . What is it?** (balloon)
10. **You can make music with this toy. . . . You usually sit down to play it. . . . What is it?** (piano)
11. **This toy is on a stick. . . . When you blow it, it spins. . . . What is it?** (pinwheel)
12. **The pieces of this toy have different shapes and colors. . . . You can stack them to make towers, houses, trains, and many other things. . . . What are they?** (blocks)

Turn all the cards facedown on the board. Turn over one card, and ask several children each to tell you something in a sentence about the toy shown. They may describe the toy's use, size, colors, parts, etc. Continue until all the cards have been described and everyone has participated.

2 Focus: pantomiming playing horns while marching to the music "Rag March" in a stop-go listening game

Stand beside the audiocassette player, with the children standing before you. Hold the music card and say:

Some toys can make music. Let's pretend that you each have a horn. Show me how you would play it.

If necessary, demonstrate by holding your hands in front of your mouth and moving your fingers as though playing a horn. Then have the children line up in single file. Designate as leaders the first child in line and the last in line. Continue:

Now let's march as we pretend to play our horns. (Lorraine) will be the first leader. Please follow (her) and play your horn with the music. When it ends, stop and turn around. When the music begins again, march behind (Gordon) in the opposite direction.

Play the song. Stop the music from time to time and check to be sure that everyone reverses direction. Encourage the children to pantomime playing horns as they march. After a short while, choose new leaders. Continue in this way as time and interest permit.

130

MATERIALS*

Audiocassette 3

Side A, Story 3, "Sounds of People – Actions"

ACTIVITY 2

Cards

Music

331

Audiocassette 2

Side B, Song 8, "Today, Yesterday, and Tomorrow"

1 Focus: brainstorming actions of people that produce sound, listening to "Sounds of People — Actions," and then naming, imitating, and describing those actions

Say:

People can make sounds with many of their body parts. I can use my hands to make the sound of clapping. (Demonstrate) **Let's think of other sounds people can make with body parts.**

Encourage each child to name such a sound. Then say:

Let's listen to some sounds made with body parts. Then we will make the same sounds together.

Play the sounds, one at a time. After each, ask:

What did you hear? (Encourage unison response) **Yes, you heard someone (walking). Let's all (stand up and walk in place).** (Pause) **Tell us in a sentence what body parts people use when they (walk), (Fiona).**

The child should answer with a sentence such as "We use our (feet and legs) to (walk)" or "We (walk) with our (feet and legs)." After all the sounds have been identified, repeat the procedure, playing the songs in random order.

2 Focus: singing, chanting, and acting out the song "Today, Yesterday, and Tomorrow"

Stand beside the audiocassette player, with the children standing before you. Hold the music card and say:

Let's sing "Today, Yesterday, and Tomorrow" about some actions that make sounds. After we sing each verse, we will act out the words together.

Play the song and refer to the music card as you sing. After the verb forms are chanted for each verse, lead the children in the action named. Continue with the song (instrumental version), using these action words:

1. cough
2. hum
3. cry
4. snore
5. laugh
6. whistle
7. sing
8. run
9. snap (fingers)

131

MATERIALS*

ACTIVITY 1

Display Board
6 ledges

Numerals & Color Shapes
294-298
304-308

ACTIVITY 2

None

1 Focus: counting shapes, and then matching pairs of cards by number

Display cards 294 through 298 in order on the board. Have 304 through 308 stacked within reach.

Point to the cards on display and say:

Let's count the shapes on each of these cards.

Point to each card in turn as the children count aloud with you. Then several children may each describe the shape(s) on a card in a sentence such as "There is (one yellow circle) on this card." When everyone seems familiar with the five cards, continue:

Now let's look at some cards with different shapes. Look at each card I hold up. Then look on the board for a card with the same number of shapes.

Hold up cards 304 through 308, one at a time, and call on individuals to answer. When a match is made, the child is to place the card beside the one it matches on the board. Repeat the procedure until everyone has had a turn. End by counting the shapes on each card aloud with the children.

2 Focus: saying and acting out a counting rhyme about bees

Ask the children to stand before you. Say:

I know a rhyme about bees that is fun to say and do. Watch as I go through it for you the first time. Then we will do it together.

Say the following rhyme with gestures. Repeat it with the children several times.

Here is the beehive;
(Cup left hand downward)
Where are the bees?
Hiding away where nobody sees.
(Hide fingers of right hand under left)
They are coming out now;
They are all alive. (Let fingers creep out)
Buzzz . . . buzzz . . . buzzz.
One . . . two . . . three . .
four . . . five!
(Touch fingers while counting)

If the children are able to understand, point to the fingers on your other hand as you continue counting to 10.

132

MATERIALS*

ACTIVITY 1

Cards

Stories

369-385

Display Board

6 ledges

ACTIVITY 2

None

1 Focus: retelling the story "P. Mooney and Zoey," and then sequencing the story cards in sets of three while stressing *first, second,* and *third*

Hold the 17 story cards and say:

P. Mooney and Zoey have been good friends ever since they met. Let's look at the story cards again and see how much of the story we can remember.

Show the story cards in order, one by one, as the children take turns telling what is happening in each picture. If necessary, ask questions such as "What else does this picture show?" or "Why did Zoey do that?" After the story has been retold, place the first three cards, out of order, on the bottom ledges of the display board. Continue:

Let's look at each picture again and decide if what it shows happened first, second, or third.

As the children respond, call on individuals to sequence the three cards on the top ledges, left-to-right as seen by the group. Continue until all the cards have been placed in order.

2 Focus: evaluating statements on actions of body parts and correcting them while stressing *not*

Say:

Now let's play a thinking game. I will ask you questions. Some of them are silly, and some are not. Please answer each question in a sentence.

Have the children answer several of the questions in unison. Then call on individuals to answer the remaining questions. The children should use sentences like "Yes, eyes do see" or "No, ears do not see; ears hear."

1. **Do eyes see?**
2. **Do legs jump?**
3. **Do knees bend?**
4. **Do tongues taste?**
5. **Do noses walk?**
6. **Do teeth chew?**
7. **Do toes hear?**
8. **Do knees skip?**
9. **Do hands clap?**
10. **Do noses sneeze?**
11. **Do arms hop?**
12. **Do ankles twist?**
13. **Do teeth wave?**
14. **Do ankles drink?**
15. **Do elbows bend?**
16. **Do noses smell?**
17. **Do knees write?**
18. **Do arms reach?**
19. **Do elbows taste?**
20. **Do ears hear?**

133

MATERIALS*

ACTIVITY 1

Fruits & Vegetables
All

Puppets
Zoey
Thinking hat

ACTIVITY 2

Cards
Music
332

Fruits & Vegetables
All

Audiocassette 2
Side B, Song 9, "Things That Go Together"

1 Focus: identifying fruits and vegetables from descriptions in riddles

Have two children help you pile the fruits and vegetables on the floor where everyone can see them.

Hold Zoey (wearing her thinking hat) and ask:

What hat is Zoey wearing today? (Encourage unison response) **Yes, she is wearing her thinking hat. I know some riddles about fruits and vegetables. Each of you will have a turn to hold Zoey and help her answer a riddle.**

Present the following riddles, one at a time, pausing between clues. The child you call on should hold Zoey and answer through her in a sentence such as "You are thinking of (strawberries)."

1. **I am thinking of a set of three fruits. . . . They are red with green leaves. . . . They each have a stem . . . . What are they?** (strawberries)
2. **I am thinking of a vegetable. . . . It is long and pointed. . . . It is orange and brown. . . . What is it?** (carrot)
3. **I am thinking of a fruit. . . . It is round. . . . It is fuzzy. . . . It is yellow and pink. . . . What is it?** (peach)
4. **1 am thinking of a vegetable. . . . It has green leaves. . . . The part you eat is yellow. . . . What is it?** (corn)
5. **I am thinking of a vegetable. . . . It is white on the inside. . . . It is brown on the outside. . . . What is it?** (potato)
6. **I am thinking of a set of three fruits. . . . They make juice that is sweet. . . . The inside is the same color as the outside. . . . What are they?** (oranges)
7. **I am thinking of a vegetable. . . . Its top is white and stringy. . . . The rest of it is white, too. . . . What is it?** (onion)
8. **I am thinking of a large fruit. . . . It has green leaves that are pointed. . . . The inside part that you eat is yellow. . . . What is it?** (pineapple)
9. **I am thinking of a set of three fruits. . . . They are large at one end and small at the other. . . . They are yellow. . . . What are they?** (pears)
10. **I am thinking of a fruit. . . . The outside peel is bumpy. . . . It is yellow. . . . What is it?** (lemon)
11. **I am thinking of a vegetable. . . . It has green leaves. . . . When it is ripe, it is red. . . . What is it?** (tomato)
12. **I am thinking of a set of three fruits. . . . They have tiny brown spots. . . . They are long and yellow. . What are they?** (bananas)
13. **I am thinking of a set of three fruits. . . . They have brown stems. . . . They can be red, yellow, or green. . . . What are they?** (apples)

Continue by having the children take turns holding Zoey and presenting their own riddles about the fruits and veyetables.

2 Focus: singing the song "Things That Go Together" to classify foods as fruits or vegetables

Give each child a fruit or vegetable. Then ask four children holding fruits to come and stand before the group. Hold the music card and say:

Let's name these four foods together.

Point to each fruit as the group names it. Continue:

What word can we use to name all four of these foods?

If no one can answer, give the word *fruits* and have the children repeat it a few times. Then say:

Let's sing the song "Things That Go Together" about these four fruits.

Play the song (instrumental version) and refer to the music card as you lead the children in singing this verse:

There are things that go together, belong together.

There are things that go together

In a group like this:

(Apple), (pear), (orange), (banana).

There are things that go together,

And they are FRUITS!

Sing new verses about other groups of four fruits. Then continue as above with groups of vegetables.

134

MATERIALS*

ACTIVITY 1

Teacher provides

Pencil & paper

ACTIVITY 2

Cards

Foods

94- 152

P. Mooney Bag

1 Focus: brainstorming foods

Say:

Let's name all the foods we can. I will write them down as you name them.

Give hints as necessary. When many foods have been named, read the list aloud and praise the children for their efforts.

2 Focus: remembering food card sequences, and stressing *first* and *next*

Put all 59 food cards into the P. Mooney bag.

Say:

Let's use the food cards to play a remembering game.

Choose two cards at random from the bag and show them, one at a time, for about five seconds each. Suggest to the children that they whisper to themselves the names of the pictured foods. Then hide the cards. Ask:

Which card did you see first?

If necessary, give clues. When the correct card is named, show it to the class. Then continue:

Which card did you see next?

If the children need help in remembering the sequence, show the two cards again, one at a time, and repeat the questions. Continue with other pairs of cards.

135

MATERIALS*

ACTIVITY 1

None

ACTIVITY 2

None

1 Focus: relating pairs of clothing to pairs of body parts

Ask:

How many feet do we have? (Pause) **Yes, we have two feet. When we have two things that are the same, we say they are a pair. Some kinds of clothing come in pairs. We wear pairs of shoes, for example. What other kinds of pairs can we wear on our feet?**

Several children should each name such pairs as boots, socks, slippers, sandals, and anklets in a sentence like "I wear a pair of (boots) on my feet." Repeat this procedure, having the children discuss the clothing worn on pairs of body parts like these:

1. **hands — gloves, mittens, etc.**
2. **arms — sleeves, bracelets, etc.**
3. **ears — earrings, ear muffs, hearing aids, etc.**
4. **legs — trousers, shorts, knee pads, stockings, leg braces, etc.**
5. **eyes — glasses, goggles, sunglasses, etc.**

2 Focus: brainstorming when to wear pairs of clothing

Say:

Let's think about when you might need to wear boots.

Help the children consider and discuss many situations when boots might be worn: walking in snow or rain, wading in water, washing a car or boat, walking over rough ground, etc. Continue as above with other pairs of clothing, such as gloves, ear muffs, and glasses.

136

MATERIALS*

ACTIVITY 1

Display Board
4 ledges

Poster 2

Audiocassette 4
Side A, Selection 2,
"Sounds of the Circus"

ACTIVITY 2

Display Board
44 ledges

Poster 2

1 Focus: listening to "Sounds of the Circus," then classifying and describing people doing activities on the poster "Circus"

Do not display the poster until asked to do so.

Say:

Close your eyes and imagine where you might be if you heard these sounds.

Play selection 2 and ask:

What place would sound like that? (Encourage unison response) **Yes, these sounds would be heard at a circus.**

Quickly use the ledges to place the poster on the board. Point to it and continue:

Look at all the people and animals! They are doing many different things. Let's find and describe everyone who is swinging.

Afterwards, have the children identify and discuss performers doing these actions:

1. balancing	**4. standing**
2. lifting	**5. sitting**
3. riding	**6. pulling**

End by having each child name and discuss a favorite performer on the poster.

2 Focus: talking about circuses and their sounds

Have the poster from Activity 1 still on display.

Point to the poster and say:

You might hear many different sounds at a big circus like this. Tell us about a sound you might hear, (Lorenzo).

Call on other children in turn. They may talk about their own experiences at circuses, or use the poster and their memory of its recorded sounds for ideas. Praise all imaginative efforts.

137 

MATERIALS*

ACTIVITY 1

Puppets

P. Mooney

Zoey

Thinking hat

ACTIVITY 2

Cards

Music

337

Audiocassette 3

Side A, Selection 3,

"Sounds of People – Actions

1 Focus: talking about possible solutions to Zoey's and P. Mooney's problems

Place Zoey (wearing her thinking hat) on your hand and have her say:

Sometimes P. Mooney and I have problems that we don't know how to solve. We are going to tell you about some problems. Please help us decide what we should do.

In each case, the puppet should describe the problem and then call on several children for solutions. Praise creative efforts.

1. Zoey: **One day P. Mooney and I decided to go on a picnic. We hiked through the woods until we found a meadow that was just right. But we couldn't reach it because of the fast river we would have to cross first. Tell me how we might have crossed the river.**
2. Zoey: **One morning when I was out walking, I saw a red balloon caught in the top branches of a tall tree. Tell me how I might have reached the red balloon.**
3. P. Mooney: **I was making bread one day. While it was baking, I discovered that I had dropped my favorite ring into the dough. Tell me how I might have gotten my ring out of the bread.**
4. Zoey: **My friends and I were rowing a boat. Suddenly we noticed that it had sprung a leak and water was pouring in. Tell me how we might have kept the boat from sinking.**
5. P. Mooney: **I was driving down a country road one afternoon. Suddenly a large rock fell off a cliff and blocked the road. Tell me how I might have continued my drive.**
6. Zoey: **Last Sunday I went for a walk in the country. I discovered a well and began dropping stones down into it, so that I could hear the water splash. Just then, a gust of wind blew my action hat into the well. Tell me how I might have gotten my hat back.**

2 Focus: imitating actions in a follow-me game to the music "Rag March," and then naming the actions

Say:

Let's play a follow-me game. When the music begins, line up behind me and do exactly what I do. I may change what I am doing, so please watch carefully.

Play the selection as you lead the children in doing a variety of actions involving the upper, middle, and lower body. Begin by doing simple actions slowly, increasing the frequency of change and difficulty of action as long as the children can keep up. Change leaders occasionally. Actions might include these:

1. **patting knees**
2. **clapping**
3. **stamping**
4. **hopping on one foot**
5. **walking backwards**
6. **waving**

Continue as long as time and interest permit. End by having the children name and discuss the actions they did.

138 

MATERIALS*

ACTIVITY 1

None

ACTIVITY 2

None

1 Focus: naming actions and body parts used to do these actions, and then brainstorming actions the hands can do

Say:

Let's see if you can figure out what I tell two of you to do.

Invite two children to stand before the group. Whisper a suggestion to each, such as "(Barbara), clap your hands" and "(Raymond), scratch your leg." When the two have done these actions, ask the class:

What did (Barbara) do? (Encourage unison response) **Yes, (she) clapped (her) hands. What did (Raymond) do?** (Encourage unison response) **Yes, (he) scratched (his) leg. What body parts did they both use?** (Encourage unison response) **Yes, they used their hands. We can use our hands to do many different things. Let's think of some actions we do with our hands.**

Each child is to name and describe a hand action in a sentence such as "I can (tie my shoes) with my hands." Have the class demonstrate or pantomime each action. If no one can respond, suggest these actions:

1. **open a door**
2. **play a piano**
3. **throw a ball**
4. **wave good-bye**
5. **squeeze a sponge**
6. **turn pages**
7. **button a shirt**
8. **hold a hot dog**
9. **take a top off a jar**
10. **brush teeth**

VARIATION: To make the activity *easier,* call on only one child at a time to perform an action.

2 Focus: saying an action rhyme about body parts while stressing *is* and *are*

Stand with the children and say:

Let's learn a new rhyme about body parts. Please listen and watch as I go through it for you the first time. Then we will do it together.

Stress the verbs is and are as you say this rhyme with gestures:

This *is* my face; (Circle face with finger)
This *is* my nose. (Point to nose)
These *are* my fingers; (Wiggle fingers)
These *are* my toes. (Tap toes)
Here *are* my hands. (Hold up hands)
Here *are* my feet. (Point to feet)
Here *is* my head; (Place hands on head)
Here *is* my seat! (Place hands on "seat")

Repeat as desired, encouraging the children to join you.

139

MATERIALS*

ACTIVITY 1

Cards

Pictures from Several Categories

13 15 19 26 34 39 42 46 47 48 50 51 56 70

Display Board

6 ledges

ACTIVITY 2

None

1 Focus: listening to and talking about the story "Jimmy and the Big Question" to consider why animals do not wear clothes

In this order, picture sides hidden, display cards 34, 50, 48, 13, 42, 56, 19, 70, 15, 46, 51, 26, 39, and 47.

Say:

Today I am going to read you a story called "Jimmy and the Big Question." Please listen carefully, so that you will learn the answer to Jimmy's big question.

Read the following story, turning over the cards as indicated. Each time a card is turned, the children are to name it in unison.

Jimmy and the Big Question

One cold morning while Jimmy was dressing, one of the buttons on his shirt fell off and rolled around on the floor. "Now I'll have to change my shirt, just when it was almost buttoned!" he grumbled. "It isn't fair! None of my animal friends have shirts to button, or shoes to tie, or pants to pull on and off. Animals don't wear clothes. I wonder why. I think I'll ask them."

So Jimmy quickly changed his shirt and finished dressing. Then after breakfast, he ran outside to ask his animal friends the big question: "Why don't animals wear clothes?"

First he called to the bushy-tailed (turn card 34 for class to name) ***squirrel*** **who lived in a tall oak tree.**

"Come down, Squirrel! I have an important question to ask you."

"What can I do for you?" asked the squirrel. "Are you hungry for nuts? I can let you have a few."

"No, thank you," Jimmy said politely. "I wanted to ask you why you don't wear clothes."

"I never thought about wearing clothes," the squirrel said, "but maybe I should; it does get very cold every winter."

"How about a nice pair of (turn card 50) ***mittens?*** **" said Jimmy.**

"Yes," said the squirrel, "and I would like a little (turn card 48) ***jacket*** **with a hood, too. Yes, I think clothes are a great idea!"**

"Then come with me," said Jimmy. "Let's go to the store and buy some for you."

So the squirrel sat on Jimmy's shoulder and they went along until they met a (turn card 13) ***duck.***

"Hello, Duck," said the squirrel. "My friend here is going to buy me some new clothes for winter."

"That's terrific!" said the duck. "I'd like a few things myself, like a pair of (turn card 42) ***boots*** **and a yellow** (turn card 56) ***raincoat.*** **May I come with you?"**

"Of course!" said Jimmy and the squirrel. So the three of them went on until they came to the pond where the (turn card 19) ***goldfish*** **lived. She swam to the surface and blew bubbles at them.**

"Where are you going?" she gurgled.

"Guess what!" said the duck. "Jimmy is taking us to get some new clothes. I'm getting boots and a yellow raincoat!"

"And I'm getting mittens and a jacket!" the squirrel added.

"Oh!" bubbled the goldfish. "I've always wanted to wear a two-piece (turn card 70) ***swimsuit!*** **May I come with you?"**

"Of course!" said Jimmy, the squirrel, and the duck. The goldfish swam into her goldfish bowl, so that Jimmy could carry it as they all went along together. Soon they came to the zoo, where the (turn card 15) ***elephant*** **was crunching peanuts.**

"Where are all of you going?" the elephant asked. "To get new clothes! I'm getting mittens and a winter jacket!" chattered the squirrel.

"And I'm getting boots and a yellow raincoat!" quacked the duck.

"And I'm getting a two-piece swimsuit!" the goldfish bubbled.

"How exciting!" said the elephant, flapping her big ears. "I think I'll come with you and get a beautiful new red (turn card 46) ***dress!"***

"How about a (turn card 51) ***necklace,* too?" the duck suggested.**

"Good idea!" agreed the elephant.

Just as they started off to the store, the animals heard someone laughing above their heads. They looked up to see the (turn card 26) ***owl* sitting on a tree branch and laughing as hard as she could. "Whoooo in the world would ever think of such a thing? Whoooo?"**

"Oh, Owl," said the elephant, "why don't you come with us and get yourself a nice (turn card 39) ***blouse* and a pair of** (turn card 47) ***glasses?"***

"Yes, do!" cried the others.

"I don't give a hoot about clothes!" said the owl. "And neither should any of you. Now, how did this silly idea get started?"

"Well," said Jimmy, "I wanted to know why animals don't have to wear clothes. And why do *I* have to wear clothes all the time?"

"That's a very good question," said the owl. "Well, why didn't one of you give Jimmy the answer?"

None of the animals had anything to say.

"You mean you don't know why?" said the owl. "Mr. Squirrel, you have thick, soft fur to cover you all winter long, and a beautiful, fluffy tail."

"It is a nice tail," the squirrel admitted.

"You don't need clothes," the owl continued. "And you, Mr. Duck, have flat webbed feet that are perfectly shaped for swimming. Boots would just get in the way. As for a raincoat, you don't need one. Your snow-white feathers do a much better job of keeping you covered, and they even keep you dry."

"I guess you're right," said the duck, sighing. "And Ms. Goldfish!" the owl scolded. "Why hide those lovely orange scales under a two-piece swimsuit? Your scales protect you and help you swim." The goldfish blew bubbles thoughtfully.

"And as for you, Ms. Elephant," said the owl, "a dress would drag on the ground and get in the way, besides being tight and uncomfortable."

"Oh, dear," the elephant sighed. "I wouldn't like that at all."

"Your tough skin is the right covering for you, because it protects you," said the owl. "Now, young man," the owl said to Jimmy, "are you beginning to understand why animals don't wear clothes? Can you guess why you have to get dressed every day?"

"Yes," said Jimmy slowly, "now I understand. The animals already have something covering their bodies, like fur or scales, or feathers, or tough skin. My skin isn't enough to protect me, so I have to wear clothes to keep warm and dry. Now I have the answer to my big question."

Discuss the story with the children. Call on several to explain the answer to Jimmy's big question, "Why don't animals wear clothes?"

2 Focus: talking about favorite clothes

Say:

Let's talk about our favorite clothes. Please tell us which clothes you like best and why they are your favorites, (Alexandra).

Prompt as necessary. If a child has trouble getting started, explain why you prefer your favorite clothes.

140

MATERIALS*

ACTIVITY 1

Cards

Numerals & Color Shapes

294-313

Fruits & Vegetables

All

ACTIVITY 2

None

1 Focus: counting shapes, and then matching fruits and vegetables to the shapes by number

Have the children sit on the floor in a semicircle before you. Give them each a number card and let them take turns counting aloud the shapes pictured on their cards. If a child has difficulty, exchange her or his card for one with fewer shapes. Place the fruits and vegetables inside the semicircle. Say:

Let's take turns choosing the same number of fruits and vegetables as we have shapes on our cards. When it is your turn, show us your card and tell us how many fruits and vegetables you are going to pick.

After each turn, put the fruits and vegetables back inside the semicircle. As needed, help the children respond correctly.

2 Focus: saying and acting out a counting rhyme

Say:

I know a number rhyme that is fun to say and do. Please listen and watch as I go through it for you the first time. Then we will do it together.

Say the following rhyme with gestures:

One, two;

Touch your shoe. (Touch shoes)

Three, four;

Sit on the floor. (Sit on floor)

Five, six;

A puppy licks.

(Stick tongue in and out and nod head as though lapping up milk)

Seven, eight;

Stand up straight. (Stand at attention)

Nine, ten;

Let's count again.

Repeat several times with the children. Then continue, encouraging the children to do the actions without you.

Keep in Mind. . .
After each lesson in the program, individuals who have difficulty demonstrating proficiency in the skills you consider appropriate and important for them to learn should be tutored. Aides could help you with this task.

141

MATERIALS*

ACTIVITY 1

Display Board
4 ledges

Magnetic Shapes
All

Container

ACTIVITY 2

Puppets
P. Mooney

1 Focus: sorting magnetic shapes by color, and then describing them

Set up the board. Use the ledges to divide the board into five columns, like this:

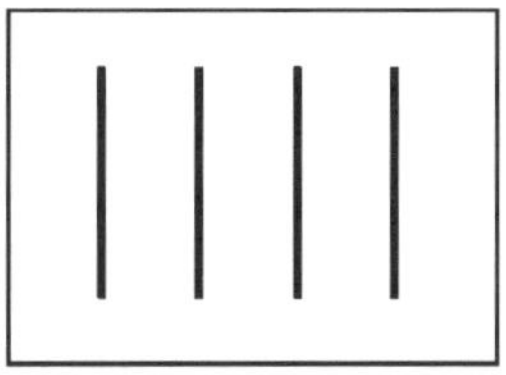

Select the five large circles, and keep the remaining shapes in the container.

Have a child who needs the experience place a large circle at the top of each column on the board. Say:

(Zachary) placed some shapes on the board. How are they alike? (Encourage several responses) **Yes, these shapes are all circles, and they are all the same size. How are these circles different from one another?** (Encourage unison response) **Yes, these circles are each a different color. Let's name the colors together.**

Point to each circle in turn as the children respond. Then pick up the container of shapes and continue:

Let's put each shape under a circle that is the same color.

Each child is to select a shape and tell its color and shape in a sentence such as "This is a (red square)" before placing it in the correct color column. Continue until everyone has had a turn or until all the shapes have been placed. Repeat if need and time suggest, calling most often on children who need the practice.

2 Focus: brainstorming things of certain colors

Place P. Mooney on your hand and have him say:

Let's play a game about colors. Please name all the things that could be the color I mention. Here's the first color: red.

The puppet should encourage every child to participate. Continue with these colors:

1. blue
2. yellow
3. black
4. green
5. white
6. brown
7. orange

142

MATERIALS*

ACTIVITY 1

Cards

Household Items (optional)

153 155 157 175
176 177 180 181
190 191 193 195
197 198

Audiocassette 3

Side A, Selection 2, "Sounds of the Home"

ACTIVITY 2

None

1 Focus: naming household items that make sounds, and then listening to "Sounds of the Home" and identifying each one

Say:

Let's think about the sounds we might hear at home. Name some of them.

Lead the children in naming as many sounds as they can. Then say:

Now let's listen to some sounds that might be heard at home. Try to figure out what might make each sound.

Play the sound effects one sound at a time. After each sound, ask, "What might make the sound?" Encourage discussion.

VARIATION: To make the activity *easier,* use the cards as cues.

2 Focus: deciding on household items needed to perform certain tasks

Have the children name a household item in answer to each of these questions:

What would I need to . . .

1. **cut some meat?** (knife or fork)
2. **drink milk?** (glass or cup)
3. **fry an egg?** (frying pan)
4. **stir some chocolate?** (spoon)
5. **sweep the floor?** (broom)
6. **wash the floors?** (scrub brush or mop, and bucket)
7. **brush my teeth?** (toothbrush and toothpaste)
8. **pick up food from my plate?** (fork and/or spoon)
9. **cut some string?** (scissors or knife)
10. **clean the rug?** (vacuum cleaner or broom)

143

MATERIALS*

ACTIVITY 1

Fruits & vegetables
All

ACTIVITY 2

Fruits & Vegetables
All

1 Focus: identifying fruits and vegetables from their descriptions

Sit in a circle with the children. Place the fruits and vegetables in the center. Say:

Let's take turns describing the fruits and vegetables. When it is your turn, tell us anything you want to say about one of them, except its name. Then we will try to figure out which one you are talking about.

Some of the time, let the person who guesses correctly have the next turn. However, slow children should also be called on to describe an item.

2 Focus: classifying fruits and vegetables by certain characteristics

Have the children sit around the fruits and vegetables. Say:

Fruits and vegetables grow in many different ways. Some grow on trees. Some grow on vines, and some grow on bushes. Let's find all the fruits and vegetables that grow *under* the ground.

As the items are named, have them grouped before you. When all the correct items (onion, potato, and carrot) have been identified, point to them and say:

Yes! These vegetables grow under the ground. Let's name them together.

Return the items to the center as they are named. Repeat this procedure with fruits and vegetables that . . .

1. **grow on trees.** (apples, bananas, lemon, orange, peach, pears)
2. **grow on bushes or small plants.** (corn, pineapple, strawberries, tomato)
3. **are sweet.** (apples, bananas, oranges, peach, pears, pineapple, strawberries)
4. **are sour.** (lemon, tomato)
5. **we peel before eating.** (bananas, carrot, corn, lemon, onion, oranges, peach, pineapple, potato)
6. **have stems.** (apples, bananas, lemon, oranges, peach, pears, strawberries, tomato)
7. **have cores.** (apples, pears)
8. **are your favorites.**

144

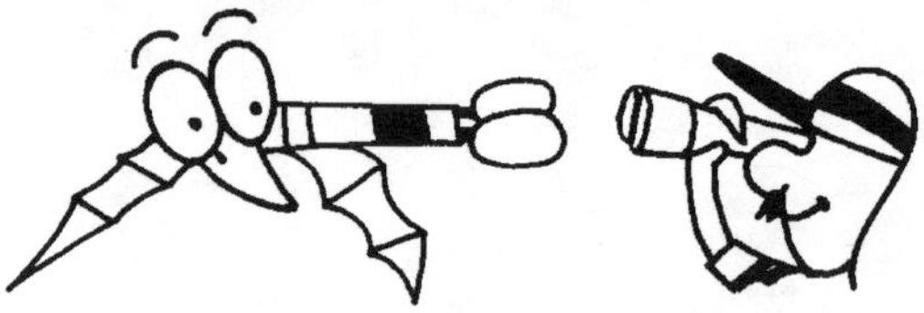

MATERIALS*

ACTIVITY 1

Cards

Face Pairs

74-93

ACTIVITY 2

None

1 Focus: describing and then matching pairs of face cards

Give each child a card, being sure to give out matched pairs. If necessary, keep a card yourself. Say:

Look at the faces on your cards. Please tell us as much as you can about the face on your card, (Sharon).

Call on everyone in turn. Each child is to describe features such as length of hair, whether the eyes are open or closed, and whether the face is frowning or smiling. Then continue:

Now let's play a game called Lost Twins. Identical twins look exactly alike, and each of us has one somewhere in this room. Please look at your card and find your twin. Then the two of you are to hold hands and sit together.

Call on each pair of "twins" to describe "their" face. Then have a child collect the cards.

2 Focus: talking about one's imaginary twin

Say:

Let's imagine that each of you has an identical twin who looks just like you. If you did have a twin, what would that person be like?

Have the children take turns describing their "twins." Suggested topics:

1. **what their twin might look like**
2. **what their twin might like to do for fun**
3. **what foods their twin might like to eat**
4. **what kinds of people their twin might like**
5. **what their twin's favorite toy might be**

145

MATERIALS*

ACTIVITY 1

Cards

Stories

386-398

ACTIVITY 2

None

1 **Focus: retelling the story "The Elephant That Did Not Know How to Listen," and then talking about the importance of listening**

Hold the 13 story cards and say:

Let's take turns telling the story of Elbert the Elephant, P. Mooney's friend who did not know how to listen.

Show the cards in sequence as the children take turns describing the action for each picture. Then lead the discussion with questions like these:

1. **Why did Elbert have trouble listening?**
2. **Do you ever have trouble listening?**
3. **What are some things that make it hard for you to listen sometimes?**
4. **Why is it important to be a good listener?**

2 **Focus: brainstorming sounds that could be heard at night, and then taking turns creating a "night sound" for the group to identify**

Say:

Let's talk about some of the sounds you might hear while lying awake in bed at night.

Encourage imaginative responses. If necessary, suggest some of these sounds:

1. **house sounds** (clicking doors, squeaking floors, rattling windows, etc.)
2. **voices** (of family, on television, on radio, of neighbors, of visitors, etc.)
3. **animals inside the house** (mouse, dog, rats, kittens, birds, etc.)
4. **animals outside the house** (cows, cats, rooster, frogs, insects, etc.)
5. **vehicles** (cars, buses, trains, trucks, sirens, bicycle bells, etc.)
6. **weather sounds** (storms, winds, thunder, etc.)
7. **sleeping sounds** (snoring, breathing, talking in sleep, etc.)

Afterwards, continue:

Now let's lie down and pretend we are in bed. (Pause)

Someone has just turned out the light, and it is very dark.

Before we go to sleep, let's be very quiet and listen to the sounds around the house. I will make the first sound.

Bark like a dog. Then whisper:

What was that? (Encourage unison response) **Yes, that was a dog barking. Now lie back. Let's listen for another sound. When I tap you, make a sound for the rest of us to name.**

Each child you tap should make a sound for the others to identify in unison. Give everyone a turn. You may wish to have the children discuss their bedtime fears. Explain that nearly everyone is sometimes afraid and that talking about our fears can help us feel less frightened.

146

MATERIALS*

ACTIVITY 1

Cards

Animals

1 3 5 8 11 12 13
15 16 17 18 20 21
23 25 26 27 29 31
32 34 35 36

Display Board

None

6 ledges

Audiocassette 3

Side A, Selection 1,
"Sounds of Animals"

ACTIVITY 2

None

1 Focus: listening to "Sounds of Animals," identifying each one, and then describing the animals

Say:

People can often name an animal by listening to its sound. Today let's see if you can name some animals from the sounds they make.

Play "Sounds of Animals," one sound at a time. After each sound, the children are to identify the animal in unison and then describe it to you. Help by asking questions about the animal's size, color, temperament, and habits.

VARIATION: To make the activity *easier,* place the corresponding animal cards on the board as each sound is identified. Remove cards as needed to make room for others.

2 Focus: identifying real and imaginary pets from descriptions, and then imitating their sounds

Sit in a circle with the children and say:

Today let's think about the sounds that pets make. Imagine one pet you would love to have. The rest of us will try to guess what your pet is from the sound you say it makes. I will describe my pet first.

Describe your pet, real or imagined, by saying:

My pet's name is (Tuppence). (She) is (small) and has (soft, curly black hair). (She) likes to (jump high in the air) and makes a sound like this: (ruff, ruff). What kind of pet might sound like that? (Encourage unison response) **Yes, my pet is a (dog), so (she barks). Let's all pretend to be (dogs) and (bark) together.**

The children should use sentences to tell about the pets they would like. Continue until everyone has had a turn.

147

MATERIALS*

ACTIVITY 1

Cards
Animals
1 5 6 9 15
25 30 33 34 38

Display Board
5 ledges

Puppets
Zoey
Thinking hat

ACTIVITY 2

Cards
Animals
(same as for Activity 1)
Music
328

Display Board
5 ledges

Audiocassette 2
Side A, Song 5,
"If and Then Go Together"

1 Focus: identifying animals from descriptions in riddles

Set up the board with ledges, and display the 10 animal cards.

Review the animal card labels with the children. Put Zoey (wearing her thinking hat) on your hand. Have her point to the board and say:

Let's use these animals to play a guessing game. I will give you some clues. Try to figure out which animal I am describing. When you think you know the animal, raise your hand.

After each clue, Zoey should pause to give the children time to think and make a choice. Give all the clues even when the correct choice has been made early.

1. **This animal is small. . . . It has feathers. . . . It has wings. . . . It lives in a tree. . . . What animal is it?** (bird)
2. **This animal is very small. . . . It has eight legs. . . . It does not have a tail. . . . It lives in a web. . . . What animal is it?** (spider)
3. **This animal is large. . . . It growls. . . . It likes to eat honey. . . . What animal is it?** (bear)
4. **This animal is large. . . . It is a golden brown color. . . . It roars. . . . Sometimes it lives in a zoo or circus. . . . What animal is it?** (lion)
5. **This animal is small. . . . It is yellow. . . . Its mother is a hen. . . . Its father is a rooster. . . . It pecks on the ground to find its food. . . . What animal is it?** (chick)
6. **This animal is very small. . . . It is brown. . . . It has no legs. . . . It lives in the ground. . . . What animal is it?** (worm)
7. **This animal is very large. . . . It is gray. Sometimes it lives in a circus. . . . It has a long nose called a trunk. . . . It has big, floppy ears. . . . What animal is it?** (elephant)
8. **This animal is small. . . . It has a long tail. . . . It has thick fur. . . . It lives in a tree. . . . It likes to eat nuts. . . . What animal is it?** (squirrel)
9. **This animal is small. . . . It has fur. . . . It has long ears. . . . It likes to eat carrots and lettuce. . . . It hops. . . . What animal is it?** (rabbit)
10. **This animal is very small. . . . It has two beautiful wings. . . . It flies from flower to flower. . . . What animal is it?** (butterfly)

End by showing the cards one at a time as the children name at least three characteristics of each pictured animal.

VARIATION: To make the activity *harder,* do not use the cards.

2 Focus: describing animals in the song "If and Then Go Together"

Stand beside the board and the audiocassette player, with the children standing facing you. Hold the music card and say:

Let's sing about some of the animals Zoey described. First we will each choose an animal and tell one thing about it. Then we will sing. I choose a bird; a bird has feathers. Now listen to my song.

Play the song (instrumental version) and sing:

If you are a bird, then you have feathers, etc.

Repeat, encouraging the children to join you. Continue in this way with verses the children suggest.

VARIATION: To make the activity *easier,* use these verses:

1. **If you are an elephant, then you have a trunk, etc.**
2. **If you are a butterfly, then you can flutter, etc.**
3. **If you are a spider, then you spin a web, etc.**
4. **If you are a bear, then you like honey, etc.**
5. **If you are a chick, then you can peep, etc.**
6. **If you are a lion, then you run fast, etc.**
7. **If you are a rabbit, then you have long ears, etc.**
8. **If you are a squirrel, then you eat nuts, etc.**
9. **If you are a worm, then you can wiggle, etc.**

148

MATERIALS*

ACTIVITY 1

Cards

Foods

98 100 101 102
104 105 111 114
123 130 144 150

Display Board

6 ledges

Magnetic Shapes

Large black circle

Large black rectangle

Large black square

Large black triangle

ACTIVITY 2

None

1 Focus: drawing shapes in the air, and then identifying shapes in pictured foods

Display the food cards in random order on the board.

Hold up the circle and ask:

What shape is this? (Pause) **Yes, it is a circle. Let's all draw a circle in the air.** (Demonstrate) **Now look at the pictures of food and see if you can find any foods that contain circles.**

Call on several children to trace the circles on the food cards as they describe what they see. Repeat the procedure with the other three shapes. Make sure everyone participates. Point out that some pictures contain more than one shape; the cheese, for example, is shaped ike a triangle and has circular holes.

2 Focus: identifying shapes of classroom objects

Have the children take turns naming the shapes of classroom objects. They are to use sentences such as "A (book) looks like a (rectangle)." They should consider objects such as these:

Circles

1. **door knobs**
2. **flower pots or planters**
3. **tops of jars**
4. **tops of cups**

Triangles

1. **musical instruments**
2. **puzzle parts**

Squares

1. **blocks**
2. **napkins**
3. **boxes**

Rectangles

1. **windows**
2. **doors**
3. **pictures**
4. **bulletin board**
5. **table tops**

149 

MATERIALS*

ACTIVITY 1

Cards

Pictures from Several Categories

201 204 208 213
217 218 221 268
269 271 272 273
277 281

Display Board

4 ledges

ACTIVITY 2

Cards

Music

328

Audiocassette 2

Side A, Song 5, "If and Then Go Together"

1 Focus: relating people and vehicles, and then talking about places to travel

Set up the board with ledges and display vehicle cards 268, 269, 271, 272, 273, 277, and 281. Stack people cards 201, 204, 208, 213, 217, 218, and 221.

Hold the seven people cards as you point to the board and say:

Let's imagine that all these vehicles are parked in the same parking lot. I will show you some pictures of people. We will pretend that they need to go somewhere. Please tell me which vehicle each person might choose.

Hold up the people cards, one at a time. If necessary, give clues. The children should respond with sentences such as "The (astronaut) would travel in the (space capsule)." Set aside each matched pair of cards. Continue:

Now that we know how the people might travel, let's talk about where they might go. (Show cards 201 and 277) **Tell me where this astronaut might go in this space capsule and what he might do when he gets there.**

Call on several children to respond. Continue in this way with the remaining pairs of cards.

2 Focus: thinking about vehicles with wheels, and then singing about them in the song "If and Then Go Together"

Hold the music card and say:

Many vehicles have wheels. Name as many as you can.

The children should use sentences such as "A (bicycle) has wheels." When the list is finished, continue:

Now let's stand up and sing a song about wheels.

Play the song (instrumental version) and refer to the music card as you sing these two verses with the children:

1. **If you are a wheel,** (Draw large circle in the air) **then you are round, etc.**
2. **If you are a wheel,** (Move hands around each other in circular motion) **then you can roll, etc.**

Repeat the verses two or three times.

150

MATERIALS*

ACTIVITY 1

Cards

Toys

228 240 241 242
247 249 250 251
252 253 254 257
261 262 265

Display Board

6 ledges

ACTIVITY 2

Cards

Toys

228* 240* 262*

Music

329

Audiocassette 2

Side A, Song 7,
"Hi Ho, Pal"

1 Focus: talking about and classifying toys by their indoor and/or outdoor use

Display the 15 toy cards in random order on the board.

Point to the board and say:

Let's think about where we might play with these toys. Some can be used only outdoors; others can be used both outside and inside. Let's talk about each one.

Point to each card in turn and ask these questions:

1. **What is this toy called?**
2. **Can it be used indoors? Why or why not?**
3. **Can it be used both indoors and outdoors? Why or why not?**
4. **What do you do when you play with this toy? Also have the children consider the size and appearance of each toy. Encourage everyone to participate in the discussion.**

2 Focus: singing the song "Hi Ho, Pal" while pantomiming the use of toys

Stand beside the audiocassette player, with the children standing before you. Hold up the three toy cards, one at a time, saying about each:

Please show me how you would play with this toy.

When the children have finished their three pantomimes, show them card 228 and continue:

Let's sing "Hi Ho, Pal" as we pretend to bounce this ball.

Play the song (instrumental version) and refer to the music cards as you lead the singing. Insert the words "bouncing balls" and have the children do the action. Repeat the verse two or three times. Then continue with the two remaining toy cards, ending the verses with these words:

Verse 2:" . . . jumping rope."
Verse 3:" . . . riding bikes."

151

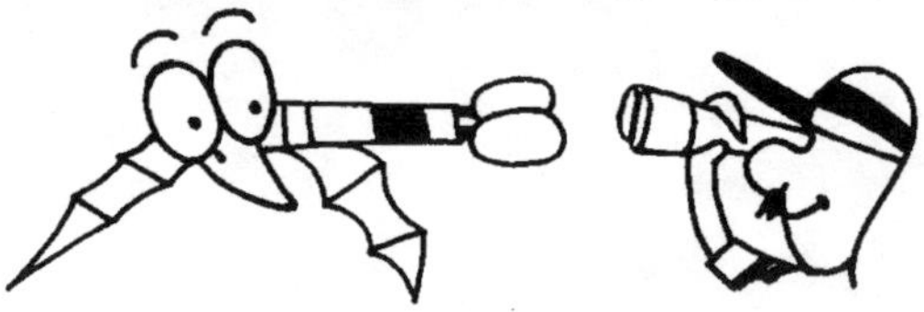

MATERIALS*

ACTIVITY 1

None

ACTIVITY 2

P. Mooney Bag

Teacher provides

An equal number of hard or soft objects, including a ball of yarn, a piece of silk or satin, a glass bottle, a smooth rock

1 Focus: brainstorming and pantomiming things that can be done with one and two hands

Say:

Let's talk about our hands again. They are very important to us, because we use them to do many things. Sometimes we do things with only one hand. At other times, we do things with both hands. Let's name some things we do with only one hand.

The children are to use sentences as they name as many activities for one hand as they can. Have the activities pantomimed as they are named. Repeat this procedure as the children brainstorm activities that require two hands.

One hand:

1. **using a fork, knife, spoon**
2. **writing with a pencil**
3. **stirring a pot**
4. **scratching an arm**
5. **writing a letter**
6. **picking up a letter**
7. **petting a dog**
8. **turning a page**

Two hands:

1. **tying shoelaces and ribbons**
2. **buttoning a shirt**
3. **holding a heavy box**
4. **cutting paper with scissors**
5. **pulling on pants**
6. **buckling a belt**
7. **washing dishes**
8. **getting a glass of water**

2 Focus: identifying hard and soft objects by touch

Put the objects into the bag.

Wear the bag and say:

When we touch something, our fingers tell us how it feels. We know whether it is hard or soft. Let's feel some *hard* and *soft* objects now.

Remove the (ball of yarn) from the bag. Emphasize that (the yarn) is soft as the children pass it around and feel it. Repeat this procedure with the (stone), pointing out that it is hard. Continue in this way with the other objects in the bag. Then return the objects to the bag and let the children take turns feeling one and describing it in sentences like "I have a (rock). This (rock) feels (hard)." Continue until everyone has had a turn.

152

MATERIALS*

ACTIVITY 1

Display Board

Manikin, Disassembled

Body parts

Curly hair

Facial features

ACTIVITY 2

Teacher provides

Mirror (optional)

1 Focus: identifying missing body parts, and then talking about how one would get along without them

Ask two children to assemble the manikin on the board. Then say:

(Bob) and (Marvina) did a good job of putting our manikin together today. Now let's play a game with it. While you cover your eyes, I will take away two of the manikin parts. Then we will talk about what we would do if we did not have those body parts.

When the children's eyes are covered, remove a leg and a foot from the manikin. After the group has identified the missing parts, lead a discussion with these questions:

1. **If you had only one leg, what might you have trouble doing?**
2. **Are there other ways that you could do those things?**
3. **Do you know anyone who has only one leg?**

Continue in this way with other body parts.

2 Focus: talking about mirrors, and then pretending to be mirrors by imitating one another's actions

Ask:

What does a mirror do? (Pause) **Yes, a mirror shows a copy of whatever is in front of it.**

Call on several children to tell where and when they have used mirrors. Then continue:

Let's play a mirror game. Find a space where you will have room to move your arms and legs. Now let's pretend that all of you are mirrors and must copy what I do.

Begin by placing your arms over your head. Check to see that every child is copying you. Then slowly change the positions of your arms. When the children understand the idea, have them pair up, face each other, and take turns being mirrors for each other. As necessary, help each pair to produce a variety of actions, including facial expressions.

OPTIONAL: Begin the activity by passing around a mirror.

153

MATERIALS*

ACTIVITY 1

Fruits & Vegetables

All

Puppets

Zoey

Thinking hat

ACTIVITY 2

Fruits & Vegetables

All

1 Focus: making up riddles about fruits and vegetables for the group to guess

Sit with the children in a circle, and place the fruits and vegetables in the center. Hold Zoey (wearing her thinking hat), and have her say:

Let's make up some riddles about these fruits and vegetables. (Hold up banana) **Is this a fruit, or a vegetable?** (Pause) **Yes, it is a fruit. Tell me what color, shape, and size it is.**

When the banana has been thoroughly described, Zoey should tie together the children's ideas into riddle form. For example:

I am thinking of something. . . . It is a fruit. . . . It turns yellow when it is ripe. . . . It is long, narrow, and shaped like a tube. . . . What is it? (banana)

Give more practice if necessary. Once the children understand, have them take tums holding Zoey and presenting a riddle for the others to solve. Help as necessary.

VARIATION: To make the activity *easier,* Zoey may need to continue to help the children make up riddles.

2 Focus: following directions that stress positional words and sequencing of actions

Give each child a fruit or a vegetable, and hold one yourself. Have the children stand about two feet apart. Stress the positional words as you give commands like those listed below. Demonstrate if necessary.

Hold your fruit or vegetable . . .

1. ***under*** **your arm; then blink.**
2. ***beside*** **your ear; then jump.**
3. ***behind*** **your back; then turn.**
4. ***between*** **your knees; then jump.**
5. ***in front of*** **your nose; then sit down.**
6. ***in back of*** **your neck; then stand up.**
7. ***next to*** **your arm; then shiver.**
8. ***below*** **your chin; then stretch high.**
9. ***on top of*** **your foot; then turn around.**
10. ***above*** **your head; then lie down as though you were dead.**

Afterwards, let individuals take turns doing the above actions for the group. After each, the group should describe what was done in a sentence like "(Joseph) held an (apple) *under* (his) arm; then (he blinked)."

154

MATERIALS*

ACTIVITY 1

Cards

Numerals & Color Shapes

294-303

Color Chips

All

P. Mooney Bag

ACTIVITY 2

Color Chips

1 chain of 10 chips

All remaining chips

P. Mooney Bag

1 Focus: counting shapes and matching color chips to shape cards, and then linking the chips while stressing *longer* and *shorter*

Put all the chips into the bag, and stack the cards in order.

Wearing the bag, hold the 10 color shape cards and say:

Please take a card and point to the shapes on it as you count them aloud, (Imogene). (Pause) **Now choose the same color and number of chips from the bag.** (Pause) **Good! Now link your chips into a chain.**

When all 10 cards have been used in this way, have the 10 chains placed in order on the floor before you. (If your group is larger than 10, have some children work together, so that everyone participates.) Then lead a discussion about how to lengthen or shorten the chains. For example, hold up a chain and ask questions like these:

1. **What could we do to make this chain *longer*?** (Pause) **Yes, we would *add* chips to it.** (Demonstrate)
2. **What could we do to make this chain *shorter*?** (Pause) **You are right; we would *take away* some chips.** (Demonstrate)

End by having the children arrange the chains in numerical order on the floor; then have everyone count in unison from one to 10 as you hold up the chains in turn.

VARIATION: To make the activity *harder,* hold up the longest and shortest chains and have the group discuss how to make them the same in length. Then ask a child to make the chains equal in length.

2 Focus: making a chain of 10 chips, and then saying and acting out a counting rhyme

Make a chain of 10 chips and put the remaining chips into the bag.

Wearing the bag, hold up the chain and say:

Look at my chip chain. Let's count the number of chips on it together. (Do this) **Now let's take turns choosing 10 chips from the bag and linking them to make chains.**

Have the children hold their chains as you count the chips aloud with them. Then continue:

Now, as I say a number rhyme, please do what I do.

Remove chips as indicated while you say this rhyme:

Ten little color chips all in a line;
One fell down (remove and drop a chip), **then there were nine.**

Nine little color chips sitting on a gate;
One fell down (remove and drop a chip), **then there were eight.**

Eight little color chips looking up at heaven;
One fell down (remove and drop a chip), **then there were seven.**

Seven little color chips sitting on some bricks;
One fell down (remove and drop a chip), **then there were six.**

Six little color chips getting ready to jive;
One fell down (remove and drop a chip), **then there were five.**

Five little color chips going through a door;
One fell down (remove and drop a chip), **then there were four.**

Four little color chips climbing up a tree;
One fell down (remove and drop a chip), **then there were three.**

Three little color chips going to the zoo;
One fell down (remove and drop a chip), **then there were two.**

Two little color chips going for a run;
One fell down (remove and drop a chip), **then there was one.**

One little color chip having no fun;
He ran home (drop chip), **then there was none.**

Repeat several times, having the children first reassemble their chains each time.

155

MATERIALS*

ACTIVITY 1

None

ACTIVITY 2

None

1 Focus: talking about funny experiences

Say:

Let's talk about things that are funny. What does the word *funny* mean? (Discuss) **Now let's talk about the funniest thing that ever happened to each of you.**

Let the children take turns describing their funniest experiences. Encourage them to question each other.

2 Focus: relating three words to make funny sentences

Say:

Let's make up funny sentences to try to make each other laugh. I will take the first turn.

Use one of the sets of words in the list below to make up a humorous sentence, like this: "Yesterday a butterfly pushed a lion down my chimney." Then let the children take turns. If necessary, use the word groups more than once.

1. **butterfly, lion, chimney**
2. **airplane, birthday, baby**
3. **dance, rainbow, rocket**
4. **snowman, orange, rabbit**
5. **school, horse, grandma**
6. **smoke, television, castle**
7. **bike, bridge, balloon**
8. **dentist, elephant, rock**
9. **engine, milk, man**
10. **sun, swing, clown**

156

MATERIALS*

ACTIVITY 1

Display Board
4 ledges

P. Mooney Stick

Poster 4

ACTIVITY 2

Display Board
4 ledges

Poster 4

Puppets
P. Mooney

1 Focus: naming and describing items on the poster "City in Summer," and talking about city life

Do not display the poster until asked to do so.

Hold the stick and say:

P. Mooney's magic is going to send us on a magical trip. Where do you think it might take us?

When several guesses have been made, have the children close their eyes. Then wave the stick as you say:

Mooney Magic, zing and zip!

Take us on a Mooney trip.

Quickly use the ledges to place the poster on the board. Then say:

Open your eyes! Where are we? (Encourage unison response) **Yes! We are in a city.**

Call on children to point out and describe those things which especially interest them on the poster, such as the following:

1. **mail carrier**
2. **pigeon**
3. **mailbox**
4. **crane**
5. **fan**
6. **birdcage**
7. **elevated train**
8. **washing machine**
9. **cat**
10. **sign painters**

If no one notices P. Mooney on the poster, ask the children to look for him there. Continue with questions like these:

1. **Have you ever lived in a city like this one?** (Encourage the children to discuss their own experiences)
2. **What kinds of work do you see people doing in this poster?**
3. **How do people get from one place to another in the city?**
4. **What are some things that city children have fun doing?**
5. **What season of the year is it in this city? How can you tell?**
6. **Would you like to live in this city? Why or why not?**

Accept all appropriate answers and add instructive comments. End by waving the stick again as you say:

Mooney Magic, do a trick!

Take us back, P. Mooney Stick!

2 Focus: identifying items on the poster "City in Summer" while using a rhyme

Leave the poster from Activity 1 on display.

Put P. Mooney on your hand and have him say:

Let's play a looking game. Look at the poster and try to find what I name.

P. Mooney should look at the poster, study it a few seconds, and say:

I went to the city and what did I see?

I saw a (jet plane), oh, zippity-zee!

Have P. Mooney call on a child to come and point to the (jet plane). That child may then hold P. Mooney and repeat the rhyme, naming another item found in the poster. Continue as time and interest permit.

157

MATERIALS*

ACTIVITY 1

Cards

Numerals & Color Shapes

314-323

Color chips

8 per child, one of each color

All remaining chips

P. Mooney Bag

Teacher provides

1 envelope per child

ACTIVITY 2

None

1 Focus: naming and matching colors in the game Color Bingo

Put a set of eight chips, one of each color, into an envelope for each child. Put the remaining chips into the bag.

Give the children an envelope apiece, and have them sit in pairs on the floor before you. Hand each pair a number card to place on the floor. Wear the bag and say:

Let's play the game Color Bingo again. Each time I show you a chip from the bag, look on your card and see if it has the same color. If it does, take your matching chips and place them upon that color on the card. The partners whose card first has two chips on every color may then say, "Bingo!"

Check to see that the children respond correctly. Ask each child of a winning pair to name the colors on their card. Then have everyone exchange cards or use the unused ones, and repeat the game with the "winners" taking turns calling out the colors. Continue in this way as time and interest suggest.

2 Focus: saying a color rhyme, and then brainstorming items of chosen colors

Gather the children around you in a circle. Say:

Listen as I say a rhyme about colors. Then we will say it together and take turns choosing the colors we like.

Read this rhyme:

Red and orange, green and blue,
Shining yellow, dark brown, too;
Black and white are quite a sight.
Choose any color that you like.

Invite the children to join you in repeating the rhyme. Name a child in the last line: "Choose any color that you like, (Hans)." When that child chooses a color, the others are to name all the things they know are (red). Repeat the procedure with seven other children, encouraging each to name a new color. Continue until all eight colors have been suggested.

158

MATERIALS*

ACTIVITY 1

Cards
People
223

ACTIVITY 2

Teacher provides
Mirror

1 Focus: talking about feeling *happy*

Show the card and ask:

How do you think this girl feels?

Encourage discussion. If no one says that the girl seems happy, suggest this. Then continue:

Let's talk about what makes each of us happy.

Encourage the children to tell about things, events, or people which make them feel happy. Accept all responses.

2 Focus: talking about and acting out being happy

Ask:

How does your mouth look when you are happy? (Discuss) **Yes, it is curved in a smile when you feel happy. Let's all smile and look at ourselves in this mirror.**

Pass the mirror around. Then continue:

We do other things that show we are happy. Sometimes we laugh. Let's all laugh together. (Do this) **What else do we do when we are happy?**

Help the children identify and carry out "happy" actions such as these:

1. **humming**
2. **dancing**
3. **singing**
4. **jumping joyfully**
5. **clapping**
6. **whistling**
7. **giggling**
8. **hugging**
9. **squealing gleefully**
10. **grinning**

159

MATERIALS*

ACTIVITY 1

Cards

Vehicles

272

ACTIVITY 2

Cards

Vehicles

267-283 (272*)

1 Focus: brainstorming ways to travel that are faster than walking

Show the card and ask:

What is this? (Pause) **Yes, it's a car. What do cars do?** (Pause) **Yes, they carry people. Why are cars important to us?**

After the discussion, say:

We can travel faster by riding in a car than we can by walking or running. There are many vehicles that move faster than we can walk or run. Let's name some of them.

Give hints as necessary. Encourage everyone to participate, and comment on imaginative responses.

2 Focus: talking about and classifying vehicles by whether they can carry *few* or *many* people

Let two volunteers distribute the cards. If necessary, two children may share a card. Say:

Some of the vehicles on your cards can carry only a *few* people, and some can carry *many* people. Let's take turns telling how many people might be able to ride in these vehicles.

After everyone has responded for his or her card, have the children holding vehicles for few passengers sit on your right side and the children with vehicles for many passengers sit on your left. Conclude by having the children identify the two groups of vehicles in unison.

160

MATERIALS*

ACTIVITY 1

None

ACTIVITY 2

Cards

Music

338

Audiocassette 2

Side B, Song 15,

"Contrasts"

1 Focus: talking about frightening experiences

Say:

We have already talked about funny things. Today let's talk about what makes us feel frightened or scared. Think of the scariest thing you can and tell us about it. Use sentences.

Let each child describe something she or he finds frightening or scary. The children should also say what they do when frightened. Encourage them to question each other.

2 Focus: listening to and talking about the music "Contrasts" while stressing *scary* and *funny*, and then moving imaginatively to the music

Say:

Now let's listen to some music. Part of it may be funny, and part of it may remind you of being scared. Listen and see if you can tell which part is funny and which is scary.

Play the song. Afterward, let the children discuss the music and what it made them think about. Accept all responses. Then continue:

Let's listen to the music again. This time, when you hear the funny part, act the way funny people do. When the music becomes scary, let's turn ourselves into scary people.

Repeat the song two or three times. Encourage imaginative responses.

Keep in Mind. . .
After each lesson in the program, individuals who have difficulty demonstrating proficiency in the skills you consider appropriate and important for them to learn should be tutored. Aides could help you with this task.

161

MATERIALS*

ACTIVITY 1

P. Mooney Stick

ACTIVITY 2

P. Mooney Stick

Teacher provides

Paper bag (optional)

1 Focus: imagining and talking about being invisible in different situations

Wave the stick as you say:

Mooney Magic, do a trick.

Make us invisible, P. Mooney Stick.

Then say:

Now everyone is invisible. What does being invisible mean? (Encourage responses) **Let's all think about where we would go if we were invisible and what we would do there.**

Discuss these ideas with the children. If they need prompting, suggest situations like this:

1. **being invisible at home**
2. **being invisible at the doctor's office**
3. **being invisible at the barber/ beauty shop**
4. **being invisible at the grocery store**

End by waving the stick and saying:

Eenie, Mooney,

Macaroony!

Now let's be

You and me.

2 Focus: identifying classmates' voices in a P. Mooney-stick game

Have the children stand in a circle. Choose a child to be "it." Have "it" stand in the center, eyes closed, one hand holding the stick and the other covering his or her eyes. The other children are to join hands and circle "it" until that child says, "The P. Mooney stick says, 'Stop!'" Without looking, "it" then points the stick. The child at whom the stick points is to say, "The P. Mooney stick is pointing at me." "It" then guesses who is talking. If the guess is correct, the two change places. Continue as time permits.

OPTIONAL: Use a paper bag to cover the eyes of the child who is "it."

162

MATERIALS*

ACTIVITY 1

None

ACTIVITY 2

Cards

Pictures from Several Categories

5 6 15 21 32 35
153 155 173 229
233 239 251 252
259 262 265 274
275 277

P. Mooney Bag

1 Focus: sequencing, describing, and pantomiming preparations for a trip from the country to the city

Say:

Let's pretend that we live on a farm in the country. Today we are going to take a special trip to the city. It is very early and we are still in bed, but we have to get ready to go. Let's think of all we have to do before we can leave. I will start. First, we must all get out of bed.

Have the children act this out.
Then say:

What must we do next, (Pei Ching)?

Call on individuals in turn to name the next preparation for the group to pantomime. If necessary, suggest activities like these:

1. **bathroom activities**
2. **dressing**
3. **packing a lunch**
4. **preparing the vehicle for travel**
5. **counting money**
6. **eating breakfast**
7. **feeding farm animals**

2 Focus: talking about funny ways to travel to the city

Put the 20 cards into the bag.

Wear the bag and say:

Now we are off to the city, but it is very far away, so we cannot walk there. Let's talk about some funny ways to make the trip. You may begin, (Timothy).

The child is to come to the front, pick a card from the bag, and say, "I would go to the city on (a broomstick)." Continue with other children until all the cards have been used. Conclude by asking individuals:

What do you think would be the funniest way to travel?

Encourage the use of sentences.

163

MATERIALS*

ACTIVITY 1

Cards

Pictures from Several Categories

5	38	42	46
50	64	69	100
109	117	119	135
157	168	169	172
173	186	187	189
223	242	249	281

Display Board

2 ledges

ACTIVITY 2

Color Chips

All

P. Mooney Bag

1 Focus: talking about the relationships between pictures and the activities associated with them

Set up the board and ledges. Stack the cards in the order listed below.

Place cards 5 and 38 on the board and say:

Let's play a thinking game. Look at these two pictures. (Point)

Now I will ask someone a question. Please listen carefully.

When I call on you, answer in a sentence.

Display each set of cards before calling on children to respond to these questions and statements:

1. 5•**bird**
38•**worm**
What do you think will happen if this bird gets hungry?

2. 42•**boots**
50•**mittens**
64•**snowsuit**
Greg is getting ready to go outside. He will put on these clothes. What do you think the weather is like?

3. 100•**cereal**
117•**orange juice**
135•**toast**
Andrea is getting ready to eat. What time of the day do you think it is?

4. 157•**scrub brush**
173•**pail**
172•**mop**
If your father were to get out these things, what do you think he would be getting ready to do?

5. 249•**sailboat**
242•**pail and shovel**
69•**boy's swimsuit**
Clemuel is packing some things to take with him. Where do you think he is going?

6. 281•**mail truck**
This truck stopped outside Elizabeth's house. Why?

7. 119•**chocolate milk**
189•**kitchen table**
186•**sponge**
Michael was trying to put a glass of chocolate milk on the table. But something happened. What do you think happened?

8. 168•**iron**
169•**ironing board**
46•**dress**
What does Sabrina's mother have to do before Sabrina goes to the party?

9. 223•**happy girl**
Juanita's grandmother and grandfather came to visit her. How do you think she feels? Why?

10. 109•**ham**
187•**spoon**
Bill will have meat for his dinner. But he has only one thing with which to cut and eat his meat. Do you think he will be able to cut the meat with that? Why not?

2 Focus: counting color chips, and then following directions involving colors and naming colored objects

Put the chips into the bag.

Wear the bag and say:

Each of you may take five color chips out of the P. Mooney bag. When it is your turn, please count the chips as you pull them out.

When all the children have five chips apiece, say:

Now please look at your chips and listen carefully. If you have a chip that is the same color as a (banana), stand up. (Pause) **Those of you who are standing are each to name one other thing that is (yellow).**

Afterwards, have the group count the standing children in unison. Then have those children return their chips to the bag. Continue as before by asking for chips that are the same color as . . .

1. **a tomato.**
2. **tires on a truck.**
3. **leaves on a tree in summer.**
4. **mashed potatoes.**
5. **a mud puddle.**
6. **a clear sky.**
7. **the P. Mooney bag.**

164 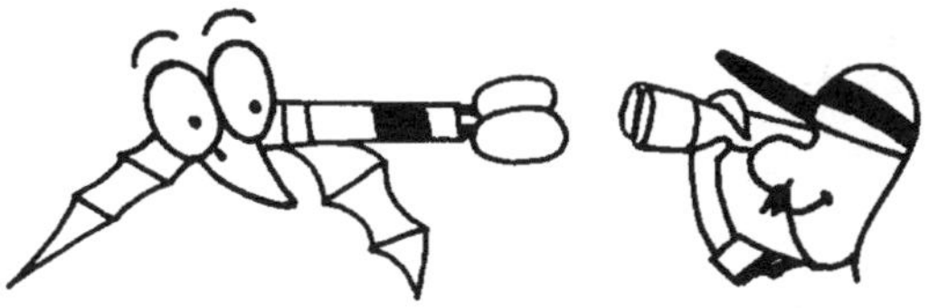

MATERIALS*

ACTIVITY 1

Display Board
4 ledges

P. Mooney Stick
Poster 5

ACTIVITY 2

None

1 Focus: naming and describing items on the poster "Winter Scene," and then talking about experiences with *snow*

Do not display the poster until asked to do so.

Hold the stick and say:

P. Mooney's stick is going to send us on a magical Mooney trip. Where do you think it might take us?

After the children have told their guesses, have them close their eyes as you wave the stick and say:

Mooney Magic, zing and zip!

Take us on a Mooney trip.

Quickly use the ledges to place the poster on the board. Then say:

Open your eyes. Where are we? (Discuss) **Yes, we are at a winter scene where it is very cold.**

Encourage the children to point out and describe the poster items that interest them. If no one notices P. Mooney on the poster, ask the children to look for him there. Continue by asking either of these questions:

1. **Have you ever played in snow like this? What was it like?**
2. **What do you think it would be like to play in snow?**

After the discussion, wave the stick as you say:

Mooney Magic, do a trick!

Take us back, P. Mooney Stick!

2 Focus: saying an action poem about a *snowman*

Stand with the children and say:

If we had a lot of snow, we could make a snowman. I know a rhyme about building a snowman. Please listen and watch me as I go through it for you the first time. Then we will do it together.

Say this rhyme with gestures:

Roll a little snowball
(Make a small circle with both hands)
Until it's big and round.
(Make a large circle)
Listen as you roll it.
(Pantomime pushing a large snowball)
It doesn't make a sound.
(Cup hand to one ear and whisper these words)
Our snowman needs two eyes.
(Point to eyes)
He also needs two ears. (Point to ears)
Here is his mouth. (Point to mouth)
Here is his nose. (Point to nose)
Here is his hat.
(Put both hands on head to make a pointed "hat")
Here are his toes.
(Point with both hands to toes)
Let's give him a broom to hold.
(Put hands to one side as if holding a broom)
I hope he doesn't catch a cold!
(Pantomime shivering)

Lead the children in saying the rhyme several times. Each time, invite a different child or pair of children to lead the group in doing the actions.

165 

MATERIALS*

ACTIVITY 1

Cards

People

224

ACTIVITY 2

Cards

Music

328

Audiocassette 2

Side A, Song 5,

"If and Then Go Together"

1 Focus: talking about feeling *sad*

Show the card and ask:

How do you think this girl feels?

Encourage discussion. If no one says that the girl seems sad, suggest this. Then continue:

Let's talk about what makes each of us feel sad.

Encourage the children to tell about things, events, or people which make them feel sad. Accept all responses.

2 Focus: talking about things we do when we feel *happy* or *sad,* and then singing the song "If and Then Go Together"

Say:

Let's name some of the things we do when we feel sad.

Encourage the children to tell what they do when they are sad. Discuss such actions as crying, going away to be by oneself, and talking to someone special. Then ask the children what they do when they feel happy, and continue as before. Encourage everyone to participate. End by playing the song (instrumental version). Refer to the music card as you lead the children in singing these verses:

1. **If you are happy, then you may smile, etc.**
2. **If you are sad, then you may cry, etc.**

166

MATERIALS*

ACTIVITY 1

Cards

Toys

226 228 235 242
247 248 251 252
253 254 255 260
262 263

Display Board

6 ledges

ACTIVITY 2

None

1 Focus: identifying *toys* from rhyming names

Set up the board with ledges and display the 14 toy cards in random order.

Review the toy card labels with the children. Then say:

Now we are going to play a rhyming game. We will give ourselves new first names that rhyme with the names of toys. Let's begin.

Choose a girl to stand beside you. Point to her and say:

This is "Jane." She likes an . . . airplane. (Point to card 226) **The words *Jane* and *airplane* rhyme.**

Lead the group in saying in unison:

***Jane* likes an *airplane*.**

Continue in this way with other children, using the sentences given below. If the children have trouble, ask them to say the names of the toys in turn until they find the one that rhymes.

1. **This is "Paul." He likes a . . . ball.** (Point to card 228)
2. **This is "Mike." He likes a . . . trike.** (Point to card 262)
3. **This is "Polly." She likes a . . . dolly.** (Point to card 235)
4. **This is "Gail." She likes a . . . pail.** (Point to card 242)
5. **This is "Jake." He likes a . . . rake.** (Point to card 247)
6. **This is "Dot." She likes a . . . robot.** (Point to card 248)
7. **This is "Kate." She likes a . . . skate.** (Point to card 251)
8. **This is "Fred." He likes a . . . sled.** (Point to card 252)
9. **This is "Clyde." He likes to . . . slide.** (Point to card 253)
10. **This is "King." He likes to . . . swing.** (Point to card 254)
11. **This is "Dee." She likes to have . . . tea.** (Point to card 255)
12. **This is "Elaine." She likes a . . . train.** (Point to card 260)
13. **This is "Chuck." He likes a . . . truck.** (Point to card 263)

2 Focus: talking about names the children would choose if they could change theirs

Call on children to tell what first names they would choose if they could change theirs. Encourage everyone to participate, and accept all responses.

167

MATERIALS*

ACTIVITY 1

Cards
Animals
3 11 12 23 37

Display Board
(optional)
3 ledges (optional)

ACTIVITY 2

Cards
Animals (optional)
6 15 17 29 30 31
33 36

Display Board
(optional)
6 ledges (optional)

1 **Focus: identifying *animals* from descriptions in riddles**

Say:

Let's play a guessing game. I will tell you a riddle in verse about an animal. Try to figure out which animal I mean.

Have the children respond in unison to each of these riddles*:

1. **I'm small and furry, and very soft to touch.**
   I think when you see me, you'll like me so much.
   I meow when I am hungry, and purr when I am glad.
   I don't like the water; it makes me look bad.
   I live around the barn, and sometimes in a house.
   My favorite dinner is a nice little mouse. (kitten)

2. **I'm big and gentle but not much fun.**
   When it's time to eat, I come on the run.
   I have two legs at the front and two at the rear.
   If you meet my brother, just call him a steer.
   My coat is smooth and soft to touch.
   I give lots of milk that you like so much. (cow)

3. **I fly through the air with my two little wings.**
   If you get in my way, I am likely to sting.
   You'll find me in the garden,
   Or in a flowering tree.
   If you are looking for honey,
   Just follow me. (bee)

4. **My tail is short; my ears are long.**
   I seldom stay where I belong.
   I have four feet and sixteen toes,
   A small black spot they call my nose.
   My back is smooth and full of hair.
   If we start to race, I'll beat you there.
   I like to run and chase a ball
   And lick your face when you have had a fall.
   I like to sleep in a patch of sun,
   Or tease the cat and watch it run,
   Go in the woods for a nice long hike,
   But what I like best is to chase a bike.
   (dog)

5. **I am small and round; my shell is hard.**
   I can crawl and walk, but cannot hop.
   I live in the water, sometimes on land.
   I am so small you can hold me in your hand.
   I have four short legs that move so slow.
   And I carry my shell wherever I go.
   (turtle)

Then continue:

Now let's see if you can guess an animal from only part of a riddle.

Read two consecutive lines chosen at random from each riddle. If the children have trouble guessing, read more lines until the animal is identified.

VARIATION: To make the activity *easier,* display the cards on the board.

2 **Focus: identifying *animals* from the first part of their names, and then describing them**

Say:

Let's play a listening game. I will say the first part of an animal's name. Try to figure out which animal I mean. Then we will name three things about the animal. Here is the first one: *roos*. . . . (Pause) **Which animal did I start to name?**

The children should respond with the sentence, "You started to say rooster." Then have three children each name in a sentence one characteristic of the animal. Continue with these word parts:

1. **pup** . . . (puppy)
2. **turk** . . . (turkey)
3. **ele** . . . (elephant)
4. **ger** . . . (gerbil)
5. **rab** . . . (rabbit)
6. **spi** . . . (spider)
7. **butter** . . . (butterfly)

VARIATION: To make the activity *easier,* display the cards and/or pronounce more of the word.

** NOTE:*
These rhymes are by Dorothy W. Barth.

168

MATERIALS*

ACTIVITY 1

None

ACTIVITY 2

None

1 Focus: relating pairs of short words to make *compound* words, and then defining them

Say:

Let's talk about words. What does the word *butter* mean? (Discuss) **Now think about the word *fly*. What is a fly?** (Discuss) **What long word can we make by putting the words *butter* and *fly* together?** (Pause) **Yes, the long word is *butterfly*. What is a *butterfly*?**

Continue as above with these compound words:

1. **haircut**
2. **airplane**
3. **sidewalk**
4. **bedroom**
5. **football**
6. **rainbow**
7. **snowsuit**
8. **cupcake**
9. **baseball**
10. **pocketbook**
11. **blackboard**
12. **pancake**
13. **shoelace**
14. **swimsuit**
15. **raincoat**
16. **moonlight**
17. **toothpaste**
18. **washcloth**
19. **playground**
20. **headlight**

2 Focus: listening to pairs of short words and identifying the resulting *compound words*

Say:

Now let's play a listening game. I will have two of you each say a short word. Try to figure out what long word is made from the two short words.

Ask two children to come to the front. Whisper half a compound word to each (*foot* and *ball*, for example). Then the two children are to say the words in the right order to the class. Have the group say the compound word in unison. Using the words listed below, continue with other pairs of children.

1. **someone**
2. **upstairs**
3. **bridesmaid**
4. **classroom**
5. **football**
6. **blackbird**
7. **snowman**
8. **sailboat**
9. **bedroom**
10. **blackboard**
11. **hairdresser**
12. **handshake**
13. **haircut**
14. **washcloth**

169

MATERIALS*

ACTIVITY 1

Color Chips
All

P. Mooney Bag

ACTIVITY 2

Color Chips
All

P. Mooney Bag

1 Focus: comparing chip chains while stressing the words *fewer* and *more*

Put the chips into the bag.

Wear the bag and say:

I am going to give you each some color chips. Count your chips and then link them together.

Give each child a different number of chips, between five and 20 apiece. Help anyone who has trouble linking his or hers. Continue:

(Sue Ann) and (Richard), please stand up and show us your chains. (Pause) **Now please look at these two chains and raise your hand if you can tell me which has more chips and which has fewer chips.**

When the children have done so, discuss the meanings of *more* and *fewer.* Then have the two children begin a line that will go from *fewest* to *most* chips per chain. Continue in this way with other pairs of children until everyone has found a position in the line. End by having the children unlink and pile their chips in the center of the activity area.

2 Focus: making a chain of 10 chips, and then saying and acting out a counting rhyme

Have the color chips piled in an activity area.

Ask the children to sit in a circle on the floor around the pile of chips. Pick up 10 chips, one by one, to link as the children count them in unison. Then hold up your chain and say:

Now each of you may take 10 chips from the pile and make a chain like mine.

Help as necessary. Have the children hold up their chains and count the chips in unison or individually. Then continue:

Now let's say the rhyme about 10 little color chips. Remember to take the chips off your chain and drop them as the rhyme says. Let's begin.

Remove the chips as indicated while you say this rhyme:

Ten little color chips all in a line;

One fell down (remove and drop a chip), **then there were nine.**

Nine little color chips sitting on a gate;

One fell down (remove and drop a chip), **then there were eight.**

Eight little color chips looking up at heaven;

One fell down (remove and drop a chip), **then there were seven.**

Seven little color chips sitting on some bricks;

One fell down (remove and drop a chip), **then there were six.**

Six little color chips getting ready to jive;

One fell down (remove and drop a chip), **then there were five.**

Five little color chips going through a door;

One fell down (remove and drop a chip), **then there were four.**

Four little color chips climbing up a tree;

One fell down (remove and drop a chip), **then there were three.**

Three little color chips going to the zoo;

One fell down (remove and drop a chip), **then there were two.**

Two little color chips going for a run;

One fell down (remove and drop a chip), **then there was one.**

One little color chip having no fun;

He ran home (drop chip), **then there was none.**

Repeat as time and interest permit.

170

MATERIALS*

ACTIVITY 1

Cards

Stories

433-450

Teacher provides

Blank cassette

Tape recorder

ACTIVITY 2

None

1 Focus: using a tape recorder to retell the story "Terrapin Turtle's Travel Troubles," and then listening to the results

Keep the 18 story cards in the right order as you give one out per child. If necessary, two children may share a card. If your class is small, place the cards in order along the chalkledge, and have children take more than one turn. Say:

Let's pretend that we are in a recording studio to record the story "Terrapin Turtle's Travel Troubles." Each of you is to tell the part of the story shown on a card. I will record what you say with this tape recorder. (Point) **Then we will play back the tape and listen to our story. Now look at your card and get ready to speak into the microphone.**

When the children have had time to prepare, begin the recording by announcing the title. Then let each child in turn tell the part of the story shown on the card. If children are sharing a card, give each an opportunity to speak. Continue until all the cards have been described. End by playing the recording for the children. Help them identify each storyteller. Comment on all efforts, especially good ones.

2 Focus: talking about places to visit and ways to travel

Say:

Let's talk about traveling. We can go to some very interesting places. What places would you like to visit?

Encourage discussion. Then, if time permits, continue:

Let's think about all the ways we can travel. How would you choose to travel to the places you want to visit?

Make sure everyone participates in the discussion. Ask questions to encourage hesitant children. Encourage the use of sentences.

171

MATERIALS*

ACTIVITY 1

None

ACTIVITY 2

None

1 Focus: talking about *negative* and *positive* feelings

Ask:

Have you ever felt like saying "No, I won't! No! No!"? (Pause) **Yes, we have all felt that way often. Tell us about something that makes you want to say that.**

Encourage the children to present their negative feelings. You may wish to begin the discussion with examples from your own experience. If the children have trouble getting started, ask if they have ever said "No! I won't!" to friends, to siblings, to teachers, or to their parents. Accept all responses. Continue as before with a discussion of positive feelings expressed by "Yes, I will!" Conclude by remarking that everyone sometimes wants to say "No! I won't!" or "Yes, I will!"

2 Focus: pantomiming *positive* and *negative feelings* using a chant

With the children standing before you, say:

Let's say and act out a chant. I will go through it for you the first time. Then we will chant these words together several times:

No! I won't!

No! I won't!

No! No!

No! I won't!

Invite the children to join you in repeating the chant. They are to use their whole bodies to express its meaning with actions like these:

1. **stamping feet**
2. **clenching fists**
3. **moving jerkily**
4. **frowning and looking stubborn**
5. **saying the chant faster and louder**

Continue as above with this chant:

Yes, I will!

Yes, I will!

Yes! Yes!

Yes! I will!

Suggested ways to express "yes";

1. **jumping**
2. **clapping**
3. **dancing**
4. **smiling and looking pleased**
5. **saying the chant faster and louder**

172

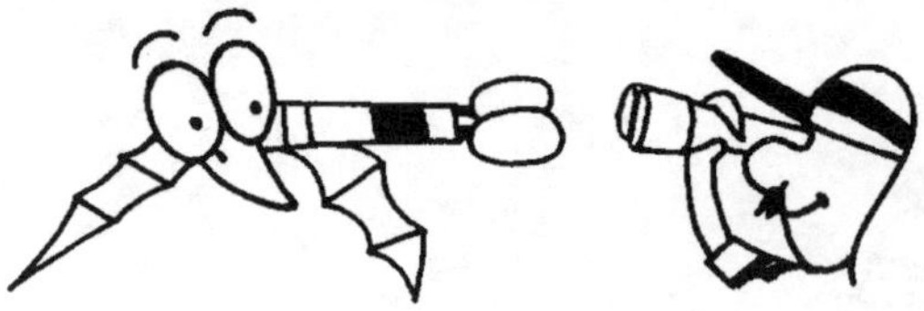

MATERIALS*

ACTIVITY 1

Cards

Vehicles

267-281

Display Board

6 ledges

ACTIVITY 2

Cards

Vehicles

(same as for Activity 1)

Display Board

6 ledges

1 Focus: talking about the energy used by vehicles

Display the 15 vehicle cards on the board.

Point to the cards and say:

All of these vehicles help us travel. Let's talk about what makes them move. (Point to card 272) **What makes this car move?** (Pause) **Yes, it has an engine which uses gasoline or some other fuel.**

Discuss the car's use of gasoline. Continue by having the class consider these vehicles and their energy sources:

1. **bicycle — human energy**
2. **airplane — gasoline (for small planes), jet fuel**
3. **train — steam, electricity, coal, diesel fuel**
4. **camping trailer — must be pulled by another vehicle**

Conclude by having the children name the type of energy or power used by each vehicle on display.

2 Focus: classifying vehicles into those that travel on *water,* in the *air,* and on *land*

Display the 15 vehicle cards on the board.

Say:

Vehicles can travel on water, in the air, or on land. (Point to board) **Let's figure out where these vehicles usually travel. Which of these travel on water?** (Pause) **Yes, a rowboat and a ship travel on water.**

Let two children hold cards 275 and 276, respectively, as you and the class discuss these water vehicles. Ask questions like these:

1. **Can a rowboat move only in water?**
2. **How would a rowboat be moved on land?**

Set the two cards aside. Continue as above with discussions of vehicles that travel in the air or on land. If time permits, end by having the children name all the vehicles they can that travel on water, in the air, or on the land.

173

MATERIALS*

ACTIVITY 1

Cards

Foods

98 99 101 106
114 116 122 123
125 135 145 146
151

Display Board

6 ledges

ACTIVITY 2

Cards

Foods

(same as for Activity 1)

1 Focus: listening to a poem and naming rhyming foods

Set up the board with ledges and display the 13 food cards in this order: 98, 106, 145, 116, 135, 123, 114, 101, 122, 99, 125, 146, and 151.

Say:

I am going to read you a rhyme about foods. Each time I pause, look at the pictures on the board for the kind of food to finish the rhyme. Then we will say the two lines together. Let's begin.

Read the rhymes given below, one by one. Each time, call on a child to point to the right card after the group has named the food that rhymes. Then reread the rhyme and ask the children to repeat each line in unison after you. Point to the card again only if the children need help.

1. **I am really hungry, for goodness sake!**
   What I need is a piece of (pause) ***cake.*** (Point to 98)
2. **I need some energy in my legs.**
   What I need are some scrambled (pause) ***eggs.*** (Point to 106)
3. **I am so hungry that I can't even reach.**
   What I need is a great big (pause) ***peach.*** (Point to 145)
4. **I am so hungry that I can't wiggle my toe.**
   What I need is some wiggly (pause) ***jello.*** (Point to 116)
5. **I am hungry for what I like most.**
   What I want is a piece of (pause) ***toast.*** (Point to 135)
6. **I am so hungry. I don't know why.**
   What I need is a piece of (pause) ***pie.*** (Point to 123)
7. **I am so hungry that I could moan.**
   What I need is an (pause) ***ice-cream cone-*** (Point to 114)
8. **I want some energy for my knees.**
   What I need is a piece of (pause) ***cheese.*** (Point to 101)
9. **I am so hungry I could almost shudder.**
   What I need is some (pause) ***peanut butter.*** (Point to 122)
10. **I am hungry for something handy.**
    Yes, I know. I want some (pause) ***candy.*** (Point to 99)
11. **I am hungry for something to pass through my lips.**
    What I need are some (pause) ***potato chips.*** (Point to 125)
12. **I am as hungry as a bear.**
    What I need is a big ripe (pause) ***pear.*** (Point to 146)
13. **I am so hungry. I am so slow.**
    What I need is a red (pause) ***tomato.*** (Point to 151)
    Oh, my goodness! Now my stomach is sore.
    I can't eat even one bite more.

2 Focus: talking about *foods*

Stack the 13 food cards, with card 98 on top.

Hold the cards and say:

Let's talk about these foods. (Show card 98) **Do you like to eat cake?**

Encourage the children to discuss whether or not they like each food. Accept all responses. For further discussion, ask questions like these:

1. **Have you ever eaten this kind of food?**
2. **What kind of (cake) do you like to eat?**
3. **When do you like to eat (cake) most?**
4. **What do you like to eat with (cake)?**
5. **What does (cake) taste like?**

OPTIONAL: End by having each child name a food he or she would choose as a special treat.

174

MATERIALS*

ACTIVITY 1

Color Chips

1 set of 8, 1 of each color

ACTIVITY 2

None

1 Focus: brainstorming objects by color

Link the eight chips into a chain.

Hold the chip chain and say:

Let's name together the colors on this chip chain.

Point to each chip in turn as the children respond in unison. Then let the children take turns naming the colors. Continue:

Now look at this (red) chip. (Point) **Let's take turns naming something that is (red).**

Have each child use a sentence to name a (red) object. Give hints as necessary. Encourage the children each to name something different. Continue in this way with the other seven colors.

2 Focus: imitating clapping patterns

Ask the children to stand before you. Say:

Please listen carefully as I clap a pattern. Then all of you together are to make the same pattern.

Clap out patterns like those given below and have the children repeat them in unison. Adjust the patterns to challenge the children. Make sure you give them enough practice to learn each one.

1. **clap, clap, clap, clap, etc.**
2. **clap, pause, clap, pause, etc.**
3. **clap, clap, pause, clap, clap, pause, etc.**
4. **clap, pause, clap, clap, pause, clap, pause, clap, clap, pause, etc.**
5. **clap, clap, pause, clap, pause, clap, clap, pause, clap, pause, etc.**

If feasible, continue by calling on individuals in turn to come up and present a pattern for the group to repeat.

175

MATERIALS*

ACTIVITY 1

None

ACTIVITY 2

Cards

People

201 203 207 208
209 210 212 213
214 215 216 217
218 220 221

Display Board

6 ledges

1 Focus: talking about what work one would like to do when one grows up

Say:

Let's talk about what kind of work you would like to do when you grow up.

Have the children take turns responding in sentences like "When I grow up, I would like to be (an astronaut)." For further discussion, ask questions like these:

1. **What would you wear for your job?**
2. **Where would you go to work?**
3. **What would you do as you worked?**
4. **What special equipment would you need to do your work?**
5. **Do you know anyone who does that kind of work?**

2 Focus: imagining and talking about vacation activities of workers

Set up the board with ledges and display the 15 people cards.

Show the cards one by one to the children, and have them name each occupation or activity pictured.
Then say:

Let's talk about what these people might do on their vacations. Imagine that you are an astronaut, like this man. (Point to card 201) **If you were an astronaut, what kind of vacation would you enjoy?**

Point to each card in turn and have the children suggest a kind of vacation for each person pictured.

OPTIONAL: End by having the children each name a favorite kind of vacation.

176

MATERIALS*

ACTIVITY 1

None

ACTIVITY 2

Teacher provides

Blank cassette

Tape recorder

1 Focus: listening to compound words, and identifying the *short words* in each

Say:

Please listen as I say some long words. Each long word is made out of two short words. Tell me the two short words you hear.

Use the list given below. If the children need help, pause between the two parts of each word. Then go through the list again, saying the words more rapidly and in random order.

1. birdhouse	**11. blackboard**
2. mousetrap	**12. cookbook**
3. backbone	**13. housework**
4. railroad	**14. toothbrush**
5. firefly	**15. schoolchild**
6. armchair	**16. horseshoe**
7. whitewash	**17. jackknife**
8. sidewalk	**18. beehive**
9. woodwork	**19. outside**
10. stairway	**20. washboard**

VARIATION: To make the activity *harder,* discuss the meanings of the short and the compound words.

2 Focus: defining *compound words,* and using them in sentences

Say:

Let's use some long words to make a tape recording. I will give you each one word to use in a sentence. After we have recorded all your sentences, we will listen to our recording and name each speaker.

Give each child a long word from the Activity 1 list to use in a sentence. Help as necessary. Record all the sentences, and then have the group listen to the recording and name each speaker.

VARIATION: To make the activity *harder,* play back the sentences in random order.

177

MATERIALS*

ACTIVITY 1

Display Board
6 ledges

Manikin, Movable

ACTIVITY 2

Display Board
6 ledges

Manikin, Movable

1 Focus: identifying *body parts,* and describing their functions

Set up the board and display the manikin on it.

Say:

Let's play a touch-and-tell game. I will point to a part of the manikin. Please touch that part on yourself and tell me what it is in a sentence. Then I will ask two or three people to tell what they can do with that body part.

Use the list given below, checking to see that the children respond correctly. Each time, have two or three children use a sentence like "I can (nod my head)" to describe a function of that body part.

1. head	**13. lower arm**
2. neck	**14. heels**
3. shoulders	**15. wrist**
4. chest	**16. fingers**
5. waist	**17. thumb**
6. stomach	**18. hands**
7. hips	**19. toes**
8. legs	**20. feet**
9. arms	**21. ankles**
10. back	**22. shins**
11. upper arm	**23. knees**
12. elbow	**24. thighs**

2 Focus: evaluating, and then imitating and describing the movable manikin's positions

Stand beside the board, with the children standing before you. Say:

Let's try to move our bodies into the same position as the manikin's.

Let a volunteer position the manikin for everyone to try to imitate. Before they move, help the children decide if the action is possible. Then have them describe either what they did or what they could not do. If anyone has trouble choosing a manikin position, suggest one of these:

1. **bend leg backwards**
2. **tilt head back**
3. **lift arms over head**
4. **touch chin to chest**
5. **bend forward at waist**
6. **nod head**
7. **touch nose with foot**
8. **stand on tiptoe**
9. **crouch on heels**
10. **lean elbows on knees**

178

MATERIALS*

ACTIVITY 1

Cards

Household Items

153 154 156 159
160 162 166 168
169 170 178 180
184 186 188 189
190 191 195 198

Display Board

6 ledges

ACTIVITY 2

Teacher provides

1 piece of rope 10 feet (3 meters) long

1 Focus: comparing pairs of household items while stressing *larger* and *smaller*

Set up the board with ledges. Stack the 20 household cards into the following pairs: 160, 154; 190, 178; 168, 162; 156, 198; 195, 191; 186, 159; 180, 153; 184, 169; 166, 188; 170 and 189.

Hold the stacked cards on your lap. Show cards 160 and 154, and say:

Let's think about how large and how small a clock and a bed really are. Look at the pictures on this pair of cards and think about which item would be smaller and which would be larger. (Pause) **Which is the smaller?** (Pause) **Which is the larger?**

When the children have answered correctly, place the cards on the board, with the smaller item on the left. Then have the children compare the sizes of the two objects by saying in unison:

1. **A (clock) is *smaller* than a (bed). and**
2. **A (bed) is *larger* than a (clock).**

Point to the cards in the right order as these sentences are repeated. Next remove the cards and repeat the procedure with the remaining pairs of cards.

2 Focus: talking about a rope, and brainstorming its uses

Hold up the piece of rope and ask these questions:

1. **What is this?**
2. **What color is this rope?**
3. **What does this rope feel like? Is it rough, or smooth?** (Let children handle rope)

Then say:

Now let's think about what we could do with a piece of rope.

Encourage the children to think of uses like these:

1. **to swing on**
2. **to climb a tree**
3. **to use as a jump rope**
4. **to hold luggage on a car**
5. **to tie wagons or tricycles together to make a "wagon train"**

179

MATERIALS*

ACTIVITY 1

None

ACTIVITY 2

Puppets

P. Mooney

1 Focus: evaluating and correcting statements on size comparisons in a true-false game

Say:

Let's play a true-false game. We will take turns telling the class something about our size. Then everyone will decide if what they hear is true, or false. I will go first. I am larger than an elephant! Is that true or false? (Pause) **It is false. I am not larger than an elephant.**

Help the children make up comparisons like those listed below. After the group has decided whether a statement is true or false, discuss any questions the children have about the comparison.

1. **I am smaller than a cup.**
2. **I am larger than a car.**
3. **I am larger than a bird.**
4. **I am smaller than a horse.**
5. **I am larger than a chicken.**
6. **I am smaller than a fish.**

2 Focus: following directions using size comparisons in the game P. Mooney Says

Have the children stand around you. Hold P. Mooney and have him say:

Let's play P. Mooney Says. When you hear the words "P. Mooney says," do what I say. If I do not begin by saying "P. Mooney says," don't move. Let's practice before we play.

Practice by having the puppet say:

1. **P. Mooney says, "Run and touch something larger than the door handle."** (Make sure everyone responds correctly)
2. **Run and touch something smaller than the door handle.** (Make sure everyone stands still and understands why)

When the children are ready, have P. Mooney give commands like these:

1. **P. Mooney says, "Run and touch something larger than a trash can."**
2. **P. Mooney says, "Run and touch something smaller than a desk."**
3. **P. Mooney says, "Run and touch something larger than a telephone."**
4. **Run and touch something smaller than the P. Mooney bag.**
5. **P. Mooney says, "Run and touch something smaller than a yardstick."**
6. **P. Mooney says, "Run and touch something larger than a pencil."**
7. **P. Mooney says, "Run and touch something larger than a windowpane."**
8. **Run and touch something smaller than a desk top.**
9. **P. Mooney says, "Run and touch something smaller than a cup."**
10. **P. Mooney says, "Run and touch something larger than a door."**

Continue as time and interest permit.

180

MATERIALS*

ACTIVITY 1

Display Board
4 ledges

Poster 5

ACTIVITY 2

Display Board
4 ledges

Poster 5

Audiocassette 4
Side B, Selection 5, "Sounds for Winter Scene"

1 Focus: talking about winter, and then describing items in the poster "Winter Scene" while stressing counting

Use the ledges to display the poster on the board.

Point to the poster as you ask:

What time of year does this poster show? (Pause) **Yes, it is a winter scene. How do we know it is winter?** (Discuss) **P. Mooney is somewhere in the poster. See if you can find him.**

After the children have done so, lead a discussion on the contents of the poster. Encourage them to describe items that interest them. Make sure everyone participates. If necessary, promote discussion with these remarks:

1. **I see some animals. How many do you see? What are they doing?**
2. **I see some vehicles. How many do you see? What are they doing?**
3. **I see some people sliding in the snow. How many are sliding? What are they using to help them slide?**
4. **Have you ever been in snow like this? When? Tell us about it.**
5. **What would you most like to do in this poster? How would you do it?**

2 Focus: identifying each of the "Sounds of the Winter Scene"

Leave the poster from Activity 1 on display.

Point to the poster and say:

If we were at this winter scene, we would hear many sounds. Let's look at the poster again as we listen to some of them.

Play the selection. Then say:

Let's listen again. This time, raise your hand if you know what is making each sound.

Play the selection again and have the sound sources named. Then have a volunteer come up and point to the correct items as you play the sounds a third time. Continue until most children are familiar with the sounds.

Keep in Mind. . .
After each lesson in the program, individuals who have difficulty demonstrating proficiency in the skills you consider appropriate and important for them to learn should be tutored. Aides could help you with this task.

181

MATERIALS*

ACTIVITY 1

Cards

Animals

1 3 8 11 12 13 20 25 26 27 31 36

ACTIVITY 2

Cards

Animals

(same as for Activity 1)

1 Focus: adding *-ing* to action words to create adjectives while naming and describing animals from their sounds

Stack the 12 animal cards in numerical order.

Hold the cards, show card 1, and say:

Let's use two sentences to name this animal and tell what sound it makes.

Have one child name the animal in a sentence like this: "That is a bear." Then say:

Now let's use another sentence to tell what sound this bear could make.

Have a child respond in a sentence like this: "That bear could make a growling sound." Then continue:

Now let's name both the animal and its sound in one sentence. I will go first: "This could be a *growling* bear." Let's say that sentence together.

Continue as before with the remaining cards, having the children take turns making up three sentences about each one. Give everyone at least one turn, even if some cards must be used more than once.

VARIATION: To make the activity *easier,* always say the third sentence for the children to repeat.

2 Focus: naming the animals and imitating their sounds in a chant

Hold the 12 stacked animal cards and say:

Now I will teach you a rhyming verse about these animals and their sounds.

Show card 1, and lead the children in saying the following rhyme line by line until they seem to know it and are producing the right animal sound.

Eenie, Mooney,
Macaroony!
What are we today?
All of us are (*growling bears*);
This is what we say:
(Grrr....)

Continue with the other cards. Have the children repeat the rhyme and sound for each animal, using this list:

1. **buzzing bees**
2. **meowing cats**
3. **mooing cows**
4. **barking dogs**
5. **quacking ducks**
6. **gobbling turkeys**
7. **clucking hens**
8. **roaring lions**
9. **hooting owls**
10. **oinking pigs**
11. **crowing roosters**

We recommend that you read again Part I of the Teacher's Guide at about this point. This should remind you of ways to teach the lessons for maximum efficiency.

182

MATERIALS*

ACTIVITY 1

Display Board
4 ledges

Poster 4

Audiocassette 4
Side B, Selection 4, "City in Summer"

ACTIVITY 2

Display Board
4 ledges

Poster 4

1 Focus: identifying "Sounds of the City in Summer," and then classifying and describing people by their actions in the poster "City in Summer"

Do not display the poster until asked to do so.

Say:

Close your eyes and imagine where you might be if you heard these sounds.

Play "City in Summer" and ask:

What place might sound like that? (Pause) **Yes, these sounds might be heard in a city. Here is a picture of a city scene for you to talk about.**

Use the ledges to place the poster on the board. Continue:

Look at all the people in this city! Let's take turns pointing to someone on the poster and describing what that person is doing.

Afterwards, point on the poster to someone splashing. Say:

This (boy) is splashing water. We could call (him) a splasher. Now let's find all the splashers.

Repeat this procedure with these groups:

1. **diggers**
2. **sprayers**
3. **riders**
4. **players**
5. **balancers**
6. **kneelers**
7. **sitters**
8. **walkers**
9. **workers**
10. **talkers**

2 Focus: thinking about "who might say that" on the poster "City in Summer"

Leave the poster from Activity 1 on display.

Point to the poster and say:

Let's play Who Might Say That? as you look at this poster. I will say a sentence that someone in the picture might say. Tell me who might say that sentence and why you think so.

Say the sentences given below, one at a time. See that everyone has a turn.

1. **"This water feels great!"**
2. **"I like your airplane. Will it fly?"**
3. **"Here, kitty. Please come back."**
4. **"I think I will play in that water, too."**
5. **"Here comes the mail carrier."**
6. **"Is that enough water, kids?"**
7. **"Breaking through the street is hard work!"**
8. **"Want to buy a newspaper?"**
9. **"This is a big sign to paint!"**
10. **"Don't fall off!"**
11. **"I hope your wing is not broken."**
12. **"Who wants to buy some popcorn?"**
13. **"Look how high in the air we are already!"**
14. **"I wish I didn't have to stay in this cage on such a nice day."**
15. **"I think the fire is out now."**
16. **"It's too hot to work today."**
17. **"My finger tastes salty from that popcorn."**
18. **"It's so hot today that I had to turn on the fan."**
19. **"I wish I could have a drink of that water."**
20. **"Let's go around once more!"**

183

MATERIALS*

ACTIVITY 1

None

ACTIVITY 2

None

1 Focus: classifying groups of four words

Gather the children around you and say:

I am going to say four words. Tell me one word or phrase that describes all four.

Use the sets of words listed below. Help as necessary, and give everyone a turn.

1. **cow, cat, horse, chick** (animals)
2. **blouse, raincoat, socks, jeans** (clothes)
3. **balloon, dolls, slide, top** (toys)
4. **cake, popcorn, rice, ham** (foods)
5. **clown, teacher, police officer, farmer** (people)
6. **apple, grapes, strawberries, oranges** (fruit)
7. **truck, train, rowboat, car** (vehicles)
8. **red, blue, yellow, green** (colors)
9. **potato, onion, pumpkin, carrots** (vegetables)
10. **saucer, plate, baking dish, cup** (dishes)

VARIATIONS: To make the activity *easier,* reduce the number of words in a set. To make it *harder,* let the children take turns making up lists for the group to classify.

2 Focus: brainstorming descriptions of people, animals, clothes, toys, foods, vehicles, and colors

Say:

Let's think as fast as we can. I will say a word like *cow.* When I point to you, use a sentence to tell us something about a cow. Everyone will have a turn. Please tell something no one else has.

Use words from the list in Activity 1. Continue with a word until the children run out of ideas; then move to another word. Increase interest by keeping the pace rapid.

184

MATERIALS*

ACTIVITY 1

None

ACTIVITY 2

None

1 Focus: listening to pairs of *short words*, and identifying the resulting *compound words*

Say:

Let's play a listening game. You will hear two short words. I want you to figure out what long word is made when the two short words are put together.

Ask two children to stand beside you as helpers. Whisper to each child one of the two short words of a compound word. For example, you might whisper the word *bird* to the first child and *bath* to the second. The two children are to say their words in turn. The group then names the compound word (*birdbath*) and discusses its meaning. Continue with other pairs of children, using words like these:

1. barnyard	**11. herself**
2. lighthouse	**12. wagonload**
3. windmill	**13. typewriter**
4. newspaper	**14. sunshine**
5. fireworks	**15. birthday**
6. wallpaper	**16. cowboy**
7. battleship	**17. rainbow**
8. schoolgirl	**18. seaside**
9. handbag	**19. snowman**
10. somewhere	**20. scarecrow**

2 Focus: listening to compound words, reversing the order of *short words* to make silly compound words, and then using the new words in sentences

Say:

It might be fun to say our big words backwards. The new words will usually sound silly. Let's start with the word *barnyard*. What two words make that word? (Pause) **Yes, the two words are *barn* and *yard*. Listen while I say *barnyard* backwards: *yardbarn*. Let's all say *yardbarn* and *barnyard*.**

Have the children do so several times. When they can easily reverse the order of the two component words, continue:

Now let's use the funny word *yardbarn* in sentences. I will say the first sentence: "I walked to the *yardbarn*, and I saw some pigs."

Call on several children to make up sentences with *yardbarn*. Continue in this way with other words from the list in Activity 1. Try to give everyone at least one turn. Encourage the children to help one another and to have fun. Comment on imaginative efforts.

VARIATION: To make the activity *harder*, have the children discuss whether each new compound word is silly, or sensible.

185

MATERIALS*

ACTIVITY 1

Fruits & vegetables
All

P. Mooney Bag

ACTIVITY 2

Fruits & Vegetables
All

1 Focus: naming fruits and vegetables from memory

Wear the P. Mooney bag and say:

Let's play a remembering game. I will show you four fruits and vegetables. Then while you cover your eyes, I will put one of the four items into the bag. You are to tell me which fruit or vegetable is missing. To help you remember, you may whisper the names of the fruits and vegetables to yourself as you look at them.

Show each group of four fruits and vegetables for 10 to 15 seconds. Call on individuals to name the missing item.

VARIATIONS: To make the activity *harder,* hide two of the four items and/or display more than four items at once. To make it easier, show two or three items at once and hide only one.

2 Focus: naming fruits and vegetables in a counting chant

Give each child a fruit or vegetable, keeping the potato for yourself. Stand facing the group, and hold up the potato. Lead the children in saying the following chant several times:

One potato, two potatoes,

Three potatoes, four;

Five potatoes, six potatoes,

Seven potatoes, more.

Then have the children take turns holding up an item for the group to name in the chant:

One (banana), two (bananas),

Three (bananas), four;

Five (bananas), six (bananas),

Seven (bananas), more.

Make sure everyone has a turn.

186

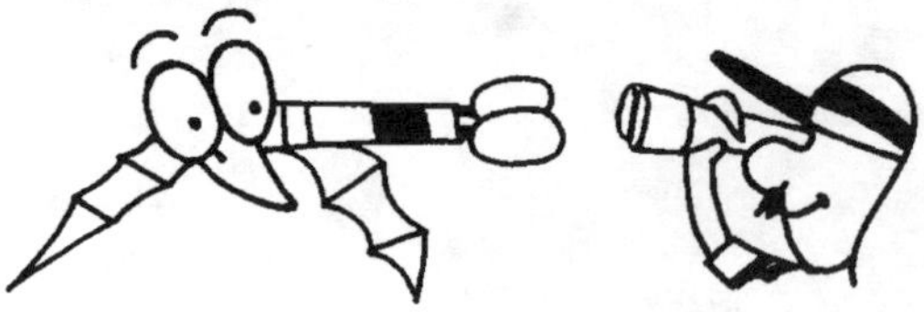

MATERIALS*

ACTIVITY 1

Cards

Stories

451-462 (optional)

463

Display Board (optional)

6 ledges (optional)

Audiocassette 1

Side B, Song 4,
"P. Mooney and the Gasless Goose"

ACTIVITY 2

None

1 Focus: listening to the story "P. Mooney and the Gasless Goose," and answering questions

Show card 463 and ask:

Who is this? (Pause) **Yes, it is P. Mooney's friend Gasless Goose. Let's listen to his story again. Then we will talk about what happened in the story.**

Play the story without showing the cards. Then lead a discussion with questions like these:

1. **What did P. Mooney see through his green goggles?**
2. **What did Gasless Goose look like?**
3. **What problem did Gasless Goose have?**
4. **How did P. Mooney help Gasless Goose?**

VARIATION: To make the activity *easier,* show the 13 story cards as the story is narrated, and display them in sequence during the discussion.

2 Focus: evaluating and answering real and absurd questions containing rhyming words, and then making up more questions

Say:

The story of Gasless Goose has many words that rhyme. Let's make up some questions using rhyming words. I will make up the first one: Did you ever see a *boat* wearing a *coat*?

The group is to respond by saying heartily, "No! I never saw a *boat* wearing a *coat!*" Continue in this way with these questions:

1. **Did you ever see a spoon flying to the moon?**
2. **Did you ever see a mouse sneaking around a house?**
3. **Did you ever see a bat wearing a hat?**
4. **Did you ever see a boy playing with a toy?**
5. **Did you ever see a rake eating a cake?**
6. **Did you ever see a light having a fight?**
7. **Did you ever see a fish lying in a dish?**
8. **Did you ever see a dog running on a log?**
9. **Did you ever see money eating honey?**
10. **Did you ever see a cot being cooked in a pot?**
11. **Did you ever see a pony eating bologna?**
12. **Did you ever hear an alligator say, "See you later"?**

Repeat the questions, calling on children to name the two rhyming words in each.

OPTIONAL: Continue by having the children make up their own absurd rhyming questions.

187

MATERIALS*

ACTIVITY 1

Cards

People

222

ACTIVITY 2

Cards

People

(same as for Activity 1)

1 Focus: imagining and talking about what might make someone angry

Show card 222 and ask:

How do you think this boy feels?

When the children have discussed how angry the boy seems, continue:

Let's think about what might have made this boy feel angry. We will take turns telling stories about what angered him.

Accept all responses. Stress the use of sentences. Summarize each story for the children, in order to show your acceptance of their attitudes towards anger.

2 Focus: talking about feeling angry

Show card 222 and say:

Now let's talk about what makes us angry.

Let the children take turns talking about situations, people, or events which anger them. If necessary, ask questions to draw out the children. Be non-judgmental about their feelings.

188

MATERIALS*

ACTIVITY 1

None

ACTIVITY 2

Cards

Toys

226-266

1 Focus: completing statements which involve analogous reasoning about the functions of body parts

Say:

Today let's think about what our bodies can do. I will say part of a sentence about body parts; please finish the sentence for me.

Pause for the children to complete each of these statements:

1. **We see with our eyes; we hear with our ______ .** (ears)
2. **We smell with our nose; we taste with our ______.** (tongue or mouth)
3. **We reach with our arms; we jump with our ______.** (legs)
4. **We have ten toes on our feet; we have ten fingers on our ________ .** (hands)
5. **We listen with our ears; we watch with our _______ .** (eyes)
6. **We draw with our hands; we dance with our ______.** (feet)
7. **We talk through our mouth; we sneeze through our _______ .** (nose)
8. **We blink with our eyes; we clap with our _______ .** (hands)
9. **We snap with our fingers; we lick with our _______ .** (tongue)
10. **We scratch with our fingers; we sniff with our _______ .** (nose)
11. **We whistle with our lips; we tap with our _______ .** (fingers or toes)

Repeat the statements in reverse order, like this: "We hear with our ears; we see with our . . . (eyes)." Have the children complete each one in unison.

2 Focus: talking about the importance of vision and hearing, and then describing a toy to an imaginary friend who is blind

Say:

Our eyes and ears are very important to us. Why?

Lead the children in talking about the importance of sight and hearing. Give each child a toy card. Then continue:

Now let's pretend that you each have a friend who cannot see; your friend is completely blind. You want to tell your friend about your new toy. When I call on you, try to describe the toy very well, so your friend can imagine what it is like.

Let the children take turns describing their toy pictures. Help as necessary.

OPTIONAL: Have the group close their eyes as they listen, and ask them to identify the toy being described.

189

MATERIALS*

ACTIVITY 1

Cards

Animals

1-38

Display Board

6 ledges

ACTIVITY 2

Cards

Animals

(same as for Activity 1)

1 Focus: classifying animals by their ability to make sound, and then comparing loudness of sounds made by pairs of animals

Display animal cards 1 through 13. Stack the remaining cards in order.

Point to the cards on display and say:

Let's look at these cards and find the animals that do not make sounds loud enough for us to hear.

When the children have named the two "soundless" animals (beetle and butterfly), remove the 13 cards from the board. Continue as before with two other groups of 13 and 12 cards, respectively. The following "soundless" animals should be identified:

1. 4•**beetle**
2. 6• **butterfly**
3. 19•**goldfish**
4. 33•**spider**
5. 38•**worm**

Remove the five pictures from the board. Then say:

Let's play a comparing game. I will show you pictures of two animals. Tell me which animal makes the louder sound.

Display cards 1 and 8, and call on a child to name the louder animal in a sentence such as "A bear is louder than a cat." Then ask:

Why is a bear louder than a cat?

Encourage discussion. Continue with other pairs of cards.

2 Focus: naming animals in a number chant

Give each child an animal card. Hold a card yourself. Say:

Now let's say a chant about the animals shown on your cards. I will go through it for you the first time. Then we will say it together.

Show your card as you say this rhyme:

One, two, three, four, five;

Once I caught a (goat) alive.

Six, seven, eight, nine, ten;

Then I let him go again.

Invite the children to join you in saying the rhyme again. Then let each child in turn lead the group in chanting the rhyme about his or her animal.

190

MATERIALS*

ACTIVITY 1

Teacher provides

Wet towel (optional)

Wire hanger (optional)

ACTIVITY 2

Cards

Music

335

Audiocassette 2

Side B, Song 10,

"Rhythm Walk"

1 Focus: talking about body parts that can twist and bend, and then imitating the actions

Say:

Today let's talk about bending and twisting our bodies, and do the actions. Let's start with bending. What body parts can bend? Name one that can, and show us how it bends, (Melissa).

Lead the children in identifying and bending these jointed body parts:

1. ankles
2. back
3. elbows
4. fingers
5. knees
6. neck
7. shoulders
8. toes
9. wrists

Continue with a discussion and demonstration of body parts that can twist. Help the children discover which body parts can both twist and bend:

1. ankles
2. back, including neck waist and hips
3. elbows
4. neck
5. wrist

VARIATION: To make the activity *easier,* illustrate *twisting* by wringing a wet towel. Illustrate *bending* by bending a wire clothes hanger.

2 Focus: bending and twisting to the music "Rhythm Walk," and then describing the actions

Say:

Let's bend and twist as we listen to "Rhythm Walk."

Play band 1, and lead the children in bending and twisting their bodies to the music. Repeat the recording as interest dictates. Call on children to describe their actions in sentences.

191

MATERIALS*

ACTIVITY 1

Cards

People

200 201 203 206
207 208 209 210
212 213 216 217
218

Display Board

6 ledges

Teacher provides

Blank cassette (optional)

Tape recorder (optional)

ACTIVITY 2

Cards

People
(same as for Activity 1)

Display Board

6 ledges

1 Focus: describing the work people do, and telling stories about people who work

Display the 13 people cards on the board.

Point to the board and say:

Let's name these workers and tell what kind of work each one does.

When the children have done so, continue:

Now let's take turns making up stones about these people.

Let the children take turns selecting a card and telling a story about that worker. Cards may be chosen more than once. Give everyone a turn, and accept all responses. Stress the use of sentences. Help as necessary by asking questions.

OPTIONAL: Record the stories and play them back at the end of the activity. Have the children identify the speaker and the card being discussed.

2 Focus: describing people from memory

Say:

Now let's play a remembering game. While I count to 10, look at all these cards. (Point) **When I say "10," I will turn one over and ask you to describe the person on it. Tell me about the person's work, appearance, and clothes.**
Let's start!

Have several children each name one or two things about the card you turn over. When its main characteristics have been identified, continue with other cards. Continue until all the cards have been described and everyone has participated.

VARIATION: To make the activity *harder,* have the children close their eyes while you turn over each picture.

OPTIONAL: Let the children take turns counting to 10 and turning over cards.

192 

MATERIALS*

ACTIVITY 1

Cards

Stories

400 401 403 404
418

Display Board

4 ledges

Audiocassette 1

Side B, Song 1,
"P. Mooney, Ophelia, and the Where-Bear"

ACTIVITY 2

None

1 Focus: listening to the story "P. Mooney, Ophelia, and the Where-Bear," and then summarizing the story

Set up the board with ledges, and display the five story cards in order, picture sides hidden.

Say:

Let's listen again to the story of how P. Mooney helped Ophelia solve her problem. Listen closely, so you will be able to summarize the story. To *summarize* means to tell in a few sentences what happened.

Play the story without showing the cards. Then say:

Now let's try to say what the story was about without telling all of it. I will go first.

Summarize the story in five sentences, like this:

1. **P. Mooney met a little girl named Ophelia, who had a problem.**
2. **Ophelia got lost because she never knew where she was.**
3. **P. Mooney solved her problem by giving her a Where-Bear.**
4. **The Where-Bear knew all directions and could take Ophelia anywhere.**
5. **The Where-Bear made Ophelia happy by taking her home, where she wanted to be.**

Now turn over the cards on the board, picture sides showing, and say:

Now let's practice summarizing the story. These cards will help you remember what happened.

Let several children each describe the action shown on the first card in no more than two sentences. Then continue with the other cards in turn until each has been described and everyone has participated.

2 Focus: following directions using positional words

With the children standing, say:

Let's play a following-directions game. I will give you directions about where to stand in a line. Listen carefully. You may go first and start the line, (Isaac). Stand in back of (Isaac), (Joanna).

Then continue with similar directions, using one of these words or phrases in each: *between, in front of, in back of, beside.* When everyone is in line, continue with directions like these:

1. **Jump *to the back,* (boys).**
2. **Jump *to the side,* (everyone).**
3. **Jump *to the front,* (girls).**

Continue as time permits.

193

MATERIALS*

ACTIVITY 1

Color Chips
All
Container

ACTIVITY 2

Color Chips
All
Container

1 Focus: talking about rainbows, and then making a color chip rainbow

Say:

Let's talk about rainbows. What does a rainbow look like?

Call on children to describe a rainbow. Next, have them tell about times they have seen rainbows. Then continue:

Now let's make a rainbow out of color chips.

Place the container of chips on the floor in front of the children. Have them find and link all the red chips. Arrange the completed chain in an arc on the floor to form the first color band of the rainbow. Repeat this process with the following colors in this sequence: orange, yellow, green, and blue. Once the color chip rainbow is complete, you may wish to ask:

What makes a real rainbow appear in the sky?

Call for responses. If the children are curious, explain that a rainbow occurs when the sun shines brightly through tiny raindrops left hanging in the air. These raindrops act as prisms to separate white light into the colors of the rainbow.

2 Focus: talking about what one would buy with the pot of gold at the end of the rainbow

Leave the color chip rainbow from Activity 1 on the floor.

Say:

An old story says that there is a pot of gold at the end of the rainbow. Do you think there really is a pot full of gold where the rainbow ends?

After the discussion, continue:

Let's pretend that there *is* a pot of gold at the end of the rainbow. In the pot is enough gold to buy anything we want. Let's take turns telling what we would buy with the rainbow's pot of gold.

Have the children answer in sentences. Accept all responses.

194

MATERIALS*

None

ACTIVITY 2

Cards

Clothing

42 43 58 65

Music

325

Display Board

1 ledge

Audiocassette 2

Side A, Song 2,
"The Is-Are Song"

1 Focus: thinking and talking about clothes appropriate to various activities

Say:

Today let's pretend that we have to get dressed for many different activities. What clothes would we wear to go swimming?

When several children have answered in sentences, ask:

What kinds of things might we take along when we go swimming?

After the discussion, continue by asking the above questions about activities like these:

1. **going to school in fine weather**
2. **walking home from school in the rain**
3. **going to bed**
4. **going to a birthday party**
5. **playing outside on a cold day**
6. **playing outside on a hot day**
7. **going on a picnic**
8. **riding a horse**
9. **going camping**
10. **playing baseball**
11. **going to a dancing lesson**
12. **going on an airplane to visit someone in a city far away**

2 Focus: evaluating and correcting the use of is and are in sentences, and then singing "The Is-Are Song"

Say:

Let's play a listening game. I will say a sentence two ways. Please tell me which way is right. Listen carefully!

Stress the plural subject and the verb as you say each of these sentences:

Three *shirts is* in the washer.
Three *shirts are* in the washer.

Then ask the children to name the correct sentence. Help if necessary. Continue as above with the sentence pairs listed below. Make sure the less able children participate.

1. **The *cap is* on the boy. The *cap are* on the boy.**
2. **The *coats is* on the hanger. The *coats are* on the hanger.**
3. **The *sweaters is* in the suitcase. The *sweaters are* in the suitcase.**
4. **The *snowsuit is* on the skier. The *snowsuit are* on the skier.**
5. **The *swimsuit is* on the diver. The *swimsuit are* on the diver.**
6. **The *shoes is* dirty. The *shoes are* dirty.**
7. **My *slip is* lost. My *slip are* lost.**
8. **The *boots is* wet. The *boots are* wet.**
9. **The *purses is* leather. The *purses are* leather.**
10. **My *jacket is* missing. My *jacket are* missing.**

End by displaying clothing cards 42, 43, 58, and 65 in order. Play band 3 (instrumental version) and refer to the music card as you lead the children in singing the four verses given below. After each, have the children point to show you where they would wear the item. Also call on a child to answer the song's question in a sentence like "You put (boots) on my (feet)."

1. **Boot is one; boots are two. Where would I put some boots on you?**
2. **Cap is one; caps are two. Where would I put a cap on you?**
3. **Shirt is one; shirts are two. Where would I put a shirt on you?**
4. **Sock is one; socks are two. Where would I put some socks on you?**

195

MATERIALS*

ACTIVITY 1

Display Board
4 ledges

Poster 6

Audiocassette 2
Side B, Selection 6, "Town in Fall"

ACTIVITY 2

Display Board
4 ledges

Poster 6

1 Focus: classifying things that can make sounds on the poster "Town in Fall," and then identifying each of the "Sounds of the Town in Fall"

Use the ledges to display the poster on the board.

Point to the poster and say:

Let's look at this poster of a town in fall, and find all the things that can make sounds.

Have the children take turns naming an item that can make sounds. If you wish, have them imitate the sound or tell what the people might be saying. Then continue:

Now let's listen to the poster sound effects. As you listen, look at the poster and try to figure out what could make each sound. Then I will play the sounds again and let you take turns naming them and pointing to the poster items.

After playing selection 3, repeat it several times, pausing to allow children to name and point out sources of sounds. Helping as needed, continue until all the sounds have been identified.

2 Focus: playing the game What Would Happen If. . . ? about the poster "Town in Fall"

Say:

Let's play a game called What Would Happen If. . . ? Please look at P. Mooney in the hot-air balloon. (Pause) **What do you think would happen if a small hole appeared in the balloon?**

Call on children to describe the outcome of this situation. Encourage full discussion and accept all responses. Continue in this way with these imaginary situations:

What do you think would happen if . . .

1. **a tire on the fruit-and-vegetable truck blew out?**
2. **the cat suddenly stopped, turned around, put up his back and hissed, and then chased the dog?**
3. **the painter on the ladder dropped his white paint?**
4. **the small plane swooped down and flew very low over the street?**
5. **the man's wheelchair had a big motor and could move very fast?**
6. **a big leak appeared in the water tank?**
7. **the telephone in the booth rang?**
8. **the girl on the tricycle ran into the blind person's seeing-eye dog?**

196

MATERIALS*

ACTIVITY 1

Cards

Vehiclesl

267-283

P. Mooney Bag

ACTIVITY 2

Cards

Pictures from Several Categories

94-103

267-283*

Numerals & Color Shapes

284-293

P. Mooney Bag

P. Mooney Stick

1 Focus: identifying vehicles from descriptions given by other children

Put the 17 vehicle cards into the bag.

Wear the bag, and have the children sit in a circle. Stand behind a child, take a card from the bag, hold the card over the child's head, and say:

Heavy, heavy hangs a card over your head. It is a picture of something in which we can travel. Try to guess what it is from clues we will give you.

Call on other children to describe the pictured vehicle while the child guesses. If necessary, add clues until the right vehicle is named. Then give the child the card to hold. Continue in this way with other children until all cards have been identified and everyone has had a turn.

2 Focus: following directions that stress counting from one to five

Select enough of the food, numeral, and vehicle cards to have one per child, with about an equal number from each category. Mix the cards and put them into the bag.

Wearing the bag, hold the stick and have the children stand in a semicircle. Say:

Now let's play a following-directions game. As each of you takes a card from the bag, the P. Mooney stick will turn you into whatever you are holding — a food, a numeral, or a vehicle. Then I will give directions. Do only what I tell your group to do.

As each child takes a card from the bag, wave the stick over her or his head and chant:

Mooney Magic, do a trick;

Make a (food), P. Mooney Stick!

Continue in this way until everyone has been "transformed." Then say:

Now look at your card and remember what you are as I give directions.

Give directions like these:

1. **All *foods,* jump three times.**
2. **All *numerals,* hop two times.**
3. **All *vehicles,* bend down and touch your toes one time.**

Continue with other commands that call for performing an action from one to five times. End by saying:

All foods, numerals, and vehicles, please sit down.

Then wave the stick over everyone and chant:

Eenie, Mooney,
Macaroony!
Now let's be
You and me!

197

MATERIALS*

ACTIVITY 1

None

ACTIVITY 2

Puppets
P. Mooney

1 Focus: talking about words that sound the same but have different meanings, and making up sentences using the words

Say:

Today we are going to talk about words that sound the same but have different meanings. Listen to these two sentences and find the word that is the same in each one.

1. **"A dog saw a squirrel and began to *bark* loudly."**
2. **"The squirrel ran up a tree, digging its toes into the tree's *bark*."**

If necessary, repeat the two sentences until the children name the word *bark*. Then call on children to give the two meanings of *bark*, helping as necessary. Continue with the list given below. In each case, after discussing the two meanings of each word, have the children make up sentences that illustrate each meaning.

1. clothes, close	**4. chest, chest**
2. bat, bat	**5. blue, blew**
3. bear, bare	**6. back, back**

2 Focus: following directions that stress positional words in the game *P. Mooney Says*

With the children standing in front of you, put P. Mooney on your hand and have him say:

Let's play the game P. Mooney Says. Please show me your thumbs. (Pause) **All right. Now listen carefully. I will tell you where to point your thumbs, but move only if I first say "P. Mooney says."**

Have the puppet omit "P. Mooney says" about half the time as he gives these commands:

P. Mooney says . . .

1. **Point your thumbs up.**
2. **Point your thumbs down.**
3. **Point your thumbs to the side.**
4. **Point your thumbs to the back.**
5. **Point your thumbs to the front.**

If the children are doing well, increase the pace to keep the game lively and to increase the level of difficulty. Continue as time permits.

198

MATERIALS*

ACTIVITY 1

Fruits & Vegetables
All

ACTIVITY 2

Fruits & Vegetables
All

1 Focus: classifying fruits and vegetables by various characteristics, and then describing and counting the items in each group

Have the children sit before you in a semicircle. Place the fruits and vegetables on the floor in front of them. Say:

Let's see how many ways we can group the fruits and vegetables. First, let's find all the fruits and vegetables that are *yellow.*

Have the children take turns doing so. As each yellow item is named, have it set aside as part of a separate group. Then call on children to answer these questions about the yellow group:

1. **How many things are in this group?**
2. **What are their names?**
3. **How many fruits are in this group?**
4. **How many vegetables are in this group?**
5. **Are any of these things the same? What are they? How many are there of each?**
6. **There is one thing that is the same about everything in this group. What is it?**

Continue as above with these groupings:

1. **all orange things**
2. **all red things**
3. **all fruits**
4. **all vegetables**
5. **all round things**
6. **all long things**
7. **all things not red, orange, or yellow**

2 Focus: brainstorming foods smaller or larger than the fruits and vegetables

Leave the fruits and vegetables from Activity 1 on the floor.

Say:

Let's think of foods that are *smaller* than these fruits and vegetables. Name them as fast as you can!

Afterwards, ask the children to name foods *larger* than the fruits and vegetables.

OPTIONAL: Keep tallies on the board for each category, and have the children compare the results.

199

MATERIALS*

ACTIVITY 1

None

ACTIVITY 2

Cards

Music

333

Audiocassette 2

Side B, Song 5, "Make a Sound" (vocal version)

Side B, Song 7, "Make a Sound" (instrumental version)

1 Focus: identifying loud and soft sounds while stressing *first* and *second*

Have one child stand before the group. Say:

Let's play a listening game. While you have your eyes closed, (Bernard) will make a loud sound and a soft sound. I will ask everyone whether the *first* sound was *loud* or *soft*. Then I will ask whether the *second* sound was *loud* or *soft*.

If the child cannot think of a sound to make, suggest one like clapping hands. When the class has identified the soft and loud sounds, call on someone to demonstrate how the sounds were made. Continue with other children, varying the order of loud and soft sounds. Try to give everyone a chance to perform, allowing them to move around the room to make such sounds as closing a drawer.

2 Focus: singing the song "Make A Sound" while stressing *loud* and *soft*

Hold the music card and say:

We can use our voices to sing both *loudly* and *softly*. Now let's sing "Make A Sound." Please sing along with me.

Play the song and refer to the music card as you lead the children in singing the four verses. Using the song (instrumental version), repeat the song as time and interest suggest. Each time the song is repeated, have one or more children lead the group.

200

MATERIALS*

ACTIVITY 1

Color Chips
All

P. Mooney Bag

Puppets
P. Mooney
Zoey
All 3 hats

ACTIVITY 2

None

1 Focus: matching color chips to colors of P. Mooney's and Zoey's clothes in a following-directions activity, counting chips, and then remembering and naming colors of the puppets' clothes

Place the puppets where the children can easily see them. Put the chips into the bag.

Have each child take five chips, all different colors, from the bag. Say:

Let's use our chips to play a following-directions game. Look at P. Mooney and Zoey. (Point) **If you have a chip the same color as P. Mooney's bag, stand up.**

When these children are standing, say:

Yes, P. Mooney's bag is orange. Now let's count the people who have orange chips.

Lead the children in counting aloud as you touch each standing child.
Then say:

(Seven) people have orange chips.

Then have the children put their orange chips back into the bag. Continue as above, calling for children with chips that are . . .

1. **the color of the buttons on Zoey's shoes.** (white)
2. **the color of the bottom stripe on P. Mooney's hat.** (red)
3. **the color of P. Mooney's moustache.** (brown)
4. **the color of Zoey's coat.** (yellow)
5. **the color of the bill of P. Mooney's hat.** (blue)
6. **the color of Zoey's thinking hat.** (green)
7. **the color of Zoey's safety pin.** (black)

When all the chips have been put back into the bag, hide the puppets and say:

Let's see if you can remember the colors of P. Mooney's and Zoey's clothes.

The children should answer these questions in unison:

1. **What colors are the stripes in P. Mooney's shirt?** (red and blue)
2. **What color is Zoey's discovery hat?** (brown)
3. **What color are Zoey's shoes?** (black)
4. **What color is P. Mooney's bag?** (orange)
5. **What color is P. Mooney's hat?** (red and blue)
6. **What color are the letters on P. Mooney's bag?** (black)
7. **What color is Zoey's coat?** (yellow)
8. **What color are the buttons on Zoey's shoes?** (white)
9. **What color is Zoey's thinking hat?** (green)
10. **What color is P. Mooney's moustache?** (brown)
11. **What color is Zoey's action hat?** (red)
12. **What color are P. Mooney's eyes?** (he has no eyes)

2 Focus: talking about favorite colors

Have the children discuss their favorite colors. Each child should name a favorite color and tell why she or he particularly likes it.

Keep in Mind . . .
After each lesson in the program, individuals who have difficulty demonstrating proficiency in the skills you consider appropriate and important for them to learn should be tutored. Aides could help you with this task.

201

MATERIALS*

ACTIVITY 1

Display Board

Magnetic Shapes

5 large circles

5 large rectangles

5 large squares

5 large triangles

ACTIVITY 2

None

1 Focus: classifying magnetic shapes by color, counting them, and then naming them from memory

Set up the board and arrange the five squares along the top. Place the remaining 15 shapes in the lower part of the board.

Say:

Today let's sort our shapes by color. Find a triangle that is the same color as the *first* square, (Oralee). (Point to square on far left, and pause) **Now put the triangle right under the square.**

Have four children each place one of the remaining triangles under the square of the same color. Continue with the circles and the rectangles until all the shapes are arranged like this:

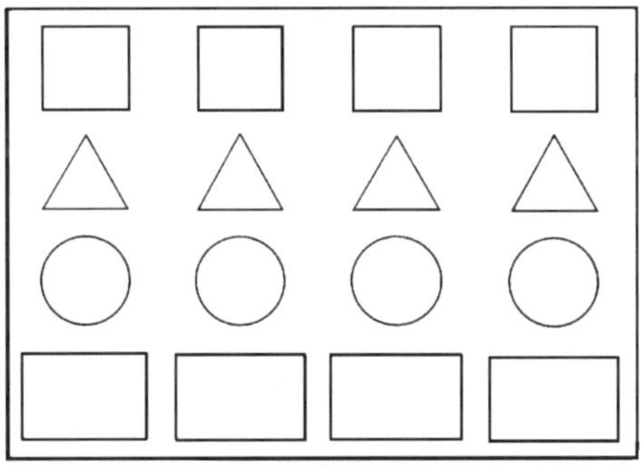

Lead the children in counting each line of shapes, saying, "One (square), two (squares), three (squares), etc." Then ask:

How many shapes of each kind do we have? (Pause) **Yes, that is right. We have five squares, five triangles, five circles, and five rectangles. Now let's count the shapes by color.**

Going from top to bottom, point to each shape in a column as you lead the children in saying, "One (red) shape, two (red) shapes, three (red) shapes, four (red) shapes." Have them tell you how many colors are in each column. Then say:

Now let's play a remembering game. Cover your eyes while I take a shape off the board. (Do this) **Now look and see if you can tell which shape is missing.**

Call on a child to identify the missing shape by both shape and color. Then put it back onto the board. If necessary, help by pointing to and naming the shapes and colors in the line from which the shape was removed. Each time, ask the child who names a shape to tell how the choice was made. Continue until everyone has identified a missing shape.

OPTIONAL: Let the children take turns removing a shape for others to identify.

2 Focus: talking about the shape of boxes, and then brainstorming things that can be made from boxes

Ask:

What shape are most boxes?

When the children have told you that boxes are usually square or rectangular, ask:

What are some of the things you could make with a very large box?

Call on children to answer. If necessary, suggest making such items as these:

1. a cave

2. a house

3. a store

4. a fort

5. a drum

6. a mask

7. a house for a pet

202

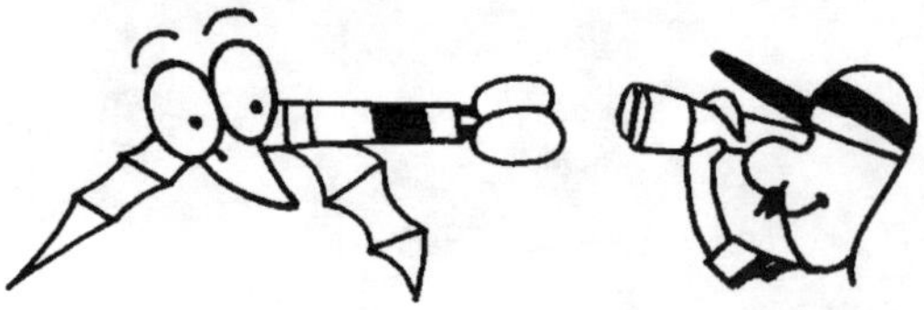

MATERIALS*

ACTIVITY 1

Cards

People

225

ACTIVITY 2

Cards

People

(same as for Activity 1)

1 Focus: talking about being surprised

Show card 225 and ask:

How do you think this boy feels?

Encourage discussion. If no one says that the boy seems surprised, suggest this. Then continue:

Try to remember something that happened which surprised you.

Encourage each child to use sentences while telling about being surprised. Accept all responses.

2 Focus: imagining and talking about what might surprise someone

Show card 225 again and say:

Pretend that this boy is a friend of yours. Imagine that you did or said something that made him look like this. Tell us how you surprised him.

Let the children take turns describing their surprises for the boy in the picture.

203

MATERIALS*

ACTIVITY 1

Cards

Household Items

155 158 160 163
171 174 175 176
178 183 190 191

ACTIVITY 2

None

1 Focus: listening to the poem "The Lost Turtle," and completing lines with rhyming words

Stack the 12 household cards in this order: 155, 158, 176, 191, 190, 171, 160, 183, 163, 174, 175, and 178.

Hold the stacked cards and say:

Today you are going to help me with a poem about a lost turtle. Listen carefully and say the rhyming word when I hold up a card.

Read the poem given below, pausing for the children to finish the line in unison as you hold up the correct card.

Where, oh, where did the turtle go?
We'll have to search for him high and low.

Let's look under the bed in my room;
Maybe I swept him there with the (show card 155) ***broom.***

He must be here in the house somewhere
Maybe he's hiding under a (show card 158) ***chair.***

Where would a turtle want to go?
Maybe he's stuck in the (show card 176) ***radio.***

Where to look next is such a decision!
Is he behind the (show card 191) ***television?***

Poor little turtle; he's all alone!
Could he be under the (show card 190) ***telephone?***

Is he lost in the basement cold and damp?
Or is he hiding behind that (show card 171) ***lamp?***

If he wanted to hear "tick-tock, tick-tock,"He might have crawled behind this (show card 160) ***clock.***

I really don't know what to think;
Maybe he fell down into the (show card 183) ***sink.***

Maybe he tried to climb 'way up,
And tumbled down inside a (show card 163) ***cup.***

See if he's hiding on top of a can;
While you look there, I'll look in this (show card 174) ***pan.***

Oh, dear me, it's getting late.
We still have to look under every (show card 175) ***plate.***

I know we'll find him sooner or later.
Oh, look! He's in the (show card 178) ***refrigerator!***

Repeat the rhyme, having the children finish the lines. Do not show the cards again unless the children cannot remember the rhyming words.

2 Focus: talking about being lost and what to do when lost

Ask:

Have any of you ever been lost? Let's talk about what it's like to be lost. If you have ever been lost, please raise your hand.

Call on children to tell about how they got lost and how it felt. After the discussion, say:

Now let's talk about what you would do if you were lost.

Each child should tell one thing to do, saying, "If I were lost, I would (ask a policeman for help)." Accept all responses, but stress the correct things to do.

204

MATERIALS*

ACTIVITY 1

P. Mooney Bag

Puppets

P. Mooney

Teacher provides

Small cards, 3 in. x 5 in. (7.62 cm x 12.7 cm) or 4 in. x 6 in. (10.16 cm x 15.24 cm). 1 per child, with a sticker or small picture pasted on one side and the child's name and address printed on the other side

ACTIVITY 2

Cards

Music

324

Puppets

P. Mooney (optional)

Audiocassette 2

Side A, Song 1, "I'm P. Mooney"

1 Focus: recognizing one's address when heard, and then describing the picture on a piece of "mail"

Put the small cards into the bag.

Wear the bag and put P. Mooney on your hand. He says:

Hello, everyone! Today let's pretend that I am your mail carrier and my bag is the mailbag. There is a letter in it for each of you. Listen carefully for your name and address.

P. Mooney should pretend to read the address on a card as he asks:

Who lives on (Woodham Road)? I have a letter for someone who lives at (31 Woodham Road).

If the right child does not recognize the address, have the puppet say:

I have a letter for someone whose last name is (Contreres). Whose last name is (Contreres)?

If the last name is not recognized, then have P. Mooney give the first name; however, always proceed in this order:

1. **the street address**
2. **the child's *last* name**
3. **the child's *first* name**

When the right child recognizes an address, have that person use a sentence to tell P. Mooney her or his name and address. If the child finds this too difficult, she or he may respond by saying only, "My name is (Elena Contreres)." Have the puppet give the card to the child and ask that it be shown to the group and its sticker or picture described. Continue as before with the remaining pieces of "mail."

VARIATION: To make the activity *harder,* add the children's telephone numbers to the cards, and have P. Mooney begin each "delivery" by announcing a telephone number.

2 Focus: describing P. Mooney from memory, and then singing and acting out the song "I'm P. Mooney"

Say:

Suppose P. Mooney were lost. Let's see how well you can describe him to someone looking for him. Raise your hand if you can tell us one thing about how P. Mooney looks.

Have the children take turns telling something in sentences about P. Mooney's appearance. Encourage them to name traits and features not previously mentioned. If they have trouble remembering, ask questions like these:

1. **What does P. Mooney wear on his head?**
2. **What does his face look like?**
3. **What are his clothes like?**
4. **What else does he wear?**

When everyone has participated, summarize the descriptions. Then stand beside the record player and continue:

Now let's sing and act out P. Mooney's song together.

Lead the children in singing and acting out the song. Repeat as desired.

OPTIONAL: Show the puppet for verification of the children's descriptions.

205

MATERIALS*

ACTIVITY 1

Cards

Pictures from Several Categories

1 30 94
103 105 107
121 127 146
150 172

ACTIVITY 2

None

1 Focus: making adjectives from nouns, and then using these words to describe cards

Stack the 11 picture cards in numerical order.

Hold the cards and say:

Let's play a word game. I will tell you something about what is pictured on one of these cards. Then we will change my words a little bit and describe the picture in a new way. (Show card 1) **I can say that this bear has lots of *hair*. Or I can say that this bear is *hairy*. This is a *hairy* bear. Let's say those sentences together.**

Lead the children in saying:

This bear has lots of *hair*. This is a *hairy* bear.

Continue as above with the remaining cards, using the following sentence pairs. Pause each time for the children to complete the second sentence.

Show: Say:

1. 30•**This rabbit has lots of fur. This is a _______ .** (furry rabbit)
2. 94•**This bacon has lots of grease. This is _______ .** (greasy bacon)
3. 103•**This corn on the cob has lots of butter. This is _______ .** (buttery corn on the cob)
4. 105•**This doughnut has lots of sugar. This is a _______ .** (sugary doughnut)
5. 107•**This fish has lots of bones. This is a _______ .** (bony fish)
6. 121•**These pancakes have lots of syrup. These are _______ .** (syrupy pancakes)
7. 127•**These pretzels have lots of salt. These are _______ .** (salty pretzels)
8. 146•**This pear has lots of spots. This is a _______ .** (spotty pear)
9. 150•**These strawberries have lots of seeds. These are _______ .** (seedy strawberries)
10. 172•**This mop has lots of strings. This is a _______ .** (stringy mop)

End by showing each card again and asking, "What kind of (bear) is this?" Have first a child and then the group respond, "This is a (hairy bear)."

VARIATION: To make the activity *easier*, omit the second sentence and ask, "What kind of (bear) is this?" The children should respond, "(Hairy)."

2 Focus: talking about when certain actions would be done, and then identifying the action words in a rhyming activity

Say:

Let's talk about when we might do some actions. First let's think about humming. When do you feel like humming?

Encourage discussion. Then continue as above with these actions:

1. **sliding**
2. **smiling**
3. **frowning**
4. **licking**
5. **sneezing**
6. **dancing**

When all the actions have been discussed and everyone has participated, continue by saying:

Now let's play a looking-and-listening game.

Hum for several seconds; then ask:

Am I humming, or am I strumming?

The children should respond, "You are humming; you are not strumming." Continue with these actions and questions:

Action:	***Ask:***
1. slide	**Am I riding, or am I sliding?**
2. smile	**Am I piling, or am I smiling?**
3. frown	**Am I frowning, or am I clowning?**
4. lick	**Am I ticking, or am I licking?**
5. sneeze	**Am I sneezing, or am I freezing?**
6. dance	**Am I prancing, or am I dancing?**
7. cry	**Am I trying, am I crying?**

206

MATERIALS*

ACTIVITY 1

Cards

People

222 225 (optional)

ACTIVITY 2

Cards

People

222* 223 224 225*

Display Board

2 ledges

1 Focus: evaluating situations and deciding whether each would cause anger or surprise

Say:

I am going to describe some situations for you. Tell me whether you would be surprised or angry if the same thing happened to you. Here's the first one: Suppose you were playing outside in the snow, and you saw someone wearing a bathing suit. Would you feel surprised, or would you feel angry?

Encourage several children to explain why they would feel surprised. Continue with situations like those listed below, asking after each, "Would you feel surprised, or angry?"

1. **Suppose a boy knocked you down into a mud puddle and then laughed at you.**
2. **Suppose your (sister, brother) took one of your toys away from you and would not give it back.**
3. **Suppose you woke up one morning to find you had grown so tall that your head bumped the ceiling.**
4. **Suppose you saw a horse roller-skating down the street.**
5. **Suppose you wanted to watch your favorite television program, but your mother made you go to bed.**
6. **Suppose you came to school one day and everyone was walking upside-down on the ceiling.**
7. **Suppose that while you were eating a great big ice-cream cone, a big dog jumped up on you and ate the ice cream.**
8. **Suppose you saw a baby pushing a big man in a baby carriage.**

OPTIONAL: Use the cards to help the children evaluate the situations.

2 Focus: making facial expressions and identifying feelings they express, and then talking about these feelings

Display the four cards on the board.

Point to the board and say:

Let's take turns pretending to feel like one of these children. When it's your turn, try to look sad, happy, angry, or surprised. The rest of us will guess how you are pretending to feel.

Call on each child in turn. When the group has named an emotion, have them ask the child, "Why do you feel (happy)?" The child should answer in a sentence such as "I am (happy) because (my aunt gave me an apple)." Give everyone a turn.

207

MATERIALS*

ACTIVITY 1

None

ACTIVITY 2

Cards

Animals (optional)

1 2 7 8 9 10
11 12 13 14 18 20
21 22 23 24 27 28
29 31 32

1 Focus: brainstorming foods, toys, and animals

Say:

Let's see how fast you can name animals, foods, and toys. I will ask you to name one, two, or three items, so please listen carefully.

Call on children with this request: "Name (three) (animals), (Stan)." Vary the number and item requested, and always put the child's name at the end. Praise good efforts.

OPTIONAL: Tally the three categories on a blackboard, and end by having the children count and discuss the items in each list.

2 Focus: using the names of adult and baby animals to complete sentences that stress *before* and *after*

Say:

Let's play a thinking game about animals. I will tell you the name of a baby animal. When I pause, tell me in unison what animal the baby will grow up to be.

Pause for the group to complete each of the statements listed below:

1. ***Before* I grow up, I am called a bear cub. But *after* I grow up, I am called a** _______ . (bear)
2. ***Before* I grow up, I am called a calf. But *after* I grow up, I am called a** _______ . (cow)
3. ***Before* I grow up, I am called a kitten. But *after* I grow up, I am called a** _______ . (cat)
4. ***Before* I grow up, I am called a chick. But *after* I grow up, I am called a** _______ . (hen, rooster).
5. ***Before* I grow up, I am called a colt. But *after* I grow up, I am called a** _______ . (horse)
6. ***Before* I grow up, I am called a puppy. But *after* I grow up, I am called a** _______ . (dog)
7. ***Before* I grow up, I am called a duckling. But *after* I grow up, I am called a** _______ . (duck)
8. ***Before* I grow up, I am called a kid. But *after* I grow up, I am called a** _______ . (goat)
9. ***Before* I grow up, I am called a lamb. But *after* I grow up, I am called a** _______ . (sheep)
10. ***Before* I grow up, I am called a piglet. But *after* I grow up, I am called a** _______ . (pig)

Repeat the exercise by reversing the two sentences, saying, "*After* I grow up, I am called a (sheep). But *before* I grow up, I am called a (lamb)."

VARIATIONS: To make the activity *harder,* have individuals respond. To make it *easier,* show the right pair of cards each time.

208

MATERIALS*

ACTIVITY 1

Display Board
4 ledges

Poster 4

ACTIVITY 2

None

1 Focus: predicting and talking about "what would happen if. . . ?" using the poster "City in Summer"

Use the ledges to display the poster on the board.

Say:

Let's play the game What Would Happen If. . . ? Please find P. Mooney in the picture. (Pause until the children have done so) **What do you think would happen if he ate all the popcorn in the wagon?**

Call on children to describe in sentences what might happen. Encourage discussion. Continue with the situations listed before, preceding each by asking, "What would happen if . . . "

1. **the bird got out of the birdcage?**
2. **the fire fighter could not turn off the water?**
3. **someone were in the house which is being knocked down?**
4. **the house collapsed into the children's playground?**
5. **the mail carrier delivered all the mail to the wrong people?**
6. **the laundry hanging on the line fell onto the head of the man sitting on the steps?**
7. **the boy's airplane landed in the water?**
8. **the cat jumped onto the dog?**
9. **the car started to roll away?**

2 Focus: listening to groups of three words, and deciding whether they rhyme

Say:

Let's play a rhyming game. I will say groups of three words. Sometimes they will rhyme and sound alike. But sometimes the three words will not rhyme. Listen carefully and tell me in a sentence whether or not the words rhyme.

Use the list below. The children should respond by saying, "Yes, those words rhyme" or "No, those words do *not* rhyme." Have them stress the word *not*. Occasionally let a single child answer.

1. **hat, cat, fat**
2. **pan, pie, put**
3. **bed, Ted, fed**
4. **hold, cold, horse**
5. **take, tool, lake**
6. **water, wing, wait**
7. **hay, may, say**
8. **get, let, net**
9. **hill, pill, fill**
10. **far, feet, find**
11. **kind, came, cake**
12. **take, cake, make**
13. **see, tree, me**
14. **fan, fake, fire**
15. **hot, not, got**
16. **car, far, tar**
17. **came, cold, keep**
18. **find, kind, bind**

VARIATION: To make the activity *harder,* either increase the speed of your presentation or add words to each group.

209

MATERIALS*

ACTIVITY 1

Fruits & vegetables
All

Teacher provides
1 paper bag per child

ACTIVITY 2

Fruits & Vegetables
All

1 Focus: identifying fruits and vegetables from children's descriptions

For each child, place a fruit or a vegetable into a paper bag.

Give each child a bag. Say:

Look at what is in your paper bag, but don't tell anyone what you have.

Each child is to stand before the group and describe the fruit or vegetable without naming it. The other children then take turns guessing the item. When it is correctly identified, the child should show it to the group.

2 Focus: following directions using descriptions of fruits and vegetables while stressing *same* and *different*

Mix all the fruits and vegetables together on the floor in front of the group. Say:

Listen carefully and raise your hand if you can follow my directions.

Give the directions listed below, calling on children to respond. Replace the fruits and vegetables after each turn.

1. **Pick up three things that have the same name but are different colors.** (three apples)
2. **Pick up three things that have the same name and the same color but are three different sizes.** (three pears)
3. **Pick up one thing that has "eyes."** (potato)
4. **Pick up three things that have the same name, but one is large and two are small.** (three oranges)
5. **Pick up three things that have the same name, but two are large and one is small.** (three bananas)
6. **Pick up one thing that is called an "ear."** (corn)
7. **Pick up three things that grow under the ground.** (carrot, onion, potato)
8. **Pick up one thing that rhymes with potato.** (tomato)
9. **Pick up one thing that makes you cry when you peel it.** (onion)
10. **Pick up three things of the same color that you must peel before you can eat them.** (three oranges)

If necessary, repeat so that everyone has a turn, or provide more directions.

210

MATERIALS*

ACTIVITY 1

None

ACTIVITY 2

P. Mooney Stick

1 Focus: talking about words that sound the same but have different meanings, and making up sentences using the words

Say:

Let's talk about some words that sound the same but have different meanings. Listen to these two sentences. Please find the word that is the same in both:

1. **Jenny likes to spin her toy *top*. The roof is on the *top* of a house.**

If necessary, repeat the sentences until the children identify the word top. Then call on children to give the two meanings of top.Have them make up additional sentences for each meaning. Continue as above with these statements:

1. **She found a big *rock* in the yard. I will sit in the chair and *rock* the baby.**
2. **What clothes will you *wear* today? Can you tell me *where* the pet shop is?**
3. **My *nose* is red because the sun burnt it yesterday. Who *knows* how I can make this box into a playhouse?**
4. **The *bear* was in the woods behind the house. The water was cold on my *bare* feet.**
5. **The *duck* was in the barnyard eating grains of wheat. The man who was cleaning windows told me to *duck* under his ladder so I wouldn't bump my head.**

2 Focus: following directions that stress the numbers one to five in a P. Mooney-stick game, and then describing the action while stressing the past tense

Stand with the children. Hold the stick and say:

We are going to play a game with P. Mooney's stick. First, let's practice the rhyme we will say. It goes like this:

(Eve), be nimble; (Eve), be quick;

Jump (three times) over the P. Mooney stick!

Repeat the rhyme until everyone seems familiar with it. Then say:

Now we are ready to play the game. I will put the P. Mooney stick onto the floor. (Do this) **Listen carefully for the number of times you are to jump. You may go first, (Eve).**

Lead the children in saying the rhyme, inserting a number from one through five. Use the child's name in the rhyme, and have her or him jump over the stick the correct number of times. Then stress the past tense as you lead the class in saying, "(Eve) jumped over the P. Mooney stick (three) times." Continue until everyone has had a turn.

211

MATERIALS*

ACTIVITY 1

Cards

Household Items (optional)

154 158 159 160
162 167 168 171
172 176 178 182
183 188 189 197
198

ACTIVITY 2

None

1 Focus: naming household items to complete sentences which describe their use, and then brainstorming other things that have the same use

Say:

Let's play a naming game. Please finish each sentence I say by naming a household item. Let's try one: We sleep in a (pause for the children to complete) **(bed).**

Continue:

Now let's think of other things on which we could sleep.

Give hints as necessary until several children have each named an item. Then sum up their suggestions like this:

Yes, we can sleep in a (bed), in a (sleeping bag), on a (cot), on a (sofa), or on the (floor).

Repeat as above with these statements:

1. **We can sit in a _______ .** (chair)
2. **We can put clothes into a _______ .** (chest of drawers)
3. **We can tell time with a _______ .** (clock)
4. **Two people can sit on a _______ .** (couch, sofa)
5. **We can drink from a _______ .** (glass)
6. **We can iron clothes with an _______ .** (iron)
7. **When it gets dark, we can turn on a _______ .** (lamp)
8. **We can clean the kitchen floor with a _______ .** (mop)
9. **We can listen to a _______ .** (radio)
10. **We can keep food cold in a _______ .** (refrigerator)
11. **We can wash our hands in a _______ .** (bathroom sink)
12. **We can wash dishes in a _______ .** (kitchen sink)
13. **We can cook on a _______ .** (stove)
14. **We can eat our meals at a _______ .** (table)
15. **We can clean the rugs with a _______ .** (vacuum cleaner)
16. **We can wash our clothes in a _______ .** (washing machine)

OPTIONAL: Use the cards, but only if the children have trouble completing the sentences.

2 Focus: talking about what one's ideal room would be like and who would be invited into it

Ask:

Have you ever wanted a room all your own, one where you could do whatever you wanted to do, and could see only those people you wanted to see? Let's imagine and talk about what your room would be like, and whom you would invite into it.

Have the children take turns talking about and describing their imagined rooms.

212

MATERIALS*

ACTIVITY 1

Display Board

Magnetic Shapes
Large black square
Medium black square
Small black square
Large black triangle
Medium black triangle
Small black triangle

ACTIVITY 2

None

1 Focus: using squares and triangles to make "houses/' and stressing largest, smallest, and medium-sized

Put the six shapes in random order on the lower half of the board.

Say:

Let's use our shapes to make houses, but let's practice first. Which shape could we use for the roof of the largest house we could make? (Pause) **That's right; this large triangle could be the roof. Which square would we use to make the rest of the largest house?** (Pause) **Yes, we would use this large square.** (Point to left side of board) **Please come and build a house on the board for us here with the largest square and triangle, (Piedro).** (Pause) **Now we have the largest house we can make with our shapes.**

Keep the "house" displayed as a frame of reference. Ask two other children to come to the board. Say to the first child:

Make the *smallest* house you can over here. (Point to right side of board)

Say to the second child:

Make the *medium-sized* house here in the middle. (Point)

Help as necessary. Then repeat the procedure with other groups of three children, using the small or medium-sized "house" as the reference from time to time. If feasible, continue until everyone has had at least one turn.

2 Focus: talking about what would happen to one's way of living if the earth were covered with water

Say:

Let's suppose the entire earth were covered with water. Let's talk about the many ways this would change the way we live.

Lead discussion of the children's ideas. If necessary, suggest topics like these:

1. **the clothes we would wear**
2. **where we would live**
3. **what we would eat**
4. **how we would move about**

213

MATERIALS*

ACTIVITY 1

None

ACTIVITY 2

Teacher provides

Blank cassette

Tape recorder

1 Focus: listening to pairs of short words presented in correct and reverse order, and identifying the correct compound word for each

Say:

Let's play a listening game. You will hear two short words. Try to figure out what long word can be made out of them.

Ask two children to stand on either side of you. Whisper the word *tooth* to the first child and *paste* to the second. The two children are then to say these words in turn to the group. The other children are to name the compound word and discuss its meaning. Continue with other pairs of children, using these words:

1. armchair	**6. horseshoe**
2. cupcake	**7. rainbow**
3. doorstep	**8. shoeshine**
4. goldfish	**9. shotgun**
5.grapefruit	**10. teaspoon**

OPTIONAL: If your children are able, continue by saying:

Now let's listen to the short words in backwards order. Try to figure out what the long words are. Saying the words backwards will usually sound silly. Let's try one: paste-tooth. Say it with me. (Do this) **What long word is made out of these two short words?** (Pause) **Yes; the long word is toothpaste.**

Continue by having pairs of children present the two short words in reverse order. Call on the group or individuals to name the correct compound word.

2 Focus: listening to compound words and the two short words in each, and then using the short words in sentences

Say:

Let's listen to the long words again. When I call on you, name the two short words and use them in sentences. I will record everyone's sentences and play them back. Then we will guess who was speaking.

Use the word list from Activity 1.

214

MATERIALS*

ACTIVITY 1

Cards

Animals

1-38

ACTIVITY 2

Cards

Animals

1-38,* 1 for each child

1 Focus: classifying animals by the presence or absence of certain body parts

Arrange the 38 animal cards on the floor or along chalkledges, so they can be seen by the children.

Point to the cards and say:

Look at all these pictures of animals! Some of these animals come *with* certain body parts and others are *without* them. *Without* means they *do not have* those parts. I will name an animal group. Tell me which of these animals belong in that group.

Use the list given below. Each time, help the children select and set aside the cards named for a group. Then point to each of these cards in turn for the children to name in a sentence like "The animals (with wings) are (bees, beetles, etc.)" The same animals may be chosen for several groups, so have the children select from the entire set of animal cards each time.

Find all the animals .

1. **with nails.**
2. **without feathers.**
3. **without tails.**
4. **with scales.**
5. **with beaks.**
6. **without wings.**
7. **with hoofs.**
8. **without fur.**

2 Focus: being assigned animal roles, and then following directions in the game Animal Exchange

Have the children stand in a circle around you. Say:

Let's play a game called Animal Exchange! I will give each of you an animal card. Pretend to be that animal. Then I will tell two of you animals to change places. When I say "All animals, exchange," then you may all change places.

Give each child an animal card. During the game, give instructions such as "(Bear) and (cat), change places." Occasionally call out, "All animals, exchange!" Continue as time and interest permit.

215

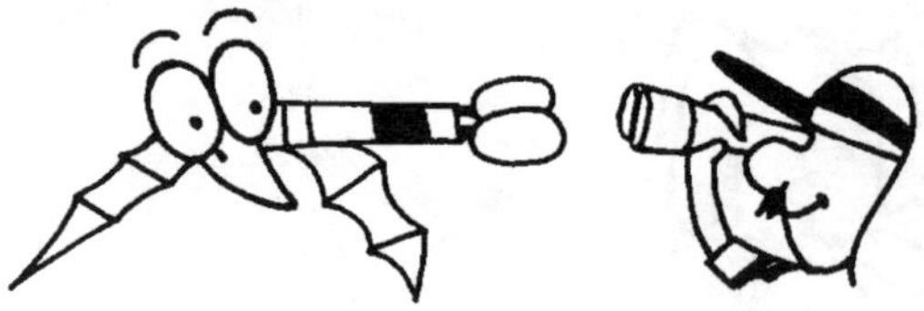

MATERIALS*

ACTIVITY 1

None

ACTIVITY 2

None

1 Focus: brainstorming animals without legs, and talking about how they move

Ask:

What does the word *without* mean? (Discuss) **Yes, to be *without* means not to have something. Now let's name all the animals we can that are *without* legs.**

Help as necessary by suggesting some of these animals: snakes, worms, and sea animals such as fish, oysters, clams, whales, porpoises, dolphins, sharks, seahorses, seals, and eels.

OPTIONAL: As each animal is named, discuss how it moves.

2 Focus: imagining being without usable legs, and talking about how one would move around without them

Say:

Let's imagine that you were *without* legs that could move. How would you get from one place to another?

Encourage discussion. Then ask:

Do you know anyone who cannot use his or her legs?

Help the children understand the special problems of such a handicapped person.

216

MATERIALS*

ACTIVITY 1

None

ACTIVITY 2

None

1 Focus: evaluating questions, deciding which are silly, and correcting them

Say:

Today I am going to ask you some questions. Some of them are silly and some are sensible. When a question is sensible, answer, "Yes." But if it is silly, tell us why.

Call on individuals to answer each of the questions given below. When an absurd question is identified, ask the child to explain why it is silly.

1. **Does a bird fly?**
2. **Does a cat meow?**
3. **Does a turtle fly?**
4. **Does an elephant meow?**
5. **Does a toad jump?**
6. **Does a bee buzz?**
7. **Does a lion fly?**
8. **Does a goat bark?**
9. **Does a worm jump?**
10. **Do dogs bark?**
11. **Does a coat talk?**
12. **Does a watch tick?**
13. **Does a dress meow?**
14. **Does a bed swim?**
15. **Does an airplane fly?**
16. **Do roller skates fly?**
17. **Does a chair say "gobble-gobble"?**
18. **Does a radio fly?**
19. **Does a ball bounce?**
20. **Does a pig bark?**

2 Focus: talking about places to visit and things to do

Say:

Let's talk about all the places you would like to visit if you were going on a trip.

Let the children talk about their favorite activities on trips. They may tell their own experiences on farms, in the cities, at the lake, on the ocean, etc. End by having the group think about where they would like to go next.

217

MATERIALS*

ACTIVITY 1

None

ACTIVITY 2

None

1 Focus: classifying groups of four words

Say:

I am going to say four words. Try to figure out one word or phrase we could use to describe all four words.

Call on individuals to name the word or phrase classifying each group listed below. Try to give everyone at least one turn.

1. **orange, brown, black, white** (colors)
2. **shoes, jeans, raincoat, socks** (clothes)
3. **lamb, duck, bear, gerbil** (animals)
4. **six, three, one, five** (numbers)
5. **eggs, hot dog, salad, toast** (foods)
6. **sink, stove, refrigerator, chair** (household items)
7. **barber, astronaut, nurse, grocer** (people, workers)
8. **peach, grapes, apple, pear** (fruit)
9. **airplane, bicycle, truck, police car** (vehicles)
10. **puzzle, roller skates, ball, robot** (toys)
11. **triangle, circle, square, rectangle** (shapes)
12. **corn, lettuce, carrots, beans** (vegetables)

VARIATIONS: To make this activity *easier,* reduce the number of words in a set. To make it *harder,* whisper categories to individuals and have them each make up a list of three or four items for the group to classify.

2 Focus: brainstorming descriptions of people, clothes, animals, foods, vehicles, toys, and household items using sentences

Say:

Let's think as fast as we can. I will name an item like shoes. When I point to you, tell me something about shoes in a sentence. Tell something no one else has said, and think quickly. Everyone will have a turn.

Use the words from the Activity 1 list, except shapes, colors, and numbers. Continue with the same item until the children run out of ideas. Vary the categories from which items are chosen.

218

MATERIALS

ACTIVITY 1

Display Board

Magnetic Shapes
All

ACTIVITY 2

None

1 Focus: sequencing magnetic shapes to complete a series

Set up the board and arrange this series of three large squares and three large circles at the top:

Say:

Let's talk about rows of shapes. (Point to shapes on board) **This is a row of squares and circles. Look and tell me which shape should come next in this row.**

After obtaining a correct response, have the children complete the series with the rest of the large squares and large circles. Then have them name the shapes in unison. Continue as above with the series given below. Be sure to use shapes of the same size unless otherwise indicated.

1. 
2. 
3. 
4. 
5. 
6. 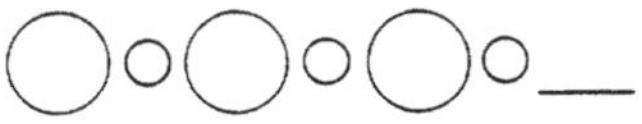
7. 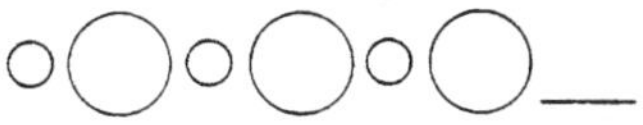
8. 
9. 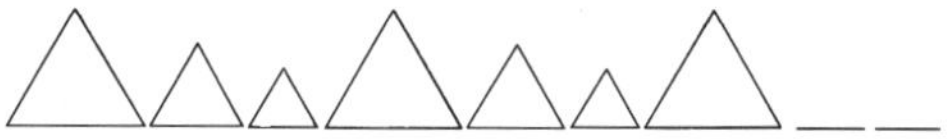
10. 

If necessary, repeat the series so that everyone has a turn.

VARIATION: To make the activity *easier,* place the ledges vertically to isolate each pattern, like this:

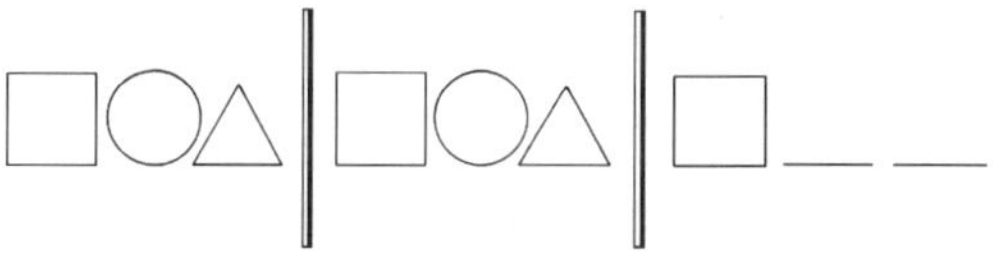

2 Focus: talking about where one would like to live and why

Say:

Let's pretend that you can live anywhere you want. Raise your hand if you are ready to tell us where you would like to ive, and why.

If necessary, start by talking about an unusual but interesting living place, like a cave or the moon. Then let the children discuss their choices. Give everyone a turn, and stress the use of sentences. Encourage and acknowledge imaginative presentations.

219

MATERIALS*

ACTIVITY 1

None

ACTIVITY 2

Cards

Foods (optional)

98 106 117 119
120 122 123 125
129 131 132 134
135 136 137 145

1 Focus: listening to names of foods with one or two words, and identifying how many words are heard

Say:

Let's play a listening game today. I will say the names of some foods you know. Sometimes you will hear one word, and sometimes you will hear two. I will say the names slowly. Please tell me if you hear one word, or two words in each name.

Use the list given below. Pause between each word in double names.

1. orange juice
2. cake
3. fried eggs
4. nuts
5. peach
6. fruit salad
7. toast
8. soda pop
9. apple
10. chocolate milk
11. soup
12. apple pie
13. peanut butter
14. potato chips
15. taco
16. roast turkey

VARIATION: To make the activity *easier,* pause noticeably between words in foods with double names.

2 Focus: describing foods in sentences

Say:

Now let's describe some foods. Think about (orange juice). Raise your hand if you can tell us something about (orange juice) in a sentence.

Use the list from Activity 1, and call on one or two children to describe each item. If necessary, ask questions about the look, color, taste, smell, texture, etc.

OPTIONAL: Use the cards only if the children have difficulty describing the foods.

220

MATERIALS*

ACTIVITY 1

Display Board

Magnetic Shapes
All circles
All squares

ACTIVITY 2

None

1 Focus: sequencing magnetic shapes to complete a series

Say:

Today we are going to talk some more about how rows of shapes can be arranged so you can tell what comes next. Look at the order in which I arrange these shapes.

Place two large circles and two large squares across the board from left to right in a row, like this:

Point to the row and say:

This row of shapes is called a *series*. Let's name the shapes in this series.

Moving left to right, point to each shape as it is named by the group. Then say:

When we put shapes into a series like this, we can tell which one should come next. Should a *circle*, or a *square* come next? (Pause) **Yes, the next shape should be a circle.**

As necessary, provide further explanation and demonstration. Before placing each shape, ask, "Which shape should come next?" When everyone seems to understand, let the children take turns completing the series of large shapes. Continue with a series of medium shapes and then a series of small shapes. End by asking the children how they knew which shape to place next in each series.

VARIATIONS: To make the activity *harder,* use a more complex pattern, such as

To make it *easier,* avoid using the word *series.*

2 Focus: talking about what one likes to do at a grocery store

Say:

Let's talk about what we like to do when we go to the store for groceries.

Lead the discussion. If necessary, help by asking if they like to do things like buying candy or a drink, looking at magazines or books, riding in a grocery cart, looking at prizes, choosing cereals with pictures to cut out, riding mechanical horses, or having their own money to spend. Each child should participate. Adjust the term *grocery store* to suit your location. For example, it may be more appropriate to use the term *supermarket.*

Keep in Mind. . .
After each lesson in the program, individuals who have difficulty demonstrating proficiency in the skills you consider appropriate and important for them to learn should be tutored. Aides could help you with this task.

221

MATERIALS*

ACTIVITY 1

Cards

Pictures from Several Categories

1 5 7 18 19
20 21 23 24 30
31 32 34 36 40
42 43 52 59 64
118 130 138 139 146
155 161 162 165 166
170 172 176 178 187
188 228 235 245 269

Display Board

2 ledges

ACTIVITY 2

Cards

Pictures from Several Categories (optional)

1* 5* 18* 21* 32*
42* 43* 59* 146*
161* 166* 172* 228*
235*

Display Board (optional)

2 ledges (optional)

1 Focus: identifying objects that do not belong in certain categories, and telling why they do not

Arrange the 40 cards in the groups of four listed below. Display cards 43, 170, 42, and 138 on the board.

Point to the cards on display and ask: **Which of these four things could you not wear, (Deirdre)?** (Pause) **Yes, you could not wear a knife or bananas. Why?** (Discuss) **Which of these things could you not eat, (Roger)?** (Pause) **You are right! You could not eat a cap or boots. Why?**

Continue as above with the groups listed below. The children you call on should answer in sentences.

Display:

1. 139•**carrots** 161•**comb** 130•**sandwich** 118•**milk**	**Which of these things could you not eat?** **Which of these things could you not drink?**
2. 36• **turkey** 146•**pear** 30•**rabbit** 32•**sheep**	**Which of these things is not an animal?** **Which of these are not fruits?**
3. 228•**ball** 52•**overalls** 245•**puzzle** 235•**dolls**	**Which of these things is not a toy?** **Which of these things are not clothes?**
4. 34•**squirrel** 24•**lamb** 230•**kittens** 19•**fish**	**Which of these things do not live in the water?** **Which of these things does not live on land?**
5. 40•**bonnet** 20•**hen** 59•**knit shirt** 640•**snowsuit**	**Which of these things are not clothes?** **Which of these things do not fly?**
6. 162•**couch** 178•**refrigerator** 7•**calf** 176•**radio**	**Which of these things does not belong in the house?** **Which of these things are not animals?**
7. 31•**rooster** 1•**bear** 21•**horse** 188•**stove**	**Which of these things would you not find in a kitchen?** **Which of these things is not an animal?**
8. 155•**broom** 172•**mop** 18•**goat** 165•**dustpan**	**Which of these things would not help your father or mother clean the house?** **Which of these things are not animals?**
9. 166•**fork** 5•**bird** 269•**bicycle** 187•**spoon**	**Which of these things could you not eat?** **Which of these things are not alive?**

VARIATION: To make the activity *harder,* after each of the second questions is answered, call on a child to tell you in a sentence which of the four cards belong together and why.

2 Focus: identifying words in which the beginning sound is separated from the rest of the word

Hold the 14 cards and say:

Now let's play a listening game. I will say some words but not as I usually do. I will stretch out each word to make it sound longer. When I call on you, tell me what word I am saying.

Separate the beginning consonant from the rest of the word as you say each word listed below. Repeat a word until the child you call on recognizes it, pausing less and less between the first and second parts. Use the cards only if necessary. Give everyone a turn, even if some words are used more than once.

1. b. . . oots
2. c. . . omb
3. p. . . ear
4. h. . . orse
5. sh. . . eep
6. d. . . oll
7. c. . . ap
8. sh. . . irt
9. b. . . ear
10. g. . . oat
11. m. . . op
12. f. . . ork
13. b. . . ird
14. b. . . all

VARIATION: To make the activity *easier,* display the cards in random order on the board, and use them as cues.

222

MATERIALS*

ACTIVITY 1

Display Board
4 ledges

Poster 1

ACTIVITY 2

Display Board
4 ledges

Poster 1

1 Focus: predicting actions of people and animals in the poster "Farm in Spring"

Use the ledges to display the poster on the board.

Point to the poster and say:

Let's talk again about the large picture of a farm in spring. Think about what some of the animals and people might be going to do.

Ask the questions listed below, encouraging the children to make predictions and tell you why they feel as they do. Have everyone participate, and make sure the right verb forms are used.

1. **What will the girl do with the fish she's holding?**
2. **What will the bird do with the worm?**
3. **What will the farmer do with the horse he is leading?**
4. **What will the young raccoon do after putting his foot into the water?**
5. **What will the fox try to do with the duck and ducklings?**
6. **What will happen after the pigs eat all the food from the feeder?**
7. **What will happen when the hawk sees the field mouse?**
8. **What will the turkeys and chickens do during the night?**
9. **What will the turtle do next?**
10. **What will P. Mooney do when he gets the hay put away?**

2 Focus: counting items on the poster "Farm in Spring" to answer "how-many" questions

Leave the poster from Activity 1 on display.

Say:

Now let's take turns counting things in the poster. Come up and count aloud all the (people) you see, (Katie). Point to them as you count.

Encourage other children to point out items that were missed.
Continue as above with these items:

1. **people**
2. **horses**
3. **turkeys**
4. **dogs**
5. **rabbits**
6. **goats**
7. **sheep**
8. **raccoons**
9. **cats**
10. **fish**
11. **birds**
12. **pigeons**
13. **ducks**
14. **buildings**
15. **geese**
16. **foxes**
17. **butterflies**
18. **chickens**
19. **turtles**

223

MATERIALS*

ACTIVITY 1

None

ACTIVITY 2

None

1 Focus: predicting and talking about what might happen in described situations

Say:

Let's play a thinking game. I will read the beginning of a very short story and then ask several of you to finish it for me in different ways. You are to tell us what you think might happen.

Present the following situations, one at a time. Each time, several children should respond in sentences. As necessary, help them use the right verb forms.

1. **Laura left her dinner on the table. Laura's cat jumped up onto the table. What do you think happened?**
2. **It snowed all night. The next day Ricardo made a snowman. Soon the sun came out. What do you think happened?**
3. **Wayne's father gave him a quarter. Wayne put it into his pocket. Wayne's pocket had a hole in it. What do you think happened?**
4. **Stacy went outside to play. It was cold and icy. Stacy began to run on the slippery ice. What do you think happened?**
5. **Bruce put a piece of bread into the toaster. He forgot it. The bread did not pop up. What do you think happened?**
6. **James had a cat. His cat saw a mouse running across the floor. What do you think happened?**
7. **A bird was sitting in a tree. The bird saw a worm on the ground. What do you think happened?**
8. **Louretta was running down the stairs. She did not see some roller skates lying on the stairs. What do you think happened?**
9. **Theodore turned on the water to fill the bathtub so he could take a bath. He forgot the water was running in the bathtub. What do you think happened?**
10. **Rachel started to pick a flower. A bee was on the flower. What do you think happened?**

OPTIONAL: Conclude each item by rereading the situations and paraphrasing the endings which the children suggested.

2 Focus: following directions which stress the word *before*

Have the children stand in front of their chairs. Say:

Let's play a following-directions game to see if you can remember what the word *before* means.

Give the directions listed below and others as desired. Explain, repeat, or demonstrate as necessary to strengthen the children's understanding of the word *before.*

1. **Before you sit down, slide your feet back and forth.**
2. **Before you stand up, smile a big smile.**
3. **Before you sit down, jump once.**
4. **Before you stand up, stamp your feet.**
5. **Before you sit down, sneeze a big sneeze.**
6. **Before you stand up, lick your lips.**
7. **Before you sit down, frown a big frown.**
8. **Before you stand up, hum a tune.**
9. **Before you sit down, turn around twice.**

224

MATERIALS*

ACTIVITY 1

None

ACTIVITY 2

None

1 Focus: brainstorming and talking about what can be seen but not heard and heard but not seen

Say:

Let's talk about things we can see but cannot hear, and other things that we can hear but cannot see. First, raise your hand if you can name something we can see but cannot hear.

Get as many responses as possible and have the children discuss each. Continue by having them brainstorm and discuss things heard but not seen. Make sure everyone participates. Suggested topics:

Things seen but not heard:

1. **snow falling**
2. **sun shining**
3. **clouds**
4. **smoke**
5. **grass or plants growing**
6. **stars**
7. **someone smiling**
8. **someone waving**
9. **someone winking**

Things heard but not seen:

1. **echoes**
2. **heart beating**
3. **thunder**
4. **stomach growling when you are hungry**
5. **joints cracking with movement**
6. **hiccups**

2 Focus: talking about when certain actions would be done

Say:

I will name some actions. Tell me when you might do each one.

Call on children to tell when they might do these actions: jump, walk, hop, turn, run, sit, write, and sing. Give everyone a turn.

225

MATERIALS*

ACTIVITY 1

Display Board

Manikin, Movable

ACTIVITY 2

None

1 Focus: imitating the position of the movable manikin, and then considering actions possible from that position

Display the movable manikin on the board.

Have the children stand facing the board. Say:

Please watch what I do with the manikin. Try to put yourself into the same position.

Use the list given below. Each time, have the children return to standing position after assuming the pose. Then call on individuals to tell the things that they could do when in that position, asking, "What might you be getting ready to do if you were in that position, (Adela)?" Encourage them to think of many possibilities.

Positions and possible actions:

sleeping
sunbathing
taking a bath
floating on water

carrying
fixing lunch
standing in a bus
lifting
pushing
pulling

jumping
climbing
driving a car

crawling
searching
hiding
moving under a table

bending over
picking up something
exercising

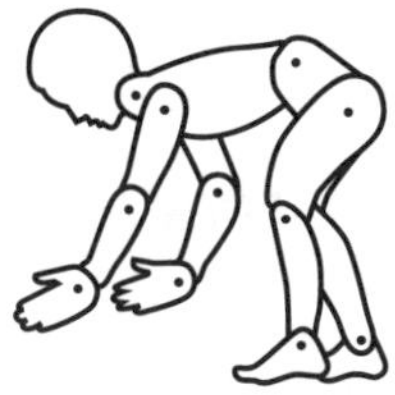

kneeling
playing with blocks
picking up something
scrubbing
rolling a ball
looking for something

2 Focus: evaluating questions, deciding which are silly, and correcting them

Say:

I have questions about some actions our bodies do. Some of these questions are silly, but some of them are sensible. Please listen carefully, and answer my questions.

Have individuals respond to each question listed below in sentences such as "Yes, legs can jump" or "No, eyes do not hear." After each absurd question has been correctly answered, ask the children to tell why it was silly.

1. **Do legs jump?**
2. **Do eyes hear?**
3. **Do ears talk?**
4. **Do teeth bite?**
5. **Do noses smell?**
6. **Do toes taste?**
7. **Do feet write?**
8. **Does hair grow?**
9. **Do fingers bend?**
10. **Do elbows hop?**
11. **Do noses sniff?**
12. **Do arms swing?**
13. **Do necks turn?**
14. **Do faces frown?**
15. **Do tongues lick?**
16. **Do knees bend?**
17. **Do mouths stand?**
18. **Do stomachs read?**

226

MATERIALS*

ACTIVITY 1

None

ACTIVITY 2

P. Mooney Stick

1 Focus: evaluating silly sentences, and talking about what is absurd in them

Say:

Let's play a listening-and-thinking game. I will read you some silly sentences. Listen and tell me what is silly about each one.

The children you call on should use sentences to say what is silly about each of these sentences:

1. **The fish walked down the road.**
2. **The elephant jumped out of the tree.**
3. **The rabbit flew through the air.**
4. **The boy was hungry, so he ate a plate.**
5. **Anne sat down on the stove.**
6. **It was dark, so I turned on the door to see.**
7. **1 picked up the fire and put it in the bag.**
8. **A horse named Gilbert went skating down the street.**
9. **Neusa put on her swimsuit to play in the snow.**
10. **Leo put on his shoes to go to bed.**
11. **It was so hot outside that everything froze.**
12. **Our dog Julia drove the car down the street.**
13. **The elephant rode on the ant's back.**
14. **It is time to go to school, so I will put on my pajamas.**
15. **One goat wore a pretty dress.**
16. **The duck said, "Meow, meow, meow."**
17. **The kitten lapped its ice-cream cone.**
18. **The pig said, "Baa-baa, I want some food."**
19. **Leslie used her toothbrush to sweep the floor.**
20. **Amos ate his soup with a knife.**

2 Focus: imagining, talking about, and pantomiming being very small

Have the children stand before you. Say:

Let's pretend that we are as small as our thumbs. Raise your hand if you can tell us what it would be like to be that small.

Lead the discussion. Help the class consider topics like these:

1. **What we might eat.**
2. **Where we would live and sleep.**
3. **The clothes we might wear.**
4. **What it would be like to walk through tall grass.**
5. **How everything would look to us.**

Then wave the stick and say:

Mooney Magic, do a trick.

Make us small, P. Mooney Stick.

Then say:

Now that we are very small, let's imagine we are trying to walk through tall grass.

Lead the pantomime by squatting and pretending to push your way through the grass. Ask the children what they might try to do. If necessary, offer ideas such as reaching up high to pick a dandelion and attempting to pick up an acorn. Praise imaginative efforts. End by waving the stick and saying:

Eenie, Mooney,

Macaroony!

Now let's be

You and me.

227

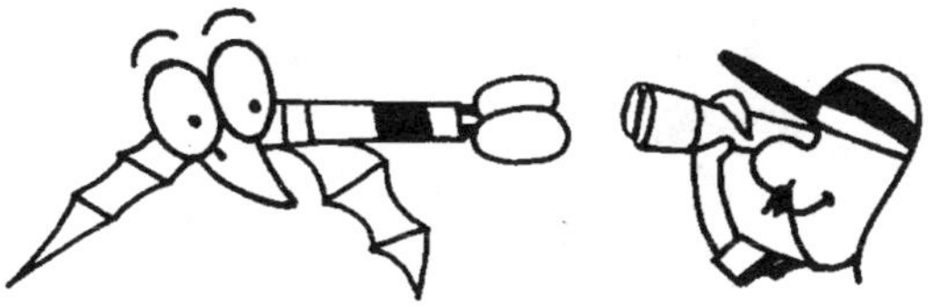

MATERIALS*

ACTIVITY 1

None

ACTIVITY 2

None

1 Focus: identifying words in which the beginning sound, m, is separated from the rest of the word

Say:

Today we are going to make words out of sounds. Listen to this sound: m-m-m-m. (Continue in a humming manner for a few seconds) **Let's make it together.**

Then say:

Now let's use the in-in-in-in sound to make words. After all of you have made the sound, I will add the rest of the word. For example, if you say "m-m-m-m" and I say "ouse," the word we make will be *mouse*. Let's begin.

Each time the class says "m-m-m-m," add one of the word parts listed below and ask, "What word is that?" Let either the class or individuals answer. Help as necessary.

1. -arch	**8. -itten**	**15. -inute**
2. -agic	**9. -ovie**	**16. -oney**
3. -ail	**10. -ad**	**17. -other**
4. -eat	**11. -agazine**	**18. -outh**
5. -ilk	**12. -ap**	**19. -ud**
6. -oon	**13. -eal**	
7. -onkey	**14. -iddle**	

2 Focus: talking about sounds one likes to hear

Say:

Let's talk about things we like to hear. We will take turns naming our favorite sounds. I will start. The sound I most like to hear is (rain falling on the roof). I like that sound, because it makes me feel (peaceful).

Have the children, in turn, describe their favorite sounds and why they like them. Stress the use of sentences.

228

MATERIALS*

ACTIVITY 1

Teacher provides
Chalk
Chalkboard

ACTIVITY 2

Audiocassette 3
Side A, Selection 1,
"Sounds of Animals"

1 Focus: brainstorming animals that have certain characteristics

Say:

Today let's play a thinking game. When I call on you, name an animal with fur.

Call on children at random until no one can name another furry animal. Tally acceptable responses on the chalkboard. Continue as before with these categories:

1. **animals with feathers**
2. **animals that swim**
3. **animals bigger than a person**
4. **animals smaller than a baby**
5. **animals that fly**
6. **animals that cannot fly**
7. **animals that make noises**
8. **animals that cannot make noises**

Praise all worthy efforts. End by leading the children in counting and comparing the number of entries in each category.

2 Focus: listening to each of the "Sounds of Animals," and describing the animals without naming them

Say:

Now let's listen to sounds of animals. Don't say the name of the animal you hear. Instead, I will ask one of you to describe the animal. The rest of us will tell you whether you are describing the right one.

Play selection 1 (bear). The child you call on should describe the animal without naming it, using sentences such as "I hear a brown and furry animal which lives in the woods. It growls and likes to eat honey." Give clues to help the speaker describe the animal in detail. The group should decide if the correct animal was described and then name the animal. Continue in a similar fashion with the remaining selections.

229

MATERIALS*

ACTIVITY 1

Cards

Stories

339-352

ACTIVITY 2

None

1 Focus: retelling the story "How P. Mooney Got the P. Mooney Stick," and talking about the importance of helping others

Hold the 14 story cards and say:

Let's retell the story about how P. Mooney got his P. Mooney stick.

Help the children briefly retell the story. If they have trouble remembering how it began, read clues from the portion printed on the back of the first card, and ask:

What did P. Mooney see as he was flying around in his High Flyer, looking for forest fires?

If further help is needed, add:

P. Mooney saw a poor little sick tree with all its branches drooping. What happened next?

Provide help only as needed. After the children have retold the story, summarize their version like this:

Yes, P. Mooney discovered a sick tree in the forest. He helped the tree get well. When it was healthy again, the tree thanked P. Mooney for his help by growing a P. Mooney stick. P. Mooney likes his stick very much and uses it often.

End by asking:

What can we learn from this story? (Pause for responses) **Yes, it makes P. Mooney feel good to help people. Like the tree in the story, people enjoy thanking whoever helps them.**

2 Focus: talking about ways one can help other people

Say:

Now let's talk about how we can help other people.

Encourage discussion. If necessary, have the children answer questions like these:

1. **What are some of the ways we can help our father?**
2. **What are some of the ways we can help our mother?**
3. **What are some of the ways we can help our brother(s)?**
4. **What are some of the ways we can help our sister(s)?**
5. **What are some of the ways we can help our grandfather(s)?**
6. **What are some of the ways we can help our grandmother(s)?**
7. **What are some of the ways we can help our teacher(s)?**
8. **What are some of the ways we can help our neighborhood friends?**
9. **How can we help people who have trouble seeing?**
10. **How can we help people who have trouble talking?**
11. **How can we help people who have trouble walking?**

230

MATERIALS*

ACTIVITY 1

None

ACTIVITY 2

None

1 Focus: adding -er to action words to create nouns

Say:

Let's name some actions we all can do.

When the children have done so, summarize by saying:

Yes, we can walk and run. We can jump and skip. We can eat and sleep. All of us do these things some of the time. But if I were to sleep *most* of the time, you could call me a *sleeper.* If I were to *run* most of the time, what would you call me?

If no one mentions the word *runner,* suggest it. Explain that -er can be added to action words to create nouns, giving examples as necessary. Then continue as above with the list given below, pausing each time for the class to complete this sentence: "If I were to (jump) most of the time, I would be a (jumper)."

1. eat	**10. paint**	**19. frown**
2. walk	**11. sit**	**20. smile**
3. play	**12. draw**	**21. sing**
4. hop	**13. count**	**22. hum**
5. skip	**14. listen**	**23. whistle**
6. slide	**15. look**	**24. think**
7. skate	**16. talk**	**25. lick**
8. swim	**17. laugh**	**26. sneeze**
9. sweep	**18. cry**	**27. dance**

VARIATION: To make the activity *easier,* say the noun and ask what that kind of person does most of the time.

2 Focus: defining *hide,* and then talking about where and when one likes to hide

Ask:

What does it mean to *hide* something? (Pause for responses) **Yes, when we hide something, we put it where it cannot be seen. Now let's talk about places where we like to hide.**

Lead a discussion of hiding places. Encourage the use of sentences. End by having children tell about when they most feel like hiding.

231

MATERIALS*

ACTIVITY 1

None

ACTIVITY 2

Color Chips

10 chips of the same color per child, using all 8 colors

1 Focus: talking about colors in the environment

Say:

Every day we see colors all around us. Let's think and talk about when we might see different colors.

Encourage the children to answer and discuss each of these questions:

1. **When does the sky usually look orange?** (at sunrise or sunset)
2. **When does the sky look blue?** (in clear weather)
3. **When might the sky look gray?** (in bad weather)
4. **When are grass and leaves green?** (in spring and summer after a rainfall)
5. **When do our faces and ears get red?** (when we are cold or hot)
6. **When do grass and leaves get brown?** (in fall and winter, and when it is very dry)
7. **When might it be black all around us?** (at night or in a very dark place)
8. **When does the ground look white?** (when it is covered with snow)
9. **What might we drink to make our tongue blue or purple?** (grape juice)
10. **What can we drink to make the outside of our mouth look white?** (milk)
11. **What could we drink or eat to make the outside of our mouth look brown?** (chocolate milk or chocolate ice cream)

OPTIONAL: Continue by saying:

Let's talk about when or where you have seen things that are yellow. Raise your hand if you want to tell us about it.

Encourage the children to respond. If time permits, continue with other colors.

2 Focus: linking and naming color chips, and then following directions in the game Color Exchange

Have the children sit in a circle. Give each child 10 color chips of the same color; be sure to use all eight colors. Say:

Each of you has 10 color chips that are all one color. Let's use them to play a game called Color Exchange. I will tell certain colors to change places. When I say, "All colors, exchange," then all colors are to change places.

Before the game, have the children link their chips and name their colors. Then give directions such as "(Red and blue), change places!" Only the children with those colors should move. From time to time call out, "All colors, exchange!" All the children in the circle should then change places.

232

MATERIALS*

ACTIVITY 1

Cards

Pictures from Several Categories

5 14 25 44 67
107 121 127 131
137 144 146 150
154 162 203 204
206 211 213 248
256 266 272 273
283 286 287 290

Display Board

2 ledges

ACTIVITY 2

Cards

Music

332

Audiocassette 2

Side B, Songs 3 & 4
"Things That Go Together"
(vocal and instrumental)

1 Focus: telling how two out of three cards go together

Set up the board and ledges. Sort the 30 picture cards into groups of three, as listed below; stack them in the order indicated.

Hold the cards and say:

Let's play a thinking game. I will put three cards on the board. Please tell me which two cards go together and why.

Display the first three cards on the board. Point to cards 248 and 14 in turn. Ask:

Which of these goes with this card? (Point to card 5)

When the children choose card 14, ask:

Why do *bird* and *duckling* go together?

If no one can answer, explain that the two go together because they both are animals. Invite the group or a child to say:

A (bird) and a (duckling) go together because they both are (animals).

Continue as above with the remaining groups of cards.

1. 5•**bird,** 248•**robot,** 14•**duckling**
2. 1•**bear,** 25• **lion,** 150•**strawberries**
3. 204•**boy,** 144•**oranges,** 211•**girl**
4. 146•**pear,** 137•**apple,** 67•**sweater**
5. 154•**bed,** 107•**fish,** 162•**couch**
6. 256•**teddy bear,** 266•**whistle,** 286•**the numeral 3**
7. 203•**barber,** 213•**mail carrier,** 127•**pretzels**
8. 287•**the numeral 4,** 290•**the numeral 7,** 283•**tow truck**
9. 273•**police car,** 272•**car,** 206•**clown**
10. 121•**pancakes,** 44•**girl's coat,** 131•**sandwich**

2 Focus: brainstorming foods, animals, toys, and other categories, and then singing the song "Things That Go Together"

Hold the music card and say:

Let's name things that go together. Name as many things to eat as you can.

When the children have named at least a dozen foods, ask:

What word can we use to describe all these things? (Pause) **Yes, they are all *foods.* Now let's sing "Things That Go Together" about foods. When I point to you, please name a food.**

Play "Things That Go Together" (instrumental version) and refer to the music card as you lead the children in singing. Point to children in turn to name a food as you sing the song's three verses. Continue as above with other categories such as animals, toys, vehicles, clothes, numbers, and colors.

233

MATERIALS*

ACTIVITY 1

Puppets

P. Mooney

Zoey

Thinking hat

ACTIVITY 2

Cards

Music

326

Puppets

Zoey

All 3 hats

Audiocassette 2

Side A, Song 4, "Zoey"

1 Focus: talking about possible solutions to Zoey's and P. Mooney's problems

Place Zoey (wearing her thinking hat) on your hand and have her say:

P. Mooney and I have some difficult problems to solve. Please help us decide what we should do to solve our problems.

Alternate puppets as indicated below. Each problem could have several interesting solutions. Encourage a spirit of fun and praise all efforts.

1. Zoey: **I was sailing in a big ship on the ocean when the wind blew my thinking hat into the water. Tell me how I might have gotten my hat back.**
2. P. Mooney: **One day I came home very dirty from work. When I went into the bathroom to take a bath, I found that the stopper to the bathtub was gone! What could I have done to keep the water in the tub?**
3. Zoey: **A very important person was coming to town for a visit. Everyone lined the streets to see her. There were so many people standing in front of me that I could not see at all. Tell me about different ways I could have seen this person.**
4. P. Mooney: **One day last winter, someone accidentally threw a snowball through my window. The cold wind came blowing through the hole. Tell me how I could have stopped the wind from blowing into my house.**
5. Zoey: **Tomorrow is my friend's birthday, but I don't have any money to buy a gift. Name some things that I could give my friend that don't cost money.**
6. P. Mooney: **I was riding above the clouds one day in my hot-air balloon when a tiny hole appeared in the balloon. Tell me how I might have patched the hole.**
7. Zoey: **P. Mooney and I wanted to go on a picnic, but our car was out of gas, and no stations were open. Please tell me how we could have gotten to the picnic park!**
8. P. Mooney: **While I was out on my Mooney skates one day, I saw a dog chasing a cat. The cat ran up a tree to escape and then couldn't get down again. How could I have helped the cat get out of the tree?**

2 Focus: singing and acting out the song "Zoey"

Stand beside the audiocassette player, with the children standing before you. Place Zoey (wearing her discovery hat) on your hand. She says:

Let's sing the song about my three hats. Please do the actions for each hat you see me wearing. Let's start by singing about my discovery hat.

Play the song and switch Zoey's hats as indicated in each verse. If necessary, rehearse the actions:

discovery hat — shade eyes with one hand and look around thinking hat — put chin in palm of hand and pretend to think action hat — run in place

Repeat the song, and have the children take turns holding the puppet and switching her hats.

234 

MATERIALS*

ACTIVITY 1

None

ACTIVITY 2

Cards
Household Items (optional)
153-199

1 Focus: listening to names of household items with one or two words, and identifying how many words are heard

Say:

Let's play a listening game. I will slowly say the name of something that belongs in the house. You are to tell me how many words you hear. You may hear one, two, or three words.

Use the list given below, pausing between each word in names with two or three. Alternate calling on the group or one child to name the words in each item.

1. **stove**
2. **tool set**
3. **cup and saucer**
4. **sewing machine**
5. **iron**
6. **vacuum cleaner**
7. **pail**
8. **kitchen table**
9. **hairbrush**
10. **broom**
11. **clock**
12. **baking dish**
13. **glass**
14. **washer**
15. **ironing board**
16. **mop**
17. **lamp**
18. **scrub brush**
19. **frying pan**
20. **sponge**
21. **scissors**
22. **chest of drawers**
23. **radio**
24. **record player**

VARIATION: To make the activity *harder,* do not pause between words, and/or speed up your presentation.

2 Focus: deciding on household items needed to perform certain tasks

Say:

Now I will describe some jobs we might need to do at home. Tell me what we would need to do the work. Suppose you were carrying a bowl of sugar and spilled it onto the floor. What would you need to clean up the sugar?

Call on several children to name and discuss items such as a broom, dustpan, wastebasket, or vacuum cleaner. Continue as above with the situations listed below. Make sure everyone participates.

1. **making a sandwich**
2. **emptying the trash**
3. **washing clothes**
4. **cleaning up spilled milk on the kitchen floor**
5. **washing hands**
6. **brushing teeth**
7. **taking a bath**
8. **cleaning the bathroom**
9. **washing and drying dishes**
10. **making breakfast**

VARIATIONS: To make the activity *easier,* display the household cards as cues along a chalkledge. To make it *harder,* have the children also decide the sequence for use of the items.

235

MATERIALS*

ACTIVITY 1

None

ACTIVITY 2

None

1 Focus: completing sentences which stress positional words and relate one body part to another

Say:

Let's play a thinking game. I will say some sentences telling where our body parts are found. I want you to finish each sentence.

The children should respond in unison to complete the sentences given below. Explain or demonstrate as necessary.

1. **My mouth is *under* my _______ .** (nose)
2. **My mouth is *above* my _______ .** (chin)
3. **My teeth are *in* my _______ .** (mouth)
4. **My ears are *at the sides* of my _______ .** (head)
5. **My nose is *in the middle* of my ______ .** (face)
6. **My hair is *on top of* my _______ .** (head)
7. **My hands are *at the ends* of my _______ .** (arms)
8. **My legs are *under* my _______ .** (body)
9. **My feet are *at the ends* of my _______ .** (legs)
10. **My arms are *at the sides* of my _______ .** (body)
11. **My neck is *under* my _______ .** (head)
12. **My neck is *above* my _______ .** (chest)
13. **My nose is *over* my _______ .** (mouth)
14. **My nose is *under* my _______ .** (eyes)
15. **My tongue is *in* my _______ .** (mouth)
16. **My skin is *around* my whole _______ .** (body)

Vary the order as you repeat the sentences for individuals to complete.

VARIATION: To make the activity *harder,* reverse the order of the sentences, saying, for example, "*Under* my nose is my (mouth)."

2 Focus: talking about what one likes to do best, and remembering what others have said in a listener-talker game

Divide the class in half. Have the groups sit in two circles, one inside the other. Say:

You are sitting in two circles for a special reason. The people sitting in the inside circle will be talkers. They will take turns telling us one thing they like to do. The people sitting in the outside circle will be listeners. Each listener will try to remember what the talker in front of him or her has said. Let's start.

When every talker has mentioned a favorite activity, say:

Now, listeners, I want each of you to tell us what your talker said.

Continue until every listener has had a turn. Praise all efforts. Then have the children change circles and repeat the procedure.

236 

MATERIALS*

ACTIVITY 1

None

ACTIVITY 2

Cards

Pictures from Several Categories

37 114 153 157
164 167 169 173
174 175 179 182
183 186 199 233
250 256 265 266
275

P. Mooney Bag

1 Focus: imagining and talking about living at the bottom of the ocean

Say:

Today let's imagine what living in another place would be like. Suppose we lived at the bottom of an ocean, with fish swimming all around us. What do you think it would be like to live underwater, (Michiko)?

Encourage every child to participate in the discussion. As necessary, expand their thinking by asking:

1. **What clothes might we wear?**
2. **What type of home might we live in?**
3. **How would we move around?**
4. **How might we eat?**
5. **How would we breathe?**
6. **What things would we have to do differently?**

2 Focus: talking about funny ways to travel to the bottom of the ocean

Put the 21 picture cards into the bag.

Wear the bag and say:

Get ready, everyone! We are off to the bottom of the ocean, but it is a long way down. Let's talk about some funny ways to make the trip. I will go first. (Pick card from bag) **I would ride to the bottom of the ocean on** (Pause) **(a turtle).**

Call on a child to pick a card as she or he says, "I would ride to the bottom of the ocean on a(n) (ice-cream cone)." Continue with other children until all cards have been used. Conclude by asking each child:

What would be the funniest way for you to travel to the bottom of the ocean?

237

MATERIALS*

ACTIVITY 1

Audiocassette 3

Side A, Selection2
"Sounds of Home"

ACTIVITY 2

None

1 Focus: identifying each of the "Sounds of the Home," and relating them to the rooms in which they might be heard

Say:

Let's play a listening game called "Rooms Where I Might Hear This Sound".

Play the "Sounds of Home", one selection at a time. After each sound, ask someone:

What sound was that, (Karen)? (Pause) **Please tell us in which room or rooms you might hear that sound.**

Encourage the use of sentences, and accept all reasonable answers. Repeat the sounds, calling on other children as above.

2 Focus: naming the various rooms in a house, and then brainstorming items that might be found in each

Say:

Let's see how fast you can think today. As quickly as you can, name all the rooms that might be in a home.

Help as necessary. Suggestions:

1. kitchen
2. laundry room
3. bedroom
4. living room
5. bathroom
6. hallway
7. closet
8. dining room
9. den
10. study
11. pantry
12. library

Then say:

I will name one of the rooms. When I call on you, tell me one thing you might see there.

Name a room and call on several children to suggest items found there. Continue with other rooms. Keep the pace lively, and go through the list of rooms several times, as necessary. Make sure everyone has at least one turn.

238

MATERIALS*

ACTIVITY 1

None

ACTIVITY 2

None

1 Focus: using opposites to complete sentences that stress *before* and *after*

Say:

Let's play a thinking game. I will read some sentences, but I will leave off the last word. Listen carefully and tell me what it should be. I will give you a hint. The last word should be an opposite.

Have the children complete each of these sentences:

1. **After I grow, I am *tall*. But before I grow, I am ______ .** (short)
2. **After I took my medicine, I was *well*. But before I took my medicine, I was ______ .** (sick)
3. **After I eat, I am *full*. But before I eat, I am ______ .** (hungry)
4. **After I cut my hair, it is *short*. But before I cut my hair, it is ______ .** (long)
5. **After I drink my milk, my glass is *empty*. But before I drink my milk, my glass is ______ .** (full)
6. **After I shut the door, the door is *closed*. But before I shut the door, the door is ______ .** (open)
7. **After I sleep, I am *rested*. But before I sleep, I am ______ .** (tired)
8. **After the sun comes up, it is *light*. But before the sun comes up, it is ______ .** (dark)
9. **After I put on my gloves, my hands are *warm*. But before I put on my gloves, my hands are ______ .** (cold)
10. **After I wash, I am *clean*. But before I wash, I am ______ .** (dirty)
11. **After I climb the tree, I am *high*. But before I climb the tree, I am ______ .** (low)
12. **After I am asleep, my eyes are *closed*. But before I am asleep, my eyes are ______ .** (open)
13. **After I blow up a balloon, it is *big*. But before I blow up a balloon, it is ______ .** (little)
14. **After I boil the water, it is *hot*. But before I boil the water, it is ______ .** (cold)
15. **After I jump into the swimming pool, I am *wet*. But before I jump into the swimming pool, I am ______ .** (dry)
16. **After I enter the house, I am *in*. But before I enter the house, I am ______ .** (out)
17. **After the band begins to play, it is *loud*. But before the band begins to play, it is ______ .** (quiet)
18. **After I fill the basket, it is *heavy*. But before I fill the basket, it is ______ .** (light)
19. **After I chew a piece of gum, it is *soft*. But before I chew a piece of gum, it is ______ .** (hard)
20. **After I climb the stairs, I am *up*. But before I climb the stairs, I am ______ .** (down)

OPTIONAL: Repeat the sentences in reverse, saying, for example, "Before I grow, I am *short*. But after I grow, I am (tall)."

2 Focus: comparing and classifying foods by taste and feel

Say:

Let's think about how foods taste or feel in the mouth. Foods can taste sweet, sour, or salty. They can feel soft or chewy, cold or warm. Please listen to my questions about foods, and answer when I call on you.

The children you call on should respond in sentences to the questions listed below. Give each child a turn by repeating the questions in random order, substituting other foods.

1. **Which food is sweeter: green beans, or cake?**
2. **Which food is saltier: watermelon, or pretzels?**
3. **Which food is chewier: jello, or carrots?**
4. **Which food is more sour: milk, or lemons?**
5. **Which food is softer: potato chips, or rice?**
6. **Which food is colder: orange juice, or an ice-cream cone?**
7. **Which food is warmer: toast, or soup?**
8. **Which food is spicier: tacos, or jam?**

End by asking the children to name the sweetest foods they have ever eaten. Continue by asking them to name:

1. **the saltiest foods**
2. **the softest foods**
3. **the spiciest foods**
4. **the coldest foods**
5. **the chewiest foods**

239

MATERIALS*

ACTIVITY 1

None

ACTIVITY 2

None

1 Focus: completing statements which involve analogous reasoning about animals

Say:

I am going to say some imcomplete sentences about animals. When I call on you, tell me what word will finish the sentence correctly.

Call on the group or individuals to complete these statements:

1. **A squirrel is covered with fur; a chicken is covered with _______ .** (feathers)
2. **A rabbit hops; a fish _______ .** (swims)
3. **A horse walks; a bird _______ .** (flies)
4. **A cow moos; a duck _______ .** (quacks)
5. **A cat meows; a dog _______ .** (barks)
6. **A bee buzzes; a cat ______ .** (meows)
7. **A rooster crows; a man _______ .** (talks)
8. **A fish is covered with scales; a bird is covered with _______ .** (feathers)
9. **A duck swims; a butterfly ______ .** (flies)
10. **A duckling is little; a horse is _______ .** (big)
11. **A hen gives eggs; a cow gives______ .** (milk)
12. **A sheep is covered with wool; a cat is covered with ________ .** (fur)
13. **A butterfly is small; an elephant is _______ .** (large)
14. **A lion roars; a kitten _______ .** (meows)
15. **A pig oinks; a turkey.** (gobbles)
16. **A kid is little; a goat is _______ .** (big)
17. **An owl flies; a toad _______ .** (hops)
18. **A rabbit moves fast; a turtle moves _______ .** (slowly)
19. **A horse is big; a colt is _____ .** (little)
20. **A bird chirps; a sheep _______ .** (baas)
21. **Goats eat grass; birds eat _______ .** (worms, seeds)
22. **Bears are covered with fur; owls are covered with ________ .** (feathers)
23. **Spiders make webs; bees make ______ .** (hives)
24. **Pigs eat corn; squirrels eat _______ .** (nuts)

OPTIONAL: Repeat by reversing the statements, like this: "A chicken is covered with feathers; a squirrel is covered with (fur)."

2 Focus: talking about having any pet one wishes

Ask:

If you could have any pet in the whole world, what animal would you choose?

The children are to take turns naming their choice in a sentence such as "If I could have any animal in the world, I would choose a (giraffe)." Encourage unusual and imaginative choices. Each time, promote discussion with questions like these:

1. **Why would you choose that animal?**
2. **What kind of living space would the animal need?**
3. **What kinds of food would it eat?**
4. **Would the animal require special care or housing?**
5. **How would your family and friends react to the animal?**

Accept all responses.

240 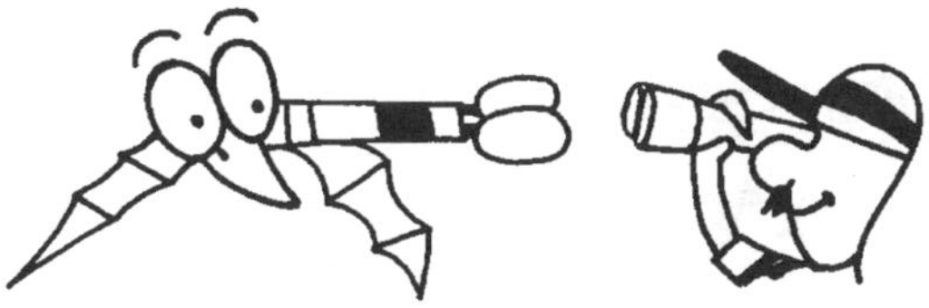

MATERIALS*

ACTIVITY 1

None

ACTIVITY 2

None

1 Focus: identifying numbers from rhyming words

Say:

We are going to play a rhyming game about numbers. First let's count aloud from one to 10.

Lead the children in doing so. Ask the questions below in sequence, letting the group respond. Then repeat the questions in random order for individuals to answer.

What number rhymes with . . .

1. sun?	***6. sticks?***
2. blue?	***7. heaven?***
3. tree?	***8. gate?***
4. floor?	***9. line?***
5. hive?	***10. hen?***

When everyone has had a turn, say:

Now I will name some numbers. When I call on you, tell me a word that rhymes with the number I have named.

In random order, name numbers from one to 10. Call on several children to name a rhyming word for each number. Give everyone a turn.

2 Focus: using groups of three words to make funny sentences

Say:

Let's try to make everyone laugh by making up ridiculous sentences. I will take the first turn. My three words are *balloon, barked,* and *banana.* Listen to my sentence: "The banana barked at the balloon."

Have the children take turns making up funny sentences with the word groups listed below. Reuse the list as needed to give each child a turn. Encourage a spirit of fun.

1. flower, food, forget

2. giraffe, giant, gloves

3. mosquito, medicine, motor

4. puppy, purse, pumpkin

5. sneeze, snake, snow

6. turtle, TV, teeth

7. witch, window, wolf

8. dinosaur, dollar, doctor

9. nickel, noise, nose

Keep in Mind. . .
After each lesson in the program, individuals who have difficulty demonstrating proficiency in the skills you consider appropriate and important for them to learn should be tutored. Aides could help you with this task.

241 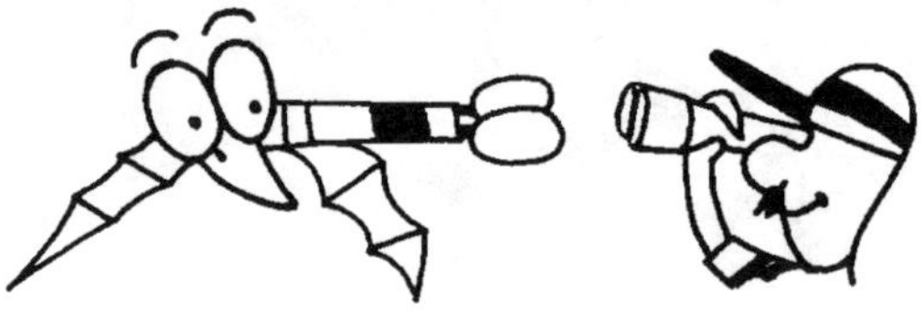

MATERIALS*

ACTIVITY 1

Color Chips
20 of each color

P. Mooney Bag

ACTIVITY 2

None

1 Focus: naming colors from memory
Link the chips into eight chains, one of each color.

Wear the bag and say:

Let's play a remembering game. I will show you four color chip chains. Then while your eyes are closed, I will put one of the chains into the P. Mooney bag. You are to look at the other chains and tell me which one is missing. To help you remember, you may whisper the names of the colors as you look at the four chains.

Show the children four chains for 10 or 15 seconds. Then have them cover their eyes. Put a chain into the bag and say:

Open your eyes! (Pause) **What did I hide?**

The children you call on should answer in sentences.

VARIATIONS: To make the activity *harder,* hide more than two of the chains. To make it *easier,* show two or three chains and hide only one.

2 Focus: naming holidays, and talking about colors associated with them

Say:

Let's talk about colors and holidays. Some holidays make us think of certain colors. First let's name all the holidays we can. Then we will talk about the colors that go with them. Raise your hand if you can name a holiday.

Be sure that Christmas, Thanksgiving, Valentine's Day, Easter, and Halloween are mentioned. Then lead the children in talking about each holiday and the colors associated with it.

242 

MATERIALS*

ACTIVITY 1

None

ACTIVITY 2

None

1 Focus: comparing heights of children, and sequencing from shortest to tallest

Say:

Today we are going to compare each other's heights. Let's line up, with the shortest person at one end and the tallest person at the other end.

Choose two children to stand beside each other in front of the group. Ask:

Who is *taller:* (Shawn), or (Lullah)? (Pause) **Yes, (Lullah) is taller than (Shawn). This means that (Shawn) is *shorter* than (Lullah).**

Ask another child to stand beside the two children. Help the class decide how the third child compares in height with the first two. Have the three line up from shortest to tallest. Continue with other children until everyone is in line. Then ask:

Who is the *tallest* person in our line? (Pause for unison response) **Who is the *shortest* person in the line?** (Pause) **Name some children who are (shorter/taller) than you, (Anthony).**

VARIATION: To make this activity *harder,* have several children, in random order of heights, stand where the others can see them. Ask questions like "Is this statement true, or false: '(Maria) is taller than (Peter)'?"

2 Focus: evaluating statements about height, and correcting them while stressing *not*

Say:

Let's play a thinking game. I will whisper a sentence to each of you. You are to repeat it to the group. Then everyone else will say in a sentence whether the sentence is true or false.

Have the children take turns standing by you. Whisper one of the statements listed below to each child. Then call on the group or individuals to answer the child in a sentence such as "No, you are not taller than a giraffe" or "Yes, you are shorter than a flagpole."

1. **I am taller than a dandelion.**
2. **I am shorter than a lighthouse.**
3. **I am taller than a tree.**
4. **I am shorter than a sugar bowl.**
5. **I am taller than a moon rocket ship.**
6. **I am shorter than a policeman.**
7. **I am taller than an ostrich.**
8. **I am shorter than a man on stilts.**
9. **I am taller than an ice-cream soda.**
10. **I am shorter than a bus.**
11. **I am taller than a chair.**
12. **I am shorter than a building.**
13. **I am taller than a turkey.**
14. **I am shorter than a ladder.**
15. **I am taller than a tower.**
16. **I am shorter than a jungle gym.**
17. **I am taller than a salt shaker.**
18. **I am shorter than an ant.**
19. **I am taller than a giraffe.**
20. **I am shorter than a bird.**

VARIATION: To make the activity *harder,* have the children make up their own statements about being tall or short.

243 

MATERIALS*

ACTIVITY 1

None

ACTIVITY 2

None

1 Focus: classifying groups of compound words, identifying the short words in each compound word, and using the short words in sentences

Say:

Tell me one word or phrase that describes these four words: *dollhouse, pinwheel, football,* and *sandbox.*

If no one says the word toys, suggest it. Then say:

Each of those four names is a long word made from two short words. Listen as I say the names again, and tell me the two short words in each toy name.

Repeat the four words, one at a time, and have the class name the component words. Then have two children each make up a sentence with one of the short words. Continue as above with these groups of compound words:

1. **watermelon, strawberry, doughnut, popcorn** (foods)
2. **snowsuit, swimsuit, wristwatch, raincoat** (clothes)
3. **airplane, rowboat, motorboat, sailboat** (vehicles)

2 Focus: brainstorming foods by type

Say:

Let's see how many different foods you can name. Call on children to name foods until about ten have been mentioned. Then say:

Now let's see how many different desserts you can name. Have five or six children each name a different kind of dessert. Continue as above with these categories:

1. **sandwiches**
2. **soups**
3. **vegetables**
4. **cereals**
5. **cold drinks**
6. **fruits**
7. **meats**
8. **candies**

OPTIONAL: End by asking several children to name their favorite food in each category. Give everyone a chance to participate.

244

MATERIALS*

ACTIVITY 1

Cards

Animals

1-38, except 2 & 13

Display Board

4 ledges

ACTIVITY 2

Cards

Animals

(same as for Activity 1)

Music

328

Audiocassette 2

Side A, Song 6 & 7
"If and Then Go Together"
(vocal and instrumental)

1 Focus: sequencing sets of three animal pictures from smallest to largest, and then describing the sequence

Set up the board with two horizontal rows of two ledges each. Have the 36 animal cards arranged in groups of three as fisted below.

Say:

I will show you pictures of three animals. Then I will ask one of you to arrange the three from smallest to largest. Let's begin.

In random order, place cards 8, 27, and 33 on the bottom row of ledges. Point to the left side of the top two ledges, and say:

Find the smallest animal and put its picture here, (Rhoda). (Pause) **Why did you put the spider first?** (Pause) **Yes, the spider is the smallest animal.** (Point to center of top two ledges) **Now find the next larger animal and put its card here, (Kurt).** (Pause) **Why did you put the cat in the middle?** (Pause) **That is right; the cat is larger than the spider.** (Point to right side of top two ledges) **Now put the picture of the largest animal here, (Hazel).** (Pause) **Why did you put the pig in the third position?** (Pause) **Yes, a pig is usually larger than a cat. The pig is the largest of the three animals.**

Continue as above with the remaining groups of three. After each group is arranged, call on a child to describe the animals in the sequence from smallest to largest. If necessary, make new groups of three cards so that everyone may have a turn.

1. 8•**cat**, 27•**pig**, 33•**spider**
2. 4•**beetle**, 23•**kittens**, 14•**duckling**
3. 3•**bee**, 9•**chick**, 31•**rooster**
4. 12•**dog**, 19•**goldfish**, 16•**fly**
5. 15•**elephant**, 21•**horse**, 24•**lamb**
6. 29•**puppy**, 34•**squirrel**, 38•**worm**
7. 11•**cow**, 18•**goat**, 35•**toad**
8. 1•**bear**, 37•**turtle**, 36•**turkey**
9. 5•**bird**, 20•**hen**, 32•**sheep**
10. 25•**lion**, 28•**piglet**, 30•**rabbit**
11. 6•**butterfly**, 17•**gerbil**, 7•**calf**
12. 26•**owl**, 10•**colt**, 22•**kid**

2 Focus: choosing the five smallest and five largest animals, and then singing the song "If and Then Go Together" about the choices

Display the 36 animal cards in random order on a chalkledge or on the floor, so the children can easily see them.

Point to the cards and say:

Now let's find the five animals which you think are the *largest* of all; then we will find the five *smallest* animals.

Help the children compare the animals. Have them choose five very large and five very small animals. Suggested choices:

Large	*Small*
1. bear	**1. bee**
2. cow	**2. beetle**
3. elephant	**3. butterfly**
4. horse	**4. fly**
5. lion	**5. worm**

Accept any reasonable choices. End by playing Song 7 (instrumental version) of "If and Then Go Together." Refer to the music card as you lead the children in singing these verses about their choices:

1. **If you are an (elephant), then you are large, etc.**
2. **If you are a (bear), then you are large, etc.**
3. **If you are a (lion), then you are large, etc.**
4. **If you are a (cow), then you are large, etc.**
5. **If you are a (horse), then you are large, etc.**
6. **If you are a (beetle), then you are small, etc.**
7. **If you are a (bee), then you are small, etc.**
8. **If you are a (butterfly), then you are small, etc.**
9. **If you are a (fly), then you are small, etc.**
10. **If you are a (worm), then you are small, etc.**

245

MATERIALS*

ACTIVITY 1

None

ACTIVITY 2

None

1 Focus: classifying groups of five words

Say:

I am going to say five words. Tell me what word or phrase we could use to describe all five words.

Use the word groups listed below. Help as necessary, and give everyone a turn.

1. **turkey, ham, rice, eggs, chicken** (foods)
2. **scissors, knife, lamp, spoon, mop** (household items)
3. **legs, chest, nose, head, arms** (body parts)
4. **seven, five, one, three, two** (numbers)
5. **Mary, Thomas, Jose, Bertha, Jason** (names)
6. **jeans, sock, boot, cap, ring** (things to wear)
7. **owl, bird, spider, worm, rabbit** (animals)
8. **apple, pear, peach, pineapple, lemon** (fruit)
9. **airplane, rocking horse, sled, truck, puzzle** (toys)
10. **baby, barber, boy, woman, girl** (people)
11. **blue, red, white, black, orange** (colors)
12. **helicopter, ship, car, bicycle, tow truck** (vehicles)
13. **onion, corn, potato, carrot, lettuce** (vegetables)
14. **chair, table, bed, couch, desk** (furniture, household items)
15. **water, soda pop, milk, orange juice, chocolate milk** (things to drink)
16. **fire fighter, mail carrier, doctor, farmer, dentist** (workers, people)

VARIATIONS: To make the activity *easier,* reduce the number of words in a set. To make it *harder,* have the children take turns making up sets of four items for the group to classify.

2 Focus: brainstorming descriptions of people, clothes, animals, foods, vehicles, toys, household items, and body parts

Say:

Let's see how fast we can think. I will say a word like corn. If I point to you, tell me something about corn in a sentence. Everyone will have a turn. Tell something no one else has said.

Use the list from Activity 1, omitting colors, numbers, and names. Continue with the same word until the children run out of ideas. Vary the categories from which words are chosen.

246 

MATERIALS*

ACTIVITY 1

Cards

People

200 202 203 204
205 206 207 209
211 212 213 214
215 217 218 219
221 222 223 224
225

ACTIVITY 2

None

1 Focus: answering questions about people while stressing the use of past, present, and future tenses

Hold the 21 stacked people cards and say:

I will show you a picture of someone doing something. Then you are to answer my questions about that person. Let's begin.

Show card 200 and ask:

What is this man doing, (Gloria)? (Pause) **You are right. He is flying through the air on his trapeze. If he does the *same* thing every day, what do you think he did yesterday?** (Pause) **Yes, yesterday he *flew* through the air. Now, if he does the same thing every day, what do you think he will do tomorrow?** (Pause) **Right! Tomorrow he *will fly* through the air.**

Continue to show card 200 as you say:

Let's suppose this man on the trapeze does *different* things every day. If he does *different* things every day, what do you think he did yesterday? (Pause) **Yes, yesterday he (drove a tractor). If he does *different* things every day, what do you think this man will do tomorrow?** (Pause) **Right; tomorrow he will (paint a house).**

Repeat this procedure with as many of the remaining cards as you consider appropriate. Help the children use past, present, and future tenses correctly in their responses.

2 Focus: imitating clapping patterns

Say:

Please listen carefully as I clap a pattern; then I will ask you to clap the same pattern together.

Clap patterns like the following for the children to repeat in unison. As necessary, repeat until the children can imitate the pattern well. After each group response, call on individuals to imitate the pattern. If your children are able, let them take turns leading the group.

1. **clap, pause, clap, clap, pause, clap, clap, clap, pause, etc.**
2. **clap, clap, clap, pause, clap, clap, pause, clap, pause, etc.**
3. **clap, pause, clap, clap, clap, pause, clap, pause, clap, clap, clap, pause, etc.**

247

MATERIALS*

ACTIVITY 1

None

ACTIVITY 2

None

1 Focus: identifying words in which the beginning sound, *sh*, is separated from the rest of the word

Say:

Today we are going to make more words with sounds. Listen to this sound: sh-sh-sh (Continue for a few seconds) **Let's make it together.**

Afterwards, ask the children what the sound makes them think about.
Then say:

Now we will use the sh-sh sound to make words. After all of you have made that sound, I will add another sound. Tell me what word the sounds make when they are put together. For example, if you say "sh-sh-sh" and I say "ut," the word we make will be *shut*. Let's begin.

Each time the class says "sh-sh-sh," add one of the word parts listed below and ask, "What word is that?" Call on a child or the group to identify the word. Help as needed by running the two parts of the word closer and closer together.

1. -eep	**7. -arp**	**13. -ore**
2. -oe	**8. -e**	**14. -ort**
3. -ape	**9. -ell**	**15. -oulder**
4. -irt	**10. -ine**	**16. -ovel**
5. -adow	**11. -ip**	**17. -ow**
6. -aker	**12. -op**	**18. -ower**

2 Focus: talking about wearing funny clothes

Say:

Suppose I were to say, "Tomorrow you are to wear funny or strange clothes to school." What would you wear?

Have everyone answer. Encourage the children to make imaginative choices and to speak in sentences.

248

MATERIALS*

ACTIVITY 1

Cards

Foods

95 100 110 112
113 114 117 121
122 130 131 132

ACTIVITY 2

None

1 Focus: counting and naming items pictured on food cards, and then grouping the cards by the number of items shown

Stack the 12 food cards in numerical order.

Hold the cards and say:

Tell me how many different things you see in each of these food cards, and then name them.

Show the cards in order, one at a time. Each child you call on should describe the pictured items in a sentence such as "There are two different things in this picture: green beans and a plate." Give everyone a turn. If there are more than 12 children, reuse the cards. End by displaying all the cards upon the floor or chalkledge. Then have the children group the foods by the number of items in each picture. This list may be helpful:

Two items

95•**green beans and dish**
110•**hamburger and bun**
113•**hotdog and bun**
114•**ice cream and cone**
117•**orange juice and glass**

Three items

100•**cereal, milk, and dish**
112•**honey, honeycomb, and jar**
122•**knife, peanut butter, and jar**
130•**bread, lettuce, and tomato**
131•**straw, bottle, and soda pop**
132•**soup, spoon, and bowl**

Four items

121•**pancakes, syrup, butter, plate**

VARIATION: To make the activity *easier,* point to the items as the children count them. Then lead the class in saying a sentence like "There are four things in this picture: two ears of corn and two pieces of butter."

2 Focus: remembering a whispered and repeated message about food

Have the children line up. If there are more than about 10 children, ask them to form two even lines facing each other. Say:

Let's send messages about what we are going to eat for breakfast, lunch, or dinner. I will whisper the first message.

Whisper to the lead child in a line, "We will eat *hamburgers* and a *salad* for dinner." That child then whispers the message to the next child, and so on down the line. When the message reaches the end, the last child should say it aloud. Then have the group compare that message with the one you whispered. Let the last child come to the head of the line and begin a new message. When breakdowns occur in a message, help those responsible.

VARIATION: To make the activity *harder,* increase the number of foods the children must remember.

249

MATERIALS*

ACTIVITY 1

Display Board
4 ledges

Poster 2

ACTIVITY 2

Display Board
4 ledges

Poster 2

1 Focus: predicting and talking about "what would happen if" using the poster "Circus"

Use the ledges to display the poster on the board.

Say:

Let's use the circus poster to play What Would Happen If. . . ? Look at P. Mooney riding his Chaincycle along the wire. (Pause) **What would happen if P. Mooney suddenly fell off his Chaincycle?**

Encourage discussion of the probable consequences. Continue with the situations listed below. Begin each by asking:

What do you think would happen if.

1. **the balls the girls are standing on were to burst?**
2. **the gorilla were to break his chains?**
3. **the tall man were to trip over the weight?**
4. **the big firecracker were to go off?**
5. **the man on the unicycle were to fall into the ring with the elephants?**
6. **the barbells were to break in half?**
7. **the bowling pin were to land in the lion's cage?**
8. **the band were to start playing very, very fast music?**
9. **the bear were to fall off and the horse were to rear up?**
10. **the girl riding on the shoulders of the high-wire motorcycle rider were to sneeze?**

2 Focus: counting items on the poster "Circus" to answer "how-many" questions

Leave the poster from Activity 1 on display.

Say:

Now let's count some of the things in our circus poster. I will tell you what to count.

After the children have scanned the poster, lead them in counting each of the items listed below. Ask how many of each item they see. They should respond in a sentence such as "There are (four clowns) in this picture."

1. **clowns**
2. **elephants**
3. **people on the trapeze**
4. **dogs**
5. **people in the band**
6. **circus rings**
7. **people on the high wire**
8. **things with wheels**
9. **people swinging**

250

MATERIALS*

ACTIVITY 1

None

ACTIVITY 2

None

1 Focus: evaluating questions, deciding which are silly, and correcting them

Say:

I have some questions to ask you. Some of them are silly, and some are not. Listen, and answer my questions.

Ask the questions listed below. Each time, the children should respond in unison with sentences such as "Yes, (clowns) are funny" or "No, (bears) do not bark." Then let someone correct the silly sentence by saying, "Bears do not bark; bears growl." Repeat as necessary to ensure that everyone understands each answer before you continue.

1. **Are clowns funny?**
2. **Do bears bark?**
3. **Do dogs jump?**
4. **Do cars think?**
5. **Do swings move?**
6. **Do horses prance?**
7. **Do gorillas grow?**
8. **Do drums dance?**
9. **Do whips snap?**
10. **Do balls breathe?**
11. **Do elephants eat?**
12. **Do lions live?**
13. **Do bicycles bite?**
14. **Do firecrackers fly?**
15. **Do people laugh?**
16. **Do chains cheer?**

2 Focus: talking about the meaning of making a promise and how it feels to have promises broken

Say:

Tell me what it means to make a promise to someone. What does "making a promise" mean?

Encourage the children to discuss what they think a promise is. Then ask:

If someone promised to do something special for you and then didn't do it, how would you feel?

Encourage the children to discuss their reactions to broken promises.

251

MATERIALS*

ACTIVITY 1

Puppets

P. Mooney

Zoey

Thinking hat

ACTIVITY 2

Color Chips

1 chain of 3 to 6 color chips (assorted colors & lengths) per child

1 Focus: talking about possible solutions to Zoey's and P. Mooney's problems

Place Zoey (wearing her thinking hat) on your hand and have her say:

P. Mooney and I need your help again today. We have some more problems to solve.

In each case, the right puppet should present the problem and lead the discussion. Have the puppets encourage fun and provide hints to help the children suggest several solutions. Praise all worthy efforts.

1. P. Mooney: **Some friends of mine have asked me to help them make a playhouse. Tell me some ways we might do so.**
2. Zoey: **I have a sick friend who must stay in bed for a week. But staying in bed with nothing to do is very boring. What are some things my friend might do to make the time seem to go faster?**
3. P. Mooney: **I want to surprise my friends at a party by dressing to look like a scary monster. Please tell me how I could make myself look monstrous.**
4. Zoey: **The leaves are dropping off the trees everywhere. There are many colored leaves on the ground. Tell me different ways I might gather up the leaves.**
5. P. Mooney: **One day as I was riding my Chaincycle across the hills to visit a friend, the chain on my Chaincycle broke. Tell me some other ways I might have gotten to my friend's house.**
6. Zoey: **Next Saturday morning I want to make chocolate-chip cookies, but the chocolate chips are on a very high shelf in the kitchen. How might I get them down from the shelf?**
7. P. Mooney: **One day the rain was coming down very fast. I looked everywhere, but I couldn't find my raincoat. Tell me how I might have gone out into the rain without getting wet.**
8. Zoey: **While I was at the fair, my ring came off my finger and rolled away. It rolled and rolled and stopped on the other side of a tall fence. Please tell me how I might have gotten my ring back.**

2 Focus: counting three to six chips in color chip chains, and then brainstorming items of the same color

Being sure to use all eight colors, make the chains listed under Materials, having about an equal number of each length of three to six chips, and put the chains into the bag.

Put on the bag. Each child you call on should withdraw a chain and count the chips aloud for the group. When everyone has had a turn, ask the children who have them to hold up the red chips in their chains. Then say:

Now let's each name something red.

Keep the pace lively and encourage the children not to repeat items. Give everyone at least one turn. Repeat this procedure for the remaining seven colors.

252

MATERIALS*

ACTIVITY 1

None

ACTIVITY 2

None

1 Focus: talking about words that sound the same but have different meanings

Say:

Let's talk about some more words that are pronounced the same but have different meanings. Tell me what word sounds the same in both these sentences:

1. **We went to *watch* the bicycle races.**
2. **Kenneth got a *watch* for his birthday.**

Repeat and help as necessary until they identify watch as the common word. Then call on children to give the two meanings of watch. Have several others make up sentences for each meaning. Continue as above with these pairs of words and sentences:

1. **The *sail* on the boat had a tear in it. There is a big *sale* at the department store.**
2. **Sonja *can* roller skate well. We need a *can* of juice for snack time.**
3. **It may get very *cold* this winter. Edward was sick with a *cold* last week.**
4. **The telephone will *ring* loud enough for you to hear it. Grace got a *ring* for her birthday.**

2 Focus: talking about things one likes to see and touch

Say:

Let's take turns telling what we most like to look at and why. Who wants to start?

Give everyone a turn, and accept all responses. Stress the use of sentences. Continue as above, talking about favorite things to touch.

253

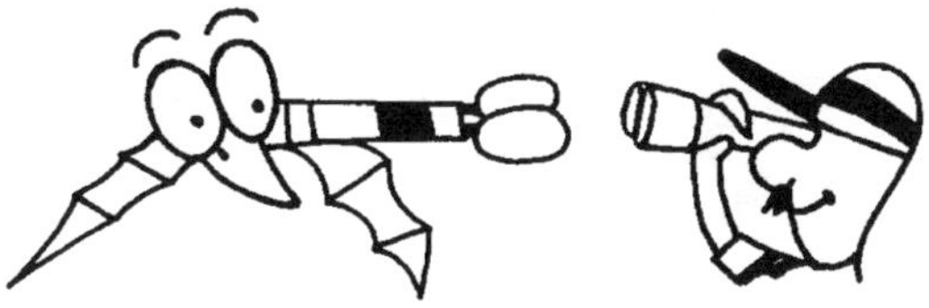

MATERIALS*

ACTIVITY 1

Display Board

Manikin, Movable

ACTIVITY 2

None

1 Focus: imitating the position of the movable manikin, and then considering actions possible from that position

Set up the board and place the movable manikin upon it.

Stand beside the board, with the children standing facing it. Say:

Please watch the manikin to see what it does. You are to do the same thing the manikin is doing.

Put the manikin into one of the positions given below, and invite the children to imitate it. Then call on children to tell what they could do in that position, asking, "What might you be getting ready to do now, (Mario)?" Encourage them to think of many possibilities.

Suggested positions and actions:

stretching
reaching a high shelf
falling
hanging

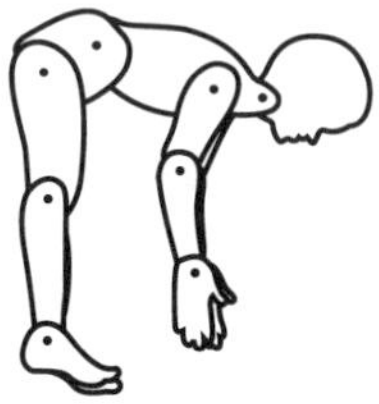

rowing a boat
exercising
tying shoes
polishing shoes

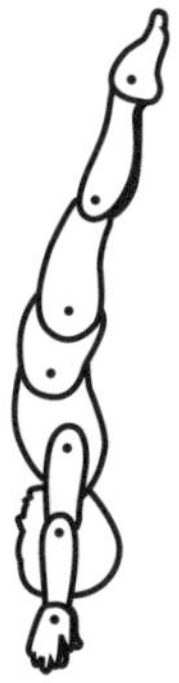

diving
sunbathing
floating
sleeping

leaping
dancing
kicking

running a race
jumping over something
walking fast

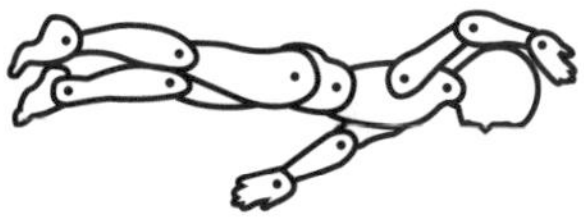

swimming

VARIATION: Have the children perform or pantomime all the actions they suggest.

2 Focus: listening to three words and deciding whether they rhyme

Say:

Let's play a rhyming game. I will say three words. Sometimes the three words will rhyme; they will all end with the same sound. But sometimes they will not rhyme. Listen carefully and tell me whether the words rhyme with one another.

Say the following groups of words in turn. The children should answer in unison with the sentence "Yes, those words rhyme" or "No, those words do not rhyme." Occasionally call on individual children to respond.

1. **ball, tall, call**
2. **can, tan, pan**
3. **brush, bread, brave**
4. **pie, lie, die**
5. **bug, tug, rug**
6. **tar, bar, car**
7. **bun, bill, big**
8. **smack, crack, rack**
9. **heel, peel, meal**
10. **red, lead, fed**
11. **but, cut, rut**
12. **cake, take, make**
13. **glad, glass, glove**
14. **cheek, week, leak**
15. **free, key, me**
16. **card, guard, lard**
17. **hide, ride, tide**
18. **join, joke, juice**

VARIATION: To make the activity *harder,* increase the speed of presentation and/or the number of words in each series.

254

MATERIALS*

ACTIVITY 1

Cards

Pictures from Several Categories

11	12	15	25
29	30	33	34
38	98	118	123
137	142	149	153
168	170	173	184
190	194	200	204
205	210	212	214
216	217	219	221
254	261	265	268
272	274	282	

Display Board

2 ledges

ACTIVITY 2

None

1 Focus: making up and telling short stories from three pictures

Display cards 30, 142, and 205 on the board. Arrange the remaining cards in groups of three, as indicated below.

Point to the cards on display and say:

Let's make up stories about this group of three pictures. Listen to my story about the rabbit, the lettuce, and this boy.

Make up a short story like this one: "The boy watched the rabbit nibble some lettuce." Call for other stories using these three pictures. Then have the children take turns making up stories about the groups of cards listed below.

1. 194•**tool set**, 216•**tree house**, 214•**man**
2. 210•**fire fighter**, 168•**iron**, 221•**older woman**
3. 11•**cow**, 118•**milk**, 173•**pail**
4. 265•**wagon**, 212•**grocer**, 149•**pumpkin**
5. 217•**police officer**, 219•**toddler**, 272•**car**
6. 282•**pickup truck**, 15•**elephant**, 25•**lion**
7. 254•**swing**, 34•**squirrel**, 12•**dog**
8. 274•**helicopter**, 216•**nurse**, 33•**spider**
9. 204•**boy**, 98•**cake**, 170•**knife**
10. 29•**puppy**, 153•**bathtub**, 184•**soap**
11. 123•**apple pie**, 38•**worm**, 137•**apple**
12. 190•**telephone**, 268•**ambulance**, 200•**acrobat**

2 Focus: talking about what might be inside an imaginary box

With the children seated in a circle with you, say:

Imagine there is a box here in the center of our circle. (Point) **The box could be very small, or it could be very large.** (Demonstrate) **Inside the box is something very surprising. What do you think it might be?**

The children are to take turns answering in sentences such as "I think there might be a baby dragon inside that box." Encourage unusual and imaginative answers.

255

MATERIALS*

ACTIVITY 1

Display Board
4 ledges

Poster 6

ACTIVITY 2

None

1 Focus: thinking about "who might say that" on the poster "Town in Fall"

Use the ledges to display the poster on the board.

Point to the poster and say:

Look at all these people and animals. I will say a sentence that one of them might say. Please try to figure out who might be speaking. Who might say, "I got this helmet for my birthday"? (Discuss) **Yes, you are right. The boy holding the helmet might say that.**

Have someone repeat, "I got this helmet for my birthday," as he or she points to the boy on the poster. Then continue with these statements:

1. **"These windows are really dirty!"**
2. **"I am going to be in a wheelchair race tomorrow."**
3. **"I can't fly very far without more wind."**
4. **"Your teeth look very healthy, Mr. Lamb."**
5. **"Would you like some freshly baked cookies?"**
6. **"There is a picture of me on the sports page!"**
7. **"I wish I could cross the street on my skates."**
8. **"When I fly over the town, I will wave to the people."**
9. **"I hope I don't spill any of this paint."**
10. **"The air smells so good. I wish I could see the pretty leaves."**
11. **"I really like ice cream."**
12. **"Oh, dear, the mail will not be picked up until 5:00."**
13. **"Whee, look at my paper airplane fly!"**
14. **"Don't cut it too short, please."**
15. **"This bag of groceries is heavy."**
16. **"What is the price of your potatoes, Mr. Coles?"**
17. **"You had better run fast, cat, or I will catch you."**
18. **"This rake works well."**

VARIATION: To make the activity *harder,* whisper statements for individuals to present to the class.

2 Focus: evaluating questions, deciding which are silly, and correcting them

Say:

Now I have some questions to ask you. Some of them are silly, but some are sensible. Listen carefully. When a question is sensible, say, "Yes." If it is silly, say, "No," and tell us why. Raise your hand if you are ready to answer.

Call on children to answer these questions:

1. **Do wheelchairs waddle?**
2. **Do balloons fly?**
3. **Do pumpkins prance?**
4. **Do rakes roar?**
5. **Do dogs chase?**
6. **Do ladders lean?**
7. **Do trucks turn?**
8. **Do mailboxes sing?**
9. **Do barbers cut?**
10. **Do painters paint?**
11. **Do tricycles roll?**
12. **Do leaves fall up?**
13. **Do streets shiver?**
14. **Do newspapers fold?**
15. **Do awnings argue?**
16. **Do roller skates spin?**
17. **Do dentists drill?**
18. **Do bicycles fly?**
19. **Do airplanes land?**
20. **Do lampposts leap?**

VARIATION: To make the activity *harder,* call on individuals to present similar questions of their own.

256

MATERIALS*

ACTIVITY 1

None

ACTIVITY 2

Cards

Foods

100 104 108 112
113 114 119 121
122 124 125 128
131 132 133 134

1 **Focus: brainstorming body parts, clothing, and household items**

Say:

Let's see how fast you can name clothing, body parts, and household items. Name (four body parts), (LaShonda).

Continue with other children. Always give the child's name last. Praise all reasonable efforts.

VARIATIONS: To make the activity *easier* or *harder,* ask for fewer or more than four items per turn.

OPTIONAL: Tally responses for each of the three categories. End by having the children count and discuss the responses in each group.

2 **Focus: using *full* and *empty* to complete sentences that stress *before* and *after***

Stack the 16 food cards in numerical order.

Show card 100 as you say:

I am going to say part of a sentence about this picture. Please complete this sentence for me: "Before I ate my breakfast, this bowl of cereal was full. But after I ate, the bowl was (Pause for unison response) **(empty)." That's right; the bowl was empty after I ate. Does this picture show the bowl before or after I ate, (Alfredo)? Yes! The picture shows the bowl of cereal before I ate.**

Continue as above with the remaining 15 cards, calling on one child to complete the sentence, and on another to answer the question.

1. 104•**After the family ate lunch, this package of crackers was empty. But before lunch, the package was _______ .**
2. 108•**Before these greens were cooked, this bowl was empty. But after the greens were cooked, the bowl was _______ .**
3. 112• **Before the beekeeper gathered the honey, this jar was empty. But after the beekeeper gathered honey, the jar was _______ .**
4. 113•**After the hot dog was cooked, this roll was full. But before the hot dog was cooked, the roll was _______ .**
5. 114•**Before I dropped this ice cream, this cone was full. But after I dropped it, the cone was _______ .**
6. 119•**Before I drank the chocolate milk, the glass was full. But after I drank it, the glass was _______ .**
7. 121•**Before we cooked the pancakes, this plate was empty. But after we cooked them, the plate was _______ .**
8. 124•**Before the movie, the bag of popcorn was full. But after the movie the bag was _______ .**
9. 125•**After lunch, the potato chip bag was empty. But before lunch, the bag was _______ .**
10. 128•**Before the rice was cooked, the bowl was empty. But after the rice was cooked, the bowl was _______ .**
11. 131•**After I drank the soda pop, the bottle was empty. But before I drank the pop, the bottle was _______ .**
12. 132•**After I filled the bowl with soup, the bowl was full. But before I filled it, the bowl was _______ .**
13. 133•**Before dinner, the plate of spaghetti was full. But after dinner, the plate was _______ .**
14. 134•**Before the man filled the taco shell, it was empty. But after he filled it, the shell was _______ .**

VARIATIONS: To make this activity *easier,* omit the question about whether the picture shows the item before or after. To make it *harder,* omit the final word in the first sentence and have the children complete both sentences in each pair.

257 

MATERIALS*

ACTIVITY 1

Cards

People

202 204 205 211
214 215 219 220
221

Display Board

6 ledges

Teacher provides

Blank cassette (optional)

Tape recorder (optional)

ACTIVITY 2

Cards

People
(same as for Activity 1)

Display Board

6 ledges

1 Focus: describing the actions of people, and then making up short stories about the people

Display the nine people cards on the board.

Say:

Look at these pictures of people. You are to tell what each of them is doing.

Call on children to name the actions of each person shown. Then say:

Now let's make up stories about these people. You may each choose someone to tell a story about.

Give everyone a turn, and stress the use of sentences. The cards may be chosen more than once. Help as necessary with questions about the person and about what may have preceded and followed the pictured activity.

OPTIONAL: Record the stories, and play them back at the end of the activity. Ask the children to identify the speaker and the card being discussed.

2 Focus: describing people cards from memory

Leave the cards from Activity 1 on display.

Point to the cards on display and say:

Now let's play a remembering game. Look at all of the people on these cards while I count from one to 10. When I say "10," I will turn over a card and then ask you to tell all you can remember about that person. Try to remember what work the person does, what he or she is wearing and doing, and what the person looks like. Let's start!

Slowly count from one to 10 as the children scan the cards. Then turn a card over, and have several children each name one or two things about it. When the main characteristics have been identified, continue with other cards. If feasible, continue until all cards have been described and everyone has participated.

VARIATION: To make the activity *easier,* have the children cover their eyes. Then turn over a card and have someone name the missing picture. Rearrange the cards between turns.

OPTIONAL: Let the children take turns counting to 10 and turning over a card for others to describe.

258

MATERIALS*

ACTIVITY 1

Color Chips
1 of each color

ACTIVITY 2

None

1 Focus: identifying colors from rhyming words

Link the eight chips into a chain.

Hold up the chain and say:

We are going to play a rhyming game about colors. First let's all name the colors in this chain.

Point to each chip in turn as the children name the colors individually or in unison. Lay the chain aside. Have the children respond in unison to these questions:

What color rhymes with . . .

1. **head?**
2. **jello?**
3. **Jean?**
4. **shoe?**
5. **town?**
6. **stack?**
7. **bite?**

Then say:

One of the colors did not have a rhyming word. What color was it?

If no one names *orange,* hold up the chain and remove the corresponding chips as you ask the questions again. Then point out that there is no word that rhymes with orange. Repeat the questions in random order for individuals to answer. When everyone has had a turn, say:

Now I will say the names of colors. Tell me some words that rhyme with each color.

Call on children to name rhyming words for every color but orange. Help as necessary, so everyone responds correctly at least once.

2 Focus: using groups of two words to make funny sentences

Say:

Let's take turns making up funny sentences that will make everyone laugh. I will go first. My two words are *jaws* and *whale.* I will try to make you laugh.

Make up a humorous sentence such as "I tried to eat a whale, but my jaws were too small." Then have the children take turns doing the same with the following word groups. If necessary, use the word list again to give each child a turn. Encourage the children to construct ridiculous sentences that may promote laughter in the group.

1. **kangaroos, knees**
2. **mosquito, ankles**
3. **turtle, toes**
4. **hippopotamus, hips**
5. **snake, head**
6. **worm, neck**
7. **giraffe, shoulder**
8. **bear, waist**
9. **monkey, elbows**
10. **caterpillar, wrists**
11. **sharks, fingers**
12. **fish, arms**

259

MATERIALS*

ACTIVITY 1

Display Board
2 ledges

Magnetic Shapes
5 medium circles
5 medium rectangles
5 medium squares
5 medium triangles

ACTIVITY 2

Cards
People
224

1 **Focus: classifying magnetic shapes into various groups, and then counting and describing the items in the group**

Place the ledges vertically to separate the left two-thirds of the board from the right one-third. Put the shapes onto the left side.

Say:

Let's see how many ways we can group the magnetic shapes. Find all the shapes that are black, (Basil). Put them over here. (Point to right side of board)

When the four black shapes have been moved, call on children to answer these questions:

1. **How many shapes are in this group?**
2. **What are the names of the shapes in this group?**
3. **How many (circles), (squares), (triangles), and (rectangles) are in the group?**
4. **There is one thing about everything in this group that is the same. What is it?**

Continue as above with the groupings listed below. Make sure everyone participates at least once.

1. **all red shapes**
2. **all green shapes**
3. **all blue shapes**
4. **all yellow shapes**
5. **all shapes with straight sides**
6. **all shapes with curved sides**
7. **all shapes with four sides**
8. **all shapes with three sides**

2 **Focus: imagining and talking about what might make someone sad**

Show card 224 and say:

Let's imagine that this girl is a friend of yours. Pretend she told you what happened to make her look so sad. When I call on you, tell us what happened to her.

Have several children relate the imagined sad event. Accept all responses.

VARIATION: To make the activity *easier,* start various sad stories and call on individuals to complete them.

260

MATERIALS*

ACTIVITY 1

None

ACTIVITY 2

None

1 Focus: answering questions about whether objects are long or tall

Say:

Today let's talk about the words *long* and *tall*. What does the word long mean? (Discuss) **When something is *long*, one end of it is far from the other end. What does the word *tall* mean?** (Discuss) **Yes, if something is *tall*, it stands high up from the ground.**

When the children seem to understand, continue:

Now I will ask you some questions about whether certain things are long, or tall. Some things are both long and tall. Let's begin. Is a flagpole long, or is it tall, (Evelyn)?

Have individuals respond in sentences. Always say the child's name at the end of your question. Present such items as these:

1. **snake** (long)
2. **lamppost** (tall)
3. **wall** (tall and long)
4. **flagpole** (tall)
5. **train** (long)
6. **pile of blocks** (tall and long)
7. **line of traffic** (long)
8. **elephant's trunk** (long)
9. **tower** (tall)
10. **scarf** (long)
11. **tree** (tall)
12. **bridge** (long and tall)
13. **giraffe** (tall)
14. **river** (long)
15. **street** (long)
16. **alligator** (long)
17. **sunflower** (tall)
18. **necklace** (long)
19. **banana** (long)
20. **caterpillar** (long)

OPTIONAL: Also have the children demonstrate the length or height of the items by using their arms and bodies.

2 Focus: imagining and talking about having arms longer than one's legs

Say:

Let's imagine that our arms are very, very long. In fact, they are even longer than our legs. Let's talk about what it would be like if our arms were longer than our legs.

Encourage the children to discuss their ideas. If necessary, ask what type of clothing they would need, what activities they could or could not do, and how they would adjust to the situation. End by having the children consider whether it would be better to have arms longer than legs.

Keep in Mind. . .
After each lesson in the program, individuals who have difficulty demonstrating proficiency in the skills you consider appropriate and important for them to learn should be tutored. Aides could help you with this task.

261

MATERIALS*

ACTIVITY 1

Cards
Vehicles
267-283

Display Board
6 ledges

ACTIVITY 2

None

1 Focus: naming parts of vehicles, and then classifying vehicles by their parts

Set up the board and stack the 12 transportation cards, with card 269 on top.

Show card 269 and say:

Look at this picture of a bicycle, and name all the bicycle parts you see.

The various children you call on should name and point to bicycle parts such as wheels, handlebars, seat, and pedals. When the vehicle has been fully discussed, place the card on the board. Continue with the remaining cards, encouraging everyone to take a turn. Then point to the 12 cards on the board and say:

Now look at all these ways to travel. Find all the vehicles that have *engines*.

When the children have done so, continue by asking them to find all items with the following:

1. **wheels**
2. **pedals**
3. **seats**
4. **wings**
5. **sirens**
6. **oars**
7. **handles**
8. **propellers**
9. **doors**
10. **rear-view mirrors**
11. **bumpers**
12. **signs**

2 Focus: remembering and repeating a whispered message about things seen on a bus trip

Have the children line up. If there are more than 10 children, have them form two lines of about equal length. Say:

Imagine we are on a bus trip. As we ride along the road, we see many interesting sights. Let's send messages about what we see on the bus trip. I will whisper the first message.

Whisper to the child who heads the line, "On the bus trip, I saw a bird, an alligator, and a man in a wheelchair." That child then whispers the message to the next child, and so on down the line. The last child in the line is to say the message out loud. Then have the group compare this message with the one they heard. The last child may then head the line. Whisper a new message to that person about three sights seen on the bus trip, and continue as above.

VARIATIONS: To change the level of difficulty, increase or decrease the number of items the children must remember.

262

MATERIALS*

ACTIVITY 1

Cards

Toys

227 232 235 236
242 246 247 250
255 260

ACTIVITY 2

Audiocassette 3

Side B, Selection 2, "Sounds of Toys"

1 Focus: counting and naming items pictured on toy cards, and then grouping the cards by the number of items shown

Stack the 10 toy cards in numerical order.

Hold the cards and say:

Tell me how many different things you see in each of these toy cards, and then name the items.

Show the cards in order, one at a time. Each child you call on should describe the pictured items in a sentence such as "There are three different things in this picture: a rake, a shovel, and a hoe." Give everyone a turn. If there are more than 10 children, reuse the cards. End by displaying all the pictures upon the floor or chalkledge. Then have the children group the cards by the number of items in each picture, as listed below:

Two Items

235•**boy doll and girl doll**

236•**drum and drumsticks**

242•**pail and shovel**

246•**race cars and race track**

Three Items

247•**rake, shovel, and hoe**

Four Items

250•**sandbox, sand, shovel, and pail**

Six Items

227•**paint box, paint brush, chalk, chalk box, crayons, crayon box**

260•**engine, coal car, boxcar, caboose, tracks, railroadcrossing sign**

255•**cups, saucers, teapot, lid, sugar bowl, creamer**

Ten Items

232•**case, eyeglasses, stethoscope, hypodermic needle, thermometer, tongue depressor, microscope, scissors, pill box, headlight**

2 Focus: listening to each of the "Sounds of Toys" and describing the toys without naming them

Say:

Now we are going to listen to some sounds of toys, one sound at a time. Don't say the name of the toy you hear. When I call on you, describe the toy without naming it. Then everyone else will decide whether you described the correct toy.

Play "Sounds of Toys". The child you call on should describe the toy in sentences such as "I hear a round rubber toy. It is a toy that bounces. You can play with this toy indoors and outside." Give clues to help the speaker describe the toy in detail. Then have the group decide if the correct toy has been described. Continue in this way with the remaining sounds.

VARIATION: To make the activity *easier,* describe the toys yourself, being right about half the time. Have the children tell whether your descriptions are correct and why.

263

MATERIALS*

ACTIVITY 1

None

ACTIVITY 2

None

1 Focus: talking about body parts that are jointed, and then moving them

Have the children stand around you. Ask:

What is a joint? (Discuss) **Yes, a joint is the place where two things or two parts are joined. Look at your wrist, where your hand and arm are joined. See how your hand can move where the joint is?** (Demonstrate) **Now let's talk about other joints in our body that allow us to bend, turn, and move. Name another joint, and show us how it moves, (Gavin).**

Lead the discussion and, as necessary, suggest these jointed body parts:

1. **ankles**
2. **elbows**
3. **fingers**
4. **jaws**
5. **knees**
6. **neck**
7. **shoulders**
8. **toes**

2 Focus: using groups of three words to make funny sentences

Say:

Let's make up funny sentences and try to make the others laugh. I will take the first turn. My three words are *pudding, prince,* and *porpoise.* I will try to make you laugh.

Make up a humorous sentence such as "The prince ate the pudding, and then the porpoise ate the prince." Then have the children take turns doing the same with the following word groups. Try to give everyone a turn, even if you must repeat or add word groups.

1. **clown, climb, clock**
2. **glue, gloves, garden**
3. **taxi, table, terrible**
4. **breakfast, brother, beast**
5. **detective, diamond, dinosaur**
6. **nest, neighbor, needle**
7. **mittens, mice, mistake**
8. **ladder, lake, lady**
9. **wagon, wave, world**
10. **grasshopper, groceries, growl**

VARIATION: To make the activity *easier,* use groups of two words.

264

MATERIALS*

ACTIVITY 1

None

ACTIVITY 2

None

1 Focus: predicting and talking about what might happen, and completing short stories

Say:

Let's do some thinking. I will start a very short story and then ask you to tell me what might happen.

Present the following situations, one at a time. Let several children respond to each in sentences. Then finish each story by paraphrasing one or more of the endings suggested by the children, stressing correct verb forms.

1. **Willie Mae went to school. It was her first day at school. She started to cry. What do you think happened?**
2. **Two boys were feeding the fish pieces of bread. One boy dropped his loaf into the pond. What do you think happened?**
3. **Russell took his brother's paints and crayons. He did not ask his brother. What do you think happened?**
4. **One night a large mosquito was buzzing around the room. Warren was in his bed. What do you think happened?**
5. **The television in Sumiko's house broke. The television repairman came and could not fix it. What do you think happened?**
6. **Conrad was going to a birthday party for his very best friend. He put on one shoe. But he could not find the other shoe. What do you think happened?**
7. **A car knocked down the sign which said "Bus Stop." The next morning, Melanie started walking to catch the bus to school. What do you think happened?**
8. **Luke was blind and had a guide dog. The dog went to school with him every day. One day the dog was very sick. What do you think happened?**
9. **The baby was sitting on the floor while Mother was washing clothes. The cabinet door was open. What do you think happened?**
10. **Rosa was using a hose to put water into a bucket. She wanted to water the new apple tree her father had planted. But the hose had a hole in it. What do you think happened?**

2 Focus: listening to groups of four words, and deciding whether they rhyme

Say:

Let's play our rhyming game again. I will say four words. Sometimes the words will be rhyming words; they will sound alike. But sometimes the four words will not rhyme. Listen carefully and tell me whether the words rhyme.

Use the word groups listed below. Individuals or the group should answer by saying, "Yes, those words rhyme" or "No, those words do *not* rhyme." Stress the use of *not.*

1. **sat, pat, cat, fat**
2. **can, tan, man, ran**
3. **big, bug, beg, bag**
4. **take, cake, make, rake**
5. **hot, not, got, cot**
6. **came, cane, come, crown**
7. **cold, mold, scold, told**
8. **see, tree, free, me**
9. **get, let, net, set**
10. **water, winter, waiter, wonder**
11. **bed, led, fed, Ted**
12. **fan, can, Dan, man**
13. **find, bind, kind, blind**
14. **just, rust, must, dust**
15. **join, Judy, jello, jolly**
16. **pail, jail, mail, sail**
17. **hold, cold, mold, sold**
18. **may, Ray, say, hay**

VARIATION: To make the activity *harder,* increase the speed of presentation and/or the length of each word group.

265

MATERIALS*

ACTIVITY 1

Cards

Pictures from Several Categories

3 11 20 53 99
106 110 111 112
117 118 121 123
132 137 144 151
153 154 156 158
161 168 169 174
180 181 189 195
196 201 205 208
210 213 216 217
273 277 280 281

ACTIVITY 2

None

1 Focus: talking about the relationship between two pictures

Stack the 41 picture cards in the order indicated below, with 195 and 196 on top.

Hold the cards and say:

Let's play a thinking game. When I show you two pictures, try to figure out how they go together. Let's try one. (Show cards 195 and 196) **How do these two things go together?** (Pause) **Yes, a tube of toothpaste and a toothbrush are both used to clean teeth.**

Repeat this procedure, showing the cards in the following pairs. Have individuals answer in sentences. Make sure everyone understands the relationship between the two objects in each pair.

1. 20•**hen,** 106•**fried eggs**
2. 110•**hamburger,** 111•**raw hamburger**
3. 53•**pajamas,** 154•**bed**
4. 168•**iron,** 169•**ironing board**
5. 3•**bee,** 112•**honeycomb**
6. 181•**sewing machine,** 180•**scissors**
7. 174•**frying pan,** 121•**pancakes**
8. 273•**police car,** 217•**police officer**
9. 153•**bathtub,** 184•**hand soap**
10. 99•**candy,** 205•**child**
11. 117•**orange juice,** 144•**oranges**
12. 213•**mail carrier,** 281•**mail truck**
13. 201•**astronaut,** 277•**space capsule**
14. 11•**cow,** 118•**milk**
15. 208•**doctor** 216•**nurse**
16. 123•**apple pie,** 137•**apple**
17. 156•**brush,** 161•**comb**
18. 280•**fire truck,** 210•**fire fighter**
19. 189•**kitchen table,** 158•**chair**
20. 151•**tomato,** 132•**soup**

2 Focus: answering riddles with body part names that have more than one meaning

Say:

Some words have more than one meaning. Today I will say some riddles about the body parts whose names also mean something else. Raise your hand if you have the answer to a riddle. Usually there is more than one good answer.

Use the list below as you ask each time, "What has (hands) but is not a person?"

1. **hands** (clock, watch)
2. **a back** (chair, book)
3. **legs** (chair, table, pants)
4. **heels** (shoes, socks, loaf of bread)
5. **fingers** (gloves)
6. **eyes** (potatoes, needles, hurricane)
7. **a coat** (animals)
8. **teeth** (comb, rake, saw)
9. **ears** (corn)
10. **nails** (animals, tool box)
11. **skin** (animals, fruits, and vegetables)

266

MATERIALS*

ACTIVITY 1

None

ACTIVITY 2

Puppets

P. Mooney

Teacher provides

Blank cassette (optional)

Tape recorder (optional)

1 Focus: comparing two items by telling how they are the same and how they are different

Say:

I am going to name two things. Tell me how they are the same and how they are different. Bird and fish; how are a bird and a fish the same?

Call on individuals until several characteristics have been named and used in sentences containing the words *same* and *because*. Then continue:

Yes, a bird and a fish are the same, because (they are both alive) and (they are both animals). Now tell me ways in which a bird and a fish are different.

Several children should answer in sentences stressing *different* and *because*. Then review by saying:

A bird and fish are different, because (a bird flies and a fish swims); and a fish and a bird are different, because (a fish has scales and a bird has feathers).

Continue with these pairs of words:

1. **butterfly, worm**
2. **ring, necklace**
3. **swimsuit, snowsuit**
4. **stove, refrigerator**
5. **bed, chair**
6. **car, ship**
7. **meat, milk**
8. **blocks, tea set**
9. **man, baby**
10. **glass, plate**

2 Focus: talking about what one would like to pull from the P. Mooney bag

Hold the puppet and say:

Now let's imagine that you could ask P. Mooney to pull anything you wanted out of his P. Mooney bag. What is pulled out can be any size. Think what it would be, and take turns telling him in a sentence.

Let everyone hold P. Mooney and tell him what to pull from the bag. Stress the use of sentences.

OPTIONAL: Record each child's response and replay the tape as you ask the group to identify each voice.

267

MATERIALS*

ACTIVITY 1

None

ACTIVITY 2

None

1 Focus: identifying words in which the beginning sound, *n*, is separated from the rest of the word

Say:

Today we are going to make words out of sounds. Listen to this sound: n-n-n-n. (Continue in a humming manner for a few seconds) **Let's make it together.**

Afterwards, call on several children to make the sound. Have them tell what the sound reminds them of. Then say:

Now let's use the n-n-n-n sound to make words. After all of you have made the sound, I will add the rest of the word. For example, if you say "n-n-n-n" and I say "ose," the word we make will be nose. Let's begin.

Each time the class says "n-n-n-n," add one of the word parts listed below and ask, "What word is that?" Let either the class or individuals answer. Help as necessary.

1. **-ine**
2. **-ew**
3. **-ever**
4. **-o**
5. **-ees** (knees)
6. **-ife** (knife)
7. **-uckle** (knuckle)
8. **-ot**
9. **-oon**
10. **-one** (none)
11. **-est**
12. **-ut**
13. **-ewspaper**
14. **-ext**
15. **-obody**
16. **-ight** (night)
17. **-oise**
18. **-ow**
19. **-ice**
20. **-othing** (nothing)

2 Focus: talking about things one likes to smell

Say:

One of the words we made with the n-n-n-n sound is the body part we use to smell. What is that word?

When the children have identified *nose,* continue:

Now let's talk about things we like to smell. We will take turns naming our favorite smells. I will start. The smell I like best is (a rose). Smelling (roses) makes me think of (beautiful flowers).

Have the children, in turn, name their favorite things to smell. Accept all reasonable responses, and stress the use of sentences.

268 

MATERIALS*

ACTIVITY 1

Cards
People
200-221

Display Board
2 ledges

ACTIVITY 2

None

1 Focus: making up and telling stories about pairs of pictures of people

Stack the 22 people cards in pairs, using this order: 211, 214; 207, 215; 204, 217; 206, 219; 212, 218; 201, 205; 202, 220; 203, 200; 213, 221; 208, 209; 210, and 216. Set up the board, and display cards 211 and 214.

Say:

Let's make up stories about the two people on these cards. (Point) **When I call on you, you may tell your story to the rest of the group.**

Give the children a little time to think. Then call on several to tell a short story about the girl and the man. Continue with the remaining 10 pairs of cards. Try to give everyone a turn, helping as necessary.

OPTIONAL: Summarize each child's story.

2 Focus: talking about how friends make one happy and telling how one makes a friend laugh

Say:

Let's talk about how our friends make us feel happy. When I call on you, tell me one thing a friend has done that made you feel happy.

Call on everyone in turn. Encourage the children to listen and not repeat others' ideas. Then continue with this question: "What are some of the ways we can make a friend laugh?" Have the speaker demonstrate when possible. Encourage the children to accept and express themselves freely.

269

MATERIALS*

ACTIVITY 1

None

ACTIVITY 2

None

1 Focus: identifying which of three words does not belong in a category, and telling why

Say:

Let's play a thinking game. I will name three things: bread, plate, and jam. Which one could you *not* eat? (Pause) **Yes, you could not eat a plate. Tell me why.** (Encourage several responses) **Which of these things could you not wash?** (Pause) **Yes, you could not wash bread or jam. Why couldn't you?**

Continue with the word groups listed below. The children you call on should respond in sentences.

Say:	***Ask:***
1. hat gloves milk	**Which of these things could you *not* wear? Which of these things could you *not* drink?**
2. broom mop book	**Which of these things could you *not* read? Which of these things could you *not* clean with?**
3. bird mosquito candle	**Which of these things *cannot* fly? Which of these things *cannot* make light?**
4. bracelet earring ears	**Which of these things *cannot* hear? Which of these things are *not* jewelry?**
5. wagon tricycle airplane	**Which of these things does *not* travel on the ground? Which of these things does *not* travel in the air?**
6. chair roof table	**Which of these things could *not* be found *in* your home? Which of these things could *not* be found *on top of* your home?**
7. ship school bus rowboat	**Which of these things could *not* be found in the water? Which of these things could *not* be found at the school?**
8. barn hous train	**Which of these things could you *not* travel in? Which of these things are *not* buildings?**
9. brush shoelace comb	**Which of these things could *not* be used to fix your hair? Which of these things could *not* be used to tie your shoes?**
10. needle thread coat	**Which of these things could *not* be used to sew a dress? Which of these things could *not* keep you warm?**

2 Focus: brainstorming different ways to protect oneself in rainy and cold weather

Say:

Suppose it were raining very hard. What are all the ways we could protect ourselves from the rain if we had to go out into it?

Call on everyone in turn. Encourage the children not to repeat others' ideas. Continue by asking, "What are all the ways we could dress to keep warm in cold weather?"

270

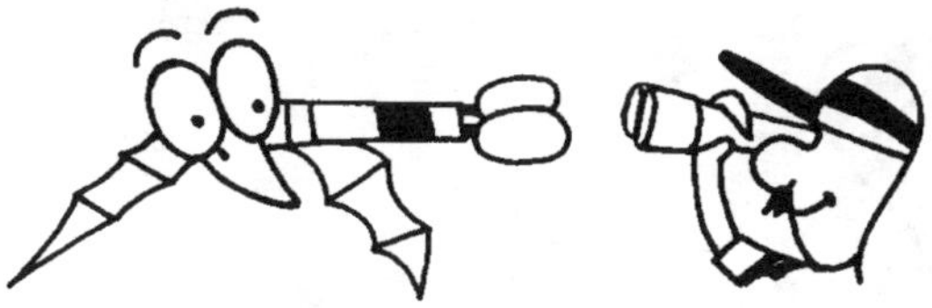

MATERIALS*

ACTIVITY 1

Audiocassette 2

Side A, Selection 3, "Sounds of People – Actions"

ACTIVITY 2

None

1 Focus: listening to and making up stories about each of the "Sounds of People — Actions"

Say:

Let's listen to some sounds people make when they do certain actions. First decide what the sound is, and then make up a short story about what might be happening.

Play the sounds, one at a time. After each, ask the group to identify the sound, and then have several children each tell a short story about the sound. Encourage imaginative responses. Try to give everyone a turn.

2 Focus: brainstorming different times when one would perform certain actions

Say:

Now let's think of all of the times when we might clap our hands. Tell me when you might clap your hands, (Sylvia).

Continue until the children run out of ideas. Then repeat the procedure with such actions as these:

1. **cough**
2. **cry**
3. **snap fingers**
4. **hum**
5. **laugh**
6. **run**
7. **sing**
8. **sneeze**
9. **shove**
10. **walk**
11. **whistle**

We recommend that you read again Part I of the Teacher's Guide at about this point. This should remind you of ways to teach the lessons for maximum efficiency.

271

MATERIALS*

ACTIVITY 1

Cards

Toys

226-266

ACTIVITY 2

None

1 Focus: classifying toys by various characteristics

Arrange all 41 toy cards on the floor or along chalkledges where the children can easily see them.

Point to the cards and say:

Look at all of these pictures of toys. I will ask you to find all the toys with a certain part or which can do a certain action.

Have individuals point out the cards showing toys with the characteristics listed below. Each time, assemble the group of cards, and then call on someone to name the toys again, like this: "The toys that (make sounds) are (drum, guitar, cap gun, piano, robot, top, and whistle)." Rearrange the cards after each group is identified.

Find all the toys . . .

1. **that make sounds.**
2. **that have wheels.**
3. **with ears.**
4. **with legs.**
5. **that have pictures on them.**
6. **that can roll.**
7. **that you get on.**
8. **that you get in.**
9. **that go up and down.**
10. **you must blow to make work.**
11. **that have more than one part.**
12. **that will slide.**
13. **that will hold other things.**
14. **that have motors or run on batteries.**
15. **that have ropes.**

2 Focus: evaluating questions about toys, deciding which questions are silly, and correcting them

Say:

I am going to ask you some questions about toys. Some of the questions are silly, but some are sensible. If a question is sensible, answer "Yes." If it is silly, say, "No," and tell us why.

Call on children to answer these questions:

1. **Do balls bounce?**
2. **Do ropes jump?**
3. **Do books read?**
4. **Do boats sail?**
5. **Do skates roll?**
6. **Do tunnels tumble?**
7. **Do swings swing?**
8. **Do jungle gyms climb?**
9. **Do robots walk?**
10. **Do balloons blow?**
11. **Do rakes rake?**
12. **Do shovels dig?**
13. **Do sleds slide?**
14. **Do pinwheels spin?**
15. **Do wagons roll?**
16. **Do slides slide?**
17. **Do whistles whistle?**
18. **Do blocks fall?**
19. **Do guitars strum?**
20. **Do cars race?**

272

MATERIALS*

ACTIVITY 1

Cards

Numerals & Color Shapes 294-303

ACTIVITY 2

Cards

Numerals & Color Shapes (same as for Activity 1)

1 Focus: counting from one to 10 the number of shapes on each of the shape cards, and then sequencing them in an ascending and descending number line

Give 10 children one card apiece. Then say:

If you have a card, stand up. (Pause) **Please count the shapes on your card. I will ask each of you how many shapes your card has.**

After doing this, continue:

Now let's arrange the cards from one to 10. "Number one," please stand here. (Point to activity area)

Have the 10 children, in turn, line up in numerical order, left to right as seen by the class. They should hold up the cards so the other children may help with sequencing. Then have everyone count aloud from one to 10 as each card is held up high. Continue by giving the cards to 10 other children or by giving different cards to different children. Say:

Now let's start with the number 10 and count backwards. "Number 10," please stand here. (Point to activity area)

Have the 10 children line up in descending numerical order. End by having everyone count from 10 to one as each card is held up.

2 Focus: counting shapes, and then clapping that number in unison

Hold the 10 cards, stacked in random order, and say:

When I show you a card, please count to yourself the number of shapes on it. Do not tell anyone the number. Then you are all to clap one time for each shape, and tell me how many times you clapped. Let's start.

Each time you show a card, give the children a few moments to count the shapes silently before they clap and name the number shown. Continue as time and interest permit.

VARIATION: To make the activity *easier,* have the children tell the number before they clap; then count aloud with them as they clap the right number of times. Or call on individuals to clap, and have the group say whether or not that person clapped the correct number of times.

273

MATERIALS*

ACTIVITY 1

Display Board
4 ledges

Poster 3

ACTIVITY 2

Display Board
4 ledges
Poster 3

1 Focus: predicting and talking about "what would happen if. . . ?" using the poster "Department Store"

Use the ledges to display the poster on the board.

Say:

You have seen this poster of the department store before. Look at it again as we play the game What Would Happen If. . . ?

Encourage the children to imagine and describe the consequences of the following situations. Encourage each child to respond, and accept all reasonable answers.

What do you think would happen if . . .

1. **the motor controlling the helicopter broke down?**
2. **the dog got inside the store?**
3. **someone tried to run down the escalator which was going up?**
4. **someone threw darts at the balloons?**
5. **the boy on the down side of the teeter-totter suddenly got off?**
6. **the boy on the jungle gym fell?**
7. **the electric power in the entire store stopped?**
8. **the store closed and some of the people were locked in?**
9. **a little child got lost from his or her parents?**
10. **all the toy animals and dolls came to life?**

2 Focus: counting items on the poster "Department Store" to answer "how-many" questions

Leave the poster from Activity 1 on display.

Say:

Let's count some of the things in our poster. Please listen carefully and look for what I ask you to count.

Use the questions listed below. Each time, give the children a few moments to scan the poster. Lead them in counting the items in unison. Then call on individuals to answer your question with a sentence such as "There are (four helicopters) in this poster."

How many . . .

1. **helicopters do you see?**
2. **people are on the jungle gym?**
3. **people are eating?**
4. **people are going up?**
5. **people are reading?**
6. **people are looking at clothes?**
7. **floors does the store have?**
8. **people are playing?**
9. **things have two wheels?**
10. **pairs of boots do you see?**
11. **castles do you see?**
12. **pairs of skates do you see?**
13. **numbers do you see?**
14. **animals do you see?**

274

MATERIALS*

ACTIVITY 1

None

ACTIVITY 2

None

1 Focus: talking about the most exciting thing that ever happened to one and how one reacted

Sit in a circle with the children and say:

We have talked about things that are funny and things that are frightening. We have also talked about being angry, sad, happy, and surprised. Today let's talk about another feeling: being excited. Think about the things that make you feel excited. Then tell us about the most exciting thing that ever happened to you and how you acted.

Let children, one at a time, describe something very exciting in their own experiences. Encourage them to tell how they act when excited.

2 Focus: brainstorming exciting things to do

Say:

Now let's think of exciting things you would like to do. When I point to you, tell us about one thing you would find very exciting. Try to think of things that have not been said before.

Let each child tell about one exciting activity. If time and interest permit, give everyone a second turn.

275

MATERIALS*

ACTIVITY 1

Cards

Pictures from Several Categories

15	17	21	23
29	52	64	177
190	191	194	204
205	206	210	211
213	215	218	220
221	228	238	251
252	255	256	257
261	264	266	270
273	274	278	283

Display Board

2 ledges

ACTIVITY 2

None

1 Focus: making up and telling stories from four pictures

Stack the cards in the order listed below. Display cards 191, 206, 228, and 15 on the board in this order.

Say:

Let's take turns making up the most interesting stories we can about groups of four pictures. (Point to board) **Listen to my story about the television, the clown, the ball, and the elephant:**

"Last night I saw a television show about the circus. It showed a clown tossing a ball into the air. An elephant got very excited when he saw the clown and the ball. Suddenly the elephant chased the ball and stamped on it. The ball popped with a large bang! Everyone in the audience cheered and clapped."

Let several children make up stories about each group listed below. Make sure everyone has a turn.

1. 21•**horse,** 64•**snowsuit,** 252•**sled,** 29•**puppy**
2. 261•**treehouse,** 256•**teddy bear,** 177•**record player,** 255•**tea set**
3. 266•**whistle,** 213•**mail carrier,** 221•**older woman,** 211•**girl**
4. 257•**teeter-totters,** 278•**camping trailer,** 220•**woman,** 273•**police car**
5. 274•**helicopter,** 218•**teacher,** 23•**kittens,** 210•**fire fighter**
6. 283•**tow truck,** 270•**school bus,** 194•**tool set,** 190•**telephone**
7. 205•**child,** 264•**tunnel,** 238•**cap gun,** 251•**roller skates**
8. 17•**gerbil,** 215•**older man,** 204•**boy,** 52•**overalls**

VARIATION: To make the activity *easier,* use sets of only two or three words.

2 Focus: following directions that stress the words *before* and *after*

Have the children stand before you. Say:

Let's play a following-directions game to see if you can remember what the words *before* and *after* mean as you carry out directions.

Give the following and similar directions. Explain, repeat, or demonstrate as necessary to help the children understand *before* and *after.*

1. **After you sit down, shake your head.**
2. **Before you stand up, clap your hands.**
3. **Before you sit down, turn around twice.**
4. **After you stand up, stamp your foot.**
5. **Before you turn around one time, clap your hands.**
6. **After you sit down, frown a big frown.**
7. **After you stand up, slide your feet.**
8. **Before you sit down, swing your arms.**
9. **Before you stand up, smile a big smile.**
10. **After you sit down, put your hands on your head.**

276

MATERIALS*

ACTIVITY 1

None

ACTIVITY 2

None

1 Focus: deciding which of three words does not belong in a category, and telling why

Say:

I am going to say three words to you. Two of the words go together, but one word does not belong with the other two. Here are the three words: *pig, cow, table.* Which word does *not* belong? (Pause for unison response) **That is right. *Table* doesn't belong with *pig* and *cow.* Why, (Rufus)?** (Pause) **You are right. A pig and a cow are animals, but a table is not an animal; it is a piece of furniture.**

Continue as above with the following groups of three words. The children you call on should respond in sentences.

1. **boots, bear, cap**
2. **pie, chair, soup**
3. **bus, truck, book**
4. **sheep, shoes, shirt**
5. **leg, chalkboard, nose**
6. **radio, TV, popcorn**
7. **clown, bicycle, train**
8. **ring, watch, worm**
9. **nine, red, five**
10. **ship, rowboat, book**
11. **turtle, taco, toast**
12. **jeans, jacket, gerbil**
13. **boy, drum, guitar**
14. **stove, range, pear**
15. **dentist, car, police officer**
16. **man, turkey, teacher**
17. **fly, bee, mop**
18. **red, snow, blue**
19. **run, jump, robot**
20. **sponge, race, soap**

2 Focus: following directions which stress the word *after*

Have the children stand in front of their chairs or seats. Say:

Now we will play a following-directions game to see if you remember what the word *after* means.

Give the following and similar directions. Provide any explanation, repetition, or demonstration needed to ensure that the children know the meaning of *after.*

1. **After you sit down, smile a big smile.**
2. **After you stand up, slide your feet.**
3. **After you sit down, stamp your feet.**
4. **After you stand up, jump once.**
5. **After you sit down, clap your hands.**
6. **After you stand up, touch the floor with your hands.**
7. **After you sit down, frown a big frown.**
8. **After you stand up, turn around twice.**
9. **After you sit down, put your hands on your head.**
10. **After you stand up, swing your arms.**

277

MATERIALS*

ACTIVITY 1

Audiocassette 1

Side B, Story 6, "P. Mooney and the Kiwi"

ACTIVITY 2

Cards

Stories 419-432

Display Board

6 ledges

Puppets

P. Mooney

Teacher provides

Cardboard "Me" buttons that will stick to clothing, 1 per child

1 Focus: listening to the story "P. Mooney and the Kiwi," and answering questions

Say:

Today let's listen again to the story of P. Mooney and the Kiwi. It has been a long time since you heard this story, so listen carefully. Afterwards, I will ask you questions about the story.

Play the recording. Then call on children to answer questions like these:

1. **What vehicle did P. Mooney ride to the picnic?**
2. **What foods did he pull out of his P. Mooney bag?**
3. **Who said, "I am bigger than an elephant"?**
4. **The Kiwi said he was smaller than what animal?**
5. **The Kiwi said he was faster than what animal?**
6. **The Kiwi said he could jump higher than what animal?**
7. **When the Kiwi realized that a bird could sing better than he, what did he do?**
8. **Why did the Kiwi say all of those things?**
9. **What did P. Mooney do to make the Kiwi feel better?**
10. **At the end of the story, how did the Kiwi feel and what did he do?**

2 Focus: acting out the story "P. Mooney and the Kiwi"

Say:

Now let's act out the story. We will look at the story cards to help us remember what happened.

Place card 419 on the left side of the top row of ledges. Let someone hold the puppet and act out the part of the story shown on the card. Continue by adding one card at a time and calling on other children to perform. End by having P. Mooney place a "Me" button on each child's chest as he says, "You're important because you are (Abigail Evans)!"

VARIATION: To make the activity *harder,* do not use the story cards.

278

MATERIALS*

ACTIVITY 1

None

ACTIVITY 2

None

1 Focus: evaluating whether activities take a short or a long time to do

Say:

Today let's think about how long it takes to do things. Watch what I do, and then tell me if it took a long time or a short time. (Clap several times) **Did it take me a short time or a long time to clap?** (Pause) **Yes, clapping takes a short time. Does it take a short time or a long time to build a house?** (Pause) **Yes, building a house takes a long time. Now I will name some other actions. Tell me whether each of them takes a long time or a short time.**

Continue, using the following and similar examples. The children you call on should answer in sentences.

Does it take a long time or a short time to . . . .

1. **swallow?**
2. **go from one birthday to the next?**
3. **jump one time?**
4. **bounce a ball once?**
5. **grow old enough to get a job?**
6. **grow as tall as your parents?**
7. **turn on a light?**
8. **clean and straighten up a messy room?**
9. **snap your fingers once?**
10. **take a bath when you are very dirty?**
11. **go to sleep and then wake up in the morning?**
12. **turn around once?**
13. **go from winter to summer?**
14. **sneeze?**
15. **start the car?**
16. **get dressed to go outside in cold weather?**
17. **look at all the pictures in a big book?**

2 Focus: counting from one to 10 first slowly and then quickly, and then chanting a counting rhyme

Have the children stand in front of you. Say:

Now let's count from one to 10. We will start counting very slowly, but gradually we will count faster and faster. Make sure you say all the numbers as you keep up with me.

Lead the children in doing this five or six times. Then say:

Now let's learn a new counting rhyme. Listen to the words, and watch what I do. Then we will do it together.

Hold up the right number of fingers as you say this rhyme:

One, two, three, four, five;
Once I caught a fish alive.
Six, seven, eight, nine, ten;
Then I let him go again.

Ten, nine, eight, seven, six;
That fish was in an awful fix.
Five, four, three, two, one;
I let him go out in the sun!

Lead the children in saying the rhyme several times. Check to see that they hold up the correct number of fingers.

OPTIONAL: Call on individuals to perform for the group.

279 

MATERIALS*

ACTIVITY 1

Cards

Animals

1 4 8 12 13 14 15
17 23 25 31 32 35

Display Board

6 ledges

ACTIVITY 2

Cards

Animals

(same as for Activity 1)

Display Board

6 ledges

1 Focus: making adjectives from nouns, and then using these words to describe animals

Stack the 13 animal cards in the order listed below. Set up the board with ledges and display card 1.

Point to the card on the board and say:

We have talked about this bear before. We called it a hairy bear, because it is covered with hair. What kind of a bear is it? (Pause) **That's right. It is a hairy bear. Now look at each picture I put on the board and answer my questions.**

Display the cards in turn. For each, give the description provided below. Help the children as necessary to answer in unison with sentences such as "It is a (hairy bear)." Leave the cards on the board.

1. 4•**This beetle's legs are covered with hair. What kind of legs does the beetle have?**
2. 8•**This cat has a lot of spots. What kind of cat is it?**
3. 12•**This dog's hair has lots of waves. What kind of hair does the dog have?**
4. 13•**This duck is covered with feathers. What kind of duck is it?**
5. 14•**This duckling is covered with fluff. What kind of duckling is it?**
6. 15•**This elephant's skin has lots of wrinkles. What kind of skin does the elephant have?**
7. 17•**This gerbil's nose has lots of whiskers. What kind of nose does the gerbil have?**
8. 23•**These kittens are covered with fur. What kind of kittens are they?**
9. 25•**This lion has a mane made out of hair. What kind of mane is it?**
10. 31•**This rooster's tail is made out of feathers. What kind of tail is it?**
11. 32•**This sheep is covered with wool. What kind of sheep is it?**
12. 35•**This toad's skin has lots of bumps. What kind of skin does the toad have?**

2 Focus: describing animals by naming four characteristics of each

Leave the cards from Activity 1 on display.

Point to the cards and say:

Now let's describe these animals by telling four things about each of them. First tell what we said about the animal a few minutes ago, and then tell three more things. I will start. (Point to card 1) **This bear is hairy and brown and big. It has big claws.**

Continue by letting the children each describe an animal. If possible, give everyone a turn.

VARIATION: To make the activity *easier,* have the children tell only one or two more features of each animal. Stress the use of and.

280

MATERIALS*

ACTIVITY 1

None

ACTIVITY 2

None

1 Focus: using opposites to complete sentences that stress *before* and *after*

Say:

Let's play a thinking game. I will read some sentences, but I will leave off the last word. Listen carefully and tell me what it should be. Here is a hint: The last word should be an opposite.

Have the children complete each of these sentences:

1. **After I went through the door, I was *inside*. But before I went through the door, I was _______ .** (outside)
2. **Before I turned on the heater, I was *cold*. But after I turned it on, I was _______ .** (warm)
3. **After we put sugar on the grapefruit, it was *sweet*. But before we put sugar on it, the grapefruit was _______ .** (sour)
4. **Before I started to get up early, I would get to school *last*. But after I started to get up early, I got to school ___________ .** (first)
5. **Before I grow up, my parents are *young*. But after I grow up, my parents will be _______ .** (old)
6. **After I climbed on the chair, I could see *over* the table. But before I climbed on the chair, I could see _______ .** (under) **the table.**
7. **Before the sun came up, it was *dark*. But after the sun came up, it was _______ .** (light)
8. **After I sanded the wood, it was *smooth*. But before I sanded it, it was _______ .** (rough)
9. **Before I cleaned up my room, it was *messy*. But after I cleaned up my room, it was _______ .** (neat)
10. **Before I walked around the house, I was in *back* of it. But after I walked around the house, I was in ______ .** (front) **of it.**
11. **After I went to bed, I was *asleep*. But before I went to bed, I was _______ .** (awake)
12. **Before I put on the monster mask, I looked *pretty*. After I put on the monster mask, I looked _______ .** (ugly)
13. **After I put my toys in the box, it felt *heavy*. But before I put my toys in the box, it felt _______ .** (light)
14. **After Dad repaired my wagon, it was *fixed*. But before he repaired the wagon, it was _______ .** (broken)
15. **After I tied my shoe, it felt *tight*. Before I tied my shoe, it felt _______ .** (loose)
16. **Before Pablo invited me to his party, I felt *sad*. After Pablo invited me to his party, I felt _______ .** (happy)
17. **Before I used the ruler to draw a line, it was *crooked*. But after I used the ruler to draw a line, it was _______ .** (straight)
18. **After the bird flew away, it was *far* from me. Before the bird flew away, it was _______ .** (near) **to me.**

2 Focus: talking about dragons

Say:

Let's think and talk about dragons. Is a dragon a real or an imaginary animal?

Lead a discussion of this imaginary creature. Have the children consider these topics:

1. **how a dragon is supposed to look**
2. **whether it is supposed to have wings**
3. **what it is supposed to eat**
4. **where it is supposed to live**
5. **how it is thought to send fire from its mouth**

Keep in Mind . . .
After each lesson in the program, individuals who have difficulty demonstrating proficiency in the skills you consider appropriate and important for them to learn should be tutored. Aides could help you with this task.

281

MATERIALS*

ACTIVITY 1

None

ACTIVITY 2

None

1 Focus: talking about the relationship between two words

Say:

Let's play a thinking game. When I say two words, please try to figure out how they go together. Here are the first two words: pencil and paper. How do a pencil and a piece of paper go together? (Discuss) **Yes, they are both used for writing or drawing. We use a pencil to write or draw on paper.**

Continue with the following pairs of words. The children you call on should respond in sentences. Make sure everyone understands the relationships.

1. **cow, barn**
2. **cake, oven**
3. **vase, flowers**
4. **straw, soda drink**
5. **watch, wrist**
6. **horse, saddle**
7. **pig, corn**
8. **cereal, bowl**
9. **seat belt, car**
10. **sewing machine, thread**
11. **dog, dog collar**
12. **horse, apple**
13. **gerbil, treadmill**
14. **ambulance, nurse**
15. **crayons, coloring book**
16. **bear, honey**
17. **table, chair**
18. **fish, fishing pole**
19. **hammer, nail**
20. **child, ice cream**

2 Focus: following directions that stress the words *before* and *after*

Have the children stand in front of their chairs. Say:

Let's play a following-directions game to see if you remember what the words *before* and *after* mean as you carry out directions. Listen closely and do what I say.

Give the following and similar directions. Explain, repeat, or demonstrate as necessary to help the children understand what *before* and *after* mean.

1. **Clap your hands *before* you sit down.**
2. **Close your eyes *after* you stand up.**
3. **Blink your eyes *before* you sit down.**
4. **Jump up *after* you stand up.**
5. **Turn around *before* you sit down.**
6. **Snap your fingers *after* you stand up.**
7. **Say hello *after* you sit down.**
8. **Stamp your feet *before* you stand up.**
9. **Hop on one foot *before* you sit down.**
10. **Clap your hands *after* you stand up.**

VARIATIONS: To make the activity *easier,* use only *before* or *after* in all the commands. Example:

1. **Clap your hands *before* you sit down.**
2. **Close your eyes *before* you stand up.**

To make it *harder,* call on individuals to give commands. Prompt as necessary.

282

MATERIALS*

ACTIVITY 1

None

ACTIVITY 2

None

1 Focus: thinking and talking about what clothes would be worn in various kinds of weather

Say:

Today let's pretend that the weather is very cold. It is freezing and snowing outside. Tell me in one long sentence three items of clothing you would wear and why.

The children you call on should respond in sentences such as "I would wear a snowsuit, a pair of mittens, and a pair of boots to keep me warm." Stress the correct use of *and* in a series. Continue by asking what clothes they would wear if the weather were . . .

1. **hot, with bright sunshine and no clouds in the sky.**
2. **cool, with very heavy rain and loud thunder.**
3. **very windy, with tree leaves falling everywhere.**
4. **very foggy and damp, with gray skies.**
5. **warm and partly cloudy, with leaves budding on the trees.**

VARIATION: To make the activity *easier,* ask for fewer than three items each time.

2 Focus: using groups of three words to make funny sentences

Say:

Let's make up funny sentences from groups of three words. I will take the first turn. My three words are *sing, sister,* and *sink*. Here is my sentence: "When I began to sing, my sister fell into the sink."

Call on everyone in turn to make up a sentence from one of the word groups listed below. Add other word groups as necessary.

1. **zebra, zipper, zoo**
2. **shadow, shot, sheep**
3. **chocolate, chin, church**
4. **jail, jungle, jump**
5. **thunder, thirsty, thumb**
6. **clown, cloud, clock**
7. **visit, vegetable, vacation**
8. **dragon, dream, dress**
9. **spank, spider, spoon**
10. **parakeet, party, package**

VARIATION: To make the activity *harder,* use more than three words.

283

MATERIALS*

ACTIVITY 1

Cards

Numerals & Color Shapes
284-293

ACTIVITY 2

None

1 Focus: identifying the numbers one to 10 from rhyming words, and then identifying rhyming words from numbers

Stack the 10 numeral cards in order.

Say:

Let's play a rhyming game with numbers. As I show you the numeral cards one by one, let's all count aloud from one to 10 and then backwards from 10 to one.

Do this with the children. Then ask the following questions. Ask them in sequence first, and have the children respond in unison. Then repeat the questions in random order for individuals to answer. Give everyone a turn.

What number rhymes with . . .

1. ***fun?***
2. ***blue?***
3. ***knee?***
4. ***drawer?***
5. ***live?***
6. ***fix?***
7. ***Kevin?***
8. ***weight?***
9. ***vine?***
10. ***when?***

Afterwards, continue:

When I call on you, tell me a word that rhymes with the number I say.

Present numbers from one to 10 in random order. Call on everyone in turn. End by placing all the cards in order, and have the children name them in ascending and descending order.

2 Focus: talking about things one once did but no longer does

Say:

Today let's talk about things we once did but don't do anymore.

Lead the children in discussing what they no longer do because of such changes as being older, living in a different location, changes in family structure, changes in interest, etc. Ask leading questions to encourage everyone to participate. Accept all responses.

284

MATERIALS*

ACTIVITY 1

None

ACTIVITY 2

None

1 Focus: deciding whether certain activities take a year or a second to do

Say:

When we talk about time, we sometimes say it takes us a *second* to do something. Or we may say that something takes a *minute*, an *hour*, a *day*, or even a *year*. Is a *year* a long time, or a short time? (Discuss) **Yes, a *year* is a long time. Is a *second* a long time, or a short time?** (Discuss) **You're right; a *second* is a very short time. Now let's talk about whether certain things take place in a *second* or a *year*.**

Have the class respond in unison to each of these questions:

Does it take a second or a year . . .

1. **to blink your eyes?**
2. **to go from one birthday to the next?**
3. **to jump one time in the air?**
4. **to go from kindergarten to first grade?**
5. **to go from one summer to the next?**
6. **to snap your fingers?**
7. **to switch on a lamp?**
8. **to go from one winter to the next?**
9. **to nod your head?**
10. **to fall down?**
11. **for a puppy to grow to be a dog?**
12. **to stand up?**
13. **for a calf to grow to be a cow?**
14. **to grow three inches taller?**

2 Focus: thinking of and naming three things from requested categories, and then classifying the items

Say:

Now let's play a thinking game. I will ask someone to tell us three words that go together. Then you are to figure out the word or phrase that describes all three words.

Have someone come to the front. Whisper to that child:

Think of three vehicles, (Elissa). Say the names to the group, and then ask, "What are they?"

When the group has identified the three items as vehicles or ways to travel, continue as above with the categories listed below. Give everyone at least one turn to appear before the class.

1. **animals**
2. **clothing**
3. **colors**
4. **foods**
5. **fruits**
6. **household items**
7. **numbers**
8. **toys**
9. **vegetables**
10. **vehicles**

VARIATIONS: To make the activity *easier*, whisper three words to each child standing before the group. To make it *harder*, request more than three words per turn.

285

MATERIALS*

ACTIVITY 1

Cards
Clothing
39-73

ACTIVITY 2

None

1 Focus: classifying clothes by various characteristics

Arrange the 35 clothing cards on the floor or along chalkledges where the children can easily see them.

Point to the cards and say:

Look at all of these pictures of things to wear. I will ask someone to find items of clothing that are the same in some way. When I call on you, name all the things that belong in the group I mention, and tell why they do. Then you are to put those cards here. (Point to chalkledge or activity area)

Use the list given below. The children you call on should name and group the cards chosen. Then have other children each name the grouped cards in a sentence like "The clothes that are (woolly) are (baby bonnet, booties, sweater, and baby sweater)." Rearrange the cards after each group is identified.

Name all the things to wear . . .

1. **that are woolly.**
2. **with checks or plaids.**
3. **with buttons.**
4. **with things to tie.**
5. **worn above your chest.**
6. **that are metal.**
7. **with sleeves.**
8. **worn at or above the waist.**
9. **with zippers.**
10. **with pockets.**
11. **worn below the waist.**
12. **with legs.**
13. **worn on or below your ankles.**
14. **worn on your wrist or hands.**

2 Focus: evaluating questions about clothing, deciding which questions are silly, and correcting them

Say:

I have some questions to ask you about clothing. Some of the questions are silly and some are sensible. If the question is sensible, answer, "Yes." If it is silly, answer, "No," and tell us why the question is silly.

Have individuals respond to these questions:

1. **Do shoes have heels?**
2. **Do rings ring?**
3. **Do caps cover heads?**
4. **Do pajamas sleep?**
5. **Do watches tell time?**
6. **Do jeans have sleeves?**
7. **Do boots have toes?**
8. **Are shorts short?**
9. **Do zippers zip?**
10. **Are mittens worn on feet?**
11. **Do shirts have shoes?**
12. **Can you see through glasses?**
13. **Do socks have sleeves?**
14. **Do suits have coats?**
15. **Are slips worn over dresses?**
16. **Do pants have legs?**
17. **Do buttons have holes?**
18. **Are snowsuits cold?**
19. **Do jackets have sleeves?**
20. **Do necklaces have necks?**

286

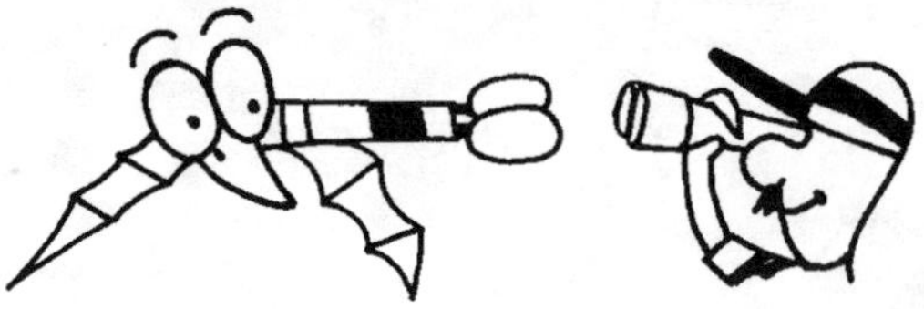

MATERIALS*

ACTIVITY 1

None

ACTIVITY 2

None

1 Focus: talking about words that sound the same but have different meanings

Say:

Let's talk again about words that sound the same but have different meanings. Please tell me what word is pronounced the same in these two sentences: "Todd filled the *pail* with water." (Pause) **"Gwen looked very *pale* and *sick.*"**

Helping as necessary, repeat the sentences until the children name the words pall and pale. Then call on children to tell the two meanings. Have several others make up different sentences to illustrate each definition. Continue with these pairs of sentences:

1. **The sick bird was too *weak* to fly.**
   This *week* we will see a movie at school.
2. **The two pages always *stick* together.**
   This *stick* can reach the ball stuck in the tree.
3. **Darrell's leg had a *break* in it, so he wore a plaster cast to help it heal.**
   The *brake* in the car was worn out.
4. **The box was made of *iron.***
   Mother used an *iron* to press the clothes.
5. **Grandfather's *watch* always had the correct time.**
   Virginia and her father went to *watch* the ball game.

2 Focus: deciding whether statements are true about the characteristics of pairs of animals, and then following directions if they are true

Ask the children to stand before you. Say:

Let's play a listening-and-thinking game. I will say something about two animals. If what I say is correct, then follow the direction. If what I say is not correct, stand still.

Give the following and similar directions to the group. If any children have difficulty, repeat the direction until everyone responds correctly.

1. **If both a chick and a cow have two legs apiece, turn around.**
2. **If both a calf and a piglet are baby animals, then stand on one foot till I count to three.**
3. **If both an owl and a duck have feathers, then bend down and touch the floor.**
4. **If both an elephant and a gerbil can fly, then snap your fingers.**
5. **If both a turkey and a puppy have fur on their bodies, then say, "Cock-a-doodle-do."**
6. **If both a butterfly and a bee have wings, then say, "Meow."**
7. **If both a bird and a squirrel live in trees, then clap your hands.**
8. **If a spider is bigger than a house, then put your hands on your head.**
9. **If both a turtle and a goldfish live in water, then clap your hands over your head.**
10. **If both a turtle and a worm have hard coverings on their bodies, stamp your feet twice.**

11. **If both a lamb and a lion live on a farm, turn around twice.**
12. **If both a cow and a goat give milk, touch your nose to your knee.**
13. **If both a bear and a pig have claws, then say, "Moo."**
14. **If a rabbit is smaller than a colt, then nod your head.**
15. **If both a hen and a rooster are chickens, then wiggle all of your fingers.**
16. **If both a cat and a kid meow, then make a happy face.**
17. **If both a sheep and a toad have four legs apiece, then shake hands with the person next to you.**
18. **If both a duckling and a beetle like to swim, then say, "Baaa."**
19. **If both a kitten and a fly would make nice pets, then cross your legs.**
20. **If both a cat and a dog can move their tails, then say, "Hooray!"**

287

MATERIALS*

ACTIVITY 1

Puppets

P. Mooney

Zoey

Thinking hat

ACTIVITY 2

None

1 Focus: talking about possible solutions to Zoey's and P. Mooney's problems

Place Zoey (wearing her thinking hat) on your hand and have her say:

P. Mooney and I need your help to solve some more problems. Please tell us what we should do.

Have the appropriate puppet present each problem listed below. Help the children suggest several solutions for each. Praise good contributions.

1. Zoey: **The ground is covered with puddles after a storm. One of my boots has a hole in it. Please tell me how I could fix my boot, so I could walk through the puddles and not get my foot wet.**
2. P. Mooney: **Yesterday I bought a new green plant. I want to watch it grow. Please tell me all the ways I could measure how much the plant is growing.**
3. Zoey: **I like to make candy apples. I need to pick apples from the very top of a tall apple tree. Tell me how I could get to those apples.**
4. P. Mooney: **Whenever I give my dog a bath, everything gets very wet. Tell me how I could keep things dry while I bathe the dog.**
5. Zoey: **The new sandbox in the playground has sand piled near it, but there is no shovel. Tell me some ways to get the sand into the sandbox.**
6. P. Mooney: **It is very late, and some of my friends want to spend the night with me. But I do not have enough beds. How can I make more places for people to sleep?**
7. Zoey: **One day I was walking along the road when I saw some children trying to catch a pet rabbit that had escaped from its cage. Tell me all the ways we could get the rabbit back.**
8. P. Mooney: **One day I decided I would go fishing in a stream, but I did not have my fishing gear with me. Tell me some other ways I could go fishing.**

2 Focus: brainstorming cold and hot items

Say:

Now we will play a thinking game. Let's see how fast you can name things that are cold or hot. First, name as many cold things as you can, as quickly as you can.

Encourage the children to name cold items as fast as they can. When no one can think of another cold item, continue by calling for things that are hot. Praise all correct contributions.

288

MATERIALS*

ACTIVITY 1

Fruits & Vegetables
All

Teacher provides
1 paper bag per child

ACTIVITY 2

Fruits & Vegetables
All

1 Focus: naming four characteristics of fruits and vegetables for the rest of the group to guess

For each child, prepare a paper bag containing a fruit or a vegetable. Pile the bags in the activity area.

Have the children sit around the piled bags. Ask one child to choose a bag. Say:

Look at what you have in your paper bag, (Justin), but don't tell anyone what it is. Tell us four things about your item without naming it. Then the group will guess what you are describing.

Let each child in turn choose a bag, stand before the group, and describe the item for the group to guess. When the item is identified, the child should remove it from the bag and show it to the group. Have the child making a correct guess take the next turn.

VARIATIONS: To change the level of difficulty, ask for more or fewer than four characteristics.

2 Focus: following directions about fruits and vegetables in the game Fruit and Vegetable Exchange

Have the children continue to hold their items from Activity 1.

With the children standing in a circle, say:

Let's use the fruits and vegetables to play a game called Fruit and Vegetable Exchange. I will tell certain fruits and vegetables to change places. When I say "All fruits, exchange," then all fruits are to change places. But if I say "All vegetables, exchange," only the vegetables are to change places. When I say "All fruits and vegetables, exchange," you must all change places.

Help anyone who has difficulty as you give directions such as these:

1. **All oranges, exchange.**
2. **All fruits, exchange.**
3. **All red fruits and vegetables, exchange.**
4. **All vegetables, exchange.**
5. **All long fruits and vegetables, exchange.**
6. **All yellow fruits and vegetables, exchange.**
7. **All apples, exchange.**
8. **All yellow fruits, exchange.**
9. **All red fruits, exchange.**
10. **All white and brown vegetables, exchange.**
11. **All fruits and vegetables of more than one color, exchange.**
12. **All fruits and vegetables, exchange.**

Continue in this manner.

289

MATERIALS*

ACTIVITY 1

Display Board
4 ledges

Poster 4

ACTIVITY 2

Display Board
4 ledges
Poster 4

1 Focus: thinking and talking about why things are happening in the poster "City in Summer"

Use the ledges to display the poster on the board.

Say:

Let's talk again about this picture of the city. I want you to think about and explain why certain things are happening in the picture.

Ask the following questions as you point to the corresponding poster items. Give everyone a chance to participate, and accept all reasonable responses.

Why do you think . . .

1. **the children are playing in the water?**
2. **the boy is showing his airplane to the police officer?**
3. **the bird is in the birdcage?**
4. **these flowers are in these containers?**
5. **the building is being torn down?**
6. **the workers are wearing hard hats?**
7. **the man who shines shoes is not there?**
8. **the buildings are so tall?**
9. **the street has white lines on it?**
10. **the fan is in the window?**
11. **the men are working on this billboard?**
12. **the child is bending down near the pigeon?**
13. **the girl is kneeling on the fire escape?**
14. **the sports car is parked by the playground?**
15. **these clothes are hanging on the line?**

2 Focus: imagining and talking about what the city in the poster "City in Summer" might have been like a long time ago

Leave the poster from Activity 1 on display.

Say:

Let's imagine what this city would have been like a hundred years ago. That is a very long time ago. Look at the picture, and let's talk about how things would have been different then.

Have the children consider topics like these:

1. **what the land might have looked like**
2. **what buildings might have been built**
3. **what types of clothes might have been worn**
4. **what vehicles might have been used**
5. **what kinds of work the people might have done**

290

MATERIALS*

ACTIVITY 1

Cards

People

200-221

ACTIVITY 2

Cards

Music

331

Audiocassette 2

Side B, Song 8, "Today, Yesterday, and Tomorrow"

1 Focus: completing stories about pictures of people

Stack the 22 people cards in order.

Hold the cards and say:

Today let's finish stories about the people in these pictures. I will tell the beginning of the story, and then ask someone to tell us how it might end.

Show the right card as you read each story beginning. Then call on several children to suggest possible endings. Encourage imaginative responses.

1. 200•**Everyone in the tent was watching the *acrobat* do his swinging act. Then the acrobat heard a strange sound. It was the sound of. . . ."**
2. 201•**While the *astronaut* was walking on the moon, he suddenly sent a radio message back to earth. The message was. . . ."**
3. 202•**The *baby* thought, "This teddy bear is very special because. . . ."**
4. 203•**Mother said that if Enoch sat still while the *barber* cut his hair, she would. . . ."**
5. 204•**A *boy* named Ned was playing ball with the boys who lived on his street, when suddenly. . . ."**
6. 205•**A *child* named Pat had been very sick in bed with measles. At last, Mother said, "Pat, you may. . . ."**
7. 206•**Crab Orchard School was having a carnival to raise money for a gymnasium. One of the teachers dressed up like a *clown,* and she. . . ."**
8. 207•**"I have to go to the *dentist,*" said Mr. Smith. "I love caramel apples, but today while I was eating one. . . ."**
9. 208•**"We must take Shalayna to the *doctor* right away!" said her mother. "While she was riding her bicycle on the street, she. . . . "**
10. 209•**A *farmer* named Mr. Phillips said, "I am driving my tractor today, and I need some help to. . . . "**
11. 210•**The *fire fighter* was high in the air. He looked down at the crowd below and shouted. . . ."**
12. 211•**A *girl* named Fern got a new leg brace. She told her mother. . . ."**
13. 212•**The *grocer* said, "Mrs. Allen, I have a special bargain today. It is. . . ."**
14. 213•**Tammy was anxiously watching for the *mail carrier.* Today she. . . ."**
15. 214•**Julio's *father* said, "If I help you pump up this tire, Julio, will you help me to. . . . ?"**
16. 215•**As my *grandfather* was painting the fence, he heard something in back of him. When he looked. . . ."**
17. 216•**The *nurse* said, "This baby is very sick. I will have to. . . . "**
18. 217•**The *police officer* sped to the scene and then radioed to headquarters, "The get-away car was a red sports car. I also see. . . ."**
19. 218•**The *teacher* told her class, "Today after we have finished work, we will. . . ."**
20. 219•**A *toddler* named Rod jumped up and down, saying, "Please! Please, I want. . . . "**
21. 220•**Monroe's *mother* was about to throw the ball. All of a sudden she looked down on the floor and gasped when she saw. . . ."**
22. 221•**Alberta's *grandmother* was cutting greenery because today was a very special day. Today was the day. . . ."**

2 Focus: singing, chanting, and acting out the song "Today, Yesterday, and Tomorrow"

Hold the music card and say:

Let's sing "Today, Yesterday, and Tomorrow" about some actions that make sounds. After we sing each verse, we will act out the words together. Make the loudest and longest sounds you can.

Play the song and refer to the music card as you sing. After the verb forms are chanted for each verse, lead the children in the action named.

Encourage a spirit of fun as you lead the group in making the longest and loudest sounds they can. Continue with the song (instrumental version), using these action words:

1. **sneeze**
2. **hum**
3. **cry**
4. **clap**
5. **run**
6. **snap (fingers)**
7. **whistle**
8. **laugh**
9. **snore**

291 

MATERIALS*

ACTIVITY 1

None

ACTIVITY 2

None

1 Focus: comparing pairs of items by telling how they are the same and how they are different

Say:

Today I will name two things at a time. When I call on you, tell us in sentences how the two are the same and how they are different.

Use the following list of pairs. Several common and dissimilar characteristics may be named in each case. Stress the use of *same* and *different.*

1. **hen, rooster**
2. **cat, lion**
3. **boots, raincoat**
4. **shoes, socks**
5. **booties, tennis shoes**
6. **mop, vacuum cleaner**
7. **chair, couch**
8. **astronaut, fire fighter**
9. **sled, wagon**
10. **newspaper, book**
11. **apple, potato**
12. **cracker, doughnut**
13. **rain, airplane**
14. **bicycle, car**

VARIATION: To make the activity *harder,* ask for reasons why the objects in each pair are the same or different.

2 Focus: brainstorming descriptions of animals, clothes, food, household items, people, toys, and vehicles

Say:

Let's think as fast as we can. I will say a word like rooster. When I point to you, tell us something about roosters in a sentence. Tell us something no one else has said.

Use the words from the list in Activity 1. Help as necessary, and give everyone a turn. Continue with the same word until the children run out of ideas. Then move to another word. Vary the categories from which the words are chosen.

292

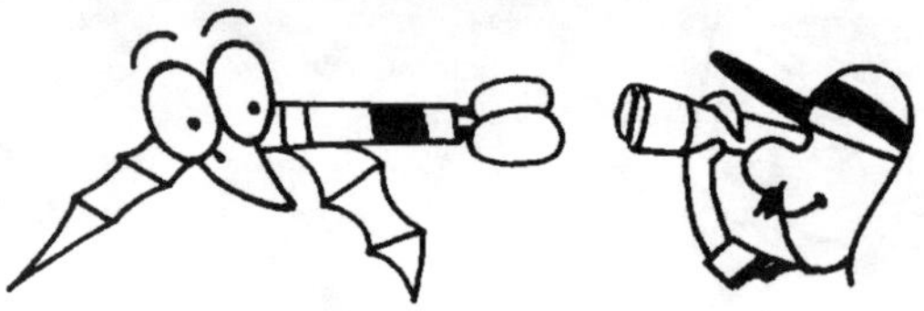

MATERIALS*

ACTIVITY 1

Audiocassette 3,
Side B, "Sounds of Vehicles"

ACTIVITY 2

Cards
Vehicles
267-283

Display Board
6 ledges

1 Focus: listening to "Sounds of Vehicles," identifying each, and then making up stories about what might be happening

Say:

Let's listen to sounds of ways to travel. After you tell me what the sound is, I will ask someone to make up a story about what might be happening.

Play the sounds, one at a time. After each, have the group name the sound, and then call upon one or more children in turn to tell a short story about that way to travel. Encourage imaginative responses. Give everyone a turn.

2 Focus: describing vehicles from memory

Display the 17 vehicle cards on the board.

Point to the pictures and say:

Now let's play a remembering game. Look at all these vehicles while I count from one to 10. When I say "10," I will turn over a card so you cannot see the picture. When I call on you, tell us everything you can remember about that vehicle — its name, color, and what it looks like. Let's start!

Each time, call on children until the main characteristics of a vehicle have been identified. Continue until all cards have been described. Encourage everyone to participate.

OPTIONAL: Have the children take turns counting from one to 10 and turning over a card.

293

MATERIALS*

ACTIVITY 1

Audiocassette 1

Side A, Story 3

"P. Mooney and Zoey"

ACTIVITY 2

Cards

Numerals & Color Shapes

314-323

Color Chips

All

P. Mooney Bag

Teacher provides

1 envelope per child

1 Focus: listening to the story "P. Mooney and Zoey," and answering questions

Say:

Today we are going to listen again to the story about how P. Mooney and Zoey first met. It has been a long time since you heard this story. Please listen carefully, because I will ask questions afterwards about what happened.

Play the recording. When the story ends, ask individuals questions like these:

1. **Who had the problem in this story?**
2. **What was the problem?**
3. **Who solved the problem?**
4. **What steps did Zoey take to solve P. Mooney's problem?**
5. **What are some other ways Zoey could have solved P. Mooney's problem?**

2 Focus: matching colors in the game Color Bingo

For each child, prepare an envelope containing a set of eight chips, one of each color. Put the remaining chips into the bag.

Give each child an envelope, and have them sit in pairs on the floor before you. Hand each pair a number card to place on the floor. Wear the bag and say:

Let's play the game Color Bingo again. Each time I show you a chip from the bag, look on your card and see if it has the same color. If it does, take your matching chips and place them on that color on the card. The partners whose card first has two chips on every color may then say, "Bingo!" They will be the winners.

Check to see that the children respond correctly. Ask each child of a winning pair to name the colors on their card. Then have everyone exchange cards, and repeat the game, with the winners taking turns calling out the colors. Continue in this way as time and interest suggest.

294

MATERIALS*

ACTIVITY 1

Cards

Pictures from Several Categories

3 97 110 111
112 115 117 118
119 123 126 135
137 144 148 150
202 205

Display Board

2 ledges

ACTIVITY 2

None

1 Focus: identifying the relationship between two or more pictured items, and then talking about what must be done to change one to the other

Set up the board with one ledge on the left side and one on the right side. Display card 118 on the left ledge and 119 on the right. Stack the remaining cards into the groups listed below.

Say:

Look at these two cards, and tell me what has to be done to change this kind of milk (point to card 118) **into this kind.** (Point to card 119 and discuss) **You are right. We must add chocolate to the white milk to make chocolate milk.**

Continue as above with the cards listed below, helping as necessary.

1. 144•**oranges**, 117•**orange juice**
2. 137•**apple**, 123•**apple pie**
3. 111•**raw hamburger**, 110•**hamburger**
4. 148•**potato**, 126•**baked potato**
5. 97•**bread**, 135•**toast**
6. 150•**strawberries**, 115•**jam**
7. 202•**baby**, 205•**child**
8. 142•**lettuce and** 151•**tomato**, 130•**sandwich**

2 Focus: using opposites to complete statements involving analogous reasoning

Say:

I am going to say sentences which will not be finished. Listen carefully, and tell me what word will finish the sentence correctly. I will give you a hint: it will be an opposite.

Call on individuals or the group to complete these sentences:

1. **A second is short; a year is _______ .** (long)
2. **Oranges are sweet; lemons are _______ .** (sour)
3. **Potatoes are vegetables; apples are _______ .** (fruit)
4. **Balls are round; boxes are _______ .** (square)
5. **An inch is short; a mile is _______ .** (long)
6. **Daytime is light; nighttime is _______ .** (dark)
7. **Jet planes are fast; rowboats are _______ .** (slow)
8. **Ants are small; elephants are _______ .** (large)
9. **Attics are high; basements are _______ .** (low)
10. **Summer is hot; winter is _______ .** (cold)
11. **A tow truck is heavy; a bicycle is _______ .** (light)
12. **A child is short; an adult is _______ .** (tall)
13. **A rock is hard; a piece of cotton is _______ .** (soft)
14. **The bark of a tree is rough; the skin of your face is _______ .** (smooth)
15. **The desert is dry; the ocean is _______ .** (wet)

OPTIONAL: Continue by reversing the two parts of each sentence.

295

MATERIALS*

ACTIVITY 1

None

ACTIVITY 2

Cards
Music
335

Audiocassette 2
Side B, Song 12,
"Rhythm Walk"

1 Focus: describing family members in a listener-talker game

Divide the class in half. Have the two groups sit in circles, one inside the other. Say:

Now let's play a remembering game. The people sitting in the inside circle will be "talkers." They will take turns telling us about someone in their family. The people sitting in the outside circle will be "listeners." Each listener must remember what the talker in front of him or her says. Let's start.

Call on someone in the inside circle to tell the group about a person in his or her family. Continue until each child in the inner circle has had a turn.
Then say:

Now, listeners, when I call on you, tell us what the talker in front of you said.

Continue until each listener has had a turn, helping as necessary. Praise good memories. Then have the children change circles and repeat the procedure.

VARIATION: To make the activity *easier,* have each listener immediately tell what his or her talker said.

2 Focus: imagining caterpillars while listening to the music "Rhythm Walk," and then moving like a caterpillar to the music

Hold the card and say:

While I play some music, close your eyes and imagine as many different kinds of caterpillars as you can.

Play the song. Then call on children to talk about the caterpillars they imagined. Accept all responses. Ask:

Does the music remind you of the way a caterpillar crawls along? (Pause) **A long time ago, we pretended that all of us together were one long caterpillar. Let's do it again! First, let's practice moving our bodies up and down.**

Play the recording and demonstrate the action: move from a standing position to a half-squat in time to the music. When the children can move correctly, line them up in single file. Each should hold the preceding child's waist. Repeat the recording as the children move up and down (not in unison) to the music, creating a wave-like effect as they imitate a caterpillar crawling around the room. Change leaders and continue as long as time and interest suggest.

296

MATERIALS*

ACTIVITY 1

None

ACTIVITY 2

Puppets

P. Mooney

1 Focus: considering and talking about the effects of not having electricity for several days

Say:

Suppose all the electricity were cut off for several days at your house or in a house that has electricity. What would be affected if this happened?

Have the children name as many things as they can. If necessary, help by asking them to consider such things as food stored in the freezer and refrigerator; the clocks, television, and radios; the heating system, air conditioner, and hot water heater; and the stove, dishwasher, and lights. Stress our heavy reliance on electricity.

OPTIONAL: End by leading a discussion on such causes of power failure as major disasters (hurricanes, floods, snowstorms, tornadoes, tidal waves) and equipment breakdowns.

2 Focus: following directions that stress counting while playing the game P. Mooney. May We?

Ask the children to stand shoulder-to-shoulder in a single line. Put the puppet on your hand, and have him say:

Let's play the game P. Mooney, May We? When I tell all of you to do something, ask together, "P. Mooney, may we?" You may move after I say, "Yes, you may." Let's begin. (Pause) Hop forward two times and count aloud as you do so.

P. Mooney should get a response of "P. Mooney, may we?" and give permission before each command is carried out. Continue with instructions like those given below, making sure the children move and count correctly. Demonstrate as necessary.

1. **Take four giant steps.**
2. **Clap your hands five times.**
3. **Take six small steps.**
4. **Turn around three times.**
5. **Pat your stomach seven times.**
6. **Take two giant steps backwards.**
7. **Stamp your feet four times.**
8. **Nod your head three times.**
9. **Jump forward five times.**
10. **Touch your toes two times.**
11. **Step sideways two times.**
12. **Take four small steps backwards.**
13. **Take five small steps forward.**
14. **Clap your hands behind your back three times.**
15. **Slide your feet four times.**
16. **Sit down two times.**

VARIATION: To make each instruction *harder,* have a child ask, "P. Mooney, may we (take two giant steps)?" Or increase difficulty by combining two instructions, like this: "Take two giant steps, and then clap your hands four times."

297

MATERIALS*

ACTIVITY 1

None

ACTIVITY 2

None

1 Focus: talking about being shy

Sit in a circle with the children and say:

We have talked about being happy and sad, frightened and excited, angry and surprised. Today let's discuss another feeling: being shy. What does the word shy mean? (Discuss) **Now let's talk about what has happened to make you feel shy.**

Have each child tell about such an experience. Stress the use of sentences.

2 Focus: deciding if situations would create feelings of happiness, sadness, excitement, surprise, fright, anger, or shyness

Say:

I am going to describe some situations. When I call on you, tell us how you might feel if the same thing happened to you. Say whether you would feel happy, sad, frightened, excited, angry, shy, or surprised. Here's the first one: Bernice and her brothers spent all afternoon building a person out of snow. Next day the sun shone brightly, and the snowperson melted. How did Bernice feel, and why?

Call on children to respond. Several emotions may be cited if they are explained. Then continue with these situations:

1. **Randall had never been to the circus before. He watched the acrobats swinging at the top of the tent. Then they began to jump from swing to swing. How do you think Randall felt? Why?**
2. **Joshua went with his father to join the Cub Scouts. It was Joshua's first day there. How do you think he felt? Why?**
3. **Gail's neighbors asked her to go to the fair with them. There were lots of people at the amusements, and Gail got lost. How do you think she felt? Why?**
4. **Rudy was certain he would receive clothes for his birthday. When he opened his birthday gift, he found it was a baseball glove. How do you think Rudy felt? Why?**
5. **Dee's daddy had an important friend come to her house. Father said to Dee, "Please come and sing us a song." How do you think she felt? Why?**
6. **Echon was shopping with her mother in a tall department store downtown. Suddenly the fire alarm went off very loudly when they were on the top floor. How do you think Echon felt? Why?**
7. **It was Stella's birthday, and she got a brand-new bicycle. Stella took her new bicycle for a ride, and then she parked it in front of her house. When she went outside again, the bicycle was gone. It had been stolen. How do you think Stella felt? Why?**
8. **Vince's grandmother came to visit. Grandmother had knitted him a new wool sweater. He tried it on, and it made him look handsome. He climbed up on her lap and gave her a hug. How do you think Vince felt? Why?**
9. **Olga was walking home from school when some neighborhood children started laughing at her and calling her bad names. How do you think Olga felt? Why?**
10. **Hiram's school was selling ornaments to raise money for the school. Hiram sold the most ornaments, and he won a portable television set. How do you think he felt? Why?**

11. Eloise's mother was very sick. One day the doctor said that her mother had to go to the hospital and stay for a few days until she got well again. How do you think Eloise felt? Why?

12. Sean was looking forward to riding in an airplane over the city. He could hardly wait. How do you think he felt? Why?

13. The children were sitting in class when another teacher opened the door and stood there holding a tray of ice cream and cake. He said, "Stop whatever you are doing! Right now we are going to have a big party!!" How do you think the children felt? Why?

298

MATERIALS*

ACTIVITY 1

Cards
Household Items
153-199

ACTIVITY 2

None

1 Focus: classifying household items by various characteristics

Arrange the 47 household cards on the floor or along a chalkledge where the children can easily see them.

Point to the cards and say:

Let's look at these pictures of household items. I will ask you to find things that are alike in some way. When I call on you, tell me which items belong in the group I mention, and explain why they do. Then I will ask you to pick out the pictures you selected and arrange them over here. (Point to chalkledge)

Use the list of questions given below. After the correct selection has been made, call on several children in turn to name the grouped items in a sentence like this: "The household items (that can hold liquid) are (bathtub, cup, baking dish, glass, pail, frying pan, saucepan, bathroom sink, kitchen sink, spoon, toilet, and wastebasket)." Rearrange the cards after each group is identified.

Find all the household items . . .

1. **that can hold water or other liquids.**
2. **that have four legs.**
3. **that have bristles.**
4. **with pillows.**
5. **used to cook.**
6. **that use electricity to run.**
7. **that cut.**
8. **used to clean.**
9. **used to eat.**
10. **that have numbers on them.**
11. **with doors.**
12. **with shelves.**
13. **with drawers.**
14. **that are pointed.**
15. **that you can squeeze.**

2 Focus: deciding whether statements are true about the characteristics of pairs of household items, and then following directions if the statements are true

Ask the children to stand before you. Say:

Now let's play a listening-and-thinking game. If what I say is correct, then follow the direction. If what I say is not correct, don't move.

Give directions like those listed below. If any children have difficulty, repeat and explain the direction until everyone responds correctly.

1. **If scissors and a knife both cut, then clap your hands.**
2. **If a frying pan and a dustpan are both used to cook, then say, "Hamburger!"**
3. **If a scrub brush and a hairbrush are both used to keep your hair neat, then make a funny face.**
4. **If a chair is smaller than a couch, then stamp your feet.**
5. **If a knife and a fork are both used in eating, then turn around.**
6. **If an iron and a stove could both burn your finger, then say, "Ouch."**
7. **If you could sleep in a bookcase and a bed, then scratch your nose.**
8. **If you could drink from both a glass and a wastebasket, then nod your head.**
9. **If you could take a bath in a bathtub and a sink, then say, "Wow!"**
10. **If a radio and a TV both make sound, then jump up once.**
11. **If a bar of soap and a toothbrush both are used to clean your teeth, then pretend to sneeze.**

12. If a sink and a bathtub both have stoppers, then say, "Hooray!"

13. If a broom and a brush both have bristles, then touch your toes.

14. If a glass and a pail both hold water, then touch your nose to your knee.

15. If a vacuum cleaner and a washing machine both make noise, then touch your nose with your tongue!

299

MATERIALS*

ACTIVITY 1

Cards

Pictures from Several Categories

12	19	21	32
49	99	124	137
149	170	173	180
181	190	191	201
203	204	205	209
211	214	217	218
221	224	241	246
247	249	252	254
260	264	265	277

Display Board

2 ledges

ACTIVITY 2

None

1 Focus: making up and telling short stories from four pictures Display cards 205, 246, 260, and 264 on the board. Stack the remaining cards in the order indicated below.

Say:

Let's make up interesting stories using these four pictures. (Point) **Listen to my story about this child, the tunnel, the race-car set, and the train:**

"Les was very excited with his birthday presents. Father gave him a tunnel to crawl through. Mother gave him a race-car set. His grandfather gave him a train."

Have several children make up stories about those four cards. Then call for stories about the following groups of cards. Give each child a turn, encouraging everyone to make up an enjoyable story.

1. 203•**barber**, 180•**scissors**, 12•**dog**, 99•**candy**
2. 217•**police officer**, 224•**sad girl**, 249•**sailboat**, 19•**goldfish**
3. 21•**horse**, 211•**girl**, 209•**farmer**, 252•**sled**
4. 247•**rake, hoe, shovel**, 221•**older woman**, 190•**telephone**, 32•**sheep**
5. 181•**sewing machine**, 49•**jeans**, 241•**jungle gym**, 204•**boy**
6. 173•**pail**, 137•**apple**, 254•**swing**, 214•**man**
7. 170•**knife**, 149•**pumpkin**, 218•**teacher**, 265•**wagon**
8. 124•**popcorn**, 191•**television**, 277•**space capsule**, 201•**astronaut**

VARIATIONS: To change the level of difficulty, use more or fewer than four words.

2 Focus: talking about a pet one would like to own and what would happen if everyone took pets to school on the same day

Say:

Imagine that we could own any kind of pet we wanted. Let's take turns telling what pets we would choose.

Have the children discuss their choices in some detail. Then continue:

Now let's pretend that one day we all brought the pets we just named to school. What might happen if we brought all of them on the same day?

Encourage every child to participate. If necessary, ask leading questions to stimulate discussion.

300

MATERIALS*

ACTIVITY 1

None

ACTIVITY 2

None

1 Focus: completing statements to name foods which can be drunk, crumbled, licked, peeled, sliced, spread, squeezed, and stirred

Say:

Please finish each sentence I say by naming a food. Finish this sentence, (Naomi): "We can drink ______ ." (Pause for response) **That's right. We can drink (milk). Finish this one, (Felix): "We can spread______ ."** (Pause for response) **Good. We can spread (jam). Now when I call on you, repeat and finish my sentence by naming a food.**

Continue with the verbs listed below. Reuse the list as necessary to give everyone at least one turn. Always give the child's name last. The children you call on should repeat the entire sentence.

1. drink	**5. slice**
2. crumble	**6. spread**
3. lick	**7. squeeze**
4. peel	**8. stir**

VARIATION: To make the activity *harder,* in each of the eight cases, have the children repeat the foods previously named and then add one more item.

2 Focus: naming and remembering a sequence of foods

Say:

Let's pretend we are making a sandwich. I will ask five people in turn to tell what they would like to put into the sandwich. Each person is to name something different. Remember to name the things already in the sandwich before you tell us what you want to add. Let's begin. My sandwich has bread. What will your sandwich have in it, (Martha Beth)?

The five children you call on should respond with a sentence like "My sandwich has (bread), (butter), (ham), (tomato), and (lettuce)." Repeat the procedure with *soup* and *salad.* Each child should have at least one turn.

VARIATIONS: To make the activity *easier,* reduce the number of items to be remembered. To make it *harder,* have the children suggest items for silly sandwiches, soups, and salads.

Keep in Mind . . .
After each lesson in the program, individuals who have difficulty demonstrating proficiency in the skills you consider appropriate and important for them to learn should be tutored. Aides could help you with this task.

301

MATERIALS*

ACTIVITY 1

None

ACTIVITY 2

Color Chips
All

P. Mooney Bag

1 Focus: comparing pairs of activities, and telling which of each pair takes a longer or shorter time to do

Say:

Let's talk more about time. Some things take a short time to do, and others take a long time. Raise your hand if you know which of these two things takes longer to do.

Read the following statements, one at a time. The children you call on should answer in sentences using the word longer. Discuss any answers which cause disagreement.

Does it take longer . . .

1. **to jump into a swimming pool, or to go grocery shopping at the supermarket?**
2. **to throw a rock into a lake, or to tie your shoe?**
3. **to say your name, or to wash a dog?**
4. **to button your shirt, or to sneeze?**
5. **to paint a picture, or to pour water out of a glass?**
6. **to paint your room, or to get dressed on a very cold day?**
7. **to take a nap, or to ride in a jet plane to a faraway city?**
8. **to walk two miles, or to feed the dog?**
9. **to brush your teeth, or to drop an egg on the floor?**
10. **to plant a tree, or to hiccup?**

Repeat the statements, asking each time, "Which of these two actions takes a *shorter* time to do?"

2 Focus: making a chain of 10 chips, and then saying and acting out a counting rhyme

With the children seated on the floor in a circle, pile the color chips in the center. Link 10 chips of various colors as the children count them in unison. Then hold up your chain and say:

Look at my chain. Let's count its chips again together. (Do so) **Now each of you may choose 10 chips of as many colors as you like and make a chain out of them.**

Help as necessary, and have the children individually count the chips on their chains. Then continue:

Now let's hold our chains and say our color chip rhyme. Remember to take the chips off your chain as the rhyme says. Let's begin.

Remove chips as indicated while you say this rhyme with the children:

Ten little color chips all in a line;

One fell down (remove and drop a chip), **then there were nine.**

Nine little color chips sitting on a gate;

One fell down (remove and drop a chip), **then there were eight.**

Eight little color chips looking up at heaven;

One fell down (remove and drop a chip), **then there were seven.**

Seven little color chips sitting on some bricks;

One fell down (remove and drop a chip), **then there were six.**

Six little color chips getting ready to jive;

One fell down (remove and drop a chip), **then there were five.**

Five little color chips going through a door;

One fell down (remove and drop a chip), **then there were four.**

Four little color chips climbing up a tree;

One fell down (remove and drop a chip)**, then there were three.**

Three little color chips, going to the zoo;

One fell down (remove and drop a chip)**, then there were two.**

Two little color chips, going for a run;

One fell down (remove and drop a chip)**, then there was one.**

One little color chip, having no fun;

He ran home (drop chip)**, then there was none.**

Repeat as time and interest permit.

302

MATERIALS*

ACTIVITY 1

Display Board
4 ledges

Poster 5

ACTIVITY 2

Display Board
4 ledges

Poster 5

1 Focus: thinking about "who might say that" on the poster "Winter Scene"

Use the ledges to display the poster on the board.

Point to the poster and say:

You have seen this big picture before. Look at all these people again. I will say a sentence that one of them might say. Please try to figure out who might be speaking. Raise your hand if you can point to the person and repeat the statement as if you were the person speaking.

Present the statements below, one at a time. The children you call on should point to the right person on the poster and then repeat the statement as if that person were speaking. Each child should have a turn.

Who might say . . .

1. **"Let me put on his hat"?**
2. **"Oh, my leg hurts"?**
3. **"Mmmm, I love toasted marshmallows"?**
4. **"I like to feel the wind blowing my hair"?**
5. **"Stand still, so I can take your picture"?**
6. **"Hey, wait for me. I fell off"?**
7. **"Whoa! Come on up. I'll give you a ride"?**
8. **"I'm going to hit that snowman with my snowball"?**
9. **"I think I've got a fish"?**
10. **"This ice feels cold"?**
11. **"Look! I can ski on one leg"?**
12. **"Look at all the skiers coming down the hill"?**
13. **"Let's use these sticks for arms"?**
14. **"I hope I don't run into that ambulance"?**
15. **"Please tell our viewers how long you have been skating"?**

2 Focus: counting items on the poster "Winter Scene" to answer "how-many" questions

Leave the poster from Activity 1 on display.

Say:

Now let's count some of the things in our poster. I will tell you what to count.

Each time, let the children scan the poster before you lead them in counting one of the items listed below. Then call on someone to respond in a sentence such as "There are (three snowmen) in this picture." Begin with this question:

How many (snowmen) do you see in this poster?

Use additional items like these:

1. **vehicles**
2. **animals**
3. **skiers**
4. **people throwing**
5. **deer**
6. **sleds**
7. **dogs**
8. **skaters**
9. **people cooking**
10. **people fishing**
11. **cats**

VARIATION: To make the activity *harder,* have the children attempt it while the poster is covered. Expose the picture for verification.

303

MATERIALS*

ACTIVITY 1

None

ACTIVITY 2

None

1 Focus: listening to compound words, and identifying the two short words in each

Say:

Let's listen to words today. I will have someone say a long word made out of two short words. Raise your hand if you can tell us what the two short words are.

Ask a child to stand beside you. Whisper one of the compound words listed below for the child to say to the group. After someone has identified the two short words, call on other children to define them. Use compound words like these:

1. wristwatch	**10. bathtub**
2. underpants	**11. dollhouse**
3. pancake	**12. rowboat**
4. birdhouse	**13. pinwheel**
5. watermelon	**14. sandbox**
6. strawberry	**15. sailboat**
7. wastebasket	**16. peanut**
8. dustpan	**17. popcorn**
9. saucepan	**18. pineapple**

2 Focus: listening to sentences containing compound words in which the order of the short words is reversed, and identifying the "backwards" words

Say:

Now let's see if you can figure out what the long words are when they are said backwards and used in sentences. Here's the first sentence: "I don't know what time it is, because I can't find my watchwrist." What word is backwards? (Pause) **You're right. *Watchwrist* is the backwards word. Now let's say the sentence correctly.**

Lead the children in saying, "I don't know what time it is, because I can't find my wristwatch." Repeat this procedure with the following sentences. Give everyone a turn.

1. **I put my *pantsunder* into the wash.**
2. **Let's eat this *cakepan.***
3. **We built a *housebird* out of old lumber.**
4. **This is a juicy slice of *melonwater.***
5. **The rabbit hopped in the *berrystraw* patch.**
6. **Please put the trash into the *basketwaste.***
7. **We need the broom and *pandust.***
8. **I need a bath. Please fill the *tubbath* for me.**
9. **For her birthday, she got a *housedoll.***
10. **Let's go out on the lake in the *boatrow.***
11. **Nicola was outside playing with her *wheelpin.***
12. **Take the bucket and shovel to the *boxsand.***
13. **That *boatsail* will be great to sail in the bathtub.**
14. **I want a *nutpea* butter sandwich.**
15. **Help me eat this bag of *cornpop.***
16. **Here's a glass of *applepine* juice.**

304

MATERIALS*

ACTIVITY 1

Cards

Numerals & Color Shapes

294-313

ACTIVITY 2

Cards

Numerals & Color Shapes

(same as for Activity 1)

Music

334

Audiocassette 2

Side B, Song 8, "Find That Shape" (vocal)

Side B, Song 9, "Find That Shape" (instrumental version)

1 Focus: describing and matching pairs of number-and-shape cards, and then following directions that stress numbers

Have the children sit around you. Give each child one of the 20 number-and-shape cards, making sure to distribute matched pairs. If necessary, take a card yourself. Say:

Look carefully at your card. When I call on you, describe your card in a sentence telling the kind of shapes, their color, and their number. (Rachel), please start.

The children you call on should respond in a sentence such as "My card shows seven red rectangles." When everyone has had a turn, have the children stand. Continue:

Now let's play a game called Lost Twins. Each of you has a "twin" whose card shows the same *number* of shapes as yours. Your "twin's" card may have different kinds and colors of shapes, but the *number* is the same as yours. When you find your "twin," stand together.

When all the "twins" are paired, give the following and similar directions in random order:

1. **Ones, turn around once.**
2. **Twos, turn around twice.**
3. **Threes, turn around twice.**
4. **Fours, turn around once.**
5. **Fives, turn around once.**
6. **Sixes, turn around twice.**
7. **Sevens, turn around once.**
8. **Eights, turn around twice.**
9. **Nines, turn around twice.**
10. **Tens, turn around once.**

2 Focus: singing and acting out the song "Find That Shape"

Have the paired children stand side by side in a large circle. In random order, spread the 20 number-and-shape cards on the floor inside the circle, picture sides up. Hold the music card and say:

Now let's sing the song "Find That Shape." At the beginning of each verse, I will point to a pair of you.
When it is your turn, the two of you are to step into the circle and each find a card that shows the number we are singing about. Hold up your card for everyone to see.

Play song 9 (instrumental version), and refer to the music card as you sing this verse:

Find a one, find a one.

Can you find a card with one?

Find a one, find a one.

Can you find that number?

Invite the children to join you as you repeat the verse. Continue with other verses using the numbers one to 10 in numerical order. At the beginning of each verse, point to a pair of children. As the verse progresses, check to be sure that the chosen pair has found and held up the correct cards. Continue with more verses about the same numbers in random order. Give everyone at least one turn.

305

MATERIALS*

ACTIVITY 1

Cards

Pictures from Several Categories

12	42	46	49
50	53	58	60
61	63	64	65
71	72	115	122
131	153	157	158
163	167	170	172
173	175	178	183
184	186	187	189
228	229	242	249
252	255	261	262
265			

Display Board

4 ledges

ACTIVITY 2

Cards

Music (optional)

328

Audiocassette 2

Side A, Song 6 "If and Then Go Together"

1 **Focus: evaluating groups of four pictures, and telling what items are missing to carry out an activity**

Display cards 115, 122, and 175 on the board.

Say:

Let's pretend that we are going to make a peanut-butter-and-jam sandwich. Look at these three cards (point), and figure out what items are missing to make the sandwich.

When the children have pointed out that bread and a knife are missing, review all the items needed to make the sandwich. Continue as above with the following sets of cards

1. 153•**bathtub**, 184•**hand soap**, 186•**sponge** — **Kevin is getting ready to take a bath. Some things are missing. What are they?** (water in the tub and a towel)

2. 46•**girl's dress**, 60•**shoes**, 63•**girl's slip**, 71•**girl's underpants** — **Christina is getting dressed to go to a party. She has forgotten something. What is it?** (socks)

3. 50•**mittens**, 64•**snowsuit**, 252•**sled** — **It just snowed, and Jason is getting ready to go sledding. Something is missing. What is it?** (boots)

4. 157•**scrub brush**, 172•**mop**, 173•**pail** — **Betty Jean is going to wash the floor. Some things are missing. What are they?** (soap and water)

5. 163•**cup and saucer**, 167•**glass**, 170•**knife**, 175•**plate**, 187•**spoon** — **Jackson is setting the table for dinner. He has forgotten something. What is it?** (fork)

6. 49•**jeans**, 52•**boy's pajamas**, 58•**boy's shirt**, 61•**tennis shoes**, 65•**socks**, 72•**boy's undershorts** — **Tommy is packing his suitcase to go on a trip. Something is missing. What is it?** (suitcase)

7. 158•**chair**, 178•**refrigerator**, 183•**kitchen sink**, 189•**kitchen table** — **Helen is putting furniture into her dollhouse kitchen. Something is missing. What is it?** (stove)

8. 12•**dog**, 42•**boots**, 262•**tricycle**, 265•**wagon** — **It is a rainy day. Erik is going outside to ride his tricycle and give his dog a ride in the wagon. Something is missing. What is it?** (raincoat)

9. 228•**ball**, 242•**pail and shovel**, 249•**sailboat** — **George is going to the beach for the day. He has forgotten something. What is it?** (swimsuit)

10. 131•**Soda pop**, 229•**balloon**, 255•**tea set**, 261•**tree house** — **Pamela is going to have a birthday party in her tree house. Something is missing. What is it?** (birthday cake)

2 Focus: using opposites to complete statements involving analogous reasoning

Say:

I am going to say some sentences, but I will not finish them. Listen carefully to each sentence, and try to figure out what word will finish it correctly. The right word will be an opposite.

Call on individuals to complete the following statements. Stress the words *if* and *then.* After each sentence is completed correctly, lead the children in repeating all of it.

1. **If it is full, then it is not _________ .** (empty)
2. **If it is open, then it is not _______ .** (closed)
3. **If it is cold, then it is not _______ .** (warm, hot)
4. **If it is wet, then it is not _______ .** (dry)
5. **If it is outside, then it is not _______ .** (inside)
6. **If it is loud, then it is not _______ .** (quiet, soft)
7. **If it is soft, then it is not _______ .** (hard)
8. **If it is up, then it is not _______ .** (down)
9. **If it is over, then it is not _______ .** (under)
10. **If it is in front, then it is not in _______ .** (back)
11. **If it is pretty, then it is not _______ .** (ugly)
12. **If it is first, then it is not _______ .** (last)
13. **If it is off, then it is not _______ .** (on)
14. **If it is thick, then it is not _______ .** (thin)
15. **If it is broken, then it is not ______ .** (fixed, repaired)
16. **If it is near, then it is not _______ .** (far)
17. **If it is crooked, then it is not _____ .** (straight)
18. **If it is tight, then it is not _______ .** (loose)

Continue by reversing each sentence, like this: "If it is empty, then it is not ________ . (full)"

OPTIONAL: End by playing the song (instrumental version) of "If and Then Go Together," and have the children sing about opposites.

306

MATERIALS*

ACTIVITY 1

None

ACTIVITY 2

None

1 Focus: identifying workers from pantomimed actions

Say:

Today let's pretend to be people with interesting jobs. I will whisper a kind of job to each of you. When it is your turn, please say and do what you think someone with that job would. The rest of the group will try to guess who that person is.

Use the following list as you call children in turn to the front of the group to perform. If necessary, help the children by acting part of the role and suggesting gestures or conversation characteristic of each profession.

1. astronaut
2. butcher
3. boxer
4. carpenter
5. cook
6. dancer
7. detective
8. doctor
9. farmer
10. judge
11. king
12. mechanic
13. movie star
14. pilot
15. president
16. sailor
17. soldier
18. teacher
19. television announcer
20. truck driver

2 Focus: remembering and repeating a whispered message about items to be taken on a trip

Have the children line up. If there are more than about 12 children, have them form two equal lines facing each other. Say:

Let's send messages about what we are going to take on a trip. I will whisper the first message.

Whisper to the child who heads the line, "On our trip, we will take a suitcase, a toothbrush, and a raincoat." That child then whispers the message to the next child, and so on down the line. The last child is to say the message out loud. Have the group compare that message with the one they heard. The last child may then head the line. Whisper a new message to that person about three other items to be taken on a trip, and continue as above.

VARIATIONS: To change the level of difficulty, increase or decrease the number of items the children must remember.

307

MATERIALS*

ACTIVITY 1

None

ACTIVITY 2

None

1 Focus: classifying groups of three words

Say:

I am going to say three words. Tell me what word or phrase describes all three.

Present the following sets of three words, one set at a time. As necessary, help the children respond correctly in each case.

1. **hat, sweater, coat** (clothes)
2. **balloon, airplane, race-car set** (toys)
3. **onion, lettuce, greens** (vegetables)
4. **mop, broom, bucket** (household or cleaning items)
5. **foot, back, chest** (body parts)
6. **Denise, Jonathan, Carmen** (names)
7. **calf, kid, piglet** (baby animals)
8. **bicycle, truck, train** (vehicles)
9. **thunder, growling, echo** (sounds)
10. **white, black, red** (colors)
11. **lemon, pineapple, watermelon** (fruits)
12. **nurse, grocer, mail carrier** (people, workers)
13. **snowsuit, sneakers, swimsuit** (clothing)
14. **week, year, second** (time)
15. **rectangle, circle, triangle** (shapes)
16. **two, 10, seven** (numbers)
17. **cookies, ice cream, candy** (sweet foods)
18. **grandmother, baby, father** (people or family members)
19. **sit, jump, walk** (actions)
20. **spring, fall, summer** (seasons of the year)

VARIATIONS: To make the activity *easier,* exclude these categories: actions, time, sounds, and seasons. To make it *harder,* have the children take turns making up lists of three items for the group to classify.

2 Focus: brainstorming descriptions of specific animals, clothes, body parts, toys, vegetables, fruits, foods, vehicles, people, and seasons

Say:

Let's think as fast as we can. I will say a word like *coat.* When I point to you, tell me something in a sentence about coats. Try to name something no one else has.

Use the words from the list in Activity 1, excluding colors, numbers, names, shapes, sounds, actions, and words concerning time. The children you point to should each make up a sentence about that word. Continue with the same word until the children run out of ideas. Vary the categories from which the words are chosen.

308

MATERIALS*

ACTIVITY 1

Display Board
2 ledges

Magnetic Shapes
5 large circles
5 small circles
5 large rectangles
5 small rectangles
5 large squares
5 small squares
5 large triangles
5 small triangles

ACTIVITY 2

None

1 Focus: classifying magnetic shapes into various groups, and then counting and describing the items in each group

Set up the board, separating the left two-thirds of the board from the right one-third by placing the ledges vertically. Place the 40 shapes in random order onto the left side of the board.

Say:
Let's see how many ways we can group the magnetic shapes. First, find all the shapes that are black, (LaTanya), and put them here. (Point to right side of board)

When the child has done so, call on children to answer questions like these:

1. **How many shapes are in this group?**
2. **What are the names of the shapes in this group?**
3. **What are the sizes of the shapes in this group?**
4. **How many (circles, squares, triangles, rectangles) are in the group?**
5. **There is one thing about everything in this group that is the same. What is it?**

Continue as above with these groupings:

1. **all red shapes**
2. **all green shapes**
3. **all blue shapes**
4. **all yellow shapes**
5. **all large shapes**
6. **all shapes with straight sides**
7. **all shapes with curved sides**
8. **all shapes with four sides**
9. **all shapes with three sides**
10. **all small shapes**

Each child should be given at least one chance to participate.

2 Focus: evaluating and correcting statements using *taller than* and *longer than* in a true-false game

Say:
Now I will whisper something to each of you. You are to tell the group what I say. Then everyone will tell you in a sentence whether what you said is true or false. Let's try one!

Have the children take turns standing by you. Use the list given below. The group should respond to each child with a sentence such as "Yes, a refrigerator is taller than a television" or "No, a watermelon is not longer than a bathtub."

1. **A refrigerator is taller than a television.**
2. **A watermelon is longer than a bathtub.**
3. **A rocking horse is taller than a jungle gym.**
4. **A slide is longer than a sled.**
5. **A tree house is taller than a dollhouse.**
6. **A fire truck is longer than a passenger train.**
7. **A mop is taller than a pail.**
8. **A potato is longer than an ironing board.**
9. **A doghouse is taller than a telephone pole.**
10. **A mop is longer than a hot dog.**
11. **A bottle of soda pop is taller than a tricycle.**
12. **A bed is longer than a toothbrush.**
13. **A sailboat is taller than a rowboat.**
14. **A bicycle is longer than a school bus.**
15. **A toddler is taller than a farmer.**
16. **A guitar is longer than a cap gun.**
17. **(Sam) is taller than a space capsule.**
18. **An airplane is longer than a roller skate.**
19. **(Clare) is taller than an ice-cream cone.**
20. **A hairbrush is longer than a teeter-totter.**

309

MATERIALS*

ACTIVITY 1

None

ACTIVITY 2

None

1 Focus: talking about the relationship between two words

Say:

Let's play a thinking game. When I say two words, try to figure out how they go together. Here are the first two: *oars* and *rowboat*. How do those two things go together? (Discuss) **Yes, oars are used to move a rowboat over the water.**

Continue as above with the following pairs of words. The individuals you call on should respond in sentences. Try to make sure everyone understands the relationship between the two objects.

1. **bird, birdseed**
2. **light bulb, lamp**
3. **plug, iron**
4. **ice cube, water**
5. **key, lock**
6. **cat, milk**
7. **soap, water**
8. **clothes, washer**
9. **sheets, pillow**
10. **cash register, money**
11. **football, football player**
12. **telephone, telephone pole**
13. **bird, worm**
14. **eyes, glasses**
15. **dog, meat**
16. **shoes, laces**
17. **boat, water**
18. **ring, finger**
19. **squirrel, nuts**
20. **school bus, child**

2 Focus: thinking of and naming three things from requested categories, and then classifying them

Say:

Now let's play another thinking game. I will ask one of you to tell the group three words that go together. The group must then name the word or phrase that describes all three words.

Choose a child to come to the front. Whisper to that person:

Think of three toys, (Larry). Say the names of the toys to the group; then ask, "What are they?"

When the group has answered correctly, continue as above with the following categories:

1. **actions**
2. **body parts**
3. **colors**
4. **foods**
5. **fruits**
6. **numbers**
7. **people**
8. **toys**
9. **shapes**
10. **vegetables**

310

MATERIALS*

ACTIVITY 1

None

ACTIVITY 2

None

1 Focus: thinking of and naming animals or foods while stressing three, four, five, and more

Say:

Let's see how fast you can name animals or foods. Name (four animals), (Debbie).

Vary your requests to challenge individuals, having children name from three to five or even more animals or foods at a time. Always give the child's name last to retain suspense. Praise all reasonable efforts.

VARIATION: To make the activity *harder,* add other categories.

2 Focus: talking about one's experiences of being in trouble

Say:

Tell me what it means to be "in trouble."

Encourage discussion of the phrase. Then say:

Let's talk about when you were in trouble. Raise your hand when you are ready to tell us about a time when you were in trouble.

Have the volunteers take turns talking about their own experiences. Accept all responses.

311

MATERIALS*

ACTIVITY 1

Display Board (optional)

4 ledges (optional)

Poster 2 (optional)

Audiocassette 4

Side A, Selection 2, "Circus"

ACTIVITY 2

Display Board

4 ledges

Poster 2

1 Focus: listening to "Sounds of the Circus," and then making up a progressive story about going to a circus

Say:

Close your eyes and imagine where you would be if you heard these sounds.

Play selection 2 and then ask:

What place would sound like that? (Encourage unison response) **Yes, these sounds are all circus sounds. Now let's make up a story about a trip to the circus. Everyone will have a turn to add a sentence in the story. Please listen very closely to the persons who speak before you do. I will take the first turn.**

Start the audiocassette player. Announce the story's title — "A Trip to the Circus" — and begin with a sentence like "One day my father surprised me by saying, 'Let's get ready to go to the circus."' Then have the children each add a sentence or two to the story. Play back the finished story, and call on children to identify each speaker.

VARIATION: To make the activity *easier,* use the ledges to display the poster "Circus" on the board after the children have heard the sound effects. If the poster is used, leave it on display for Activity 2.

2 Focus: talking about the number of wheels on unicycles, bicycles, and tricycles, and telling which one would be easiest to ride, using the poster "Circus"

Use the ledges to display the poster on the board.

Say:

There are three kinds of cycles: tricycles, bicycles, and unicycles. Let's see which of these three kinds of cycles is shown in the poster.

Help the children identify the unicycle, the bicycle, and P. Mooney's Chaincycle. Then ask:

How many wheels does a tricycle have? (Pause) **That's right; a tricycle has three wheels. How many wheels does a bicycle have?** (Pause) **Good; a bicycle has two wheels. How many wheels does a unicycle have?** (Pause) **Yes, a unicycle has one wheel. *Uni* means one, *bi* means two, and *tri* means three. Now, let's talk about which kind of cycle would be the hardest and easiest to ride and why.**

Lead the discussion, using questions to encourage every child to participate. End by reviewing the meanings of *tri, bi,* and *uni,* but don't pressure the children to use these terms.

312 

MATERIALS*

ACTIVITY 1

Cards

Animals

3 4 6 16 33

Display Board

2 ledges

ACTIVITY 2

None

1 Focus: describing and talking about beetles, spiders, flies, butterflies, and bees

Display the five animal cards on the board.

Point to the cards and say:

Let's talk about each of these small creatures.

Point to each picture in turn. Have each creature named and described, adding instructive comments. Then ask:

What word could we use to name all five of these?

Discuss what word would be appropriate. Explain that all except the spider are *insects,* that all five could be called *bugs,* and that all are *animals.* Then say:

Now let's find out how these animals are the same, and how they are different. Tell me how many legs each one has. (Discuss) **Yes; a bee, a fly, a beetle, and a butterfly each have *six* legs, but a spider has *eight* legs.**

Lead a discussion about these and other small animals by asking questions like these:

1. **How are these animals different from most farm animals?**
2. **Where might you find small animals like this?**
3. **Have you ever seen any small animals? If so, where?**
4. **Did you ever catch any? If so, how?**
5. **Which of these animals can spin? Fly? Bite? Swim? Crawl? Roll up? Produce something we eat?**
6. **What do these animals eat?**
7. **What season of the year do you see these animals most often?**
8. **How do these small animals help us?**
9. **How do you feel about animals like this?**

Stress the fact that plants and animals depend on one another. Encourage the children to be curious and to explore for bugs and insects on their own.

2 Focus: talking about seasons and the activities that are fun to do during each of the four seasons, and then completing statements about the sequence of seasons by stressing *before* and *after*

Say:

Now let's talk about what is fun to do during different seasons of the year. What do you like to do in winter?

Lead a discussion on the indoor and outdoor winter activities available in your community. Call on children to name their favorites. Continue with discussions of spring, summer, and fall activities. Then say:

Now let's talk about what season you like best and why it is your favorite.

Call on everyone in turn. End by asking the group to complete the following statements:

1. **After winter, it is** _______ . (spring)
2. **After spring, it is** _______ . (summer)
3. **After summer, it is** _______ . (fall)
4. **After fall, it is** _______ . (winter)
5. **Before winter, it is** _______ . (fall)
6. **Before fall, it is** _______ . (summer)
7. **Before summer, it is** _______ . (spring)
8. **Before spring, it is** _______ . (winter)

313

MATERIALS*

ACTIVITY 1

Teacher provides

Pieces of string, each about 3 feet (1 meter) long, 1 for each child & 1 for self

ACTIVITY 2

None

1 Focus: comparing the length, width, and height of classroom objects to a piece of string about three feet (one meter) long while stressing *shorter than, longer than,* and *same as*

Give each child a piece of string; hold one yourself.

With the children standing before you, hold your string out to full length and say:

This piece of string is one meter long. Let's find some classroom items that are about as long, or tall, or wide as a meter.

Help them find several such items by calling on children to measure possibilities with their strings. Each child should describe the object he or she measured in a sentence like "The table is longer than the string" or "The chair is shorter than the string" or "The door is the same width as the string." Stress the use of *shorter than, same as,* and *longer than.*

Continue by asking children to predict whether other items are the same as, shorter, longer, taller, or wider than a meter. Each child you call on should verify the estimate by comparing the object's length with the string's.

VARIATION: To make the activity *easier,* choose items obviously shorter than a meter, and help children measure them with the string. Then continue with items that are longer than a meter.

2 Focus: completing sentences which stress opposites and the words *if* and *then*

Say:

I will say some sentences, but I will not finish them. Listen carefully to each sentence, and try to figure out the opposite that will finish it correctly.

Call on children to complete the following statements. After each is completed correctly, lead the group in repeating the entire sentence.

1. **If it is not small, then it is _______ .** (large)
2. **If it is not short, then it is _______ .** (long)
3. **If it is not narrow, then it is _______ .** (wide)
4. **If it is not thick, then it is _______ .** (thin)
5. **If it is not low, then it is _______ .** (high)
6. **If it is not slender, then it is _______ .** (fat)
7. **If it is not big, then it is _________ .** (little)
8. **If it is not light, then it is _______ .** (heavy)

Continue by reversing each sentence, like this: "If it is not large, then it is ________ (small)."

314

MATERIALS*

ACTIVITY 1

None

ACTIVITY 2

None

1 Focus: talking about possible solutions to school problems

Say:

Let's talk about problems we might have to solve in school someday.

Lead discussions of solutions to the following school situations. To encourage everyone to participate, hint at possible solutions. Praise all creative efforts.

Problem Situation	*Possible Solutions*
1. Suppose our whole group wanted to sit around a table to do a project, but the table was not large enough for everyone. What could we do to solve this problem?	**a. Have everyone sit on the floor.** **b. Find more chairs and squeeze close together.** **c. Push several tables together.**
2. Suppose that when it was time to go home from school, we found out that all our gloves and mittens were lost or mixed up. How could we solve this problem?	**a. Put strings on mittens and attach to jacket.** **b. Everyone have different colors and designs.** **c. Put our gloves into coat sleeves or pockets.** **d. Put names on them.**
3. When another class came to visit ours, it was raining outside. We did not have enough coat hooks for everyone. What could we do to solve this problem?	**a. Put more than one coat on the hooks.** **b. Put extra coats on chairs.** **c. Make a neat pile of coats.**
4. Suppose it were our morning snack time, and we did not have enough plates for everyone. What could we do to solve this problem?	**a. Use napkins.** **b. Cut the paper plates in half.** **c. Share a plate.** **d. Cut up art paper.**

2 Focus: imitating clapping and stamping patterns in the game Copycat

Ask the children to stand before you. Say:

Let's play the game Copycat. I will clap and stamp different patterns. Please watch and listen carefully as I make a pattern. Then all of you are to be copycats and make the same pattern together.

Use your hands and feet to make patterns like those given below. Have the children repeat them in unison. Adjust the patterns to challenge the children.

1. **clap, clap, stamp, stamp, clap, clap, stamp, stamp**
2. **stamp, clap, clap, clap, stamp, clap, clap, clap**
3. **clap, clap, clap, stamp, stamp, clap, clap, clap**
4. **clap, clap, pause, stamp, pause, clap, clap, pause**
5. **stamp, clap, clap, pause, stamp, clap, clap, pause**
6. **stamp, stamp, stamp, clap, stamp, stamp, stamp, clap**

VARIATIONS: To make the activity *harder,* call on individuals to repeat the pattern and/or to make up patterns for the group to imitate. To make it *easier,* reduce the length of the pattern from eight actions to about four.

315

MATERIALS*

ACTIVITY 1

None

ACTIVITY 2

None

1 Focus: talking about being proud

Sit in a circle with the children and say:

We have talked about how we sometimes feel happy, sad, frightened, excited, shy, angry, or surprised. Today let's talk about another feeling: being proud. What does the word *proud* mean?

Lead a discussion until everyone understands that feeling proud means feeling good about something done well. Call on volunteers to describe experiences that made them feel proud.

VARIATION: To make the activity *easier,* do not define *proud.* Simply give examples that illustrate its meaning.

2 Focus: evaluating situations and deciding if they would create feelings of happiness, sadness, excitement, surprise, fright, anger, shyness, or pride

Say:

I will describe some situations. For each one, tell me how you might feel if the same thing happened to you. Tell whether you would feel happy or sad, frightened or excited, angry or shy, surprised or proud. Let's begin.

Read the situations listed below. Encourage discussion, and accept all reasonable responses.

1. **Mark had been feeling happy about going to his friend's birthday party. But on the day of the party, he woke up with the measles. How do you think Mark felt?**
2. **Francesca felt sad because her bicycle had a flat tire. Her brother fixed it for her. How do you think Francesca felt then?**
3. **William took his dog for a hike in the woods behind his house. After he had walked a long way, he noticed it was getting dark and decided to start home. When he started back, he couldn't find the path he had been following. How do you think William felt?**
4. **Sheila had a part in the school play. She had worked very hard to learn her part, and on the day of the play, she remembered all her lines perfectly. After the play, her mother and father said, "Sheila, you did a fine job!" How do you think Sheila felt?**
5. **Rodney saw some big boys bullying his friend Joanie. They threw Joanie's books on the ground and pushed her. How do you think Rodney felt?**
6. **Vernon got a sled for his birthday, but he had not been able to use it because there was no snow. One day his mother called to him, "Vernon, come quickly and look out the window. It is snowing!" How do you think Vernon felt?**
7. **Mother was meeting with some people in the living room. There was a phone call for Mother. Sarah had to go into the living room where all the adults were to tell' her mother about the phone. How do you think Sarah felt?**
8. **Jimmy John heard the doorbell ring, but when he opened the door, no one was there. How did Jimmy John feel?**
9. **Mei-Ling saw a tall ladder leaning against the house, so she started to climb it. When she got almost to the top, she looked down. How do you think Mei-Ling felt?**
10. **Rocco likes to visit his aunt and uncle. Today is the last day of his visit, and tomorrow he will go home. How do you think Rocco feels?**
11. **Joyce had a big chocolate cookie. She shared part of her cookie with Yvette. How did Yvette feel?**

12. Emilio took his lunch to school. At lunch time he went to get his lunch, and someone had taken it. How did Emilio feel?

13. Malita and Ruth were very good friends. One day Malita invited Ruth to come with her after school and to spend the night. How do you think Ruth felt?

14. Adam had a great big red balloon. Suddenly it popped with a loud bang! How did Adam feel?

15. Stewart had just moved to town and was going to a new school. At recess some boys decided they would play football. Stewart wanted to ask to join them, but he didn't know any of the boys. How do you think he felt?

16. Everyone in Cameron's class had been working very hard on art pictures because Ms. White, the teacher, said she was going to give a prize for the best picture. When the day to give the prize came, Ms. White said, "First prize for a fine picture goes to Cameron." How do you think Cameron felt?

VARIATION: To make the activity *easier,* select the situations involving the feelings easiest to describe.

316

MATERIALS*

ACTIVITY 1

None

ACTIVITY 2

Cards

Music

335

Audiocassette 2

Side B, Song 10, "Rhythm Walk"

1 Focus: naming and counting parts of the arms, legs, and head

With the children standing in a circle, say:

Look at my arms move. (Shake both arms) **Now shake your arms.** (Pause) **Let's name as many parts of our arms as we can.**

Point to the parts in turn and call on individuals to identify them. Then lead the group in naming in unison the nine parts of the arm from the fingernails to the shoulder: fingernails, fingers, thumbs, knuckles, hands, wrists, elbows, arms, and shoulders. Have the children count the parts aloud in unison. Repeat this procedure with the following body parts:

1. **legs (toenails, toes, knuckles, heels, feet, ankles, knees, legs, thighs, etc.)**
2. **head (hair, ears, forehead, eyes, eyebrows, eyelashes, nose, lips, teeth, jaw, cheeks, chin, etc.)**

2 Focus: performing an Mrican dance to the music "Rhythm Walk"

With the children standing in a circle with you, say:

All over the world, people dance. Today we are going to learn a dance which comes from Africa. It is called "Ring Shout" First we move around the circle in this direction (point), **shuffling our feet like this.** (Demonstrate) **It is very important *not* to lift your feet off the floor. Let's try shuffling our feet along the floor together.**

Play the song, and lead the children in the shuffle action in time to the music. When the children can shuffle in a circle correctly, continue:

Now let's do some actions with other parts of our bodies as we shuffle. Do any action you like in time with the music. You might raise both arms, or nod your head, or bend at your waist. Remember, keep your feet on the floor all the time; do not lift them off the floor.

Repeat the music; the children are to shuffle as they move other body parts (not in unison) to the music, creating a wave-like effect. Suggest another movement to a child only if necessary. Encourage them to have fun. Continue as time and interest suggest.

317

MATERIALS*

ACTIVITY 1

Fruits & vegetables
All

P. Mooney Bag

ACTIVITY 2

None

1 Focus: brainstorming what can be made from real fruits and vegetables

Put the fruits and vegetables into the bag.

With the children sitting in a circle, wear the bag and say:

I am going to give each person a fruit or a vegetable. Please think of all the things that could be made from your fruit or vegetable if it were real.

Let each child take an item from the bag. Keep an apple for yourself. Hold it up and say:

I have an apple. Apples can be used to make many foods, which often have the word *apple* in the name. I can think of one: We can make apple juice from apples. Can you think of another?

Call on children to name in sentences such foods as apple pie, apple jelly, apple sauce, candy apples, apple cider, etc. Then let the children take turns naming foods made from their fruit or vegetable. If necessary, suggest some of these:

1. **banana - *banana* split, *banana* pudding, *banana* sandwich**
2. **carrot - *carrot* sticks, *carrot* juice, *carrot* for a rabbit, *carrot* cake**
3. **corn - fried *corn*, *corn* on the cob, *corn* fritters, *corn* bread, pop*corn*, *corn* oil, *corn* dogs, *corn*meal, *corn*flakes, *corn*starch, *corn* chips**
4. **lemon - *lemon*ade, *lemon* juice, *lemon* tea, *lemon* flavoring**
5. **onion - *onion* soup, fried *onion* rings**
6. **orange - *orange* juice, *orange* cake, *orange* tea, *orange* marmalade**
7. **peach - *peach* jam, *peach* pudding, *peaches* and cream, stewed *peaches***
8. **pear - *pear* honey, *pear* salad, stewed *pears***
9. **pineapple - *pineapple* juice, candied *pineapple*, *pineapple* ice cream, *pineapple* upside-down cake, canned *pineapple* chunks.**
10. **potato - french-fried *potatoes*, *potato* chips, mashed *potatoes*, baked *potato*, *potato* soup, roast *potato***
11. **strawberry - *strawberry* jam, *strawberry* ice cream, *strawberry* cheesecake, *strawberry* shortcake**
12. **tomato - *tomato* juice, *tomato* soup, *tomato* salad, *tomato* sauce, *tomato* catsup, lettuce-and-*tomato* sandwich, stewed *tomatoes***

2 Focus: naming and remembering the sequence of fruits and vegetables in a planting-a-garden game

Say:

Let's pretend we are going to plant a vegetable garden. I will ask each of you to name a vegetable you would plant. When it is your turn, name the vegetables in the order already chosen, and then add yours to the list. Let's begin. I'll start: "In our garden, let's plant (corn)." Now, (Rebecca), say what I said and add another vegetable.

Continue until an error is made. Then start again, calling on other children. Give every child at least one turn, calling most often on those who need help.

318

MATERIALS*

ACTIVITY 1

None

ACTIVITY 2

None

1 Focus: identifying workers from pantomimed actions

Say:

Today let's pretend again to be people with interesting jobs. I will whisper a kind of job to each of you. When it is your turn, please say and do what you think someone with that job would. The rest of the group will try to guess who that person is.

Use the following list. If necessary, help shy children by playing part of the role. Suggest gestures and conversation appropriate for each profession.

1. **babysitter**
2. **barber**
3. **boxer**
4. **bus driver**
5. **cook**
6. **dentist**
7. **doctor**
8. **fire fighter**
9. **gas station attendant**
10. **grocer**
11. **house painter**
12. **lion tamer**
13. **mail carrier**
14. **nurse**
15. **police officer**
16. **school principal**
17. **singer**
18. **teacher**
19. **television weather reporter**

2 Focus: talking about what one would do or change if one were a teacher for a day

Say:

Now pretend you could be a teacher for one day. Raise your hand when you are ready to tell us what you would try to do or change during the day you were the teacher.

Encourage all children to have a turn.

319

MATERIALS*

ACTIVITY 1

Cards

Stories (optional)

355 361 362 363 364 365 366 367 368

Teacher provides

Blank cassette

Tape recorder

ACTIVITY 2

None

1 Focus: retelling the story "P. Mooney and Mr. Nobody," and then telling the story backwards

Say:

One story we have not talked about for a long time is "P. Mooney and Mr. Nobody." Let's take turns telling it now.

When the plot of the story has been retold, say:

Suppose Mr. Nobody forgot to take his blue medicine one day, and his body parts began to disappear in the opposite order from which they appeared. Let's make up and record a story about what happened. Then we will listen to our story.

Choose a child to start the story as you record it. Continue calling on children until as many as possible have contributed. Then play the recording for the group to hear. Praise all reasonable efforts.

VARIATION: To make the activity *easier,* display in reverse order the cards listed under Materials.

2 Focus: evaluating and correcting statements about body parts in a true-false game

Say:

Let's play a true-false game. I will whisper something to each of you. You are to tell the group what I say. Then everyone will tell whether what you say is true or false.

Have the children take turns standing by you. Use the statements given below. Then have the group or individuals answer in a sentence such as "No, a finger is not part of the foot" or "Yes, a finger is part of the hand."

1. **A finger is part of the hand.**
2. **A foot is part of the arm.**
3. **A nose is part of the face.**
4. **A head is part of the body.**
5. **An ankle is part of the leg.**
6. **A fingernail is part of the foot.**
7. **A heel is part of the foot.**
8. **An ear is part of the hand.**
9. **A knee is part of the arm.**
10. **An elbow is part of the arm.**
11. **A thumb is part of the foot.**
12. **A wrist is part of the arm.**
13. **Eyes are part of the face.**
14. **Teeth are part of the mouth.**
15. **A shoulder is part of the leg.**
16. **A tongue is part of the mouth.**
17. **A thigh is part of the arm.**
18. **A leg is part of the body.**
19. **A face is part of the head.**
20. **A knuckle is part of the nose.**

VARIATION: To make the activity *harder,* have the children make up their own statements.

320

MATERIALS*

ACTIVITY 1

None

ACTIVITY 2

None

1 Focus: brainstorming actions, vehicles, and workers

Say:

Let's see how fast you can name actions, vehicles, and people who are workers.

Call on children by saying, "Name three (actions), (Brady)." Vary the requests for actions, vehicles, and workers. Always give the child's name last, and praise all reasonable efforts.

VARIATIONS: To change the level of difficulty, request more or fewer than three items per turn.

2 Focus: talking about not being able to open one's mouth for an entire day

Ask:

What would it be like if you couldn't open your mouth for a whole day? Think about the things you would not be able to do or would have trouble doing. Raise your hand when you are ready to answer.

Lead a discussion of this situation. See that everyone has a chance to participate. Stress the use of sentences.

VARIATION: To make the activity *harder,* have the group discuss what would be good, bad, and dangerous about this situation.

Keep in Mind . . .
After each lesson in the program, individuals who have difficulty demonstrating proficiency in the skills you consider appropriate and important for them to learn should be tutored. Aides could help you with this task.

321

MATERIALS*

ACTIVITY 1

Cards

Foods

95 97 103 106
107 120 123 124
125 126 129 130
135

ACTIVITY 2

None

1 Focus: naming prepared foods and describing how they originally looked

Stack the 13 food cards.

Show card 106, and say:

Let's think about this picture. What does it show? (Pause) **Yes, it shows two fried eggs. What did these eggs look like before someone decided to fry them?** (Discuss) **What was done to make them look like this picture?**

Summarize the main points discussed before showing the next card. Continue with the remaining cards.

2 Focus: completing statements which relate parts of things to wholes

Say:

Let's do some more thinking. I will read some sentences about parts of things, but I will leave off the last word of each sentence. Listen carefully and tell me what the last word should be.

Call on individuals to complete the sentences listed below. From time to time, repeat those with which the group had difficulty.

1. **A leaf is part of a _______ .** (plant, flower, tree)
2. **A page is part of a _______ .** (book, paper)
3. **A knob is part of a _______ .** (door)
4. **A window is part of a _______ .** (house, building)
5. **A sleeve is part of a _______ .** (coat, blouse, dress, shirt)
6. **A pedal is part of a _______ .** (bicycle, tricycle)
7. **A feather is part of a _______ .** (bird)
8. **A branch is part of a _______ .** (tree)
9. **A wing is part of a _______ .** (bird, airplane)
10. **A wheel is part of a _______ .** (vehicle, car, truck, etc.)
11. **An oven is part of a _______ .** (stove)
12. **A zipper is part of a _______ .** (jacket, pants, coat)
13. **A seed is part of a _______ .** (plant)
14. **Whiskers are part of a _______ .** (cat, animal, a man's face)
15. **A sail is part of a _______ .** (boat)
16. **A propeller is part of an _______ .** (airplane)
17. **An engine is part of a _______ .** (car, truck, airplane, lawnmower)
18. **A crust is part of a _______ .** (pie, loaf of bread)
19. **A pocket is part of a _______ .** (coat, jacket, pants)
20. **A blade is part of a _______ .** (knife)

322

MATERIALS*

ACTIVITY 1

Display Board
4 ledges
Poster 5

ACTIVITY 2

Display Board
4 ledges
Poster 5

1 Focus: talking about why various things might be happening on the poster "Winter Scene"

Use the ledges to display the poster on the board.

Point to the poster and say:

Let's talk again about this winter scene. I want you to think about and explain why certain things are happening in the picture.

Point to the item mentioned as you ask each question listed below. Call on individuals in turn to answer. Accept all reasonable responses.

Why do you think . . .

1. **the cat is on the fence?**
2. **the ambulance is there?**
3. **the man is carrying the little child on his shoulders?**
4. **the girl at the fire is wearing dark glasses?**
5. **the two people are helping the other person work?**
6. **there are so many birds flying?**
7. **the house has bells around it?**
8. **the TV truck and crew are there?**
9. **the boy pulling the sled threw a snowball at the girl?**
10. **the skier has only one leg?**
11. **the people on the snowmobile have stopped?**
12. **there is a basket next to the fire?**
13. **the girl's dog is wearing a sweater?**
14. **the man is taking a picture?**
15. **the boy fell off the toboggan?**

2 Focus: counting items on the poster "Winter Scene" to answer "how-many" questions

Leave the poster from Activity 1 on display.

Say:

Now let's count some of the things in our poster. How many (rabbits) do you see in this poster, (Lydia)? Tell us in a sentence.

The child should respond in a sentence like "There are (two rabbits) in the poster." Then lead the group in counting the (rabbits) as you point to them. Continue as above with these pictured items:

1. **snowmen**
2. **people wearing jackets or coats with hoods**
3. **people wearing hats**
4. **things with four legs**
5. **things that move on runners**
6. **things with wheels**
7. **animals with hoofs**
8. **people riding**
9. **people cooking**
10. **people skating**
11. **people throwing**
12. **people skiing**

323

MATERIALS*

ACTIVITY 1

None

ACTIVITY 2

Audiocassette 3

Side A, Selection 5, "Sounds of People – Actions"

1 Focus: making up and telling stories about pairs of sounds

Say:

Today let's make up stories. I will mention two sounds that you might hear. Think about them for a minute, and then make up a short story about what might have happened. When I call on you, tell us your story. Here are the first two sounds: a jet airplane taking off (imitate the sound) **and then a loud crash of thunder.**

Call on several children to tell different short stories about these two sounds. Then repeat this procedure, using the following or other pairs of sounds. Encourage each child to take a turn, giving hints as necessary. Praise all reasonable efforts.

1. **a door creaking and then soft footsteps**
2. **the wind howling loudly and house shutters banging**
3. **fire-engine siren wailing and the loud crackling of a fire**
4. **a bumping sound and a knock at the door**

OPTIONAL: Summarize each story after the child finishes.

2 Focus: listening to "Sounds of People — Actions," identifying each, and talking about why each sound might happen

Have the children sit on the floor or on rugs. Say:

Let's pretend that you are asleep in a strange house. Lie down, everyone. (Pause) **Everything in the house is very dark. It is the middle of the night. Suddenly you wake up. You heard a sound like this. . . .**

Play the first sound effect. Then whisper in a surprised voice:

Sit up! (Pause) **What was that?** (Encourage several responses) **Yes, it was the sound of someone clapping. Why would someone be clapping in the middle of the night?** (Discuss) **Now lie back, everyone. Let's listen for another sound.**

Continue with the remaining sound effects. End by asking the children whether they have ever heard any of these sounds in the middle of the night, and talking about their experience if they have.

324

MATERIALS*

ACTIVITY 1

Cards

Numerals & Color Shapes

284-293

ACTIVITY 2

Display Board

4 ledges

Poster 5

1 Focus: identifying numbers from one to 10 from rhyming words, then identifying rhyming words from numbers

Stack the 10 numeral cards in order.

Say:

Let's play our rhyming game with numbers again. First, let's look at the number cards and count aloud from one to 10.

Hold up the cards in order, one by one, as you lead the children in counting. Then continue:

Now let's count backwards from 10 to one as we look at the number cards.

Lead the class in doing so. Then present the following questions in random order, calling on individuals to answer:

What number rhymes with . . .

1. ***run?***
2. ***glue?***
3. ***bee?***
4. ***snore?***
5. ***dive?***
6. ***mix?***
7. ***heaven?***
8. ***late?***
9. ***pine?***
10. ***pen?***

Continue by saying:

When I call on you, tell me a word that rhymes with the number I say.

Present numbers from one to 10 in random order. The children you call on should respond by naming a rhyming word in a sentence.

2 Focus: talking about what the poster "Winter Scene" would look like in summer

Use the ledges to display the poster on the board.

Point to the poster and say:

Look at this picture of a winter scene. Let's talk about how the scene on this poster would look if it were summertime.

Ask the following questions as you point to the appropriate items on the poster. Give everyone a chance to participate, and accept all reasonable responses. Stress the use of sentences.

What do you think . . .

1. **the hillsides and the lake would look like?**
2. **the people would be wearing?**
3. **the people would be doing? What kinds of sports and games might they be playing?**
4. **the people might be eating?**
5. **the vehicles would be?**
6. **the trees, plants, and animals would look like?**

325

MATERIALS*

ACTIVITY 1

None

ACTIVITY 2

None

1 Focus: listening to compound words, and identifying the two short words in each

Say:

Today let's take apart some more long words that each contain two short words. Raise your hand when you can tell me the two short words in each long word my helper says.

Ask a child to stand beside you as a helper. Whisper a word from the list below for the child to say to the group. When someone has identified the two short words, call on other children to define each of them.

1. afternoon	**10. footprint**
2. anyone	**11. grasshopper**
3. bathroom	**12. homework**
4. basketball	**13. indoors**
5. baseball	**14. seesaw**
6. firecracker	**15. sometime**
7. fireman	**16. somebody**
8. flashlight	**17. suitcase**
9. football	**18. upstairs**

2 Focus: listening to sentences containing compound words in which the order of the short words is reversed, identifying the "backwards" words, and correcting the sentences

Say:

Now let's try to figure out long words that are said backwards and used in sentences. Here's the first one: "I must do my workhome tonight." What word is backwards? (Pause) **You are right. *Homework* is the backwards word. Now let's say the sentence together correctly.**

Lead the group in saying, "I must do my *homework* tonight." Continue as above with the following sentences. Give everyone a turn.

1. **In the *noonafter*, my little brother takes a nap.**
2. **Is there *oneany* here who can jump rope?**
3. **There's a bug in the *roombath*!**
4. **My big sister is a *ballbasket* player.**
5. **I have lost my *ballbase* glove.**
6. **The *crackerfire* went off with a loud bang!**
7. **The *fighterfire* used the hose to spray the burning building.**
8. **I used a *lightflash* to look in the dark closet.**
9. **The *ballfoot* soared between the goalposts.**
10. **He spied a mysterious *printfoot* in the mud.**
11. **I found a *hoppergrass* in the bucket.**
12. **When we go on vacation, I pack my *casesuit*.**
13. **There is a *sawsee* at the park playground.**
14. **I would like to go to the beach, *timesome*.**
15. **Will *bodysome* please pass the milk?**
16. **When it rains, we have to play *doorsin*.**
17. **Go *stairsup* and bring me a blanket.**

If more practice is necessary, repeat items from Activity 2 of lesson 303.

326

MATERIALS*

ACTIVITY 1

Cards

Pictures from Several Categories

12 15 21 251 252 265

267-283

ACTIVITY 2

Cards

Pictures from Several Categories

12* 15* 21* 251* 252* 269* 265* 275*

1 Focus: classifying kinds of transportation which do and do not require gasoline or diesel fuel

Display the 23 picture cards in random order on a chalkledge.

Point to the cards and say:

These pictures all show ways to move from one place to another. Let's figure out which ones use gasoline or diesel fuel, and which do not.

Discuss each pictured item, separating the cards into users and non-users of gasoline and diesel fuel. Then point to the fuel-using vehicles and continue:

Now let's talk about how much fuel these vehicles need. Tell me which vehicle would need the most fuel, and why you think so.

Call on several children, and accept all reasonable responses. Then continue with these questions:

Which vehicle . . .

1. **uses the least fuel? Why?**
2. **could carry the most persons? Why?**
3. **could go the longest distance? Why?**
4. **have you traveled in? Why?**

2 Focus: talking about how non-users of gasoline or diesel fuel move, and then brainstorming other ways of moving

Display the eight cards in random order on a chalkledge.

Point to the cards and say:

Now let's talk about how each of these items moves. Think about what kinds of energy they use.

Discuss each card in turn with the children. Then continue:

Now let's talk about other ways to travel that do not use gasoline or diesel fuel.

Lead the children in brainstorming such means of transportation as walking, skis, snowshoes, canoes, gliders, hang gliders, skateboards, and balloons.

327

MATERIALS*

ACTIVITY 1

None

ACTIVITY 2

None

1 Focus: completing short stories by predicting what might happen in a variety of situations

Say:

Let's do some thinking. I will read part of a very short story. When I call on you, tell us what might happen to finish the story.

One at a time, present the following situations. The children you call on should respond in sentences and use the right verb forms. Encourage a variety of endings in each case.

1. **Carlotta went to play at her friend's house. She took her shoes off because it was hot. When she got ready to go home, she could not remember where her shoes were. What do you think happened?**
2. **Steve had to use a wheelchair because he couldn't walk. His class took a trip to a bakery. Steps led up to the front door. What do you think happened?**
3. **Bethany had borrowed a picture book from the school library. On the day the book was supposed to be returned, Bethany could not find it. What do you think happened?**
4. **The teacher announced that all the quiet children in the room were going to have a snack. Alvin was busy talking to Charles. What do you think happened?**
5. **Margaret accidentally locked the door to her house, and she could not get inside because she did not have a key. What do you think happened?**
6. **It was a cold day. Philip put on his jacket, but the zipper was broken. What do you think happened?**
7. **It was Mother's birthday. Coretta was going to wrap Mother's gift. She discovered there was no wrapping paper. What do you think happened?**
8. **All of the children were going to make a decoration for the class party. Donald did not listen to the teacher's directions. What do you think happened?**
9. **Mother was going to make sandwiches for lunch. There was not enough bread. What do you think happened?**
10. **Some children were playing ball beside a busy street. The ball rolled into the street. What do you think happened?**

2 Focus: brainstorming living and non-living things

Say:

Let's play a thinking game about things that are living. A living thing uses food and grows. Plants and animals are living things. Let's see how fast you can name things that are *living*. When I point to you, name a living thing.

Call on children in random order. Give everyone at least two turns. Then continue by calling for things that are not living.

VARIATION: To make the activity *easier,* name animals, plants, and non-living objects for children to identify in a sentence as living or non-living.

328

MATERIALS*

ACTIVITY 1

None

ACTIVITY 2

None

1 Focus: comparing units of time and talking about whether it takes a year or a minute to do certain activities

Say:

Let's talk about time again. Sometimes we say that it takes us a minute to do something. Other times we say it takes us a year. Which is longer — a year or a minute? (Pause) **Yes, a year is longer than a minute.**

Discuss. Then have the children respond in sentences to questions like these:

Does it take about a minute or a year . . .

1. **to rinse an apple?**
2. **to go from one birthday to another?**
3. **to turn to the right television station?**
4. **for a kitten to become a cat?**
5. **to tie your shoes?**
6. **to go from one summer to the next?**
7. **to light a candle with a match?**
8. **for you to grow two or three inches?**
9. **to button your shirt?**
10. **to look at a birthday card?**
11. **to clean the windshield of a car?**
12. **for you to grow out of a jacket?**
13. **to zip your jacket?**
14. **to dial a telephone number?**
15. **to grow tall enough to reach the water faucet?**
16. **to put on a pair of shorts?**
17. **to fill a glass with milk?**
18. **for the legs of your jeans to be too short?**

2 Focus: describing what one usually is doing at certain times of the day

Say:

We usually do certain things at the same time each day. Let's think about what we usually do at 12 o'clock noon.

The children you call on should respond in sentences such as "At noontime we usually eat our lunch." Continue with questions like these:

What are we usually doing at . . .

1. **12 o'clock midnight?**
2. **9 o'clock in the morning?**
3. **2 o'clock in the afternoon?**
4. **6 o'clock at night?**
5. **4:30 o'clock in the afternoon?**
6. **3 o'clock in the morning?**
7. **7:30 o'clock in the morning?**
8. **9 o'clock at night?**

VARIATION: To make the activity *easier,* don't specify the hour when you ask children what they do at various points in the day.

329

MATERIALS*

ACTIVITY 1

Display Board

4 ledges

Poster 1

ACTIVITY 2

Cards

Animals

7 8 9 10 11 12
13 14 18 20 21 22
23 27 28 29 31 32
36

Music

336

Audiocassette 2

Side B, Song 11, "Round Dance"

1 Focus: predicting and talking about "what would happen if. . . ?" using the poster "Farm in Spring"

Use the ledges to display the poster on the board.

Say:

Let's use the poster "Farm in Spring" to play the game What Would Happen If. . .? Look at P. Mooney pitching hay from the hayloft. The loft is the attic or top floor of the barn. (Point) **What would happen if he lost his balance and slid down into the loft?**

Encourage discussion, and accept all responses. Continue with these imaginary situations:

What do you think would happen if . . .

1. **the dog chased the cat?**
2. **the dragonfly flew into the spider's web?**
3. **the goat tried to butt the calf?**
4. **the fox tried to catch the duckling?**
5. **the baby raccoon played with the hornets' nest?**
6. **the butterfly landed on the turtle's nose?**
7. **the frog jumped into the boy's overalls?**
8. **the tractor rolled backwards downhill?**
9. **lightning struck the barn?**
10. **the goose tried to catch the turtle?**
11. **the horses stopped and wouldn't let the farmer lead them?**
12. **the turkey pecked the colt?**
13. **the hen laid an egg outside?**
14. **the bull broke through the fence?**

2 Focus: imitating barnyard noises to the music "Round Dance" in a stop-go listening game

Display the 19 animal cards on a chalkledge.

Let each child choose a card. Have the children stand in a circle as you hold the music card and say:

Let's play a game called "Barnyard Noises." I will be the farmer, and you will be the barnyard animals. Put your animal card on the floor in front of you. When the music begins, join hands and circle the barnyard animals. When the music ends, stop and look at the card in front of you. Make the noise which that animal makes. When the music starts, circle the cards again.

Play the music as the children move. Then lift the needle, and have the children all make their sounds at once. Then go around the circle and have each child in turn make his or her sound. Encourage the children to enjoy themselves. Continue as time and interest suggest.

330

MATERIALS*

ACTIVITY 1

None

ACTIVITY 2

None

1 Focus: evaluating whether certain things can happen *anytime, sometimes,* or *never*

Say:

Today let's talk about things that happen *all the time, sometimes,* or *never.* These words and phrases tell us how often certain things take place. I will name something that happens. Tell me if it happens *all the time, sometimes,* or *never.*

Use the statements listed below. For the first two or three, have the group respond. Then let individuals answer in sentences such as "We breathe all the time." The children you call on should explain those statements for which the correct answer is "sometimes" or "never."

1. **We breathe.**
2. **We play in the snow.**
3. **We climb stairs.**
4. **We hear.**
5. **We can read when we are born.**
6. **We ride in a car.**
7. **A leopard has spots.**
8. **Trees lose their leaves.**
9. **A baby grows.**
10. **We smell with our nose.**
11. **A cat has kittens.**
12. **A hen lays eggs.**
13. **We fly using our arms as wings.**
14. **We sleep.**
15. **Water is wet.**
16. **The wind blows.**
17. **It's dark at night.**
18. **We know how to talk, when we are born.**
19. **We see.**
20. **The earth stops turning.**

2 Focus: using riddles to identify words that have multiple meanings

Say:

Today let's talk about words that sound the same but have more than one meaning. I will tell you the two meanings of each word. You are to tell me what word I am talking about.

Here's the first one: It is the outer covering of a tree. It is the sound a dog makes. What word is it? (Pause) **You are right! The word is *bark.***

Continue as above with the following statements. Each child should participate.

1. **It is a word that describes the highest part of something. It is a toy that spins around very fast. What word is it?** (top)
2. **It is something very hard which you can find on the ground. It is the word for what you do in a rocking chair. What word is it?** (rock)
3. **It is an animal that swims and quacks. It is the word for what you do when you walk under something low. What word is it?** (duck)
4. **It is a front part of your body between your shoulders and your waist. It is a piece of furniture in which you put clothes. What word is it?** (chest)
5. **It is the part of your body which is behind your chest. It is a word which is the opposite of the word *front.* What word is it?** (back)
6. **It is an animal that looks like a mouse with wings. It is a strong wooden stick with which you can hit a ball. What word is it?** (bat)
7. **It is a large growly animal with thick brown hair. It is a word that describes you when you have no clothes on. What word is it?** (bear, bare)

8. **It is the color of the sky. It is the word for what you might have done yesterday to make a balloon bigger. What word is it?** (blue, blew)

9. **It is a word that means to have something on your body. It is a word that tells you the place that something can be found. What word is it?** (wear, where)

10. **It is the part of your body which helps you smell. It is a word that tells you someone is very sure about something. What word is it?** (nose, knows)

VARIATION: To make the activity *harder,* have the children make up and say sentences using the different meanings of the words.

331 

MATERIALS*

ACTIVITY 1

Cards

Music

327

Stories

386-398

Audiocassette 1

Side A, Story 4, "The Elephant that Did Not Know How to Listen"

Audiocassette 2

Side A, Song 5, "Elbert's Song"

ACTIVITY 2

Cards

Stories

386-398

Display Board

6 ledges

1 Focus: listening to the story "The Elephant That Did Not Know How To Listen," answering questions, and singing "Elbert's Song"

Hold the 13 story cards and say:

Today I am going to read the story of Elbert the Elephant. Who is Elbert? (Pause) **You're right. Elbert is the elephant that did not know how to listen. Please listen closely, because I will ask you questions afterwards.**

Read the story from the backs of the cards, and then call on children to answer questions like these:

1. **What was Elbert's problem?**
2. **How did P. Mooney help Elbert?**
3. **Why is it important to be able to listen and to understand?**
4. **How would we look if we all wore ear elevators? After the discussion, end by playing song 5 and having the group listen to "Elbert's Song" and sing the chorus. Repeat as time and interest permit.**

VARIATION: If you prefer, play the recorded story instead of reading it aloud.

2 Focus: acting out the story "The Elephant That Did Not Know How To Listen"

Hold the 13 story cards and say:

Now let's act out Elbert's story. Looking at the story cards will help us remember what happened.

Place card 386 on the far left side, top row, of the board. Choose a child to act out the action shown on that card. Continue with the remaining cards in order. Praise all efforts.

VARIATION: To make the activity *harder,* do not use the story cards.

332

MATERIALS*

ACTIVITY 1

None

ACTIVITY 2

None

1 Focus: completing statements which relate parts of things to wholes

Say:

Let's do some thinking. I will read a sentence about parts of things, but I will leave off the last word. Listen carefully, and tell me how the sentence should end.

Call on children to complete these statements:

1. **A paddle is part of a _______ .**
   (canoe, rowboat)
2. **A lid is part of a _______ .**
   (pan, box)
3. **A stem is part of a _______ .**
   (flower, plant)
4. **A button is part of a _______ .**
   (shirt, blouse, coat)
5. **A faucet is part of a _______ .**
   (sink, bathtub)
6. **A siren is part of a(n) _______ .**
   (ambulance, police car)
7. **A page is part of a _______ .**
   (book)
8. **A floor is part of a _______ .**
   (room, building)
9. **A leaf is part of a _______ .**
   (flower, plant, tree)
10. **A bristle is part of a _______ .**
    (brush)
11. **A burner is part of a _______ .**
    (stove)
12. **A caboose is part of a _______ .**
    (train)
13. **A trombone is part of a(n) _______ .**
    (band, orchestra)
14. **A horn is part of a(n) _______ .**
    (animal, vehicle, band)
15. **A bulb is part of a _______ .**
    (lamp, light fixture, flower)
16. **A roof is part of a _______ .**
    (building)
17. **An eraser is part of a _______ .**
    (pencil)
18. **A root is part of a _______ .**
    (plant, tree)
19. **Frosting is part of a _______ .**
    (cake, cookie)
20. **A frame is part of a _______ .**
    (picture)

VARIATION: To make this activity *harder,* have the children name other parts for each item.

2 Focus: brainstorming things that have handles

Say:

Many things have a part called a *handle*. Let's see how many of them we can name. When I point to you, tell us one thing that has a handle. Try to name something no one else has named.

Help as necessary.

OPTIONAL: Tally responses on a chalkboard, and end by having the children count the items named and discuss the results.

333

MATERIALS*

ACTIVITY 1

Fruits & vegetables
All

ACTIVITY 2

None

1 Focus: comparing fruits and vegetables by *texture, length, shape, color,* and *size*

Spread out the fruits and vegetables on a table or the floor. Have the children sit around the items. Say:

Let's talk about these fruits and vegetables. I have some questions to ask about them.

The children you call on should use sentences to answer these and similar questions:

1. **Which is longer — the banana, or the carrot?**
2. **Which has more prickly leaves — the pineapple, or the strawberry?**
3. **Which is smoother — the tomato, or the onion?**
4. **Which is rounder — the apple, or the orange?**
5. **Which has more colors — the pear, or the tomato?**
6. **Which is seedier — the onion, or the strawberry?**
7. **Which is rougher — the orange, or the pineapple?**
8. **Which is fuzzier — the peach, or the lemon?**
9. **Which is thicker — the carrot, or the corn?**
10. **Which is more pointed — the carrot, or the lemon?**
11. **Which is wider at the bottom — the apple, or the pear?**
12. **Which is bumpier — the corn, or the potato?**
13. **Which is sweeter — the apple, or the lemon?**
14. **Which is thinner — the corn, or the banana?**
15. **Which is smellier — the lemon, or the onion?**
16. **Which is shorter — the carrot, or the banana?**
17. **Which is smaller — the potato, or the pineapple?**
18. **Which is redder — the strawberry, or the tomato?**
19. **Which is leafier — the tomato, or the corn?**
20. **Which is softer — the banana, or the potato?**

2 Focus: talking about other possibilities for P. Mooney's first name

Say:

P. Mooney's name has two parts: "P." and "Mooney." Do you think his first name might be something different from "P"? (Pause) **Let's talk about what it might be.**

Accept all responses. Then ask the children to tell as many names as they can that start with the sound of "P," such as Paul, Pedro, Patrick, Peter, etc. Lead the group in saying each suggested first name with the last name, like this: "Patrick Mooney."

334

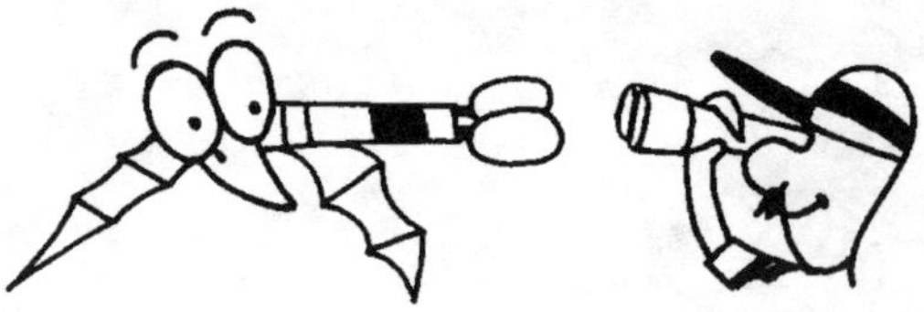

MATERIALS*

ACTIVITY 1

None

ACTIVITY 2

None

1 Focus: thinking of and naming four things from requested categories, and then classifying them

Say:

Let's play a thinking game. I will ask someone to tell you three words that go together. Try to figure out what word or phrase describes all four words.

Choose a child to stand beside you. Whisper to that person:

(Linda), tell everyone the names of four animals. (Pause) **Class, what word or phrase describes the four things that (Linda) named?**

Help as necessary. When the group has responded correctly, continue with other children, using the list given below. Each child should have a turn.

1. animals
2. actions
3. body parts
4. cars
5. colors
6. foods
7. fruits
8. household items
9. names
10. numbers
11. people
12. toys
13. shapes
14. vegetables
15. vehicles

2 Focus: talking about flying like a bird

Say:

Let's suppose everyone could fly the way birds fly. What would it be like?

Encourage everyone to participate in the discussion. As necessary, help by asking questions like these:

1. **What would you be able to see?**
2. **Where would you go if you could fly?**
3. **What games would you play if you and all your friends could fly?**
4. **Where might you sleep and eat if you flew far away?**
5. **What kind of traffic rules would be needed if everyone could fly?**
6. **What other things would we do differently from the way we do them now?**

335

MATERIALS*

ACTIVITY 1

Cards

Foods

94-152

ACTIVITY 2

None

1 Focus: classifying foods by various characteristics

Arrange the 59 food cards on the floor or along a chalkledge where the children can easily see them.

Point to the cards and say:

Look at all of these pictures of foods. I will ask you to go up and pick out the pictures of foods that are alike or the same in a certain way. After you have arranged them together over here (indicate area of chalkledge), **I will ask you to name them and explain why they belong in that group.**

Use the list given below. After the correct selection has been made, call on several children in turn to name the items in a sentence like this: "The foods that are (salty) are (bacon, ham, popcorn, potato chips, and pretzels)." Return the selected cards to the full group each time.

1. **buttery**
2. **cold**
3. **cooked**
4. **crunchy**
5. **fruit**
6. **hot**
7. **leafy**
8. **liquid**
9. **meat**
10. **raw**
11. **salty**
12. **seedy**
13. **sticky**
14. **sweet**
15. **vegetables**

2 Focus: deciding whether a statement about foods is true, and then following directions if the statement is true

Ask the children to stand before you. Say:

Now let's play a thinking-and-following-directions game. I will say a sentence. If what I say is correct, then follow the direction. If what I say is not correct, then stand still.

Use the list given below. If any children have difficulty, repeat the direction until everyone responds correctly. Each time, call on individuals to explain what they did and why.

1. **If bacon, ham, and hamburger are meat, then cross your legs.**
2. **If tomatoes, strawberries, and bananas all are red, then put your hands on your head.**
3. **If candy, jam, and honey all taste sweet, then nod your head.**
4. **If oranges, peaches, and peanut butter all are juicy, then put your hands on your feet.**
5. **If you can drink milk, soda pop, and spaghetti, then clap your hands.**
6. **If nuts, carrots, and potato chips are crunchy, then make a happy face.**
7. **If soup, pancakes, and fried eggs all are served warm, then turn around.**
8. **If a taco, an onion, and a pear all are fruits, then say, "Super!"**
9. **If you can drink chocolate milk, jello, and orange juice, then close your eyes.**
10. **If popcorn, pretzels, and potato chips all are salty, then raise your arms over your head.**
11. **If milk, ice cream, and butter all are stored in the refrigerator, then touch your nose to your knee.**
12. **If pineapples, watermelons, and peaches all are fruits, then wiggle your fingers.**
13. **If cheese, crackers, and soda pop all come in a bottle, then snap your fingers.**
14. **If pineapples, watermelons, and pumpkins all have hard outer coverings, then touch your toes with your hands.**
15. **If potatoes, cookies, and cake all can be baked in the oven, then say, "Hooray!"**

16. If grapes, bananas, and apples all grow in bunches, then nod your head.

17. If onions, carrots, and lettuce all are vegetables, then say, "Wow!"

18. If pumpkins, corn, and oranges all are orange, then stamp your feet.

19. If soup, milk, and juice all are liquid, then jump up.

20. If you like ice cream, then say, "P. Mooney."

VARIATION: To make this activity *easier,* reduce the number of foods in each command from three to two.

336

MATERIALS*

ACTIVITY 1

None

ACTIVITY 2

Audiocassette 3

Side B, Selection 2, "Sounds of Toys"

1 Focus: making up and telling stories about pairs of sounds

Say:

Today let's make up stories. I will tell you two sounds we might hear. Think about them for a minute, and then make up a short story about what might have happened. When I call on you, tell us your story. Here are the first two sounds: a telephone ringing and someone running.

Have several children each tell a short story about these two sounds. Continue with the following pairs of sounds. Each child should have a turn.

1. **police sirens, screeching tires**
2. **a band playing, a puppy yelping**
3. **skates swishing, a loud crack**
4. **a man snoring, a door closing very softly**
5. **a bell ringing, a child running**

OPTIONAL: To set good storytelling models, summarize the children's efforts.

2 Focus: listening to "Sounds of Toys," identifying each and talking about how one would play with each of the toys if one could not see

Say:

Pretend you are blind and cannot see your toys; you can only hear them. Now close your eyes and pretend that you are playing with your toys. Try to figure out which toy would sound like this.

Play the "Sounds of Toys". Then ask:

What was that? (Encourage unison response) **Yes, it was a ball. How would you play with a ball if you could not see?** (Encourage imaginative responses) **Let's close our eyes again and listen to another sound.**

Continue with the remaining sound effects.

337

MATERIALS*

ACTIVITY 1

Display Board
4 ledges

Poster 4

ACTIVITY 2

Display Board
4 ledges

Poster 4

1 Focus: talking about how things on the poster "City in Summer" work

Use the ledges to display the poster on the board.

Point to the poster and say:

Look at this picture of the city in summer. Let's talk about how certain things work that we see in this big picture.

Ask the following questions as you point to the right items on the poster. Give everyone a chance to participate, and accept all reasonable responses. Stress the use of sentences.

How do you think . . .

1. **the mail carrier gets the mail out of the box?**
2. **the fire escape works?**
3. **the fire fighter's mask works?**
4. **the jackhammer works?**
5. **the flowers in the containers are watered?**
6. **the painters get up to the sign and back down to the ground?**
7. **the merry-go-round goes around?**
8. **the clothes get hung up and taken down?**
9. **the streets are kept clean?**
10. **the people get to their work places in the top floors of the skyscrapers?**
11. **the fire fighter turns the hydrant on and off?**
12. **the used furniture gets into the store?**
13. **the street-light bulbs are changed?**
14. **the windows get cleaned on the tall buildings?**
15. **the crane works?**

2 Focus: remembering and naming what is on the poster "City in Summer"

Leave the poster from Activity 1 on display.

Say:

Now let's play a remembering game. (Fold poster to back of board) **Name four things you remember are on the poster "City in Summer," (Scott).**

Call on children in random order. Encourage everyone to name items not already cited. End by displaying the poster as the children name things they had not remembered.

VARIATIONS: To change the level of difficulty, ask for more or fewer than four items per request.

338

MATERIALS*

ACTIVITY 1

None

ACTIVITY 2

None

1 Focus: talking about riding on a cloud

Ask:

What is a cloud? (Discuss) **Yes, a cloud is made of tiny drops of water, and it floats high in the sky. Do you think a person could float on a cloud?** (Encourage responses) **Well, just for today, let's pretend that we are light as a feather and are floating on a cloud. If you looked down from your cloud, what might you see far below?**

Call on several children to respond. Continue with questions like these:

1. **What do you think the people and animals would look like?**
2. **Would you be able to see cars and buses?**
3. **What would houses and buildings look like?**
4. **What kind of land might you see below?** (ocean, desert, mountains, islands)
5. **What might it be like to meet another cloud?**
6. **How would you make the cloud come down to earth so you could get off?**

2 Focus: following directions which stress the words *before, after,* and *while*

Have the children stand in front of their chairs. Say:

Let's play a following-directions game to see if you remember what the words *before, while,* and *after* mean. Listen carefully to my directions.

Give the following and similar directions. Explain, repeat, or demonstrate as necessary to aid the children in understanding *before, after,* and *while.*

1. **Clap your hands *before* you sit down.**
2. ***While* you are sitting down, breathe fast.**
3. **Close your eyes *after* you stand up.**
4. **Blink your eyes *before* you sit down.**
5. **Rub your hands *while* you are sitting.**
6. **Jump up *after* you stand up.**
7. **Turn around *before* you sit down.**
8. **Snap your fingers *after* you stand up.**
9. ***While* you stand, nod your head.**
10. **Say hello *after* you sit down.**
11. **Stamp your feet *before* you stand up.**
12. ***While* you stand, smile.**
13. **Hop on one foot *before* you sit down.**
14. **Clap your hands *after* you stand up.**
15. **Slide your feet back and forth *while* you stand.**

VARIATION: To make this activity *easier,* always place *before, after,* or *while* at the beginning of the commands.

339 

MATERIALS*

ACTIVITY 1

None

ACTIVITY 2

None

1 Focus: imagining and talking about being absent from Earth for many years and then coming back

Say:

Let's imagine that you traveled in a rocket ship to a star so far away that you needed many years to go there and get back. When you returned to Earth, you had grown into an adult. Let's think about what things here on Earth might be like then. How old would you be, and what might you look like?

Encourage everyone to join in the discussion. As necessary, help with questions like these:

1. **What might have happened to your family?**
2. **How might your home have changed?**
3. **What kinds of programs might be shown on TV?**
4. **How might you travel?**

2 Focus: listening to sentences containing compound words in which the order of the short words is reversed, identifying the "backwards" words, and correcting the sentences

Say:

Now let's play a listening game. Try to figure out what long word is being said backwards in this sentence: "The cat quietly watched the *trapmouse*." What word is backwards? (Pause) **You're right. *Trapmouse* is the backwards word. Now let's all say the sentence correctly.**

Lead the children in saying, "The cat quietly watched the *mousetrap*."

Continue with the sentences listed below.

1. **I ate some *fruitgrape* for breakfast.**
2. **When I was sick, I took a *spoontable* of medicine.**
3. **The *boycow* jumped onto his horse.**
4. **We had a *cakecup* for dessert.**
5. **The children ran to the *groundplay* to play ball.**
6. **Use your *clothwash* to get your face clean.**
7. **I used my children's *bookcook* to make dinner.**
8. **We trained our dog to go get the *papernews*.**
9. **We went outside at night to try to catch a *fly fire*.**
10. **The bear tried to get honey out of the *hivebee*.**
11. **Patrick fell down the *waystair*.**
12. **My sister works in an office and uses a *writertype*.**
13. **The *shinesun* came through my window and woke me up.**
14. **I have a new electric *roadrail* train.**
15. **My brother used his *knifejack* to sharpen the stick.**
16. **I love to *skateroller* on the *walkside*.**

If more practice is needed, repeat the items from Activity 2 of lesson 325.

340

MATERIALS*

ACTIVITY 1

Display Board
2 ledges

Magnetic Shapes
All

ACTIVITY 2

Display Board (optional)

Magnetic Shapes
(optional)
1 large circle
1 large rectangle
1 large square
1 large triangle

1 Focus: classifying magnetic shapes into various groups, and then counting and describing the items in each group

Use the ledges to divide the display board so that two-thirds of it is to the left and one-third is to the right. Place the 60 shapes in random order on the left side of the board.

Say:

Let's see how many ways we can group the magnetic shapes. First find all the shapes that are red and put them on the empty side of the board, (Judy).

When the 12 red shapes have been selected, call on children to answer questions like these:

1. **How many shapes are in this group?**
2. **What are the names of the shapes in this group?**
3. **How many (circles, squares, triangles, rectangles) are in the group?**
4. **Are there some things that are the same in this group? What and how many of each?**
5. **There is one thing about everything in this group that is the same. What is it?**

Continue with these groupings:

1. **all blue shapes**
2. **all green shapes**
3. **all yellow shapes**
4. **all black shapes**
5. **all shapes with straight sides**
6. **all shapes with curved sides**
7. **all shapes with three sides**
8. **all shapes with four sides**
9. **all large shapes**
10. **all small shapes**

Give everyone at least one turn.

2 Focus: brainstorming things shaped like circles, rectangles, squares, and triangles

Say:

Now think of all the things you can that are shaped like circles. Name them as fast as you can.

Encourage quick responses. Continue by asking the class to name rectangular, square, and triangular items, respectively.

VARIATION: To make the activity *easier,* display the four large shapes listed under Materials as clues.

Keep in Mind . . .
After each lesson in the program, individuals who have difficulty demonstrating proficiency in the skills you consider appropriate and important for them to learn should be tutored. Aides could help you with this task.

341

MATERIALS*

ACTIVITY 1

Cards

Household Items

155 156 157 160
161 165 168 170
171 172 176 177
178 180 181 186
188 190 191 193
194 195 197 198

ACTIVITY 2

None

1 Focus: talking about household items and the kind of energy they use

Display the 24 household cards in random order on the chalk/edge.

Point to the cards and say:

Look at these pictures. Let's talk about which of these things use electricity.

Lead the discussion. Divide the cards into two groups: users and non-users of electricity. Then point to the non-users and say:

These household items do not use electrical energy. So let's talk about how they work.

Lead the discussion. Point out that these items depend on human energy. Then discuss questions like the following:

1. **If we did not have electricity, what things would be affected? How might we have light? How might we wash our clothes?**
2. **Which things would we be unable to do?**
3. **Can you think of other electrical household items which we have not talked about?**

If necessary, suggest such possibilities as electric mixer, electric blanket, electric knife, electric toothbrush, electric tools, etc.

2 Focus: imagining and describing new machines

Ask:

What is an inventor? (Pause) **Yes, an inventor is someone who designs or *invents* new things. An inventor of machines designs and builds new machines. Suppose a great inventor of machines were here today. This inventor will build each of us a machine. Think about what kind of machine you would ask the inventor to make for you. When I call on you, tell us what your machine would do and how it might work.**

Encourage imaginative requests.

342

MATERIALS*

ACTIVITY 1

None

ACTIVITY 2

None

1 Focus: deciding whether statements about living things are true, and then following directions if they are true

Say:

Let's play a following-directions game about living things. I will say a sentence which names something which may or may not be alive. If the thing named is living, then do what the sentence tells you to.

Use these sentences:

1. **If a rock is a living thing, then clap your hands.**
2. **If a tulip is a living thing, then shake your head.**
3. **If a turtle is a living thing, then turn around once.**
4. **If a chair is a living thing, then smile a big smile.**
5. **If a toy teddy bear is a living thing, then swing your arms.**
6. **If candy is a living thing, then swing your arms.**
7. **If an ostrich is a living thing, then put your hands on your head.**
8. **If an astronaut is a living thing, then frown a big frown.**
9. **If a window is a living thing, then blink your eyes.**
10. **If a fish is a living thing, then touch your toes.**
11. **If a tree is a living thing, then say, "Yeah."**
12. **If a barn is a living thing, then make a funny face.**
13. **If a cactus is a living thing, then touch your nose.**
14. **If snow is a living thing, then blink your eyes.**
15. **If a camel is a living thing, then wiggle your fingers.**
16. **If a snowperson is a living thing, then stamp your feet.**
17. **If a candle is a living thing, then say, "Bumblebee."**
18. **If a toad is a living thing, then wave your arms over your head.**
19. **If an eraser is a living thing, then pretend to sneeze.**
20. **If a record player is a living thing, then sit on the floor.**

VARIATION: To make the activity *harder,* reverse the two parts of each sentence, like this: "Clap your hands if a rock is a living thing."

2 Focus: brainstorming living and non-living things

Sit in a circle with the children and say:

Now let's think more about living things and things that are not alive. When I say "living things," we will take turns naming things that are alive. But listen very carefully, because when I say "non-living things," you must then name something that is not alive. Let's begin: "living things."

Have the child next to you name a living thing. Then ask the next person to do the same. When four or five children have responded, call for things that are not alive. If feasible, continue until everyone has had at least three turns.

343

MATERIALS*

ACTIVITY 1

Cards

Stories

346

ACTIVITY 2

None

1 Focus: talking about how a tree looks in summer, fall, winter, and spring

Hold card 346 and say:

Look at this tree. What season of the year does this picture show?

After summer has been named, ask:

How do you know it is summer? (Discuss) **What season comes after summer?** (Encourage unison response) **Let's talk about what this tree would look like in the fall.**

Encourage the children to discuss how trees look in autumn. Continue with discussions of winter and spring. End by having the group name the four seasons in sequence: summer, fall, winter, spring.

VARIATION: To make the activity *easier,* discuss only summer and winter. If a discussion of summer, fall, winter, and spring is not applicable to your area, then discuss the seasonal changes that do occur where you live.

2 Focus: imagining and talking about a truckload of objects

Say:

If you could have a truck loaded with anything in the world, what would you choose to fill up the truck? When I call on you, name a choice and tell why.

If necessary, suggest such ideas as candy, shells, marshmallows, toys, money, jewels, or decorated eggs. Encourage the children to use their imaginations and enjoy themselves.

344

MATERIALS*

ACTIVITY 1

Display Board (optional)

4 ledges (optional)

Poster 3 (optional)

Audiocassette 4

Side A, Selection 3, "Department Store"

Teacher provides

Blank cassette

Tape recorder

ACTIVITY 2

None

1 Focus: listening to "Sounds of the Department Store," and then making up a progressive story about a department store

Say:

Close your eyes and imagine where you might hear these sounds.

Play the sounds and ask:

What place would sound like that? (Encourage unison response) **Yes, these sounds are all department store sounds. Let's make up a story about the department store. Everyone will add a sentence to the story. Listen carefully to the persons who speak before you. I will take the first turn.**

Start the tape recorder. Announce a title, and begin the story with a sentence such as "One day my mother surprised me and said, 'Let's get ready to go to the department store.'" Then have each child add one or two sentences to the story. End by playing back the story, and have the group identify each speaker.

VARIATION: To make this activity *easier,* display the poster after the group has identified the recorded sounds.

2 Focus: brainstorming things that can be bought in a department store

Say:

Let's pretend that we are going shopping in a big department store. Think about all the different things you could buy there. When I point to you, tell us your choice. Let's start in the furniture department! What would you buy in that part of the store, (Megan)?

Have several children respond. Continue with other departments such as those listed below. If necessary, define the department names.

1. **book department**
2. **children's clothes department**
3. **jewelry department**
4. **bathroom supplies department**
5. **kitchen utensils department**
6. **restaurant**
7. **luggage department**
8. **china and silverware department**
9. **shoe department**
10. **candy department**
11. **toy department**
12. **sporting supply department**
13. **ladies' clothes department**
14. **gardening and plants department**
15. **hobbies and games department**
16. **men's clothing department**
17. **auto supply department**

345

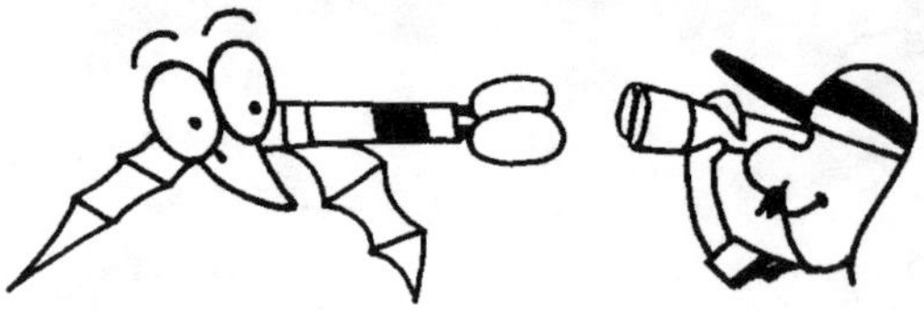

MATERIALS*

ACTIVITY 1

Cards
Stories
451-463

ACTIVITY 2

None

1 **Focus: listening to the story, "P. Mooney and the Gasless Goose," and then summarizing the main points**

Hold the story cards and say:

Let's listen again to the story of P. Mooney's friend Gasless Goose. I will read a little bit of the story, and then I will ask you to tell me that part in your own words.

Look on the back of card 451 and read the first verse of the story. Then call on children to summarize it. Continue with the remaining verses, helping as necessary. Review the meanings of unfamiliar words.

VARIATIONS: To make the activity *harder,* have the children tell the story from memory, assisting only when necessary. To make it *easier,* show the story cards.

2 **Focus: evaluating questions containing two rhyming words, deciding which questions are silly, and answering them**

Say:

The story of Gasless Goose has many words that rhyme. I will ask you some questions using rhyming words. You are to answer each one with a sentence. Here is the first question:

"Did you ever see a *goat* sailing a boat?"

Lead the children in heartily responding, "No, I never saw a goat sailing a boat!" Continue in this way with the questions given below, calling for unison and individual responses. Help only as necessary.

Did you ever see . . .

1. **a *rose* with a *nose*?**
2. **someone *look* at a *book*?**
3. **a *bat* lying on a *mat*?**
4. **a *toy* playing with a *boy*?**
5. **someone getting ready to *bake* a *cake*?**
6. **a *fish* making a *wish*?**
7. **a *dog* running in the *fog*?**
8. **a *pig* wearing a *wig*?**
9. **a *pot* cooking a *dot*?**
10. **a *sight* under a *light*?**
11. **a *bat* wearing a *hat*?**
12. **a *cook* reading a *book*?**

OPTIONAL: Repeat the questions, calling on children to name the two rhyming words in each.

346 

MATERIALS*

ACTIVITY 1

Display Board
4 ledges

Poster 4

ACTIVITY 2

None

1 Focus: evaluating whether certain things can happen *anytime* or only *sometimes,* using the poster "City in Summer"

Use the ledges to display the poster on the board.

Say:

Today let's talk about things that could happen *anytime* and things that can happen only *sometimes.* These two words tell us *when* something might happen. Look at the flowers in this window box and hanging from the street lamp. (Point to items on poster) **Raise your hand if you can tell me in a sentence whether these flowers might bloom *anytime* or only *sometimes.* Please tell us why.**

As necessary, help individuals answer in sentences such as "Flowers can bloom only sometimes." The children you call on should explain their reasoning in sentences such as "Flowers bloom only when the weather is warm." Call on children to give reasons for their answers as you ask questions like these:

1. **Could a jet plane take off anytime or only sometimes? Why?**
2. **Would the mail carrier deliver mail without his jacket anytime or only sometimes? Why?**
3. **Would the workers repair the street anytime or only sometimes? Why?**
4. **Would the fan in the room be running anytime or only sometimes? Why?**
5. **Would the people wear clothes with no sleeves anytime or only sometimes? Why?**
6. **Can people buy a newspaper anytime or only sometimes? Why?**
7. **Would the children ride the merry-go-round anytime or only sometimes? Why?**
8. **Would someone hang the clothes outside on the line anytime or only sometimes? Why?**
9. **Would people use the fire escape on the building anytime or only sometimes? Why?**
10. **Could someone mail a letter in the mailbox anytime or only sometimes? Why?**

2 Focus: using riddles to identify words that have multiple meanings

Say:

Today let's talk about words that sound the same but have more than one meaning. I will tell you two meanings of each word. You are to name the word.

The group should name the right word for each pair of definitions given below:

1. **I am the sickness you have when you sneeze and blow your nose. I am the word for how you feel when you are not warm.** (cold)
2. **I am a round metal container that holds trash. I am the word for being able to do something.** (can)
3. **I am a large piece of cloth that catches the wind for a boat. I am something a store uses to get customers to buy things.** (sail, sale)
4. **I am something you wear on your finger. I am the sound a bell makes.** (ring)
5. **I am the word for not being strong. I am a word that names seven days.** (weak, week)
6. **I am a word for how your face sometimes looks when you are sick. I am another word for bucket.** (pale, pail)
7. **I am a fallen piece of tree. I am the word for what tape does to paper.** (stick)

8. **I am the part of a car which makes it stop. I am the word for what happens to a dish dropped onto the floor.** (brake, break)
9. **I am something that gets very hot and is used to smooth wrinkles out of clothing. I am a strong metal.** (iron)
10. **I am a word that means to look at something. I am something worn on your wrist to show you the time.** (watch)

VARIATION: To make this activity *harder,* end by calling on children to define each word.

347

MATERIALS*

ACTIVITY 1

None

ACTIVITY 2

None

1 Focus: pantomiming everyday actions for the rest of the group to guess and repeat

Say:

Please watch as I pantomime an action we do every day. Try to figure out what I am doing. Then you may take turns pantomiming everyday actions for the group to guess.

Pantomime an everyday action such as putting on socks and shoes. Make sure your pantomiming is a clear model. Then ask:

What did I do? (Encourage children to respond in sentences) **Yes, I (put on my socks and shoes). Let's do it together.**

After this has been done, call on individuals to pantomime other actions, whispering instructions as necessary. In each case, have the rest of the group guess and repeat the pantomime. Here are some actions you may wish to suggest:

1. **brushing teeth**
2. **getting into bed and going to sleep**
3. **opening a door and walking through it**
4. **raking leaves into a pile**
5. **pouring milk into a glass**
6. **opening a bottled drink and putting a straw into the bottle**
7. **spreading bread with butter and jam**
8. **cracking an egg and putting it on to fry**
9. **turning on the television and finding the right TV program**
10. **answering the telephone**
11. **opening a package**
12. **setting the table**
13. **peeling a banana**
14. **opening a jar**
15. **putting on a jacket and zipping it**
16. **opening an umbrella**
17. **reading a book**
18. **using a pencil to write**
19. **climbing stairs or steps**
20. **filling a fuel tank**

2 Focus: brainstorming objects associated with common actions

Say:

Now let's think of all the things we might use to clean our teeth. Name as many of them as you can. (Lead brainstorming) **Yes! (A toothbrush, toothpaste, and a glass) are all things we use to clean our teeth. Can anyone name anything else?** (Pause) **That's right, (Juan); we might also use (water and dental floss).**

Continue with actions such as those listed in Activity 1.

348

MATERIALS*

ACTIVITY 1

None

ACTIVITY 2

None

1 Focus: talking about the relationship between two words

Say:

Let's play a thinking game. When I say two words, please try to figure out how they go together. Here are the first two: *milk* and *glass*. How might milk and glass go together? There may be more than one way. (Discuss) **Yes, you might drink milk from a glass. You might buy milk in a glass bottle.**

Continue with the following pairs of words. The children you call on should respond in sentences. Make sure everyone understands the relationship between the two objects. More than one correct answer is possible for each pair.

1. **toothbrush, toothpaste**
2. **water, pool**
3. **shoes, laces**
4. **stopper, bathtub**
5. **seatbelt, buckle**
6. **bee, honey**
7. **bucket, mop**
8. **cup, saucer**
9. **wheel, tire**
10. **iron, ironing board**
11. **soup, spoon**
12. **seeds, plant**
13. **ice, refrigerator**
14. **train, tracks**
15. **rabbit, carrots**
16. **kitten, cat**
17. **traffic officer, whistle**
18. **soda pop, straw**
19. **tow truck, car**
20. **sandwich, bread**

2 Focus: naming root words in a series of longer words

Say:

Now I am going to say a word you may not know. It is made from a word you probably do know. Try to figure out what that word is. Let's begin: *monstrous*. Do you hear a familiar word in *monstrous*? (Repeat word slowly several times as necessary, emphasizing the root word) **Yes, the word *monstrous* comes from the word *monster*. What does *monstrous* mean?**

When the children have learned that *monstrous* means "like a monster," ask several of them to use the word in a sentence. Continue with words like these:

1. **laughable**
2. **selfish**
3. **collection**
4. **wishful**
5. **lovable**
6. **announcement**
7. **preparation**
8. **likeable**
9. **tonsillitis**
10. **exaggeration**

VARIATION: To make the activity *easier,* do not emphasize the meanings of the longer words.

349

MATERIALS*

ACTIVITY 1

Display Board
4 ledges

Poster 5

ACTIVITY 2

None

1 Focus: predicting and talking about "what would happen if. . . ?" using the poster "Winter Scene"

Use the ledges to display the poster on the board.

Say:

You have seen this poster of the winter scene before. Look at it again as we play the game What Would Happen If. . .?

Encourage the children to imagine and describe the consequences of the following situations. Each child should have a turn. Accept all responses.

What would happen if . . .

1. **someone lit a firecracker under the horse?**
2. **P. Mooney's sled tipped over?**
3. **the little girl got too close to the fire?**
4. **the snowman began to sing?**
5. **the dog got into the picnic basket?**
6. **one of the skiers could not stop at the bottom of the hill?**
7. **the boy on the man's shoulders threw his snowball?**
8. **the snowmobile ran into the ambulance?**
9. **the sun came out, and it became very warm?**
10. **the dog in the red sweater grabbed the snowball in his mouth?**
11. **the big dog running down the hill jumped onto the toboggan?**
12. **the ice on the pond suddenly melted?**
13. **the TV truck got stuck in the snow?**
14. **the rabbit turned around and chased the cat?**
15. **the man with the camera forgot to put film into his camera?**
16. **the ice fisherman caught a very large fish?**

2 Focus: comparing pairs of items, and deciding which is warmer

Say:

I will name two things. Tell me which one is warmer. Let's begin. Which is warmer — a glass of water, or a glass of ice? (Encourage unison response) **Yes, a glass of water is warmer than a glass of ice. Now I will name other pairs of things. When I call on you, tell us which one is warmer.**

Continue with the following and similar examples. The children you call on should answer in sentences using the phrase "is warmer than."

Which is warmer —

1. **frying bacon, or a glass of orange juice?**
2. **inside a refrigerator, or inside an oven in which a cake is baking?**
3. **an ice-cream cone, or a hamburger?**
4. **a bowl of soup, or a peanut-butter sandwich?**
5. **a snowball, or a rubber ball?**
6. **taking a shower, or standing in the rain?**
7. **a piece of bread, or some toast from the toaster?**
8. **a snowman, or a doll?**
9. **holding an icicle, or toasting a marshmallow?**
10. **sunshine, or winter wind?**
11. **taking a bath, or swimming in a lake?**
12. **corn on the cob, or fruit salad?**
13. **playing with a hose, or sitting in front of a fire?**
14. **stepping into a puddle, or stepping into bathwater?**
15. **a hot dog, or a plate of jello?**
16. **a bottle of soda pop, or a cup of cocoa?**

17. being under a blanket, or being under a sheet?

18. an igloo, or a brick house?

19. going ice-skating, or lying in the sun?

20. lemonade, or a cup of coffee?

If time permits, repeat by asking children which item in each pair is cooler.

VARIATION: To make the activity *harder,* ask the children to use a sentence to give the reasons for each choice.

350

MATERIALS*

ACTIVITY 1

None

ACTIVITY 2

Teacher provides

Blank cassette

Tape recorder

1 Focus: brainstorming words and phrases associated with spiders

Say:

Today let's talk about spiders. What does the word spider make you think about? (Pause) **Raise your hand when you are ready to describe what spiders remind you of. Try not to repeat what anyone else has said.**

Call on children at random. Give clues if necessary.

OPTIONAL: End the activity by summarizing the children's responses.

2 Focus: imagining spiders, and then making up a progressive story about them

Say:

Close your eyes and imagine that you are looking at some spiders. (Pause) **Now let's make up a story about spiders. Each person will have a turn to add a sentence to our story, so please listen carefully to those who speak before you. I'll start.**

Turn on the tape recorder. Begin the story with a sentence such as "One day while I was taking a bath, my grandmother said, 'Look! A big black spider is right behind you!"' Then let each child add a sentence or two. End by playing back the story as the children identify each speaker.

OPTIONAL: Have the children suggest a title for their story.

351

MATERIALS*

ACTIVITY 1

Teacher provides
Blank cassette (optional)
Tape recorder (optional)

ACTIVITY 2

None

1 Focus: making up and telling stories about two sounds

Say:

Today let's make up stories about sounds. I will tell you two sounds you might hear. Think about them, and make up a story about what might have happened. Then you may tell your story to the group.

Let each child tell a different story about a pair of sounds like these:

1. **band music getting louder and louder, and the sound of marching**
2. **a jet airplane taking off, and then the loud sound of thunder**
3. **a bathtub being filled, and a knock on the door**
4. **a chair rocking, and a child singing**
5. **scissors cutting, and then a sewing machine stitching**
6. **children screaming and laughing, and then a door slamming**
7. **toad croaking, and a boat being rowed through the water**
8. **rooster crowing, and a tractor engine starting**
9. **glass breaking, and a broom sweeping**
10. **fire-truck siren, and an ambulance siren**
11. **a buzzing bee, and a person saying, "Ouch!"**
12. **wind blowing, and a wolf howling**
13. **sound of TV, and a person snoring**
14. **a sheep baaing, and a dog barking**
15. **a music box playing, and a baby cooing**
16. **a horse galloping, and a gunshot**
17. **hard rain falling, and a person running**
18. **angry voices shouting, and a child crying**
19. **a vacuum cleaner, and then a clanking sound**
20. **a bird chirping, and a cat meowing**

OPTIONAL: Record the stories and play them back, or summarize what each child says.

2 Focus: brainstorming *happy, sad, quiet,* and *scary* sounds

Say:

Let's talk about sounds: happy sounds, sad sounds, scary sounds, and quiet sounds. Tell me a happy sound, (Juan). (Pause) **Yes, (laughing) reminds me of being happy, too. Now name a scary sound, (Louise).** (Pause) **I agree; (the sound of thunder) makes me feel a little scared.**

Continue by having the children each name a sound that is happy, sad, quiet, or scary. Vary the type of sound called for, and keep the pace lively. Try to give everyone at least two turns.

Keep in Mind . . .
After each lesson in the program, individuals who have difficulty demonstrating proficiency in the skills you consider appropriate and important for them to learn should be tutored. Aides could help you with this task.

352

MATERIALS*

ACTIVITY 1

Teacher provides

Blank cassette (optional)

Tape recorder (optional)

ACTIVITY 2

None

1 Focus: brainstorming things that have windows

Say:

Many things have windows. Let's see how many of them you can name. When I point to you, tell us one thing that has a window. Try not to repeat what anyone else has named.

Give cues as necessary so each child names at least one thing.

OPTIONAL: Record the responses and end by replaying them.

2 Focus: imagining and talking about what might be happening inside a castle with many windows

Say:

Imagine that you are standing outside a castle that has many windows. Suppose you could see inside all the castle windows. Raise your hand when you are ready to tell us some things you might see inside one window.

If feasible, have each child describe at least one thing for the group. As necessary, give clues that will stimulate imaginative responses and a spirit of fun.

353

MATERIALS*

ACTIVITY 1

None

ACTIVITY 2

None

1 Focus: talking about words that sound the same but have different meanings

Say:

Let's talk again about words that sound the same but have different meanings. Tell us one meaning of the word *bark,* (Darcey). Yes, *bark* is the sound a dog makes. Now tell us another meaning for *bark,* (Miranda). That's right. *Bark* can also be the covering of a tree.

Continue as before with the following list:

1. bat, bat	**11. sail, sale**
2. bear, bare	**12. can, can**
3. chest, chest	**13. cold, cold**
4. blue, blew	**14. ring, ring**
5. back, back	**15. week, weak**
6. clothes, close	**16. pale, pail**
7. top, top	**17. stick, stick**
8. rock, rock	**18. brake, break**
9. nose, knows	**19. iron, iron**
10. duck, duck	**20. watch, watch**

2 Focus: talking about the imagined meanings of nonsense words

Say:

Now let's talk about some nonsense words. Think about what they might mean if they were real words. The first word is *wigwog.* What do you think about when you hear the word *wigwog*? What do you think *wigwog* might mean if it were a real word?

Encourage several children to suggest imaginative meanings. Accept all responses. Continue with nonsense words like these:

1. snoozle	**6. skrungle**
2. thigamajig	**7. lollapalooza**
3. dolloping	**8. zingerelly**
4. shrubbly	**9. puddlian**
5. thubberelli	**10. pickle-lilly**

354

MATERIALS*

ACTIVITY 1

None

ACTIVITY 2

Color Chips

All

1 Focus: identifying the short words of compound words, saying the two words in reverse order to create a silly compound word, and then making sentences out of each silly compound word

Say:

Today let's think about the two small words in many bigger words. What two words are in the word *milkman*, (Bud)? (Pause) **Yes, the two words are *milk* and *man*. Now say *milkman* backwards, (Bud). It will be a silly word.** (Pause) **Yes, the backwards word is *manmilk*. Use *manmilk* in a silly sentence.**

Continue as above with compound words like these:

1. football	**11. strawberry**
2. mousetrap	**12. wastebasket**
3. birdhouse	**13. rainbow**
4. barnyard	**14. shoeshine**
5. fireworks	**15. horseshoe**
6. wallpaper	**16. armchair**
7. snowman	**17. sunshine**
8. scarecrow	**18. battleship**
9. campground	**19. woodwork**
10. peanut	**20. chalkboard**

2 Focus: remembering a number and following directions in the game Number Exchange

Have available for each child a color chip chain of three to 10 chips, with two or three children having chains with the same number of chips.

Have the children sit in a circle, and give each child a chain. Ask them to count their chips. Then say:

Let's play a game called Number Exchange. Remember how many color chips you have. I will tell certain numbers to change places. When I say "All numbers, exchange," then all numbers are to change places.

Give directions like "Threes, exchange." The children with chains of three chips should then exchange places. From time to time, call out "All numbers, exchange!" All the children should exchange places.

VARIATION: To make the activity *harder,* call for two numbers to exchange, saying, "Fives and sevens, exchange."

355

MATERIALS*

ACTIVITY 1

Display Board
4 ledges

Poster 4

ACTIVITY 2

Display Board
4 ledges

Poster 4

1 Focus: imagining and talking about how the city in the poster "City in Summer" would look in winter

Use the ledges to display the poster on the board.

Point to the poster and say:

Let's talk again about this picture of a city in summer. Suppose this poster showed the city during a very cold winter. It is freezing and snowing. Tell how things would be different then.

If necessary, help by asking how each of these things would change:

1. **children playing by fire hydrant**
2. **clothing and uniforms of all people**
3. **windows of buildings open and people talking**
4. **fan in window**
5. **blooming flowers in flower box and plant on lamppost**
6. **color of sky**
7. **car with top down**
8. **truck washing the street**
9. **clothes hanging out of window**
10. **P. Mooney's popcorn stand**
11. **sign painter**
12. **workers using jackhammer in street**

2 Focus: counting items on the poster "City in Summer" to answer "how-many" questions

Leave the Poster from Activity 1 on display.

Say:

Now let's count some of the things in our poster. When I call on you, come to the poster and point to the items I name.

Each time a child has done so, lead the group in counting the objects. After that, let another child respond in a sentence such as "There are (seven vehicles) in the poster." Use the following format and items:

How many (vehicles) do you see in this poster?

1. **vehicles**
2. **people**
3. **workers**
4. **animals**
5. **buildings**
6. **street lights**
7. **mailboxes**
8. **stores**
9. **birds**
10. **street corners**
11. **lights**
12. **people with hats**
13. **children**
14. **sets of stairs**

356

MATERIALS*

ACTIVITY 1

Cards

Toys

226 228 229 230
231 233 236 237
239 241 242 243
244 247 248 251
252 253 257 259
260 262 263 264
265

ACTIVITY 2

None

1 Focus: describing the front, back, top, and bottom of toys

Hold up card 226 and say:

Let's look closely at this airplane and talk about it. (Pause) **Does this airplane have a back and a front?** (Discuss) **How do you know?**

Have someone describe the difference between the back and the front of the airplane. Then ask:

Does this airplane have a top and a bottom? (Pause) **How do you know?**

Have other children describe the top and bottom of the toy. Continue with the remaining toy cards, stressing the positional words *front, back, top,* and *bottom.* Help anyone who has difficulty learning them.

2 Focus: identifying classroom objects by using positional words

Say:

I will ask each of you to use a certain word as a clue to finding something. Raise your hand when you are ready to describe in a sentence what you see that is *under* something else. (Pause) **That is right, (Jane); the (box) is under the (table).**

The children you call on should respond in sentences.

Give everyone at least two turns, being sure no one uses the same positional word twice. Use these words:

1. **over**
2. **beside**
3. **between**
4. **behind**
5. **in front of**
6. **around**
7. **in**
8. **on**
9. **over**
10. **above**
11. **under**

357

MATERIALS*

ACTIVITY 1

None

ACTIVITY 2

Teacher provides

Blank cassette

Tape recorder

1 Focus: brainstorming words and phrases associated with fire

Say:

Today let's think and talk about fire. When I point to you, name something you think about when you hear the word *fire*. Try not to repeat what anyone else has said.

Call on children in random order, giving clues if necessary.

OPTIONAL: End by summarizing the children's responses.

2 Focus: imagining a fire, and then making up a progressive story about it

Say:

Close your eyes and imagine that you are watching a fire. (Pause) **Now let's make up a story about a fire. Each person will have a turn to add a sentence to our story, so please listen carefully to the persons who speak before you. I will start.**

Turn on the tape recorder. Begin the story with a sentence such as "After cooking their dinner over a campfire, the campers left the fire and went for a long walk." Then let each child add a sentence or two. End by playing back the story as the children identify each speaker.

OPTIONAL: Have the children suggest a title for their story.

358 

MATERIALS*

ACTIVITY 1

None

ACTIVITY 2

Fruits & Vegetables
All

Teacher provides
1 transparent plastic bag per child

1 Focus: brainstorming living and non-living things that make sounds

Sit in a circle with the children and say:

Let's think some more about living and non-living things that make sound. When I say "*living* things that make a sound," we will take turns naming one. But when I say "*non-living* things that make a sound," you must name one of those. Let's begin.

Have the child beside you name a sound-producing living thing. Then ask the next person to continue. When four or five children have responded, call for non-living things that make a sound. Continue until everyone has had several turns.

VARIATION: To make the activity *harder,* also ask for living and non-living things that have legs.

2 Focus: following directions stressing *and* and *or,* using the fruits and vegetables

With the children still sitting in a circle, place the fruits and vegetables in its center and say:

Today I am going to give everyone a bag you can see through. (Do this) **Now I will ask each of you to put certain fruits and vegetables into your bag and hold it up. Listen carefully to the two words *and* and *or* in my directions. Please put into your bag the apple *and* the orange *and* the onion *and* the carrot, (Matthew).**

When the child has done so, have the group tell whether (the) choices were correct. Put the fruits and vegetables back into the center. Stress the difference between and and or as you continue with these directions:

Please put into your bag . . .

1. **the apple *and* the orange *and* the pineapple and the banana.**
2. **the onion *and* the carrot or the corn *and* the potato.**
3. **the pineapple *and* the small banana *or* the orange *and* the large banana.**
4. **the pineapple *and* the large orange *and* the tomato *and* the strawberry.**
5. **the strawberry *and* the red apple *or* the large pear *and* the peach.**
6. **the carrot *and* the onion *or* the potato *and* the green apple.**
7. **the lemon *and* the tomato *and* the yellow apple *and* the red apple.**
8. **the pineapple *and* the onion *or* the large banana *and* the small pear.**
9. **the small orange *and* the yellow apple *and* the potato *and* the corn.**
10. **the corn *and* the large banana *and* the lemon *and* the onion.**
11. **the large orange *and* the small banana *or* the lemon *and* the pineapple.**
12. **the onion *and* the carrot *or* the red apple *and* the peach.**
13. **the small pear *and* the strawberry *and* the small banana *and* the peach.**
14. **the tomato *and* the pineapple *and* the lemon *and* the small banana.**
15. **the large banana *and* the yellow apple *and* the potato *and* the red apple.**
16. **the green apple *and* the large orange *or* the yellow apple *and* the peach.**
17. **the small orange *and* the onion *or* the corn *and* the carrot.**
18. **the peach *and* the pineapple *and* the potato *and* the strawberry.**
19. **the yellow apple *and* the small banana *or* the pineapple *and* the strawberry.**
20. **the lemon *and* the corn *and* the green apple *and* the red apple.**

359

MATERIALS*

ACTIVITY 1

None

ACTIVITY 2

None

1 Focus: imagining and talking about what it would be like if no one could talk or hear

Say:

Let's imagine that no one in the world could hear or talk. How would people share their ideas?

Lead the children in discussing ways of communicating besides speaking and listening. Then say:

Now let's talk about how our lives would be different if no one could talk or hear.

Give everyone a chance to participate. If necessary, ask questions like these:

1. **Would there be (telephones, radios, television, horns)?**
2. **How might we send messages to people far away?**
3. **Would there be traffic lights and road signs?**

2 Focus: comparing and describing the difference between the front and the back of objects

Say:

Now let's talk about the words *front* and *back*. Is there a difference between someone's front and back? (Discuss) **How can you tell the difference between the front and the back of a person?**

Encourage the group to describe a person seen first from the front and then from the back. Continue with

1. **dog**
2. **shoes**
3. **wagon**
4. **desk**
5. **car**
6. **house**
7. **robot**
8. **book**
9. **television**

these items:

VARIATIONS: To make the activity *easier,* display the available items listed above (shoes, desk, book) for the children to view as they describe the front and back of each. To make it *harder,* end by having the children each name an object which does not have a front and a back.

360

MATERIALS*

ACTIVITY 1

Cards

Stories

352 366 374
396 417 432
450 463

Display Board

4 ledges

ACTIVITY 2

Cards

Music

324 325

Puppets

P. Mooney

Zoey

All 3 hats

Audiocassette 2

Side A, Song 4, "Zoey"

Side A, Song 1, "I'm P. Mooney"

1 Focus: talking about P. Mooney's friends in the P. Mooney stories

Place the eight story cards on the ledges, picture sides hidden.

Say:

We have learned about many of P. Mooney's friends in his stories. Let's see how many of his friends you can remember and name.

List on the chalkboard as many of the following characters as the children can name:

P. Mooney

Mr. Nobody

Zoey

Elbert the Elephant

Ophelia

Where-Bear

Kiwi

Terrapin Turtle

Gasless Goose

Then turn over the cards, and have the children identify each character as you read the list. Give clues as necessary to help them name the characters not listed. Then point to the characters in random order and call on children to summarize the story for each. End by asking the children each to name her or his favorite character and tell why.

2 Focus: remembering and talking about enjoyable times spent with P. Mooney and Zoey, and saying good-bye to them

Hold P. Mooney and Zoey (wearing her discovery hat), and say:

Now it's time to say good-bye to P. Mooney and Zoey. If you wish, you may tell Zoey and P. Mooney something you enjoyed doing with them when you say good-bye.

Have the children take turns doing so. Then let two children hold the puppets as you continue:

Let's sing our songs about P. Mooney and Zoey. First let's sing Zoey's song. We will sing P. Mooney's song last of all.

Play Zoey's song and ask the child holding the puppet to change her hats as indicated in the song. Then play P. Mooney's song and lead the children in singing. End the program by having the two puppets wave and say, "Good-bye."

Appendices

Appendix A: Acknowledgments

Since its original publication in 1968, Level P of the PLDK series has been used by many people who have suggested ways to improve, expand, and revise the program. Because literally hundreds of you have written to us, we cannot thank persons individually; we hope this revision will do that for us, as we have incorporated many of your suggestions and were guided by your advice. We are especially grateful to Connie Davies and to the teachers of Noble School for the Retarded in Indianapolis for their extensive field testing of the original lessons.

This revision was truly a joint venture between the authors and the very capable staff of American Guidance Service. AGS policy does not allow us to mention staff members by name. Most were in the Program Development department, which was responsible for editing our lessons and organizing the art. The contributions of the staff of the Product Development department are also recognized for securing the high-quality components and packaging of this revision. Special thanks go to Gene Roeckers of Wayzata, Minnesota, for the overall packaging design.

During a period of three years, the original lessons were thoroughly revised and expanded several times. Those persons contributing to this effort were Patsy Casey, Mary Craighead, Margie Donnelly, Susan Gorrell, Lydia Horton, Kathi Oster, and Jo Von Neida. Lynette Hardie Wills worked closely with the authors from the beginning of the revision, which has greatly benefited from her talent, her organization, her international perspective, and her dedication.

We are grateful to the following free-lance illustrators, whose talents were responsible for the new picture cards and posters: Jan Waide, Leighton Fossum, Richard Gravender, Charles Hooper, J. William Myers, Jr., Rosalie Pearson, and Denise Saupe. Mark Ascerno from the University of Minnesota critiqued the artwork of insects. We also thank Pony Maples of Nashville, who worked with us in developing the art work for the posters and in critiquing "Sounds of the Environment."

Level P's puppets were created by several persons. Special thanks are due to Charles Hooper and Charlie Walton for helping to develop Zoey. P. Mooney remains the same in this revision, but again we thank Charlie Walton and Dorothy Barth for their part in his creation. Animal Fair, Inc., of Chanhassen, Minnesota, deserves credit for the production of both puppets.

The four new pieces entitled "Music for Movement" were composed by Libby Larsen of Minneapolis. AGS staff revised both the music and lyrics of the original "Songs for Language Development" and added new material for this revision. Bob Schultz of Voiceworks, Inc., and Jerry Stenstadvold at Sound 80 Studio, both of Minneapolis, engineered the recordings for both the songs and stories. The P. Mooney stories have been enhanced by the creative narrations of Irving Fink and Harriett Lee, both of Minneapolis.

In the manual to the first edition, we recognize many of the original contributors. Some of the key figures involved in this revision are cited here. But any venture the size and scope of this revision has many contributors, and we thank them all. We also thank the children who have responded to and learned from the original lessons.

Special thanks are due to the persons who typed and retyped lessons and this Teacher's Guide: Chris Beam, Donna Campbell, Eileen Cloyd, Polly Delzell, Debbie Griffin, Loretta Harris, Cheryl Orloff, and Lindsay Sale. Finally, the staff of the Nashville-based 1101 Group has been involved in the development of this revised program in many different ways. Their interest, ideas, reactions, help, and encouragement throughout the revision are gratefully acknowledged.

K. B, H./L. M .D./J OS. 1/81

Appendix B: Manipulative Materials

COLOR CHIPS, 240

30 black	30 orange
30 blue	30 red
30 brown	30 white
30 green	30 yellow

COLOR CHIP CONTAINER, 1

MANIKINS, 2

1 Disassembled Manikin (20 parts)

13 Body Parts

2 arms	1 head
2 ears	2 legs
2 feet	1 neck
2 hands	1 trunk

4 Facial Features

2 eyes and eyebrows
1 mouth
1 nose

3 Hairstyles

1 curly hairdo
1 long hairdo
1 short hairdo

Movable Manikin

DISPLAY BOARD, 1

Ledges, 6

MAGNETIC GEOMETRIC SHAPES,* 60

15 Circles	*15 Rectangles*
5 large	5 large
5 medium	5 medium
5 small	5 small

*5 colors: black, blue, green, red, yellow; each shape in each size is represented in each color

15 Squares	*15 Triangles*
5 large	5 large
5 medium	5 medium
5 small	5 small

PLASTIC FRUITS AND VEGETABLES, 23

3 apples (1 green, 1 red, 1 yellow)
3 bananas
1 carrot
1 corn
1 lemon
1 onion
3 oranges
1 peach
3 pears
1 pineapple
1 potato
3 strawberries
1 tomato

PUPPETS, 2

P. Mooney Zoey

PUPPET ACCESSORIES, 5

P. Mooney bag
P. Mooney stick
Zoey's action hat
Zoey's discovery hat
Zoey's thinking hat

Appendix C: Visual Materials

CARDS, 463

Art Picture Cards

Animals

1. bear (r)*
2. bear cub
3. bee(r)
4. beetle
5. bird (robin) (r)
6. butterfly
7. calf
8. cat
9. chick
10. colt
11. cow(r)
12. dog (r)
13. duck (r)
14. duckling
15. elephant (r)
16. fly (r)
17. gerbil (r)
18. goat (r)
19. goldfish
20. hen (r)
21. horse (r)
22. kid
23. kittens (r)
24. lamb
25. lion (r)
26. owl (r)
27. pig (r)
28. piglet
29. puppy (r)
30. rabbit
31. rooster (r)
32. sheep (r)
33. spider
34. squirrel (r)
35. toad (r)
36. turkey (r)
37. turtle
38. worm

Clothing and Accessories

39. blouse (girl's)
40. bonnet (baby's)
41. booties
42. boots
43. cap
44. coat (girl's)
45. coveralls (baby's)
46. dress (girl's)
47. glasses
48. jacket
49. jeans
50. mittens
51. necklace
52. overalls
53. pajamas (boy's)
54. pajamas (girl's)
55. purse
56. raincoat
57. ring
58. shirt (boy's)
59. shirt, knit
60. shoes, saddle
61.shoes, tennis
62. shorts
63. slip (girl's)
64. snowsuit
65. socks
66. suit (boy's)
67. sweater
68. sweater (baby's)
69. swimsuit (boy's)
70. swimsuit (girl's)
71. underpants (girl's)
72. undershorts (boy's)
73. wristwatch

*Note: (r) indicates accompanying recording in sound books 1, 2, or 3

*Face Pairs**

74. & 75. face smiling, short hair
76. & 77. face frowning, short hair
78. & 79. face smiling, long hair
80. & 81. face frowning, long hair
82. & 83. face smiling, right eye closed, long hair
84. & 85. face smiling, right eye closed, short hair
86. & 87. face smiling, both eyes closed, short hair
88. & 89. face frowning, both eyes closed, short hair
90. & 91. face smiling, both eyes closed, long hair
92. & 93. face frowning, both eyes closed, long hair

Foods

94. bacon
95. beans, green
96. beans, red
97. bread
98. cake
99. candy
100. cereal
101. cheese
102. cookies
103. corn on the cob
104. crackers
105. doughnut
106. eggs (fried)
107. fish (baked)
108. greens
109. ham
110. hamburger
111. hamburger (raw)
112. honey with comb
113. hot dog
114. ice-cream cone
115. jam
116. jello
117. juice, orange
118. milk
119. milk, chocolate
120. nuts
121. pancakes
122. peanut butter
123. pie, apple
124. popcorn
125. potato chips
126. potatoes (baked)
127. pretzels
128. rice
129. salad, fruit
130. sandwich
131. sodapop
132. soup
133. spaghetti with sauce
134. taco
135. toast
136. turkey, roasted

fruits and vegetables

137. apple
138. bananas
139. carrots
140. grapes
141. lemons
142. lettuce
143. onion
144. oranges
145. peach
146. pear
147. pineapple
148. potato
149. pumpkin
150. strawberries
151. tomato
152. watermelon

*sets of identical cards

Household Items

153. bathtub (r)
154. bed
155. broom (r)
156. brush, hair
157. brush, scrub (r)
158. chair
159. chest of drawers
160. clock
161. comb
162. couch
163. cup and saucer
164. dish, baking
165. dustpan
166. fork
167. glass
168. iron
169. ironing board
170. knife
171. lamp
172. mop
173. pail
174. pan, frying
175. plate (r)
176. radio (r)
177. record player (r)
178. refrigerator
179. saucepan
180. scissors (r)
181. sewing machine (r)
182. sink, bathroom
183. sink, kitchen
184. soap, hand
185. soap, laundry
186. sponge
187. spoon
188. stove
189. table, kitchen
190. telephone (r)
191. television (r)
192. tissues, facial
193. toilet (r)
194. tool set
195. toothbrush (r)
196. toothpaste
197. vacuum cleaner (r)
198. washer (r)
199. wastebasket

People

200. acrobat
201. astronaut
202. baby (r)
203. barber
204. boy (r)
205. child
206. clown
207. dentist
208. doctor
209. farmer
210. fire fighter
211. girl(r)
212. grocer
213. mail carrier
214. man (r)
215. man, older (r)
216. nurse
217. police officer
218. teacher
219. toddler
220. woman (r)
221. woman, older (r)

emotional expressions

222. angry boy
223. happy girl
224. sad girl
225. surprised boy

Toys

226. airplane
227. art set
228. ball (r)
229. balloon (r)
230. blocks
231. book
232. doctor/nurse
233. doll buggy
234. dollhouse
235. dolls
236. drum (r)
237. guitar (r)
238. gun, cap (r)
239. horse, rocking
240. jump rope (r)
241. jungle gym
242. pail and shovel
243. piano and stool (r)
244. pinwheel
245. puzzle
246. race-car set
247. rake, hoe, and shovel
248. robot (r)
249. sailboat
250. sandbox
251. skates, roller (r)
252. sled
253. slide
254. swing
255. tea set
256. teddy bear
257. teeter-totters
258. top (r)
259. tractor
260. train set (r)
261 . tree house
262. tricycle
263. truck
264. tunnel
265. wagon
266. whistle (r)

Vehicles

267. airplane, jet (r)
268. ambulance (r)
269. bicycle
270. bus, passenger (r)
271. bus, school
272. car (r)
273. car, police (r)
274. helicopter (r)
275. rowboat (r)
276. ship (r)
277. space capsule
278. trailer, camping
279. train, passenger (r)
280. truck, fire (r)
281 . truck, mail
282. truck, pickup
283. truck, tow (r)

Miscellaneous Cards

Numerals and Color Shapes

numerals

284. 1
285. 2
286. 3
287. 4
288. 5
289. 6
290. 7
291. 8
292. 9

color shapes

294. 1 yellow circle
295. 2 blue squares
296. 3 brown triangles
297. 4 orange rectangles
298. 5 green circles
299. 6 white squares
300. 7 red rectangles
301. 8 black circles
302. 9 yellow squares
303.10 blue triangles

color shapes, mixed

304. 1 brown shape
305. 2 orange shapes
306. 3 green shapes
307. 4 white shapes
308. 5 red shapes
309. 6 black shapes
310. 7 yellow shapes
311. 8 blue shapes
312. 9 brown shapes
313. 10 orange shapes

colors and numerals

314. brown, blue, red, green
315. yellow, green, blue, brown
316. orange, red, green, yellow
317. yellow, white, orange, brown
318. black, red, white, blue
319. white, yellow, brown, blue
320. green, black, white, orange
321. red, orange, green, black
322. black, brown, yellow, red
323. blue, orange, black, white

Music

songs for language development
(listed in order of appearance)

324. I'm P. Mooney (r)
325. The Is-Are Song (r)
326. Zoey (r)
327. Elbert's Song (r)
328. If and Then Go Together (r)
329. The Not Song (r)
330. Hi Ho, Pal (r)
331. Today, Yesterday, and Tomorrow (r)
332. Things That Go Together (r)
333. Make a Sound (r)
334. Find That Shape (Color, Number) (r)

music for movement
(listed in order of appearance)

335. Rhythm Walk (r)
336. Round Dance (r)
337. Rag March (r)
338. Contrasts (r)

Story Cards With Narratives"
(listed in order of appearance)

339.-352. How P. Mooney Got the P. Mooney Stick (r)
353.-368. P. Mooney and Mr. Nobody (r)
369.-385. P. Mooney and Zoey (r)
386.-398. The Elephant That Did Not Know How to Listen (r)
399.-418. P. Mooney, Ophelia, and the Where-Bear (r)
419.-432. P. Mooney and the Kiwi (r)
433.-450. Terrapin Turtle's Travel Troubles (r)
451.-463. P. Mooney and the Gasless Goose (r)

POSTERS**, 6

(listed in order of appearance)

Farm in Spring (poster 1)
Circus (poster 2)
Department Store (poster 3)
City in Summer (poster 4)
Winter Scene (posterS)
Town in Fall (poster 6)

*Each illustration has the corresponding story part on its reverse side

**3 sheets printed on both sides

Appendix D: Auditory Materials

(four audiocassettes)

Audiocassette 1:

P. Mooney Stories	Playing Time
Side A	
How P. Mooney Got the P. Mooney Stick	6:15
P. Mooney and Mr. Nobody	6:54
P. Mooney and Zoey	7:40
The Elephant That Did Not Know How to Listen	7:50
Side B	
P. Mooney, Ophelia, and the Where-Bear	7:14
P. Mooney and the Kiwi	6:33
Terrapin Turtle's Travel Troubles	8:04
P. Mooney and the Gasless Goose	6:40

Audiocassette 2:

Songs for Language Development and Music for Movement	Playing Time
Side A	
I'm P. Mooney (vocal)	1:04
The Is-Are Song (vocal)	:57
The Is-Are Song (instrumental)	:57
Zoey (vocal)	1:35
Elbert's Song (vocal)	1:23
If and Then Go Together (vocal)	:43
If and Then Go Together (instrumental)	:43
The Not Song (vocal)	:45
The Not Song (instrumental)	:45
Hi Ho, Pal (vocal)	:29
Hi Ho, Pal (vocal-instrumental)	:29
Hi Ho, Pal (instrumental)	:29
Side B	
Today, Yesterday, and Tomorrow (vocal)	1:12
Today, Yesterday, and Tomorrow (instrumental)	1:12
Things That Go Together (vocal)	1:43
Things That Go Together (instrumental)	1:43
Make a Sound (vocal)	2:12
Make a Sound (vocal)	1:50
Make a Sound (instrumental)	1:06
Find That Shape (vocal)	2:08
Find That Shape (instrumental)	2:08
Rhythm Walk	1:48
Round Dance	1:31
Rag March	1:28
Contrasts	2:08

SOUNDS

Audiocassette 3:

SOUNDS OF THE ENVIRONMENT

Side A

Sounds of Animals 1	Playing Time
bear	:09
bee	:10
bird	:06
cat	:09
cow	:10
dog	:05
duck	:10
elephant	:06
fly	:10
Sounds of Animals 2	
gerbil	:09
goat	:06
hen	:08
horse	:08
kittens	:09
lion	:13
owl	:11
Sounds of Animals 3	
pig	:11
puppy	:12
rooster	:09
sheep	:07
squirrel	:08
toad	:06
turkey	:07
Sounds of the Home	
bathtub being filled	:09
broom, sweeping	:10
brush, scrub	:10
plates,stacking	:05
radio	:12
record player	:12
scissors	:11
sewing machine	:08
telephone	:08
television	:13
toilet	:07
toothbrush	:05
vacuum cleaner	:12
washer	:12

Sounds of People—Actions	Playing Time
clapping	:07
coughing	:06
crying	:09
finger snapping	:10
humming	:06
laughing	:11
running	:05
singing	:08
sneezing	:04
snoring	:12
walking	:12
whistling	:07

Side B

Sounds of People-Voices

baby cooing	:08
boy talking	:12
girl talking	:12
man talking	:10
man (elderly) talking	:23
woman talking	:15
woman (elderly) talking	:27

Sounds of Toys

ball	:05
balloon	:09
drum	:14
guitar	:11
gun, cap	:12
jump rope	:05
piano	:14
robot	:11
skates, roller	:08
top	:20
train set	:08
whistle	:04

Sounds of Vehicles

airplane, jet	:06
ambulance	:05
bus, passenger	:12
car	:16
car, police	:11
helicopter	:12
rowboat	:13
ship	:10
train, passenger	:13
truck, fire	:16
truck	:20

Audiocassette 4: SOUNDS OF PLACES

Side A

Sounds for Poster 1, Farm in Spring — **Playing Time** **1:53**

1. cow mooing
2. pigs grunting
3. robin singing
4. tractor motor idling
5. owl hooting
6. bees buzzing
7. horse whinnying
8. rooster crowing

Sounds for Poster 2, Circus — **1:51**

1. band fanfare
2. elephant trumpeting
3. crowd applauding
4. miniature clown car
5. ringmaster announcing
6. horses hoofs
7. lion roaring and whip cracking
8. acrobat over drum roll: "Hup! Hup!"

Sounds for Poster 3, Department Store — **1:49**

1. man: "Jimmy, how do you like those blue shoes?"
2. sipping soda
3. child on teeter-totter: 'Up . . . down."
4. toy racing cars on track
5. child: "Mama, may I please have this book?"
6. carousel music
7. little dog whimpering

Side B Sounds for Poster 4, City in Summer — **2:05**

1. air hammer
2. elevated train
3. kitten meowing
4. children laughing and playing
5. jet plane
6. footsteps on cement sidewalk
7. pigeon cooing
8. steam (scoop) shovel and falling debris

Sounds for Poster 5, Winter Scene | **Playing Time**

1. sleighbells, horse neighing **1:39**
2. boy: "Careful! Don't knock the broom down."
3. footsteps in snow
4. large dog barking
5. older man to child: "Would you like to go for a ride, too?"
6. child on toboggan coming down hill: 'Whe-ee-ee!"
7. announcer: "This is our live-action news team, and today we're talking to people having fun on the ice."
8. crackling fire
9. snowmobile

Sounds for Poster 6, Town in Fall **2:08**

1. cash register
2. dentist drill
3. scissors clipping
4. tricycle bell
5. boy: "Hey, Steve, how do you like my blue helmet?"
6. baby cooing and laughing
7. little dog barking
8. roller skates
9. single engine airplane

Appendix E: Classification of PLDK-P Activities by 25 Skill Areas

Definitions

Assembling: Putting together the parts of a whole object.

Brainstorming: Generating as many responses as possible in answer to a question or command, by contributing ideas spontaneously.

Chanting: Reciting a rhyme or a phrase in a rhythmic manner.

Classifying: Sorting items into appropriate categories.

Comparing: Examining the attributes of two or more items in order to determine how they are alike and how they are different.

Counting: Naming numbers in order. Enumerating items.

Describing: Listing the attributes of an item or giving an account of an event.

Discussing: Sharing ideas on a topic by talking in detail or answering questions.

Dramatizing: Assuming the character and actions of a person, animal, or object.

Following Directions: Performing an action in response to a command.

Identifying: Selecting from a collection of items (the) one that answers the question or fits the description.

Imagining: Forming a mental picture not based on direct experience.

Labeling: Naming a stimulus item.

Listening: Hearing with thoughtful attention.

Matching: Grouping items on the basis of identical attributes.

Pantomiming: Conveying a story, event, or emotion by expressive bodily or facial movements.

Predicting: Foretelling an event by reasoning and observing.

Problem Solving: Evaluating possible solutions to a hypothetical problem in order to arrive at a satisfactory answer.

Reasoning: Drawing logical conclusions from known or presented information. Relating: Determining connections between two or more items,

Remembering: Bringing to mind images, ideas, or information from the past. Storing images, ideas, or information in the mind.

Sentence Building: Generating sentences based on a given model.

Sequencing: Determining and demonstrating the proper order of a series of items or events.

Storytelling: Telling or retelling a story or part of a story.

Vocabulary Building: Learning the definitions of specific words.

Index

Appendix F: Classification of PLDK-P Activities by 41 Subject Areas

Absurdities: 37.2, 41.1, 52.1, 98.1, 102.1, 112.2, 128.2, 132.2, 162.2, 177.2, 179.1, 184.2, 186.2, 216.1, 225.2, 226.1, 236.2, 242.2, 250.1, 255.2, 260.2, 271.2, 285.2, 345.2

Actions and Functions: 2.2, 5.2, 14.1, 14.2, 23.1, 29.1, 52.1, 63.2, 64.1, 64.2, 66.1, 66.2, 68.2, 72.2, 79.2, 81.2, 85.2, 93.1, 93.2, 101.2, 102.1, 107.1, 107.2, 111.2, 117.2, 121.2, 128.2, 130.2, 136.1, 138.1, 151.1, 152.2, 158.2, 177.1, 177.2, 182.1, 190.1, 190.2, 205.2, 223.2, 224.2, 270.1, 270.2, 274.2, 275.2, 276.2, 281.2, 290.2, 300.1, 301.1, 314.2, 316.2, 318.1, 320.1, 330.1, 335.2, 338.2, 347.1, 347.2

Analogies: 188.1, 239.1

Animals: 7.2, 16.1, 16.2, 17.2, 18.1, 18.2, 22.1, 22.2, 26.1, 26.2, 27.1, 27.2, 34.2, 35.1, 35.2, 39.1, 62.2, 73.1, 73.2, 74.1, 74.2, 78.2, 87.1, 87.2, 89.2, 95.2, 100.1, 100.2, 107.1, 107.2, 109.1, 126.1, 126.2, 139.1, 146.1, 146.2, 147.1, 147.2, 167.1, 167.2, 181.1, 181.2, 189.1, 189.2, 207.1, 207.2, 214.1, 214.2, 215.1, 228.1, 239.1, 239.2, 244.1, 244.2, 279.1, 279.2, 286.2, 299.2, 310.1, 312.1, 329.2, 350.1, 350.2

Body Parts: 14.1, 14.2, 15.1, 15.2, 23.1, 23.2, 36.1, 36.2, 37.1, 37.2, 41.1, 41.2, 52.1, 52.2, 63.1, 64.1, 79.1, 79.2, 80.1, 80.2, 93.1, 93.2, 98.1, 101.1, 101.2, 102.1, 104.1, 104.2, 130.1, 132.2, 135.1, 138.1, 138.2, 144.1, 151.1, 152.1, 177.1, 188.1, 190.1, 214.1, 215.1, 215.2, 235.1, 256.1, 260.2, 263.1, 265.2, 316.1, 319.1, 319.2, 320.2

Cause and Effect: 264.1, 349.1

Clothing and Accessories: 24.1, 24.2, 33.1, 33.2, 76.1, 76.2, 103.1, 103.2, 104.1, 104.2, 112.1, 112.2, 135.1, 135.2, 139.1, 139.2, 194.1, 247.2, 256.1, 269.2, 282.1, 285.1, 285.2

Colors: 11.2, 34.2, 48.1, 58.1, 58.2, 59.2, 60.1, 60.2, 61.1, 61.2, 70.1, 83.2, 90.1, 90.2, 94.1, 103.1, 106.1, 106.2, 113.1, 115.1, 115.2, 141.1, 141.2, 154.1, 157.1, 157.2, 174.1, 193.1, 200.2, 201.1, 209.2, 231.1, 231.2, 241.1, 241.2, 251.2, 258.1, 259.1, 293.2, 333.1, 340.1

Directional Terms: 4.2, 55.1, 55.2, 56.2, 94.2, 98.2, 125.2, 153.2, 192.2, 197.2, 235.1

Emotions: 86.1, 86.2, 102.2, 155.1, 158.1, 158.2, 160.1, 160.2, 165.1, 165.2, 171.1, 171.2, 187.1, 187.2, 202.1, 202.2, 203.2, 206.1, 206.2, 250.2, 259.2, 268.2, 274.1, 274.2, 297.1, 297.2, 310.2, 315.1, 315.2, 351.2

Energy: 172.1, 296.1, 326.1, 326.2, 341.1

Environment: 17.1, 30.1, 34.1, 35.1, 39.1, 39.2, 51.1, 51.2, 81.1, 82.1, 89.1, 99.1, 100.1, 100.2, 105.1, 105.2, 106.1, 120.1, 120.2, 121.1, 126.1, 128.1, 136.1, 136.2, 145.2, 148.2, 156.1, 156.2, 162.1, 164.1, 180.1, 182.1, 182.2, 195.1, 195.2, 208.1, 211.2, 212.2, 216.2, 218.2, 220.2, 222.1, 222.2, 231.1, 236.1, 237.2, 249.1, 249.2, 255.1, 273.1, 273.2, 289.1, 289.2, 302.1, 302.2, 311.1, 314.1, 318.2, 322.1, 322.2, 324.2, 329.1, 337.1, 337.2, 338.1, 342.1, 342.2, 344.1, 344.2, 346.1, 349.1, 355.1, 355.2

Foods: 11.1, 12.1, 12.2, 25.1, 25.2, 38.1, 38.2, 47.1, 47.2, 48.1, 48.2, 53.1, 53.2, 54.1, 54.2, 76.2, 84.1, 84.2, 88.1, 88.2, 110.1, 110.2, 111.1, 111.2, 133.1, 133.2, 134.1, 134.2, 140.1, 143.1, 143.2, 148.1, 153.1, 153.2, 173.1, 173.2, 185.1, 185.2, 196.2, 198.1, 198.2, 207.1, 209.1, 209.2, 219.1, 219.2, 238.2, 243.2, 248.1, 248.2, 256.2, 288.1, 288.2, 294.1, 300.1, 300.2, 310.1, 317.1, 31 7.2, 321.1, 333.1, 335.1, 335.2, 358.2

Handicaps: 152.1, 188.2, 215.2, 336.2, 359.1

Household Items: 50.1, 50.2, 57.1, 57.2, 60.1, 68.1, 68.2, 75.1, 75.2, 110.1, 114.1, 114.2, 142.2, 178.1, 203.1, 211.1, 234.2, 237.2, 256.1, 298.1, 298.2, 341.1

Machines: 123.2, 341.2

Numbers and Numerals: 58.1, 71.2, 84.1, 89.1, 89.2, 103.1, 126.2, 131.1, 140.1, 140.2, 154.1, 154.2, 169.1, 185.2, 196.2, 207.1, 209.2, 210.2, 240.1, 248.1, 249.2, 251.2, 259.1, 262.1, 272.1, 272.2, 278.2, 283.1, 284.2, 296.2, 301.2, 302.2, 304.1, 304.2, 308.1, 310.1, 311.2, 316.1, 324.1, 340.1, 354.2

Opposites: 95.2, 199.1, 199.2, 238.1, 256.2, 280.1, 287.2, 294.2, 305.2, 313.2

Parts and Wholes: 69.1, 261.1, 321.2, 332.1, 332.2, 352.1, 356.1, 359.2

People: 97.1, 121.1, 123.1, 149.1, 182.1, 191.2, 246.1, 257.1, 257.2, 268.1, 270.1, 290.1, 294.1, 323.2

- **Family Members:** 44.1, 144.2, 295.1
- **Workers:** 45.1, 45.2, 175.2, 191.1, 306.1, 318.1, 320.1
- **Voices:** 122.1, 161.2

Personal Identity: 1.2, 19.2, 44.2, 77.2, 108.2, 117.1, 161.1, 166.2, 175.1, 204.1, 211.2, 216.2, 218.2, 229.2, 230.2, 235.2, 239.2, 252.2, 267.2, 268.2, 274.1, 283.2, 310.2, 318.2, 334.2, 343.2

Places (see Environment)

Posters: 17.1, 34.1, 35.1, 39.1, 39.2, 51.1, 51.2, 81.1, 89.1, 99.1, 100.1, 100.2, 105.1, 105.2, i28.1, 136.1, 136.2, 156.1, 156.2, 164.1, 182.1, 195.1, 195.2, 208.1, 222.1, 222.2, 249.1, 249.2, 255.1, 273.1, 273.2, 289.1, 289.2, 302.1, 302.2, 322.1, 322.2, 324.2, 329.1, 337.1, 337.2, 349.1, 355.1, 355.2

Rhymes: 9.2, 11.2, 12.2, 18.2, 36.2, 43.2, 54.2, 79.1, 85.2, 89.2, 93.2, 99.2, 126.2, 131.2, 138.2, 140.2, 154.2, 157.2, 164.2, 167.1, 169.2, 173.1, 181.2, 185.2, 186.2, 189.2, 203.1, 21 0.2, 278.2, 301 .2

Riddles: 16.2, 60.1, 71.1, 90.2, 97.1, 109.1, 112.1, 114.1, 123.1, 129.1, 133.1, 147.1, 153.1, 167.1, 265.2, 330.2, 346.2

Appendix G: Summary of Activities

1.1 INTRODUCING: Puppet (P. Mooney)

1.2 LABELING: Personal identity (introducing oneself to P. Mooney)

2.1 DESCRIBING: Puppet (P. Mooney)

2.2 FOLLOWING DIRECTIONS: Actions (movement game)

3.1 INTRODUCING/REMEMBERING: Song ("I'm P. Mooney"); Puppet (P. Mooney)

3.2 DISCUSSING/REMEMBERING: P. Mooney bag; song ("I'm P. Mooney")

4.1 ASSEMBLING/CHANTING: Color chips; Traditional song

4.2 FOLLOWING DIRECTIONS: Words (positional-directional words)

5.1 IMAGINING/DESCRIBING: Imaginary contents of P. Mooney bag

5.2 IDENTIFYING: Actions pantomimed by teacher

6.1 LISTENING/REMEMBERING: Story ("How P. Mooney Got the P. Mooney Stick")

6.2 REMEMBERING/PANTOMIMING: Song ("I'm P. Mooney")

7.1 INTRODUCING/DISCUSSING: P. Mooney stick

7.2 DISCUSSING/PANTOMIMING: Animals

8.1 DISCUSSING: Magnetic shapes and magnetism

8.2 DISCUSSING/MATCHING: Shapes

9.1 REMEMBERING/STORYTELLING: Story ("How P. Mooney Got the P. Mooney Stick")

9.2 CHANTING/FOLLOWING DIRECTIONS: Rhyme (P. Mooney-stick game)

10.1 ASSEMBLING/DESCRIBING: Shapes

10.2 LISTENING/PANTOMIMING: Music for movement ("Rhythm Walk"); Moving like a caterpillar

11.1 DESCRIBING/DISCUSSING: Foods (apples)

11.2 CHANTING/IDENTIFYING: Rhyme; Finding red objects

12.1 COMPARING: Foods (apples); Senses (sight, smell, touch)

12.2 DISCUSSING/CHANTING/ PANTOMIMING: Foods (apples); Rhyme

13.1 LISTENING: Story ("P. Mooney and Mr. Nobody")

13.2 REMEMBERING/STORYTELLING: Story ("P. Mooney and Mr. Nobody")

14.1 PANTOMIMING/IDENTIFYING: Actions of body parts

14.2 CHANTING/PANTOMIMING: Traditional song; Body parts and their functions

15.1 DISCUSSING/ASSEMBLING: Body parts (disassembled manikin)

15.2 CHANTING/PANTOMIMING: Traditional song; Body parts and their functions

16.1 LABELING: Animals

16.2 REASONING/IDENTIFYING: Riddles about animals

17.1 LABELING/DISCUSSING: Environment (poster "Farm in Spring")

17.2 LISTENING/REASONING: Song ("The Is-Are Song"); Words (singular/plural); Sounds of animals

18.1 DRAMATIZING: Song ("The Is-Are Song"); Words (singular/plural); Sounds of animals

18.2 CHANTING/PANTOMIMING: Rhyme about a dog

19.1 LISTENING/REMEMBERING: Story ("P. Mooney and zoey")

19.2 INTRODUCING/DESCRIBING: Puppet (zoey); Personal identity (appearance)

20.1 INTRODUCING/IDENTIFYING: Song ("Zoey"); Zoey's hats

20.2 VOCABULARY BUILDING/DISCUSSING/PANTOMIMIN G: Words for Zoey's hats

21.1 REMEMBERING: Song ("Zoey")

21.2 REMEMBERING/STORYTELLING: Story ("P. Mooney and Zoey")

22.1 LABELING: Animals

22.2 CLASSIFYING: Animals that make sounds

23.1 REASONING/IDENTIFYING: Actions of body parts

23.2 CHANTING/FOLLOWING DIRECTIONS: Traditional song; Body parts

24.1 LABELING: Clothing and accessories

24.2 LABELING/REMEMBERING: Clothing and accessories; Song ("The Is-Are Song")

25.1 MATCHING/CLASSIFYING: Foods (fruits)

25.2 LABELING/REMEMBERING: Foods (fruits)

26.1 LABELING/DESCRIBING/RELATING: Animals and their young

26.2 LABELING/REMEMBERING: Animals; Song ("The Is-Are Song")

27.1 LISTENING/IDENTIFYING: Sounds of animals

27.2 FOLLOWING DIRECTIONS: Sounds of animals

28.1 LISTENING/STORYTELLING: Story ("The Elephant That Did Not Know How to Listen")

28.2 LISTENING/PANTOMIMING: Music for movement ("Rhythm walk"); Moving like elephants

29.1 IDENTIFYING: Sounds of actions

29.2 INTRODUCING/DISCUSSING: Song ("Elbert's Song")

30.1 LISTENING/REMEMBERING/ DISCUSSING: Environment

30.2 PANTOMIMING: Song ("Elbert's Song"); Moving like elephants

31.1 LISTENING/IDENTIFYING: Sounds (classmates' voices)

31.2 REASONING: Word analysis (rhyming)

32.1 LABELING/DESCRIBING: Toys

32.2 FOLLOWING DIRECTIONS: Music for movement ("Rag March"); Toy parade

33.1 LABELING: Clothing

33.2 CLASSIFYING/IDENTIFYING: Clothing

34.1 MATCHING/RELATING: Color (red); Environment (poster "Farm in Spring")

34.2 BRAINSTORMING/PANTOMIMING: Song ("If and Then Go Together"); Animals; Size

35.1 CLASSIFYING/IDENTIFYING: Animals; Environment (poster, "Farm in Spring")

35.2 BRAINSTORMING/PANTOMIMING Animals

36.1 IDENTIFYING: Single and multiple body parts

36.2 CHANTING/PANTOMIMING: Rhyme about functions of body parts

37.1 MATCHING/RELATING: Body parts of disassembled manikin to one's own body parts

37.2 REASONING/DESCRIBING: Absurdities about body parts

38.1 LABELING/MATCHING: Foods

38.2 LABELING/REMEMBERING: Foods; words (linking words)

39.1 COMPARING: Sizes; Animals; Environment (poster "Farm in Spring")

39.2 CLASSIFYING/PANTOMIMING: Song ("If and Then Go Together"); Animals; Sizes; Environment (poster "Farm in Spring")

40.1 LISTENING/REMEMBERING: Story ("P. Mooney and Zoey")

40.2 REMEMBERING/PANTOMIMING: Song ("Zoey")

41.1 ASSEMBLING/REASONING: Absurdities; Body parts

41.2 CLASSIFYING/PANTOMIMING: Song ("The Not Song"); Body parts; Words (negation)

42.1 LABELING/DESCRIBING: Toys

42.2 CLASSIFYING/PANTOMIMING: Song ("The Not Song"); Toys; Words (negation)

43.1 LISTENING/IDENTIFYING: Sounds of toys

43.2 CHANTING/FOLLOWING DIRECTIONS: Rhyme (P. Mooney-stick game)

44.1 SEQUENCING/DISCUSSING: People; Time (age)

44.2 LISTENING: Song ("Hi Ho, Pal"); Personal identity (names)

45.1 LABELING/DISCUSSING: People (workers)

45.2 IDENTIFYING/PANTOMIMING: Workers from pantomimed actions

46.1 LISTENING/ASSEMBLING: Story about shapes (circle, triangle)

46.2 LISTENING: Song ("Hi Ho, Pal"); Shapes

47.1 LABELING/DESCRIBING: Foods

47.2 LABELING/REMEMBERING: Foods

48.1 MATCHING/RELATING: Colors; Foods

48.2 LISTENING/LABELING: Music for movement ("Round Dance"); Foods

49.1 DISCUSSING: Toys

49.2 FOLLOWING DIRECTIONS/PANTOMIMING: Toys

50.1 LABELING/DESCRIBING: Household items

50.2 PANTOMIMING: Song ("Hi Ho, Pal"); Uses of household items

51.1 DISCUSSING: Environment (poster "Department Store")

51.2 LABELING/MATCHING: Environment (poster "Department Store"); Toys

52.1 REASONING/DESCRIBING: Absurdities about body part functions

52.2 CLASSIFYING/PANTOMIMING: Song ("The Not Song"); Body Parts; Words (negation)

53.1 LABELING/DESCRIBING: Foods

53.2 LABELING/REMEMBERING: Foods

54.1 DRAMATIZING/LABELING: Foods

54.2 CHANTING/COUNTING: Rhyme about foods

55.1 LISTENING/REMEMBERING: Story ("P. Mooney, Ophelia, and the Where-Bear"); Words (positional-directional)

55.2 FOLLOWING DIRECTIONS: Game about words (positional-directional)

56.1 STORYTELLING: Story ("P. Mooney, Ophelia, and the Where-Bear")

56.2 FOLLOWING DIRECTIONS: Game about words (positional-directional)

57.1 LABELING/DESCRIBING: Household items

57.2 PANTOMIMING: Song ("Hi Ho, Pal"); Household items

58.1 MATCHING/RELATING/COUNTING: Colors of color chips to classroom objects; Numbers

58.2 CHANTING: Traditional song; Colors

59.1 LISTENING/ASSEMBLING: Story about shapes

59.2 IDENTIFYING: Colors; Shapes

60.1 IDENTIFYING/REASONING: Riddles about household items; Colors

60.2 ASSEMBLING/FOLLOWING DIRECTIONS: Colors (oolor chip game)

61.1 DISCUSSING: Colors; Safety

61.2 FOLLOWING DIRECTIONS: Colors (traffic light game)

62.1 LISTENING/REMEMBERING: Story ("The Elephant That Did Not Know How to Listen")

62.2 LISTENING/IDENTIFYING/RELATING: Sounds of animals to animal cards

63.1 COMPARING: Body parts (disassembled and movable manikins)

63.2 DESCRIBING/PANTOMIMING: Actions (copying movable manikin poses)

64.1 BRAINSTORMING/DESCRIBING: Actions; Body parts

64.2 LISTENING/PANTOMIMING: Song ("Today, Yesterday, and Tomorrow"); verb tenses; Actions

65.1 CLASSIFYING/COMPARING: Shapes; Words (negation)

65.2 IDENTIFYING: Shapes; Senses (touch)

66.1 LISTENING/IDENTIFYING: Sounds made by actions

66.2 PANTOMIMING: Song ("Today, Yesterday, and Tomorrow"); verb tenses; Actions

67.1 STORYTELLING/DESCRIBING: Story ("P. Mooney, Ophelia, and the Where-Bear"); Words (positional-directional)

67.2 CHANTING/PANTOMIMING: Traditional song; Words (positional-directional)

68.1 CLASSIFYING/LABELING: Household items by location

68.2 CLASSIFYING/FOLLOWING DIRECTIONS: Actions; Household items; Words (positional-directional)

69.1 CLASSIFYING: Parts and wholes; Toys with wheels

69.2 LISTENING/PANTOMIMING: Song ("If and Then Go Together"); Shape (circle)

70.1 IDENTIFYING: Shapes; Colors

70.2 LISTENING/DISCUSSING/PANTOMIMING: Music for movement ("Contrasts"); Shapes (circle, triangle)

71.1 IDENTIFYING/REASONING: Riddles about toys

71.2 FOLLOWING DIRECTIONS/COUNTING: Number game

72.1 ASSEMBLING: Size (length of color chip chains)

72.2 LISTENING: Music for movement ("Rag March"); Actions (stop-go listening game)

73.1 CLASSIFYING/LABELING: Animals

73.2 LABELING/REMEMBERING: Animal game

74.1 LISTENING/IDENTIFYING/DISCUSSING: Sounds of animals

74.2 CHANTING/PANTOMIMING: Animals

75.1 IDENTIFYING: Household items

75.2 FOLLOWING DIRECTIONS/ PANTOMIMING: Household items

76.1 SEQUENCING/DISCUSSING: Clothing; Words (describing words)

76.2 LISTENING/CLASSIFYING: Song ("Things That Go Together"); Clothing;Toys; Foods

77.1 LISTENING: Story ("P. Mooney and the Kiwi")

77.2 REMEMBERING/DISCUSSING: Story ("P. Mooney and the Kiwi"); Personal identity

78.1 REMEMBERING/COMPARING: Story ("P. Mooney and the Kiwi"); Words (comparatives)

78.2 LISTENING/PANTOMIMING: Song ("If and Then Go Together"); Animals

79.1 DESCRIBING/CHANTING/ PANTOMIMING: Rhyme about face parts

79.2 DESCRIBING/PANTOMIMING: Actions; Body parts

80.1 CLASSIFYING/IDENTIFYING: Body parts

80.2 REMEMBERING/PANTOMIMING: Song ("The Is-Are Song"); Body parts

81.1 LABELING/DISCUSSING: Environment (poster "Circus")

81.2 PANTOMIMING: Actions (tightrope walker)

82.1 RELATING: Statements of circus performers to poster illustrations; Environment (poster "Circus")

82.2 LISTENING/IDENTIFYING: Sounds ("Sounds of the Circus")

83.1 CLASSIFYING/SEQUENCING: Shapes; Sizes

83.2 LISTENING/DESCRIBING: Music for movement ("Round Dance"); Shapes; Colors

84.1 DRAMATIZING/COUNTING: Foods; Numbers

84.2 CLASSIFYING: Foods needing refrigeration

85.1 LISTENING/STORYTELLING: Story ("P. Mooney and the Kiwi")

85.2 BRAINSTORMING/CHANTING: Actions; Rhyme

86.1 DISCUSSING: Emotions

86.2 REMEMBERING/PANTOMIMING: Song ("The Not Song"); Emotions; Words (negation)

87.1 IDENTIFYING: Animals; Word synthesis

87.2 CLASSIFYING: Song ("Things That Go Together"); Animals

88.1 CLASSIFYING/LABELING: Foods (fruits and vegetables)

88.2 IDENTIFYING: Foods; Senses (touch)

89.1 IDENTIFYING/COUNTING: Environment (poster "Circus"); Numbers

89.2 DISCUSSING/CHANTING/ PANTOMIMING: Animals; Rhyme; Numbers

90.1 BRAINSTORMING/COMPARING: Color (orange)

90.2 IDENTIFYING/REASONING: Riddles about orange items

91.1 LISTENING/IDENTIFYING: Sounds ("Sounds of People — Actions")

91.2 LISTENING/SEQUENCING: Song ("Make a Sound"); Words (comparatives)

92.1 BRAINSTORMING/DISCUSSING: Toys

92.2 LISTENING/PANTOMIMING: Music for movement ("Round Dance"); Toys

93.1 LABELING/DESCRIBING: Body parts; Actions

93.2 CHANTING/PANTOMIMING: Rhyme; Actions; Body parts

94.1 MATCHING/RELATING/DESCRIBING: Colors; Toys

94.2 ASSEMBLING/FOLLOWING DIRECTIONS: Color chips; Words (positional-directional)

95.1 LISTENING/REMEMBERING: Story ("Terrapin Turtle's Travel Troubles"); vehicles

95.2 LISTENING/PANTOMIMING: Music for movement ("Contrasts"); Animals; Opposites

96.1 BRAINSTORMING/COMPARING: vehicles; Words (comparatives)

96.2 PANTOMIMING: Song ("Make a Sound"); Words (comparatives)

97.1 IDENTIFYING/REASONING: Riddles about people

97.2 PANTOMIMING: Song ("Make a Sound"); Words (comparatives)

98.1 ASSEMBLING/REASONING: Absurdities; Body parts

98.2 FOLLOWING DIRECTIONS: Words (positional-directional)

99.1 LISTENING/IDENTIFYING/RELATING: Sounds ("Sounds of the Farm in Spring"); Environment (poster "Farm in Spring")

99.2 CHANTING/PANTOMIMING: Rhyme

100.1 MATCHING/RELATING: Animals; Environment (poster "Farm in Spring")

100.2 RELATING/DRAMATIZING: Song ("The Is-Are Song"); Sounds of Animals; Environment (poster "Farm in Spring")

101.1 LISTENING/IDENTIFYING: Story ("P. Mooney and Mr. Nobody"); Body parts

101.2 FOLLOWING DIRECTIONS: Actions; Body parts

102.1 COMPARING/PANTOMIMING: Absurdities; Actions; Body parts

102.2 LISTENING/PANTOMIMING: Music for movement ("Contrasts"); Emotions

103.1 DESCRIBING: Clothing; Colors; Numbers

103.2 FOLLOWING DIRECTIONS/REASONING: Clothing

104.1 CLASSIFYING/RELATING: Clothing; Body parts

104.2 RELATING/DRAMATIZING: Song ("The Is-Are Song"); Clothing; Body parts

105.1 LISTENING/IDENTIFYING/RELATING: Sounds ("Sounds of the Department Store"); Environment (poster "Department Store")

105.2 DRAMATIZING/COUNTING: Environment (poster "Department Store"); Counting (color chips)

106.1 MATCHING/RELATING: Colors (brown); Environment (classroom)

106.2 IDENTIFYING: Colors; Word analysis (rhyming)

107.1 BRAINSTORMING: Actions; Animals

107.2 DESCRIBING/PANTOMIMING: Actions; Animals

108.1 IDENTIFYING/STORYTELLING: Story ("How P. Mooney Got the P. Mooney Stick")

108.2 IDENTIFYING/REASONING: Personal identity (names); Word analysis (rhyming)

109.1 IDENTIFYING/REASONING: Riddles about animals

109.2 LISTENING/DISCUSSING: Song ("I'm P. Mooney")

110.1 DISCUSSING/RELATING: Foods; Household items

110.2 CLASSIFYING: Song ("Things That Go Together"); Foods

111.1 SEQUENCING/REMEMBERING: Foods (fruits)

111.2 PANTOMIMING: Song ("The Is-Are Song); Foods (fruits); Actions; Words (singular-plural)

112.1 IDENTIFYING/REASONING: Riddles about clothing; Word analysis (rhyming)

112.2 REASONING/PANTOMIMING: Clothing; Absurdities

113.1 CLASSIFYING: Colors; Shapes

113.2 IDENTIFYING: Song ("Find That Shape")

114.1 IDENTIFYING/REASONING: Riddles about household items

114.2 IDENTIFYING/PANTOMIMING: Household items

115.1 LABELING/MATCHING/RELATING: Colors

115.2 FOLLOWING DIRECTIONS: Song ("Find That Color"); Colors

116.1 STORYTELLING/DISCUSSING: Story ("P. Mooney and Mr. Nobody")

116.2 STORYTELLING/SEQUENCING: Pictures to story ("P. Mooney and Mr. Nobody")

117.1 IMAGINING/DISCUSSING: Personal identity (being invisible)

117.2 CLASSIFYING/PANTOMIMING: Song ("Things That Go Together"); Actions

118.1 LISTENING/IDENTIFYING: Sounds ("Sounds of vehicles"); vehicles

118.2 REASONING/RELATING: vehicles for certain trips

119.1 IMAGINING/DISCUSSING: vehicles; Travel

119.2 PANTOMIMING: vehicles

120.1 LABELING/DISCUSSING: Environment (poster "Town in Fall")

120.2 MATCHING/RELATING/COMPARING: Environment (poster "Town in Fall")

121.1 CLASSIFYING/DESCRIBING: Environment (poster"Town in Fall"); People

121.2 PANTOMIMING: Song ("Today, Yesterday, and Tomorrow"); verb Tenses; Actions

122.1 LISTENING/IMAGINING: Sounds ("Sounds of People — voices"); People

122.2 BRAINSTORMING/FOLLOWING DIRECTIONS: Song ("Make a Sound")

123.1 REASONING/RELATING: Riddles about people

123.2 DISCUSSING/PANTOMIMING: Musicfor movement ("Rhythm Walk"); Machines

124.1 LISTENING: Story ("P. Mooney and the Gasless Goose")

124.2 VOCABULARY BUILDING: Story ("P. Mooney and the Gasless Goose"); Words

125.1 ASSEMBLING/CLASSIFYING: Size (length of color chip chains)

125.2 FOLLOWING DIRECTIONS: Size; Words (positional-directional)

126.1 CLASSIFYING/RELATING: Animals; Environment

126.2 CHANTING/COUNTING/ PANTOMIMING: Animals: Rhyme; Numbers

127.1 LISTENINGNOCABuLARY BUILDING: Story ("P. Mooney and the Gasless Goose"); Word analysis (rhyming)

127.2 DRAMATIZING/FOLLOWING DIRECTIONS: Story ("P. Mooney and the Gasless Goose")

128.1 REASONING/RELATING: Environment (poster "Department Store"); Poster illustrations to statements

128.2 CLASSIFYING/FOLLOWING DIRECTIONS: Absurdities; Actions

129.1 REASONING/IDENTIFYING: Riddles about toys

129.2 LISTENING/PANTOMIMING: Music for movement ("Rag March"); Parade of horn "players"

130.1 BRAINSTORMING/LISTENING: Sounds ("Sounds of People — Actions"); Body parts

130.2 PANTOMIMING: Song ("Today, Yesterday, and Tomorrow"); verb Tenses; Actions

131.1 COUNTING/MATCHING/RELATING: Numbers; Shapes

131.2 CHANTING/COUNTING/ PANTOMIMING: Rhyme about bees

132.1 STORYTELLING/SEQUENCING: Story ("P. Mooney and Zoey")

132.2 REASONING/RELATING: Absurdities; Body parts; Words (negation)

133.1 REASONING/IDENTIFYING: Riddles about foods (fruits and vegetables)

133.2 CLASSIFYING: Song ("Things That Go Together"); Foods (fruits and vegetables)

134.1 BRAINSTORMING: Foods

134.2 REMEMBERING/SEQUENCING: Foods

135.1 REASONING/RELATING: Body parts; Clothing

135.2 BRAINSTORMING/RELATING: Clothing (pairs); Weather

136.1 LISTENING/CLASSIFYING: Environment (poster "Circus"); Sounds ("Sounds of the Circus"); Actions

136.2 DISCUSSING: Sounds; Environment (poster "Circus")

137.1 PROBLEM SOLVING: Situations involving P. Mooney and Zoey

137.2 FOLLOWING DIRECTIONS/ PANTOMIMING: Music for movement ("Rag March"); Game

138.1 BRAINSTORMING/PANTOMIMING: Actions; Body parts

138.2 CHANTING/PANTOMIMING: Rhyme; Body parts; Words (singular/plural)

139.1 LISTENING/DISCUSSING: Story ("Jimmy and The Big Question"); Clothing; Animals

139.2 DISCUSSING: Clothing

140.1 COUNTING/RELATING: Numbers; Foods

140.2 CHANTING/COUNTING/ PANTOMIMING: Rhyme; Numbers

141.1 CLASSIFYING/DESCRIBING: Colors; Shapes

141.2 BRAINSTORMING: Colors

142.1 LISTENING/IDENTIFYING: Sounds ("Sounds of the Home")

142.2 REASONING/RELATING: Household items to tasks

143.1 DESCRIBING/IDENTIFYING: Foods (fruits and vegetables)

143.2 CLASSIFYING/RELATING: Foods (fruits and vegetables)

144.1 DESCRIBING/MATCHING: Body parts

144.2 IMAGINING/DISCUSSING: People (family members)

145.1 STORYTELLING/DISCUSSING: Story ("The Elephant That Did Not Know How to Listen")

145.2 BRAINSTORMING/LISTENING/IDENTIFYING: Environment; Sounds

146.1 LISTENING/IDENTIFYING/DESCRIBING: Sounds ("Sounds of Animals"); Animals

146.2 DESCRIBING: Animals (pets)

147.1 IDENTIFYING/REASONING: Riddles about animals

147.2 DESCRIBING: Song ("If and Then Go Together"); Animals

148.1 REASONING/RELATING: Shapes to pictured foods

148.2 IDENTIFYING/RELATING: Shapes; Environment (classroom objects)

149.1 RELATING/DISCUSSING: People; vehicles; Travel

149.2 BRAINSTORMING/DESCRIBING: Song ("If and Then Go Together"); Vehicles

150.1 CLASSIFYING/DISCUSSING: Toys

150.2 PANTOMIMING: Song ("Hi Ho, Pal"); Toys

151.1 BRAINSTORMING/PANTOMIMING: Actions; Body parts

151.2 IDENTIFYING (TOUCHING): Senses (touch)

152.1 REASONING/DISCUSSING: Body parts; Handicaps

152.2 DISCUSSING/PANTOMIMING: Actions

153.1 DESCRIBING/IDENTIFYING: Riddles created by the children about foods

153.2 FOLLOWING DIRECTIONS/SEQUENCING: Foods; Words (positional-directional)

154.1 RELATING/ASSEMBLING: Colors; Numbers; Words (comparatives)

154.2 CHANTING/COUNTING: Rhyme; Numbers

155.1 DISCUSSING: Emotions (what makes one laugh)

155.2 SENTENCE BUILDING/RELATING: Funny sentences about three specified items

156.1 DESCRIBING/DISCUSSING: Environment (poster "City in Summer")

156.2 CHANTING/IDENTIFYING: Environment (poster "City in Summer"); Rhyme

157.1 MATCHING/RELATING: Colors

157.2 CHANTING/BRAINSTORMING: Rhyme; Colors

158.1 DISCUSSING: Emotions (feeling happy)

158.2 RELATING/PANTOMIMING: Actions; Emotions (feeling happy)

159.1 BRAINSTORMING: Vehicles

159.2 CLASSIFYING/DISCUSSING: Vehicles

160.1 DISCUSSING: Emotions (what frightens one)

160.2 LISTENING/PANTOMIMING: Music for movement ("Contrasts"); Emotions

161.1 IMAGINING/DISCUSSING: Personal identity (being invisible)

161.2 LISTENING/IDENTIFYING: Classmates' 162.1 SEQUENCING/PANTOMIMING: Environment; Travel

162.1 SEQUENCING/PANTOMIMING Environment; Travel

162.2 LABELING/REASONING: Absurdities; Travel

163.1 REASONING/RELATING: Determining situations from pictured items

163.2 MATCHING/RELATING: Color chips to specified items

164.1 DESCRIBING/DISCUSSING: Environment (poster "Winter Scene")

164.2 CHANTING/PANTOMIMING: Rhyme about building a snowperson

165.1 DISCUSSING: Emotions (feeling sad)

165.2 DISCUSSING/DESCRIBING: Song ("If and Then Go Together"); Emotions (feeling happy and sad)

166.1 IDENTIFYING/RELATING: Toys; Word analysis (rhyming)

166.2 DISCUSSING: Personal identity (names)

167.1 IDENTIFYING/REASONING: Rhymed riddles about animals

167.2 REASONING/RELATING: Word synthesis; Animals

168.1 REASONING/RELATING: Words (compound words)

168.2 LISTENING/RELATING: Words (compound words)

169.1 COMPARING: Numbers; Size (color chip chains)

169.2 ASSEMBLING/CHANTING: Rhyme about color chips

170.1 STORYTELLING/LISTENING: Story ("Terrapin Turtle's Travel Troubles")

170.2 DISCUSSING: Travel; Vehicles

171.1 DISCUSSING: Emotions (negative and positive feelings)

171.2 CHANTING/PANTOMIMING: Emotions (positive and negative feelings)

172.1 DISCUSSING: Energy used by vehicles

172.2 CLASSIFYING: Vehicles

173.1 LISTENING/IDENTIFYING: Rhyme; Foods

173.2 DISCUSSING: Foods

174.1 BRAINSTORMING: Items of specified colors

174.2 REMEMBERING/SEQUENCING: Sounds

175.1 DISCUSSING/IMAGINING: Personal Absurdities; Rhymes

175.2 DISCUSSING/IMAGINING: People (workers); Travel

176.1 LISTENING/IDENTIFYING: Words (compound words)

176.2 SENTENCE BUILDING/LISTENING: Words (compound words)

177.1 IDENTIFYING/DESCRIBING: Actions; Body parts

177.2 DESCRIBING/PANTOMIMING: Absurdities; Actions (copying movable manikin poses)

178.1 COMPARING: Household items; Size

178.2 DESCRIBING/BRAINSTORMING: Uses for a piece of rope

179.1 COMPARING/REASONING: Absurdities; Size

179.2 FOLLOWING DIRECTIONS: Size

180.1 DISCUSSING/DESCRIBING: Environment (poster "Winter Scene"); Seasons

180.2 LISTENING/IDENTIFYING: Sounds ("Sounds of the Winter Scene")

181.1 RELATING/REASONING: Animals; Word Analysis; Words (describing words)

181.2 LABELING/CHANTING: Animals; Rhyme; Words (describing words)

182.1 LISTENING/IDENTIFYING: Sounds ("Sounds of the City in Summer"); Environment (poster "City in Summer"); Actions; People

182.2 IDENTIFYING/RELATING: Environment (poster "City in Summer"); Statements to poster illustrations

183.1 CLASSIFYING: Groups of four items

183.2 BRAINSTORMING/DESCRIBING: Characteristics of specified items

184.1 LISTENING/IDENTIFYING: Words (compound words)

184.2 SENTENCE BUILDING/LISTENING: Words (compound words); Absurdities

185.1 LABELING/REMEMBERING: Foods (fruits and vegetables)

185.2 CHANTING/LABELING: Foods (fruits and vegetables); Rhyme; Numbers

186.1 LISTENING/REMEMBERING: Story ("P. Mooney and the Gasless Goose")

186.2 LISTENING/REASONING:
187.1 DISCUSSING/IMAGINING: Emotions (feeling angry)
Absurdities; Rhymes

187.1 DISCUSSING/IMAGINING: Emotions (feeling angry)

187.2 DISCUSSING: Emotions (feeling angry)

188.1 REASONING/RELATING: Analogies; Body parts

188.2 DISCUSSING/DESCRIBING: Senses (sight, sound); Handicaps

189.1 CLASSIFYING/COMPARING: Animals; Words (comparatives)

189.2 LABELING/CHANTING: Animals; Rhyme

190.1 DISCUSSING/PANTOMIMING: Actions; Body parts

190.2 PANTOMIMING/DESCRIBING: Music for movement ("Rhythm Walk"); Actions

191.1 DESCRIBING/STORYTELLING: People (workers)

191.2 DESCRIBING/REMEMBERING: Memory game about people

192.1 LISTENING/STORYTELLING: Story ("P. Mooney, Ophelia, and the Where-Bear")

192.2 FOLLOWING DIRECTIONS: Words (positional-directional)

193.1 DISCUSSING/ASSEMBLING: Colors; Weather

193.2 IMAGINING/DISCUSSING: What one would buy with the rainbow's pot of gold

194.1 REASONING/RELATING: Clothes to activities

194.2 REASONING: Song ("The Is-Are Song"); Words (action words, singular/plural)

195.1 RELATING/LISTENING/IDENTIFYING: Sounds ("Sounds of the Town in Fall"); Environment (poster "Town in Fall"); Sounds to poster illustrations

195.2 PREDICTING: Environment (poster "Town in Fall")

196.1 DESCRIBING/IDENTIFYING: Vehicles

196.2 CLASSIFYING/FOLLOWING DIRECTIONS: Foods; Numbers; Vehicles

197.1 LISTENING/REASONINGNOCABULARY BUILDING: Words (homonyms)

197.2 FOLLOWING DIRECTIONS: Words (positional-directional)

198.1 CLASSIFYING/DESCRIBING: Foods

198.2 BRAINSTORMING: Foods; Size

199.1 LISTENING/IDENTIFYING: Sounds; Opposites (loud/soft)

199.2 REASONING: Song ("Make a Sound"); Opposites (loud/soft)

200.1 FOLLOWING DIRECTIONS/MATCHING/RELATING: Color chips to P. Mooney's and Zoey's outfits

200.2 DISCUSSING: Favorite colors

201.1 CLASSIFYING/REMEMBERING: Shapes; Colors

201.2 BRAINSTORMING: Shapes; Uses for boxes

202.1 DISCUSSING: Emotions (being surprised)

202.2 IMAGINING/DISCUSSING: Emotions (being surprised)

203.1 LISTENING/REASONING: Rhyme; Household items; Word analysis (rhyming)

203.2 DISCUSSING/REASONING: Emotions; Safety (what to do when lost)

204.1 LISTENING/REMEMBERING: Personal identity (names and addresses)

204.2 REMEMBERING/PANTOMIMING: Song ("I'm P. Mooney")

205.1 DESCRIBING/REASONING: Words (describing words)

205.2 DISCUSSING/IDENTIFYING: Actions; Word analysis (rhyming)

206.1 REASONING: Emotions (surprise and anger)

206.2 PANTOMIMING/DISCUSSING: Emotions

207.1 BRAINSTORMING: Specified numbers of animals, foods, and toys

207.2 RELATING: Animals; Time (age); Words (describing words)

208.1 PREDICTING/DISCUSSING: Environment (poster "City in Summer")

208.2 LISTENING/REASONING: Word analysis (rhyming)

209.1 DESCRIBING/IDENTIFYING: Foods (fruits and vegetables)

209.2 CLASSIFYING/FOLLOWING DIRECTIONS: Foods (fruits and vegetables); Colors; Numbers

210.1 LISTENING/REASONING/VOCABULARY BUILDING: Words (homonyms)

210.2 CHANTING/FOLLOWING DIRECTIONS: Rhyme; Numbers

211.1 IDENTIFYING/BRAINSTORMING: Household items

211.2 IMAGINING/DISCUSSING: Personal identity (a room of one's own); Environment

212.1 ASSEMBLING: Shapes; Size

212.2 IMAGINING/DISCUSSING: Environment

213.1 LISTENING/REASONING: Words (compound words)

213.2 LISTENING/IDENTIFYING: Words (compound words)

214.1 CLASSIFYING: Animals; Body parts

214.2 FOLLOWING DIRECTIONS: Animals

215.1 BRAINSTORMING/DISCUSSING: Animals; Body parts

215.2 IMAGINING/DISCUSSING: Body parts; Handicaps

216.1 REASONING: Absurdities

216.2 DISCUSSING: Environment; Personal identity

217.1 CLASSIFYING: Groups of fourwords

217.2 BRAINSTORMING/DESCRIBING: Characteristics of specified items

218.1 SEQUENCING: Shapes

218.2 IMAGINING/DISCUSSING: Personal identity (where one would like to live); Environment

219.1 LISTENING/IDENTIFYING: Foods; Word analysis

219.2 DESCRIBING: Foods

220.1 SEQUENCING: Shapes

220.2 DISCUSSING: Environment (grocery stores)

221.1 IDENTIFYING/RELATING: Words (negation)

221.2 LISTENING/IDENTIFYING: Word synthesis

222.1 PREDICTING: Environment (poster "Farm in Spring")

222.2 COUNTING: Environment (poster "Farm in Spring")

223.1 PREDICTING: Consequences of specified actions

223.2 FOLLOWING DIRECTIONS: Actions; Time

224.1 BRAINSTORMING: Senses (sight, sound)

224.2 DISCUSSING: Actions; Time

225.1 REASONING/PANTOMIMING: Poses of movable manikin

225.2 LISTENING/REASONING: Absurdities

226.1 LISTENING/REASONING: Absurdities

226.2 IMAGINING/DISCUSSING/ PANTOMIMING: Size (being very small)

227.1 LISTENING/IDENTIFYING: Word synthesis

227.2 DISCUSSING: Sounds one likes

228.1 BRAINSTORMING: Animals

228.2 LISTENING/IDENTIFYING: Sounds ("Sounds of Animals")

229.1 STORYTELLING/DISCUSSING: Story ("How P. Mooney Got the P. Mooney Stick")

229.2 DISCUSSING: Personal identity (relationships)

230.1 REASONING: Words (action, naming)

230.2 DISCUSSINGNOCABULARY BUILDING: Words (action); Personal identity (where one likes to hide)

231.1 DISCUSSING: Colors; Environment

231.2 ASSEMBLING/FOLLOWING DIRECTIONS: Colors

232.1 REASONING/RELATING: Groups of illustrations

232.2 BRAINSTORMING/CLASSIFYING: Song ("Things That Go Together")

233.1 PROBLEM SOLVING: Solutions to P. Mooney's and Zoey's problems

233.2 PANTOMIMING: Song ("Zoey")

234.1 LISTENING/IDENTIFYING: Words (compound words)

234.2 PROBLEM SOLVING/RELATING: Household items needed for specified tasks

235.1 REASONING/RELATING: Body parts; Words (positional-directional)

235.2 DISCUSSING/REMEMBERING: Personal identity (what one best likes to do)

236.1 IMAGINING/DISCUSSING: Environment

236.2 DISCUSSING: Absurdities; Travel

237.1 LISTENING/IDENTIFYING/RELATING: Sounds ('Sounds of the Home") to rooms in which they might occur

237.2 BRAINSTORMING: Environment (home); Household items

238.1 RELATING: Opposites

238.2 COMPARING/CLASSIFYING: Foods; Senses (taste)

239.1 RELATING/REASONING: Animals; Analogies

239.2 IMAGINING/DISCUSSING: Animals; Personal identity (what pet one would choose)

240.1 LISTENING/IDENTIFYING: Numbers; Word analysis (rhyming)

240.2 SENTENCE BUILDING/RELATING: Funny sentences about three specified items

241.1 LABELING/REMEMBERING: Colors

241.2 RELATING: Colors to holidays

242.1 COMPARING/SEQUENCING: Size (heights)

242.2 REASONING: Absurdities; Size (heights); Words (comparatives)

243.1 CLASSIFYING/REASONING: Words (compound words)

243.2 BRAINSTORMING: Foods

244.1 SEQUENCING/DESCRIBING: Animals; Size

244.2 COMPARING/CLASSIFYING: Song ("If and Then Go Together"); Animals; Size

245.1 CLASSIFYING: Groups of five words

245.2 BRAINSTORMING/DESCRIBING: Words (describing words)

246.1 DESCRIBING: People; Verb Tenses

246.2 LISTENING/REMEMBERING/SEQUENCING: Sounds clapped in patterns

247.1 LISTENING/IDENTIFYING: Word synthesis

247.2 IMAGINING/DISCUSSING: Clothing

248.1 LABELING/COUNTING/CLASSIFYING: Foods; Numbers

248.2 LISTENING/REMEMBERING: Foods

249.1 PREDICTING: Environment (poster "Circus")

249.2 COUNTING: Environment (poster "Circus"); Numbers

250.1 REASONING/DESCRIBING: Absurdities

250.2 DISCUSSING: Emotions (how it feels to have a promise broken)

251.1 PROBLEM SOLVING: Solutions to P. Mooney's and Zoey's problems

251.2 COUNTING/BRAINSTORMING: Numbers; Colors

252.1 LISTENING/REASONING/VOCABULARY BUILDING: Words (homonyms)

252.2 DISCUSSING: Senses (sight, touch); Personal identity (what one most likes to see and touch)

253.1 REASONING/PANTOMIMING: Poses of movable manikin

253.2 LISTENING/REASONING: Word analysis (rhyming)

254.1 SENTENCE BUILDING/RELATING: Sentences about three specified items

254.2 IMAGINING/DISCUSSING: Contents of an imaginary box

255.1 IDENTIFYING/RELATING: Environment (poster "Town in Fall"); Statements to poster illustrations

255.2 REASONING: Absurdities

256.1 BRAINSTORMING: Body parts; Clothing; Household items

256.2 REASONING/RELATING: Foods; Opposites; Time

257.1 DESCRIBING/STORYTELLING: People

257.2 DESCRIBING/REMEMBERING: People

258.1 IDENTIFYING/REASONING: Colors; Word analysis (rhyming)

258.2 SENTENCE BUILDING/RELATING: Funny sentences about two specified items

259.1 CLASSIFYING/COUNTING/DESCRIBING: Shapes; Numbers; Colors

259.2 IMAGINING/DISCUSSING: Emotions (being sad)

260.1 DISCUSSING/REASONING: Size

260.2 IMAGINING/DISCUSSING: Absurdities; Body parts

261.1 LABELING/CLASSIFYING: Vehicle parts and wholes

261.2 LISTENING/REMEMBERING: Travel

262.1 COUNTING/CLASSIFYING: Numbers; Toys

262.2 LISTENING/IDENTIFYING/DESCRIBING: Sounds ("Sounds of Toys"); Toys

263.1 DISCUSSING/PANTOMIMING: Jointed body parts

263.2 SENTENCE BUILDING/RELATING: Funny sentences about three specified items

264.1 PREDICTING: Consequences of situations

264.2 LISTENING/REASONING: Word analysis (rhyming)

265.1 RELATING/DISCUSSING: Relationship between two pictured items

265.2 REASONING/RELATING: Body parts; Riddles

266.1 COMPARING: Same/different

266.2 IMAGINING/DISCUSSING: Imaginary items from the P. Mooney bag

267.1 LISTENING/IDENTIFYING: Word synthesis

267.2 DISCUSSING: Senses (smell); Personal identity (favorite smells)

268.1 IMAGINING/STORYTELLING: People

268.2 DISCUSSING: Emotions (feeling happy); Personal identity (friends)

269.1 CLASSIFYING/DISCUSSING: Words (negation)

269.2 BRAINSTORMING: Clothing; Weather

270.1 LISTENING/IDENTIFYING/ STORYTELLING: Sounds ("Sounds of People — Actions"); Sounds; Actions; People

270.2 BRAINSTORMING: Actions

271.1 CLASSIFYING: Toys

271.2 REASONING/DESCRIBING: Absurdities; Toys

272.1 COUNTING/SEQUENCING: Numbers; Shapes

272.2 COUNTING: Numbers; Shapes

273.1 PREDICTING/DISCUSSING: Environment (poster "Department Store")

273.2 COUNTING: Environment (poster "Department Store")

274.1 DISCUSSING: Emotions (being excited); Personal identity (one's most exciting experience)

274.2 BRAINSTORMING/DISCUSSING: Actions; Emotions (being excited)

275.1 IMAGINING/STORYTELLING: Stories from groups of four pictures

275.2 FOLLOWING DIRECTIONS: Actions; Time (before/after)

276.1 CLASSIFYING/DESCRIBING: Words (negation)

276.2 FOLLOWING DIRECTIONS: Actions; Time (after)

277.1 LISTENING/REMEMBERING: Story ("P. Mooney and The Kiwi")

277.2 DRAMATIZING/REMEMBERING: Story ("P. Mooney and The Kiwi")

278.1 REASONING: Time (duration)

278.2 COUNTING/CHANTING: Numbers; Rhyme

279.1 REASONING/DESCRIBING: Animals; Words (describing words)

279.2 DESCRIBING: Animals

280.1 REASONING/RELATING: Opposites

280.2 IMAGINING/DISCUSSING: Dragons

281.1 RELATING/DISCUSSING: Words

281.2 FOLLOWING DIRECTIONS: Time (before/after); Actions

282.1 RELATING/DISCUSSING: Clothing; Weather

282.2 SENTENCE BUILDING/RELATING: Funny sentences about three specified items

283.1 LISTENING/IDENTIFYING: Numbers; Word analysis (rhyming)

283.2 DISCUSSING: Personal identity (things one no longer cares to do)

284.1 REASONING: Time (duration)

284.2 REASONING/CLASSIFYING: Numbers; Words (naming words)

285.1 CLASSIFYING: Clothing

285.2 REASONING/DESCRIBING: Absurdities; Clothing

286.1 LISTENING/IDENTIFYING: Words (homonyms)

286.2 REASONING/FOLLOWING DIRECTIONS: Animals; Words (describing words)

287.1 PROBLEM SOLVING: Solutions to P. Mooney's and Zoey's problems

287.2 BRAINSTORMING: Opposites (hot and cold items)

288.1 DESCRIBING/IDENTIFYING: Foods (fruits and vegetables)

288.2 FOLLOWING DIRECTIONS: Foods (fruits and vegetables)

289.1 REASONING/DISCUSSING: Environment (poster "City in Summer")

289.2 IMAGINING/DISCUSSING: Environment (poster "City in Summer")

290.1 IMAGINING/STORYTELLING: People

290.2 PANTOMIMING: Song ("Today, Yesterday, and Tomorrow"); Actions

291.1 COMPARING: Same/Different

291.2 BRAINSTORMING/DESCRIBING: Characteristics of specified items

292.1 LISTENING/IDENTIFYING/ STORYTELLING: Sounds ("Sounds of Vehicles"); Vehicles

292.2 REMEMBERING/DESCRIBING: Vehicles

293.1 LISTENING/REMEMBERING: Story ("P. Mooney and Zoey")

293.2 MATCHING/RELATING: Colors

294.1 REASONING/RELATING: Foods; People

294.2 RELATING: Opposites

295.1 DESCRIBING/REMEMBERING: People (family members)

295.2 LISTENING/PANTOMIMING: Music for movement ("Rhythm Walk"); Moving like a caterpillar

296.1 DISCUSSING: Energy (electricity)

296.2 COUNTING/FOLLOWING DIRECTIONS: Numbers

297.1 DISCUSSING: Emotions (being shy)

297.2 REASONING/DISCUSSING: Emotions

298.1 CLASSIFYING: Household items

298.2 REASONING/FOLLOWING DIRECTIONS: Household items

299.1 IMAGINING/STORYTELLING: Stories about groups of four items

299.2 DISCUSSING/IMAGINING: Animals (pets)

300.1 REASONING/RELATING: Actions; Foods

300.2 SENTENCE BUILDING/REMEMBERING: Foods

301.1 COMPARING: Actions; Time (duration)

301.2 COUNTING/CHANTING: Numbers; Rhyme

302.1 REASONING/RELATING: Environment (poster "Winter Scene"); Statements to poster illustrations

302.2 COUNTING: Environment (poster "Winter Scene"); Numbers

303.1 LISTENING/IDENTIFYING: Word analysis; Words (compound words)

303.2 LISTENING/REASONING: Word analysis; Words (compound words)

304.1 MATCHING/FOLLOWING DIRECTIONS: Numbers

304.2 PANTOMIMING: Song ("Find That Number"); Numbers

305.1 REASONING/RELATING: Words

305.2 REASONING/RELATING: Opposites

306.1 PANTOMIMING/IDENTIFYING: People (workers)

306.2 SENTENCE BUILDING/REMEMBERING: Travel

307.1 CLASSIFYING: Words

307.2 BRAINSTORMING/DESCRIBING: Characteristics of specified items

308.1 CLASSIFYING/COUNTING/DESCRIBING: Numbers; Shapes

308.2 REASONING/COMPARING: Size (length/height); Words (comparatives)

309.1 RELATING/DISCUSSING: Words

309.2 BRAINSTORMING/CLASSIFYING: Groups of specified items

310.1 BRAINSTORMING/COUNTING: Animals; Foods; Numbers

310.2 REMEMBERING/DISCUSSING: Emotions; Personal identity; Safety

311.1 LISTENING/STORYTELLING: Sounds ("Sounds of the Circus"); Environment (poster "Circus")

311.2 VOCABULARY BUILDING/DISCUSSING: Numbers: Word analysis

312.1 DESCRIBING/DISCUSSING: Animals

312.2 DISCUSSING/RELATING: Time (seasons)

313.1 COMPARING: Size; Words (comparatives)

313.2 REASONING/RELATING: Opposites

314.1 PROBLEM SOLVING: Environment (classroom)

314.2 LISTENING/REMEMBERING/SEQUENCING: Actions (patterns clapped out)

315.1 DISCUSSING: Emotions (being proud)

315.2 REASONING/RELATING: Emotions to situations

316.1 LABELING/COUNTING: Body parts; Numbers

316.2 LISTENING/PANTOMIMING: Music for movement ("Rhythm Walk"); Actions

317.1 BRAINSTORMING: Foods

317.2 SENTENCE BUILDING/SEQUENCING/REMEMBERING: Foods

318.1 RELATING/PANTOMIMING: People (workers) to pantomimed actions

318.2 IMAGINING/DISCUSSING: Environment (classroom); Personal identity (what one would do as teacher)

319.1 STORYTELLING/SEQUENCING: Story ("P. Mooney and Mr. Nobody"); Body parts

319.2 REASONING/RELATING: Body parts

320.1 BRAINSTORMING: Actions; Vehicles; People (workers)

320.2 IMAGINING/DISCUSSING: Body parts (what not being able to open one's mouth would be like)

321.1 RELATING/DESCRIBING: Foods (cooked to uncooked)

321.2 RELATING: Parts and wholes

322.1 REASONING/DESCRIBING: Environment (poster "Winter Scene")

322.2 COUNTING: Environment (poster "Winter Scene")

323.1 IMAGINING/STORYTELLING: Sounds

323.2 LISTENING/IDENTIFYING/DISCUSSING: Sounds ("Sounds of People — Actions"); People

324.1 LISTENING/IDENTIFYING: Numbers; Word analysis (rhyming)

324.2 IMAGINING/DISCUSSING: Environment (poster 'Winter Scene"); Seasons

325.1 LISTENING/IDENTIFYING: Word analysis

325.2 LISTENING/REASONING: Word analysis

326.1 CLASSIFYING: Vehicles; Energy

326.2 BRAINSTORMING/DISCUSSING: Energy; Travel

327.1 PREDICTING/STORYTELLING: Various situations

327.2 BRAINSTORMING: Living and non-living things

328.1 COMPARING/DISCUSSING: Time (duration)

328.2 DESCRIBING/DISCUSSING: Time

329.1 PREDICTING/DISCUSSING: Environment (poster "Farm in Spring")

329.2 LISTENING/PANTOMIMING: Music for movement ("Round Dance"); Animals

330.1 REASONING/RELATING: Actions; Time

330.2 LISTENING/REASONING/VOCABULARY BUILDING: Riddles; Words (homonyms)

331.1 LISTENING/REMEMBERING: Story ("The Elephant That Did Not Know How to Listen")

331.2 DRAMATIZING: Story ("The Elephant That Did Not Know How to Listen")

332.1 RELATING: Parts and wholes

332.2 BRAINSTORMING: Parts and wholes (things that have handles)

333.1 COMPARING: Foods (fruits and vegetables); Size; Color; Senses (touch)

333.2 DISCUSSING: Puppets (P. Mooney)

334.1 BRAINSTORMING/CLASSIFYING: Groups of specified items

334.2 IMAGINING/DISCUSSING: Travel; Personal identity (what being able to fly would be like)

335.1 CLASSIFYING: Foods

335.2 FOLLOWING DIRECTIONS/REASONING: Foods; Actions

336.1 STORYTELLING: Sounds

336.2 LISTENING/IDENTIFYING: Sounds ("Sounds of Toys"); Handicaps; Toys

337.1 REASONING/DISCUSSING: Environment (poster "City in Summer")

337.2 REMEMBERING/LABELING: Environment (poster "City in Summer")

338.1 IMAGINING/DISCUSSING: Environment; Travel

338.2 FOLLOWING DIRECTIONS: Actions; Words (before, while, after)

339.1 IMAGINING/DISCUSSING: Travel; Time

339.2 LISTENING/REASONING: Word analysis

340.1 CLASSIFYING/DESCRIBING: Colors; Numbers; Shapes

340.2 BRAINSTORMING: Shapes

341.1 DISCUSSING: Household items; Energy

341.2 IMAGINING/DESCRIBING: Machines

342.1 REASONING/FOLLOWING DIRECTIONS: Environment (living things)

342.2 BRAINSTORMING: Environment (living and non-living things)

343.1 DISCUSSING: Time (seasons)

343.2 IMAGINING/DISCUSSING: Vehicles; Personal identity (what one would choose to fill up a truck)

344.1 LISTENING/IDENTIFYING/STORYTELLING: Sounds ("Sounds of the Department Store"); Environment

344.2 BRAINSTORMING: Environment

345.1 LISTENING/STORYTELLING: Story ("P. Mooney and the Gasless Goose")

345.2 REASONING: Absurdities; Word analysis (rhyming)

346.1 REASONING: Environment (poster "City in Summer"); Words (anytime, sometime)

346.2 LISTENING/IDENTIFYING: Riddles; Words (homonyms)

347.1 PANTOMIMING/IDENTIFYING: Actions

347.2 BRAINSTORMING/RELATING: Actions to objects

348.1 RELATING/DISCUSSING: Words

348.2 LISTENING/REASONING: Word analysis